TEXAS DIVIDED

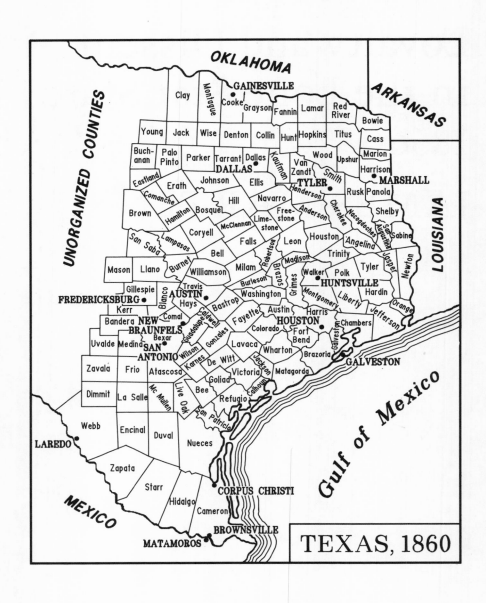

TEXAS, 1860

TEXAS DIVIDED

Loyalty and Dissent in the Lone Star State 1856-1874

JAMES MARTEN

026492

THE UNIVERSITY PRESS OF KENTUCKY

Frontispiece: Adapted by Lawrence Brence from map
by Liz Conrad in *Secession and the Union in Texas,*
by Walter L. Buenger (Austin, 1984).

Scholarly publisher for the Commonwealth,
serving Bellarmine College, Berea College, Centre
College of Kentucky, Eastern Kentucky University,
The Filson Club, Georgetown College, Kentucky
Historical Society, Kentucky State University,
Morehead State University, Murray State University,
Northern Kentucky University, Transylvania University,
University of Kentucky, University of Louisville,
and Western Kentucky University.

Editorial and Sales Offices: Lexington, Kentucky 40506-0336

Library of Congress Cataloging-in-Publication Data

Marten, James, 1956-
    Texas divided : loyalty and dissent in the lone star state,
1856-1874 / James Marten.
        p.   cm.
    Includes bibliographical references.
    ISBN 0-8131-1700-3 (alk. paper)
    1. Texas—History—Civil War, 1861-1865.   2. Reconstruction—
Texas.   3. Texas—History—1846-1950.   4. Dissenters—Texas—
History—19th century.   5. Sectionalism (United States)   I. Title.
E532.9.M37   1990
973.7'09764—dc20   89-48256
                                                              CIP

This book is printed on acid-free paper meeting
the requirements of the American National Standard
for Permanence of Paper for Printed Library Materials. ♾

To Linda

Contents

Acknowledgments

This book is no different from any other in that a number of individuals and institutions aided in its completion. Financial aid was provided by the Texas Chapter of the Colonial Dames of America, by the Daughters of the Republic of Texas, by a Dora Bonham grant from the Department of History and a Texas Studies Dissertation Fellowship from the College of Liberal Arts at the University of Texas at Austin, and by a Faculty Development Award from the Graduate School of Marquette University. The staffs at the Barker Texas History Center and the Perry-Castenada Library at the University of Texas at Austin, the Texas State Archives, the Austin History Center at the Austin Public Library, and the Marquette University Memorial Library sped research with their competence and courtesy. In addition, although the notes barely show it, I was also welcomed by the able archivists at the Southern Historical Collection at the University of North Carolina at Chapel Hill and at the Duke University Library.

The guiding hand of Robert H. Abzug is evident throughout the work. He delivered inciteful and extensive comments on several drafts of the 1986 dissertation on which this book is based and on a subsequent draft long after his duties as my dissertation director had officially ended. I will always value his scholarship, confidence, and continuing friendship. Reid Mitchell volunteered to read the entire manuscript and I profited enormously from his wit and shrewd suggestions. I also benefited from the comments and cooperation of my dissertation committee at the University of Texas at Austin—George B. Forgie, Robert A. Divine, Norman D. Brown, and Omer Galle—and from the remarks willingly offered on parts of the manuscript by Walter Buenger, Frank Klement, Grady McWhiney, and Tim Machan. F. E. Abernethy, Carl Moneyhon, Randolph B. Campbell, Col. Harold B. Simpson, Liz Conrad, and William Gist all generously corresponded with me on large or small aspects of my research. A number of friends and fellow graduate students at UT-Austin helped with suggestions and favors, including James Boyden, Judith Kaaz Doyle, Sally Graham, Brian Hosmer, Richard McCaslin, and James B. Martin. At the

University Press of Kentucky, Wm. Jerome Crouch and the staff made the publishing process much less of a puzzle to this novice. Any surviving errors of fact or of judgment remain, of course, solely mine.

On a more personal note, I would like to thank my family. Roy and Mary Lou Marten have always been encouraging and proud parents. Many of my own feelings of self-worth and confidence stem from their enthusiastic support; I firmly believe that my cherished memories of their determined attendance at years of high school and college sporting events, concerts, and other miscellaneous occasions will continue to contribute in some way to whatever success I achieve in life. My younger sister Jane, a small-town music teacher, has overcome her disdain at my professor's teaching schedule to express her satisfaction that at least I finally have a paying job. Her interest has always been appreciated. Another intangible acknowledgment goes to my four-year-old daughter Lauren Ruth, who during her brief life has unknowingly and happily put graduate school and my own career, to say nothing of the Civil War, in proper perspective.

I dedicate *Texas Divided* to my wife, Linda Gist Marten. Marriage into the Gist clan has allowed me to claim as shirt-tail in-laws southern dissenters from the Gist and McCracken families. During the Civil War, Joe McCracken, one of Linda's great-great-great uncles, hid in a Boone County, Missouri, apple cellar for two years to avoid conscription into the Confederate army (not to mention the Union army), while several great-great-uncles on the Gist side served in the Union army, although they lived in Confederate Arkansas during the war. Linda, on the other hand, endured five Texas summers and supported our little family through six years of graduate school with only a few murmurs of dissent; dedicating this slim volume to her attests—albeit meagerly—to my appreciation for the faith, patience, and love she has demonstrated throughout a dozen years of marriage.

Introduction:
Drawing the Line

The Civil War hardly scratched the Confederate state of Texas. Thousands of Texans died on battlefields hundreds of miles to the east, of course, but the war did not destroy Texas's farms or plantations or her few miles of railroads. Her long border with Mexico neutralized the effect of the federal blockade on Texas, and the battles fought inside her borders were mere skirmishes compared to the sanguinary struggles in Virginia and Tennessee. Although unchallenged from without, Confederate Texans faced challenges from within—from fellow Texans who opposed their cause. Dissension sprang from a multitude of seeds. It emerged from prewar political and ethnic differences; it surfaced after wartime hardships and potential danger wore down the resistance of less-than-enthusiastic rebels; it flourished, as some reaped huge profits from the bizarre war economy of Texas.

The geographic location—indeed, isolation—of the Lone Star state caused her domestic struggle to overshadow the fight with the Yankees more than in perhaps any other southern state. Nevertheless, all the satellites in the Confederate constellation fought their own internal civil wars between 1861 and 1865. The surprising amount of unity with which Texans and their corevolutionaries marched against the Yankees obscured for a time the divisions within southern society. Many southerners had long objected to the principles espoused by the secessionists or had opposed secession. Despite this opposition, passion usually overcame ideology, sparking widespread support for southern fire-eaters and winning votes for secession in Texas and all over the South. Fiery campaign speeches against "Black Republicans" in 1860 and "Union shriekers" in 1861 helped spawn a Confederate patriotism among Texans that reached its zenith in the months immediately following the attack on Fort Sumter, before beginning a decline that would not reach its nadir until the end of the war.

Prewar and wartime conditions produced a wide range of dissenting styles among Texans that lasted well into the Reconstruction. The sometimes volatile dynamics among the major social, political, and ethnic groups in antebellum Texas, produced a spectrum of dissent, which I have traced from the origins to the Reconstruction fates of groups and individuals who refused to support the southern and Confederate causes. In many ways, the real civil war in Texas was fought not over the state's relationship with the federal government, but over relationships among Texans. These battles, blending race, politics, and economics, gave birth to a turbulent era of strife and conflict. That those who did not support the Confederacy generally did not emerge victorious from the Civil War, despite its outcome, makes the story even more compelling, and sheds light on the course of events in Texas and in the South for the rest of the nineteenth and much of the twentieth century.

The question of loyalty—to the South, to the Confederacy, to the Union, to one's ethnic group—provides one key to understanding this story of a society at war with itself. Many of the people included in this book were not conscious of any disloyalty. Some were not dissenting against anything in particular; they merely wanted to protect their own interests. Others no doubt resented accusations of disloyalty. They saw themselves as perfectly loyal—but to governments or entities other than the Confederate States of America or state governments that carried out Confederate policies. Their loyalty to the South, or at least the way they demonstrated that loyalty, required them to commit actions other southerners eagerly labeled "disloyal." Walter L. Buenger examines the dual results of Texans' goals, expectations, and loyalties in his persuasive article, "Texas and the Riddle of Secession." He argues that similar attitudes about slavery, for instance, could lead to opposite responses to secession, as supporters of the institution disagreed not over its value and its justice, but over how best to preserve it.[1]

"Loyal" Texans had many ways of eliminating dissent and dissenters, which I have presented here because their perceptions of and attempts to curb dissent were vital elements in the course of events. Vigilant southerners helped to create the attitudes and institutions that the "disloyal" resisted. The waxing and waning of the many forms of wartime suppression provide a useful counterpoint to the varieties of dissent.

The study of loyalty and vigilance provides one vantage point for examining the structure and dynamics of Texas society during a crucial period in its history. The question of loyalty loomed very large to Americans—and especially to southerners—during the mid-nineteenth century, as the United States joined other Western nations in enforcing notions of national loyalty. The nation had come to be defined as an entity worthy of devotion and had achieved the power to unify a society by enforcing the loyalty of its members. American "Patriots" had enthusiastically purged their society of disloyal American "Loyalists" in the 1770s and 1780s. After the American and French revolutions, legal enforcement of loyalty became formalized, and social pressure to be true to one's country mounted. "To be traitorous had long been a crime," writes Boyd C. Shafer, "to be a national traitor became the most heinous of crimes." As a result, patriotism—an "individual necessity and moral duty"—became a standard by which "all men could be judged."[2]

Texans were certainly judged by that standard during the sectional conflict, and many were found wanting. The perception of loyalty often hinged on attitudes about personal liberty, race relations, economic development, and states' rights. These were, of course, central issues during the Civil War and Reconstruction; the rationale behind dissent and that behind attempts to suppress it reveal much about the aspirations of the several ethnic groups and political parties of Texas, including how they viewed the state of their society and what elements of that society they wanted to preserve or to change.

My definition of dissenters is not restricted merely to people who opposed the Confederacy for political or constitutional reasons, but includes those people whose "disloyalty" to the South and to Texas stemmed from deeper, cultural origins, or, contradictorily, from shallow reasons of self-interest or simple lack of interest. No single definition of dissent would have allowed me to trace the evolution of dissent and conformity over the course of a generation.

In order to portray and to analyze the myriad reactions of Texans to the circumstances that led to the Civil War and Reconstruction, I have used a number of methodologies. Sometimes the book resembles a collective biography of prominent Texans; their words and lives must represent the thoughts and actions of men who were more obscure or less articulate but who nevertheless shared the ideologies, hopes, or fears of their leaders. At other times I focus on groups—Germans, Mexicans, slaves, freedmen, Travis County Unionists, Texans in the Union army—in hopes of drawing generalizations out of their experiences. Analyses based on traditional sources such as manuscript collections, newspapers, and government documents mingle with occasional forays into rudimentary quantification.

I have also relied heavily on the works of other historians in my attempt to bridge the gap between the antebellum years and Reconstruction. Previous books, with a few notable exceptions, have tended to compartmentalize both the chronological periods of the sectional conflict and the categories of dissenters in the South.[3] Georgia Lee Tatum's *Disloyalty in the Confederacy*, for instance, is concerned primarily with organizations who opposed the Confederacy and with "peace" societies. Other classic studies, such as Ella Lonn's *Desertion during the Civil War* or Albert Moore's *Conscription and Conflict in the Confederacy*, examine those subjects narrowly and fail to consider their pre- or postwar ramifications. National, regional, and state historical journals have published scores of interesting although limited articles or collections of primary sources dealing with Unionists, and an astonishing number of other works have intensively examined such topics as the various strands of Unionist ideology, southern nationalism, wartime states' rights controversies, and race relations. Several generations of state studies have generally neglected dissent, although they usually offer chapter-length narratives or dramatic vignettes of desertion, speculation, or resistance to the Confederacy.

Texas historians have also examined the period extensively, yet, except for Randolph Campbell's analysis of Harrison County and Vera Lea Dugas's unpublished 1963 dissertation on the period's economic history, they generally have not attempted to unite the pre- with the postwar years. Walter L. Buenger and Frank H. Smyrl have looked at antisecessionism; Robert P. Felgar, Stephen B. Oates, Claude Elliott, Robert L. Kerby, and a host of other authors have written about various aspects of the war years; and Charles Ramsdell, James Baggett, and Carl H. Moneyhon have offered useful interpretations of Reconstruction. I have depended on these and many other articles, monographs, theses, and dissertations to flesh out my own research for the entire period.[4]

Although I have hardly approached the comprehensiveness or, no doubt, the eloquence of Carl Degler's *The Other South*, his work has informed much of what follows. Like Degler, I have sought in this book to "illustrate concretely . . . that the South is not and never has been a monolith." I have also found a continuity in ante- and postbellum dissent and in the efforts by southerners to stamp it out. If few Texans actually advocated the eradication of slavery, many opposed the more extreme strategies for preserving it. Although race was an ever-present factor in the process, the participants' loyalties—to country, region, or state—remained the most important constant in the dissension in Texas. In the end, as in other parts of the South, dissenters "who sought to escape their southern past" and tried to overcome the South's preoccupation with race, failed.[5]

The editor of the *Brownsville Ranchero* wrestled with the complexities of loyalty in an editorial written during the dark days of late 1864. "Where shall the line be drawn," he asked, "between loyal and disloyal subjects of the Confederate States?" He worried over this "thoroughly hairsplitting" issue, one which must be redefined by the participants of "every revolution, struggle for liberty, civil or belligerent war." "The difference between the worst good man on the road to salvation," wrote the editor, "and the best bad man, on the highway to endless perdition, is no more intricate than this loyal, disloyal question." Many Texans drew lines during the years before and after the Civil War, deciding how far they would go in supporting the Union, how much they would sacrifice in supporting the Confederacy, and what ends justified which means in enforcing Texans' loyalty to the Confederate States and to the South. The long sectional conflict also revealed deep fissures in southern and in Texan society, creating contours that would become battle lines in the fight over the shape that Texas society would take after the smoke had cleared. Loyal and dissenting Texans participated in the rocky process that Drew Gilpin Faust describes in *The Creation of Confederate Nationalism.* "Independence and war," she writes, "reopened unfinished antebellum debates, intensified unresolved prewar conflicts, and subjected some of the most fundamental assumptions of the Old South to public scrutiny." This is neither the history of the Civil War in Texas, nor of secession or Reconstruction, although those events obviously provide the necessary backgrounds for the drama. Rather, it is the history of men dealing with the sometimes fragmented southern society in which they lived—some fighting to change it, others to preserve it—and an examination of the lines that divided Texas and Texans during the sectional conflict of the nineteenth century.[6]

1

Southern Vigilantism and the Sectional Conflict

During the night of September 13, 1860, a Fort Worth vigilance committee hanged a Methodist minister named Anthony Bewley for plotting to incite an insurrection among Texas slaves. Bewley was no meddling New England abolitionist, but a Tennessean who had spent his entire career working in the slave states of Missouri, Arkansas, and Texas. His nativity failed to save him, however, and in a letter to his family from a jail cell in Fayetteville, Arkansas, a week before his death, he seemed resigned to his fate: "I expect when they get us we will go the trip." He protested that none of the abolitionist sentiments with which he was charged "have ever been countenanced in our house," and offered his wife the faint comfort "that your husband was innocent." Nevertheless, Bewley realized that, as a member of the hated Northern Methodist Episcopal Church, he was fair game for any sort of vigilante activity, especially during "these times of *heated* excitement," when "mole hills are raised mountain high." It seemed "enough to know that we are 'North Methodists,'" and the Fort Worth vigilantes "had sworn vengeance against *all such folks.*"[1]

That hunger for vengeance had risen from the ashes of a July 8 fire in Dallas that caused an estimated $400,000 worth of damage and destroyed most of the city's business establishments. Fires struck several other North Texas towns on that hot summer Sunday; Texans blamed their slaves and marauding abolitionist "emissaries" for the wave of arson. Charles R. Pryor, the editor of the *Dallas Herald*, described the plot and the growing alarm in the northern counties of the state in a letter to the *Austin State Gazette*. "I write in haste," he wrote, "we sleep upon our arms, and the whole country is most deeply excited." The print shop of the *Herald* lay in ashes, and Pryor asked the *Gazette* to "warn the country of the dangers that threaten it. . . . All is confusion, excitement and distrust. . . . There never were such times before."[2]

Throughout the rest of the summer, reports of burnings, poisonings, attempted murders, and other evidence of a widespread plot bred rumors all over the state. According to one source, the slaves had planned a general uprising on August 6, and "the whole country was in arms." Newspapers castigated masters for "laxity and indifference" in the management of their slaves and blamed the uprising on "unwise indulgence and foolish charity" toward northern incendiaries. Public meetings passed resolutions condemning Black Republicans or other northern conspirators for corrupting otherwise faithful negroes. Texans in more than two dozen counties formed vigilance committees. Citizens of Rush Creek directed its committee to keep "a strict watch over the action of every stranger coming in our midst." They vowed "to hang or burn" anyone trafficking in ideas, pamphlets, or poison among the slave population. Members of the Chatfield Vigilance Association pledged to defend their families, as well as their "honor and property," against the "robbers, murderers, assassins, traitors, the incendiaries . . . and thieves" at large in the land; "believing that all the crimes condemned by God and man flow from [abolition] principles as naturally as bitter waters from bitter fountains," they promised to "discard and ignore all smaller punishments" and to "inexorably execute our deliberate decree—DEATH!" The "people of Guadalupe" would assume to be enemies all northerners "whose antecedents are not known, and whose means of support are not visible." The *Matagorda Gazette*, while boasting that "everything here is quiet and orderly," declared that "the white man who is caught tampering with slaves in this community had better have his peace made with God . . . for if he don't swing, it will be because there is no hemp in the South."3

Hemp was apparently plentiful, for a Long Point physician wrote in mid-August that "a good many of these . . . negro lovers have already been hung up." Vigilantes around the state hanged at least ten white men and nearly thirty blacks, although a contemporary estimate put the numbers even higher, at twenty-five and fifty, respectively. Most of the blacks were suspected of poisoning wells or some other kind of homicidal plotting; most of the white victims were northerners, although some of them had lived in Texas for years. Scores of slaves and several whites were whipped or banished from the state, or both, for their alleged transgressions. A young peddler found with several copies of Hinton Rowan Helper's antislavery polemic *The Impending Crisis of the South* was allegedly burned alive in Buchanan. The woods near Bastrop seemed "to be alive with runaway slaves" apparently seeking to escape similar fates. Even innocent white men worried that their vigilant neighbors might suspect them of wrongdoing. Edward Burrowes, a young immigrant from New Jersey, asked his mother to "tell the folks sending me [northern] papers to stop, for I am afraid that it might get me in a tight place the way things is going now.

Thair was two men hung in some of the upper counties for takin northern papers, and I might get in the same fix if they keep on coming."[4]

The violence climaxed in September with the hanging in Fort Worth of the fifty-six-year-old Bewley. At the time of his death he was a missionary in the Arkansas Mission Conference of the Northern Methodist Episcopal Church. Texans had long associated Northern Methodist ministers with abolitionism, and a mob had broken up their 1859 annual meeting in Bonham. The events of the next year raised even more suspicions. "As is the custom in the worlds [sic] history of such matters," Gideon Lincecum sarcastically wrote to his nephew, "the insurrection was conducted in the name of the Lord. Poor Lord, he stands a bad chance to sustain a good character, for the damndest rascals perform their villainies in his name universally." Assigned to Texas less than two months before the insurrection panic erupted, Bewley arrived at a time when Texans were desperately casting about for "dangerous" characters. Despite his apparent moderation in regard to slavery, Bewley fled Fort Worth in mid-July. Bewley's vocation, the timing of his appearance in Texas, and a letter that he supposedly lost under a haystack outlining plans for an abolitionist conspiracy "convicted" him in his absence. The local vigilance committee's offer of a $1000 reward inspired a posse of Texans to track Bewley all the way to Missouri, drag him back to Texas, and hang him without a trial.[5]

Bewley's ordeal reveals the most drastic way that southerners punished those they perceived to be disloyal. Indeed, the decades after 1820 produced many crises similar to the Texas "insurrection" of 1860, during which southerners could perfect means of enforcing standards of loyalty. Vigilance associations and mass-produced justice were not invented by Texans, however; they were an American tradition during the antebellum period, and appeared whenever dissent reared its disloyal head in the south. The members of the mob who lynched Bewley simply played out the southern ritual of eliminating ideas that posed a threat to a way of life that by 1860 seemed to face enemies from all sides, particularly from the North. Lynching was, of course, the most extreme method of extending discipline to faithless southerners; it was complemented by equally effective political, rhetorical, and social versions of censorship and punishment. Such methods of ensuring sectional loyalty demonstrated a growing southern defensiveness in the face of the rising power of the North, along with a commitment to protecting slavery and providing for its expansion. These ideas created a sense of loyalty to the South that encouraged southerners to lash out at any external or internal enemy that challenged southern values or interests. Of course, northerners also employed mob violence to enforce community standards and to express political opinions. Ironically, the same ideas about slavery that angered southerners often led northern rioters to attack abolitionists.[6]

Southerners usually underestimated northern antiabolitionism, however, and their intolerance of challenges to southern society from within often coincided with periods of sectional friction. W.J. Cash, in his classic analysis of the southern mind, asserted that conflict with "the Yankee" inspired "the concept of the South as something more than a matter of geography, as an object of patriotism, in the minds of Southerners." The old loyalties to states and communities, Cash wrote, "would be rapidly balanced by rising loyalty to the new-conceived and greater entity—a loyalty that obviously had superior sanction in interest, and all the fierce vitality bred by resistance to open attack." As a result, every revival of the northern threat to southern institutions caused defensive southerners not only to oppose northern aggression, but also to punish those who failed to meet their responsibilities as loyal southerners. A southern man's most pressing obligation of course, was to defend slavery, and most cases of perceived disloyalty involved some sort of violation of this element of the southern code. Economic interest and the need for social stability combined to make "slavery . . . no abstraction—but a *great* and *vital* fact," wrote Arthur P. Hayne of South Carolina. "Without it our every comfort would be taken from us. Our wives, our children, made unhappy— education, the light of knowledge—all *all* lost and our *people ruined forever.*" That religion became one of the rocks on which slavery stood encouraged southerners to enforce sanctions against anyone who in some way threatened slavery.[7]

The deepening rupture between the sections redefined southern loyalty so that it encompassed more than just a proper reverence for slavery. As southern extremism grew, southern Whigs, National Democrats, and Unionists, among others, risked the same sort of public censure as the few antislavery men who lived in or passed through the South. By the beginning of the Civil War, southern radicals commonly applied the epithet *abolitionist* to political enemies who resisted secession or any other expression of southern rights. The same methods for punishing racial disloyalty proved popular in punishing political disloyalty, and vigilant southerners organized associations to enforce loyalty during sectional crises, important elections, and after the secession process had begun.

John Brown's futile expedition to Harpers Ferry in 1859 deepened the South's commitment to vigilance and raised the stakes in its drive to eliminate dissent. The raid set off a wave of panic and led southerners to practice the stern vigilante measures they had used against aliens or disloyal natives for years. Residents in every parish and district in South

Carolina held public meetings and organized vigilance committees charged with protecting the public from rabid abolitionists. Vigilantes in Columbia, South Carolina, captured, whipped, and tarred and feathered an Irish stonecutter for allegedly using "seditious language" against slavery. In North Carolina, "a wave of panic approaching hysteria" caused concerned authorities to censor the mail, step up slave patrols, and eye suspiciously free blacks and northern teachers, peddlers, and Methodist ministers. Mississippians withdrew their sons from northern colleges, kicked out Yankee teachers, and imposed an "intellectual isolation" upon themselves that shut down all communication between this crucial southern state and the North. The fear spawned by Brown's raid swept many previously cautious southerners into the radicals' camp and provided the southern nationalist movement with a much needed momentum.[8]

A year later the North and the South reaped the harvest of four decades of sectional strife, as Lincoln's election set in motion the chain of events that culminated in secession. The southern campaigns of the Constitutional Unionists, the Southern or Breckinridge Democrats, and the National or Douglas Democrats, revealed how few political and philosophical options were open to politicians and individuals in the slave states by 1860. Every party promised to guarantee southern rights and to resist the incursions of meddling Yankee abolitionists. In many cases, according to one historian, the campaign degenerated to "a shouting match to see who could call the Republicans blackest." Differences between Garrisonian radicals and moderate Republicans were ignored; anyone who failed to defend southern rights must oppose them. The realities of politics in the South forced politicians of many stripes into a narrow range of options, and no one who hoped to win—outside the sparsely populated and frequently Unionist mountain regions—could espouse any creed that challenged southern orthodoxy. Voters were similarly restricted, and vigilance committees mobilized in many areas to ensure the appropriate balloting. The *Nashville Union and American*, like many southern papers, called on its readers and the entire South to unite behind the Southern Democrat John C. Breckinridge, for only he had a chance to prevent the election of Abraham Lincoln. "Can any true Southern man calmly contemplate such a result without horror and the deepest humiliation?" asked the *Union and American*. "If he does not feel humiliated for himself he must feel so for his children's sake. If this be so, has the South lost her manhood? Is she so weak, imbecile and distracted that her sons cannot unite and strike one good, strong, healthy blow for her independence and equality[?] . . . Every true Southern patriot will say, 'strike the blow.'"[9]

Southerners who refused to strike the particular blow advocated by the Nashville paper were excoriated, as many southern dissenters had been before. One of the men that nationalistic southerners loved to hate during the campaign was Georgia's Herschel V. Johnson, a Unionist who was also Stephen A. Douglas's running mate. Throughout the South, particularly in Georgia, crowds hissed Johnson, hanged him in effigy (once just outside his hotel room in Macon), and threatened him with violence. When his train stopped in Georgia towns on the way home from the national nominating convention, Johnson recalled, people "would gather at the windows to get a glance at the man who dared to stand boldly in opposition to the sectional disunion movement of the Breckinridge democracy." Johnson knew that Georgians did not crowd depot platforms to catch a glimpse of a favorite son: "They eyed [me] not as a hero they wished to admire, but as some curious specimen of the genus homo, who deserved the gallows, for alleged treason to the rights of the South."[10]

Loyalty to the South was not an issue that suddenly appeared in 1861. Obviously, not every southerner worried about his neighbor's politics or his allegiance to slavery. But the rising concern of a growing minority of antebellum southerners reveals much about the ways that southerners perceived their interests, defined loyalty, and purged from their society people or opinions that they believed threatened slavery, southern political institutions, or the conservative social system. The months following the Harpers Ferry incident saw the frantic creation of one of the few regionwide campaigns to drive dissenters out of the South. More often, local vigilantes, spurred to action by slave insurrections, sectionalized political campaigns, or other emergencies, flushed from the system individuals who became scapegoats for southern disappointments and fears.

Mere chance cannot explain why some dissenters suffered the slings and arrows of vigilantism while others remained to a greater or lesser degree unmolested. Economic status, social position, and geography all played a part. Hapless Methodist missionaries, for instance, were more vulnerable to expulsion or violence than prominent politicians, attorneys, or planters, who usually had to contend only with angry epithets and editorials. Vigilant southerners used a wide variety of techniques to suppress heresy, or to convince their friends and colleagues of the error of their ways. In addition, although the persecution of individual dissenters never failed to receive a lot of attention and usually a fair amount of public acclaim, the southern gospel of individual liberty usually kept the newer doctrine of southern loyalty from overcoming justice, common sense, and the normal functioning of partisan politics.

The act of secession and the formation of the Confederacy at least temporarily changed all that, as it institutionalized antebellum vigilance and suddenly labeled men who had considered themselves good southerners as traitors to the South. Decades of a rather erratic enforcement of southern values suddenly became Confederate policy. Many men who, even after the events of 1860 and 1861, still could not tolerate southern radicalism, faced an abrupt transition in public sentiment, as for a short time the South united in its contempt for the North and for anyone who did not support the Confederate cause. Benjamin Hedrick had experienced this phenomenon five years earlier, when he lost his professorship at the University of North Carolina for supporting John C. Fremont for president. In a letter to university official Charles Manly, he wrote that, as a native of North Carolina, he had "always endeavored to be a faithful law abiding member of the community. But all at once I am assailed as an outlaw, a traitor, as a person fit to be driven from the State by mob violence, one whom every good citizen was bound to cast out by fair means or foul. This was more than I could bear." Thousands of southern men accused of treason, disloyalty, or disaffection during the war could have written those words. Few Unionists or antislavery southerners considered themselves outsiders; most no doubt believed that their ideas held out the best hope of progress and security for the South's future. Yet that vision of the future did not mesh with the ideas of the other good southerners who controlled the southern states after late 1860.[11]

When Texas joined the Union in 1845, she inherited a history of sectional tension that helped determine her course over the next sixteen years. In a state dominated by immigrants from the Southern states and with an economy increasingly dependent on slave labor, the political and economic interests of most Texans placed them solidly within southern traditions. As a result, the vigilante heritage of the South found an application in Texas, and the development of the idea of southern loyalty spread to Texas after the Mexican War. This vigilance, combined with the violence endemic to frontier Texas, created a place where, according to one Galveston resident, "a man is a little nearer death . . . than in any other country."[12]

Texans generally kept pace with their southern compatriots in ferreting out and disciplining individuals or groups who violated their perception of loyalty to the South. As in the other slave states, most instances of prewar enforcement of loyalty involved defending the peculiar institution. Texas law mandated prison sentences of at least two years for "free persons" who publicly claimed that men had no right to own slaves, who tried to bring the institution "into dispute in the mind of any free inhabitant of this State," or who encouraged a slave to be "discontented with his state of slavery." Postmasters could turn abolitionist literature received in their offices over to local authorities—in fact, they could be charged with a misdemeanor if they did not—and anyone who subscribed to such liter-

ature could be fined $500 and confined for six months. The Texas legis-
lature and the courts squelched a short-lived attempt by a group of Texans
and Mexicans to establish the "Republic of the Rio Grande" in South Texas
in 1850, at least partly because they feared the movement might be the
beginning of an abolitionist campaign. The *State Gazette* warned that
"some ramifications of northern fanaticism may have extended there," and,
if allowed even this small toehold, the abolitionists might grow strong
enough to "command the South." In 1854, a vigilance committee in Austin
expelled at least twenty Mexican families, and Austin businessmen
pledged not to hire Mexican laborers because their presence inspired
"false notions of freedom" among the slaves, making them "discontented
and insubordinate." A military expedition against the Indians a year later
turned into an attempt to recapture the estimated four thousand fugitive
slaves living in northern Mexico. Finally, during the three-and-a-half
decades between the Texas Revolution and the Civil War, Texans deter-
minedly narrowed the rights of free blacks, pushing them outside the
"black belt" in eastern Texas and, indeed, out of the state; they numbered
only about 350 by 1860.[13]

Local communities also stepped up their vigilante activities. In East
Texas in the mid-1850s, a citizen's group calling themselves "Moderators"
committed a number of murders and other depredations. They sought to
drive out the large number of free blacks and mulattoes who lived in the
county, but they directed much of the violence at those whites who refused
to aid the Moderators in their crusade. The tourist Frederick Law
Olmsted reported that thirty families had left the county, and that the
sheriff, deputy sheriff, and two strangers passing through the county had
been killed. Adolf Douai, a friend of Olmsted's and the editor of the *San
Antonio Zeitung*, left Texas after his abolitionism cost him many of his
advertising patrons, most of his friends, and all of his credit. These
examples of Texas vigilantism led the New Englander George S. Denison,
a teacher in San Antonio, to write, "I have become a very little disgusted
with this country. . . . Slavery is the grand Golden Calf, and everyone who
don't believe and maintain that it is an institution established by God itself
[*sic*], and is the only hope and object of our common country, is denounced
as a traitor to the South & to Republican Institutions."[14]

Politics, slavery, and loyalty to the South were further intertwined
when in the fall of 1856 an insurrection scare began in Tennessee and
Kentucky and spread by the end of the year throughout the slave states.
Most southerners attributed the uprising, allegedly scheduled to begin on
Christmas Day, to the growth of the Republican party and especially to the
sparks set off by that autumn's presidential campaign between John C.
Frémont and James Buchanan. In Texas, a Colorado County vigilance

cmmittee discovered in early September that the county's blacks planned to kill all the whites, steal their horses, and fight their way to Mexico. Slaveowners promptly hanged three blacks, whipped two others to death, and ordered all Mexicans—who were also implicated—out of the county, while the state legislature restricted slaves' rights to possess weapons, a moribund slave patrol system found new life, and vigilance committees surfaced in many towns around the state. One of their victims, a David O. Hoover, owned a thousand acres of land but no slaves, and voted for Frémont in the fall election. Threatened with lynching, he fled the state with his family and fifty-five cents. In October, a plot in Hallettsville implicated two white men.[15]

The scare induced a rash of vigilant rhetoric. The *State Gazette* hoped that the instigators of these revolts "may yet pay for their villainous deeds by the forfeiture of life itself.—Prompt and efficient punishment is demanded in these cases." The editor added that he had always favored law and order, but that in times such as these, it was proper that "the popular vengeance may be meted out to the criminal with as much necessity as we would strike down an enemy in self-defense, or shoot a mad dog in our path." Like many southerners, he blamed the threat on the fanatical rhetoric produced during the recent campaign: "We hope that this will be the last Presidential contest in which Southern institutions are alone to be the stake to be lost or won." Anson Jones, a former president of the Republic of Texas, also indicted Frémont and the Republicans. In a July speech at Washington, Jones called Frémont "a renegade southerner, envious of the fame of Benedict Arnold," and asserted that an abolitionist "must of necessity be either a knave or a fool" and refused to extend much charity to either. The former ought to be hanged "for high treason," while the latter would benefit from the scriptural axiom, "A rod for the fool's back." Jones warned that Black Republicanism had become synonomous with abolitionism and that only southern unity and a strict adherence to the constitution could save the Union from this threat.[16]

The people of Texas found other sources of danger between the insurrections of 1856 and 1860 and quickly stamped them out. Wood County vigilantes ran two journalists out of the state in 1857 for printing "grossly libelous . . . infamously false and . . . ridiculously absurd" abolitionist opinions. In 1859, an "Indignation meeting" of Gainesville citizens resolved greater vigilance—which they executed with a vengeance three years later—after a local man named E.C. Palmer, who had recently been convicted of "gaming with a negro slave," was discovered to be an abolitionist. Palmer wisely headed for safer pastures in California before Gainesville residents could act, but the meeting resolved that the "residence in our midst" of persons entertaining those sentiments was "dangerous and fatal to the interest and institutions of the South," and pledged "to use every means in our reach, to remove such persons from among us." Finally, in April 1860, the State Democratic Convention in Galveston expelled W. W. Leland of Karnes County because of his "Black Republican proclivities." Leland admitted to voting for Frémont in 1856, but protested that he had done so only because he, like the Republican candidate, favored a southern route for the Pacific railroad. According to the *Brownsville Ranchero*, Leland resembled "the fox who, on his return from a thieving excursion, minus his tail, which had been left in the jaws of a trap, as a memento . . . tried to make his old comrades believe that 'no tails' was the latest and only fashion." This "new doctrine" found believers among neither the foxes nor Karnes County voters, and Democrats in Leland's home county promptly endorsed the state convention's action.[17]

By 1860, the southerners' fears of isolated abolitionists inciting slaves to rebellion had grown to the belief that a substantial number of northerners, led by Black Republicans, were conspiring to overthrow the institution of slavery and to deprive the South of her rights. In Texas, the 1860 insurrection scare prompted a sharp exchange between moderate Unionists and the supporters of southern rights that hinged on the question of loyalty. The former hardly approved of slave insurrections, but believed they were the work of marauding individuals, not of abolitionist groups in the North, and that secessionists had exaggerated the danger in order to fire public passions. The latter associated the insurrection with an alarming pattern of attacks against southern institutions spearheaded by growing groups of northern fanatics.

"Rumor has burned almost every town in Texas this season," quipped the *Galveston Civilian*. The *Texas Republican* warned against such unfounded and exaggerated rumors regarding the slave insurrection, while the *Paris Press* protested "against the spirit, manifested by some persons, to take advantage of the present excitement to revenge personal injuries, and vent their spite upon those against whom they may be prejudiced." All this talk of hangings and mobs would tarnish the state's image, the Unionist *Southern Intelligencer* predicted. Its editor complained that "because this paper did not give way to the madness of the hour, and flood the country with . . . infernal falsification . . . we are denounced by fools and madmen as being 'unsound on the slavery question,' as if soundness implied nothing but capacity for falsehood and misrepresentation." James Newcomb, of the *Alamo Express* in San Antonio, came even more to the point: "If this whole matter of incendiarism was whittled down to the truth, it would result in the disclosure of the fact that it has been the work of a few miserable black-hearted Abolitionists . . . gratifying a private revenge, and have [sic] no connection with any one beyond the State."[18]

Many editors disagreed with such moderate opinions, and the *Houston Telegraph* struck an unusually bloodthirsty pose when it declared, "It is better for us to hang ninety-nine innocent (suspicious) men than to let one guilty one pass, for the guilty one endangers the peace of society." The Democratic organ, the *State Gazette*, led the campaign in Texas for Breckinridge and against those newspapers that denied any link between the 1860 insurrection crisis and the conflict between the North and South. Those same people who denounce "our suffering citizens for exposing the abolition incendiaries," asserted the *Gazette*'s editor, propose "unconditional submission to the principles of the Black Republican party." The *State Gazette* accused the Unionist "clique" that supported Gov. Sam Houston of bowing to Republican wishes so that, in the event of a Republican victory, they would be rewarded with lucrative offices. These men, in turn, "are in the habit of denouncing as treason every manly southern sentiment." The *Gazette* summarized the opinion of most vigilant southerners when it manfully declared early in 1861 that "Helperism, its aiders and abettors, should be strangled by the hangman's knot, and crowned with an infamous martyrdom."[19]

Interestingly, only one ex-slave commented on the 1860 "insurrection." Joe Oliver recalled many years later that "to dis day I thinks hit wuz de work of de Abolition preachers dat cum to work up de nigger's against de w'ite folks." Oliver, a teenager in 1860, believed that the "abolition preachers" started the fires, then "put hit on de slaves." The slaveowners responded by organizing vigilance committees "whose business hit wuz to arrest dese folks dat is tryin' to git de slaves to rise up agin' de w'ite folks." When the war came, however, southern whites "forgit all 'bout dese troubles, for de slaves did'nt rise up agin' de w'ite folks like dey had been told to do by dese abolition preachers, or whoever dey wuz." The agitators also forgot about the slaves, for "dey had gained dey purpose to work up de feelin's 'bout de war."[20]

By 1860, southerners and Texans had for a generation enforced loyalty to the South. Men who challenged slavery—whether they hailed from the North or the South—were silenced, exiled, or, in extreme cases, killed. Of course, southerners traditionally discovered the need for vigilance during times of sectional conflict; however, as crisis crowded upon crisis during the 1850s, and as new threats to the South and radical solutions to its problems surfaced, dissenters found themselves increasingly isolated. Vigilant southerners soon linked the old distrust of those rare southerners who opposed slavery to the large minority who opposed radical southern nationalism. "This charging of want of fidelity to the South," cried James Newcomb of the *San Antonio Alamo Express*, against "a man or set of men because of his or their devotion to the Union is palpably wrong . . . and decidedly ungenerous and un-American like."21

Nevertheless, in Texas, those individuals or groups who had for years lived outside the political or cultural mainstreams of Lone Star society, found their Unionism, or antislavery sentiments, or disaffection from Texans in general, lumped together under the category of disloyalty to the South and, later, to the Confederacy. Men who opposed secession could be labeled abolitionists and were subject to the same sorts of sanctions and violence as any other traitor to southern communities. The peculiar color-blindness of southerners led them to consider a challenge to any aspect of southern life or values a challenge to the doctrine of white supremacy. The Civil War did nothing to dilute that attitude, and by the Reconstruction period, it proved even more damaging to the survival of dissent in Texas.

2

Antebellum Dissenters in Texas

Amelia Barr stood "on a vast plain, dark and lovely, with the black clouds low over it." She waited in a pouring rain "with clasped hands" but "without the power to pray," watching as "a great white arch grew out of the darkness . . . as high as heaven, and wide as the horizon." Amelia "wondered at its beauty and majesty," but soon a black line bisected the arch. The arch finally split in two and half of it collapsed, "amid groans and cries, far off, but terrible." Then "a *Presence* of great height" suddenly appeared, "dim and shadowy, standing beside the ruined arch, and he cried for the *birds of prey* in a voice that filled all space. Turning north, and south, and east, and west, he cried, '*Come! and I will give you flesh to eat!*'"[1]

Late in life, Mrs. Barr, an English-born popular novelist and widow of Unionist-turned-Confederate Robert Barr, wrote that her 1859 dream foreshadowed the Civil War. Those Texans who suffered for failing to support the Confederate war effort would probably have agreed with her. Opposition, on constitutional grounds, to secession and the dogma of states' rights; devotion to the Union; disapproval of slavery; political or economic self-interest; ethnic antipathy; or simple lack of interest all contributed to the motivations of a motley band of dissenting Texans during the decades of antebellum strife and Civil War. Various combinations of these attitudes were exhibited by old-line Whigs, Know-Nothings, and National Democrats; by a minority of the immigrant German population residing in the state; and by most Mexican-Americans living along the Rio Grande border. In one sense, theirs were the "groans and cries" that mourned the destruction of the Union. Despite frequent but highly localized attempts to suppress dissent during the antebellum period, the existence of these groups proves that the growing pressure to conform failed to create a homogeneous southern populace, and that there still existed in the South people whose allegiance to the institutions upon which southern society was based seemed questionable. How a man viewed the existing state of Texas society and politics and how he believed future progress could be accomplished, frequently determined whether his neighbors would label him a "loyal" or "disloyal" southerner.[2]

In Texas, political resistance to secession and to the Confederacy grew out of the 1850s struggle by Whigs and renegade Democrats to maintain an organized opposition to the state's Democratic party. Ironically, however, the events of that decade only strengthened the Democracy's dominance in Texas. The rise of the Republican party, the highly publicized bloodshed in Kansas, John Brown's raid on Harpers Ferry, and the election of Abraham Lincoln, along with crises exclusively Texan—an escalation of Indian attacks along the frontier, unrest on the Rio Grande, the 1860 slave "insurrection"—made the Democrats' increasingly sectional solutions to these problems appear sensible and necessary. As a result, Unionist strength dwindled, and Texas was transformed from a state overwhelmingly in favor of remaining in the Union in 1859 to one decisively in favor of secession in 1861. Secession fever came late to Texas, but it struck with considerable force and urgency.[3]

The Democratic party in Texas had evolved out of the pro- and anti-Houston partisanship of the Texas republic. Most immigrants to Texas were southerners and Democrats, and the national party's support for the annexation of Texas and for the Mexican War confirmed Texas's status as a Democratic state. Even so, factionalism plagued the Texas Democrats; in 1853, for instance, seven Democrats ran for governor. Despite repeated attempts to establish central committees and hold unifying conventions, only competition from Whigs and, later, Know-Nothings, forced the two competing factions together. The Know-Nothing opposition siphoned off many Union Democrats from the state Democratic party, which fell into line with the southern wing of the National Democracy, denying Congress's power to interfere with slavery in the territories, demanding the acquisition of Cuba, endorsing the Dred Scott decision, and flirting with reopening the African slave trade. Although Texans had not suffered through the stormy decade of debate over secession experienced by older, more radical states such as South Carolina and Mississippi, by the end of the 1850s many leading Texans had adopted the Southern Democrats' ideas about secession.[4]

Southern nationalism was a major issue in the gubernatorial elections of 1857 and 1859. The Democrats victoriously pitted Hardin Runnels against the Independent Democrats' Sam Houston and, as the majority faction in the state legislature, also spiked Houston's bid for a United States Senate seat. The next two years witnessed a further radicalization of Texas Democrats and the first significant discussion of secession in the

state. Unfortunately for Runnels, neither his administration nor the federal government could deal effectively with the Comanche raids on the western and northern frontiers. Houston's vigorous 1859 campaign for governor capitalized on the Indian problem and on Runnels's radical states' rights position to win the election. Outside events soon pushed Texas toward secession, however. Houston hardly had time to warm the governor's chair before John Brown invaded Virginia, and the next year's slave insurrection in Texas helped to make the Opposition party's victory short-lived.[5]

Lincoln's election in November accelerated Texas's exit from the Union. Early in the disunion campaign, many secessionists advocated resurrecting the old Republic of Texas, and merchants in Gonzales, Houston, and Galveston soon sold out their stocks of Lone Star flags. John T. Allan wrote from Austin to his friend D. G. Osborn that "the post office is beseiged every morning for news" on the election, and reported that men had raised a Texas flag over "the principle [sic] hotel" in town. At a public meeting in front of the Calhoun County courthouse, secessionists sang the *Marsellaise*, passed resolutions urging the state of Texas to act, and paraded transparencies that read "Texas is Sovereign," "None But Slaves Submit," and, significantly, "Who is not for us is against us." Residents of Houston and Galveston wore blue cockades, and martial Galvestonians formed the Lone Star Rifle Company. The *Navarro Express* declared, "The North has gone overwhelmingly for *Negro Equality* and Southern Vassalage! Southern men, will you submit to the Degradation?" Less than a month after the election, the *Indianola Courier* scoffed at the commonly expressed Northern opinion that Unionism still survived in the South. "If there are any such, having affinity in principle," the editor wrote, "*they* are the 'traitors' in our midst, the spies in our camps, the *Tories* of our times. But [northerners] have no 'Southern brethren' unless they are the secret abolition emissaries who are prowling about the country for the purpose of inciting servile insurrections."[6]

Over Governor Houston's strenuous objections, an election for representatives to a convention to consider secession occurred January 8, 1861, and secessionists won a comfortable majority of the delegates. At the moment the polls closed in Austin, one Union-loving diarist recorded, the 130-foot secession pole and its Lone Star flag collapsed before a strong northern wind. Despite this omen, the convention began in Austin on January 28. Its proceedings lacked the agonizing self-searching and delay of those held later in Arkansas and Virginia, and on February 1 its members voted 166 to 8 to secede. A suggestion to submit the ordinance to a popular referendum aroused the only real debate, but even this proposal passed overwhelmingly. Delegate John Henry Brown supported such an election so that all those men who had previously opposed secession could demonstrate their loyalty to Texas and to the South by casting favorable votes. Many former opponents, Brown believed, now saw it as "the only safe course." A vote would allow them to show that "they are at heart as true to the cause of the South" as the men who had always seen separate state secession followed by confederation as "the only path of safety."[7]

During the three weeks between the first session of the convention and the referendum on February 23, secessionists and Unionists canvassed the state. Although the *State Gazette* urged everyone to go "to the polls and vote our honest sentiments . . . like friends and neighbors," it refused to extend its openmindedness to the small number of "demagogues" whose "pestilential heresies" rendered them incapable of nonpartisan interest in the welfare of the South or of Texas. These men "are maddened by disappointment and defeat. For them, we have nothing to say." The editorialist foreshadowed the later intolerance toward such men when he offered to "raise the window and bid the noisy little fellows to fly away in peace and safety." Unionism, at least in the minds of some, had already become heresy, and its proponents were unwelcome in a state on the verge of secession.[8]

Unionist "heretics" found themselves overwhelmed, as "the people rose in their sovereignty" and endorsed the secession ordinance by a vote of 46,153 to 14,747. Only 18 of the state's 132 counties—mostly in the north and west—rejected the ordinance. Unionists all around the state accused the secessionists of fraud and intimidation. The *San Antonio Alamo Express* applauded San Antonio voters for defeating the secession ordinance "in the face of threats, bullying, menaces, and brow beating." Secessionist election officials forced long-time citizens to prove their eligibility and compelled foreign-born residents to prove their citizenship. In Brownsville, the Unionist postmaster recalled shortly after the war that "under whip and spur every secessionist was lashed to the polls"; "threats and inducements" convinced many to vote for secession "who believed neither in its right or policy." Armed men—including the district judge and county clerk—patrolled the polling places. They "slapped their hands on their revolvers" and "told me significantly never again to vote in Texas." Anson Mills, an Indianan living in El Paso, had to wear guns to the polls to cast one of the city's handful of negative votes.[9]

James P. Newcomb, the fiery young editor of the Unionist *Alamo Express*, wrote later during the war that lies, intimidation, and fraud had played a large role in the secessionists' victory. Yet, he complained, "we cannot escape the humiliating fact, that [Union men] stood by with folded arms and allowed the conspirators to presume their opinions, and commit them, soul and body, to the work of treason." Despite such accusations, the

Dallas Herald proudly declared, "Our citizens have acted nobly and have placed themselves 'all square.' We believe the Conservative men will defend the State of Texas when she consummates the act of secession, as warmly as the secessionists." The secession convention reassembled, ended all talk of a reborn Texas republic by joining the rest of the Lower South in the Confederate States of America, and promptly declared the governor's office vacant when Houston refused to take an oath to support the Confederacy.[10]

Secession in Texas, as in the other Confederate states, made southern rights and an acceptance of secession the bases of a new national loyalty, while confederation created an institution to which all Texans suddenly owed their allegiance. The absence of a powerful opposition to secession in Texas encouraged militant secessionists to crack down harshly and confidently whenever dissent surfaced during the months and years that followed. In many instances the men who were accused of disloyalty belonged to groups in Texas whose loyalty to southern principles—including secession—had always been suspect. Once the war began, they found it difficult to swear to uphold a government that they believed had usurped the powers of the United States. The course of events ran against them, however; by March 1861, in the words of an Austin Unionist: "Every man that is not willing to support the Southern Congress is to be beheaded."[11]

The opposition to this sudden explosion of southern nationalism grew out of several diverse political traditions. When a number of prominent Texans met in May 1859, under the loose heading of National Democrats, the *Clarksville Standard* was not too far from the truth when it called these future antisecessionists a "promiscuous, heterogeneous conglomeration . . . of Old Line Whigs, Know-Nothings, Independents, Renegades, Bolters, Faggots, Stubs and Tail-ends of all parties."[12] Most antisecessionists in the state, however, emerged from one of two backgrounds: the Jacksonian minority in the Democratic party and the less-than-cohesive Whig opposition to the Democrats.[13]

Life-long Democrats such as Sam Houston and United States Congressman Andrew Jackson Hamilton called themselves Union Democrats by late in the 1850s. They worshipped the original Democrat, Andrew Jackson, and the Union he had preserved against the constitutional heresy of nullification. Houston, one of "Old Hickory's" protégés, declared in 1860 that "I have lived since early life a Jackson Democrat, and as such I shall live as long as I am on the soil of freedom, which has been baptized by the blood of better men than those who seek to inflict upon its vitals a wound no skill can ever cure." Shortly after Texas had seceded, Hamilton appeared before the Congressional Committee of Thirteen during its search for a compromise to the secession crisis. He lamented the breakup of the

Union and said that he had refused to leave Washington "until I [could] lay hold of the altar of my country, and implore Heaven" to end this conflict and restore the United States government, "the noblest structure yet devised by man."[14]

Less-well-known Texans shared Hamilton's sentimental devotion to the Union. "I have been raised in the South and as amatter [sic] of Course am Identified with the South," A.B. Burleson wrote in November 1860, "but I am also Identified with this Government and I am oposed to its over throw." An officer in the Texas Rangers, Burleson had already promised Governor Houston his help in putting down treason. In addition, the enthusiastic young Unionist had, in the true spirit of Jackson, nearly gotten into a fight with a neighbor over the issue of secession. "Dam him I will whip him if he does attempt to stope me from speakeing my sentiments at any place or time."[15]

As Burleson's letter indicates, the extent to which Texans espoused allegiance to the Union often hinged upon the extent to which they admired and were willing to follow Sam Houston, the state's most famous citizen. His bold leadership and Jacksonian rhetoric had in the past attracted disciples as well as voters; unfortunately for Houston, many Texans found his course during the 1850s unpalatable and turned from the teachings of Jackson to those of John C. Calhoun and the "regular" Democrats of Texas. A small contingent rallied behind Houston, however, and they provided a significant opposition to southern radicalism and secession in Texas.[16]

The second branch of opposition to secession had its origins, ironically, in the "conservative" camp of the Democrats' enemies. Old-line Whigs furnished the Democrats in Texas with their initial competition in the late 1840s and early 1850s.[17] When the Whig party's fragile system of alliances collapsed under the weight of internal disputes over slavery, many members experimented with the Know-Nothing party as a Unionist foil to the growing radicalism of the Democrats. Predictably, their relationship with northern antislavery Know-Nothings proved difficult to maintain and impossible to defend, and the party quickly folded after the 1856 election. Many of the Texas Know-Nothings then drifted into an alliance with the renegade Democrats in the "Opposition Clique," which in 1859 temporarily made inroads into the regular Democrats' control of the state when they managed to elect Sam Houston to the governorship. Finally, opponents of secession formed a Texas branch of the Constitutional Union party during the 1860 presidential contest in one last effort to head off radicalism in the state. The 1860 campaign motto of the *McKinney Messenger*—printed on the masthead throughout the fall—spoke for many of these men when it advocated "a union of conservatives, and the defeat of sectionalism." A meeting of Constitutional Unionists in San Antonio late in August resolved that the disruptive issue of slavery should be removed from national politics and urged that the Constitution and laws of the United States—including fugitive slave laws—be strictly obeyed. The resolutions also included a Whiggish reminder that the Union could "be preserved as a fountain of perennial blessings" only if "reconciliation, fraternity, and forbearance" characterized the actions of Americans at this crucial juncture in their history. By the beginning of 1861, their common response to the sectional crisis had blurred the boundaries between Union Democrats, Whigs, and Know-Nothings; each group desperately sought conservative answers to radical questions.[18]

Members of this Unionist coalition issued an "Address to the People of Texas" in January 1861, in an attempt to persuade Texans that secession was not in their best interests and that the convention that would soon meet to debate the question of secession was illegal. Southerners, said the proclamation, should not destroy a government "which is, in most respects, the best in the world," merely because of a difference of opinion on "one or two subjects." Rather than solving all of the South's problems, secession would create new ones—such as high taxes, discriminatory legislation that would divide slaveholders and nonslaveholders, and the need for a large standing army to keep the ever-increasing slave population under control. The Unionists urged Texans to "act with calmness, with dignity, and with a proper appreciation of the momentous issues before them," and to reject the bold but foolhardy course promoted by the secessionists.[19]

Conservatives and other Unionists suffered their final defeat when Texans ignored their advice and overwhelmingly approved the secession ordinance in February, but a few Texans launched their own small counter-revolutions. A groundskeeper complained to convention president O.M. Roberts that someone had attempted to tear down the Texas flag flying over the capitol. The Unionist *Southern Intelligencer* changed its front-page motto from "The World is too Much Governed," to "Texas is too Much Governed by Conventions." James W. Thomas, Unionist editor of the *McKinney Messenger*, promised to carry on the fight against "tyrants and usurpers . . . so long as freedom of opinion is tolerated." Perhaps the most spontaneous act of resistance came in March during the Confederate oath-taking ceremony at the capitol. When Gov. Edward Clark, Houston's lieutenant governor and successor, rose to swear his allegiance, a young woman spat from the gallery directly onto the Ordinance of Secession lying on the podium before him.[20]

Yet such displays were the exception. Loyalty to section usually prevailed over loyalty to nation, and most Unionists ruled out any sort of challenge to the new order. Some came to believe that the federal govern-

ment under the control of the Republicans actually endangered their way
of life, others turned into fire-eaters in response to the federal government's decision to force the seceded states back into the Union, and many
others simply resigned themselves to accepting the South's fate as their
own. Doubtless many agreed with Collin County's Abraham Enloe, who
in January wrote, "I am a Union man I was born under the United States
Constitution I have staid under till I am in my 59th year I am satisfyed to
remain so if we can Enjoy our usual Lights & liberties if not do as our fore
fathers Has done before us fight for liberty liberty or death I must have."
These were the conditional Unionists, men whose loyalty to the United
States had never wavered until the federal government actually threatened
southern rights, southern security, or slavery. By the spring of 1861, they
had joined the majority of Texans in resisting federal coercion and in
shifting their loyalty to a government that seemed dedicated to protecting
the rights and principles of southerners.[21]

This transformation from Unionism to secessionism reveals the delicate nature of the loyalty of many southerners and the way that most of
them gradually edged toward conformity. In Texas, the change was demonstrated by Henry A. Maltby, editor of the *Corpus Christi Ranchero*. In
January 1860, Maltby artfully linked the sectional crisis with the current
problems on the Rio Grande, and urged politicians in the United States to
end the debate over slavery and to join forces to conquer Mexico. This
would solve the border problem, provide markets for northern manufacturers and land for southern slaveholders, and take everyone's mind off the
sticky slavery question. "To cut each other's throats for niggers is certainly
absurd," he wrote, "and we have come to the very banks of the Rubicon
which only madmen would attempt to pass." In June, Maltby urged his
readers to "Pay no attention to demagogues and we are safe, listen to them,
do as they bid, and the Union is doomed." In the same issue, the paper
endorsed the Southern Democrat Breckinridge for president as the only
candidate with a prayer of defeating Lincoln.

The conditional nature of Maltby's Unionism surfaced after Lincoln's
election. On November 10, an editorial deplored the growing spirit of
disunion in the southern states. A fortnight later a report appeared of "an
unmistakable disposition" to "never . . . submit to the humiliation which
now threatens the South." A long list of wrongs committed by the Republicans against the South accompanied it, but conspicuously absent was
Maltby's usual plea to ignore fanatics. By early January, articles in the
Ranchero promoted secession and warned that any delay would be disastrous. On February 2, the *Ranchero* declared that separation was a matter
of self-preservation, if nothing else, and two months later it predicted that
separation would be peaceful, permanent, and prosperous. By April 20,

when news of the fighting at Fort Sumter reached Texas, Maltby had completed his 180-degree turnabout. "Those who are not for us, are against us," he proclaimed. "Is there a man in the south who . . . can proclaim himself an ally, confederate or apologist of the Black Republicans, or a passive submissionist to their doctrine of coercion? We hope not." The editor of the *Corpus Christi Ranchero*, like many other Texans, had made the transition from a legitimate dissent against southern extremism to an acceptance of the logic, necessity, and patriotism of disunion. Those Texans who refused to make that change found the road they traveled during the next four years littered with obstacles that tested their loyalty to the Union and guarded by vigilant sentries eager to punish them for their heresies.[22]

Fellow travelers along that road came from the state's blacks, Germans, and Hispanics—the largest groups of "outsiders" in Texas society in 1861. Together they amounted to well over a third (37.4 percent) of Texas's 1860 population of 604,215. Blacks—182,566 slaves and 355 free negroes constituted 30.3 percent of the population—were inextricably connected to the questions of how southern society should be shaped and of whites' loyalty to the South. Although they did not participate in the politics of Texas, they obviously did not support slavery and were frequently suspected of mounting insurrections against the institution. Their imagined roles as rebels in 1860 had helped push Texans toward secession, and the response of whites to slavery often determined whether or not they would be considered loyal or disloyal. As a result, even at a time when blacks enjoyed no tangible power within the larger society, they cast a very long shadow over the thoughts and deeds of Texans. The relatively small but geographically concentrated and highly visible groups of Germans and Mexicans enjoyed normal political and legal rights, but as "outsiders" they had to work harder than Anglos to prove their loyalty to the South and to Texas. Mexicans rarely fit into southern or even Texan society, and by the time the war began some no doubt hoped for the defeat of their age-old enemies. These attitudes led white Texans to question the loyalty of Mexican-Texans to their adopted state—or, more accurately, to the state and the nation that had unilaterally "adopted" them. A minority of Germans, however, created unfavorable perceptions of all Germans by publicly challenging the institution of slavery. Although most Germans denied affiliation with this group, suspicion of their loyalty lingered and made their situation difficult during the Civil War and Reconstruction.[23]

After several decades of immigration, by 1860 the 30,000 Texans of German stock accounted for 7 percent of the state's free population and 5 percent of its total population. For most of the 1840s, colonizers lured Germans to southern and eastern Texas. Many settled in San Antonio,

Galveston, and Houston, while others formed rural communities that for generations reflected their German heritage. After 1848, a new wave of immigration brought a different strain of German immigrant to Texas. These "Forty-eighters," refugees from the failed German revolution of 1848, settled on the western frontier in the counties of Gillespie, Mason, Kerr, and Medina. The first contingent of German immigrants was provincial and conservative and had accepted with few reservations the predominant states' rights philosophy in Texas. Their revolutionary experiences in Europe had shaped the opinions of the second group, however. As republicans, nationalists, and liberals, these intellectuals were accustomed to challenging authority and the existing state of society. Some of these later German colonies went so far as to ban slavery.[24]

Despite the presence of abolitionism among Germans, the actions of most foreign-born settlers gave Texans no reason to suspect their loyalty. The thrifty and industrious Germans cemented their interests to those of other Texans and quickly fit into the Texas economy as small farmers or as craftsmen in the larger towns. Most of them indicated their willingness to abide by Texas political norms by following their American neighbors into the Democratic party. The actions of the more recently arrived and less predictable liberals, however, led Texans to suspect the loyalty of all Germans. In May 1854, the liberals met in San Antonio during the annual *Saengerfest* and issued a series of resolutions later called the "San Antonio Platform." The platform contained a number of progressive social, political, and religious reforms, but its most volatile plank—as well as its most publicized—declared "that slavery is an evil, whose final removal is essential to the foundation of democracy" and urged southern state governments to take steps to eliminate the institution.[25]

The San Antonio meeting inspired a storm of criticism and sparked a scramble by the majority of Germans to divorce themselves from the abolitionism of a few of their countrymen. Several hundred Germans met in New Braunfels to disapprove "in the highest degree" of the actions taken by the San Antonio convention. The meeting closed with three cheers for the Constitution and for Texas, followed by an enthusiastic parade through town. Alexander Rossey informed the *Dallas Herald* that the delegates at San Antonio did not speak for the majority of the Germans in Texas. This is not to say that most Germans favored slavery. Rossey admitted that "the German population . . . is very delicately situated with reference to this question, socially and politically," and, in fact, most Germans opposed slavery. Frederick Law Olmsted, the Yankee who toured Texas before the controversy, confirmed Rossey's assertion and contended that most Texans were wary of the Germans' antislavery views. On the other hand, he wrote, Germans were "sensitive to the overbearing propensities" of planters "accustomed to regard all neighbors out of their own class as White Trash."26

The difference between the minority who approved of the San Antonio platform and the majority who tried to disassociate themselves from it was that the former—as often as not revolutionary refugees—hoped to turn their beliefs into actions, while the latter—often people who had lived and worked in the South for over a decade—believed it was impractical as well as impolitic to express opinions antagonistic to the slaveholders who dominated Texas.

The Germans' internal debate provided ammunition for the fledgling American party in Texas. The San Antonio platform seemed to verify the party's nativist arguments and at the same time offered the generally Unionist Know-Nothings a chance to establish their proslavery credentials. The platform suggested that the Germans in Texas represented a threat to slavery and to southern institutions, despite the conservative Germans' violent denunciations of the minority's actions. When Adolf Douai, liberal editor of the German-language *San Antonio Zeitung*, came out in support of the San Antonio platform, his colleagues around the state denounced him as a Free-Soiler and suggested that he be banished, tarred and feathered, or even drowned. His enemies finally forced him to leave Texas in 1856. The debate raged through the election of 1856, when the Know-Nothings faded from Texas politics. The attack ultimately confirmed the Germans' membership in the Democratic party and enforced an orthodoxy among them on the question of slavery that had not previously existed, an orthodoxy that was strengthened during the insurrection scare of 1860.27

Significantly, during the election of 1860, the editors of two of the state's leading German-language newspapers sounded like any other pair of Texan editors who disagreed over secession. Neither Ferdinand Flake of the Galveston *Die Union* nor Ferdinand J. Lindheimer of the *Neu Braunfelser Zeitung* considered himself an abolitionist, and both defended the right to own slaves. Like many Texans, however, they differed over the value to the South of the Union. Both were Democrats, but supported different presidential candidates in 1860. Flake favored Douglas and shared with the diminutive Illinoisan a sentimental Jacksonian love for the Union. Lindheimer endorsed Breckinridge and, like many Southern Democrats, stressed the practical benefits the Union offered. Both approached secession cautiously, but after Lincoln's election Lindheimer asserted that the question had become a matter of sacrificing "the South to the Union or the Union to the South." Flake refused to give up, and even after the secession convention adjourned he wrote that he still hoped "in the last hour, to see the Union saved." Flake's stubbornness led an angry mob to destroy his press in early January 1861. By spring, Flake had reluctantly pledged his support to the Confederacy.[28]

Even though these two influential Germans remained well within the southern mainstream in their approach to slavery and the Union, a suspicion of Germans lingered among Anglo-Texans. One rumor alleged that the Germans were involved in the slave insurrection of 1860, and the somewhat less-than-enthusiastic reception of secession by the Germans in 1861—four German-dominated counties in West Texas voted against the secession ordinance—seemed to underscore their tenuous loyalty to the southern cause. The reactions of many Germans to wartime pressures would amplify these doubts and perceptions and bring down on Texas Germans the wrath of vigilant Confederates.[29]

The antebellum and wartime persecution of the 12,443 Mexican-born residents of Texas (2.1 percent of the total population) had little to do with politics, although the traditional bloc voting of Mexicans in Texas border towns and in San Antonio drew much criticism from Anglo opponents. Rather, the Anglos' exaggerated perception of Mexican disloyalty was a function of the complex relationships among Mexicans, Anglos, and Afro-American slaves. Ever since American settlers began arriving in Texas in the 1820s, racism, economic conflict, and the frequent warfare between Texas and Mexico had poisoned relations between Anglos and Mexican residents of Texas, or *tejanos*. Exceptions came out of a tiny minority of tejanos, represented by the Benavides family of Laredo and a few other wealthy landholders, who sought the economic benefits stability would bring to the borderlands. As a result, they identified more with the Anglo population than with the Mexican, and to a fairly large extent were exempt from the penalties normally associated with their race in Texas.[30]

Despite such highly visible examples, to white Protestant Texans, Catholic Mexicans appeared lazy, ignorant, immoral, shiftless, dirty, superstitious, and doomed to subservience. The latter's wretched economic position—caused in part by the Anglo practice of seizing Mexican land through complicated legal maneuvers or by forcing sale at ludicrously low prices—encouraged racial arrogance. The primary conflict lay, however, in the Mexicans' antipathy toward slavery and their friendly acceptance of blacks as equals. "Not only [do Mexicans] consider a nigger equal with themselves," complained the *Corpus Christi Ranchero*, "but they actually court the company of the Negroes." Worse still, white Texans believed that Mexicans often helped slaves to escape, and they usually blamed the Mexicans for instigating slave rebellions. In the mid-1850s, Texans mounted an expedition that drove across the border in search of fugitive slaves.[31]

Frederick Law Olmsted accurately portrayed Texans' attitudes toward

Mexicans when he wrote that the latter "were regarded in a somewhat unchristian tone, not as heretics or heathen to be converted with flannel and tracts, but rather as vermin, to be exterminated." He characteristically emphasized the Mexicans' "abhorrence" of slavery and noted that "they consort freely with the negroes, making no distinction from pride of race." This inspired a "standing joke" in Texas taverns that he claimed to have heard at least fifty times. The gist of it was: "a nigger in Mexico is just as good as a white man, and if you don't treat him civilly he will have you hauled up and fined by an alcalde [mayor]." Listeners always greeted the notion that a black person deserved the same legal rights as a white with "great amusement." A former slave named Felix Haywood attested to the Mexicans' compassion for black slaves. "In Mexico," he declared, "you could be free. They didn't care what color you was, black, white, yellow or blue." Haywood claimed that hundreds of slaves escaped to Mexico. The tejanos' lack of prejudice against blacks seemed to endanger the institution of slavery, and Olmsted found that whenever slaveholders moved into a region, "it has been found necessary to treat [the Mexicans] as outlaws," to drive them from their homes, and to forbid them "on pain of no less punishment than instant death, to return to the vicinity of the plantations." A woman near Victoria summarized the attitudes and wishes of white Texans when she told Olmsted that, "white folks and Mexicans were never made to live together, anyhow, and the Mexicans had no business here." Since the law protected them so well, "the Americans would just have to get together and drive them all out of the country."[32]

Texans did, in fact, drive a good many Hispanics out of Texas in the years after the Texas Revolutionary War. Even Juan Seguín, a hero at San Jacinto, had to leave after his life was threatened in the 1840s. In 1857, American teamsters murdered seventy-five Hispanic competitors in the famous "Cart War"; their violence succeeded in driving most Mexican cartmen out of San Antonio. In the Rio Grande Valley, Anglo ranchers established their dominance just as surely as their central-Texas counterparts, but in a different way. Rather than eliminating Mexican rivals, Americans tended to assume the traditional roles of the Mexican elite and worked out a patriarchal accommodation with their *peones* and *vaqueroes*—their manual laborers and cowboys.[33]

A generation of racial struggles culminated in the fall of 1859. That autumn, a landed tejano named Juan Cortina gathered a large band of Mexicans from both sides of the border and terrorized the region around Brownsville. Cortina's men burned ranches, murdered several Anglos, and actually occupied Brownsville for a short time, while Texans grew hysterical. The *Corpus Christi Ranchero* called Cortina's supporters in the Rio Grande Valley "idle, vicious, depraved, thievish, ignorant and fanatical," and predicted that unless the legislature put a stop to such brigandism, "an endless war of the races will be the result." The *Navarro Express* in Corsicana recalled the previous instances of war between Texas and Mexico, when "an American expected none, neither did he ask any quarter from a Mexican." During those "dark days of Texas . . . an empire was wrested from their grasp." The *Express* warned "the nondescript and *priest ridden* Government of Mexico" to "look well to its territory! A day of reckoning is close at hand . . . when the nationality of Mexico will have 'gone glimmering,' and its name and race be numbered among the things that were." The Mexican government managed to survive, and a contingent of Texas Rangers finally defeated Cortina. But the episode symbolized the decades of what amounted to a cold war along the Rio Grande, served to further embitter Texans against Mexicans, and raised serious doubts about the loyalty of the Mexicans living in Texas.34

To be sure, many Germans and Mexicans later distinguished themselves in the Confederate army or in state militia organizations, endured wartime taxes and privations, and fulfilled their "duty" in a number of other ways. But like the minority of white, American-born Texans who refused to bear allegiance to the Confederacy, the minority of Germans and Mexicans who actively dissented based their dissent on prewar experiences. In the same fashion, Texans drew on ideas and attitudes formulated before Texas had seceded from the Union and before any shots were fired at Fort Sumter to create their perceptions of disloyalty among the "foreigners" in their midst.35

But not all disloyal southerners or Texans came from political or ethnic minority groups. Indeed, only wartime conditions can explain the dissidence of many Texans. As what Morton Grodzins characterizes as indolent patriots, they went along with secession and remained nominally loyal to the Confederacy and to their state until their lives were somehow adversely affected by this relationship. Only when their "life-situations" warranted a change did they withdraw their loyalty from the Confederacy and, in effect, become free agents, loyal only to themselves and hoping only to get through the war with life, limb, and property intact. Even the sanctions exerted against them by the various government authorities proved incapable of enforcing the loyalty of the entire population.36

Dissent against southern values and against the Confederacy originated from a number of sources in Texas. A common denominator, however, was the explicit or implied criticism of southern society reflected in the reasons some Texans dissented. Virtually none of the Unionists advocated the end of slavery or of any other important southern institutions, but they did fear that secession—or the implementation of any of a number of radical southern proposals—would threaten the economy and security of southern society. Blacks played a rather passive role in all of this, but their mere presence, and the knowledge among even the most enthusiastic supporters of slavery that they would, if possible, change their status, informed the perceptions and actions of other Texans. A large minority of Germans approved of very little in the social, economic, and political systems of the South; their statements earned all Texans of German stock the enmity of the state's Anglo-Saxons. Finally, most of the state's tejanos, as outsiders in their native land, had no reason to support slavery or any other southern bulwark. The society over which everyone was fighting held few opportunities for them. By the same token, few Mexican-Texans shared the Germans' love for the Union, since they enjoyed few kinship or political ties to the rest of the Union.

The groundswell of apparent unanimity among Texans during their surge toward secession put these anti- and nonsecessionists on the defensive and kept them there for four years. Some reluctantly joined the Confederate cause, others defied the rebels and actively worked for a Union victory, while many simply kept their heads down and stayed out of the way of their local vigilance committees and provost marshalls. John T. Allan seemed to understand the confusion and danger that faced Unionists and other non-Confederates. "Fogs and mists envelope the future," he wrote a few days after the war began at Fort Sumter. "Yet I hope for the best, while attempting to peer through the gloom." The war years would further heighten differences among Texans, and provide even greater opportunities for demonstrations of loyalty and vigilance.[37]

3

The Confederate Unionists
and the War

James W. Throckmorton begat a legend when he rose to cast his vote on the Texas secession ordinance in February 1861. "In the presence of God and my country—and unawed by the wild spirit of revolution around me," he declared to the assembled delegates in the Austin convention, "I vote 'no!'" When secessionist hisses drowned out the scattering of Unionist cheers in the gallery, Throckmorton added, "Mr. President, when the rabble hiss, well may patriots tremble!" Convention president O.M. Roberts finally quieted the noisy mixture of outrage at and admiration for Throckmorton's courage, and the roll call continued. During the celebration that followed the one-sided vote of 166 to 8, Throckmorton and six of the other men who voted against secession slipped out of the capitol and posed for a group portrait. The photograph of the seven stern, weary men was neither printed nor displayed in Texas for sixty-six years.[1]

Throckmorton represented those southern men who clung to the Union until the last possible moment, then reluctantly gathered their courage and honor to follow their states into civil war. Not all Confederate Unionists matched Throckmorton's indignation over secession and subsequent grim service to the Confederate cause, but many shared his desire to preserve southern institutions and society—especially the liberties of individual southerners—from Rebels as well as Yankees. Like Throckmorton, many Confederate Unionists had been Whigs, and they carried their Whig conservatism with them into their careers as Confederate politicians, soldiers, or citizens. And like Throckmorton, they were alarmed by the fatal political factionalism that soon divided the Confederacy, by the waning spirit of the southern people in the face of shortages and hardships, by the flagging enthusiasm of prewar fire-eaters during the dark years of fire and death, and by what they believed was a growing disregard within the Confederate government for the civil rights of southern citizens.

It is not surprising that these steadfast Unionists turned into Con-

federates. Their Unionism was a condition of their southernism, and
although their ideals lodged them solidly between the proverbial rock and
a hard place, they could not turn their energies against home and kin.
Their state and region needed their talents and experience, and they
naturally took their places as leaders and public servants. They opposed
secession, but their hatred of radicalism also led them to condemn abolitionism. In their fight against the latter, they refused to acquiesce to what
they saw as abuses by men who initiated the former. They acquired roles as
watchdogs of the Confederacy, trying to keep the war on a course consistent with their own perceptions of the southern cause.

In 1860 and 1861 they expected fellow conservatives in the North to
slow the sectional strife sown by Republicans, but were disappointed.
Reluctantly, they went to war, expecting Confederate leaders to hold on
course the revolution they had made. They were disappointed in those
hopes, too. In many ways, these men who at times explored the frontiers of
loyalty to the South were more loyal than men who had never questioned
the necessity or wisdom of secession; they hated the sunshine patriots who
had led the South into war and then carefully got out of the line of fire when
the shooting started. They mourned the destruction of their union, and
resented having to choose between their country and their homes. The
agony of that decision made them determined rebels fighting, in the end,
for a cause they had not made.

James Throckmorton delivered his "no" vote against secession on his
thirty-sixth birthday. A native of Tennessee, he moved with his family to
Arkansas and then to Texas, settling in Collin County in 1842, near what
became McKinney. After schooling in Kentucky and army service in the
Mexican War, Throckmorton practiced medicine in Texas until 1851, when
he was elected as a Whig to the state house of representatives from Collin,
Johnson, Baccus, and Denton counties. His constituents reelected him
twice and in 1857 sent him to the state senate.[2]

Throckmorton devoted much of his career in the legislature to promoting railroads and to untangling old land-claim controversies in his district.
As a Whig and a Unionist, Throckmorton helped lead the Opposition party
in Texas, and by 1859, he followed Sam Houston's lead in believing that
slavery and southern rights could best be protected within the Union.
Throckmorton tried to prevent the holding of a secession convention, then
won election as a Unionist delegate from Collin County. After he voted
against secession at the convention, he campaigned to defeat the ordinance in the state referendum and opposed the adoption by the convention of the Confederate Constitution. Nevertheless, when the convention
reassembled in March to execute the will of the people, Throckmorton

accepted the results. "The die is cast," he said grimly, in words echoed by Unionists all over the South, "the step has been taken, and regardless of consequences I expect and intend to share the fortunes of my friends and neighbors." Residents of his home county of Collin mirrored his actions. They defeated the secession ordinance by more than a two-to-one margin, and at a public meeting in McKinney in late April denounced all of the actions of the Austin convention. Nevertheless, now that a war "which we had no part in bringing on" had broken out, Collin County accepted her collective duty as "citizens true and loyal," and marched to war with Throckmorton.[3]

Throckmorton did not promise to share his friends' fortunes lightly. He promptly took the oath of allegiance to the Confederacy, helped raise a regiment of volunteers, and led his men into combat in the Indian Territory, at Elk Horn Tavern in Arkansas, and in Louisiana; he sat in the state senate during a crucial wartime session; he received brigadier's stars from the state and Confederate governments; and he finished the war as a Confederate Indian commissioner.[4]

Despite his steady service to the Confederacy, Throckmorton believed that the cause had been lost from the beginning, despaired at the death and destruction inflicted upon his section, and seethed at the incompetence, corruption, and inconstancy demonstrated by Confederate leaders. He conveyed many of these thoughts in a January 1862 letter to his friend and fellow Unionist, Benjamin H. Epperson of Red River County.[5] Throckmorton mourned the death in the 1850s of "the good old Whigh [*sic*] party and its principles," and wistfully remembered his vision of a bright future. But corruption crept into the federal government and the major political parties; the people "suffered themselves [to be] lead [*sic*] hither & thither by demagogues, until suddenly they now find themselves involved in a bloody civil war & difficulties out of which there is no pathway or passage but what is marked with ruin & blood."

Throckmorton attacked those arch secessionists who in 1861 had foolishly predicted a peaceful withdrawal from the Union, "who have reviled & slandered and traduced" those who opposed secession. Yet, while Throckmorton and other true patriots endured the "cold & merciless storms of winter," the very men who had led the South to war were "nestling close to comfortable fiers [*sic*] with their household idols around them." For those men, who had forsaken "the flag of that section which they professed to love so well," Throckmorton had nothing but contempt. "I regard them not—and only regret that our country's air should be polluted by their poisonous breath—which stinks in the nostrils of evry [*sic*] patriot."

Throckmorton voiced his dismay at the rumors of corruption and factionalism that had already surfaced in the infant Confederacy. He was not sure where the problems lay, "but certain it is [that] their [sic] is imbicility or corruption some where." The presence in the Confederate government of the factionalism and the malfeasance that he believed had ruined the old Union angered Throckmorton. "Surely it can not be so," he protested. "The man or men must be corrupt indeed who would, at such a time as this when we are groaning under the burthens of war, forget a patriots duty and seek self aggrandizement at the expense of, perhaps, the very existence of our Nationality."

Throckmorton failed to exorcise all his demons of despair in the twelve-page jeremiad, and later letters to Epperson revealed more of his Whiggish, Unionist concerns with the conduct and loyalty of his fellow southerners. In February 1864, Throckmorton—at this time a state senator—confessed that recent war news "has given me the real blue devils all over." He attributed the "depression & want of confidence" in the southern people at this depressing stage of the war to the fact that "the great heart of the southern people was not in this contest at the beginning" and to their lack of confidence in the Confederate leaders, who were now "astounded & overwhelmed with the difficulties allready encountered" in the war for independence.[6]

Throckmorton demonstrated the characteristic Unionist concern about civil rights violations, even when they stemmed from the Confederate government's attempts to prosecute the war. In June 1864, he approved the dissenting opinion of Associate Justice James H. Bell of the Texas Supreme Court, who denied the constitutionality of conscription. "It is of pure metal," he wrote, "and will stand high in future as among the ablest papers in exposition of our form of government, and in vindication of the rights of the people." He protested to Gov. Pendleton Murrah the illegal arrest and mistreatment of one Isaac Ward later in the year. "This species of outrage, and of a much more serious & reprehensible character," he complained, "have been continually practiced upon the people of the frontier." Throckmorton hated these activities because they violated the constitutional liberties of the people, but on a more practical level he feared that the victims of such abuses "cannot be relied upon or expected to sustain the cause of our country."[7]

Throckmorton also attacked the Confederacy's treatment of its citizens on the floor of the state senate. In the fall of 1864, the senate considered declaring that only the Confederate government had the power to make peace with the North and that Texas would never consent to reconstruction. Throckmorton substituted a set of resolutions that refused to dismiss a negotiated end to the war. When Sen. Chauncey Shepard of Brenham declared that "blood would flow & any man who talked of reconstruction would be hanged," Throckmorton retorted with a long speech that began with a review of the course of the war thus far. He described the early enthusiasm of the southern people, and "how they flocked to the standard in the beginning." But ever since that time, the Confederate government had done nothing but rob them of their liberty and property. He castigated the conscription laws, the suspension of habeas corpus, the currency and impressment acts, the mismanagement of military matters, and sundry other "unconstitutional burdens & petty exactions heaped upon the people." If the war ended in Confederate defeat, he declared, "these were the causes that would lead to it." Throckmorton reminded the senate of the immense amount of territory lost by the Confederate army and of the gradually rising maximum conscription age, and predicted that one day the Confederate armies, manned by 100-year-old men, would be driven all the way to the Gulf coast. And even then, after so much hardship, suffering, and death, if a survivor—an old man, or widow, or "blood stained soldier who had fought from Manasas to Gettysburg's bloody field"— should happen to let slip that he favored some sort of reconstruction in order to end the carnage, he would "be set upon by a mob of fanatics, who had contributed neither blood nor treasure, and be treated to a rope & a limb because he dared to express himself as a freem[a]n." Throckmorton finally finished, and sat down, in what he remembered as a "death like stillness."

His eloquence went for naught, as the legislature passed a number of tough-sounding resolutions. They reminded Texans that northern aggression had started the war, denied that the South was fighting merely to preserve slavery, stated that the terrible atrocities committed by northern armies eliminated any hope of reunion, and declared, "we are forbidden to admit a thought of further association with the people of the North." Nevertheless, Throckmorton wrote Epperson that his two-hour speech had opened "a new era . . . in this revolution," when "one man was found who dared speak out, and who had the temerity to lay bare the hiddeous gaping wounds that were festering & cankering in the public heart." With a trace of perverse pride he believed that the colleagues who avoided him after the speech actually thought he might be arrested for sedition.[8]

Throckmorton's contempt toward the vigilance with which some Texans planned to enforce Confederate loyalty and his dissent against the policies of the Confederate government betrayed his own flirtation with what many of his colleagues would have labeled disloyalty. His passion for protecting the rights of Texans—even those who dissented from the southern gospel—sprang from his own agonizing decision to submit to secession, from his acute awareness of the weaknesses of the southern military position, and especially from his distrust of southern leaders whose decisions to become Confederates had been much easier for them than Throckmorton's had been for him. Although his prewar conservatism led him to oppose revolutions against both the United States and the Confederate States, it also inspired him to oppose violations of the liberty that his new country fought to protect. Throckmorton and others like him validated their loyalty to the Confederacy—a loyalty to which they clung tightly because of their difficult personal decisions to become rebels—by attempting to keep the South true to its original goals of guaranteeing individual liberties and freedom from meddling outsiders.

Throckmorton represents those southerners who could not join in the wild celebrations that accompanied secession in many southern states and towns. For them, pledging their loyalty to the new government was a matter of duty, not choice. The South Carolinian Alfred Huger wrote Benjamin Perry "that my life had been prolong'd beyond what my own happiness would have required as its end," but vowed to stand with his state. If she was invaded, or "her soil saturated with the blood of her children! whether she be right or wrong, where can I be, but in the middle of her desolation! meeting her destiny & sharing her Sorrows?" Other Unionists were less morbid, believing that they must make the best of a bad situation. North Carolina Congressman Zebulon Vance wrote from Washington, D.C., that "we are swallowed up and hurried along the rushing tides of time." Now was the time to "prepare . . . for our safety and honor, by steering with, and not against the rushing volume. Unable to do as we wish, we must do as we can." An Arkansas diarist contributed money to a local volunteer company, admitting that "the trouble is on us and . . . we must defend our own borders at all events. Wicked men have brought it on us but it is too late now to look to that, we must make the best fight we can." Alexander Stephens stated succinctly in February 1861, that "we are now in the midst of a revolution. . . . It is bootless to argue the causes that produced it. . . . The wise man—the patriot and statesman in either section—will take the fact as it exists, and do the best he can under the circumstances."9

In swallowing the bitter pill of secession, most Unionists grimly granted their support and service to their states and to the Confederacy. Vance became colonel of a volunteer regiment and later served two terms as wartime governor of North Carolina, while Stephens, of course, accepted the vice presidency of the Confederate states. Even the life-long Unionist Benjamin F. Perry of South Carolina found ways to contribute to the southern war effort. When his state seceded, he wrote, "the American People seem demented. . . . They are exulting over the destruction of the best and wisest form of government ever vouched by God to man. Fools &

wicked fools they know not what they do." Nevertheless, Perry acted as a lieutenant of a home guard company, as a state legislator, and as a Confederate confiscation agent, recruiter, and district judge.[10]

Perhaps the most reluctant rebel on record in Texas was Walter Hyns, the son of a Smith County planter and slaveowner. A family slave called her master "the most hard hearted man I ever seen" for sending Walter to war against his wishes. "Walter was the best one of the family and his father just hated him cause he would take up for us niggers, so he made him go to war." Walter defiantly told his father the morning he left "that he wasn't fighting to keep the slaves, he was fighting to free them, that he wanted to be killed." The boy's mother "told him [if] he thought so much of the niggers he would be better off dead." Sure enough, "he was killed, just blowed to pieces, they could not find enough to send him home."[11]

Of course, Texas Confederates rarely went so far as Walter Hyns in their opposition to the war. In fact, the reactions of Texas Unionists to secession varied widely. Few contributed so much to and at the same time dissented so bitterly against the Confederacy as James Throckmorton. But a number of the state's leading Unionists—like antisecessionists all over the South—entered the Confederate service when it became apparent that their only alternative was to commit treason against their state and their region. The federal government's aggressive policies following the attack on Fort Sumter removed the last doubts from the minds of many former Unionists. At least two of the men who voted with Throckmorton against secession at the Austin convention—Thomas P. Hughes and Lemuel Hardin Williams, both of Lamar County—joined the army and fulfilled their duty as loyal Texans and southerners. Another active Lamar County Unionist, E. L. Dohoney, believed that secession had been accomplished only "by a species of fallacious reasoning, and by bulldozing," but chose state loyalty over national loyalty and recruited his own company of rebels. He ended the war as a captain, but not without objecting to the conscription act as "one of the most despotic laws ever enacted." His stand on civil rights was not as consistent as it might have been, however; he also collected the hated Confederate tax-in-kind.[12]

Robert H. Taylor, a Bonham lawyer and legislator, had early in 1861 pleaded with the special session of the legislature to halt Texas's march toward secession. "I want my people to wake up, think for themselves, act like men who have rights to lose," he shouted, "we must forget partisanship & personal gain and save the Union." Nevertheless, when secession finally occurred, he wrote to Benjamin H. Epperson, "let it not be said that you & I were laggard." He urged Epperson to join the war effort, so that "in the future none can say th[at] we led the opposition to secession

& then stood by and saw the country go to the Devil without staying the tide of war." Taylor followed his own advice, and despite his ardor for the union, he raised three regiments for the Confederate service. [13]

Epperson, James Throckmorton's best friend and fellow Unionist, followed Throckmorton into the Confederacy. A game leg kept him out of the army, but he willingly granted the South his political and economic support. A Texas resident since the early 1840s, Epperson was a Red River County lawyer, railroad promoter, and state representative. In politics he was, consecutively, a Whig, a Know-Nothing, and a candidate for Constitutional Union presidential elector in 1860, as well as a confidant of Governor Houston, Throckmorton and most of the other prominent Unionists in Texas. [14]

With Throckmorton, Epperson fought secession in North Texas (45 percent of the citizens in his Red River County voted against secession), but when Texas finally seceded, he reluctantly but firmly made the transition to Confederate Unionist. He participated in public meetings and helped organize and outfit local militia companies. Epperson demonstrated his commitment to the Confederacy in the fall of 1861 when he ran for the Confederate Congress from Texas's Sixth District, but his close association with the antisecession movement in Texas cost him the election. Epperson returned to his law practice in Clarksville after his defeat, and took no more part in Texas politics during the war, although he contributed funds to the Confederate cause. [15]

Other noted Texas Unionists served the Confederacy in less notable ways. The third Lamar County delegate to vote "no" at the secession convention, George W. Wright, acted as an agent, arms buyer, and provost marshall for the Confederacy. Several men who had fought for Texas independence became reluctant Confederates who once again served their national government—the fourth under which they had lived. The most famous of these was Thomas F. McKinney, one of Stephen F. Austin's "old three hundred" and a staunch supporter of the Union. He had ordered the first shot of the Texas Revolution and was an important financial benefactor of the Republic of Texas. Just after Lincoln's election he wrote that the violation of the fugitive slave law was the South's only real grievance, but that problem "has existed for years, and we have born it, why now fly off all at once because Mr. Lincoln has been constitutionally elected?" He urged fellow southerners to "hold on for all time to come to the glorious Union . . . and that celestial flag, the Stars and Stripes," and, if other southerners or northerners chose to commit treason, "let us hurl them out." Nevertheless, when Texas withdrew from the Union, the sixty-four- year-old pioneer went with it and signed on as an agent for the Confederate government. [16]

Some Unionists, although they submitted to secession and to Confederation, gave only a gruding allegiance to the Confederacy. The best known Texan trapped in this nightmare of conflicting loyalties was Sam Houston. As the most famous hero of the Texas Revolution, as president of the Republic of Texas, and as senator and governor of Texas after it became a state, Houston, despite frequent criticism, dominated Texas politics for a quarter of a century. In 1852, the state's Democratic party platform boosted Houston for the national party's presidential nomination, reminding Democrats everywhere that he was "the hero of San Jacinto" and "a patriot, chieftain, and statesman eminently worthy to be the standard bearer of the party." Nine years later, however, a Texas newspaper labeled Houston's attempts to prevent the secession of his beloved state as "a labored effort to bamboozle the people, whom he has tried to lead by the nose in the present crisis."[17]

Houston's unyielding adherence to Jacksonian Democracy—all he "ever professed, or officially practised"—caused this dramatic turnaround in the public's perception of him. Unfortunately for the old warrior, the Unionism implicit in his political stance became increasingly unfashionable in the South as the events of the 1850s unfolded. Although his rough-and-tumble style and personal popularity helped him upset the incumbent Hardin Runnels in the 1859 governor's race, his belief that secession was both unconstitutional and unnecessary reflected the opinions of fewer and fewer of his constituents. Houston hated northern extremists, but the evil promulgated by them was matched, he said, by southern radicals "who foolishly joined in the quarrel and hurled epithet for epithet." He also deprecated the "great many very gaseous gentlemen in the South" who spend "a great deal of time . . . play[ing] the demagogue," with their talk about reopening the African slave trade. They merely wished to "widen . . . the breach between the North and the South," and to prompt the North into a rash action that would justify the South's secession. Houston denied that the election of Abraham Lincoln was sufficient cause for destroying the Union, as his oath as president would force him to protect the rights guaranteed to the South by the Constitution. Furthermore, the destruction of one government required the building of a new and better one, "and if patriots yield now to the rash and reckless, who only aspire to military glory, or for anarchy and rapine, they may find that in the wreck of one free government, they have lost the power to rear another." Houston doubted that the southern people could fight a successful civil war. As the basic principle upon which the new nation rested, the right of secession "must inevitably lead to disunion, conspiracy and revolution, and at last anarchy and utter ruin."[18]

Fear of war and destruction shadowed Houston throughout the secession winter and informed his every action. His delaying tactics resembled his unpopular, long retreat to the Texas coast during the revolution, but this time there was no San Jacinto to salvage the Union. He hesitated to summon a special session of the legislature, and, when he finally spoke to the assembled legislators, he emphasized the problem of frontier defense. At the same time, he refused to call a convention to consider secession, and when it met anyway he did not recognize it until it promised to submit its resolution to a vote of the people. When the secession ordinance passed, he refused to take the requisite oath to the Confederacy and forfeited his office. Finally, he considered—but declined—an offer from the federal government for troops to keep Texas in the Union.[19]

Hounded by severe criticism from all over the state, the old man retired from public life, more or less resigned to his and his country's fate. He had always said that he would bow to the wishes of the majority of his constituents, and the landslide victory for secession in February confirmed what the secessionists had been saying for months. As a result, Houston accepted the fact, if not the justice or the legality, of secession. In a declaration to the people of Texas in mid-March, he asserted his "determination to stand by Texas in whatever position she assumes." He had for many years linked his fortunes to those of his adopted state, "follow[ing] her banners . . . when an exile from the land of my fathers." He had returned to the Union with the people of Texas, and now would "go out from the Union with them; and though I see only gloom before me, I shall follow the 'Lone Star' with the same devotion as of yore." Two months later he spoke at Independence, where he said, "the time has come when a man's section is his country. I stand by mine."[20]

Houston never quite completed his conversion to the Confederate cause, however. He apparently toyed with the idea of declaring himself governor, removing Texas from the Confederacy, and forming an independent republic. He never professed much hope for a southern victory, and when his friend William Pitt Ballinger talked with him in March 1862, Houston complained of the bad generalship that plagued the Confederate army and expressed his dislike for Jefferson Davis. The rest of the conversation left Ballinger a bit bewildered. "Couldn't really fathom what the old fellow would like to be at," the Galveston attorney wrote later that night. "Says he feels as young as at 25—I think he believes we will be overpowered, & subdued." Houston told Ballinger that he had files full of clippings from Texas newspapers "to show any of Lincoln's officers that come about him that he has been a better Black Republican for 2 yrs past then old Abe himself."[21]

But for the most part, Houston stayed at home, tending to his business interests and worrying about his son, who had enlisted in the Confederate army. He occasionally visited Union prisoners of war incarcerated in nearby Huntsville, and his Unionism apparently paid off when a Yankee chaplain, remembering a kindness from Houston when the latter was a senator in the 1850s, nursed Sam Houston, Jr., back to health after the battle of Shiloh. When Sam Sr., died on July 26, 1863, he had not had the opportunity to show his clippings to an invading army, and his Union had not yet been reconstructed. The dead hero remained a symbol of the tension between that spirit of resistance to extremism and that loyalty to one's section and state that was so tragically played out in the lives of many southern conservatives and Unionists during the Civil War. 22

Houston was not alone among this most reluctant class of Confederate Unionists. A contemporary of his, George Washington Smyth, had come to Texas in 1830 and held jobs ranging from teaching school to surveying land for the republic; he later represented Texas in the United States Congress. As the sectional crisis heated up during the late 1850s, Smyth deplored the "little issues"—which for him included the questions of slavery in the territories and the African slave trade—with which demagogues sowed discord between the sections. "We live under the best government and the happiest institutions in the world," he wrote to Thomas McKinney in 1859, "and we have nothing to mar our future prospects, were it not for those restless spirits north and south who seem to do nothing but brood over mischief and hatch evil." Smyth maintained that the "bad faith" of a few northern states did not relieve Texas of her obligations to the Union under the Constitution. By the spring of 1860, Smyth, a life-long Democrat, had become so disgusted by the sectionalism of the Texas Democrats that he was willing to seek election as a presidential elector for Sam Houston. Secession came despite his efforts—he had favored making Texas an independent republic in the event of the dissolution of the Union—and, too old to serve his state himself, he permitted George W. Smyth, Jr., to join the Confederate army. 23

Hamilton Stuart, a Kentuckian who had edited the *Galveston Civilian* for decades, had equally mixed emotions about southern sectionalism. As an editor, he supported slavery and the reopening of the slave trade; as a Douglas Democrat and federal customs collector for the fifteen years preceding secession he opposed disunion. He eventually came around to supporting Breckinridge for president as the South's only hope against the Republicans. He declared his support for Breckinridge at a meeting in Galveston, but admitted that the Southern Democrat had little chance of winning the election. The next speaker blasted Stuart for his caution and elicited cheers from the crowd when he told the editor that "he had better join the enemy if he had no better aid or comfort to give his friends." After Lincoln's election, Stuart indicated that he would submit to the will of the people, since "all political power is inherent in the people and . . . they have at all times the inalienable right to alter, reform, or abolish this form of government." Stuart continued editing the *Civilian* until the blockade cut off his paper supply and forced him to temporarily retire in 1862.[24]

Josephus Cavitt, a long-time resident of Robertson County, exhibited the profound reluctance with which many Unionists fulfilled their duty to the Confederacy. He also demonstrated the common impulse among such men to dissociate themselves from the Confederacy after the war, particularly when they applied for presidential pardons. Cavitt had not recognized the right of a state to secede from the Union, he maintained, but failed to vote against secession in the February referendum because "the numbers in favor of the act" were so large that disagreeing with them "was often calculated to involve those who were opposed to secession in unpleasant and frequently dangerous altercations." As a "peaceable and quiet man," Cavitt obeyed the laws, paid his Confederate taxes, and eventually served in the state militia—although he emphasized in his application for pardon that he was "never in the actual military service of the Confederate States or of the State of Texas." Most of his military duty consisted of being detailed to work his own ranch. He even admitted to having been a lieutenant in the state militia, but stressed throughout his application that his wartime support of the Confederate States did not mean that he accepted its principles or its sovereignty[25]

Some Unionists who at first threw in their lot with the Confederacy changed their minds during the course of the war and went even further than Throckmorton in protesting abuses committed by secessionists. W.R. Bellew had been elected captain of a volunteer company at the beginning of the war, despite his opposition to secession and his work to defeat it in his home county of Collin. However, "When they got to Hanging Union men in Northern Texas" in 1862, he wrote Provisional Governor A.J. Hamilton after the war, "I denounced it . . . and urged [subdistrict commander Henry] McCulloch to stop those acts of lawlessness." When friends warned Bellew that enemies planned to assassinate him, he escaped to Kentucky and sat out the remainder of the war. Reading Wood Black, the founder of the South Texas town of Uvalde, opposed secession, although his Republican father back in New Jersey had disinherited him for denouncing Abraham Lincoln's "radicalism." He dutifully took the Confederate oath after the war began, but when overvigilant rebels persecuted Germans in West Texas, Black protested by crossing the border into Mexico and staying there for the rest of the war, carrying on extensive trading, milling, and stock-raising activities.[26]

Another man who came to regret his painful decision to support the Confederate war effort was Reece Hughes, who had settled in Cass County in 1839. By 1861, Hughes owned 25,000 acres of land, 200 slaves, and an iron foundry, and he believed that his property and southern rights could best be preserved in the Union. Nevertheless, Hughes generously fed Confederate soldiers marching by his house and aided the needy families of neighbors who were in the army. His prewar Unionism had earned him many enemies, however, and late in the war some of them petitioned Lt. Gen. E. Kirby Smith, the commander of the Trans-Mississippi Department, to have Hughes "executed as a public enemy." His own friends in high places prevented it, but they could not stop the Confederates from seizing his iron foundry, which federal soldiers later occupied. The war ruined Hughes financially, but neither government ever reimbursed him.[27]

The experiences of two long-time friends, William Pitt Ballinger and James H. Bell, reveal the extremes of loyalty to the Confederacy displayed by Confederate Unionists. Ballinger, a prominent Galveston attorney and behind-the-scenes Whig politician, and Bell, a Democratic associate justice of the Texas State Supreme Court, both worked against secession but accepted it when Texas finally seceded in March 1861. Ballinger served as Confederate sequestration receiver and wrote editorials promoting the war effort for coastal newspapers. Bell continued as supreme court justice until he lost a reelection bid in 1864. They responded to the war quite differently, although each served the Confederacy and remained within the boundaries of what was considered loyal behavior in Texas.

Ballinger came to Texas from Kentucky in 1843, enlisted in a volunteer company during the Mexican War, and married Hallie Jack, the daughter of Texas Revolutionary War hero William H. Jack. By 1860, Ballinger, partnered with his brother-in-law Thomas McKinney Jack, was a successful attorney who was well known throughout the state. A life-long Whig, he supported John Bell for president in 1860 and opposed secession.[28]

During the 1860 campaign and the secession crisis, Ballinger shared other Unionists' disgust with the political passions engendered by secessionist demagogues, worried about the consequences of withdrawing from the Union, and hoped that southern grievances could be resolved within the Union. As 1860 drew to a close, the prolific diarist recorded his "deep distrust of the future" and his belief that "the signs of the times are evil—and there are great dangers before us." Ballinger supported slavery and believed that southerners had legitimate complaints against the government and particularly against the Republican party, but he also felt that solutions to the many problems facing the Union must "be sought peacefully & within the Union & that the disruption of the Union without such

efforts is treason to humanity." Like all good Unionists, he hoped "that
public order & prosperity will not be weakened & that security will be
given to the institution of slavery." However, he wrote, "I have strong fears
to the contrary, and my best judgment is that we are doing an unwise &
may be a fatal thing."[29]

Ballinger's conservatism seems to have paralyzed him during the
crucial two years of sectional controversy in Texas between 1859 and 1861.
He was a friend, sometime attorney to, and supporter of Sam Houston, but
he neglected to vote in the 1859 gubernatorial election. He refused to run
as a Unionist presidential elector or to campaign actively for the John Bell
and Edward Everett electors in Texas. He grudgingly delivered a Constitutional Union speech in August 1860—"It has cost me far more time &
trouble than I was willing to have devoted in that way & it is a poor
business"—but he gave up his attempt to reach the speaker's stand at a
Galveston public meeting–turned secession rally in mid-November. The
day after the meeting, Ballinger reported a "deep apprehension, if not the
positive conviction that our Govt. will be overthrown & the Union dis-
olved." Although this turn of events made him physically ill and cost him
several sleepless nights, he skipped a Union gathering three weeks later.
For the most part, Ballinger did what he did best: listen to his Unionist and
secessionist friends and record their conversations in his diary. An excerpt
from his mournful entry on New Year's Eve characterized the feelings of
many Unionists as events spiraled out of their control: "I feel more than
ever excommunicated from public affairs & politics."[30]

When it became apparent to Ballinger that the Union would be
sundered, he wrote that he had "no heart in the [Southern] cause," and
added peevishly, "Its responsibility & its glory I leave to others." For the
most part, he did. His friends convinced him that he would be more useful
at home than in the army, so he remained in Galveston as a Confederate
sequestration receiver and continued to practice law. He helped to secure
several batteries of heavy guns for the defense of Galveston and wrote
articles for the *Houston Telegraph*. Occasionally he voiced some of the
concern for civil rights that typified Unionists during the war. When he
accepted his appointment as receiver of confiscated enemy alien property,
he feared that "there will be an odium attached to the office," and promised
to "execute it in a just spirit—in maintenance of the policy of the Govt. but
not vindictively or oppressively." He also revealed a flexibility in disposing
of disloyalty cases. After a small federal force captured Galveston in the fall
of 1862 only to evacuate it early in 1863, a number of the residents of the
town were brought up on charges of trading with the enemy. Ballinger
thought this "very injudicious"; the "doctrines of allegiance in Galveston
during its occupation . . . are not such as it wd. be judicious to settle

accurately now." On the other hand, Ballinger wrote up several indictments at Confederate district court "against parties for their connexion with the enemy whilst they occupied Galv."[31]

Ballinger described his own odyssey from Unionist to Confederate in a letter he wrote to his friend and colleague, George W. Paschal, a Unionist who would spend several days in an Austin jail on charges of disloyalty. Ballinger intended this letter—which he never sent—to defuse the "bitterness and vindictiveness" Paschal felt toward the secession leaders. "You have worked yourself morbid," Ballinger wrote, "which distorts your views of the [Confederate] government." He testified to his late-developing conviction that the civil war he and Paschal had feared and hated stemmed from very real causes. He recalled that never before the fall of 1860 had he "passed . . . sadder, gloomier days of deeper truer reflection and self-communing." Ballinger had been "Whiggish even unto federalism" before the war, believing that Democrats were "without property, drunkards, licentious, demagogues . . . fatally bent on mischief" and that "Satan [was] not more the Archfiend of wickedness, the foe to peace, harmony & good order in Heaven, than was Jno. C. Calhoun on earth."

Nevertheless, as events hurried by and as Ballinger came to better understand the position of southern radicals, his mind changed. "For a long time," Ballinger wrote, "I thought the talk against the Union a mere Sham, clap-trap, meant by no body, a tinkling cymbal of a grandiloquent sound, locofoco effervescence, grateful only to a few of the most diabolical ears, out of the lower regions." Then he read John C. Calhoun's "*Book on Government*," which did not convince him of the righteousness of nullification or of secession, but did seem to be an able and perceptive exposition on "the essential dangers of Democratic government" and on the "control of the popular majority." Calhoun helped to convince Ballinger that dissatisfied southerners, even disunionists, were sincere and were not merely spouting radical doctrines for party or individual gain. Of course, neither the North nor the South would budge from the national "superstition" of the "perfection of the American Constitution," and war became inevitable. Americans' "admission of failure in the government, . . . afforded the only hope of its Salvation."[32]

The surprisingly one-sided vote on secession shocked and saddened Ballinger. Nevertheless, with a growing respect for the purposes of the secessionists, a mounting fear that the Republican party posed a danger to southern rights, and a commitment to the idea of creating "further guards against sectional majorities," Ballinger reconciled himself to secession, and ultimately, to civil war.[33]

James H. Bell never quite got used to the idea that his section was at war with the federal government. Bell was the son of Josiah Bell, one of

Stephen F. Austin's lieutenants. Born in 1825—supposedly the first white baby in Brazoria County—Bell had fought against the Mexicans who invaded Texas in the early 1840s, studied law at Harvard University and with Ballinger's father-in-law, William H. Jack, and won election to the Texas Supreme Court in 1858.[34]

Bell had as a Democrat voted for Breckinridge in 1860, but he shared many of Ballinger's views regarding the nature of politics and of political parties. He denied that the question of slavery in the territories was a practical one and believed that the war was brought about by the fatal corruption of rational political processes by politicians who could see only as far as the next election. In a speech at the capitol in Austin on December 1, 1860, Bell detailed his theory of how the country had descended into its present conundrum. Typical of many formal speeches of the day, it ranged over many centuries and several continents, and outlined one man's version of the history of the sectional crisis. Bell argued that legitimate disagreements between the North and South had been magnified all out of proportion by southern radicals obsessed with the specter of northern abolitionism. More important, a "spirit of party" had come to dominate sectional controversies. Northerners were less interested in stopping the spread of slavery than in preventing the creation of more slave state votes in Congress. Nevertheless, southerners, inspired by Calhoun, had focused on slavery, the least important and most dangerous aspect of the sectional conflict, which had only made matters worse. Party feeling had eclipsed patriotism, and now threatened to destroy the Union.

Like a true Unionist, Bell advised his fellow Texans not to "rush hastily into revolution." He recommended holding a southern convention in order to "counsel calmly and deliberately" on how to respond to the emergency. He urged Texans and southerners to remember that the Constitution did protect them, that, although "no one looks with greater abhorance than I do" upon the attitudes and plans of the Republicans, Lincoln was powerless to do anything to the South. The North had not yet committed a single crime against the South. "There are imaginary and future ones without number," Bell declared, "but what are the real ones, upon which a man can put his finger?" Bell could think of none, except the refusal by some northern states to enforce the fugitive slave law. But no one had ever been able to adequately enforce the law; it was not a new grievance that justified revolution, and it did not affect Texas slaveowners, whose runaway slaves usually sought freedom in Mexico.

Bell deplored the illegal meetings, conventions, and proclamations currently sweeping Texas and the rest of the South. These only encouraged the passions that interrupted rational thought and obscured reasonable solutions. "All history attests that appeals to the passions are a thousand

times more powerful than appeals to reason," Bell warned. "Let us, in this
hour of gloom, take counsel of reason." War would be inevitable if disunion
was undertaken hastily. "Let us be true to ourselves," Bell pleaded, "let us
not be made to believe that it is timidity or cowardice to use all honorable
means to shun the fearful evils of Disunion."[35]

Unlike Ballinger, Bell never changed his mind and never accepted the
leadership of Calhoun's disciples. In a February 1865 letter to B.H.
Epperson, the recently unseated former justice wrote that he had always
believed that the restoration of the Union, "was the inevitable result of the
war in which we are engaged." As a result, he had withheld his support
from "the men and principles that have been in the ascendant for now
nearly four years of woe and blood." By 1865, Bell believed that the best
course for Texas would be to pursue a separate peace with the federal
government and suggested that agreeing to gradually emancipate the
slaves would win friends in the North. To that end, Bell urged Texas
Unionists to support "conservative and thoughtful men" in the coming
state elections. With a victory at the polls, conservatives "might perhaps
smooth the wrinkled front of war, reanimate expiring liberty, and restore
order and law to an exhausted people."[36]

Although Ballinger and Bell attributed the war to many of the same
causes, their dissimilar responses to conscription, martial law, and various
other war powers assumed by the Confederate government reveal the
range of opinions that existed within the Confederacy's most conscientious
class of loyal citizens. Ballinger hesitantly accepted Brig. Gen. P.O.
Hebert's proclamation of martial law in Texas in the spring of 1862, but
denounced the general's forced evacuation of the threatened island of
Galveston in May. "The patriotism of poor people left at home," Ballinger
confided to his diary, "will be much better able to sustain itself against the
influence of the enemy, than against the pressure of poverty & exile."[37]

Ballinger did support the suspension of habeas corpus and the high
wartime taxes levied by the Confederate government. "I hope this legislation may do good," he wrote in March 1864, "it is certainly very rigid &
extreme." But despite this "first impression . . . of disapprobation," he
published an editorial in the *Houston Daily Telegraph* that supported
suspension. The constitutions of the United States, the Confederate
states, and of Texas all authorized the suspension of habeas corpus during
periods of rebellion or invasion, he argued. Although the situation in the
eastern states of the Confederacy obviously met these preconditions,
Ballinger also deemed it necessary in the trans-Mississippi region, where
"factions, disloyal and traitorous persons, plotting our subjugation," posed
"really and truly dangerous" threats that demanded harsh measures to
guarantee the safety of Texas. Ballinger, ever the Whig, also justified

suspension because it ensured that civil law would be enforced by the military, which would eliminate the "unorganized, irresponsible mob patriotism" that too often replaced the legitimate, orderly functioning of the law during times of crisis.[38]

Predictably, James Bell denied the right of the Confederate government to deal so severely with its citizens. When the Texas State Supreme Court upheld the Confederate conscription act in 1863, he wrote a minority opinion justifying his lone dissenting vote. Bell based his opinion on the theory that the war powers delegated to Congress by the Constitution were not unlimited, so that while the government did have the power to carry on a war, it was "sheer nonsense" to say that Congress "can use force, or require the Executive Department to use force to compel a citizen voluntarily to enlist." The Constitution limited the government to recruiting volunteers or to calling state militia units into federal service; it could put down rebellions by force, but could not use force to muster an army. Bell asserted that the government formed by the Confederate (or United States) Constitution "was not instituted with a view to the greatest possible efficiency in war," and could not exercise unlimited powers in conducting a war. Furthermore, since the sort of centralization of power entailed in conscripting men for the army smacked of Federalism, it could not possibly be the sort of interpretation of the Constitution that the leaders of the southern rebellion had in mind when they led their states out of the Union in 1861.[39]

Ballinger disagreed with the dissenting justice, and spent an entire day writing a letter that contested Bell's opinion. Ballinger's and Bell's clash over federal power demonstrates their different degrees of conversion to the Confederate cause. Bell stuck to his prewar guns; his Unionism led him to protest the exercise of what he believed to be illegitimate powers by the secessionists' government. Ballinger, no less a Unionist than Bell before the war, came to identify rather closely with the Confederate cause, and accepted many of the programs initiated by the government to win the war. Ballinger's grim commitment to the Confederate cause may also have stemmed from his tragic personal life during the war, when four of his children died of disease and his wife suffered a miscarriage. Ballinger was separated from his family for most of the war because of his official duties and because of the potential danger to them of living in Galveston; his guilt over his absences in such trying times may have stirred him to yearn for the success of the cause for which he had, in a way, sacrificed so much.[40]

The two old friends seem to have talked about the war whenever they saw each other. Early in 1862, Bell told Ballinger of his belief that the Confederacy would lose the war, that the Union would be reconstructed,

and that "the better judgt. of the people [would] return to them—in time."
During a long walk through Houston one Sunday afternoon soon afterward, Bell complained to Ballinger that he had been "ostracised" because
of his political views, and mentioned that he might speak out and tell "the
people what he thinks of public affairs" in order to "vindicate his own
record." He would tell them that the cause was hopeless, that the "best
they could do is to secure honorable terms" from the northern government. [41]

With all the zeal of a convert, Ballinger scolded the unhappy Bell. "I
told him I thought every man's feelings & efforts shd now be to put forth
our utmost strength to whip the enemy & maintain our independence, &
that any discussion now of our inability to do this & of terms with the
enemy shd justly incur all the odium possible." Ballinger said that he
would "prefer to receive the victor's terms after a last blow was spent,"
rather than restore the Union "because of our apprehended weakness." He
once again stressed his dismay at secession, and reiterated his opposition
to it. But it was now too late. If the southern people were forced back into
the union, whether through defeat or through negotiation, "it will be
because they are whipped back, & it will be with a sense of inequality,
dishonor, humiliation & future political insecurity & degradation worse
than that of any people of the globe." Drawing his text from Ecclesiastes,
Ballinger declared that the old Union would never be restored: "the silver
cord is loosd—the golden bowl broken, the pitcher broken at the fountain—the wheel broken at the cistern." If the government is reestablished,
"it will be by force and we will be practically a conquered vassal people."
Ballinger did not record Bell's response to this recitation of the former's
new commitment to the Confederacy, but Ballinger wrote in his diary that,
although "I love him dearly, & I think him . . . the most gifted man of all
my acquaintance . . . I intend to deal with Bell in the strictest candor."[42]

Although not all Texas Unionists supported the southern cause as
firmly as Ballinger, most shared James W. Throckmorton's resignation at
the destruction of the Union. "Now, and since the war commenced,"
Throckmorton wrote early in 1862, "I would not consent to reunite with the
north." He claimed that "the struggle is over with me." The North and
South "had better be separate—Our interests—pursuits & habits are too
diversified ever to be made to harmonize." Two years later, although he
still doubted that the South would win the war, he wrote to B. H. Epperson
that "we have no hope but in stern bitter resistance to the end, let it be
what it may." J. Walker Austin sounded a similar note in September 1861.
"We are all now ground down and can hear nothin[g] else but (War, War),"
he wrote during the war's first autumn. "I have whiched [*sic*] myself

thousands of times in some remote place in the mountains w[h]ere I could be clear of such excitement." Austin had always considered war "one of the greatest evils ever afflicted on the human family." However, there seemed to be no alternative but to fight the North, "since they have got to stealing and arming the Negroes against us." Austin, who enlisted as a scout in a Texas cavalry regiment, finished his thought with a question often pondered by Unionists: "What will be the end God only knows."[43]

These southern Unionists accepted the fate of more confirmed secessionists as their own, but their experiences differed from those of most other southerners, fire-eaters and dissenters alike. The doubts they expressed from the beginning of the war foreshadowed the fears of more and more southerners as the war dragged into its disheartening third and fourth years. Unlike other loyal southerners, their choice—although perhaps inevitable—had been an uncomfortable one, and many retained a bitterness about having been forced to make it. This led some of them to demand of other southerners the same standard of loyalty that they asked of themselves, and to condemn those southerners who failed to live up to it. It also contributed to their accepting roles as the collective conscience of the Confederacy. As southerners first and Americans second, they went to war against the United States. Yet their fidelity to the South led them to resist the ways in which confederation and war threatened to alter the South; their conservatism in the face of secession extended to their resistance to the radical measures undertaken by the Confederate states. As a result, they opposed attempts to destroy the traditional civil liberties of their citizens through martial law, conscription, the suspension of habeas corpus, and through a number of other petty or large infractions of the Constitution. Their close ties to southerners who were not so loyal—Ballinger's friendships with Bell and Paschal, for instance—reveal the thin line that separated loyal and dissenting southerners during the Civil War. Finally, although they were sometimes exposed to criticism for their prewar opinions and wartime conscientiousness, these proudly conservative Texans were in reality determined soldiers in the southern cause, loyal citizens of the Confederacy and of Texas, and steadfast protectors of southern society—this despite the fact that their own cause had been lost the moment southern guns fired on northern soldiers at Fort Sumter.[44]

4

Unionists as Dissenters

Austin Episcopalians fought a civil war in miniature five years before the batteries ringing Charleston Harbor silenced the guns of Fort Sumter. Despite the recent completion of a new church building, political dissension split the Church of the Epiphany into Unionist and states' rights factions that ultimately led the former to break away in April 1856 and establish Christ Church. The seceding congregation called New England-born Charles Gillette, formerly a rector in Houston, to lead the Unionist flock. Gillette doubled the membership of his little congregation during the next few years, and when the Church of the Epiphany lost its pastor to a wealthy widow, its vestry invited the members of the younger church and their rector to rejoin the old congregation. The Unionists accepted the offer, and in July 1859, members of the new Church of St. David worshipped together for the first time.[1]

The reorganization of the Episcopal Church coincided with the arrival in Austin of the new Bishop for Texas, Rev. Alexander Gregg of South Carolina, whose presence during the war would have an important effect on St. David's—and on Charles Gillette. The intensifying sectional crisis during the fall of 1860 resurrected the tensions that had previously divided the congregation. Although several leading states' rights men belonged to the church, the congregation was most notable for the number of men who would later remain loyal to the Union. Among them were S.M. Swenson, George W. Paschal, John and George Hancock, A.J. Hamilton, Thomas H. DuVal, and former Gov. E.M. Pease. Gillette naturally included himself in the Unionist contingent. When the war finally broke out, his failure to submit to his superior's demands would cost him his rectorship; the splintering of his congregation became a microcosm of the way that the Civil War fragmented southern society.[2]

Bishop Gregg's aristocratic background as a South Carolina planter's son, as a slaveowner, and as the grandson of a Revolutionary War officer

who had been persecuted by Loyalists molded his reaction to the Civil
War. When the fighting began, Gregg's son enlisted in John B. Hood's
Brigade, and his daughter presented a flag to one of Austin's first volunteer
companies. Gregg's spiritual contribution to the southern war effort
launched the controversy between the bishop and Gillette. In the spring of
1861, Gregg ordered the clergy in his bishopric to alter the liturgy in order
to make it "comformable . . . to the civil establishment." One of the
changes entailed asking God to grant a speedy end to "the unnatural war
which had been forced upon us." The northerner Gillette opposed the
politics represented by the prayer, and Gregg at first permitted him to
omit it from services at St. David's. Nevertheless, as the war went on, as
tolerance toward dissent in Texas dwindled, and as Gregg became increasingly committed to the Confederate cause—a process hastened by
the death of his son—the prayer issue came to symbolize the demands
made by Confederate Texans on the loyalty of their Union-leaning neighbors.[3]

Lucadia Pease reported as early as April 1861, that "Mr. Giletes [sic]
very prosperous parish is about being broken up." Although the bishop
"claims to be no politician," his prayer had angered many parishioners. "As
all the most respectable and wealthy members of the Church here are
Union men," Mrs. Pease wrote her sister, "they are unwilling to listen to
such a prayer." Many stopped attending worship services altogether, while
others came "only out of respect to Mr. Gillette who is a Union man." In
the summer of 1863, former member and Unionist Judge Thomas DuVal
complained that he had not been to church in over two years, but added
that he did not "think I ever shall again until the commandments of Christ
are better practiced by his so called followers."[4]

The controversy soon embroiled the entire diocese. Gillette argued
that only God knew who had been at fault in starting the war. Referring to
"the unnatural war" forced upon the South seemed to establish an "historical fact" that not even southerners unanimously believed. In addition,
Gillette posited, Gregg had unfairly withdrawn his approval to leave the
prayer out of Gillette's services. Gregg's retort included an attack on the
North, "the hotbed of infidelity on this continent" and the place where
"Unitarianism, Universalism, transcendentalism, Mormonism, spir-
itualism, and higher-lawism" flourished. Northerners had deliberately
disobeyed the scriptures by conducting a crusade against slavery. The
South was "a ravaged land" where "there should be but one sentiment
prevailing." A pastor must "set forward . . . quietness, peace, and love
among all Christian people, and especially among those that are . . .
committed to his charge." He could not fulfill that duty by contradicting
the actions of a majority of the people—or the decisions of his bishop.[5]

Gillette could not win. His base of support within his own congregation melted away, as many Unionists fell quiet or left Texas. In August
1864, the church vestry asked for and received his resignation. Unable to
collect the $1500 that the church owed him, he remained in Austin until
October 1865, when he left Texas and never returned.[6]

The Civil War shattered Austin's Episcopal community as well as the
South, as secessionists devoted to slavery and states' rights clashed with
Unionists determined not to sacrifice their precious family of American
states. The latter reversed the priorities of the Confederate Unionists,
whose primary loyalty was to their section. Unconditional Unionists condemned their state's course not because they were abolitionists or unsym-
pathetic to the South, but simply because the Union meant more to them
than their region. They judged Texas's worth in terms of its condition as an
American state, not as a southern state. In other words, their southernism
was a function of their Americanism and derived its value from the benefits
and status that the Constitution extended to member states. Another
factor that separated them from the men who most closely resembled
them—the Confederate Unionists—was political affiliation. In Texas,
many of the latter came out of the Whig tradition, while unconditional
Unionists had usually considered themselves Jacksonian Democrats before the war. The former Whigs—including James W. Throckmorton and
William Pitt Ballinger—seemed more likely than the Union Democrats to
resign themselves to the will of the majority and less likely to continue the
fight to preserve the United States after secession. This may be at least
partly attributable to the fact that the Whigs in Texas, unlike their fellow
conservatives in North Carolina, had no stable party organization to draw
them together and effectively resist secession. Thus isolated, Whigs followed their region and state out of the Union. The Union Democrats, on
the other hand, could call on the legacy of Andrew Jackson to oppose the
destruction of their party and their country. Differentiating themselves
from the Southern Democrats—many of whom also traced their origins
back to Jackson—the Democratic Unionists of Texas, despite their minority status, could still brace themselves and their Unionism against the
traditions of the National Democratic party. This gave them the strength to
champion the Union war effort, and furnished them with a motivation
missing in most Whigs for preserving the system to which they clung.[7]

Many Texans initially opposed secession, but only a fraction of them
actively worked to defeat the Confederacy. Some joined the federal army
and literally fought against friends and neighbors; some accepted positions
in the United States government as treasury agents or in some other
bureaucratic assignment; some attempted to stay quietly at home until
conscription or popular disapproval forced them out of the state; a few

somehow managed to avoid army service as well as vigilance committees and remained in Texas throughout the war. Charles Gillette's actions probably surprised few people because of his northern origins, but the attitudes of many of the southern-born, slave-owning members of his congregation reveal how divisive was the issue of whether or not to remain in the Union.

The Confederates' treatment of those men who chose the Union varied widely, but always reflected the former's determination to protect their society from internal threats as assiduously as they fought the Yankees. Events outside Texas often governed the responses of the government and its citizens to the disloyalty of friends, colleagues, and relatives. Many Unionists had shared their fellow southerners' apprehension over a future in which the Republican party controlled the government, and most, at least in 1860 and 1861, supported the institution of slavery in principle as well as in practice. Their espousal of the Union became obnoxious to other southerners only when they refused to accept secession as the best way of preserving slavery and southern rights. A number of men fell away from the Union cause as a consequence of the fighting at Fort Sumter and Lincoln's call for troops, but even then many unconditional Union men persevered in their loyalty to the United States.

The escalation of secession to war tried Texans' patience. A northerner captured during the takeover of federal forts in the spring of 1861 and held in San Antonio for nearly a year found that the battle of First Bull Run in July changed everything. Before, he reminisced after the war, "we were treated very well indeed, in fact it hardly seemed that we were prisoners." After the war's first major fight, however, "the people became bitter, and it was not so pleasant for us." Such feelings worsened in the spring of 1862, when a series of Confederate defeats in Tennessee, the bloodbath at Shiloh, and the Union capture of New Orleans jarred complacent Confederates into a renewed determination to win the war and to rid their state of its disloyal elements. These Confederate defeats, according to the *San Antonio Herald*, had emboldened Yankee sympathizers to make their sentiments known; they must be watched, and if federal forces invaded the state, "it will be necessary to dispose of the lurking enemies in our midst," who will be treated in the ways that "tories, spies and traitors are treated by all nations in times of war." The *Austin State Gazette* announced that Texans "cannot permit an element of disaffection to remain among us, to assail us with its insidious and treacherous weapons," and urged its readers "to destroy every element of treason in Texas by the most prompt and efficient means." An Austin secessionist wrote O.M. Roberts that "the lurking, dormant treason in our midst" had revealed itself "under the tidings of our reverses." As a result, he declared approvingly, "the toleration of an indulgent people will cease to be a virtue,—indeed toleration will become a positive crime." The first Confederate Conscription Act, passed in March, also encouraged men who refused to fight against the United States to leave Texas, and the first wave of forced emigration began soon after. Late in May, Brig. Gen. Paul O. Hebert declared martial law throughout Texas and in July convened a military court to try civilians suspected of disloyalty. The court passed judgment on dozens of Texans until the Confederate government in Richmond closed it down on October 10, 1862.[8]

Tolerance of Unionists varied widely throughout the rest of the war, and Unionists who left the state or merely withdrew their support from the Confederacy picked their own times to act. The disastrous military defeats of 1863 once again increased many Texans' intolerance of Union men and another wave fled the state or took to the brush. For others, the worsening economic situation, the shortages of everyday necessities, or poor treatment by military or civil officials convinced them finally to abandon their homes. Some, however, remained in Texas for the duration of the war, sequestered in their houses and often retired from business and public life.

Whatever their motivations or experiences, political dissenters faced ambivalence from both southerners and northerners. Their treatment at the hands of Confederate neighbors ranged from murder to neglect; some were hanged, some were merely ostracized, others were able to live uneasily normal lives—a few were actually ignored. Southern dissenters who went over to the side of the Union experienced a similar mixture of reactions. Unsure of whether to treat southern Unionists as allies or foes, federal troops and authorities commonly failed to treat them as either. As a result, those southerners whose self-image included a strong devotion to the Union, found themselves doubted by representatives of both sections.

The *Marshall Texas Republican* confidently asserted in late 1860 that "all political distinctions have been abandoned" in Texas, that everyone had accepted the right of secession and agreed that it was "the duty of the State to take deliberate action" to protect the South from the "Black Republicans." Nevertheless, during the four years that followed, disloyalty to the Confederacy survived and sometimes flourished all over Texas. Many communities around the state responded by reactivating ante-bellum vigilance committees to crush threats to the local Confederate power structure or to a more abstract vision of southern society.[9]

The effectiveness of these groups and of others around the Confederacy is debatable, but a popular form of Yankee propaganda during and shortly after the war—the Confederate atrocity story—related extraordinary tales of cruel vigilance. Among the most famous were the Rev. John

H. Aughey's bitter *The Iron Furnace; or, Slavery and Secession*, and
William Brownlow's politically incendiary *Parson Brownlow, and the
Unionists of East Tennessee*. Aughey claimed that the persecution of
Unionists in Mississippi, from which he had escaped early in the war, was
"only equalled, in its appalling enormity, by the memorable French
Revolution," and depicted sadistic rebels torturing, starving, and execut-
ing hundreds of loyal Union men. Brownlow, who would later serve as a
Reconstruction governor of Tennessee, told similar tales, including an
instance when Confederates hanged two Unionists from a tree near a
railroad track. For the next four days, passing trains slowed so passengers
could kick the bodies and "wave . . . their white handkerchiefs in triumph
through the windows of the car."10

Texas lacked its own well-known atrocity writer, but a Texas refugee
named R.L. Abarr published a letter in an 1863 edition of a Kansas
periodical, the *Western Journal of Commerce*, in which he described the
"Persecution of Union Men in Texas." The author had left his family in
Hays County in February 1863, when the possibility of conscription forced
him to choose "between the halter and a soldier fighting for the rebellion
against his country." Abarr estimated that vigilantes had murdered a total
of 180 men in Hays, Blaine, and Gillespie counties. Like Aughey, Abarr
compared the widespread violence against Unionists in Texas to the "reign
of terror" in France following the French Revolution. He asserted that
most southerners did not favor disunion; a few leaders had forced secession
upon the people and now controlled the South. He claimed that secessionists had murdered over two thousand Texans "for the crime of loving
the flag of Washington." So evil were the secessionists, that they would
shoot "Union men to see which way they would fall"; slit the throats "of
loyal men, that they might listen to the music of the death rattle"; and
lynch "crowds of faithful citizens just to observe the varieties of the death
gasp."11

The *Western Journal*'s correspondent overestimated the number of
deaths attributable to mob violence in Texas, but the spirit of vigilance
grew very strong in the state and throughout the South. Accustomed to
forming committees devoted to protecting the institution of slavery from
internal as well as external threats—a similar machinery had recently been
mobilized to put down the 1860 slave "revolt"—Texans organized vigilance
associations early in the war to protect southern institutions once again,
but also to perform the equally pressing duty of enforcing loyalty to the
Confederacy.

To these ends, public meetings echoed resolutions passed during the
recent slave insurrection panic. A Hopkins County meeting directed its
vigilance committee to "keep a vigilant eye on all strangers, or any one

passing through our precinct, and tampering with our negroes, or in any way exciting discord among us." Grayson County vigilantes would "wait upon every transient person in and around the vicinity . . . and examine into their characters, and the nature of their errand." Red River County formed a committee so that it might "be vigilant in guarding against . . . persons of suspicious character . . . and in ridding our county of all enemies, traitors and spies." The committee would examine suspicious persons and suspected traitors by swearing in witnesses, hearing evidence, and, if necessary, handing those suspects over to the legal authorities. The *Marshall Texas Republican* applauded the formation of local loyalty-enforcing groups: "those who are not for us and our country should be considered and treated as against us." This mania for vigilance persisted in many parts of Texas and among many groups of people throughout the war, although late in the conflict its influence shrank with the morale of war-weary Texans. The *Austin State Gazette* suggested in 1863 that alert Texans should "keep a vigilant eye on the suspicious element in our midst, and spare not the traitors. 'Eternal vigilance is the price of Liberty!'"[12]

In reality, of course, Unionists paid the true price of Confederate vigilance, and vigilantes struck often enough to keep the possibility of retribution before every Texas dissenter. Early in 1861, Harrison County residents voted overwhelmingly in favor of state representative George Whitmore's resignation. A mass meeting called Whitmore's support for the Unionist "Address to the People of Texas" "repugnant," "incendiary," and "treacherous." The Hamilton County Vigilance Committee delivered a blow for liberty later that spring when it called James McBarron, the county's chief justice, an abolitionist and demanded that he leave the county within five days, "or else abide the verdict of an indignant community." In July a Mound City committee hanged a watchman on a Red River steamer after it found him "determined and malignant" in his espousal of the Union and his declaration that "he would rather die than live in the Southern States." Sometimes the tables were turned. In June 1861, a band of "Abolitionists and outlaws," hiding out in the forks of the Sulphur River in Lamar County, broke up a public meeting before it had a chance to appoint a vigilance committee.[13]

For the most part, however, formally organized vigilance committees had little to do with the violent ends met by Texas Unionists. Most of the men murdered for their alleged disloyalty in Texas were the victims of mobs or individuals who acted without any authority beyond that sanctioned by community standards and attitudes. A Lamar County mob, for instance, hanged five men early in the war for crimes ranging from giving a Union speech before secession to setting off fireworks to celebrate a Confederate defeat. Two Burnet County landmarks—Dead Man's Hole and Hubbard Falls—obtained their names after self-proclaimed vigilantes made them the final resting places for executed Unionists. Early in 1864 a squad of Confederate soldiers lynched a seventy-five-year-old Collin County resident because his two sons served in the Union army and because the soldiers believed he was a spy. His two daughters buried him under a headstone inscribed, "Murdered by a band of traitors because of his devotion to the federal government." James Luckey, a fallen seces- sionist and militia captain who by 1864 believed the Confederate cause hopeless, was arrested for corresponding with federal troops in Indian territory. A judge released him on a writ of habeas corpus, whereupon a small group of masked men lynched him while lawyers and military authorities debated his legal status. Vigilante justice prevailed often enough in Texas to inspire the macabre joke about a new variety of tree growing around the state, whose limbs often bore a half dozen or dozen Unionists.[14]

Letters from mistreated Unionists flooded into the capitol after A.J. Hamilton took office as governor in June 1865. A Smith County man protested that the sheriff recently appointed by Hamilton had kept a pack of dogs during the war to hunt down deserters and Union men. A refugee in Ohio wrote Hamilton that "theire was a greate amount of wicked deeds done," including those committed by a man who had boasted in the writer's presence that he had "hong and helped to hang 34 of the damed union abolition." A petition from Goliad County residents warned Hamilton to be careful who he appointed to offices in that county, as many "vindictive, malicious, unprincipled" former secessionists were maneu- vering for office. During the war, they had "worked unceasingly and energetically to bring to bear all the appliances . . . they could possibly command, to annoy, harrass, distress and destroy those who differed with them in political opinions." The loyal petitioners asked Hamilton to ap- point only men who could prove their loyalty to the Union during the war.[15]

Despite the not-infrequent hangings and murders, death was only one of a number of penalties faced by disloyal Texans. The severity of the punishment depended on the seriousness of the offense, the part of the state in which the disloyalty was discovered, and the extent to which it threatened the property, lives, or sensibilities of loyal southerners. As a result, simply being "disloyal" to the Confederacy in some way rarely earned one an intimate acquaintance with the business end of a hangman's noose. At the same time, however, the infractions that attracted attention and were found worthy of punishment were often quite minor. The case against William W. Gamble, tried before the Confederate Military Com- mission in San Antonio during the summer of 1862, shows how minute

details, rumors, and the crisis atmosphere engendered by the war sometimes combined to get a quiet man with few friends deported from the
South.

During five days of testimony, the prosecution tried Gamble, a twen-
ty-two-year-old San Antonio book seller and a native of the North who
hardly spoke English, for "Keeping and circulating Abolition Books." Most
of the argument concerned an obscure English book that allegedly cast a
poor light on slavery in the South; the case hinged on whether Gamble had
knowingly kept such a dangerous book in his store. The defense asserted
that Gamble did not realize that any of his stock contained "that false,
unjust and slanderous vituperation of Southern Institutions, with which
Cockney English writers are accustomed to cater to the jealous appetites
of . . . their countrymen." Nevertheless, the court found the defendant
guilty and banished him from the Confederate States. Three days later,
Brig. H. P. Bee directed the court to reopen the case and to find out more
about Gamble's political beliefs, his family, and his "influence in the
Community." One prosecution witness testified that Gamble's father was a
"strong Union man," but also stated his belief that Gamble "seems to have
been peculiarly selected as an object of suspicion." Another defense
witness, who lived in the same boarding house with Gamble, proved more
cooperative. He testified that he considered Mr. Gamble to be a Union
man because of "his manner" and his apparent friendship and agreement
with an avid Unionist who boarded in the same house. The defense
assembled a battery of witnesses to prove that Gamble posed no threat to
the Confederacy, and he eventually went free.[16]

Some Unionists seemed to invite attack by unwisely publicizing their
political opinions and their contempt for the Confederacy. The Military
Commission found John C. McKean guilty of several charges of "Disloyalty" when witnesses testified to McKean's refusal to cooperate in any way
with the Confederate war effort. One afternoon in a shop in Lockhart he
compared Confederate soldiers to "a parcel of Negroes with Overseers,"
while another time he brandished a revolver and swore that he would
never take the oath of allegiance to the Confederacy. One witness called
McKean "a quarrelsome man," who "always goes armed and has a good
many difficulties," and avowed that "his reputation is that of a Disloyal
Citizen." Worse still, McKean had accompanied the noted Unionist A.J.
Hamilton to the Rio Grande when the latter made his escape to Mexico.
The commission sentenced McKean, who could have expected worse from
a less formal body, to prison for the duration of the war.[17]

Even men who actually committed treason, as defined by Confederate
and state law, could escape with their lives. In September 1863, a one-page
broadside named "Common Sense" appeared in Texas. Signed only by

"one who was at Vicksburg," it argued that the Confederacy was already on its last legs, asserted that the sacrifices and hardships already endured by southerners had been in vain, and urged the people of Texas to question the policies of the Confederate government. "Ruin is coming upon us, and staring us in the face . . . Destruction is coming upon our land with as certain a tread as the night follows the day." The war, begun with such high hopes, had brought only military defeat, poverty, and tyranny. Texans must not "sit down with folded hands and let chains be riveted and ruin be saddled upon us." Thomas DuVal recorded in his diary that he had seen the handbill, and wrote, "these are the first *healthy* symptoms I have seen. If we only had freedom of speech & of the press as formerly, we would soon have peace again."18

By late October, Maj. Gen. John B. Magruder had arrested five suspected authors of the broadside. Despite two unsuccessful attacks by mobs, the men never came to trial. For ten months they shuffled between jails in Houston and Austin, while state officials, military authorities, and lawyers for the accused bickered over legal jurisdictions, habeas corpus technicalities, and security for the prisoners. Finally, in August 1864, Magruder banished to Mexico three of the alleged promulgators of "Common Sense"—D.J. Baldwin, E. Seelinger, and Dr. Richard Peebles. The experience ruined the health of the sixty-three-year-old Peebles—who had fought for Texas independence during the Texas revolution—and he spent the rest of the war in New Orleans.19

These cases shed light on the ways that vigilant Texas Confederates frequently rose against men who they believed to be threats to southern institutions and to the Confederacy. Men could be attacked on the street or along back roads or, if they were lucky, formally prosecuted for uttering a seditious phrase, neglecting to fulfill some sort of minor patriotic duty, publicly agreeing with a suspicious person, or accidentally possessing a book that somehow challenged southern institutions.

Such men abounded in Austin and San Antonio. The latter was second among Texas cities only to the state capital as a center of prewar Unionist activity. In San Antonio, according to a Union soldier who waited there for his parole, "there were . . . at the commencement of the Secession Movement, a great many Union men." One of them even tried to talk the Yankee officer into leading an attack against the Confederate arsenal; he guaranteed that enough men would rally to the Union flag to capture the city. Nothing came of the plan, however, and as in most parts of the South, "as soon as the fighting began in earnest," San Antonians underwent "a gradual change of sentiment. . . . Many who were outspoken Union men at first, became bitter Secessionists." A Unionist named William McLane wrote his attorneys that he wanted to help alleviate the "suffering among the poore" by making a donation to some sort of relief society. "I should prefer relieving those that voted agains [sic] Secession but I presume those that voted for it will suffer enough when they see the mischief they have done." Public suspicion of the residents of San Antonio never died out, especially toward the many Germans living in the city. In fact, early in the war two local newspapers, the *Herald* and the *Ledger and Texan* fought a war of words over the issue of the loyalty of San Antonians. The latter challenged the loyalty of local German merchants and also questioned the enthusiasm for the southern cause of the *Herald's* management.[20]

The most prominent San Antonio Unionist was also one of the first Unionist refugees to leave Texas. James P. Newcomb, a twenty-four-year-old Nova Scotian who had lived in the state most of his life, had fought disunion through the columns of his *Alamo Express* from the beginning of the Texas secession movement. He believed that the "disolution of this Union would precipitate the people into a state of anarchy" comparable to the chaos in Mexico. After the Austin convention passed its secession ordinance, Newcomb wrote, "talk to a man now-a-days of patriotism and the glory of his country, and he hoots at you." "Truly," he lamented, "as a people, we deserve adversity for having lost sight of the old landmarks." The young editor expressed his devotion to the South, and attributed his so-called "mistaken . . . opinions" to "the free government that has taught us to think and act as a Sovereign, and to believe that the right opinion was sacred, and as free as the sunlight from Heaven."[21]

Newcomb's views had become increasingly unpopular during the secession spring, and in May, less than two weeks after Newcomb's final issue, a mob led by Knights of the Golden Circle destroyed his *Express* office. The *Indianola Courier* rejoiced that this "Black Republican paper" had been "squelched out." The *Courier's* only "objection to the proceeding is that it was done too late. . . . We are and always have been opposed to unlawful violence—but tories must be dealt with." Newcomb, the Tory in question, left for Mexico during the summer and edited newspapers in California for the duration of the war.[22]

Austin teemed with men who shared Newcomb's sentiments. "It is treason," announced "Truth Seeker" in a letter to the *State Gazette* in September 1861, "for a small clique of citizens to assemble daily in the city of Austin and by their conversation attempt to impair the confidence of all who come within the sphere of their influence, in the Confederate Government." Unfortunately for "Truth Seeker" and for the Confederate government, the "clique" of Unionists who lived in Austin was not so small. A former resident of Texas estimated that three-quarters of the residents of

Austin remained loyal to the United States. As the state capital and the home of many conservative lawyers and merchants, the city provided the Union cause with more leaders than any other place in Texas.[23]

Unionists in Travis County had made trouble for the secession movement ever since the crisis began. The county delivered over 40 percent of its vote to the Constitutional Unionist candidate John Bell in the 1860 presidential election, although the state as a whole gave him less than 30 percent, and Travis County joined only seventeen other Texas counties in voting against the secession ordinance. After the election of representatives to the secession convention, 261 Austin Unionists petitioned the Travis County delegates, urging them to boycott the convention and asserting that "a majority of the voters of the country [sic] are opposed to said convention." The delegates—John A. Green, H.N. Bundett, and George H. Flournoy—took their seats at the convention and voted in favor of secession.[24]

The Unionists' petition offers several insights into the makeup of rank-and-file Unionists in Texas—or at least in Travis County—late in the secession crisis. Census data indicate, not surprisingly, that men who supported the Union to the extent that they signed the petition were more likely to have been born in the Upper South than the average Travis County resident (53.3 to 44.6 percent). Signers tended to work as craftsmen, clerks, merchants, or lawyers, rather than as farmers or planters, and owned real and person property in amounts far above average ($10,563 to $8,689, and $6,010 to $4,534, respectively). Far fewer Union men owned no property (around one-third, compared with 46 percent of all Travis County men), and they boarded in other families' homes at a much lower rate than normal (27 to 10 percent). Slaveowning, however, was one of the few categories that did not differentiate petitioners from the typical county resident. The percentage of Unionists who owned slaves was barely lower than that of secessionists (29.6 to 33 percent), and slaveholders in both groups owned an average of just over seven slaves each—about half of each group owned three or fewer blacks.[25]

Numbers and percentages cannot enable a historian to read the minds of men who lived and died over a century ago, but they do offer hints as to why those men acted the way they did. Travis County Unionists were not hill-country yeoman with no stake in the slave system, nor were they poor outlanders with no future in the southern economy. Rather, they shared in the economic opportunities provided by the South and participated fully in the institution of slavery; in short, they had invested as much if not more in the southern economy and had as much at stake in preserving southern society as the non-Unionists with whom they disagreed. They were older, more settled, and more economically independent than their secessionist counterparts. They rejected southern nationalism not because they rejected the South and wished it ill, but because they believed disunion would destroy a southern economy and society that had been very good to them, because they distrusted the motives of secessionists, and because they refused to acquiesce in the destruction of their Union.[26]

Even after the convention severed Texas's ties with the Union, many Travis County Unionists refused to submit. At the farewell ceremonies for Sam Houston in late March, the deposed governor and A.J. Hamilton spoke so harshly against the excessive authority assumed by the secession convention that one Houston supporter "thought for a while we would have the Battle to fight in Austin instead of the North." Despite one secessionist's prediction that Lincoln and "his Black Republican crowd" would "wretchedly fail" if they came to Texas "and try to enlist from the so-called Union men a corporal's guard to oppose secession," a group of those Union men formed a company of "home guards" during the spring and summer of 1861. They drilled the manual of arms in the second story of the dry goods store at Pecan Street and Congress Avenue owned by Unionists George Hancock and Morgan Hamilton. This organization included A.J. Hamilton, Thomas DuVal, John Hancock (George's brother), John T. Allan, and William P. De Normandie among many others. These men would later demonstrate their opposition to the Confederacy by leaving Texas and actively aiding the United States. Other members—former governor E.M. Pease, George Hancock (the company's captain), Morgan Hamilton (A.J.'s older brother), and George W. Paschal—would stay in Austin during the war, but would refuse to cooperate with the Confederates. A few, including James Bell, remained only tenuously loyal to the Confederacy. One former Unionist turned Confederate, Alexander W. Terrell, told E.B. Burleson, Jr., that this informal militia unit had "never reported to the Governor—they march under no flag, and their organization is the cause of much bad feeling." That feeling no doubt worsened later in the war, when some of these men escaped to Mexico and put their drilling to practical use by joining the Union army. Those that remained behind allegedly held "a night festival" when they received news of a Confederate defeat, betrayed looks of "joy . . . upon their countenances" after the fall of Fort Donelson, and paid the war tax "only upon conpulsion."[27]

This large coterie of Travis County Unionists represents the stratum of experiences of most Texans who remained true to the Union. A.J. Hamilton and John L. Haynes, prominent Opposition politicians before the war, fled Texas and joined the Union army. Thomas DuVal and John Hancock remained civilians, but nevertheless left their homes; they found their unintentionally meager contributions to the war effort disheartening. George Washington Paschal, the well-known editor and lawyer, never left Austin during the war, but found his fortune and his reputation damaged beyond repair by his steadfast loyalty to the Union.

Perhaps none of the men who opposed secession in Texas inspired so much admiration and so much hatred as A. J. "Colossal Jack" Hamilton. A man with whom Hamilton had served in the state legislature in the early 1850s wrote to Hamilton while the latter was exiled from Texas late in 1862. "I can not say how cheering and grateful your example has been to me, and has doubtless to thousands of others," he gushed, "God bless you, my dear Sir, for all you have done, and all you have dared." Salmon P. Chase, the United States Secretary of the Treasury, wrote that Hamilton might some day "be remembered as the faithful Texan who clung to the Union and his Country when even Houston deserted both." Another Texas expatriate, George Denison, wrote to Chase that "Mr. H. is to Western Texas, what Brownlow, Maynard and Johnson are to East Tennessee." Finally, shortly after the war, Enos Woofter of Castroville welcomed Hamilton back to Texas and expressed his gratitude that the voice of "Colossal Jack" once again "reverberates o'er the Prairie." It "causes verry many honest hearts to rejoice & Evil doers to skulk from the light of day trembling as they go."28

The *Dallas Herald*, a passionately Confederate newspaper, summed up Hamilton for many Texas rebels when it congratulated Hamilton on his escape to the North, where "he has found a community of bigger fools than himself, and almost as great rascals." The editorial painted an unflattering picture of an opportunistic, hypocritical politician notorious for seducing married women. "The fanatical politicians of the north are extremely fortunate in the acquisition of Jack Hamilton," the article declared, "they love to be humbugged, and he is peculiarly qualified to humbug them." Another article remarked on Hamilton's alleged weakness for liquor: "Judging from his habits, he will need . . . the assistance of two or three sober Yankees to enable him to navigate the streets of New Orleans, right side up."29

Hamilton's path to notoriety resembled in many ways that of his fellow Jacksonian, Andrew Johnson of Tennessee. A former Austin lawyer, acting attorney general, and state representative, Hamilton went to Congress in 1859 as an Independent Democrat, Houston ally, and Unionist. He favored Douglas during the election of 1860, and when Texas seceded, remained in Washington and searched for a compromise on the House Committee of Thirty-three. Hamilton later won a special election to the state senate and stayed in Texas—"bullying about the State capitol," in the words of the *Texas Republican*—until the spring of 1862, when he fled to the hills west of Austin, where he administered federal loyalty oaths to other beleaguered Unionists. Hamilton eventually made his way with fourteen others—including his brother-in-law, George Gray, chief justice of Travis County—to Matamoros, Mexico, despite the large reward offered for his capture and a botched kidnapping attempt.[30]

As an example of the determination of Southern Unionists to help their northern friends save the Union, Hamilton became a hero all over the North. During the fall of 1862, he preached on the inevitable conflict between slave society and democracy in New York, Ohio, New England, and occupied New Orleans. He expounded the strength of Unionism in Texas, explained the diabolical plans of the slave power aristocracy to rob nonslaveholders of their rightful political power, denounced any sort of negotiated peace that recognized secession, and stressed the necessity of ending slavery in order to establish a postwar South in which everyone, not just a small minority of slaveowners, would prosper. Northern audiences, particularly Republicans, lionized Hamilton for his courage and his principles. "Of those sturdy and irrepressible patriots who ennoble their race by devotion to their country," rhapsodized the *New York Times*, "Andrew Jackson Hamilton, of Texas, should stand at the forefront." By November the Texan held commissions as a brigadier general in the Union army and as military governor of Texas, with the authority to raise troops, commission officers, and "re-establish the authority of the Federal Government in the State of Texas." Secretary of War Stanton reminded Hamilton that "upon your wisdom and energetic action much will depend."[31]

Hamilton found little opportunity to utilize his wisdom and energy. He joined Maj. Gen. Nathaniel Banks in New Orleans late in 1862, but did not reach his home state until Banks's invasion of Texas in 1863. Hamilton accompanied the troops to Texas and set up headquarters in Brownsville, but he and his Yankee allies occupied Texas for only a few months before they returned to New Orleans. There he hatched plans to win the war and to make money. His association with cotton speculators from the North led Banks to complain that members of his entourage were in New Orleans "for the basest mercenary purposes. . . . The strongest government in the world would break down under such a system of plunder as they desire to organize."[32]

Hamilton never achieved his war aims or financial goals, although he stayed in New Orleans until the summer of 1865; his accomplishments during the war never matched his fame, and personal tragedies made his war a hard one. His young daughter Katie died just before he fled Austin, his house and everything in it burned in July 1864—the *State Gazette* reported that "we have not been able to learn whether it was the work of an incendiary, or occurred through accident"—and his wife and family, four daughters and two sons, were unable to leave Texas until late in the same year.[33]

Despite his largely inconsequential wartime career, Hamilton represented for many Texans the most dangerous sort of disloyalist. A former slaveowner, Hamilton gradually metamorphosed from a Jacksonian Democrat to an advocate of emancipation and a postwar Republican. From the Unionists' standpoint, Hamilton was typical in that his devotion to the Union stemmed from his prewar political and constitutional beliefs. Unlike many other southern Unionists, however, Hamilton easily converted to the antislavery cause—although his later enthusiasm for the civil rights of freedmen was limited. He emphasized the inequities in southern society and the natural antagonism between the interests of slaveowners and nonslaveholders, echoing many of the ideas of that southern anti-Christ, Hinton Rowan Helper. As a result, unlike those Confederate Unionists who found themselves without a cause or those Unionists who merely hoped to reconstruct the Union as it had been before 1861, Hamilton and those few men who were able to adopt northern war aims considered the war to be a victorious one, at least temporarily.[34]

John L. Haynes shared many of the views of his mentor, A. J. Hamilton. A state representative from the heavily Mexican-American Starr County, a member of the Democratic Opposition in Texas, and a supporter of Sam Houston, his advocacy for Hispanic Texans made him even less popular than most other Texas Unionists. He had first antagonized the state Democratic establishment, not to mention many of his Southwest Texas constituents, when he suggested that the border crisis of 1859–1860—during which Juan Cortina terrorized Anglos along the Rio Grande—might have been caused by land frauds perpetrated upon Mexican citizens by Texans. Brownsville residents responded by hanging an effigy of Haynes, and the *Brownsville American Flag* published a poem that satirized Haynes's efforts on behalf of "that greaser band / Who shed his country's blood." Another edition ran a bogus election banner that touted Juan Cortina for president and Haynes for vice president.[35]

Haynes followed up his defense of Hispanics with a spirited defense of the Union. Despite his apparently enlightened racial outlook, he was no abolitionist, but he was, like any loyal Jacksonian Democrat, devoted to the Constitution and to the Union. "No man nor any majority of the people of this State," he wrote in an "Address to the People of Starr County," published in the *Southern Intelligencer*, "can absolve me from the superior allegiance due to the Constitution and Government under which I was born, and through which I inherit my present liberties and rights as an American citizen." On a more practical level, Haynes was convinced that secession would put the South in an untenable position. A southern Confederacy could not sustain itself, frontier protection in Texas would prove prohibitively expensive, and the destruction of the Union would pave the way for the seizure of power by a military despot.[36]

Haynes combined the issues of sectionalism and anti-Mexican feeling among Anglo Texans in a June 1859 address published in Spanish. In it, Haynes urged his "Fellow Citizens of Starr County" to support Sam Houston for governor and A.J. Hamilton for United States Congress, and to oppose the candidates put forth by the state's regular Democrats. Haynes linked the radicals' attempts to reopen the African slave trade with their anti-Mexican attitudes and accused them of scheming to resurrect a system of peonage in order to employ and control the large class of unwanted Mexicans. Haynes also reminded his constituents of Travis County's 1854 exclusion of transient Mexicans. Several of the men who participated in those proceedings, including John Marshall of the *State Gazette* and W.S. Oldham, were now among the most important radical Democrats in the state. Haynes urged his readers to "go united to the polls to vote in favor of our true friends and to bury our enemies in disgrace and confusion." Three years later Haynes had become even more of a maverick in Texas politics. Sometime in 1862 he left Travis County—where he had lived since the summer of 1860—to become lieutenant colonel of the First Texas Cavalry, eventually rising to colonel of the Second Texas Cavalry.[37]

Thomas H. DuVal enjoyed far less notoriety than either Hamilton or Haynes, and was able to tarry in Austin until the fall of 1863, living an uncomfortable but relatively safe existence on his acreage near the capital city. When he finally left, his reasons had little to do with physical dangers or with a yearning for the military life. Rather, DuVal left because of pressing financial difficulties and because it appeared that he would finally be forced into active duty with the state militia. A former secretary of Florida Territory and the brother of two heroes of the Texas Revolutionary War, the fifty-year-old federal judge for the Western District of Texas had arrived in Austin in 1846. A confirmed Jacksonian Democrat—Andrew Jackson had appointed his father governor of Florida Territory—and a friend of most of the other Unionists in Travis County, DuVal dismissed secession as a "sinful and suicidal act on the part of the State." Indeed, when "madness ruled the hour, and treason triumphed," he refused to resign from the federal bench. Instead, he remained in Austin, working briefly in the state land office and for the county surveyor in order "to keep my family from starving" and to avoid conscription. With "poverty pressing sore upon" him, and when it became apparent by October 1863, that if he stayed in Texas, he would have to "take up arms against my country," he left his family and made the long journey to Washington, D.C.[38]

DuVal's rather strange existence in Austin during the first two years of the Civil War demonstrates the surprising—though never predictable—tolerance displayed toward Unionists in some parts of the South, including heavily Unionist Travis County. Although Travis countians had chased A. J. Hamilton into the central Texas hill country, for the most part Austin Confederates left DuVal and his other friends alone. With his federal court in permanent recess, DuVal spent much of his time gardening, fishing, and talking politics with S. M. Swenson, George Paschal, E. M. Pease, and other Unionists. This "tory lot" drank brandy at a Barton Creek fishing hole, chaperoned swimming parties, and met in Austin several times a week, as hungry for war news as the secessionists. They often debated the accuracy of the notoriously unreliable reports from the east. "Hurrah for humbug," DuVal wrote in April 1863, after a newspaper reported yet another imaginary rebel victory. "I fully expect to find out, when the truth is known, that *the boot is on the other leg.*"39

But the lives of Austin Unionists were not as carefree as they appeared. As the war progressed and as other Unionists were killed, imprisoned, or forced to emigrate, DuVal's deepening poverty alarmed him. "I don't know what to do," wrote the melancholy judge. "I am very unhappy here doing nothing for myself or family and [with] no prospect of anything in the future." Worse, as the Confederate need for manpower grew, DuVal realized that he might be liable to conscription. In that case, he wrote in an uncharacteristically dramatic passage in his diary, "I shall be called out by a higher power than the Governor." He had already made up his mind "to take no part in this revolution on the side of the Confederacy." Before he would submit to military service "to aid in breaking up the Government of my fathers, I will sacrifice all—even life itself." Nevertheless, DuVal dutifully attended a militia muster in August at which only half of the men called showed up. By September 30, DuVal had made the painful decision to leave his family in Austin.40

DuVal's wartime service was far less eventful than his month-long journey to Washington, and his contribution far smaller than he had hoped. After a distasteful round of "dancing attendance in the anti chambers of the great," he finally received $5,500 in back pay for his salary as district judge. Like many other southern refugees, the judge from Texas unsuccessfully urged upon President Lincoln, Secretary of State Seward, and anyone else who would listen, his own plan for the conquest of Texas, the gradual emancipation of the slaves there, and the utilization of what he believed was a powerful Unionist majority in the state. After he finished his business in Washington, DuVal traveled to New Orleans and then joined many other Texas refugees at the headquarters of the federal expeditionary force in Brownsville. He spent a frustrating few months there with the newly commissioned Brigadier General Hamilton, then accompanied the expedition back to New Orleans, where he sat out the rest of the war. Early in 1864, he complained in words undoubtedly echoed by Unionist refugees throughout the South, "the sort of existence I am leading here is very wearying."[41]

Another Austin lawyer and Unionist home guardsman, John Hancock, avoided that existence until the fall of 1864, when pressure from Confederate conscriptors finally convinced him to leave. The Alabama-born attorney was thirty-seven years old when the war began. A slaveowner who, even after the war ended, showed no inclination to change the status of southern blacks, Hancock was A.J. Hamilton's law partner, a state district judge, and a Democratic legislator. Hancock had opposed secession, predicting that "the little oligarchy down south would wither and crisp before the march of the Federal Army like a piece of paper in a flame." When Hancock refused to take the required oath to the Confederate government, he lost his seat in the legislature and spent the next two and a half years breeding livestock and defending Unionists who ran into trouble with Confederate authorities. The Confederate John Ford recalled that Hancock would warn prospective clients about his political inclinations in order to prevent future problems. Hancock struck a more or less neutral pose for most of the war, hoping to remain in Texas as a noncombatant, and he lasted far longer than most of his Unionist colleagues. However, in early 1864, he told Ford that Confederate authorities were trying to force him into the army, and by May he was giving speeches to the federal troops in Brownsville. Hancock's departure prompted the *Dallas Herald* to approvingly report—in a pointed reference to the capital city's large population of unsavory characters—that "Austin is undergoing purification." Hancock's brother George, too old for Confederate service, stayed behind, although he had flown a United States flag from a flagpole above his store in Austin until after the battle at Fort Sumter.[42]

Hancock spent most of the last ten months of the war in New Orleans recruiting troops, trying to organize the trade in Texas cotton, and aiding other refugees from his home state. Hancock found his work profoundly unrewarding and the quality of the men who fled Texas late in the war unimpressive. Many, he wrote in his diary, "have staid as long as they found it profitable or safe and no[w] come away to let others settle [the] difficulties" after which "they will return." He complained of wasting time on "air castles, mostly constructed of cotton," and doubted the abilities of the men who hoped to set up a system for getting cotton out of Texas. His generosity toward other refugees threatened to impoverish him. "I am constantly spending money," he wrote. "There is a constant drain on me by the Texans here in destitution. It is hard to refuse those who have no means or employment, and yet I shall be in that condition in a short time." His life in New Orleans bored him; "I have always had a partiality for uniformity in most things," he confided to his diary, "but the life of a loafer, or a Texas Refugee without business, which is about the same thing, has a uniformity that is becoming not only tiersome [sic] but disgusting."[43]

Not all of Travis County's principled Unionists were forced to live the "disgusting" life of a Texas loafer. The dedicated National Democrat, former governor, and prominent member of St. David's, Elisha Marshall Pease, was a Connecticut-born attorney who had fought in the Texas Revolution. In the 1850s, he denounced the state party's overtures toward reopening the African slave trade and the leadership's attempt to ostracize dissenting members. Although he owned slaves himself, he once told his friend, William P. Ballinger, that slavery could not last fifty more years. After his campaign against secession failed, he retired to his estate near Austin and refrained from giving out any legal or political opinions. His resistance to the Confederacy resulted in a Confederate tax collector confiscating his horse and buggy in lieu of payment in 1862. He did not return to public life until after the war.[44]

One of the most noted, eloquent, and hated stay-at-home Unionists was George Washington Paschal, the epitome of a southern dissenter who remained devoted to the South. Paschal edited the *Southern Intelligencer* in the late 1850s, married Thomas DuVal's sister, and was one of the dozens of lawyers practicing in Austin before the war. A Georgian who had become chief justice of Arkansas in his twenties, Paschal moved to Austin in 1848. A benevolent slaveowner, he wrote shortly after the war of his "hearty devotion to every measure which extended the area of slavery" proposed before the war, and believed that "the institution was religiously, morally and economically right, wise and just." An ardent Democrat, he hated Know-Nothings, Republicans, and abolitionists, but nevertheless opposed the radical activities of Texas Democrats to the point of nearly fighting a duel with the secessionist John Marshall of the *State Gazette* in 1859.[45]

In a letter to George W. Smyth in the spring of 1860, Paschal denounced the recent state Democratic convention for adopting an "open secession platform" and swore to "battle for the National Democracy and the Union." When he accepted an invitation to run as a Bell-Everett elector later that year, he repeated his pledge in a letter printed in many newspapers around Texas. He argued that Lincoln must be defeated, but continued, "with those who believe no union is necessary, I have no sympathy. I am not prepared for a dissolution of this great and glorious government." Paschal predicted that disunion would result in civil war, and declared that "whatever battles I might fight would be for the preservation of the Constitution and the Union, not for the destruction of the latter because the former has been violated."46

Although in 1862 Paschal publicly claimed to have "acquiesce[d] in [Texas's] fortunes for weal or woe," he never really accepted the fact that his state now waged war against his country. William Pitt Ballinger found Paschal "very bitter on the political divisions" shortly after Lincoln's election, and in 1863 Paschal told James Bell that he could see "nothing but misery before the country." Paschal spent most of the war years opposing conscription, defending conscript evaders in court, and beginning his life's work of codifying the laws of Texas. The *Texas Republican* reported in the fall of 1862, that Paschal had finally paid his Confederate taxes after authorities threatened to turn his house into a military hospital. Early in 1864 a squad of local militiamen broke into Paschal's home and arrested him. Despite his daughter's determined attack on one of the intruders— she drew blood when she bit his hand—his arresters held Paschal in a local jail for several days without charging him with a crime. When DuVal heard of Paschal's arrest from a party of refugees in Brownsville, he "fully expect[ed] to hear that the Judge was murdered," but Paschal eventually went free.47

Although Paschal stayed in the Confederacy throughout the war, he refused to serve its government or hope for its success, and two of his sons and a stepson—G. W., Jr., and Ridge Paschal, and W. D. Price—fled Texas to join the Union army.48 In an 1863 letter he told his colleague and friend William P. Ballinger the reasons he opposed the Confederacy. He hated the powers that the Confederate government had assumed in order to prosecute the war and the Know-Nothingism that appeared in the Confederate Constitution. Paschal's primary target was conscription, which had "effectually destroyed the spirit of volunteering" among the men of the South and the evasion of which had led some areas of the Confederacy to the brink of civil war. The policy of conscription, Paschal wrote, "declare[s] that every free man belongs body, soul and blood" to the Confederacy. Southerners now "have no choice as to whether they shall be soldiers or not"; they could no longer select their own officers or their own regiments, much less choose "for or against what cause they shall fight." Southerners no longer knew "who may be arrested any day by martial law," or "whose property may be taken by any corporal['s] guard without law." Commerce was no longer controlled by Congress, but by military officers, and Confederate citizens "are subject to be taxed without limit, and . . . forcibly denied the right of immigration." Casualties, enemy occupation, and disaffection had deprived the Confederacy of many soldiers; immigration restrictions prevented the utilization of immigrants as citizens and soldiers. In sum, Paschal predicted doom for the Confederacy and its people in both the military and the constitutional senses. "The disease is at the root," Paschal lamented, "the northern armies can never subjugate us. But we have subjugated our own people."

Paschal applauded Ballinger's course since he "fell in with the revolution," and betrayed a trace of envy toward Ballinger's southern patriotism. Yet Paschal could not bring himself to support the Confederacy as loyally as Ballinger. "That ardent patriotism which you feel," he told Ballinger, "cannot be infused into the masses by the great army of office holders who have turned Speculators." Ballinger must use his influence "against the abominable listlessness, which submits to all kinds of subjugation." Paschal wearily closed his letter with the wish that he and Ballinger could meet. "I never talk," he complained, "because I should not be understood. Like you I look not to the past right or wrong; but I look the facts square in the face."[49]

The differences between Paschal's and Ballinger's interpretations of those facts reveal the point at which the spectrum of allegiance to the Confederacy shaded from loyalty to disloyalty. The Whig Ballinger and the Democrat Paschal both loved the South and agreed on many aspects of the sectional conflict. Neither celebrated the emancipation of the slaves, both decried the South's decision to secede, and both, at least early in the secession crisis, thought that the people would eventually come to their senses and allow society to return to normal. Once the war began, however, Ballinger and Paschal followed increasingly divergent courses. The former, inhibited by his Whiggish conservatism, served the new order as an appointed official and with his writing, while the latter, sparked by his Jacksonian love for the Union and states' rights, did everything he could to foil the assumption of what he considered to be unconstitutional powers by the Confederate government. Both men sought to protect the southern society they loved, but responded to the Confederacy very differently. As a result, some of the most ardent secessionists respected Ballinger and considered him a loyal rebel. Paschal, on the other hand, was arrested, deprived of his property, and forced into a wartime retirement. Paschal, and to a greater or lesser extent many of the other political Unionists, had before the war participated in all aspects of southern society and in the economy and government of Texas. Yet, when the war began, they rebelled against the Confederacy because to support it would be to deprive their state of what they believed to be one of its most important virtues: its membership in the Union.

At the opposite end of the Unionist spectrum from Paschal were those Texans who actually joined the federal army.[50] Refugees—especially those who had migrated to Texas from the free states—often found their way into northern army units early in the war. At least thirty-nine men who later enlisted in federal regiments from Texas had previously been in other units; over half served in New England outfits, while a handful were veterans of the United States regular army and a few others came from Union regiments in Louisiana. Five men volunteered for duty in black regiments either before or after their service for Texas.[51]

Confederates jailed Charles Anderson, an Ohioan before he bought a horse ranch near San Antonio in 1858, because of his outspoken opposition to secession. Anderson nevertheless escaped, became colonel of the Ninety-third Ohio, and in 1863 won election as lieutenant governor of his home state. The Mills brothers of Indiana, Anson and William, led El Paso's Unionist refugees and soldiers. Anson, who had attended West Point for a few terms, headed east after the local vigilance committee threatened his life, and rendered distinguished service in the Army of the Cumberland. Anson's younger brother William—the future husband of A. J. Hamilton's daughter, Mary—shared his brother's political beliefs and defiant attitude. After a brief imprisonment as a spy by Confederate authorities in El Paso, he served rather erratically with the federal troops in New Mexico until the fall of 1862, when he became a Federal Customs Collector for New Mexico with his headquarters in Union-occupied El Paso. Unlike Anderson and the Millses, Rev. Thaddeus McRae had grown up in the South. McRae's belief that secession was unconstitutional estranged him from his Louisiana congregation and, thinking Texas to be outside the "region temporarily abandoned by God to its own devices," McRae accepted a call from a church in Port Lavaca. Unfortunately, McRae arrived in Texas at about the same time as secession fever, and "there I was again with a bastard flag, floating over me." As the war grew bloodier, the efforts of some members of his congregation to keep the local vigilance committee at bay proved unsuccessful. The reverend "took the occasion to leave and retire to 'Abraham's Bosom,' " in the words of a Houston newspaper, when federal troops raided Port Lavaca in late 1863. He eventually made his way to New Orleans, where he became a chaplain in a military hospital for black troops.[52]

A survey of the "Index to the Compiled Service Records of Union Soldiers from Texas" reveals that more than two thousand Texans (2164) enlisted in federal forces. Most joined the First and Second Texas Cavalry Regiments. The former, organized in the fall of 1862, found recruits among the Unionist refugees in New Orleans, while the latter took shape very late in 1863 along the lower Rio Grande Valley. They saw extended field duty and combat in the swamps of Louisiana, and participated in federal expeditions into Texas in 1864. Plagued throughout the war by poor mounts, irregular issues of uniforms, and short rations, these Texans nevertheless contributed more to the Union war effort than any other group of Texas Unionists.[53]

Edmund J. Davis, the only Texas field officer to attain a brigadier's star in the federal army, commanded the First Texas at its mustering in and later headed a brigade to which the First belonged. He was yet another Unionist product of the Opposition wing of the Democratic party. A Florida native and originally a Whig, Davis moved to Corpus Christi in 1849 and soon won admission to the bar. As the Whig party disintegrated, Davis gravitated toward the Democracy, a move accelerated by his distaste for the Know-Nothing party. After a tour of duty as district attorney for Cameron County, he became judge of the state's twelfth district in 1856 and was, according to the Englishman R.H. Williams—with whom Davis would cross paths during the war—"popular with a certain section of the people." Local political parties in the lower Rio Grande Valley, called the Reds and the Blues, had grown out of land-title disputes. Davis belonged to the latter faction, the members of which were usually Unionists by 1860.[54]

Despite his prewar Unionism, Davis did not begin the war as a rebel against the Confederacy. In a speech at the Corpus Christi courthouse late in April 1861, Davis accepted the decision of the people of Texas, and urged Texans to unite to defend their honor and rights. In the same speech, however, he attacked the secession convention's unseemly and illegal adoption of the Constitution of the Confederate states; denounced the rashness of the secessionists' actions, which could only lead to a huge public debt; and claimed that the Confederate constitution's three-fifths clause would discriminate against Texas because of her relatively small slave population. Despite his profession of support for secession, Davis followed Sam Houston's lead in refusing to take the oath of allegiance to the Confederacy, and his state district court soon fell into disarray. After an uneasy year in Texas, the conscription act and clashes with local vigilantes prompted Davis to leave for Mexico in May 1862. After a flying trip to Washington, Davis returned to New Orleans with a colonel's commission and the authority to raise the First Texas Regiment. Davis served the federal government ably but unspectacularly, spending most of his war in Louisiana, where he sometimes commanded up to two thousand troops. Late in 1864 he became a brigadier general of volunteers.[55]

Unfortunately, the rank-and-file members of the First and Second Texas, like the privates and noncommissioned officers of most armies, left few written documents. Many volunteers came from the hundreds of destitute refugees who flowed into Matamoros and New Orleans, who took to heart A.J. Hamilton's cautionary advice to them: "If you are not willing

to fight to reclaim your home, then you deserve no aid, and will get none."
Some had deserted from the Confederate army while stationed along the
border; some were Germans or Hispanics anxious to seek vengeance for
injustices committed against them by Texas Confederates; many doubtless
shared the ideals of officers such as Davis and Haynes and were truly
committed to the Union cause.[56]

The reactions of the families of Texas Yankees have not survived. But at
least some no doubt responded in the same way that the family of Capt.
Charles Steedman of South Carolina reacted to his announcement in late
1860—after his state had seceded from the Union—that he would remain
loyal to his country and continue to serve it in the United States Navy.
Charles's brother James reminded him that "there is not one of your
relations but who are strong supporters of South Carolina . . . and we all
expect you to do your duty to your God, your State, and Truth." When his
sister Eliza heard of his decision, she "felt that my blood was cold in my
veins" and cried out "no, not my Brother a Traitor to his Mother Country,
where he first drew breath & saw the light of Reason, & most of all where
lie the bones of his Father, Mother, & many dear relatives." She "could not
persuade myself that a Brother . . . true Southern in soul & body, could
ever allow Northern principles to contaminate his pure soul." Steedman's
wife, a Pennsylvanian, bolstered his convictions. "Be prudent," she wrote
in April 1861, "and don't let any excitement carry you out of your steady
course."[57]

Despite family and social pressures, hundreds of Texans, including a
large number of Mexican-Americans, signed on with the Union army. On
the basis of a crude analysis of surnames, it can be estimated that Anglos
and Germans made up 46.3 and 13.1 percent of the Texas regiments,
respectively, but that tejanos made up fully 40.6 percent, far above their
share of the civilian population. This is especially true of John L. Haynes's
Second Texas. Over half of the original six hundred or so enlistees in the
junior regiment were Hispanic. Vidal's Partisan Rangers—largely deserters from the Confederate army—and most of the over four hundred
Mexicans already serving in the First Texas later transferred to the Second,
creating a unit in which perhaps three-fourths of the troopers were Mexican-Americans. Anglos, Germans, and Mexicans fought in nearly every
company of the First and Second Texas, but there was a strong element of
segregation in the regiments. About 75 percent of the First Texas's Hispanics, for instance, served in Companies H, J, K, L, and M—compared
with about 12 and 7 percent for the Germans and Anglos, respectively—
before moving over to the tejano-dominated Second Texas. Exactly one-
third of the Texas Germans in the Union army (ninety-four men) joined
Company E of the First Texas, including Adolph Zoeller, their captain,

while thirty-four found themselves in the Second Texas. Anglos, of course, made up the majority of many companies; the four-score-and-five members of the elite "Hamilton's Bodyguard" included no Mexicans and only fourteen Germans.

The two regiments from Texas generally drew scouting or garrison duty, although they occasionally found themselves in the middle of sharp skirmishes against Confederate forces that sometimes included friends, relatives, or enemies from Texas. Their lives resembled the lives of all Texas refugees during the war, with the responsibilities and dangers of military service added to the worries and homesickness spawned by separation from loved ones. Despite their backgrounds and their unique role in the federal army, their service seems to have differed very little from that of other Yankee soldiers—except, of course, for the very large fact that they were not Yankees. Their route to dissent—at least the route taken by their officers—resembled that taken by nearly every other Texas Unionist. Their convictions, or ambitions, or personalities, however, carried them to the far end of the spectrum of loyalty to the Union—they actually took up arms against their native region to defend a government and a constitution that a majority of their fellow southerners had come to believe threatened the way of life of that region. The extent to which they became outcasts in their own state was rather ludicrously exhibited early in the war when the legislature briefly considered a bill making service in the Union army sufficient grounds for divorce.[58]

This is not to say that all of these southern-born Yankees served the United States unflinchingly. About a quarter of the total number of Texans in the federal army eventually deserted. One Yankee officer recorded the desertion of two men from the First Texas in July 1864; they had gotten themselves admitted to the post hospital by feigning illness, but took advantage of an exercise period to "vamoose . . . the ranch." Lt. Benjamin McIntyre of the Nineteenth Iowa did not "think any notice was taken of it so common has become the desertions of Texas Cavalry." The federal commander at Brazos Santiago complained that "no dependence can be placed upon the detachment of First Texas Cavalry" assigned to him, as "they desert at every opportunity." He could not even send other troopers after the deserters, as only the Texans were familiar with the territory, and he could not trust them to return to camp. Despite such lapses, many Texans steadfastly performed their military duties throughout the war.[59]

The plight of Texas refugees—at least those who did not serve in the First or Second Texas—demonstrates the mixed reception they received from the federal government. Some government officials welcomed them with open arms and showed remarkable compassion, transporting them to safe quarters in New Orleans and providing them with jobs, provisions, and sympathetic ears. Nevertheless, refugees could never count on such positive treatment, and their needs and plans were rarely considered. Their situation resembled in many ways that of freedmen, whose experiences as contraband or as soldiers were decidedly mixed.[60]

Some prominent political refugees from Texas—including several of Thomas DuVal's old fishing companions—weathered the war rather well, because of their wealth or their ability to find work. S.M. Swenson, a Swede who was shipwrecked off Galveston in 1838 and who eventually became a prosperous Austin businessman and crony of Sam Houston, feared for his life and decided to leave Texas in the autumn of 1863. He secured a pass from the provost marshall of Travis County to go to a health resort in Arkansas, then headed in the other direction to Mexico, reaching Brownsville on October 31. Swenson spent the remainder of the war in Mexico and New Orleans, accumulating a fortune in the cotton trade. Amos Morrill, another Barton Creek tory, accompanied Swenson. A descendant of an old New England Puritan family and a Whig, he had lived in Texas since the 1830s and for a time shared a law office with A.J. Hamilton. His northern political connections earned him a job in the New Orleans customs house during the last year of the war. Yet another Travis County refugee, Anthony B. Norton, earned the rancor of secessionists before the war as the Unionist editor of the *Southern Intelligencer* and as a conservative lawmaker. In a speech to the legislature in January 1860, Norton urged Southerners to look to their friends in the North, to turn away from those southern radicals who "seek to proscribe, and read out, and 'place at the foot' their own countrymen—bone of their bone, and flesh of their flesh." After Norton's flight from Texas in the first year of the war, the *Marshall Texas Republican* castigated him as an "Ohio abolitionist" and "vile demagogue" whose vices were tempered only "by his being a man of feeble abilities." Norton spent most of the war in the Midwest, where he worked to alleviate harsh conditions for Texans in Union prisoner-of-war camps.[61]

The northern-born missionary Melinda Rankin fled Brownsville and her Rio Grande Female Seminary in September 1862, when the southern Presbyterian ministers with whom she worked ordered her to abandon the school because of her contacts with northern missionaries and her lack of sympathy for the Confederate cause. During the next year she taught school in Matamoros, and nursed Union soldiers and conducted a school for freedmen in New Orleans. She accompanied the federal invasion force to Brownsville in 1864 and rebuilt her school, only to return to New Orleans when the federals abandoned the Rio Grande expedition.[62]

Another South Texan, Reading W. Black of Uvalde, departed Texas in 1862 to protest the Confederates' mistreatment of Texas Germans. In his absence, he left the management of his half interest in a shipping firm to his partner, N.L. Stratton. He warned Stratton that he had "no idea of working for the Rebels in any way." When his partner ignored Black's wishes and contracted a profitable business with the Confederate government, Black urged him not to be "too sure of your ill gotten gains." Even if the Confederacy succeeded in its revolution, "it is the easiest thing in the world with a $100 to hire one of your brother Confeds to hang you before you would get 10 miles from Brownsville." Remember, threatened Black, "it was no idle oath that I swore before I left Uvalde that I would exterminate any man woman or child who would injure me to the value of a three day old chicken."[63]

Of course, most of the hundreds of refugees from Texas did not have the resources of well-known politicians, businessmen, lawyers, or civic leaders. Many were deserters from the Confederate army or conscript evaders, others were persecuted Germans from West Texas, and many were men who had in one way or another attracted the unwelcome attention of vigilance committees or military authorities in their home towns. An overwhelming number of them shared at least one characteristic, however: observers constantly emphasized the poverty into which their exile had thrust them. Late in 1864, E.D. Etchison, United States consul at Matamoros, sent a message to Gen. W.A. Pile that included a poignant, if somewhat melodramatic, description of the plight of the refugees and a plea on their behalf for aid. The refugees "daily coming in from Texas," Etchison wrote, were "destitute & forlorn, hungry and naked, sick and emaciated." They were "thousands of miles from their native hills & friends at home," isolated "here on the Mexican Rio Grande, begging for food to appease their hunger, for garment to hide their nakedness." Etchison could not get them out of his mind. "Their pale faces & haggard looks, their sunken and glasing [sic] eyes haunt me in my dreams. I hear them exclaim My God! My God! hast thou forsaken me."[64]

Although early in the war a number of Unionists journeyed by wagon train to California, most refugees chose the shorter trip to Mexico. United States consuls in Matamoros and Monterrey sent a steady stream of Texans to New Orleans—at government expense—and usually did all they could to help the refugees. The acting consul at Monterrey told Secretary of State William Seward in June 1863, that "I am seldom without some Texas refugees on my hands. They come to me destitute of money and often nearly naked." After his resignation as consul at Matamoros, Leonard Pierce submitted a bill for $24,000 to the State Department for the care of refugees. In Brownsville, refugees with families were placed in houses recently evacuated by Confederate sympathizers and issued army rations in return for any sort of work they might be able to do for the government.[65]

The evacuation of that border town by Union forces in the summer of 1864 eliminated federal protection for those refugees—not to mention the other benefits of life within the Yankee lines—and sparked a frantic exodus. A member of the retreating army reported that "the citizens [of Brownsville] generaly [sic] are very much excited." Many had sworn allegiance to the United States government. "We have given them protection and very many aids and secured them every privilege a free people could ask and a bright future seemed dawning upon them." Now, however, they "feel that their hopes and expectations are blasted—the future to them is dark and dreary with not a ray of light to dawn upon them." They could not stay in Brownsville, "for certain death await[s] them." On the other hand, "if they leave they go as beggars for they must sacrafice [sic] every possession of home and the comforts surrounding it." A "stampede" across the river to Matamoros ensued. "The landings upon both sides of the river is [sic] piled with household goods of every description," wrote the northern officer. The Unionist citizens "seem to swarm out like bees from an interupted [sic] hive."[66]

The experiences of the Brownsville expatriates underscore the inability or unwillingness of federal authorities to guarantee protection or sustenance to their southern allies. This extended to those men who had sought refuge in New Orleans, which overflowed with them. John Hancock wrote in his diary that one morning late in 1864, "at an early hour, Refugees appeared about the hotel, and several came into my room." They seemed "to feel a sad sort of pleasure in talking over their trials, hardships and wrongs." He believed that these people deserved the help of the federal government. "Not a thought seems to have been given to the condition of these unfortunate Refugees, who, because they remain true to the Federal Government, have been driven from their homes . . . in a state of great destitution." They work at menial jobs for low wages "barely sufficient to procure them the cheapest . . . clothing." They endured persecution, the hardships of life as fugitives, and "daily suffer unutterable mental suffering" over the condition of destitute families left back home, "subject to all the abuse and outrages of brutal soldiers who are persuaded that to tyrenise over unionists is meritourious." The government must do something, according to Hancock, to relieve their plight.[67]

Thomas DuVal, for one, resented the treatment he received at the hands of government representatives. When he arrived in New Orleans on Christmas Day, 1863, he was sent to the office of George Denison, a customs official who had lived in Texas for several years before the war. Denison had to certify DuVal's loyalty to the Union before the Texan would be allowed to join the federal invasion force at Brownsville. "I felt acutely this treatment," DuVal fumed in his diary. "The idea that I should go to hunt up a stranger to endorse my character and my loyalty was something hard to brook."[68]

A newspaper briefly published by Union soldiers in Brownsville also angered DuVal. The *Loyal National Union Journal* supported "the army, the people, and the [re]election of ABRAHAM LINCOLN." The editors provided news, gossip, and less-than-flattering comments about the Texas refugees flocking into occupied Brownsville. "Everybody is a refugee," reported the *Union Journal*, "or, as they more properly say, renegade." In Brownsville, one could find the "best and meanest of mankind," including "the sneak in the most profound perfection, who deserted the rebels . . . of whom, he was the most blatant and persistent." Now, however, he was "cringing and willing to take any oath that will get him a voucher for a pair of mules or a bale of cotton." Other articles castigated those refugees, who "having sneaked out of rebeldom . . . now want to hide or remain neutral." Some had the "impudence" to think "they ought to have a pension for laying down their [Confederate] arms." DuVal, not surprisingly, felt insulted at the insensitivity of the paper's editorial generalizations. "It is calculated to make loyal men desperate," he wrote, and would give refugees "the most erroneous impressions about the good sense and intelligence" of Yankee soldiers.[69]

Another refugee complained in a petition to the commander of the Brownsville forces that the federal occupation had not benefited those Texans who had steadfastly supported the Union, but had instead profited speculators who pledged the federal oath in order to make a killing in the cotton market. If such men "are to amass wealth in the service of Rebellion while we are made poor because of our loyalty" and regain power over "the destinies of the community," then bona fide loyal men "shall wake up to the fact that Loyalty is a crime to be persued [sic] with penalties while Treason is to be protected and rewarded as a Virtue." The author, G.D. Kingsbury (alias F.F. Fenn, a name he had assumed upon arriving in Texas years earlier), the former postmaster of Brownsville, closed by declaring, "Either loyal men or Rebels are to be benefitted by the triumph of the Union army."[70]

Even Union soldiers from Texas could not escape the ambiguity in the federal government's dealing with Texas Unionists. In March 1863, Col. Edmund Davis and another Texan, Maj. W.W. Montgomery, went to the booming border town of Matamoros to entice Confederate deserters into the Union army. Rebel tempers flared as Davis and Montgomery's new recruits (estimates of their numbers varied from 120 to 300), while waiting for transportation to New Orleans, taunted Confederate soldiers across the Rio Grande. One rebel reported that "their boasting talk . . . had riled the boys very much," and a party of volunteers crossed the river on the night of

March 14, killed several of the "renegades," chased the rest of them off, and carried Montgomery and Davis back into Confederate territory. By dawn, Montgomery lay dead and the raid had become an international incident.[71] The federal government, however, did little to defuse the situation.

The crisis ended when Albino Lopez, governor of the Mexican state of Tamaulipas, threatened to suspend trade between Texas and Tamaulipas unless the raiders returned the surviving captive to Mexican soil. Citizens of Matamoros, finding another reason to distrust the Anglos on the north bank of the river, took to the streets to protest the violation of neutrality. Brig. Gen. H.P. Bee, commanding southern Texas, ordered Davis's release, and by March 18 Davis and three other captives were back in Matamoros. Montgomery's body, which apparently remained in its makeshift grave for months and served as a rather grisly tourist attraction for at least one European visitor, was not recovered until federal forces invaded the lower Rio Grande later in the year. They interred Montgomery's remains with full military honors that included a eulogy by A.J. Hamilton.[72]

Confederate Texans took advantage of the event to attack all those "renegades" who had gone over to the other side. "Alas, poor Davis!" moaned the editor of the *Brownsville Flag*, "he came back with a bogus commission as Colonel, and is now trying to steal what he promised to capture." The *Flag* found it hard to believe "that we ever thought this man Davis honest; but his hypocrisy has furnished us with another lesson as to the depths of human wickedness. . . . Nature quit her work about the most delicate point in making him." In a later article the *Flag* called Montgomery "a very desparate [sic] character, who had made himself notorious and objectionable to the Confederate citizens on this frontier." The leading newspaper in the valley also questioned the accuracy of reports regarding the alleged anti-Confederate demonstrations in Matamoros after the capture. The "respectable portion" of the city's residents understood the raid to be a personal matter not reflecting on them. But the "renegades" filling the city "took it in high dudgeon and got up a torchlight procession" consisting mainly of runaway slaves, renegade Texans, "a few barefooted Mexicans and any number of children." The *Flag* scoffed that "the same crowd could have been hired to turn out for any disreputable purpose either to attend the funeral of a thief, or the orgies of a prostitute."[73]

John Haynes found in the anemic federal response to the Montgomery incident—Maj. Gen. Banks refused to retaliate against captured Confederates—a bitter symbol of the frustration felt by Unionists who were neither completely trusted nor given much to do by the United States

government. In a letter to Hamilton after the incident, he told about the
capture and hanging of Montgomery. "Such is the fate of this bravest of the
brave," he wrote about the crude treatment of the major's body. Haynes
contrasted the reaction of the federal authorities in this matter to their
severe treatment of Louisianans on the Red River who had ambushed and
killed a Yankee officer. The latter "was from Massachusetts, Capt. [*sic*]
Montgomery was but a Union man from Texas who had breasted the storm
of secession with unyielding loyalty." The angry Texan asked "is not this a
charter to the traitors to hang us all as tories and traitors to their unholy
cause?" Haynes lamented the "hard" fate of Texas refugees: "Insulted,
mocked at, deceived, and dishonored before our enemies—and then left
to the vengeance of those enemies with their ready halters." Haynes
demanded that the federal government take steps to make sure that the
commissions given to Union men guaranteed them the appropriate treatment as prisoners of war, "otherwise our commissions have simply dishonored us, making us the laughing stock of our enemies and bringing us into
contempt with every one."[74]

That the United States provided very little aid to the refugees—
beyond the rations, jobs, and protection given to some of them by individual federal commanders and representatives—highlights the fact that the
agents of the United States government did not know what to do with
them. Federal officials and army officers did not quite trust southern
Unionists; the former seemed to think of the latter as southerners first and
Unionists second. One member of the Unionist First Arkansas Cavalry
wrote a book during the war that described the problems of loyal men in
Arkansas, hoping to convince the northern invaders not to treat all southerners as though they were "the inhabitants of a conquered province." The
experiences of destitute refugees illustrate the tragic dimensions of this
distrust and lack of concern. The always unsatisfactory and often frustrat-
ing roles played by men such as John Hancock, Thomas DuVal, and A.J.
Hamilton in the Union war effort reveal how little was expected of them
and how federal authorities often perceived them as being in the way.
Abraham Lincoln wrote that Hamilton's "long and painful . . . exile" had
elicited from him "a deep sympathy," and he was instrumental in making
the Texan a brigadier. Nevertheless, federal commanders never gave top
priority to Hamilton's plans—not to mention those of his fellow Texans and
many other southern Unionists. Far more than any other group of dissenters, the wartime Union men of Texas envisioned a southern society in
keeping with northern war aims. They distrusted radical southern nationalists and often joined northern Republicans in perceiving the sinister
workings of a conspiratorial slave power; they sought to preserve the

primacy of the federal government; and although few became confirmed abolitionists, all accepted the necessity of ending slavery. Nevertheless, most found their loyalty unrewarded and their contribution to the Union war effort unsatisfying. [75]

5

Speculators, Deserters, and Bandits

Shortly after the southern defeats at Gettysburg and Vicksburg, Lt. Gen. E. Kirby Smith called the residents of his Trans-Mississippi Department "a lukewarm people, the touchstone to whose patriotism seems beyond my grasp." They appeared to be "more intent upon the means of evading the enemy and saving their property than of defending their firesides." Smith ordered the commander of the northern subdistrict of Texas, an area notorious for its disaffection, to crack down on deserters and other disloyalists. "Any enemies in our midst who by their acts and public expressions clearly evince their disloyalty," he wrote, "must be disposed of." The campaign to stamp out disloyalty failed, and less than six months later the military commander of Texas, Maj. Gen. John B. Magruder, notified Smith's chief of staff that news from North Texas was "most gloomy." He reported "that the public mind is in a most unsatisfactory condition, that a large portion of the people is disloyal." The situation worsened over the next year. James W. Throckmorton wrote from Wise County very late in the war that "the distrust as to the condition of affairs is not confined to croakers or those who never really wished us success." Disaffection "pervades every [sic] section and community, and is wide spread throughout the army."[1]

The conditions described in these letters were nurtured by long casualty lists, high taxes, impressment, and conscription. These factors could erode any man's loyalty, and many southerners withdrew whatever support they had given to the Confederacy and retreated into a neutrality or noninvolvement that Confederate officials defined as disloyalty. Those same conditions encouraged many forms of economic disloyalty on the home front—depreciating Confederate currency, trading with the enemy, speculating in cotton or any other commodity—and led to the high rates of desertion and draft evasion that plagued Confederate, state militia, and home guard units. Some members of this extremely disparate group based their actions on a foundation of Unionism, or at least antisecessionism, but the "dissent"—if it may be called that—of most surfaced only after hardships and sacrifices destroyed their spirit, or after opportunities for economic gains or self-preservation led them to compromise their loyalty to the Confederacy. That they succumbed to weakness, weariness, greed, or even common sense, showed just how precarious was the unity with which the South had gone to war in 1861.

Southerners seemed to fear this class more than other types of dissenters. Unlike political dissenters such as A. J. Hamilton or John Haynes, these enemies undermined the Confederate war effort from within. They threatened southern society by rejecting their duty to protect it. Southerners hated them for their lack of principles or clear-cut loyalties and attributed the worst character traits to them, including cowardice, opportunism, and deceitfulness. The objects of this hatred, however, rarely sought to overturn a society in which they had little at stake; their disaffection was not against southern principles or institutions as such, but against the sacrifices demanded of them by the struggle to preserve those institutions. They simply refused to fight or to support a war in which they had nothing to gain or to protect. Perhaps the particular loathing that some southerners felt for them stemmed from the fact that their presence came as a complete surprise. The solidarity with which the South had begun the war had made southerners believe that their only internal enemies were the few who had publicly campaigned against secession; this "Fifth Column" caught everyone else off guard.

For all their tough talk, loyal Confederates neither classified nor treated all these pragmatists, opportunists, and shirkers alike. Southerners reserved their worst rhetoric and treatment for deserters and draft evaders, but even they were often shielded or at least tolerated by a large segment of the population. In a few instances, vigilant Rebels drove from their towns speculators or businessmen who had merely refused to accept Confederate money, but they more typically used pointed editorials or boycotts to shame violators of the Confederate ethic. Finally, although refugees and other citizens with suspect loyalties frequently endured vicious rhetorical attacks, they were seldom exposed to any physical violence and sometimes managed to win acceptance from the communities in which they lived.

A critical factor in most disaffection and much disloyalty was the poor morale that infected the Confederacy as its conflict with the North wore down the resources and energy of southerners. Enthusiasm for the war dwindled in stages, and different segments of society grew tired of the conflict for different reasons. The war had always dismayed former Unionists, and they were the first to reject the demands of Confederate citizenship. Hill-country yeomen who had no stake in preserving the plantation economy and no reason—beyond a potent racism—for supporting slavery found themselves fighting for a way of life in which few of them participated. Conscription and its accompanying exemption clauses seemed unreasonably burdensome to them. Other southerners, even those committed to slavery and the plantation economy, disliked the fact that the Confederacy impressed their slaves and taxed their produce. Ardent states' righters, including some leading secessionists, lost their enthusiasm for the Confederate government when Jefferson Davis and other southern nationalists moved to centralize power in ways that, to them, made a mockery of states' rights. Still other previously loyal southerners became disenchanted after they concluded that the cause was lost and that further bloodshed was immoral. Some combination of these reasons led many to turn away from the Confederacy, and disaffection and outright disloyalty sprouted and grew in every Confederate state.[2]

The accelerating declension in southern loyalty late in the war seems, in hindsight, to have been inevitable. With the Confederacy's paucity of resources and men, with the mixed emotions—temporarily obscured by the passion of secession—of the mass of the population toward secession, and with the effect on southern institutions of the governmental centralization necessitated by the war, it would have been remarkable if the southern population could have retained the apparent unanimity with which it went to war in the bright, confident days following the attack on Fort Sumter. But loyal Confederates expected and even demanded the dedication of everyone, of course, and those southerners who fell or leaped off the Confederate bandwagon during the war often fared no better, and sometimes worse, than those Unionists whose principles had placed them in active opposition to secession from the start.

A wide range of activities raised the suspicions of loyal Texans against men whose actions—guided by cowardice, a lack of will, or hopes for personal gain—identified them as disloyal. Early in 1862 the *Dallas Herald* remonstrated against several local men who sought "to alarm the timid, to discourage the faltering, to injure our cause, prevent men from volunteering, and to afford encouragement and comfort to the enemy." The state legislature soon made it illegal to discourage men from enlisting in the army. Dock workers in Galveston flirted with disloyalty—at least in the minds of fervent Confederates—simply by refusing to remove government stores from the island when it was threatened with attack in the spring of 1862. After Brig. Gen. P. O. Hebert declared martial law over all of Texas, the men came back to work. The *Houston Telegraph* approved, and assured its readers that the provost marshalls would "guarantee that . . .

[neither] oppression on one hand [n]or treason on the other will be suffered."3

A lengthy controversy developed early in the war over rumors about the possible dismissal of officials at the state penitentiary in Huntsville. As appointees of the dethroned Sam Houston, many had followed his lead and only reluctantly acquiesced in secession. A.P. Wiley wrote Houston's successor that some men "of the radical stamp . . . are for decapitating . . . without benefit of clergy" anyone who was "lukewarm or laggards in the glorious cause of secession." Superintendent Thomas Carothers defended himself to Governor Clark by writing that he had supported Houston in everything but the general's *"seeming opposition"* to secession. Carothers underscored his loyalty by declaring that Jefferson Davis was his *"'beau ideal'* of a Statesman, a General, *a Man . . . I* would follow, to the Devil, if *He* lead the way."4

Amid their intrigues over the loyalty of neighbors and competitors, Texans also found time to target out-of-staters as suspicious characters, particularly refugees fleeing from the federal occupation of Missouri during the first year of the war. In October 1861, the *Dallas Herald* welcomed the large number of Missourians passing through town. Two weeks later, however, the *Herald* suspected that some of the refugees were not, in fact, from Missouri, as "everybody who comes down from the Red River country now, claims to be a Missourian, fleeing from the wrath of Lincoln." Even some of the legitimate refugees seemed to be dodging their obligations as loyal southerners. The *Herald's* editor counted a dozen "able bodied men, who . . . could do as good fighting as any in Price's gallant army."5

Other refugees experienced similar problems in Texas and doubtless shared the plea of a Louisianian temporarily residing in Kaufman County. "We are strangers in a land of strangers," he wrote to Governor Murrah, with "none to appeal to but you." Nevertheless, Texas enrolling officers sometimes conscripted refugees, despite their status as nonresidents. According to one refugee, a Dallas County conscription officer managed to draft every displaced person who happened to be in the county, contrary to the conditions of the conscription act. The widowed head of a refugee family from northern Louisiana also ran afoul of enrolling officers, who several times attempted to draft their overseer into the militia. The woman's twenty-year-old daughter, Kate Stone, kept a journal during her family's journey from their large cotton plantation northwest of Vicksburg to the isolated farms and villages of Lamar and Smith counties in northeast Texas, in which she described the suspicion directed toward refugees by the rough Texans she met. Residents of Tyler, for instance, called the many refugees gathered there "renegades"—the same term applied to turncoat

Texans. Kate unwittingly revealed one possible source of antagonism when she attributed the "strange . . . prejudice that exists all through the state against refugees" to "just pure envy." The refugees, she wrote, "are a nicer and more refined people" than most Texans, "and they see and resent the difference." Even after spending several months in Tyler, Kate reported in March 1864, that "we have refugee visitors but the natives . . . still hold aloof." Although later in the war the Stones became friends with some of the natives of Tyler, their Texas hosts never completely accepted them.[6]

Just as Texans accused some refugees of disloyalty for economic reasons—their contribution to the war effort seemed to take a poor second to preserving as much of their property and wealth as possible—they did not hesitate to accuse nonrefugees of committing economic treason. The Austin secessionist and Episcopal bishop, Alexander Gregg, assailed "The Sin of Extortion" in a sermon delivered in the capital city in March 1863. The war had brought great hardships, challenges, and opportunities to southerners, the bishop declared, and many citizens had risen to the occasion to perform their patriotic duties. Unfortunately, "the spirit of *Mammon*" in the form of speculation had reared its ugly head. This was "a development more dangerous to our peace, and more hostile to our welfare, than foes of flesh and blood." A holy war must not be polluted by pedestrian avarice, and Gregg warned his listeners against the "insidiousness of the evil, the temptations to its indulgence," and "its radically demoralizing tendencies."[8]

Some Texans took Gregg's exhortations to heart. "JWH" of Austin wrote a letter to a Houston newspaper, calling on the "men of Austin, [to] arise!!!" He demanded that they "mark forever with a brand of infamy" those extortionists, "who no longer crawl like the slimy reptiles that they are, but boldly stalk through your streets, grinding at every step with their iron heels, deeper and deeper down, the poor man, the widow and the orphan." The Texas legislature responded rather mildly by passing "an act to punish speculations in certain cases," on January 13, 1862. The law set a punishment of from two to five years in prison for buying provisions—after falsely representing oneself as a representative of the army, state, or Confederate states—"with an intent to make a profit upon such purchase." Later attempts to toughen the law failed to pass, as the states' rights and antiregulatory bent of southerners joined with the desire to avoid restricting business development to inhibit other state legislatures as well as the Confederate Congress.[9]

All sorts of activities came under the definition of economic disloyalty in Texas, including charging high prices for the necessities that became more and more scarce as the war dragged on, refusing to accept inflated Confederate currency, speculating in the booming cotton market in

Matamoros or other neutral Mexican border towns, and trading with the enemy. As early as November 1861, the *San Antonio Weekly Herald* alerted its readers to the "treason" practiced by many San Antonio merchants of refusing to exchange gold and silver for Confederate Treasury Notes. A Confederate soldier stationed in the city in May 1862, wrote in his diary that San Antonio, which had been heavily Unionist before the war, was "a town noted for extravagant prices and extortion." Merchants "will not change a Confederate note unless the soldier takes one half in goods at 3 times their price. . . . Don't think there are many good honest Southern people in Town." The prices of salt and flour doubled after a few Houston merchants cornered the market late in 1861. The next year the *New Braunfels Zeitung* offered to publish a blacklist of persons who refused to accept Confederate money. In 1863 the citizens of Lamar County petitioned the state legislature to stop interest on loans when lenders rejected payments in Confederate money. The San Antonio Military Commission shared this dim view of such goings-on when it sentenced Frederick Lochthe of Fredericksburg to thirty-five days in prison and fined him $100 for refusing to accept Confederate paper for a $20 debt. Some Texans tried to take advantage of the public's disgust at economic opportunism; the commissioners dismissed charges against William McLane, who had accepted paper money in payment for interest accrued on $8,000 in loans issued before the war, but refused to take paper as payment against the principal. Apparently the court decided McLane's accusers were themselves guilty of a form of economic disloyalty by trying to take advantage of the war to pay off their peacetime debts in depreciated currency.[10]

Vigilance committees and public meetings clearly defined fiscal dissent as treason. In an April 1862 drive against depreciators of Confederate currency, the San Antonio Committee of Public Safety cracked down on "every little sharper, to whom a dollar is more important than national independence, every croaker, who has no faith in the success of our cause—and every Lincoln sympathizer." Their names, occupations, and addresses would be published in order to expose them to "the sudden, summary and condign punishment to be inflicted upon them by an aggrieved and outraged people." The provost marshall of Dallas County condemned the high prices charged the families of Confederate soldiers by those who "would extort from the government, army and people." He took advantage of that spring's statewide martial law decree to fix reasonable prices for necessities. An 1863 public meeting in Harrison County planned to publish a list of local violators of economic loyalty, so that each of them might be identified "as a traitor to his country, that his infamy may be remembered and its consequences visited on him through all coming time." Finally, an 1863 public meeting in Travis County—perhaps influenced by Bishop Gregg's recent denunciation of extortion—passed resolutions supporting the currency and deprecating speculation. Any person who refused "to conform to the foregoing resolutions, is hereby declared an enemy to the country and [will be] treated accordingly."[11]

Grayson County women protested economic hardship in dramatic fashion during the winter of 1864. A mob of 125 armed women descended on the Confederate commissary in Sherman to collect the meat, coffee, tea, and other provisions meant for the use of soldiers' families that they believed officers had been selling illegally. They found no provisions, but promptly began looting local stores. Legend has it that William C. Quantrill, the notorious Missouri guerrilla then wintering in North Texas, stalked into the midst of the women, reminded them of the hardships endured by the uncomplaining soldiers at the front, and said, "What would your husbands think of you if they could see you?" The mob quieted, repaired the doors they had broken down, and went home. A year later the Second Texas Infantry dispersed a mob of citizens and soldiers who had marched on the home of the Confederate commander at Galveston, demanding a share of the provisions stored in the city. One rioting soldier died accidentally in the volley fired over the heads of the mob.[12]

Trading with the enemy and speculation posed the most serious violations of economic allegiance to the Confederacy. Reports of speculators began coming into the governor's office as early as May 1861, when citizens of Fannin County petitioned Edward Clark to halt cattle drives from Texas "to any of the Northern Markets," where they would be slaughtered "to feed our 'Black Republican' enemies." San Antonio businessmen had arrived in Grayson County by October of that year and were "strongly suspected here of abetting Lincoln" by purchasing flour and sending it out of Texas. Two months later, when New Orleans speculators flocked to the state to buy up every commodity that cash-poor Texans could sell them, one Houston resident asked Governor Lubbock to stop this "set of sharp speculators" from draining the state of provisions. "What good will bushels of gold do us," he asked, "if we are without food. . . . We must be protected or these Shylocks will Starve us." It is not surprising, given the religious prejudices of nineteenth-century America, that Texans often accused Jews of disloyal opportunism. R.H. Williams made a typical remark when he wrote, "How wonderfully keen is the Hebrew's scent of a profit!" Williams reported that many Jews had appeared in West Texas, selling provisions to frontier soldiers at "exorbitant" prices; "as the buzzards wind carrion, so they scented the corruption which was so rife in the state, and saw their profit in it." The *Houston Telegraph*, on the other hand, offered a back-handed compliment to Jewish merchants when it documented "the fashion of our contemporaries to charge all the extortion of the country upon the Jews"; they were no "more extortionate than the Christians."[13]

Too often, at least for the taste of loyal Confederates, speculation led to trading with the enemy, which the Texas and Confederate governments seemed utterly unable to prevent.[14] The *Brownsville Flag* announced in mid-1863 that "the town is crowded with merchants and traders from all parts of the world, and the side-walks are blocked up with goods." Men from New York and Boston stalked Brownsville streets, gathering up cotton in return for "all manner of explosive and destructive things." Yankee traders eagerly bought all the cotton they could get in Mexican markets, aided by Mexican merchants who acted as intermediaries between them and Texas cotton speculators. Texans whose financial opportunism outweighed their loyalty to the South made many fortunes along the Rio Grande. The Englishman Thomas W. House of Houston, a well-known dry goods merchant, banker, and cotton factor since 1838, continued shipping cotton to Liverpool after the war started. He avoided Confederate currency and built up his gold reserves in English banks. Another Houston merchant, William Marsh Rice, greatly expanded his considerable fortune by trading cotton through Matamoros.[15]

Even so committed a Unionist as George W. Brackenridge, a close friend of A. J. Hamilton, earned the hatred of Confederate Texans more for his dealings in cotton during the war than for his unpopular political leanings. With his several brothers serving in the Confederate army, George stayed home, running a lucrative cotton trading operation with Charles Stillman, a merchant and shipper whose ties with New York City merchants proved unvaluable. During the war's first year, most of George's neighbors and acquaintances cared little about his speculative projects. By late spring of 1862, however, after several months of Confederate defeats, such questionable dealings—especially by a young man whose duty, according to loyal Texans, lay in the army—came under closer public scrutiny. The fact that George and his partners demanded gold payments rather than Confederate paper also damaged their reputations. Many years after the war, Brackenridge recalled the transition in public opinion toward him. Early in the conflict, while the Confederates were winning, "the home folks hurrahed me about being a Yankee." After the Confederate armies lost a few battles, however, "people who had been my friends passed me without speaking. Then I could hear them talking about me when I passed." He fled Texas for Mexico in the summer of 1863 after a gang of Confederates threatened to hang him. He spent the rest of the war as a federal treasury agent in New Orleans and with the federal invasion force in Brownsville.[16]

John Warren Hunter, a Hopkins County teenager when the war

began, remembered "a never ending stream of cotton" that "poured into Brownsville," from late 1861 until the end of the war. Hunter vowed never to serve the Confederacy after local vigilantes murdered one of his friends. In order to reach a Mexican haven from Confederate military service, he drove one of the oxen-drawn wagons that "wended their weary way to the commercial mecca of the Southwest" from all over Texas, Arkansas, and Louisiana. Each year, during the spring, summer, and fall, thousands of wagons laden with cotton converged at the King Ranch 125 miles north of Brownsville. "This long stretch," Hunter later wrote, "became a broad thorofare along which continuously moved two vast unending trains of wagons; the one outward bound with cotton, the other homeward bound with merchandise and army supplies." Hunter was hardly the only driver whose choice of occupation had little to do with affection for the slow-moving trains of oxen, as even "school teachers, college professors, [and] society dudes" joined the wagon trains for the junket to the border, over which they could easily escape conscription. Not surprisingly, few drivers signed on for the return trip north.[17]

As Hunter's reminiscences indicate, speculators sometimes benefited from the disloyalty of men who had no stomach for army service. The same sort of apathy toward the Confederate war effort that led men to commit acts of economic disloyalty often caused them to desert from the army or to evade the draft. Of course, as the war became harder, bloodier, and more hopeless, and as military service lost its charm for the men who had eagerly volunteered in 1861, the problems of desertion and conscript evasion worsened. Many Texas soldiers no doubt shared the disappointment of the Louisiana private who wrote in September 1861, "how I wish this war was over, there ain't a bit of fun in it." At least 4,664 Texans deserted from the Confederate army.[18]

A letter to the *Houston Tri-Weekly Telegraph* late in 1862 outlined the causes of dissatisfaction among Texas soldiers. The Second Texas Infantry had not been paid in months, according to the author, although the officers had received their wages. "When we ask why the privates are not paid, all the satisfaction we get is, 'No money for the soldiers yet.' Yes, the poor soldier, who finds himself far away from home and friends, who risks his life for his country, is neglected, he falls sick, is sent to the hospital with not a dime in his pocket to buy any of the luxuries that a sick man requires. Vegetables are paraded before him, No money he says, and turns over and suffers. Week after week he lingers, and then fills an unmarked grave." Pvt. H.C. Medford blamed the "fraud and perfidy practiced upon the private soldier by the functionaries of the government" for the soldiers' discontent. He also exclaimed—to his diary—that most officers were "damnable pop squirts and coxcombs" whose treatment of their men

would soon "demoralize and ruin our army." William Zuber, an enthusiastic forty-two-year-old volunteer in the spring of 1862, found his ardor
dampened when he realized that even after his three-year enlistment
expired, the conscription act would require him to remain in the service.
"I began to fear," he wrote years later, "that . . . I was being used as a
permanent *slave* and would never again be permitted to enjoy the society
of my family or to provide for them." Theophilus Perry, a soldier from
Harrison County, directed his anger toward the rear, where poor morale
and profiteers undercut the army's efforts. He declared in a letter to his
wife, "every little editor and stump speaker ought to be put under a
musket and a rucksack."[19]

Hundreds of miles to the east, in Tennessee, an officer in Granbury's
Texas Brigade bitterly condemned Gen. John B. Hood after the battle of
Franklin with words no doubt echoed by many deserters from the Army of
the Tennessee. "The wails and cries of widows and orphans made at
Franklin . . . will heat up the fires of the bottomless pit to burn the soul of
Gen J B Hood for Murdering their husbands and fathers at that place that
day," he wrote. "Gen. Hood has betrayed us. . . . This is not the kind of
fighting he promised us . . . when he started into Tennessee." Other
Texans preferred not to fight outside their home state. Men deserted by
the dozens when Texas state units marched into Louisiana late in 1863,
forcing camp guards and provost marshalls to constantly patrol the camp
perimeters. One Texas soldier who stayed wrote his family that "absolute
demoralization" had set in.[20]

The demoralization reached far behind the front lines. By the summer
of 1863, Col. John S. Ford reported that in the counties north of Austin
"bodies of men are assembling, armed and equipped, to resist the enrolling officers." Deserters and conscript evaders from the southern counties
had been "increasing daily the strength" of these "squads," which, "if
unnoticed, will eventually become formidable." Three months later, Brig.
Gen. H.E. McCulloch, commanding the northern subdistrict of Texas,
estimated that at least one thousand deserters hid "in the woods, ready to
take to the brush" in North Texas. One group of at least two hundred men
guarded every road leading to their camps so closely "that not a man,
woman, or child goes near them" undetected. The men "have sympathizers all through their country, and, if they can't be induced to come
out peaceably, we will have trouble and bloodshed enough in this section
to make our very hearts sick.[21]

The situation could only get worse, and it did. By February, Mc-
Culloch had to write that "there are deserters in nearly every county" in his
district who were aided by "sympathizers who give them information and
feed them on the sly or let them steal from them." The deserters had

organized into bands of up to thirty men, and moved their camps every two or three days to avoid capture. "If the true men of this country would swear what they know," McCulloch claimed, "I could send several hundred men to the penitentiary for treason." To make McCulloch's task of retrieving deserters even more difficult, the state and federal enrolling officers, "as well as the most of the people, exhibit . . . more ignorance and knavery than any other people in the world." McCulloch also complained to Kirby Smith, the trans-Mississippi commander. "Circumstances go far to satisfy me . . . that disloyalty is widespread," he wrote, "that my brush men are deep in it, and the troops not entirely free from it." McCulloch reiterated his fear "that some good troops must be sent here or this section of country goes up." Only three months before, McCulloch had won a small victory when he persuaded over six hundred deserters and and absentees to come out of the brush in exchange for a fifteen-day furlough and permission to serve in frontier regiments. The beleaguered McCulloch claimed that if he had refused the latter condition, it would have "involved us in a domestic war."[22]

South Texas, where many of the state troops were stationed, also suffered from widespread desertion and conscript evasion, especially late in the war. Charles Lovenskold of Corpus Christi wrote Gen. J.E. Slaughter in Brownsville in November 1864, that conscription laws went unenforced in Goliad, Bee, Karnes, Refugio, San Patricio, Live Oak, McMullen, and Nueces counties. He counted three hundred "able-bodied" men lounging about, and at least two hundred absentees and deserters. "The Civil Law and authorities afford no protection to persons and property," Lovenskold reported. Robbers and thieves went unpunished, and "disloyalty and incipient if not open treason seem to be unreproved, if not protected, in many instances."[23]

The unwilling Rebels who abounded in Texas used a large assortment of techniques to escape military service. Some stayed off the line by securing exemptions from friendly physicians. Others managed to avoid the draft by claiming to join a regiment organizing some distance away from their home towns. When the state filled its quota and the new regiments marched away, the less loyal men returned to safety behind the lines. Some scrambled to find government jobs or other positions that exempted them from conscription. Other ways of avoiding duty included bribery, securing long furloughs immediately upon entering the army, and getting detailed for necessary duties back home. Job descriptions in newspapers for necessary industries—such as saltpeter and niter works— took pains to point out that men employed at those places would be exempt from active military duty. A Confederate soldier from Grimes County reported that, by the end of the war, "most of our people would sign any petition presented to them" for detailing men to public works, "whether such work were needed or not, and whether the men . . . were capable of performing it or not." Even slaves could tell when their masters were shirking. Lizzie Jones's master went to the war, "but he came home sho'tly, an' say he wuz sick wid the [con]sumption, but he got well real quick after surrender."24

One of the most notorious methods of avoiding Confederate service was to join a home guard or frontier defense unit, whose Indian patrol and deserter-chasing duties exposed men to fewer hazards than the combat they were more likely to see in the regular army. The frontier regiments went through several incarnations during the war, but were basically designed to allow men living on the frontier to protect their families from marauding Indians and to maintain a buffer zone for more settled areas of the state. Only men in counties designated by the governor could join these militia units. However, some home guard regiments harbored deserters from units sent east of the Mississippi, and the status of home guardsmen became a major source of friction between the civil and military authorities in Texas by 1864.25

The state troops were attacked from all sides. Major General Magruder protested to Governor Murrah that the army, "already much demoralized by desertions and the insidious efforts of demagogues and traitors," looked "with jealousy and discontent upon the favored class of conscripts, who have thus far been permitted to remain in the State Troops." In Pendleton Murrah's message to the legislature in May 1864, he noted that many of the men in the frontier regiments were not "bona fide" residents of the counties in which the units were recruited. All of these men, he declared, "should be expelled from the organization and placed in service under Confederate authority," tried, and "when found guilty of conspiracy and treason," punished. The families of men in the Confederate service, not surprisingly, resented the presence of so many home guard companies in the state. As early as June 1861, Charles Besser's wife complained of the "misfortune" that so many of the companies forming near their home in Enterprise were "Home Companies." She wanted more of those men "to be like someboddy—not show thiere cowardice so plane." The sister of a Confederate soldier captured at Vicksburg scorned home guardsmen as "feather beds."26

Despite the magnitude of the problem, Col. John S. Ford, Superintendent of Conscripts for Texas, issued a broadside in July 1862, declaring that "the man who opposes, in any way, the execution of the Conscript Act, has no claim to be a patriot." Most Confederate civil authorities, military men, and ardent editors agreed, and urged harsh punishments for desertion and conscript evasion. The *San Antonio Herald* applauded the conscription act, because "it is not right that the most patriotic of our citizens should alone fight our battles." With conscription, "the hardships and dangers of the war will fall alike upon all classes, including speculators, croakers and resident foreigners." The *Brownsville Fort Brown Flag* urged all government agencies to follow the lead of the General Land Office by replacing all conscriptable young men with old men, and declared that "if the young men will not go to war then, they ought to be precluded from ever holding office afterwards." The Bexar County Court punished deserters by rejecting their families' applications for county relief, while the state senate passed a bill that would have prevented deserters from voting. The *Texas Repuplican* went several steps further by suggesting that the legislature should not allow deserters to own property or to marry in Texas. Governor Murrah agreed with many of these suggestions. In a message to the legislature late in 1863, the governor said that deserters and those participating in "the harboring, concealing, and screening [of] men guilty of outrages against their country" must be forced to learn "that the way of the transgressor is hard."[27]

Deserters could learn that lesson only if they were found, and newspapers frequently published the names and descriptions of men absent without leave—and sometimes of the horses and equipment they carried off with them—while the army offered rewards ranging from thirty to sixty dollars for the "delivery" of wayward soldiers. The *Texas Republican* indulged in wishful thinking when it declared in 1863 that merely printing the names of deserters would help stem the problem. "Who can bear to contemplate the overwhelming grief and sorrow that will be experienced by those, true to our cause, who recognize in this list the name of a relative, neighbor, or friend?" Public outcry apparently did little to encourage deserters to rejoin their regiments, and most deserters went unpunished.[28]

At least one Texas Confederate officer shared the civilians' severe attitude toward deserters. Capt. Elijah Petty wrote of deserters from Walker's Texas Division, "I hope the scoundrels will be caught and shot. I dont want our Southern society disfigured with the slime of deserters or traitors." When four men received death sentences for desertion while the division campaigned in Arkansas in the late winter of 1863, Petty wrote to his wife, "I am hard hearted enough to want to see a military execution." He got his wish, and he faithfully described the death scene to his wife, calling it "a melancholy and tragic end for them." He refused to extend any sympathy to the dead men, however; "it is the just doom of the deserter," he wrote. "I had rather see a hundred killed in battle than these poor devils here." Two days later he again wrote, "I saw them shot down as stoically as I would a hog," because "they had abandoned or forfeited all claim to life or respect."[29]

As the war dragged on, it became increasingly difficult to entice men into the service. One recruiter near Hempstead found "a reaction among the people, and but few were disposed to enlist." Men willing to join up for the duration of the war "could scarcely be obtained on any terms, and feeling disgusted with the apathy of the people, I gave up the business and returned home." Even those men who ended up in the army found military as well as public opinion turned against them. An officer in the Second Texas Infantry complained that the group of remarkably sickly replacements that he was accompanying to Mississippi consisted of "the most pitiful shirks and invalids" who were "so mean that they say they dont want to fight." He insisted that "their pitiful, mean, disloyal spirit is more contemptible than their diseases are disabling." The commander of the Second Texas declared that he would rather accept a demotion to major and turn his depleted regiment into a battalion rather than "command men who have been passed by law into the ranks—no give me the brave men who made a free offering of their services to their country." William Zuber believed that the presence of conscripts actually harmed a regiment, for such men "were dissatisfied murmurers, whose clamor weakened the patriotism of others, engendered a mutinous spirit, and dampened zeal."[30]

Few deserters recorded their reasons for committing what many southerners labeled treason. But some would no doubt have concurred with the sentiments expressed in "The Confederacy," a poem written in 1864 by a Lavaca County deserter. The novice poet was "tired of Confederacy / Confound her I may say!" He complained of losing his property, of receiving no pay for his service, and of having no "chance to save my life" except "to run away." The former volunteer revealed perhaps the most important motivation in his third verse, "It will not do," he wrote, "To save the country yet / Tried our best until of late / Too many Yankees met." The "revolution is nearly past," he admitted; the "Yankees got the most and best." J.A. Cain, a veteran subject to the draft, tried to procure a substitute to take his place. The man he employed however, "will not Swear to more than 36 years old." Cain decided to rejoin the army, but bitterly wrote, "I have done my part in this war, and mine is a hard case, but such is the Law! I feel more like backsliding and giving up everything than ever before in my life."[31]

Like the young poet-soldier, most deserters merely wanted to get out of the war alive. An English traveler overheard a drunken "Texas . . . *renegado*" when he "gave up his sentiments" at the English consulate in

Matamoros. The man finished a glass of brandy with the toast "'them as wants to fight, let 'em fight—I don't.' " John Hancock found out that even those men who left Texas and traveled all the way to New Orleans usually had no plans for serving the United States. "The fact is," he wrote in his diary, "these men, have no fixed notions on the subject, had about as soon serve one side as the other, but if left to their own inclination would serve neither." They "have merely grown tired [*sic*] of the Rebel service and pay & left it."[32]

Other disaffected Texans often joined with bands of deserters to resist attempts by the Confederate government to force them into the military. Few of the members of these bands sought to defend exalted notions of United States citizenship or constitutional scruples against secession; they were usually guided by what they believed was best for themselves or their families. As early as March 1862, just before the first conscription act was passed, Unionists and conscription evaders organized to protect them- selves in Fayette County. James Sweet of Burnet forwarded to Governor Lubbock copies of letters from a set of cousins to a young man named Ferguson. Apparently the Ferguson living in Burnet planned to move to Missouri to avoid the draft. His brother, R. J. Ferguson, urged him to come instead to Fayette County, where the Union men and other draft evaders "have the power and . . . are going to use it." R. J. asked his brother to bring with him all the powder and lead he could get his hands on. The Fayette County cousin, N. B. Ferguson, invited his cousin to "come down and cast your lot with us. We are as civil as reprobates." He also asked him to bring a six-shooter "or a half dozen." Apparently N. B. believed that he and his comrades controlled the county, for he wrote, "I was in hopes that we would have a little fun but they wont buck us." He added a postscript: "Uncle Tom says come Bob says come and I say Come so do so." The Fergusons' confidence was misplaced, as the Burnet County brother wound up in the army and his Fayette County cousins soon found them- selves in jail.[33]

As in disaffected areas throughout the Confederacy, bands of desert- ers, draft dodgers, and others often preyed upon Texas civilians, Unionists and secessionists alike. In October 1863, the *State Gazette* warned Aus- tinites against going outside the city limits unarmed, "as there are jay- hawkers all around us, hiding in the mountains, who have been frequently seen close by." One former slave remembered years later that parents warned their children not to wander into the nearby woods near Jasper alone. "Dey was deserters hidin' in de woods, an' I 'spose dey thought de chillen would tell on 'em. So dey ketch dem an' whip dem an' scare dem an' sen' dem home so dey wouldn' come back no mo!" On the frontier northwest of Austin, loyal men and "Tories" exchanged atrocities; the latter tried to deflect the blame for at least one of their killings by riddling their victim with arrows. Many other counties in the state could report similar congregations of disaffected persons. A Unionist refugee ventured into Lavaca County from Mexico in 1864, only to be captured by Confederate authorities. He escaped into a network of friends and relatives of deserters hiding in a thicket on the Lavaca River. At least thirty of "the hardest looking set of men" the Unionist had ever seen were led by an honorably discharged veteran who had been wounded at Shiloh and later deserted from his home guard company when the unit was called up for active duty. Another gang of outlaws and deserters gathered in northern Bell County under the leadership of a deserter named Lige Bivens. They found refuge in a well-hidden cave in a cedar brake called "Camp Safety" by locals during and after the war, from which they mounted expeditions against soldiers' helpless families. Just before the war ended in Texas, a score of mounted deserters appeared at the funeral of a New Braunfels youth shot and killed by Confederate soldiers.[34]

One disaffected Texan exhibited his opportunism outside Texas. Martin D. Hart had practiced law, promoted railroads, and served as a state senator from North Texas before the war. He opposed secession and had signed the Unionists' "Address to the People of Texas." But when the war began he donned a Confederate captain's uniform and raised his own company. He led his command toward Arkansas, where he allegedly planned to campaign as a Rebel partisan. His recent conversion to the Confederacy apparently lacked sincerity, however, and in the fall of 1862 he switched sides and accepted a Union army commission. After a flurry of recruiting, he and the mixed bag of Unionists, deserters, and outlaws who had joined him campaigned as the "First Texas Cavalry."[35]

Although at first Hart had apparently acted out of sympathy for the Union cause, his war quickly deteriorated into the pattern set by so many other partisan units and guerrilla fighters. Hart's small band of irregulars occasionally attacked legitimate military targets, but they increasingly turned to plundering Arkansas farms and plantations and murdering men who got in their way. Hart made enemies among Yankees and Rebels alike, but the Confederates caught up with him first in January 1863. The *Marshall Texas Republican* applauded the capture of "the notorious Texas traitor," who even before his foray into crime had been "a unionist of the stripe" that venture[s] to the very borders of open treason." Hart had crossed that border, of course, and the *Republican* assured its readers that he and his men "have fallen into hands that will make short work of them." A court martial convicted Hart and his first lieutenant of murder and hanged them early in February. Shortly after, Hart's former colleagues in the Texas legislature passed a resolution congratulating the officer in

charge of the expedition for "capturing and hanging the traitor and scoundrel Martin D. Hart and his followers."[36]

A few men went far beyond these attempts at self-defense or plunder.
Perhaps the most notorious disaffected Texan was Cullen Montgomery
Baker. Baker grew up on the banks of the Sulphur River in far northeastern
Texas, near the Arkansas state line. By 1861, Baker had already murdered
three men, including a witness instrumental in convicting Baker of horse-
whipping a young boy. He deserted soon after being drafted into the
Confederate service, and spent his war hiding out in the Sulphur River
swamps, robbing and murdering black and white residents of Texas and
Arkansas. In 1864, pursued by Confederate authorities, Baker joined a
"partisan" outfit in Perry County, Arkansas, which terrorized the region
and caused many residents to migrate. When the war ended, Baker, still
untouched by Confederate authorities, returned to Texas.[37]

The surrender of the Confederate armies changed nothing for Cullen
Baker; his wartime lawlessness and violence continued. He soon gained a
reputation for fighting and often killing federal occupation troops, unruly
freedmen, and scalawags. Among his victims were two freedmen's bureau
agents and a United States tax assessor, whose deaths prompted the *New
York Tribune* to report "The New Rebellion" in Texas. The governors of
Texas and Arkansas placed rewards on his head, and federal troops scoured
both states for him and his gang. His father-in-law finally ended Baker's
violent life by poisoning him in 1869; he died with a personal body count of
twenty-seven men.[38]

Despite his years of criminal activity, some residents of the region
terrorized by Baker remembered him rather fondly. Baker, they recalled
for T. U. Taylor, would often storm into Texas and Arkansas stores, take
clothes and provisions, and shout "Charge it to the Confederacy" over his
shoulder on the way out. More important, Baker won at least limited
approval for his deeds in his self-appointed role as a local "regulator." This
amounted to terrorizing "impudent and shiftless" freedmen to make sure
they worked hard enough and left white women alone. Years later several
former slaves could still conjure up the terror Cullen Baker inspired. "I
would run my las' limit if I heard he wuz in the neighborhood," Ransom
Rosborough—a child during Reconstruction—remembered. According to
Alex Humphrey, Baker "killed Niggers like they was dogs, and if you want
to put my people on the run just say 'Cullen Baker was seen in a neighboring community last night.' They'd hide out for two days." He also spe-
cialized in protecting the "helpless" South from unscrupulous carpetbaggers and United States troops and in disciplining local scalawags, "the
most contemptible creature that ever walked the earth." On one of his
regulatory missions he killed two black men who had asked permission to

escort two white girls home. On another he shot and killed a white farmer who shared his house with two daughters and two black employees. Federal troops became favorite targets after a squad broke into his house and stole some of the jewels from a shrine Baker had built to his deceased second wife. At other times he played the part of a local Robin Hood by distributing the contents of captured federal supply trains to his neighbors.[39]

Despite his somewhat improved reputation during Reconstruction, the Civil War had not changed Cullen Baker into a man fighting for the public good; it had merely widened the scope of his crimes. His Civil War career fit perfectly into the pattern of his life, for Cullen Baker never did anything he did not want to do. His desertion from the Confederate army was not a public display of principle, but a successful attempt to escape any sort of duty that did not lie strictly within his own self-interest. The informal, violent, potentially lucrative life of a "Confederate" partisan suited him much better, as Baker swore allegiance to neither a government nor an idea. His sociopathic protection of his own interests challenged a South struggling to form a nation; even his racial vigilantism during Reconstruction was less an acceptance of the values of the larger southern society than the logical culmination of his violent life.

Not surprisingly, the largest number of lawless deserters and hangers-on centered in North Texas, many miles west of Cullen Baker's stomping grounds. Late in 1864, residents of Collin County petitioned Governor Murrah to provide a regiment of troops to preserve order in the county, in order to avoid a repetition of "the history of last Spring," when "Lawless men prowled over our farms & Prairies and held our country terror-stricken." James W. Throckmorton, himself a resident of Collin County, recommended retaining the frontier defense force in the area. It had already gone a long way toward "purging that section of deserters & dodgers & traitors." If the regiment disbanded, "the frontier would soon be overrun with this class of persons," the "settlements also would recede, and a new line of counties would be the outside."[40]

The most ambitious crackdown against disaffected elements took place in the North Texas town of Gainesville against a secret organization whose members generally understood that they were banding together merely to resist the draft. A few of their leaders, it appears, and most loyal Confederates, however, believed the "clan" to be engaged in "wicked and abominable designs" against the Confederacy and against the peaceful and loyal citizens of Cooke County, designs that combined Unionism with more self-interested forms of disloyalty. The *Texas Republican* reported that the organization had three progressively treasonous levels of membership: initiates in the first "degree" pledged themselves to secrecy and to "avenge a brother member's blood," while the second degree was committed to "robbing, jayhawking, &c," and the third "contemplated the re-establishment of the old Union." The official chronicler of the episode in Gainesville claimed that this Union club actually planned to wrench North Texas out of the Confederacy and to reenter the United States. Help would come from their Union army allies in Kansas and from "every hostile tribe of Indians then in arms against the South, and especially against Texas." The Unionists "openly denounced the Government, and vowed organized resistance to the Conscript Law"; they refused to work for "southern men," and "became a terror to their southern neighbors . . . while their conduct evinced a spirit of hate and revenge too intolerable to be borne." They allegedly had gone so far as to plan the murders of all loyal southerners, including women and children—except for young marriageable girls—and the division of their property.[41]

This "strange affair" resulted in the lynching of at least forty-four men in October 1862. When a drunken member of the club—called by many a "peace plot," although it was apparently unrelated to other "peace associations" around the South—boasted about the existence of the group to a loyal Confederate, the latter notified local authorities, who on October 1, slogged through a downpour to arrest between sixty and seventy known members. Militia units from surrounding counties and elements of several Confederate regiments hurried to Gainesville, and soon a mob of several hundred armed men gathered outside the courthouse. After an informal "town meeting" had selected a jury, the "trial" began on October 2. Over the course of the next two weeks, the citizens' tribunal executed thirty men—the murder from ambush of a leading secessionist revived a badly lagging spirit of vengeance about half-way through the proceedings—and another fourteen died at the hands of the angry mob. A few others were murdered without benefit of trial, and three members who belonged to military companies were later court-martialed and hanged.[42]

Similar episodes took place elsewhere in Texas. James W. Throckmorton prevented an orgy of lynching in Grayson County by persuading a mass meeting to turn their prisoners over to military authorities. A Collin County legend—unconfirmed in official documents or newspapers—tells about the capture and hanging from a cottonwood tree on the town square of forty-two "bushwhackers" and conscription evaders in 1864. Col. John S. Ford called such incidents "deplorable affairs . . . accounted for as a result of the passions engendered by an unfortunate Civil War." In North Texas, those passions were fueled by conflict between nonslaveholding Unionists and slaveholding secessionists—who were usually the most powerful men in the region. With the memory of the slave "insurrection" of 1860 fresh in their minds, and wary because of their very real exposure to Indian raids and their perceived vulnerability to Yankee invasion, vigilant North Texans leaped to defend home and family from an organization made up of men whose disaffection and disloyalty to the Confederacy stemmed primarily from their desire to have no part in the war.[43]

Maj. Gen. John B. Magruder, commanding the District of Texas, indicated the extent of disloyalty in Texas when late in 1863 he wrote his superior, Lt. Gen. E. Kirby Smith, that "my difficulties here would be as nothing, if the troops could be made to stay in the ranks and the people true to themselves." Magruder felt himself "surrounded . . . by traitors, [and] harassed by deserters and mutineers." Many of the "traitors" about which the general complained were merely pragmatists looking out for their own interests. A few, like Cullen Baker, relished the chaos spawned by the war; some enjoyed unprecedented prosperity because of shrewd, if unethical, business practices; most merely wanted to be left out of the war altogether. Edward T. Austin spoke for many when he wrote E. M. Pease after the war, "I opposed secession until the act was consumated." After that, however, "opposition . . . would have been treated as treason to the State; and I have too large a family to make myself a political martyr." During the war, Austin "attended to my own business and left war and politics to others." With such sentiments no doubt widespread, it is hardly surprising that Magruder seemed to see traitors all about him. Unattached in any meaningful way to the southern economy or, to a greater degree, society—or at least unwilling to risk much to sustain either—and often lacking an ideological justification for their actions this sizeable minority was often deemed by Confederates to be the greatest internal threat facing the South. Although this perception was, of course, exaggerated, by April 1865, it was painfully clear that many Texans could muster no tears when the southern cause was finally lost.[44]

6

Ethnic Texans and the War

At the end of his famous account of a "saddle-trip" through Texas in 1856, Frederick Law Olmsted summarized the "Regional Characteristics" of Texas and the prospects for settlement in West Texas. Geography and Indians would inhibit the expansion of cotton agriculture and of slavery, but perhaps more important, according to Olmsted, was the "incongruous foreign element of Mexicans and Germans" on the frontier, which would "hinder any rapid and extensive settlement of Western Texas by planters." The Yankee tourist explained that neither of these ethnic groups participated in the slave economy. The Germans opposed slavery and often competed as craftsmen and laborers against slave labor, while few tejanos could afford slaves and many treated blacks as equals. "The manners and ideals of the Texans and of the Germans are hopelessly divergent," Olmsted posited, "and the two races have made little acquaintance, observing one another apart with unfeigned curiosity, often tempered with mutual contempt." Germans enjoyed little of the political power their numbers and abilities warranted, and often "remained apart . . . content[ing] themselves with the novel opportunity of managing, after republican forms, their own little public affairs." They rarely participated in politics beyond voting, but would occasionally "move together against slaveowners as their natural enemies." A Texas planter was "by no means satisfied to find himself in the neighborhood of the German. He is not only by education uncongenial, as well as suspicious of danger to his property . . . but finds . . . a direct competition of interests" with the Germans.[1]

Even worse was the relationship between Anglos and the Mexican-Americans living in Texas. "The mingled Puritanism and brigandism" that Olmsted believed "distinguishes the vulgar mind of the South, peculiarly unfits it to harmoniously associate with the bigoted, childish, and passionate Mexicans." Long decades of conflict with whites caused the latter to "fear and hate the ascendant race" and to "associate and sympathize with the negroes." Planters commonly believed that escaping slaves found ready allies in tejanos, and as slavery extended into new areas, "the whole native population of county after county has been driven, by the formal proceedings of substantial planters, from its homes, and forbidden, on pain of no less punishment than instant death, to return to the vicinity of the plantation."[2]

As Olmsted understood, the condition of the slaves and the conflicts between the dominant white culture and the Mexicans and Germans doomed the state's three largest non-Anglo ethnic groups to share an uneasy and often dangerous status during the antebellum period. The very nature of the blacks' participation in the slave economy forced them into an adversary relationship with southern planters, as the 1860 "insurrection" had so recently shown. Germans and Mexicans found themselves allied with blacks—at least in the minds of Anglos—because of their frequently unhappy economic and political conflicts with other Texans, as well as their well-known opposition or indifference to slavery. History and race— especially for blacks and Hispanics—inevitably led to conflict between Anglo Confederates and the other ethnic groups in Texas. Their roles as dissenters were created when many of them chose to change their traditional relationships with Anglos and, perhaps, their places in the larger society around them. Although Confederates in Texas readily acknowledged that these "outsiders" had little interest in the outcome of the war for southern independence, they nevertheless measured the loyalty of Germans and Hispanics by the same standards used to judge native-born, slave-holding Texans. In addition, despite the fears that blacks aroused in whites, masters counted on the steadfast allegiance of their bondsmen and the continuation of the traditional relationship between the races. Since Confederates in Texas warred less against invading Yankees than against values, ideals, and interests that threatened the besieged slave society of the South, the issue of loyalty among blacks, Hispanics, and Germans loomed large behind the lines in Texas.

Texas slaves shared their masters' civil war. Blacks found themselves thrown along with their white "families" into the anxiety, the hardships, and sometimes the danger spawned by the war. Long after the fighting ended, James Hayes showed how intimately the crisis intertwined the experiences of slaves and whites when he told a Work Projects Administration (WPA) interviewer of his obvious affection for the "women folks" on his plantation and of his concern for them after his master and his master's son marched off to the army. James usually picked up the mail in nearby Marshall, and whenever he returned from town, "dey run to meet me, anxious like, to open de letter, and was skeert to do it." One day the faithful slave "fotcher a letter and I could feel it in my bones, dere was trouble in dat letter." Young Master Ben—the eldest son—had been killed. "When de body comes home, dere's a powerful big funeral and . . . powerful weepin's and sadness on dat place."

Hayes maintained that during the war day-to-day life on the plantation went on "like always, 'cept some vittles was scarce." The slaves "didn't know what de War was 'bout,'" and apparently were not particularly interested. "I guess we was too ign'rant," Hayes said, "De white folks didn' talk 'bout it 'fore us." When the war ended and their master returned home, the slaves joined in the celebration, singing and dancing with the "white folks." According to Hayes, when they learned that they were free to leave, "none of us knows what to do, dere warn't no place to go and why would we 'uns wan' to go and leave good folks like de marster? His place was our home." Most of the slaves chose to stay until the master died in 1866.[3]

Hayes's example may not be representative of slave life during the Civil War in Texas, but it demonstrates one way that blacks and whites were forced to interact. Hundreds of thousands of slaves in other parts of the South flocked to areas occupied by northern armies, seeking long-denied education in missionary schools, proving themselves in the federal army, and carving out new economic lives.[4] Far from the liberating Union lines, Texas slaves endured a different kind of war than blacks east of the Mississippi. Although many black Texans extended the boundaries of their bondage, they usually had no choice but to wait out the war with their masters, while masters had no choice but to rely on their slaves even more than they had in peacetime. Texans did not often discuss the faithfulness of their slaves; perhaps the latent but ever-present potential for violence within the slave system—brought to life so recently in the wave of violence and arson in 1860—caused them to reassure themselves with silence.

Many Texas slaves performed faithfully during the war. "The negroes, as a general thing," reported the *Marshall Texas Republican* soon after Appomattox, "have acted very well towards their owners and the white residents of the South, during the disturbed condition of the country for the last four years." A few joined "the invaders," but only because of their "ignorance and the superior control of the white man." With a confidence that belied whites' later reactions to blacks during Reconstruction, the *Republican* asserted that the "war has demonstrated . . . that the idea of negro insurrections, once so prevalent, is a humbug."[5]

A few slaves met their masters' highest hopes and expectations. The slave members of a Marshall Methodist church hosted a supper, complete with singing and praying, for the minister and other guests. Blacks in Houston raised forty dollars for sick soldiers with a "grand ball" in July 1862, which they "conducted with the utmost propriety and decorum" and two "highly amusing" Negro tableaux held in Austin in April 1863, raised

$450 for Texas soldiers. Many slaves went to war to tend horses, nurse the sick and wounded, or act as personal servants to their masters. Rube Witt claimed to have enlisted in the Confederate army as a teenager, while James Cape suffered a shoulder wound while fighting in Tennessee. Some slaves provided dramatic evidence of their loyalty. When federals captured his master, William Byrd walked all the way from Virginia to Texas and waited until after the war to be freed. Henry Smith marched with the Texas Brigade through the siege of Petersburg, where his master's son was killed. Henry buried him and carried his belongings back to the plantation in Texas, where he continued working after freedom until his white family died.[6]

Back home, slaves frequently "kept de work on de plantations going, for dey had to keep on livin' an' some one had to do dis work." The slaves on Burke Simpson's plantation "jis stayed an' took keer of things for de Master while [he] wuz away to de war." When Union troops invaded South Texas and tried to entice slaves away from the King Ranch, a Houston newspaper proudly reported that they "remained with their mistress, and came away with her, proving true to the last." One LaGrange planter felt so confident in the loyalty of his servants that he left his wife and four girls alone with ninety-eight slaves in 1864. "They were all good negroes," the eldest daughter testified years later, adding that "my father would never own a vicious negro—mean horse or dog." Few blacks considered escaping from the Bexar County ranch on which Felix Haywood worked, because "we was happy." Life "went on jus' like it always had before the war. . . . We get layed-onto time on time, but gen'rally life was . . . just as good as a sweet potato." Slaves were not unaware of the threat they posed to southern society, however. "If every mother's son of a black had thrown 'way his hoe and took up a gun to fight for his own freedom along with the Yankees," Haywood believed, "the war'd been over before it began." Nevertheless, "we couldn't help stick to our masters. We couldn't no more shoot 'em than we could fly." Martin Jackson's father offered a grimly prophetic argument for remaining faithful: "He kept pointing out that the War wasn't going to last forever, but that our forever was going to be spent living among the Southerners after they got licked."[7]

Other slaves found routines upset and provisions scarce, and many suffered at the hands of cruel overseers hired to replace absent masters. In Galveston, overcrowding, shortages, and hard labor on Confederate fortifications caused illnesses to flourish and mortality rates to skyrocket.[8] In the face of these hardships, most Texas slaves could hardly ignore the war, although at least one told his WPA interviewer, "White man, we 'uns didn't know dere am de war. We seed some sojers at de star[t], but dat all." Nevertheless, many slaves knew all about the war from personal experience or after listening in on the white folks' conversations. One plantation mistress remembered that "the white men didn't talk the situation around where the niggers could hear . . . knowing that the nigger is a natural news ferret, and the biggest gossiper that ever was." J.W. King said that "some of de men on de plantation would slip up to a open winda at de big house at night and . . . lissen whut was read f'om a letter." Bad news for the Confederacy fueled the slaves' hopes. Despite their distance from the battlefields on which Mr. Lincoln's army fought, they instinctively grasped what was at stake in the white men's war. Around late-night fires, Abram Sells recalled, the older men would crouch, "stirrin' the ashes with the pokes and rakin' out the roas' taters. They's smokin' the old corn cob pipe and homemade tobacco and whiperin' right low and quiet like what they's gwineter do and whar they's gwineter go when Mister Lincoln, he turn them free."9

A minority of Texas slaves became dissenters by challenging their own status and, in so doing, the institution of slavery. Some hurried the day of freedom by escaping from their masters, and a handful—forty-seven—joined the Union army, but most rebellious slaves chose less daring forms of resistance. Wartime conditions and hardships inspired slaves to rearrange their relationships with masters and mistresses. Some slaves on a Williamson County plantation ran away—despite the nearly automatic "whippin' at de stake" that would greet them if caught—when a harsh overseer took over for their master, who had gone to fight in the war. Susan Ross's brother—after refusing to go to the army—fled his master's plantation after a beating so severe that "you couldn't tell what he look like." Although the war years did see an apparent escalation in the number of runaway slaves, escape held little chance of success, at least according to one Burleson County ex-slave. "I never seen any slaves that tried to run away until after the war," said John Mosley, "but . . . they never got very far at that." Punishment was sure and swift. Lee McGillery saw "a few slaves try to run away to the north after the war started and when the white folks of the south find them they would most of the time jest shoot them. Some few they never did find."10

Some runaways exploited the traditional sympathy between Mexicans and blacks by making their way to Mexico, thus confirming vigilant Texans' contempt for Hispanics. At one point, Mexicans on the south bank of the Rio Grande rigged up a flatboat in the middle of the river. Once a fugitive reached the boat he could easily pull himself across to freedom. Jacob Branch reported that "de white folks rid[e] de Mexican side [of] dat river all de time, but plenty slaves git through, anyway." Sallie Wroe's father was sent to the border with a load of Travis County cotton. When he reached the river, he and a number of other drivers paddled a bale of cotton over to

Mexico. Upon his return home after the war, he told them "he done git 'long fine with Mexico. He learnt to talk jes' like them." Similar instances led the *Houston Telegraph* to warn its readers against taking even "their trusty negroes" to Matamoros on business. Although everyone believed that his own slave was too attached to his master to run away, Matamoros was "overrunning with these trusty, now insolent negroes." "Loose colored women" and escaped slaves with plenty of spending money would lure otherwise faithful slaves into the welcome anonymity of the city. Once there, according to one Union army officer, some blacks enlisted in the Corps d'Afrique in the occupation force at Brownsville.[11]

Many Texas Confederates also detected surliness among those slaves who did not attempt to escape. A Houston newspaper complained in January 1865, about the insolence of the city's blacks. They uttered obscenities in the presence of children, refused to yield roads or sidewalks to white ladies and puffed "vile" cigar smoke in their faces, and bought illicit liquor from white merchants. The editor accused masters of being "altogether too lenient . . . and too regardless of their [slaves'] behavior." Likewise, the *San Antonio News* reported in mid-1864 that blacks were "pulling on important airs" on that city's streets. A "general negrow row" ensued in Nueces County when a female slave stole about $2,000 and distributed it among her black and Hispanic friends. Authorities recovered only $700. A Harrison County black allegedly plundered the home of a Mrs. Manson, whose husband was off fighting the war, then burned it down to escape detection. A few whites also reported aberrant behavior among slaves on their plantations. "Jack," a slave on John B. Walker's plantation, ran away three times during the summer of 1864. Once he left after having "refused Authority," and on another escapade he "borrowed" a mule.[12]

Mrs. Lizzie Neblett recorded the deterioration of slave behavior on her Grimes County plantation in a series of letters to her husband, Will, who was away in the army for much of the war. Lonely, burdened with a colicky baby, and often ill, Lizzie frequently complained about life in general and the slaves in particular. "I could not begin to write you," she moaned in late 1863, "how our negroes do all the little things." She could trust only a few slaves, and only two would give her any news from the quarters. She groused that most would not do anything unless they were told, and that *"I find I must think continually for them."* Several slaves resisted whippings from the overseer or ran away, part of a disturbing trend of insolence and misbehavior among slaves in the neighborhood. The situation had gotten so bad that "a great many of the people are actually afraid to whip the negroes." One slave, threatened with a beating by one of Lizzie's elderly neighbors, "cursed the old man all to pieces, and walked off in the woods." He came back only after his master promised not to punish him. Another neighbor's slaves rode his horses all over the county during their nocturnal adventures, and Lizzie doubted whether her own slaves were much better. "I believe if I was to tell [the overseer] to whip one of the negroes they would resist & it would make matters no better so I shall say nothing, and if they stop work entirely, I will try & feel thankful if they let me alone." For perhaps the first time in her life, fear also entered her relationship with the slaves: "I won't sleep with my doors open, any more, & if they break open either door or window I'll have time to be better prepared for them & will fight til I die." She continued in this vein in a later letter when she wrote, "I would not care if they killed me, if they did not do worse."13

As noncitizens, even the most untrustworthy slaves could not legally be charged with disloyalty. A Confederate district judge ruled in May 1863, that since slaves "are not members of the body politic—& do not owe allegiance to the Govt.," they could not be tried for treason. Nevertheless, southerners depended on their loyalty—whether it was given voluntarily or under duress—and the southern system of swift, brutal punishment for slaves who violated community standards would have made any application of disloyalty statutes largely superfluous. Late in 1864, three railroad workers took eight hours to beat a black man to death for allegedly stealing three yards of homespun cloth, while enforcers at Tyler burned at the stake a slave suspected of murdering his master. Vigilant Texans near La Grange hanged an escaped slave named Yorick—two weeks after Lee surrendered at Appomattox—when he was found "endeavoring to accomplish a purpose too horrid to mention" upon a "German girl." The state legislature responded to the potential threat of rebellious slaves and northern invaders by passing several laws aimed at preventing slave insurrections—especially those instigated by marauding Yankee troops or their emissaries. In addition, "any person of color" captured while invading Texas could be enslaved, a fate suffered by at least a few black Yankees, and it was illegal to leave slaves alone without "free white" supervision or to allow a slave to pretend to own or to control property. Towns also tried to prevent future trouble. The Austin city council ruled that three or more blacks could not "congregate on the streets or off the owners [sic] premises." The penalty for that "crime" was ten to twenty-five lashes.14

Despite the problems caused by slaves during the Civil War, neither the war nor the behavior of their chattel property led Texas Confederates to question the desirability of retaining the peculiar institution. Early in 1863, a Huntsville resident found it impossible to purchase a slave girl, for "the country has been full of negro-buyers for months." Some masters hurried to the Texas frontier very late in the war, hoping to outrun the

Yankees and establish themselves far beyond the effective boundaries of emancipation. Elvira Boles came to Texas with her master in 1865, "a dodgin' in and out, runnin' from de Yankees" all the way from Mississippi. Late in the war, a Travis County slaveowner relocated his slaves and himself in Robertson County, hoping to hide from the advancing Union forces. As late as May 1865, owners of runaway slaves still offered rewards of up to $500 in Confederate currency, and J.L. Maxwell of Collin County offered to exchange his small farm for "Negro property."[15]

Even after the war ended, some Texans believed that slavery would survive. The *Marshall Texas Republican* predicted that the thirteenth amendment would not be ratified. Emancipation would be a social, economic, and moral disaster for both races, and would "naturally" be followed by "vagrancy, filth, disease, and crime" among the freedmen. The *Republican* asserted that Texans should be allowed to keep their slaves, especially since most owners, "actuated by an attachment for the race," still held them as late as mid-June 1865. Doubtless other Texans, even slaveowners, held no such illusions or even sentiments. Nevertheless, as events during the next decade revealed, few were ready to give up their old relationship with their slaves—a relationship upon which their entire society was based in favor of a brave new life of black and white equality. This attitude made it apparent that Texas blacks had only begun their fight for freedom; Reconstruction would find many more of them "dissenting" against centuries of servitude and tradition in their struggle to forge their own lives and their own destinies.[16]

That a sizable number of German-Texans dissented against the Confederacy surprised few Texans. They had suspected their German neighbors' loyalty since the mid-1850s, despite the fact that only a minority of Germans had agreed with the principles or the politics displayed in the "San Antonio Platform" with its noxious antislavery plank. Nevertheless, the actions of those German liberals shaped the views of "Americans" in Texas toward all Germans. The votes against the secession ordinance in several West Texas counties and the well-publicized actions of individual or groups of Germans during the war further tarnished their reputation as southerners and Confederate citizens. It probably did not help that northerners, including a former resident of Texas, George Denison, believed that "the Germans can be relied on almost without exception" to support the Union war effort. All of these factors contributed to the Confederate perception that the German element among them lacked sympathy for the southern cause because of certain principles—a hatred of slavery, a devotion to the Union—that conflicted with Confederate goals.[17]

One such shaper of the Texans' perceptions of Germans was a San

Antonio saloon keeper named Saddour, "a Union man to the backbone."
During the early days of the war, while soldiers belonging to the surrendered Union regiments waited in San Antonio for their paroles and transportation north, Saddour opened his saloon to the bored Yankees, who
enjoyed a remarkable freedom to roam around the city. Under the protection of Saddour's hospitality, they drank, sang patriotic songs, and cheered
one another and Abraham Lincoln. The German publican served Yankees
three pints of beer for the same amount—a nickel—at which he sold a
much smaller amount to Confederates. When challenged, Saddour explained his prices by tossing a large "Union" and a small "Secesh" glass
onto the floor. The former bounced off the floor unharmed, while the latter
burst into hundreds of pieces, proving what Saddour believed to be an
obvious point about the nature of the Union and that of the Confederacy,
respectively. Local authorities soon forced Saddour out of business.[18]

A more serious case arose in Bandera County, a heavily German area,
where residents apparently paid no taxes, circulated a petition demanding
a reunion of the states, threatened prominent secessionists, and stole the
buggy wheel of a Confederate judge and threw his seat cushions into a
river. The German postmaster opened the mail of leading secessionists,
and local Unionists had chosen to form a home guard company rather than
join the county militia. This extensive disaffection was all the more fright-
ening, according to a local fire-eater, because "our Southern boys have
almost all joined Capt. Adams [sic] Company and the Secessionists are in a
minority in the County at this time."[19]

Concerned Texans grew alarmed when large groups of Germans
organized in other parts of the state. An Austin County planter pleaded for
help from Governor Lubbock in March 1862, because "credible, reliable
information" revealed that two hundred Germans had vowed to resist the
Confederate draft, to aid Lincoln and the northern war effort, and, even
worse, "to *countenance* and *assist* the negroes in case of an invasion to
rebel against their owners." Col. (later Brig. Gen.) Henry McCulloch
urged Governor Lubbock to declare martial law in San Antonio in order to
thwart the anticipated seizure of the local arsenal by a company of Unionist
Germans. Guadalupe County residents petitioned the governor to exempt
an important local slaveowner from military duty because so many men in
the area had already been drafted. Only a large number of Germans who
"are not safe, or loyal citizens" remained; the drafting of any more loyal
slaveholders would be "ruinous . . . [to] the slave holding community."
Shortly after Union forces captured Galveston in the fall of 1862, C.G.
Wells wrote William P. Ballinger that the Germans in that city "are very
false to us." In order to protect themselves from the nighttime raids of

vengeance-minded rebels, "every night they go to the end of Nichols' Wharf for safety, taking up the planking behind them."20

So widespread was the real and the perceived disloyalty of the Texas Germans that vigilant Texans seemed to take special delight in persecuting them. One Union soldier believed that the "principal duty" of a regiment purportedly raised to protect the frontier "seemed to be to hunt down Union men, and hang them, especially the Germans in the settlements North of San Antonio." The English traveler Fremantle reported that the partisan rangers he talked to near Brownsville reserved their most severe hatred for Unionists. "Nothing could exceed the rancor with which they spoke of these *renegados,* as they called them, who were principally Germans." A Confederate soldier who rather sympathized with the persecuted Germans, R.H. Williams, visited the camp of a frontier regiment along the Rio Grande and found a human skull hanging from a pole on top of their commissary hut. He discovered that it had belonged to a German killed while trying to cross the Rio Grande. The rebels were "quite indignant" when Williams suggested that a proper burial might be more appropriate for this "poor remnant of humanity," than "regarding it as a trophy to be proud of."21

The Germans themselves certainly believed that they had been singled out for special mistreatment. A San Antonio resident claimed to speak for "thousands of loyal citizens of German origins" in a petition sent to the United States Congress in December 1861. It stressed the Union and antislavery sentiments of the Texas Germans, and urged an invasion to relieve the loyal citizens and slaves in the state. "It would be flattering and congenial," said the memorialist, if part of the invading force could be composed of Germans. Another German reported to A.J. Hamilton after the war that "the ruling party" had been waiting "only for the success of the rebellion to make the 'damned Duchmen' [*sic*] feel the full power of their oppression."22

One of the best-known "damned Dutchmen" was Edward Degener, a Forty-eighter and delegate to the 1854 San Antonio Convention. A former member of the German National Assembly, Degener had came to Texas after the failure of the liberal revolution in his country and had taken up farming near Sisterdale.23 By the beginning of the Civil War, Degener had earned a reputation as a dedicated Unionist and antislavery man. His actions during the first year of the war earned him a court date before the Military Commission in San Antonio on the charge that he was "hostile to the Government of the Confederate States, and is a dangerous and seditious person and an enemy to the government of the Confederate States." His main crime was to help obtain arms and supplies for a German

Unionist militia company in West Texas—a company that would, in August 1862, fight a pitched battle on the Nueces River with state troops in which two of Degener's sons, Hugo and Hilmer, would die.

Witnesses testified (although their exact words have not survived) to Degener's Unionism and disaffection from the Confederacy, and C.S. West, the Judge Advocate General—and, ironically, Thomas H. DuVal's son-in-law—stressed Degener's sons' presence in the Unionist company, his participation in the controversial *Saengerfest,* and a letter written by Degener that complained of the Confederates' tyrannical use of martial law, conscription, and the suspension of habeas corpus. Degener wrote that if the South actually won its war for independence, "it may become necessary for the Germans to emigrate again." Degener claimed in the letter that a San Antonio newspaper had recently suggested that a planter should be reimbursed for each runaway slave by "giving him two Hessians to cultivate his land." This was ridiculous, of course, but it proved that every southerner despised all Germans as "Black Republicans" and abolitionists.

Interestingly, a number of defense witnesses claimed that Degener had, in fact, ignored politics since the war had started, had tried to prevent his sons from fighting against the Confederacy, and had actually wished out loud that he had the resources to buy a slave or two. Such testimony belied Degener's later Reconstruction career was a Radical Republican congressman and San Antonio alderman and his ardent defense of the civil rights of freedmen. The court ordered him to pay a $5000 bond to guarantee his "good and loyal" behavior for the remainder of the war. 24

Other "dangerous" Germans included Jacob Kuechler, a German scientist and socialist who helped lead the ill-fated march of German Unionists to the Nueces, and Thomas Hertzberg, a San Antonio physician. Kuechler, seriously wounded in the fight with the Confederates, painfully made his way to Mexico and remained there until 1865. He, too, became a leading Reconstruction Republican. Hertzberg reported, in a postwar letter to A.J. Hamilton, that he had been "compelled to leave Texas" for Mexico in 1861. Later in the war the United States consul at Monterrey sent him to Piedras Negras, a village just across the border from Texas, to aid Unionist refugees and to recruit "our german boys into the Federal service."25

Three more West Texas Germans who appeared before the Military Commission contributed to the impression that the German population was as a rule disloyal. Witnesses accused Philip Braubach, a farmer, stage driver, and sometime law officer near San Antonio, of using his office to aid Union men, of recruiting only Union-loving Germans for a frontier defense company, of depreciating Confederate currency, and, according to one witness, of associating "with the party who halloes for the Union." Julius Schlickum also allegedly depreciated Confederate currency and, in the words of a Confederate sergeant, "never had any good news on our side, but generally had something bad to tell." More seriously, Schlickum allegedly knew and approved of certain groups of disloyal citizens who had banded together to resist conscription. The third member of the trio was Fredericksburg's own disloyal saloonkeeper, Ferdinand Doebbler. Witnesses labeled his tavern "the place of rendezvous for people calling themselves Union men" and claimed that "none of the loyal Citizens would visit his house any more." He also sold a "Black Republican newspaper" in his store. The court considered all three men doubly dangerous because of their influence over their friends and neighbors and sentenced them to prison for the duration of the war.[26]

The Degeners, Kuechlers, and Braubachs monopolized the public's perception of Texas Germans; the behavior of German Liberals in the 1850s, the outcome of the balloting on secession, and the writings of travelers such as Frederick Law Olmsted confirmed the apparent untrustworthiness of German-Americans living in Texas. Nevertheless, hundreds of Germans served loyally in Confederate or state military organizations, and a number of German leaders became Confederate officers. One of Edward Degener's lawyers, for instance, the German-born Jacob Waelder, was a Confederate major. Carl William von Rosenberg, the son of a Prussian noble, had served as a lieutenant in the Prussian army and as a Royal Architect for Frederick William IV. His liberal views made advancement difficult, and he journeyed to Texas in 1849, where he rose to chief draftsman in the General Land Office. Unlike most German political refugees who opposed slavery, however, he voted for secession and joined the Confederate army as a topographical engineer. Another German liberal, Gustavus Schleicher, speculated in West Texas land, promoted railroads, published a German-language newspaper, and worked as a surveyor in the 1850s; after winning election to the state senate in 1859, he became an advocate of secession and later entered the Confederate Army as a captain of engineers.[27]

The best-known German-Confederate was Col. August Buchel, who eventually commanded the Third Texas Cavalry. Buchel grew up in the German province of Hesse, where he graduated from a military academy and served as a lieutenant. Between 1831 and 1845, he fought for Germany and in the French Foreign Legion, and worked as an instructor in the Turkish Army. An avid duelist, he apparently killed a man in Germany and quickly sailed to Texas. He continued his military career in his new home, raising a company of Texas volunteers to fight in the Mexican War and serving on Gen. Zachary Taylor's staff at the battle of Buena Vista.

Following the Mexican War, Buchel received an appointment as Collector of Customs at Port Lavaca. When Juan Cortina raided Brownsville in 1859, he leaped at the chance to serve his state and organized a company of Indianola volunteers who helped drive Cortina out of the Rio Grande Valley. Apparently unconcerned with politics and uninterested in the slavery question, Buchel adapted well to southern society. As one of the most exerienced soldiers in Texas, Buchel naturally sought to contribute to the Confederate war effort. Late in 1861, he became lieutenant colonel and later colonel of the Third Texas Infantry, stationed in South Texas. Two years later he took command of the Third Texas Cavalry and led them through the fighting in Louisiana. He died in combat at the battle of Pleasant Hill in the spring of 1864, a well-respected and admired professional soldier.[28]

Other Germans who entered the Confederate army came from decidedly less militaristic backgrounds than Buchel. Joseph Bruckmuller, for instance, had lived in Marshall, Texas, for only three years when the war broke out. His shoemaking and grocery business fell off in the slump that followed secession, and "to live up to my duties toward my chosen country," he joined the Seventh Texas Volunteers. The regiment fought in Kentucky, Tennessee, Mississippi, and Louisiana, and Bruckmuller ended up a prisoner of war twice (once after the surrender of Fort Donelson). Frequently ill, the young German survived a bout of cholera and worked for a while as a hospital orderly. After his second escape from the Yankees, in the fall of 1863, he went back to work as a shoemaker. His occupation may have earned him an exemption from conscription; nevertheless, for the remainder of the war he was "scared to be drafted again."[29]

The letters of another German enlisted man, Rudolf Coreth, reveal some of the problems experienced by Germans in the Confederate service. Rudolf, the son of a Tyrolean count who had settled near New Braunfels in the late 1840s, joined an all-German company from Galveston in the fall of 1861 and served throughout the war in Louisiana and in garrisons in South Texas. Two of his brothers died of disease while in the Confederate army, and Rudolf apparently never regretted having volunteered to fight for his adopted country. The Coreths owned no slaves, but Rudolf hired black servants to cook and do laundry in camp and, in scores of letters to his parents, he never questioned the justice of slavery.[30]

According to one prewar German Unionist, before 1862, "it was a rare exception for a German to join the Confederate movement out of conviction," and even those who served the Confederacy, "were friends of the Union in spite of their grey jacket." This seemed not to be the case with Rudolf and many of his comrades. In spite of their reputation, young Coreth claimed that most of the German-speaking soldiers in his regiment remained faithful to the Confederacy. When the news broke that the command would soon be campaigning in Louisiana, many soldiers deserted and several officers resigned. Nevertheless, "our Germans from up there are still holding up quite well"; only three men out of the two German companies with which Rudolf was familiar had deserted. Although he personally remained loyal, Rudolf seemed aware of the attitudes of many Texans and remained as much of a German as a southerner, occasionally challenging the Confederacy's centralizing tendencies. Rudolf complained about the "dictatorship" of Brigadier General Hebert when he proclaimed martial law in the spring of 1862, and when Rudolf heard rumors that some southerners favored turning the Confederate states into a monarchy he wrote that it could probably happen. "If the planters think they can keep their Negroes under a regent," he wrote to his family, "surely they will be for it." For himself, he would try to get out of the army if the Confederacy chose to institute a monarchy.[31]

Rudolf also betrayed a hint of resentment when an "American" defeated him in an election for company lieutenant. Although the unit consisted primarily of German-Texans, many members thought that "it would make the company look very fine if we elected an American." Even though he never renounced his allegiance to the Confederacy, Rudolf distanced himself a bit from other southerners. In a letter in early 1862, he wrote to his family about "another opinion of the Southerners . . . that reached our ears here and that you may not have heard. They say about the German Northerners whom they beat in a battle, that they had stood quite still and exposed themselves to their fire and did nothing but keep loading and shooting because they were too stupid to run away."[32]

Matters came to a head for those Texas Germans who refused to adapt to the Confederacy as well as Rudolf Coreth on August 10, 1862, in a one-sided fight on the Nueces River, which the *Dallas Herald* dubbed "The Battle with the Traitors." The "battle" marked the climax of a summer-long campaign by Confederate authorities to break resistance to the Confederacy, especially to the conscription act, in the German-dominated hill country west of Austin. Opponents of the war and the draft in and near Fredericksburg had formed a "Loyal Union League." The league publicly announced that it intended to protect this exposed part of the frontier from Indians and outlaws, but Confederate officials believed—not without reason—that its genuine purpose was to resist conscription and other Confederate programs. In May 1862, a detachment of Confederate troops marched to Fredericksburg to restore order and to ensure the loyalty of the area's citizens to the Confederacy.[33]

The Confederate troopers arrested citizens, burned a few Unionists' farms, ousted a local militia captain, and generally intimidated most of the population of Gillespie and the surrounding counties. Elements of the Thirty-second Texas Cavalry joined the roundup, scouting the rough country around Fredericksburg, guarding the town day and night, and hunting "bushwhackers." Cavalryman Thomas Smith recorded in his diary that when a suspected Unionist "chances to fall into the hands of the C. S. soldiers he is dealt pretty roughly with and generally makes his last speech with a rope around his neck." According to Smith, "hanging is getting to be as common as hunting," and "the creeks in this vicinity are said to be full of dead men!!" Proof came one day when Smith witnessed "a sight which I never wish again to see in a civilized & enlightened country"—four dead bodies floating in a water hole. They had been "thrown in and left to rot, and that too after they were hanged by the neck [until] dead."[34]

Early in August, a party of just over sixty men, mostly German members of a "Union League," determined to escape exactly that kind of fate by going to Mexico. The strangely unsuspecting refugees set a leisurely cross-country pace and failed to take the necessary defensive precautions. A company of about one hundred Texas Partisan Rangers under Lt. C.D. McRae caught them after tracking them for a week through the rugged, unsettled, and sweltering South Texas frontier. The Confederates attacked before dawn on August 10, and their superior firepower overcame the outnumbered Germans after a sharp fight in which two Confederates died and eighteen were injured. Thirty Germans were killed, and about twenty were wounded. No captives survived; shortly after the firing stopped, a squad of Confederates shot to death the nine injured Unionists who had surrendered. The wounded Lieutenant McRae merely stated in his official report that the Germans "offered the most determined resistance and fought with desperation, asking no quarter whatever; hence I have no prisoners to report."[35]

News of the massacre on the Nueces sparked violent protests in San Antonio and other towns to the north that authorities soon put down. One vigilant hill country Confederate claimed that the "Union League" had been organized to "murder and pillage" loyal Texans and believed that the "bloodthirsty bushwhackers and villians disgracing the North and the Union flag by calling themselves Union men" had got what they deserved. Rudolf Coreth attributed the ugly rumors that wounded men had actually been murdered after the battle to Unionists in San Antonio. The Military Commission in San Antonio sentenced Ferdinand Simon, taken into custody after fighting against the Confederates, to death.[36]

The massacre culminated the official campaign against disloyal Germans in Texas, although for the remainder of the war hill country Unionists would be terrorized by what the Germans appropriately called the *Haengerbande*—gangs of Confederates who warred on civilian Unionists.

After the Nueces massacre, however, Germans would never again be perceived as a serious threat to the Confederate war effort. Some of the dissenting Germans had been killed, while many had escaped to Mexico, ohers had found some sort of safe hiding place, a good number had found refuge from Confederate service in the companies formed by the state to defend the frontier, and still others had settled into an uneasy accommodation with the Confederate authorities. All in all, German resistance in east-central Texas quickly dwindled, although late in 1862, large groups of Germans met in Fayette, Washington, Colorado, and Austin counties, threatening to arm themselves in order to resist conscription and causing all sorts of consternation among the apparently outnumbered residents of those counties. They signed petitions, held meetings (with as many as six hundred in attendance), and drove off enrolling officers. By late January 1863, however, the problem had disappeared, and most of the men meekly submitted to enrollment for the draft—perhaps with the specter of the Nueces incident haunting them. Fremantle reported from San Antonio a few months later that many Germans had been "at first by no means loyal to the Confederate cause," but that "it is said they are now reconciled to the new regime." One rather bloodthirsty Confederate wrote home after the Nueces incident that "the tories in this part of the country is getting somewhat scarce." He attributed their scarcity to the violence that had left disloyalists "lying and hanging all over the woods."[37]

As a whole, Germans came closer than any of the other outsiders in Texas to sharing southern values; although few owned slaves, many who had arrived before 1848 had become involved in the Texas economy and fully supported the Confederate cause. The Confederate army was sprinkled with companies or even regiments made up largely of Germans. The historian of the Thirty-second Texas Cavalry wrote that anyone riding into the camp of Company F—recruited in Comal County—"might . . . guess . . . that he had entered an encampment of the Prussian Guards, fresh off the fields of the Austro-Prussian War." Nevertheless, a large minority, unable to reconcile themselves to slavery or to secession, tried to resist or at least to ignore the Confederacy. They paid the price in blood and in the lingering suspicion with which many Texans regarded Germans.[38]

Mexicans—who also generally desired to remain apart from the Civil War—were categorized with the "treasonous" Germans in the mind of at least one Confederate officer when H. E. McCulloch, at the time a colonel, wrote to Gov. Francis Lubbock in 1862 that "if ever Lincoln's army penetrates Texas from the South or West," German refugees in Mexico "will return with all the Mexicans they can bring with them." The attitude of white Texans toward Hispanics living in Texas had not changed since

Frederick Olmsted wrote in the mid-1850s that Texans considered Mexicans "to be heathen; not acknowledged as 'white folks.' " The decades of fear, hatred, and tension between Anglos and tejanos influenced both the latter's reaction to the Civil War and the former's wartime attitude toward Mexicans.[39]

Not even the example of Cuban-born José Augustín Quintero convinced Anglos to trust their Hispanic neighbors. Quintero had practiced law and edited the *San Antonio El Ranchero*, a Spanish-language newspaper, before the war. After the attack on Fort Sumter, the thirty-two-year-old Quintero marched with his Texas regiment to the front in Virginia. Soon, however, he entered the Confederate foreign service, and in June 1861, he arrived in Monterrey to establish friendly relations with Santiago Vidaurri, the most powerful man in Northern Mexico. He had a hand in most Confederate foreign policy initiatives in Mexico, and played an active role in buying arms and supplies, in securing the Texas-Mexican border, and in establishing trade between the countries. Despite Quintero's efforts, however, Texans were much more likely to remember incidents such as an emergency in Brownsville in the fall of 1863, when the government desperately tried to round up as much transportation as possible. Mexican teamsters, according to the *Brownsville Flag*, "skeedaddled for the woods and hid their drays in the brush." The *Flag* urged Texans to "treat as aliens those who shun all the duties of citizenship and practice all the vices common to the enemies of the state."[40]

Although Hispanics served in both the Confederate and Union armies, most attempted to avoid the war between the Anglos. The principles for which the war was being fought meant very little to them, and they had neither an economic nor a political stake in the conflict. The North and the South both rather feebly endeavored to win Mexicans over to their respective sides, but memories steeled the Hispanics against most offers. Neither the United States nor the state of Texas had ever tried to protect the property or political rights of Mexican-Texans, and when both governments hypocritically tried to enlist the support of Hispanics, the latter demonstrated their resentment by leaving the gringos to kill one another.

Nevertheless, nearly nine hundred Mexican-Texans served in the Union army, many of them in John L. Haynes's Second Texas Cavalry. Some confederates, John Ford, for example, believed that these Mexicans opposed secession and fought on the side of the federals because they "looked upon the government of the United States as the most perfect of any in the world." While that sentiment may have animated a few Union tejanos, many entered federal service in order to pay back old political and economic debts. This seemed to be the case in Zapata County where, in April 1861, about forty armed Mexicans marched on the county seat of

Carrizo to keep county officials from swearing allegiance to the Confederate states. Texas troops turned them away, inflicting heavy casualties, and Ford wrote Governor Clark that "it is the only aproppriate way to treat traitors, who arm against the authorities of the state." He suggested that Juan Cortina, long the scourge of Anglo-Texans, might have been responsible for the incident. Border raids by Mexicans from both sides of the Rio Grande also plagued the Confederacy. A group of raiders operating out of Mexico under Antonio Zapata called themselves the "First Regiment of Union Troops," but seemed to content themselves with plundering Texas ranches rather than fighting Confederate troops. A Nueces County Unionit named Cecilio Balerio led a company of cavalry that preyed on the cotton trade along the border. The actions of these men led Confederate authorities to fear that the United States consul in Matamoros, Leonard Pierce, would provide arms to the Mexican refugees from conscription and initiate a race war along the border.[41]

Nearly three times as many Mexican-Texans served the Rebels as served the Yankees. Roughly 2550 of them, many from Webb, Refugio, and Bexar counties, enlisted in Confederate or state militia regiments. Santos Benavides, the wealthy Mexican-born rancher, merchant, and Rio Grande Valley power broker, achieved the highest level of any Confederate tejano, reaching the rank of colonel in command of his own largely Mexican regiment.[42]

Although some Hispanics seemed eager to fight for their adopted state, Confederate commanders rarely trusted their Mexican soldiers. At the same time, low and usually months-late pay, poor supply systems, and a profound lack of interest in the outcome of the war encouraged Hispanic volunteers to take their equipment and horses and steal across the Rio Grande. Like the German Confederates, Mexicans generally enlisted in companies or regiments made up largely of their own race, and only two Mexican-dominated southern regiments, including the one commanded by Santos Benavides, exhibited a large degree of constancy to the Confederate cause.[43]

In fact, neither side expected or received the steady allegiance of its Mexican troops. August Buchel, then lieutenant colonel of the Third Texas Cavalry at Fort Brown, complained to a superior that his Mexican soldiers, "like all their countrymen, are susceptible to bribes and corruption, and cannot be depended upon." Texans usually treated Mexicans in the same ways they had always treated them. R.H. Williams, the Confederate Englishman who empathized more than most Texans with Unionists and other disloyalists, refused to arrest and turn over to the military authorities in San Antonio four Mexican deserters he had captured. He knew that "it was a hundred to one that the bloodthirsty mob would seize them . . . and hang them in the plaza." With attitudes like these in common circulation among Confederates, it is not surprising that the Confederate cause—the cause of their long-time antagonists—inspired little enthusiasm among Mexican-Texans. In 1863 Brig. Gen. H. P. Bee, commanding the Department of Texas, proved to be more prescient than most Anglos when he protested that enforcing the conscription law on the southern frontier of Texas "would have had but the effect of driving the Mexicans across the Rio Grande and made them our enemies." Wherever it was attempted, "it . . . proved useless." Bee enjoyed some success, however, in recruiting tejanos into short-term enlistments in state units. Unlike most commanders on either side, Bee realized that the Confederate cause—or the Union cause, for that matter—was unimportant to most Mexican-Americans; he also knew that in order to win them over to the Confederate states, the government must protect their "rights and immunities as citizens."[44]

Federal officers had no better luck with—nor more confidence in— their Mexican recruits. Despite the presence of large numbers of tejanos in the Union army, few rose above the rank of sergeant. Hispanics commanded only five companies in the First or Second Texas, although they constituted a majority of the enlisted men in at least ten companies and served as noncommissioned officers in roughly the same percentage as the Mexican-Americans' overall contribution to the Union ranks. Racism no doubt played a role in this, but the fact that many Anglos commanded "Mexican" companies also suggests that the language barrier, managerial inexperience, and a lack of political savvy may have posed insurmountable obstacles to a tejano rising through the ranks. While stationed at Brownsville early in 1864 a lieutenant in the Nineteenth Iowa remarked that the Second Texas Cavalry was "a peculiar institution and rather a hard operation to keep in proper running condition." The troops were "dishonest, cowardly and treacherous and only bide their time to make good their escape." They deserted so frequently that a guard had to be placed "around them to prevent their carrying out their roving propensities." As if to validate such skepticism, more than two hundred tejanos deserted from the Union's Second Texas Cavalry during the first half of 1864.[45]

The reactions of Santos Benavides and Adrian J. Vidal to the Civil War represent opposite points on the spectrum of tejano behavior. Benavides, a descendant of the founder of Laredo, belonged to one of the wealthiest and most influential families—Anglo or Mexican—in the Lower Rio Grande Valley. His father had been a Mexican army officer, and his uncle, Bacilio Benavides, had been a chief justice and Texas Republic Congressman for Webb County, and was the only Hispanic delegate to the 1861 secession convention (he voted in favor of secession). Santos's brothers, Refugio and

Cristóbal, achieved fame and influence in their own right, as Indian fighters, businessmen, politicians, and Confederate officers.[46]

For the first two decades of his life, Santos considered himself a Mexican citizen, and as a teenager commanded a company of forty men through the bloody guerrilla fighting in the Federalist wars of 1838–1840. When United States troops occupied the disputed Nueces strip during the Mexican War, Santos chose American citizenship because he believed the United States offered a safer environment for his business and political interests. Tired of a remote, inefficient government, unfair taxes, and vulnerability to Indian attacks, Santos hoped the United States could provide the stability so desperately needed along the border.

In fact, Benavides's career revolved around his efforts to secure stability for his region. He grimly fought Indians and chased outlaws— including Juan Cortina, a tejano of the same age and background but with a startingly different perspective on race relations—and expanded his holdings and power. The patriarch of the Benavides family owned no slaves, but accepted slavery so that he, in turn, would be accepted by his Anglo neighbors. His own rule in the valley economy led him to identify with the hierarchical structure of southern society; his disdain for far-away, unresponsive governments led him to sympathize with secession. As a result, when war broke out, he assumed his accustomed place of leadership among valley Hispanics.

By the fall of 1863, Major—soon-to-be Colonel—Benavides commanded the Thirty-third Texas Regiment, leading them against Mexican raiders and against the Yankee invaders at Laredo and Brownsville. Ironically, during these skirmishes with the federals, his own largely Hispanic unit collided with the tejano-dominated Second Texas. Benavides succeeded in most of his campaigns, and earned the respect of his Confederate colleagues. Even his loyalty was questioned occasionally, however. Rumor had it, late in 1863, that he had deserted across the river with twenty of his men, while in April 1865, it was reported—apparently inaccurately—that he had unilaterally pledged to stop fighting the United States.[47]

Benavides represents those Mexican-Texans who for one reason or another felt a responsibility to Texas, if not to the South, and who perceived their interests to be identical to those of the Anglos who dominated Texas economic and political life. Unfortunately for Texas Hispanics, even his efforts on behalf of the Confederacy failed to change most Texans' minds about the mass of tejanos.

Adrian J. Vidal's experience during the war differed dramatically from Benavides's and symbolizes the way that many Hispanic Texans found a niche in neither the Confederate nor the Federal cause; his behavior during the war met the low expectations—by southern standards—that most Texas Anglos had for tejano residents. The seventeen-year-old son of a Mexican woman and a wealthy Anglo merchant, Vidal had at the age of twenty secured a Confederate captain's commission and the command of a company by the middle of 1863. At least one Confederate compatriot thought very little of this "young, half-bred Mexican." R.H. Williams found him "a vain, trifling fellow without any experience, who cared for nothing but gambling and drinking." Perhaps this attitude was so widespread among Vidal's fellow Confederates that he tired of the constant remarks about his age and race; whatever the case, Vidal killed two Confederate couriers and deserted with nearly ninety men—primarily Mexican nationals—in October 1863. After briefly threatening Brownsville, Vidal retreated up the Rio Grande Valley, robbing ranches as he went.[48]

Following a course of action different from that of most tejano deserters, Vidal accepted a captaincy from the recently arrived federal forces and returned to Brownsville, now occupied by the Yankees. There he married "the accomplished and beautiful" Anita de Chavero, and led his men on scouting expeditions throughout the Rio Grande Valley. But, after a few months of arduous duty, weary of army rules and regulations, angry at the tardy pay and poor provisions given his men, and complaining about the difficulty of fulfilling his administrative duties when he could neither read nor write English, Vidal asked for an honorable discharge. He eventually received it, but not before he and most of his men once again deserted. Lt. Benjamin McIntyre expressed no surprise that "the gay fancy little Mexican" had left the army. "It is a great pity that the country ever accepted these men for soldiers," he wrote in his diary, "and still a pity that every *yaller belly* of them has not been permitted to desert."[49]

Vidal escaped into Mexico, where he joined the Juaristas and fought against the Mexican Imperialists. In 1864, at the age of twenty-one, he was captured, court-martialed, and executed. His brief career showed how little stake Mexicans living in Texas had in the affairs of their state and country. Ill-treated in both of the armies in which he served, not committed to the principles espoused by either side, and unwilling to abide restrictions and hardships for causes that did not seem to apply to him, Vidal rejected Texas for his mother's homeland. The chief irony of his short life is that, not even in Mexico, could he find a country in which he was either safe or happy.[50]

Vidal provides an extreme, though telling, example of the shortcomings of the Confederacy's policy toward the "outsiders" living in Texas. Although with great effort men such as Santos Benavides and August

Buchel could overcome their foreign birth and live comfortably in Texas, long years of political, economic, and cultural antagonism poisoned relations between Texans and tejanos and forced a vocal minority of Germans into rebellion against the Confederacy. Although most blacks had no choice of role during the war, they shared with the other outsiders an ambiguous and sometimes dangerous position in wartime Texas. Uncommitted to the structures of a slave society fighting for its life against northern "aggression," the loyalty of black, German, and Mexican Texans became immediately suspect, as it had been even before the war started, and as it would be after the war ended.

7

Loyalty and Reconstruction 1865-1874

When news of the evacuation of Richmond reached New Orleans in April 1865, a band of exiled Texas Tories celebrated the imminent end of the war at Victor's Restaurant on Canal Street. A.J. Hamilton, Thomas H. DuVal, S.M. Swenson, George W. Brackenridge, and others feasted on wine, beef, crab, and sheepshead. These "very merry and patriotic" gentlemen thoroughly enjoyed the prospect of Confederate defeat. "Hurrah for the triumph of democracy vs aristocracy," DuVal wrote in his diary, "of freedom o['e]r slavery—of *the people* vs the Copperheads & secessionists." DuVal's "faith in the people," temporarily shaken by his wartime experiences, "is now firmer than ever. The American people will be more than ever one people, *one nation*, and . . . [will] work out a great destiny."[1]

Three months later, the first issue of the first volume of the resurrected *Southern Intelligencer* entered Reconstruction with far less confidence. "It overwhelms us to think," wrote its editor, "that out of this chaos, produced by so terrible a failure at revolution, society has to be moulded and re-turned; a state recreated; a people reorganized; industry and commerce re-established; and law and order re-enacted."[2]

The debates that raged over this re-creation of the South, no less than the war itself, hinged on the question of loyalty to the Union and to the South. To understand them we must follow the postwar course of antebellum and wartime dissent. The war had strained and often ruptured seams in southern society; whether to support the Union or secession—and, later, the Confederacy—provided only one source of tension. Attitudes concerning slavery and the southern economy, ethnic differences, political ideologies, and the willingness or reluctance to persevere in the face of extreme hardship further tested southerners and fractured their communities. The onset of Reconstruction hardly eliminated these points of contention. Rather, the postwar decade presented even starker disagreements among southerners, as they reacted to military defeat and cultural crisis. One area of conflict arose over who would rule in the South: those who had fought for the Union or those who had fought with equal sincerity for southern independence. Another crucial and related question concerned the shape postwar society would take. How would the freedmen fit into the lives of southerners unaccustomed to sharing equal rights, much less political power, with those they perceived to be inferior?[3]

Although Texas Unionists of both Confederate and Unionist persuasions briefly tried to resurrect the old prewar Opposition party, the radicalization of northern requirements for southern loyalty scuttled their efforts, as different segments of the party melted away and finally joined their old rivals, the Democrats. Even in exile, divisions among Union men had foreshadowed the dangerous factionalism of Reconstruction. According to John Hancock, "two parties" had arisen "among the Refugees—one very extreme & radical—the other conservative."[4] Each of these sects viewed the war, the South, and the Union in a different way; each formulated its own definition of loyalty to its party and to the national government; each had its own ideas about how the conquered rebels should be treated; and each sprinkled its speeches, letters, and editorials with frequent references to patriotism and loyalty. As Congress's program of Reconstruction embraced Negro suffrage, disfranchisement of thousands of former Confederates, and the sometimes arbitrary and always centralized rule of the military and the Radical Republican government, fewer and fewer Texans could comply with the escalating demands Radicals made on their loyalty. As a result, the Opposition's attempt to finally gain control of the Texas political system failed. For many former dissenters, the price of political power, as set by the northern and southern Radicals, was simply too high. Torn again by conflicting loyalties to their region and their nation, this time most of them chose the South.

For a time, all of the former Unionists rejoiced in the end of the war and hoped that Texas's return to full membership in the Union would be a speedy one. Lucadia Pease breathed a sigh of relief in a letter to her sister in the North. "It has been so long since we have been free to speak or write our sentiments," she wrote, "that I can hardly realize that I can do so now." A formal celebration early in August welcomed A.J. Hamilton, the recently appointed provisional governor, to the capital city. A large escort met Hamilton at the ruins of his burned-out home about two miles east of Austin on the morning of August 2. The procession continued into Austin and up Congress Avenue to the capitol. A battery of federal artillery boomed a welcoming salute, the crowd sang the national anthem, and E.M. Pease delivered a two-hour speech, to which Hamilton responded "with his old-time force and eloquence." Later, an "entirely impromptu" levee celebrated the Hamiltons' first night in the executive mansion.[5]

As the events that followed this disarmingly optimistic celebration would soon reveal, Hamilton needed more than eloquence to shepherd Texas smoothly back into the Union, while at the same time ensuring that only truly "loyal" men controlled the state government. As Sam Houston's heir to the Opposition's leadership, as a nationally known Texas Unionist, and as the first of the four Reconstruction governors of the state, Hamilton established the policies and attitudes against which Texans would react throughout the Reconstruction period. To conservative Unionists such as James W. Throckmorton, Hamilton's relative moderation seemed radical; to Radicals such as E.J. Davis and Hamilton's brother Morgan, A.J.'s course veered too far toward the rebellion-stained camp of the conservatives. Old political wounds, sectional antagonisms, and economic competition within the state—all exacerbated by the war—made Hamilton's thankless job even more difficult.[6]

Hamilton believed, with a Unionist logic that shows how important the question of loyalty remained during Reconstruction, that those men who had opposed secession before the war should form the basis of a restored, loyal government in Texas. He wished to monitor carefully who would be allowed to participate in rebuilding Texas government, and to that end pursued a tough policy regarding special pardons, especially for large planters. He refused to endorse most of the early applications for pardons, he told President Johnson, "because they [came from] a class who yield to what they cannot help," who "retain all the bitterness of heart which induced them in the outset to raise their hands against their Government, intensified by the dethronement of their God, the institution of Slavery." Hamilton expected repentance from the defeated rebels, but none of the applicants "seem to think it necessary to make the slightest apology for the past, but rather seem to think they place the Government under great obligations when they say with a lofty sadness 'I submit.' " The former Texas renegade believed that such men could not be relied upon to help form a loyal government.[7]

Hamilton's primary objective—which he believed could be accomplished by allowing only men of unquestionable loyalty to take part in Reconstruction—was to achieve the speedy readmittance of Texas to its full rights as a state in the Union. Nevertheless, he delayed calling a convention to make the necessary changes in the state constitution until he could be sure that Texans would select "loyal" men as delegates. The provisional government needed to administer the amnesty oath to the necessary number of registered voters, combat "treasonous" newspapers, indoctrinate the masses with the correct loyalties, and put the courts into operation so that they could "inspire a proper sense of the crime of treason in the public mind." Hamilton predicted to President Johnson that "the action of Texas will meet the public expectation if not forced too soon." By November, satisfied that "the public mind is working slowly, but . . . steadily, in the right direction," he set January 8 as election day.[8]

When the convention met in Austin on February 7, 1866, Hamilton told the delegates what he believed they must accomplish in order to win federal recognition—a program with only a modest restructuring of Texas society that foreshadowed the moderate Republicanism of later years. He recommended that the delegates declare the 1861 act of secession null and void, admit the unconstitutionality of the principle of secession, repudiate Texas's war debts, ratify the Thirteenth Amendment to the United States Constitution and promise never to reestablish the institution of slavery, and guarantee the civil and property rights of freedmen, including their right to testify in court cases involving white men. Despite the governor's optimistic report to President Johnson that the delay in holding the convention had resulted in "an evident daily improvement in the temper of the members upon all the essential questions," those members, with the conservative James W. Throckmorton presiding, deeply disappointed Hamilton. Although the convention did repudiate the war debt, its actions promoted the conservative view of how postwar society and politics should operate. The delegates rejected the Thirteenth Amendment, failed to nullify the secession of Texas, and passed an ordinance that exempted persons from legal prosecution for any of the consequences of their wartime acts. Clearly the conservatives were stalling, hoping to preserve their political influence and racial dominance in Texas while at the same time avoiding most of the controversial issues before them so as not to antagonize Congress.[9]

When it came time to elect a governor the following summer, a number of prominent conservatives, in an open letter published in many newspapers around the state, called on Throckmorton to run. "Knowing you to be opposed to the radicalism of the day" and to "the hasty and inconsiderate elevation of the negro to political equality," the signers asked Throckmorton to help perpetuate an image of society to which many conservative Texans had been quite attached before the war. They needed the former Confederate general, for recent events "speak, trumpet-tongued, to every patriot in the land" to take action. Throckmorton accepted, and after a long summer campaign, routed the Union candidate, E. M. Pease—a rather unlikely adherent of any brand of Radicalism—in a landslide, and took office on August 9. Three weeks later President Johnson ended the first round of Reconstruction in Texas by declaring the insurrection at an end in the state.[10]

But the fight was far from over, as the conservative governor, legislature, and local appointed officials proceeded to institute their own versions of Reconstruction. It was ironic that Throckmorton, one of the most reluctant rebels in Texas, became the instrument of the conservative reaction against Hamilton's moderate Republicanism. Throckmorton had anticipated joining his former Unionist colleagues in governing the state after the war was over, and Hamilton had confidently told President Johnson late in July 1865, that "the Union men of the state are a unit." Nevertheless, shortly thereafter Throckmorton led the conservative Unionists out of the fledgling Union party when it quickly became apparent that Hamilton did not include former Confederates in his definition of "Union men."[11]

As early as June, Throckmorton wrote Benjamin Epperson of his fear that "Radicalism will prevail in the fedral [sic] councils" and that "none of our sort will be elected." An August trip to Austin, during which he met with Hamilton, Pease, James Bell, and other leading Unionists, confirmed Throckmorton's fears. "I saw and heard nothing at Austin calculated to cheer the patriot," he lamented, "or that would stimulate him to renewed exertion & sacrifice for his country." Before his visit to Austin, Throckmorton had hoped that the past would be forgotten and that normal relations between the states and the federal government would soon be restored. Unfortunately, he now believed, the new government would be formed "in a spirit of petty malice" by "that class of servile creatures who had not the courage to come out at first and exert themselves against Secession." Once "war was upon us," however, they "remained here & claimed protection of that people and government to whom they were traitors & enemies." Ironically, Throckmorton and other Confederate Unionists had refused to condone the persecution of such men during the war, and had acted as "the protectors of these curs who dodged service & did nothing but curse the Confederacy in their hearts."[12]

Epperson, Throckmorton's confidant and best friend, agreed with the former Confederate general and believed that conservatives had to begin shaping postwar society immediately after the shooting ended. As early as June 1865, he called for a meeting of Texas conservatives and wrote Throckmorton that "if Hamilton is military governor, he must be controlled—Now is the time to do it." He urged his conservative colleagues to "get control of the government and lead the public mind and not wait to be led by it." Even though Epperson briefly ran as E.M. Pease's running mate in the 1866 gubernatorial election—he quickly dropped off the ticket to avoid becoming too closely associated with the burgeoning Radical branch of the Texas Unionists—he was elected to the United States

Congress in the fall of 1866. By 1870, this former old-line Whig had aligned himself with the Democratic party.[13]

The suspected "copperhead" John Hancock, the antebellum Democrat and former recruiter for the Union army, joined the early defections from the Unionist coalition. Even while a refugee from Confederate persecution in New Orleans, Hancock had pondered the turn of events caused by the war in a rather wistful diary entry. The life-long Democrat found the jubilation following Lincoln's reelection in 1864 a "striking" contrast with the election of 1860. "Then to oppose slavery was not tolerated, and to have favored the election of Mr. Lincoln . . . would have been deemed a crime." Now, however, "abolitionism is boasted a merit, and Lincoln's election the subject of rejoycing." Hancock believed "there is much food for serious, yea sad reflection for all who really love the south," especially when they considered "the low order of men, morally, socially and intellectually who occupy places of authority." For a time, Hancock's seeming betrayal of the South, combined with his scrambling to avoid service in the Confederate army, encouraged neither the Conservatives nor the Republicans to trust his loyalty. He defeated Pease as the Travis County delegate to the 1866 Constitutional Convention by campaigning against Pease's "radicalism" on the race question, but failed in his race for the United States Senate in the same year. Like many moderate Unionists, his Unionism did not extend to wishing upon his southland a harsh reconstruction. In a speech in San Antonio late in 1865 he told his audience that "we should let the past bury the dead, seize the present, and calmly and dispassionately consider the future." In the same appearance he uttered his oft-quoted remark that he was about as likely to extend the vote to Negroes as he was to mules. That and similar statements apparently confirmed his Conservative credentials, and in 1871 he won election to the United States Congress as a Democrat.[14]

Unlike Hancock, Throckmorton came to the problems of Reconstruction as a former Confederate. Yet he reached similar conclusions in weighing the choices facing southerners. Despite his love for the old Union and the Whig party before the war, his four years of fighting Yankees had obviously deeply affected him. It was only natural that he suspected Hamilton from the beginning, as the provisional governor had worn the uniform of and been placed in office by the government that Throckmorton had come to despise. He joined many other southern conservatives who had not been secessionists before the war and had only reluctantly supported the Confederacy, but who, in stubbornly refusing to yield to northern radicalism, somewhat unnaturally went over to the side of the die-hard southern "rebels." It also angered him when other prewar Unionists attacked him for his reluctant decision to support the Confederacy. "It makes me feel bitter & almost like a devil," he wrote after his election as a delegate to the 1866 Constitutional Convention, "to think that I have spent a whole life in favor of the Union—that I sacrificed my peace of mind & property & left my family allmost penniless & without help & risked my life in a cause I did not love or approve, in order that I could protect & be of service to just such men." And now, after all that, they questioned his loyalty. "D——mn them I say—I begin to despise and loathe them."15

Despite his bitterness, Throckmorton sought a rapid, painless restoration of Texas's rightful place in the Union, only a mild restructuring of southern race relations, and a magnanimity toward former Confederates. He also urged caution. A few months after assuming the governorship, he wrote that "never in the history of any people . . . was so much prudence and discretion required. . . . We must court harmony and good feeling." Nothing would be accomplished "by the bitter abuse of those who would oppress us." Throckmorton knew that practicing moderation would not be easy, however. To Epperson he railed during the Hamilton administration that the Unionists in power were "radical, bitterly and uncompromisingly proscriptive," and, in a rhetorical link to the antebellum long-ago, "just as revolutionary in their conduct . . . as the men who deposed [sic] Genl Houston." Rather than lubricating the machinery of restoration by forgetting old grudges, they sought to "keep up past issues—keep open old sores—and inflame old wounds that ought to be allowed to heal." Furthermore, this waving of the bloody shirt led these men to believe "that everybody who does not agree with them & endorse their policy is disloyal."16

The decidedly conservative state legislators elected with Throckmorton generated more than enough of the "disloyalty" predicted by Hamilton and his supporters. Their efforts to limit the political power of former Union men and to deny freedmen many basic liberties reflected the attitudes of most southern legislatures during Presidential Reconstruction.17

Throckmorton, who allegedly hung portraits of Robert E. Lee and Jefferson Davis in the executive mansion, favored these initiatives and, not surprisingly, found his own loyalty questioned. The Executive Colored Committee of Travis County, in a May 1867, letter to the governor, declared that "your whole action from the day you deserted the union cause, and took up arms against the United States Government to the present time has been one struggle against the loyal Sentiments in this State." A series of disagreements with federal military authorities regarding the protection of freedmen and Unionists and the prosecution of their attackers finally convinced Gen. Philip Sheridan, commanding the Fifth

Military District of Louisiana and Texas, to remove Throckmorton as an obstacle to reconstruction. The deposed governor doubtless had mixed emotions about losing such a difficult job; in a letter to his wife fairly early in his administration, he had complained "How miserable do we ourselves make life!" He wished that he had "been born under some other Star," rather than the one that had propelled him into public life. "Sometimes I almost wish the Radicals would turn me out," he wrote prophetically, "so that I could be a freeman once more."[18]

Throckmorton's freedom gave Texas Republicans a chance to make what had threatened to become a hollow military victory over the secessionists into a vindication for their own Reconstruction policies. One of their own, former governor E. M. Pease, took office for what turned out to be a two-year stint under the auspices of the three Reconstruction Acts passed by the Radical Congress between March and July of 1867. Contrary to the Republicans' early expectations, his administration would see the further fracturing of the Unionist coalition, as Republicans formed their own opinions on how they should respond to Congressional Reconstruction and exhibited varying ways of demonstrating their loyalty to the South. A. J. Hamilton had given the conservatives something to react against, James W. Throckmorton provided a foil for his increasingly radical opponents, and now E. M. Pease and his fellow moderates would force Republicans to make more choices about the future of Texas. The results would further polarize the conservatives and radicals in the state, as the actions of each party fed on the attitudes and hatreds of the other.

Perhaps nothing symbolized so well the divergent interpretations of the current state of Texas society than the loyalty-tinged debate over the issue of violence. Republican Unionists bitterly complained that the antebellum and wartime persecution of dissenters had continued beyond the end of formal hostilities. Conservatives, on the other hand, shrugged off such suggestions and claimed that Republicans were disloyally exaggerating the violence and the danger to which they were exposed for political reasons. No one seemed aware of the irony that Texans had made many of these same arguments during the 1860 slave "insurrection"; this time, however, the opinions and labels of "Radicals" and "Conservatives" were reversed.

The impetus to form a Texas Republican party stemmed partly from the Unionists' fear of Conservative retaliation against loyal men after the former came to power in 1866. The political and physical danger in which they and other Unionists found themselves—or in which they believed themselves—rubbed salt in the wound of losing control of the state government and no doubt awakened memories of prewar and wartime vigilance committees. Determined to rebuild the state in ways consistent with their political views and ambitions, Union men had been concerned about the alarming retention of power by secessionists since the beginning of Hamilton's provisional administration. Thirty citizens from North Texas sent Hamilton an eight-page petition in September 1865, arguing that "it is political Suicide" to place in office secessionists who, "taxing their wits to their utmost tension," had attempted to "overthrow this great and glorious Union of liberty and equality." The authors of the petition asked Hamilton to investigate a number of appointments that, because of the political inclinations of the officials, "have given general dissatisfaction to the Union men of our section." S. J. Baldwin, who the rebels had banished from Texas in 1863, wrote from Houston two years later that former rebels were going about saying, " 'when these god damned Yankee soldiers are gone we'll hang [Union men] as we ought to have done in the days of the Confederacy'!" Only military force, claimed Baldwin, could preserve the peace of the country and the lives of Union men. As if to prove the point, a letter to *Flake's Weekly Bulletin* in April 1866 told of the murder of a man in Jack County by a band of "rebel desperadoes, instruments of the [conservative] party," for the crime of demanding payment for a horse stolen while he was exiled during the war. "While I am writing," "M" penned despondently from Weatherford, "two of this party are riding through the streets, firing their pistols, inquiring and searching for Union men."[19]

A battery of witnesses testifying before the Congressional Joint Committee on Reconstruction confirmed these reports. Brig. Gen. W. E. Strong warned of a "fearful state of things" in Texas, where "gallant cavaliers," still displaying Confederate uniforms and guns, "would collect in groups and talk, in a tone particularly intended for our ears, of the deeds they had performed, and the number of Yankees they had slain." Maj. Gen. David S. Stanley observed during the summer of 1865, that former Confederate soldiers who served in the East had generally accepted their defeat, but those who had served far behind the lines in Texas "were insolent and overbearing where they dared to be . . . cursing the government and the Yankees." Another witness believed that no loyal man would be safe in Texas after federal troops were withdrawn. "Even now," testified Maj. Gen. George A. Custer, "there is no friendly feeling, and very little intercourse, between the loyal and the disloyal portion of the inhabitants." So great was the hostility, "a loyal man engaged in business receives no patronage except from loyal men." If the former secessionists "were left to themselves," an Austin Unionist told the committee, they "would seek to return to the old order of things, because they consider the present condition of things the greatest misfortune that has ever befallen them."

Another man declared in a letter to A.J. Hamilton "that I had as soon be in Hell as Texas."[20]

Texas rivaled hell for at least some Texans, according to statistics compiled and submitted to Congress by Governor Pease's office early in 1868. His "message" alleged that outlaws had committed 411 mostly unsolved or unprosecuted assaults and murders during the previous year, and listed names, dates, and other pertinent details for many of the cases. The crimes ranged from two former Confederate majors shooting it out over "unsettled accounts and jealousy," to the whipping and hanging of Wade Hampton, a freedman accused of stealing a knife, to the shooting death of a former Confederate colonel by a Unionist revenue collector. Some of the victims were Unionists (although one Dallas County man shot and killed the rebel who had murdered his Unionist father during the war), a few crimes (twelve) were perpetrated by blacks upon whites, and forty concerned blacks committing one form of atrocity or another upon other blacks. Murders, beatings, assaults, or attempted assaults by white men on freedmen amounted to nearly half (188) of the cases.[21]

Pease wrote that while "there no longer exists here any organized resistance to the authority" of the federal government, "a large majority of the white population . . . are embittered against the government by their defeat in arms and loss of their slaves." They "consider the government now existing here, under the authority of the United States, as an usurpation upon their rights," and "look upon the enfranchisement of their late slaves and the disfranchisement of a portion of their own class as an act of insult and oppression." These attitudes, the "demoralization and impatience of restraint by civil authority that always follow the close of great civil wars," and the great distances involved in Texas had created a situation in which it was nearly impossible to enforce the law at any level. Pease therefore requested that federal military authorities be empowered to do "what experience has proved cannot be effectually done by the civil officers of Texas."[22]

Despite evidence to the contrary, conservatives denied that desperadoes had overrun Texas, that the violence that did exist was politically motivated, or that the state needed federal aid to enforce the law. The *State Gazette* lambasted the "Pease Conspiracy" and expressed its surprise that "an old Texan" frequently honored by his fellow Texans could stoop so low. Apparently, the *Gazette* concluded, Pease "hated the people of Texas because, having found him to be an ingrate and a traitor to his benefactors, they rejected him over whelmingly" in the 1866 gubernatorial election. A convention of conservative delegates from twenty-one counties met in late July 1866, and resolved, among other things, that "a plot and conspiracy are on foot, and being carried out by the Radicals of Texas, to falsify and defame the people of this state to the people of the Northeastern states." Stories leaking to the outside world of violence and intimidation gave northerners the mistaken impressions that Texans were "hostile to the Constitution and Government of the United States," "vindictive and violent towards Northern citizens and adherents to the Federal Union during the late war," and "unjust and oppressive towards the freedmen in our midst." Such slanderous, obviously political statements were meant to "inflame and embitter the North against Texas" and to encourage the federal government to institute a military regime in the South. Even the Republican Ferdinand Flake, of Galveston, doubted that the violence had any political overtones. "The war has educated a class of men into idleness and into a familiarity with deadly weapons," he wrote in his *Bulletin,* "that prompts them to resort to the revolver whenever it suits their drunken vagries [*sic*]." These men "care no more for the Confederate cause than they do for the Federal"; their "only desire is for a life of idleness, vice and plunder." Flake counseled his readers in a later editorial that statements exaggerating violence "prevent immigration, hinder our trade, destroy our good name, and mar our general prosperity. . . . Let us all refrain from sowing the seeds of discord and opening still wider the breach that wise patriots are striving to close."23

Less moderate Union men found the political climate in Texas more discouraging and attributed the problem to a resurgence of southern radicalism, open disloyalty to the Union, and a throwback to antebellum vigilance. John L. Haynes reported to E. M. Pease, who was vacationing in New England, in October 1866, that the Texas legislature had passed a number of bills regulating the labor, self-defense, and travel of freedmen that would "reenslave the negroes." The Conservatives meant to prevent the election of Union men to any office, and had appointed judges who "vie with the Legislature in their hate of everything loyal to the government"; their courts were "nothing more nor less than rebel vigilance committees." Thomas H. DuVal wrote Pease that "the devilish spirit of secession is as defiant and hostile as ever," and wryly commented that the only entertainment to be found in Austin was the "occasional tableau, for the benefit of some Confederate general's widow or family." According to Morgan Hamilton, many "original union men" had gone over to the rebels because of the lack of action by the federal government, because the conservatives had finally overcome their resistance, or out of self-interest. "The sternest and strongest only," he wrote Pease, "have been able to weather the storm and keep the faith."24

Convinced that they were in danger of losing the peace after winning the catastrophic war for Union, Texas Unionists turned to the Republican Party as the safest vessel on which to weather the storm and to achieve their goals for reconstruction.[25] In formulating their response to the intransigence of Texas conservatives, Hamilton and his Unionist colleagues took their cue from the Radical Republicans who by the spring of 1867 controlled Congress. The Joint Committee on Reconstruction— although not dominated by Radicals—helped to inspire the new offensive against stubborn secessionists with the report it issued in 1866 containing the recommendations that would later surface in the Fourteenth Amendment to the Constitution. The committee suggested that the former Confederate states must not yet be allowed congressional representation, that adequate protection for loyal citizens of the South must be provided, that laws must be passed to provide for the equitable administration of civil rights, and that the gvernment must take actions that would "fix a stigma upon [the] treason" of former Confederates.[26]

A.J. Hamilton shared the northern Radicals' disgust at the course of events in the South, and his strategy for attaining the goals of Union men was considerable toughened—the first of several shifts in his opinions— during the months after he left the governor's office. Although he had always advocated basic civil rights for blacks, he had told the 1866 Constitutional Convention, "I thank God that this is a White man's Government; and I humbly trust that the time will never come when it shall cease to be so." By late in 1866, however, he could argue in a speech to the Boston Impartial Suffrage League that the freedmen had earned the right to vote with their wartime faithfulness to their masters and their postwar diligence, morality, and obedience of the law. Furthermore, if Reconstruction was to succeed and if former rebels were to be kept from permanently regaining control of southern state governments, the Republican party would have to mobilize black voters. Hamilton also insisted that military protection accompany the enfranchisement of blacks and that rebel leaders be punished; the latter's seizure of state governments "clearly demonstrated" that at this time in the South "traitors only are . . . worthy of the public confidence." Hamilton urged the president—who was rapidly losing the support of southern Unionists—to stop practicing partisan politics and to ignore the traitors surrounding him, and asked Congress to declare the former Confederate states once again out of the Union.[27]

Although many Unionists would soon back away from black enfranchisement and Confederate disfranchisement, Hamilton's words set the tone for the program of the Texas Republican party, which John L. Haynes, the party's first state chairman, had instigated in April 1867. E.M. Pease, finally—and temporarily—accepting the Republican principle of black suffrage, presided over the first state convention in Houston in July. One of the primary aims of the party was to recruit black voters, and to this end they formed secret Loyal Union Leagues all over the state. With the replacement of Throckmorton with Pease in late July, the Republicans seemed to have things going their way, as the new governor began removing Conservative officeholders and the Republicans planned a new constitutional convention that would implement their own vision of the future.[28]

In February 1868, Texans elected delegates to their second constitutional convention in less than three years. The convention met in Austin from June 1 to August 31, and then again from early December to February 8, 1869. Contrary to the optimistic expectations of the new ruling party of Texas, its deliberations revealed deep fissures among the leading Republicans in the state. When push came to shove, many discovered that their loyalty to the South was stronger than their allegiance to the Union or to the Republican party, and that they could not condone the drastic measures their more radical colleagues suggested.

Controversies developed around almost every issue, ranging from whether or not former rebels should be disfranchised to whether Texas should be divided into two states by creating a stronghold for a loyal government in West Texas. The doctrine of ab initio, whereby all acts passed by the state legislature since 1861 would be nullified, caused perhaps the most bitter disagreement among the assembled Republicans. Old economic rivalries among the planter elite, West Texas farmers, and men who favored internal improvements and state aid for railroads complicated these feuds over Reconstruction issues. By the end of the convention at least two factions had crystallized: the Moderates, led by Governor Pease, James H. Bell, and A.J. Hamilton, who controlled the state party machinery, and the Radicals, led by E.J. Davis, James P. Newcomb, and Morgan Hamilton, who controlled the state's Union Leagues. Each faction formed its own Executive Committee, and in 1869 each sent its own delegation—each headed by one of the Hamiltons—to Washington to confer with President Grant. Clearly, the situation in Texas was far less simple than Newcomb's inexplicable 1871 comment that "we have no fence-stradlers [sic] in Texas—they are either Rebel or Republican."[29]

Now that the Republicans were no longer a not-so-loyal opposition to the Conservatives, but the dominant party in the state, they could not content themselves with taking pot shots at Democratic policies and worrying about their personal safety. Rather, they now had to develop and implement their own solutions to the problems of Reconstruction. This process underscored the major divisions within their ranks. When it came time to write legislation, deal with sticky racial problems, and devise viable policies for rebuilding the state, they discovered the issue of loyalty—to the South or to the Union—cast a long, almost irresolvable shadow over every issue.

Between 1867 and 1874, a rash of defections plagued the "regular" Republican party, which accelerated during the Radical administration of Gov. Edmund Davis. E.M. Pease, always squeamish about building a party based on black votes, resigned the governorship in the summer of 1869 after the military removed many of his moderate appointees from office. Two years later, moving even further from his short-lived Radicalism, he led a taxpayers' rebellion against the allegedly profligate spending of the Davis government. James Bell, A.J. Hamilton's provisional secretary of state, opposed every major Radical program and returned to the Democratic fold. A.J. Hamilton, who represented to many Conservatives all that was evil in the Republican camp, eventually rejected the Radicals' plans for Texas and, as a delegate to the 1868 Constitutional Convention, successfully led the fight against the disqualification of former Confederates. Even Morgan Hamilton, who was Pease's Radical state comptroller and a United States senator under the Radicals, finally repudiated the Davis administration because of what he believed to be unnecessary spending, unwise support for railroads, and unfair patronage practices.[30]

John L. Haynes proved to be the most unpredictable Republican in Texas; at different times he supported all three Republican governors. He chaired the Moderates' state committee and worked against the disfranchisement of many rebel voters in order to attract a wider acceptance of the party among whites. Removed by President Grant—at the recommendation of E.J. Davis—from his sinecure as collector of customs at Galveston, Haynes lost to the Radical Republican Edward Degener in the 1869 Fourth District Congressional race, and a year later flirted with the Democrats in the Liberal Republican-Democrat fusion movement. He soon tired of the fusionists' states' rights platform, however, made an about-face, and turned to the Davis administration. Davis eventually rewarded the prodigal Republican by successfully recommending him for the collector of customs job at Brownsville.[31]

E.J. Davis and J.P. Newcomb headed the faction whose hard-nosed approaches to Reconstruction and to loyalty turned away so many Republicans. Newcomb, the former editor of the antisecessionist *San Antonio Alamo Express*, returned to Texas from his vigilante-inspired California exile in the late summer of 1867. He longed to help build a "government of the people . . . not a loose disjointed concern that can neither enforce its laws or protect its citizens at home or abroad," but a "stern unflinching just pure government that will not tolerate insult or contempt from a foreign foe or domestic enemy." Newcomb prophesied that "the avenging hand of God cannot long be stayed. . . . Justice will begin its reign, and peace will follow." The newspaperman served as secretary of state under the Radical governor E.J. Davis and managed the black-dominated Union Leagues, which provided much of the electoral support for the Radicals in Texas.[32]

Davis became Newcomb's avenging angel by winning the gubernatorial election in November 1869. He had assumed the leadership of the Texas Radicals when he chaired the 1868 constitutional convention and manipulated parliamentary procedure in an attempt to ensure passage of the Radical program. His election in November 1869, assured the Radicals—for which he became the hated symbol in Texas—of four years in which to work their magic on what they considered a still largely disloyal state.[33]

Although Conservatives spent much time and ink blasting the Republicans—the *Texas Republican*, for instance, called southerners who cooperated with northern Radicals "the most mean, dispicable, and licentiously depraved character of humanity that can be well conceived"—the steadily unraveling Republican party self-destructed in an orgy of infighting, personal attacks, and violent factionalism. On the floor of the 1868–1869 Constitutional Convention, controversies had erupted into at least four fistfights, with James P. Newcomb and George Ruby, the leading black delegate, among the combatants. Radicals often complained about "Haynes and his gang," or the "Bell & Haynes crowd," and Newcomb attacked the South Texas Republican for having come too slowly to the support of Congress because he feared it would cost him his position in the federal bureaucracy. "Haynes is certainly a diplomat," Newcomb wrote in an editorial, but "we want manliness and patriotism." Haynes countered by accusing the Radicals of being "unscrupulous in the use of means," and called their 1869 convention "a slim attendance of soreheads." The former Union colonel never refrained from bringing up his own Unionist credentials. In a letter to James P. Newcomb he accused rival Morgan Hamilton of "toasting his shins before a good fire . . . whilst I was in camp with my Regiment." Haynes did not "admit the right of these gentlemen to question my loyalty at all, and when they presume to do so, they are guilty of an impertinence."[34]

Impertinent or not, the Radicals eagerly cast aspersions on the loyalty and motivations of their erstwhile colleagues with all the fervor with which Confederates had attacked suspiciously unenthusiastic neighbors during the war. One of Haynes's fellow Union veterans, A.J. Hamilton, endured a hefty share of the Radicals' abuse. George Rives suggested to Newcomb that it would be "extremely damaging" to Hamilton's 1869 gubernatorial campaign if the Radicals would "publish to the World . . . that all the out-and-out Rebel Ku-Klux papers in the State are supporting Hamilton," while A.J. Burnett offered for publication his story of a very drunken and boisterous Hamilton and his "revolutionary crowd" during the final days of the 1868–1869 Constitutional Convention. A Union League circular during the 1869 election blasted the campaign of "our rebel, so-called Conservative, enemies under the leadership of the apostate, ex-military Governor A.J. Hamilton," and made it the duty of members to vote for "an honored brother, the soldier, hero, and statesman, General E.J. Davis, for Governor." Editor Newcomb asked what Hamilton had "ever done deserving the name of patriot or statesman? . . . A demagogue from the beginning [sic] and he will remain one to the end of the chapter."35

Threats to the Republican party stemmed from Democratic infiltration of local party organizations and from the less-than-loyal opportunism of other members. "The Republican party of Texas," declared H.C. Manning in an 1870 letter to James Newcomb, "is full of Time Servers traitors and disorganizers persons who care not what becomes of it so they can get place and profit." The postmaster, district clerk, and sheriff of McLennan County called themselves Republicans but, according to a self-proclaimed "Ex Rebel Republican," refused to cooperate with the party and were, "actual incumberance [sic] & dead weight to us." Calvert County's "loyal people" had "much to suffer, owing to the incursions of the rebels into the Republican ranks," and a regular party member in Fayette County attended a local meeting of the "white portion of Republicans," but "at times could not determine its political complexion—it was so much like a Democratic assemblage" in "its denunciation of *every* and *all* State measures." Even the state office of the Union League acknowledged the difficulty facing local Republicans when in an 1871 circular it cried "Brothers, rally! We have enemies without, spies and traitors within."36

Some men recognized the danger in the ruthlessness with which Republicans assailed one another. George C. Rives interrupted his own barrage of rhetorical barbs to write that he was "sick at heart & in despair" at the state of the Republican party in Texas. "For Gods [sic] sake," he demanded of Newcomb during the 1869 campaign, "tell me the difference between the Jack Hamilton party & our party . . . the only difference is who shall have the 'loaves & fishes' of office—There is no issue between Jack Hamilton & Davis or the rebels that I can see." "Our situation," J.G. Tracy told Newcomb in the spring of 1872, "is truly unfortunate. We ought all to be friends, working for the same great object . . . but instead we find many at sword points, hating each other worse than we do the Democrats." Newcomb seemed less worried, however. He declared in the *San Antonio Express* that men who complained about extremists on "both sides," who sought the middle, were "the lowest class of trimmers" and "traitor[s]."37

The Democrats delighted in the suicidal tendencies of the Republicans. "How pleasant 'tis to see," a piece of Democratic doggeral began,

"The rads all disagree / Each in his proper station move, / And each the other rascal prove." The *Democratic Statesman* reported happily that "escaped convicts, noted thieves and sneaking pickpockets,' are the epithets being applied by the belligerent radicals of this State to each other."38

Not surprisingly, Davis's election in November 1869, failed to end the fighting among the various groups of Republicans in Texas. Rather, the policies pursued by the Radical state government strengthened the Democrats and alienated even more Republican dissidents, as many white Republicans seemed to swing into the camp of Hamilton's moderates. A number of factors led to the decline of the Davis faction. White Texans identified it too closely with the black voters in the state, a perception strengthened by the hated state police, which, despite its generally adequate restoration of order, could not overcome the fact that the former slave population furnished many of its recruits. His enemies also attacked Davis for financing railroad development and a public school system, and there was always the federal military presence in Texas to castigate, despite its less-than-tyrannical administration by the early 1870s.39

By 1871, surviving Republicans had much more to worry about than the treachery of their former allies, as the Democrats mobilized to overthrow the "nondescript despotism" represented by E.J. Davis. The inaugural issue of the *Austin Democratic Statesman*, a party organ that went to press in July 1871, called loyal southerners to arms against the Republican program, which had tried "to belabor [the South] with the outrages and indignities of its brutal soldiery, with political disabilities, with defamation and contumely, with violence to their social life, with the mockery of republican government without representation, and with the horrid rule of a service race instructed in demoniac oppression by the basest scurf and offscourings of its myrmions." In order to "save the State and the people" the *Statesman* asked that "each man be a patriot and sacrifice on the altar of his country . . . his own private personal advancements." Democrats— including John Hancock in the Fourth District—seized all four of the state's Congressional seats at the October election.40

The disastrous Congressional election marked the beginning of the end for Radical Reconstruction in Texas, as race once again plagued the Republican party. All Radicals must have winced when a *Gilmer Sentinel* writer called a Radical "a thing that would / Be a nigger if he could." Consequently, in the 1872 state elections the besieged Radicals tried to attract white voters by trimming the budget and downplaying the campaign for law and order, but rather than gaining strength among whites, the administration undercut its support among blacks, who feared the loss of their influence with the party of emancipation. State Senator Matt

Gaines, a freedman, accused the Radicals of caring little for blacks, although "they set themselves up as the BIG GODS of the negroes,"
expecting "worship, offices, money and power from us, while deep down
in their hearts they hate and despise us." Blacks rarely received patronage,
Gaines argued. "They treat us as bad as . . . the worst Democrats, and yet
they call themselves our friends."[41]

The rapid unraveling of the Republican party allowed the Democrats
to "redeem" the legislature in 1872 and recapture the governor's office in
1873 by a margin of two to one. The *Democratic Statesman* rejoiced when
the legislature arrived in Austin in early 1873. "For six years Texas has had
no legislature that represented the people of the State," it declared. "For
six years tyranny, fraud, corruption and villainy in high and low places have
held a saturnalia of vice." Texans had "patiently submitted to robbery and
insult, hoping for the day when the people's true representatives would
again assemble in the Capitol of the State." Now, "our patience, long
suffering and forbearance under great provocations are bearing their good
fruit." The *Statesman* claimed with a certainty characteristic of newspapers of the time that "it is not too much to affirm that no Legislature that
has ever assembled in this State has had so many men of ability as that
which is about to throttle Radicalism and restore the government to its old
time purity."[42]

When the Democratic governor, the Confederate veteran Richard
Coke, took office after Davis's quixotic legal and military defense of the
state capitol, Reconstruction in Texas finally ended. The *Dallas Herald*
announced that "the tyrant's chains have fallen from [Texans'] limbs. . . .
The storm has spent its force—the clouds have lifted—and the sun of
peace, liberty and good government is risen to shed his benign light over
us as a people." Republican governments collapsed all over the South; in
Texas, the once significant and confident Unionist coalition had been
reduced to a small core of stubborn Radicals without influence or, after
1874, office. A year later, yet another Constitutional Convention erased
Radicalism from Texas by writing an inflexible and highly detailed document that limited the power, terms of office, and salaries of government
officials. For many decades afterward, the Republican party, with only
one-fourth of the state's voters, was reduced to negotiating with third
parties, fighting over federal patronage, and wrestling with the question of
whether its black majority should be allowed to control the party.[43]

Ethnic Texans continued to occupy uneasy positions in Texas politics
and society during Reconstruction. The temporary readjustment of the
power structure in Texas failed to change the status of the German and
Hispanic elements of the population. By the end of Reconstruction,

bruised by their wartime persecution and by the political reverses of the early 1870s, they generally receded into the background and picked up their lives where they had been interrupted by the war. Nevertheless, many members of the second and third largest ethnic groups in Texas continued to dissent from southern values during the postwar period, and Anglos continued to look upon them with suspicion, often measuring their worth in terms of which party they chose to support.

Many Germans, especially those in West Texas, joined the Republican party during Reconstruction. Edward Degener, now a leader of San Antonio's Germans, announced to E.M. Pease in 1866 that his city's Germans had all voted the Republican ticket, and the Joint Committee on Reconstruction learned from a Union general who had been stationed in Texas that the Germans had remained loyal to the United States and were, in fact, "radical; they go beyond the Americans in Union sentiment vastly." Only Germans seemed disposed "to treat the freedpeople kindly" in Bastrop County, according to an 1867 Freedmen's Bureau report, and the *Democratic Statesman* chided Texas Germans for "duly obey[ing] the great Radical darkey" Matt Gaines. [44]

Several Germans labored valiantly for the Radical cause in Texas, providing for conservative Anglos evidence of the "unreliability" of all German Texans. August Siemering, through the columns of the *Freie Presse Feur Texas* in San Antonio, celebrated the emancipation of the slaves and claimed that the German population had been solidly Unionist during the war. Degener, who the San Antonio Military Commission had convicted of disloyalty in 1862, was perhaps the best-known German Radical. As a member of the committee studying black suffrage, he submitted a minority report to the 1866 Constitutional Convention that justified extending the vote to freedmen on constitutional, moral, political, and historical grounds. "Let us . . . learn wisdom from the past," he wrote, "and without compulsion from any quarter, cheerfully accord to our own freedmen, rights and privileges, long unjustly withheld, thus insuring our peace and prosperity, and their gratitude and friendship forever more." Three years later he defeated John Haynes in a close race for Congress, where he served a single term. Jacob Kuechler of Gillespie County—also tried by the Military Commission—became a Radical delegate to the 1868 Constitutional Convention and later served as Davis's controversial Commissioner of the General Land Office. Because of the publicity given to these men and to the wartime disloyalty and persecution of Germans in Texas, the stereotype of an overwhelmingly Radical Germanic population in the state prevailed in the North, and former Confederates in Texas frequently considered them unreliable and disloyal. [45]

In truth, most German-Texans were not so radical. Matt Gaines angered Germans when he scolded them for not cooperating with blacks; apparently he was disappointed that the two groups could not cooperate more closely. A Freedmen's Bureau official reported that Llano County Germans, despite their wartime Unionism, steadfastly opposed granting suffrage to blacks. Louis Constant complained that many Austin County Germans, many of whom had voted against secession and suffered persecution at the hands of vigilant rebels, had after the war fallen under the influence of the secessionists. Constant attributed this to the fact that the German element of this southeastern Texas county "came from an environment, where the word 'Liberty' towards their superiors would have been punished." In addition, "we had here some 'so-called Unionists', who, during the rebellion spied on their people, and even now fulfill the orders of their old masters when they try to oppose all valuable suggestions, and to smear the outstanding men." As a result, the "masses had been lulled down," and unrepentant rebels controlled the local offices.[46]

Ferdinand Flake, an ardent prewar Unionist and editor of *Flake's Bulletin* in Galveston, represented the moderation of many Republicans and Germans. At the same time that he wrote that secession was, "in theological language, original sin," he dismissed the work of the Freedmen's Bureau as an "anomalous affair" and opposed granting suffrage to freedmen because "we do not think them qualified to exercise it discreetly." Many other Republicans joined Flake in this mixture of Radical rhetoric and conservative racial philosophy. The Galveston editor summarized the moderates' overriding hope for an early Reconstruction in his Christmas meditation for 1866. Inspired by the season, Flake wrote that "All that we need is peace and faith. . . . It is said that love begets love, and faith begets faith." The common men of both the North and the South were tired of war. "We think," opined Flake optimistically, "the dawn of a lasting peace not far distant—a day when the whole nation will not only be united in one government, but be a band of brothers, each supporting and supported by the other." Flake's refusal to support Radical Republican policies earned him an invitation to leave the party in the late 1860s.[47]

In other parts of the state, Democratic Germans opposed the Republican party for a variety of reasons. Germans in West Texas complained of their unmet demands for frontier protection; the bloc voting of black Republicans angered Germans along the Gulf coast; friction with United States troops occupying the state—a common complaint all over the South—disturbed Fayette County Germans; while others joined the Democrats in opposing the spendthrift Davis government and the state police organization. Competition among Germans, blacks, and Anglos for party patronage antagonized all three groups. By the early 1870s, even Degener had fallen out with the Davis administration.[48]

A document issued in 1873 reveals what may have been the attitudes of a good many Germans in Texas. A public meeting in La Grange, Fayette County, called for the organization of a "People's Movement"—its similarity to the Populism of the 1890s went beyond its name—that would replace the old parties that had thus far been useless in reconstructing Texas. Following such a terrible war, "the people should have joined as freedmen to co-operate in the great and glorious work of building up again what the war had mutilated or destroyed." This was not to be; "how disgraceful is the struggle in which the politicians of the two parties were engaged since the war." Corruption, the unfair influence of monopolies and corporations, and the dominance of "carpet baggers and political adventures" plagued the people of Texas. Both major parties contributed to the problem. The Republicans "wage war upon the people and upon our free institutions," while the Democratic party had become "a negative, a mere opposition party, too feeble, without vitality." As a result, the public meeting resolved to choose the best and wisest leaders from among the Republicans and Democrats, and form a new "people's party" based on a platform that ignored racial issues but called for a strict construction of the Constitution, the "repression" of the influence of business on government, the reform of education, law enforcement, and the civil service, and the mitigation of "public excitement and partisan spirit" that currently dominated the government.[49]

Enthusiasm for the Republican party, therefore, dwindled among Germans just as it had among other Texans as Reconstruction ground to its conclusion in 1873. Edward Degener lost his seat in Congress to the Democrat John Hancock in 1871, and other Radical Germans lost their jobs or jettisoned their Radicalism during the next two years. Nevertheless, Germans remained in the party in far greater numbers than other Texans, and many of the latter continued to harbor long-nurtured suspicions about the loyalty of Germans. Just as the minority of liberal Germans—such as those who had issued the infamous 1854 San Antonio platform or the men who had resisted conscription in West Texas—had poisoned the minds of Texans against the rest of their countrymen in the 1850s and during the war, the Radical element among German-Texans during Reconstruction came to dominate the public impression of this largely conservative ethnic group. Consequently, nondissenting Germans continued to pay for the political sins of the liberals after the war, just as they had before and during it.[50]

The social and political relationships between Hispanics and Texans following the war duplicated the distrust and hatred of the antebellum period. Mexican-Americans were as pragmatic during Reconstruction as they had been during the Civil War, and former Confederates and Unionists both resented the Mexican-Americans' lack of enthusiasm for their respective causes. Radicals could count on tejanos in El Paso to vote the Republican ticket, and many northern Republicans believed that the Hispanic population was as loyal as the supposedly Unionist Germans. San Antonio Mexicans, however, split their vote between the Democrats and the Republicans, while Rio Grande Valley Republicans—led by Governor Davis—could count on the support of Hispanic voters. The Democrats disingenuously appealed to the tejanos on the basis of race, and convinced many that their best interests lay with their fellow white men rather than with the freedmen. A few Radical leaders among the Mexicans accepted black suffrage wholeheartedly and advocated the Republican program for Reconstruction.[51]

Of course, with few exceptions, Hispanics had no more at stake in the political or economic systems of Texas during Reconstruction than they had ever had, and few of them took the arguments of the Anglo politicians seriously. The leading tejano secessionist and Confederate officer, Santos Benavides, served as a conservative state legislator from 1879 to 1884, and Mexican-Americans frequently served in city and county offices in San Antonio and in South and West Texas. Most others, however, continued the pragmatic participation in politics that many of them had practiced during the antebellum period, as the force of numbers and illiteracy prevented them from undertaking any sort of independent political action. The "Red" and "Blue" parties in Brownsville both "voted the Mexicans" during the last third of the nineteenth century. On the day before an election, Hispanics from both sides of the border would be rounded up, "corraled," and given food and mescal. The next day they were ushered to the balloting place, where they picked up the appropriate ballot at one table and a silver dollar from a Red or Blue representative at the next. One San Antonio Radical complained that the secessionists had marched the "Mexican rabble" to the polls where they sold their votes "to the highest bidder." James Newcomb could hardly approve of such widespread Hispanic support of the Democratic party, but he did ironically suggest that "if we can find an honest, competent Mexican we can easily command him and will find them glad to go with us."[52]

In 1871, John L. Haynes, long a liaison between the Anglo and Mexican interests in Texas, published a letter in Spanish to the tejano voters of the Rio Grande Valley in which he urged them to organize into Republican clubs in order to ensure their best representation in the Texas legislature and in the federal government. He promoted the candidacy of Edward Degener for Congress—Haynes's victorious opponent in 1869 for the same Congressional slot—against John Hancock, the former Know-Nothing who still had not renounced his membership in that "barbarous and cruel party." During the remainder of the nineteenth and into the twentieth century, however, Mexican-Texans were known more for their vulnerability to manipulation by Anglo political bosses than they were for their allegiance to any particular party.[53]

More important to most Mexicans were the economic exploitation and bloodshed that shaped their dealings with Anglos. The chronic violence in the state during Reconstruction, combined with the unsettled conditions along the western and southern frontiers of Texas, created a situation in which tejanos had to talk softly and try to stay out of the way of their Anglo neighbors. Predictably, however, many Mexicans ran afoul of white vigilante injustice. Texas Rangers, law officers, and civilians all blamed Mexicans for murders, rapes, rustling, and sundry other crimes in South and Central Texas. In the 1870s, for example, whites indiscriminately killed over forty Mexican-Texans after an unknown assailant murdered an unpopular local rancher. Whites living along the border often suspected Hispanics of plotting raids on Anglo towns or other crimes against the state, and the discovery of these "conspiracies" always created a quickly satisfied demand for doses of prophylactic lynch law. An army officer reported during this period that "there is a considerable Texas element in the country bordering on the Nueces that think the killing of a Mexican no crime," and a significant body of "Mexican thieves and cut-throats who . . . think the killing of a Texan something to be proud of." Any sort of eruption in the volatile politics of Mexico alarmed Texans living along the border and caused them to suspect the loyalty of the tejanos among them; the outbreak of the Spanish-American war in 1898 recalled the "subversion" practiced by Mexicans during the Civil War, and Texans watched the actions of their neighbors closely as the heritage of racial antagonism between these two ethnic groups continued to taint their relationship.[54]

As the climax of the sectional conflict, Reconstruction had narrowed the bounds of acceptable political and social behavior in Texas. The *Dallas Herald* compared men who refused to subscribe to what by 1873 had become the views of an overwhelming majority of voting Texans to "the locusts of Egypt, Judas, Benedict Arnold, the Santa Fe traitor, William P. Lewis, and all the other characters who have afflicted countries in past times."[55]

Men who had opposed radical states' rights stands and secession, men who had gone so far as to flee the state during the war and even fight against the Confederacy, now joined the most faithful rebels in rejoicing over the impotence of the Republican party in Texas and in the preservation of the values and social structure of the South. Many merely found themselves instinctively protecting their state and region from what they believed to be outside influences, while others could not tolerate the way that Unionism and loyalty as defined by the Yankee Congress and local Republicans had come to include support for programs unpalatable to them. For men such as E.L. Dohoney, the proscription and opportunism they had detested in the state Democratic party of the 1850s had surfaced in the Republican party of the 1870s. Although Dohoney, a Democrat, had fought strenuously against secession and opposed slavery before the war, he had served his state in the Confederate army. After the war, still a Democrat, he favored the Thirteenth and Fifteenth Amendments for pragmatic reasons and won election to the state senate in 1869, with support from moderate Republicans. There he opposed the Radicals, who "precipitated upon the State" the state police, martial law, expensive schools, "and other equally obnoxious measures." Dohoney's seemingly contradictory devotion to the Union and hatred of Republican policies stemmed from his opposition to despotism perpetrated by any political party.[56]

Some Texans did remain in the Republican party, and not all dissenters turned their backs on the past. Blacks obviously had no other realistic political choice than to vote Republican—despite Democratic attempts to woo them into the Democratic fold—and many Germans, especially in the culturally isolated counties in the Texas hill country west of Austin, stubbornly clung to the principles and the party of reform. Republican leaders such as James P. Newcomb, E.J. Davis, John L. Haynes, and Thomas H. DuVal, remained constant out of loyalty, but also because their livelihoods—as state or federal Republican appointees—depended on it. No doubt many local leaders and rank-and-file members continued their membership in the party because it provided the only means of organized opposition to the party in power.

The bottom line for many of those southerners who remained or became Democrats during Reconstruction was, of course, race. Historians have argued for over half a century that the primary unifying factor for white southerners was the doctrine of "White Supremacy." The resurgence of the Democratic party and decline of the Republican party—in the South and in Texas—was due to a large extent to the unwillingness of most whites, even the most dedicated dissenters, to grant blacks full social and political equality. As a result, the southern branch of the Democratic party attracted a heterogeneous mix of representatives of a number of political persuasions, not so much because of its minimalist, agrarian policies, but because it served as an umbrella organization for those diverse segments of the white political community who could at least agree on the need for whites to retain their traditional racial supremacy. On the other hand, northern Republicans practically forced most of their ostensible southern allies into the arms of the Democrats with their racial policies, their economic ideology, and their "bloody shirt" campaign tactics. By the end of Reconstruction, too loyal to their race and their region to remain Republicans, most white antebellum and even Reconstruction dissenters had returned to the mainstream of Texas politics and society.[57]

8

Black Texans
during Reconstruction

The Civil War and Reconstruction changed the lives of black Texans forever. Unfortunately for them, however, their futures lay largely in the hands of whites, who were at first hopelessly divided over what they should "do with" the newly freed blacks.[1] Their own expectations and ambitions heavily influenced how they would respond to black demands and needs. Suprisingly, one of the most generous attitudes expressed by a white Texan came from a Confederate veteran of the desperate fighting in the East. During his postsurrender trek back to Live Oak County, Capt. Samuel T. Foster encountered a group of black children on their way to school. "Such a thing [n]ever cross[ed] my mind," he wrote in his diary. He stopped a twelve-year-old girl and tested her briefly on reading and arithmetic. Despite her giggling—no doubt she had hardly expected a quiz from a ragged Confederate soldier so early in the day—she answered his questions quite satisfactorily. "I never was more surprised in my life!" exclaimed Foster, "the idea was new to me." In camp that evening, Foster envisioned black and white children receiving equal educations and competing as doctors, lawyers, teachers, and merchants. "The smartest man will succeed without regard to his color. . . . Our children will have to contend for the honors in life against the negro in the future." "Perhaps," Foster wondered on another occasion, "we were wrong, and . . . the negroes ought to have been freed at the start."[2]

No doubt many freedmen envisioned just such a society of good will, free competition, and merit-based progress. If all whites had shared Foster's at least temporarily open-minded approach to the restructuring of southern society, Reconstruction would have been much less violent. Of course, events followed a drastically different course. George W. Paschal, one of Austin's most prominent Unionists, revealed just how difficult it would be to reconstruct the racial attitudes of even supposedly sympathetic Texans. After a war in which he had suffered slander and poverty, had been arrested for his Union views and, ironically, had been labeled an "abolitionist," Paschal welcomed the United States troops entering the capital in July 1865, with a speech that foreshadowed the future of the several hundred freedmen in his audience. Paschal reminded them that freedom was not, contrary to what he believed most of them thought, "like heaven to the poor woman—a place where there is a great deal of singing and nothing to do." He told them that they would "have to pay the doctors to kill you, and the sextons to bury you, just as white people do." The freedmen would now be penalized for their "cursed awkwardness and carelessness, which have generally ruined your masters." He finished by telling his black listeners to "go to your homes, and make your arrangements to do better work for less pay."[3]

Paschal's version of what would probably happen to blacks—at least the attitude toward blacks it demonstrated—came much closer to reality than Foster's. Yet, it took several years of bitter political debate, frequent confrontations, and occasional magical hints of what could have been, before blacks had been forced into their "proper" roles in society. Their Reconstruction experience differed from those of the other major non-Anglo ethnic groups in Texas. The Germans and Hispanics, bruised by their wartime persecution, receded into the background and generally picked up their lives where they had been interrupted by the war. Blacks, on the other hand, became the center of attention in ways they had never been, even during the 1860 "insurrection" scare. Now, however, they were not feared as belligerent or even dangerous slaves, but as economic competitors and political rivals—roles unthinkable to most white southerners before 1865. Most of the political, economic, and social issues that contributed to the partisanship and violence of Reconstruction revolved around the freedmen and the arguments over how they should be integrated into the postwar South. The fights over the freedmen's rights to the franchise and to economic and civil equality fueled Reconstruction politics; internal disagreements over the status of blacks contributed to the eventual ruin of the state's Republican party and allowed the resurrected Democratic party to "redeem" Texas.

Blacks often ignored Paschal's conservative advice and challenged the status quo throughout the Reconstruction period. Their efforts to live independently sparked controversy when they became entangled in the forlorn attempts of other dissenters to break free from southern orthodoxy. At the most basic level, black freedom itself threatened most whites, who shuddered at the thought of sharing civil and economic rights with a race that they had long held in physical and ideological bondage. In the political arena, the definition of loyalty to the South and to Texas partially hinged on one's stance in regard to the former slave population. The destruction of an effective Republican party in Texas owed much to the inability of most Texas Republicans, even the most determined Union men, to forsake their region and their race. Finally, white conservatives alternately loathed and courted their black "friends," swearing vehemently that they would amount to no good while at the same time attempting to win their votes for the Democratic party. As a result, the whites' definition of black loyalty acquired a new political dimension, as the freedmen emerged from their roles as shadowy, potentially dangerous participants in the sectional crisis into the spotlight of Reconstruction politics.

Whites retained old patterns of race relations and vigilance, and blacks had to contend with the fact that most whites measured their worth against a simple standard: how willing they were to accept an inferior status that retained many characteristics of the antebellum status quo. Just as whites had expected their slaves to remain loyal during the war (while at the same time fearing the consequences if they did not), during Reconstruction, whites encouraged, goaded, and intimidated blacks into behaving as closely as possible to the obedient and manageable plantation stereotype. When blacks failed to submit to these restrictions, whites struck with all the suddenness and violence of the old vigilance committees. Conservatives interpreted the blacks' efforts to live free lives as a sign that the freedmen needed to be reminded of where their loyalties ought to lie. Texas freedmen also played a vital role in the issue of white loyalty during Reconstruction. Both Conservatives and Republicans sought the blacks' help in establishing once and for all whether loyalty to the United States or to the South would predominate in Texas. At the same time, whites had to make personal decisions about loyalty, and their attitudes about what place blacks should occupy in Texas society were often a function of where they chose to place their allegiance.

The scene occurred, with some variations, all over the South. The master called his remaining slaves to the big house and announced the most important news they would ever hear: they were free. In Texas, the process began on June 19, 1865—"Juneteenth" forever after—when the general commanding the District of Texas, issued General Order Number Three, which declared that "all slaves are free." It went on to state that "this involved an absolute equality of rights and rights of property between former masters and slaves"; their relationship now "becomes that between employer and free laborer." The order also advised freedmen to remain at their present homes, working for wages. "They will not," it announced, "be allowed to collect at military posts" nor "be supported in idleness" by the government.[4]

Strict reminders of the limits of government generosity meant far less to suddenly free men and women than the news that their long bondage had ended. As the word slowly filtered out through the settled southeastern portion of Texas and into the frontiers of North and West Texas, slaveowners grimly gave up their bondsmen. A Goliad County slaveowner held his slaves for another month, but abruptly released them after a stern warning from federal soldiers. Steve Williams remembered, "he come out and he say, 'You all git, I mean git from here!' " Jacob Branch recalled many years later that "Massa Tucker brung de freedom papers and read dem. He say us all am free as Hell." According to one of his former slaves, Travis County's Tom Washington read from "de big paper" and said "you is free to live and free to die and free to go to de devil, if you wants to."5

Slaves greeted freedom with a wide range of emotions, but most relished their freedom and immediately began expanding their worlds and multiplying their prerogatives. Frank Adams overheard one fellow exclaim how he would exert his new freedom in perhaps the most basic way: "Don' know w'at I's gwinter do," he cried, "but I know one t'ing, I's gwine git 'nuf sleep fo' onct." Seventeen-year-old Isom Norris made good on a wartime vow he had made to "Little Massa Joe," his owner's son and Isom's boyhood friend. One day toward the end of the war, Joe had told him, "you is goin' to be free as I is wen de war is over." Isom doubted it, but jokingly boasted that "if I gits to be free as you is, de fus' thing I'se goin' to do is give you a whipping." When the day of freedom came, "De fus' thing I 'new I jumped right straddle of Little Massa Joe, and threw him down and give him a few licks wid my fist. Den I sed, 'you 'members what I tol' you?' " Joe "tuk it as a big joke, and did not do a thing to me, but he laughed at me gettin' so happy cause I wus free as he wus."6

Some freedmen stretched their horizons and their souls by leaving the only homes and lives they had known. Susan Ross's oldest brother, upon hearing that he was free, "give a whoop, run and jump a high fence, and told mammy good bye. Den he grab me up and hug and kiss me and say 'Brother gone, don't 'spect you ever see me no more.' I don't know where he go," Susan said long afterwards, "but I never did see him 'gain." One former slave remembered that, although he and his fellow bondsmen could have stayed on their old plantation, "dare didn't none of us stayed. . . . Why de niggahs dey just scatter like quails dey goes in every dereckshun, and none of dem knows what dey is goin, dey was jus goin dats all." The *Southern Intelligencer* commented on the number of blacks moving about after the war. The "predominate" trait of blacks in the months following emancipation, it observed, was their "desire to 'go somewhere.' " Many Bastrop freedmen headed thirty miles west to Aus-

tin, where "they expect to get high prices for labor . . . see a heap of people
. . . hear the band that brays the best music . . . [and] above all . . . meet
and shake hands with '*Massa Jack, the Governor and the Givernment*.' "
Blacks moved in great numbers to Galveston, San Antonio, and
Houston—where nearly 40 percent of the population was black five years
after the war—and founded at least thirty-nine all-black communities by
the 1870s.[7]

Despite their propensity to take to the road immediately after emancipation, many former slaves eventually returned or settled fairly close to
their old homes; there was no massive population shift from one part of the
state to another between the end of the war and 1870. Some gratefully
continued working for their former owners for wages or for a share of the
crops. Hannah Jameson, for instance, realistically stayed on her master's
plantation because "when surrender broke, you could tie all a Nigger
family had in a bed sheet. They had nothing 'cept a house full of Niggers
and no where to go." Slaves who had been fond of their masters often
stayed until they could buy homes nearby. Even some of the blacks who
moved far away struggled to retain old ties. Theresa Moore moved with her
husband from central Texas to a West Texas farm after the war, but in 1869
she wrote to her old mistress, Mary Polley, scolding her for not writing and
asking for news about friends and family members, white and black.
Theresa promised that she would soon come for a visit and extended an
open invitation for anyone in the Polley family to visit her. "Mistress,"
Theresa pleaded at the end of her letter, "please answer my letter right
away for it is almost a year since I have heard a word from home and I do
want to hear from you all so bad."[8]

No matter how close to their slave lives they remained physically,
freedmen eagerly sought the education that they believed would help
them get ahead in a white man's world. "Nearly every darkey in town has
got a primer or spelling book," the *Southern Intelligencer* reported conde-
scendingly, "and gone to work learning to spell." Lucadia Pease wrote from
Austin that "I meet the darkies every day in the street with their books and
slates, and they seem to be very proud of the opportunaty [*sic*] to attend
school." During the five years that the Freedmen's Bureau administered
schools in Texas, over twenty thousand blacks learned at least rudimentary
reading and writing skills. Bureau schools encountered many obstacles,
ranging from white opposition and book, building, and teacher shortages,
to a severe yellow fever outbreak in the summer of 1867. Furthermore, few
freedmen could afford the fifty-cent a month tuition charged after March
1867. The bureau's best year was its last; in 1870, it reported sixty-six
schools in Texas (with forty-three of them owned by freedmen), 3,248

students, and sixty-three teachers (including twenty-seven blacks). This still represented only a small fraction of the 70,000 or so school-age black children, but marked a hopeful beginning for black education in the state.[9]

Freedmen channeled their energies into other areas of society as well, trying to participate fully in their communities and jealously guarding their new-found rights. Many whites found all of this strange and alarming, and much of the social and political unrest and violence that characterized reconstruction in Texas and elsewhere stemmed from the fact that whites and blacks had two entirely different views of how postwar southern society should operate. A black from Prairie Lea discovered this when he asked to see some cattle he was about to buy from a white rancher; the white man gave the black man a beating for his presumptuousness. Whites could not get used to blacks behaving in ways that would have been inconceivable in the past. Stephen Paschal, a freedman living in Galveston, rose during a Republican meeting and declared that if he had had the advantages of a white man, "he would have been as smart a man as . . . ever trod Texas." According to a Freedmen's Bureau teacher in attendance, a northern soldier in the crowd called Paschal a " 'damn liar,' whereupon a general disturbance took place and a number of shots were fired, wounding two men."[10]

The Republican *Southern Intelligencer* bemusedly reported that freedwomen in North Austin "have gone to house-keeping in regular style." The women behaved just like white housewives: "They receive the visits of their friends, talk largely, gossip some, we suppose, in imitation of other people, wash clothes, and vegetate generally." Unfettered by laws restricting their rights to congregate, freedmen participated in the sorts of social activities previously reserved for whites or held under white supervision. The biggest celebration of the year took place on Juneteenth— Liberation Day—but Independence Day also witnessed blacks enjoying their new freedom. Church and school picnics, railroad excursions, harvest festivals, fund raisers, baseball games (with white umpires), dances, and band concerts all marked attempts by blacks to live free lives. Freedmen further exerted their freedom by accelerating their antebellum secession from white congregations. In separate churches, blacks could develop their own religious beliefs, learn how to manage money and institutions, and hone leadership skills. Finally, blacks began, by mid-1867, serving on juries—indeed, dominating them, in districts where few white men could swear the "ironclad oath."[11]

Freedmen also claimed a freedom long denied them in slavery—the right to protect themselves. Their efforts were one of the reasons some whites suspected an uprising among freedmen on Christmas Day, 1865. In response to random and organized violence against blacks, some established local militia companies. A minor "riot" between the races in Tyler erupted when about twenty blacks drilled on the streets after dark, with drum, bugle, and firearms. A freedman from near Jefferson named Dick Walker raised "a cullud militia to keep the Klux off the niggers," which met regularly at the local African Methodist Church. A company of planters attacked, killing and wounding several of the black militiamen. White vigilantes near Jefferson also broke up a group of freedmen allegedly led by white outsiders because nearby citizens had been "apprehensive of an outbreak among the negroes. The report is, that the negroes . . . contemplated a general massacre and robbery of the neighborhood." Former slaves frequently remembered the ways that individual freedmen dealt with the Ku Klux Klan; their sometimes violent resistance no doubt puzzled and enraged whites accustomed to slave subservience. Nancy King's brother-in-law out-maneuvered a squad of "Ku Kluxers" who were chasing him by tying a grapevine across the road "'bout breast high to a hoss." When the night riders "hit that grapevine, it throwed them every which way and broke some their arms."[12]

Violence or the threat of violence frequently erupted when whites failed to live up to the blacks' perceptions of justice. A dozen armed freedmen rescued two alleged cattle rustlers from a deputy sheriff in July 1868. In the same month, a similar phenomenon with an unusual racial twist occurred in Waco, where a black was arrested, but not incarcerated, for assaulting another freedman. Armed negroes "rioted" until authorities put him in jail. The *Texas Republican* responded in the only way whites could to the blacks' assertion of their rights. "Negro riots, under radical rule," declared the *Republican* a few months before Radical Republicans actually took over the state government, "are becoming common throughout the State, and unless something transpires to change the feelings of the blacks, localities in which there are large negro populations, will be visited with the horror of a 'conflict of races.'" Up to a hundred freedmen gathered at Eagle Lake to prod local authorities into investigating the disappearance of two blacks. Their "riotous demonstrations" threw the "whole town . . . in[to] a state of extreme excitement." The missing men's bodies were found soon afterwards. In late 1871, a black state policeman pumped three bullets into a white suspect. Whites and blacks in the community armed themselves, and a black civilian wound up dead. A particularly interesting episode with political overtones occurred in Houston in June 1868, when a black named George Noble angered the city's freed community by voting the Conservative ticket in an election. Noble had recently been acquitted of murdering a black man, but on June 13 he shot another at a Negro dance. Once again, he was taken into custody but not to jail. A black lynch mob gathered, fighting broke out, and two blacks suffered wounds. Clanging church bells and couriers soon brought in blacks from all over the city and outlying areas. By late that night, five to six hundred blacks and nearly that many whites roamed the streets of Houston with guns in hand. Authorities averted more violence when they finally lodged Noble in jail.[13]

The Radical Davis administration helped blacks explore previously uncharted territory when it organized the State Police and the State Militia. A burgeoning crime rate, especially of violent crimes—over a thousand homicides were reported in Texas between 1865 and 1868, while only five killers were convicted—inspired the Radicals to set up an integrated State Police force in 1870. During its three-year existence, officers made seven thousand arrests and began to make a dent in the criminal population of the state. Its racial makeup—about 60 percent of its 160 to 200 officers were black—rendered it politically vulnerable. Unaccustomed to blacks wielding any sort of authority over them, and calling it "The Standing Army of the Texas Autocrat," Conservatives associated the State Police with "nigger rule" and blamed it for several controversial incidents during the Davis era. Blacks also served in large numbers in the Texas Militia, another short-lived and unpopular Radical effort to enforce the law, and black militiamen joined Davis in his last-ditch effort to hold the state capitol in early 1874.[14]

Nowhere was the "war of races"—not to mention white astonishment and revulsion at the efforts of blacks to enter Texas society as equals—more apparent than in Reconstruction politics. Many whites had difficulty adjusting to blacks casting votes, and few found it within themselves to accept magnanimously the fact that former slaves now had the right to join political parties, make public speeches, and run for office. On July 4, 1868, attendance at Marshall's Independence Day celebration "was confined . . . entirely to the sons and daughters of Ham." Four years before, such a congregation of blacks in one place would have been illegal. Now, however, "the negroes flaunted their blue ribbons, and shouted to their hearts' content." Late in 1868, a "Radical" torchlight procession wound its way through Austin to the state capitol. Americans participated in boisterous political demonstrations all over the nineteenth-century United States, but these Americans were almost entirely black (supposedly, only one white man, a German "who looked frightfully out of place and must have been lost," took part). The *Hempstead Countryman* called it "a disgrace to the city of Austin." Whites found public demonstrations by blacks bad enough, but even less palatable were the now frequent political speeches by blacks. In 1867, not long after black Americans obtained the right to vote, a freedman in Crockett "mounted a goods box" and delivered an hour-long speech in which he declared himself a candidate for governor.

During the dark—for Conservatives—days of the Davis administration, a black man from Galveston threw his hat into the race for Congress at a Radical caucus. Ferdinand Flake reported that the candidate "was severe on the white folks—told the negroes that they ought to vote for none but their own color for office."[15]

Many blacks followed that advice; by early 1868, fifty thousand freedmen had registered to vote, and in February over 80 percent turned out to cast their ballots almost unanimously in favor of what everyone predicted would be a Radical-dominated constitutional convention. Nine black men, out of a total of ninety delegates, attended that convention, and fourteen blacks—two senators and twelve representatives—won election to the Twelfth Legislature in 1870.[16]

These black legislators came from a number of different backgrounds. They included the well-educated, New England-born Sen. George Ruby, a former journalist and Freedmen's Bureau teacher who had begun serving in local and appointed offices for Texas Republicans in 1867. Also among them was Richard Allen, a former slave who during and after emancipation earned a reputation in Houston as a reliable carpenter and bridge builder; he also had served as a Freedmen's Bureau agent. Matt Gaines—the other black state senator—was a diminutive former slave from Louisiana who preached the religious and political gospel to the freedmen of Washington County. These legislators formed a nucleus of black leadership in Texas. Several had participated in the 1868 Constitutional Convention, while others had been voter registrars or filled other local Republican offices. Three of them were illiterate. Five new faces appeared in the next legislature—the Thirteenth—including the colorful S. Meshack Roberts. Roberts had been a loyal Upshur County slave who had protected his owner's home during the war; his master rewarded him with a plot of land. He survived an 1867 whipping by the Ku Klux Klan to serve in the Texas legislature for six years. These black leaders formed a solid alliance with Radicals in Texas.[17]

For Democrats, the most upsetting aspect of this alliance was the obvious absence in blacks of loyalty toward their former masters. Virtually all blacks voted for white Republican candidates—men who sought to overturn, in the eyes of old Confederates, the only viable system of race relations. The latter complained that the Freedmen's Bureau, Loyal Union Leagues, and the state Republican party manipulated the politically naive freedmen during elections, and in many cases they were correct. A circular letter issued during the gubernatorial campaign of 1869 by Ruby, the Grand President of the State Council, Union League of America, made it clear that the league expected the freedmen to pledge their allegiance to the Republicans and cast their votes for the Radical candidate, E.J. Davis.

The "vows" of league members, he declared, "imposed upon them . . . grave duties." The success of the Republican party, "the loyal reconstruction of the State, and the restoration of peace, prosperity, and happiness to our people" depended on "the vigor and efficiency of our organization." Ruby directed members to subscribe to "sound Republican journals" and to stay in close touch with their Republican leaders, so that the "efforts of cajolery, bribery, and intimidation by the rebel enemy are rendered abortive." An Austin woman reported that blacks there were "ambitious to show by their good behavior that they deserve to be free." Many accomplished this by voting for the party that had freed them; to prevent those who could not read "from being imposed upon, their ballots have a likeness of Abram [sic] Lincoln on them." Blacks in Marshall reported to the local Loyal Union League headquarters to receive their instructions before going to the courthouse to vote. Alex Jackson remembered "companies" of Loyal Leaguers led to the polls by their precinct "captains," their double-file columns stretching for two blocks. The bureau agent stationed in Sterling reported that "if the freedmen have a fair opportunity to vote with sufficient protection, they will vote as the Bureau Agent instructs them. They believe in him—know what he is sent among them for—and will obey him in every respect." M.H. Goddin, posted in Polk County, "the worst hole in the country," found a "feeling of disperation [sic] . . . against me and the freedmen, because it is clear to see that all the freedmen will vote just as I tell them."[18]

Conservative whites feared such steadfast loyalty to the Republicans. As late as 1873, the *Dallas Herald* predicted that the "sable supporters" of Governor Davis in the Loyal Union Leagues "will be organized and the old flag be made to do impious duty in fluttering over the kinky heads of the leaguers as they march" to the polls, "shouting the name and praises of the man who deserted Texas in her darkest hours." The *Texas Republican* announced in June 1867, that "fanaticism is rampant." Recently a black registrar in Harrison County declared "himself a radical, and informed his sable brethren that they should and *must* regard the Southern white man as their enemy, and that they must prepare themselves to vote the radical ticket, or they would be severely punished." The freedman also warned that "every white man who advised a negro to vote a conservative ticket would be subjected to some dreadful torture." To whites, blacks who subscribed to such views had "forsaken the people amongst whom they have been raised." Every step freedmen took or attempted to take away from their former bondage seemed to take them farther from their subordinate position and the obligations it entailed. Their expressions of freedom appeared as a kind of treason to whites who, while doubting that blacks possessed the intelligence or initiative to pose a threat on their own, nevertheless feared that they would join the assault on southern society and institutions by northern Radicals and southern scalawags. That whites considered many black actions during Reconstruction as a breach of their communal responsibilities and as examples of failed loyalty goes far in explaining their reactions to the freedmen.[19]

The new order of things alarmed many Anglo-Texans, who constantly commented on the behavior and attitudes of the freedmen. The "spectacle" of blacks voting drew much comment from whites, who seemed drawn and repulsed in equal measures to the novel phenomenon. Lucadia Pease, not surprisingly, was fairly sympathetic to the blacks living in Travis County. She wrote her sister early in 1868 that freedmen voting on whether or not to hold another constitutional convention "have been as quiet and orderly in their demeanor as if this was not the first time their manhood had been acknowledged by the whites." Two hundred mounted Webberville blacks had entered town with "the stars and stripes at the head of the column, and singing 'rally round the flag!' " Mrs. Pease reported that the "rebels" were "like madmen in their indignation that the negroes should vote." A year-and-a-half later, the editor of the *State Gazette* observed blacks voting in another election, and predictably described a far different scene. "There was pulling and hauling, and tearing up and changing of tickets," he wrote for other disfranchised "rebels" who would not have the privilege to vote, "and shouting for Hamilton and Davis and voting they knew not how and evidently did not care." The blacks "were having a glorious time with electioneering and whiskey and loud talk and voting some how or other."[20]

Whites were also dismayed when blacks began serving on juries and reacted with surprise and condescension when they "deported themselves in a creditable manner." Many whites involved in legal proceedings, however, waived their right to a jury trial and presented their cases directly to judges. The *Bastrop Advertiser* announced that the "Judge or Justice of the Peace, that would sit on the bench with a negro jury is no better than a nigger himself," while the *Crockett Sentinel* said that it was "the duty of all patriotic judges" to resign rather than supervise courts in which "the jury boxes must be filled by negroes" and in which white citizens no longer "have any security for life, liberty, or property."[21]

Whites expected no good from their former human property at the polls or in court, and newspapers and individuals seemed to delight in reporting the immoral, criminal, or foolish behavior of freedmen. The *Marshall Texas Republican*, one of the state's best newspapers, copied articles and editorials from all over Texas that proved to conservative whites, at least, that freedom had ruined the morals of most freedmen. In Waco, a black nearly destroyed a local hotel when he tried to set fire to his wife after a quarrel, while the *Millican News Letter* reported late in August 1867 that "Saturday night seems to have been eventful with the freed folks," as a "general row" had broken up a freedmen's dance. The *Trinity Advocate* found evidence of black criminality and Radical corruption in an episode in which a freedman knifed a one-legged Confederate veteran and wounded one of the men sent to arrest him. When he turned himself in the next day, he "was turned loose upon the community without any trial or without giving bond for his appearance hereafter!" A black woman living in Rusk County allegedly murdered her infant and buried it in a garden. She then escaped to Tyler, taking refuge, according to the *Rusk Observor*, in "a low bawdy house." A local "agent of the negro bureau . . . prevented her arrest." Early in the first autumn after emancipation, the *Texas Republican* printed a report that two thousand negro prostitutes plied their trade in Richmond, Virginia, and complained that every Southern city had suddenly become a "den . . . of negro prostitution." Occasionally, even worse violations of community morality developed between blacks and whites. The editor of the *Sherman Courier* was "humiliated and disgusted" when he saw a "nigger school marm" from Bonham "beastly drunk" on a Sherman sidewalk. "The last we saw of her," the newspaperman shuddered, "she was being escorted to some nigger cabins near town, between two colored gentlemen," one of whose arm was "encircling her waiste [*sic*] in a familiar and affectionate manner. To what lower depths of degradation can human nature fall."22

Whether or not freedom led to a decline in the morals of blacks in Texas is, of course, highly debatable—but it is also irrelevant. Conservative Texans certainly thought so, or at least they wanted to think so, and this belief contributed to their attitudes toward blacks and toward the defunct institution of slavery, as well as to their political campaigns during Reconstruction. Blacks who went too far in exerting their freedom would soon learn the cost of deserting their former masters and ignoring the kindnesses with which they had been treated. They must learn where to place their loyalties, determine whom they could trust, and discover their proper place in a free society. At the same time, white Texans must realize that support of the Republican party and their radical racial programs would encourage the freedmen in their decadence and their apostasy. Only by opposing such disturbing tendencies—and by rejecting the Republican party—could whites demonstrate their loyalty to the South.

For whites, the rights, considerations, and freedom expected by the freedmen went far beyond the bounds of possibility or decency. Their world had at least temporarily turned upside-down, and they did their utmost to right it—in politics and in their "social relations" with blacks. Whites had generally feared the worst as it became clear that slavery would be extinguished with the Confederacy. Soon after the war lurched to its end, the *Marshall Texas Republican* asked editorially, "What is to Become of the Negro?" The paper urged masters to retain influence over their slaves, and predicted that a system of compulsory labor would eventually be instituted, "which will make the negro useful to society and subordinate to the white man." When Texans envisioned the future, they—like most white southerners—did not see a new world of racial equality, but a world that resembled the one in which they had lived before the war. The *Houston Telegraph* assured its readers that the social system of the South would not be radically altered, but cautioned that for a time, "occurrences will continually take place that will shock all our sensibilities. . . . We shall be disgusted with a thousand things heretofore unheard of." Nevertheless, the watchword of the times must be "that what cannot be cured must be endured."[23]

Anglos endured some of the freedman's "shocking" and "disgusting" actions, but generally responded aggressively to protect their interests and their vision of society. The *State Gazette* revealed the incredulousness shared by many whites at the turn of events in the three short years since the war, when a headline announced "The Reign of Niggerdom" in June 1868. "We have now in Texas negro voters and negro officials. Negro juries sit upon the rights of white men, and settle vexed questions of law and land titles. Negroes go to political meetings and crowd around respectable white ladies, elbowing their way every where. Negro balls are held in the capitol, and Negro schools are examined there. Negro processions parade our streets, by day and by night, with bands of music and flags. Negroes are in the hall of the House of Representatives, to make a constitution for the white people. They threaten the white members with their 40,000 voters. They boldly say that they are to rule the country." Surely, the *Gazette* mourned, "the reign of niggerdom has commenced."[24]

White Texans exhibited two contradicatory reactions to the postwar racial situation. Many abused the freedmen and ridiculed their attempts at building new lives. Some whites wanted to exterminate the blacks living in their midst—literally, or, more often, figuratively—by making them into nonpersons, with few legal, civil, or economic rights. Accompanying this gut-level, highly individual reaction, however, was a more calculating, politicized version of the same reluctance to give up their former relationship with the black race. Whites believed that the new loyalties of freedmen had to be reversed and the old loyalties recreated; they must be made to see their former masters as their true allies. After blacks became a potent political force in the late 1860s, some whites sought to win them over to the Democratic party—or at least to neutralize their support for the

Republicans—by recalling images of slavery's paternal past. These dual reactions were actually opposite sides of the same racial coin. At times repulsed by the freedom-spawned actions of their former slaves and loath to have anything to do with blacks on an equal basis, whites nevertheless sought to use friendship and political manipulation in enlisting the unwitting aid of blacks in rebuilding in a more subtle form their pre-emancipation racial relationship.

Violence and abuse characterized the initial reactions of many whites to the end of that relationship; ironically, such behavior indicated an end to the oft-claimed loyalty of paternalistic masters to their slaves. Blacks often told of masters and mistresses giving the new class of free men and women short shrift or washing their hands of them entirely. Andy McAdams's master "was far from forcing us to stay on as servants after the war." When word came that the peculiar institution no longer existed, his master simply told him he would have to leave. It was as though "they opened the gate and set the dog after us—just like you would a bunch of wild cattle that you were going to turn loose in a large pasture to graze or rustle for their living." Eli Davison recalled that his master vowed "if he got up next morning and found a negro on his place that he would horse whip him." Minerva Bendy summed up the experience of many black Texans when she said, "After us free dey turn us loose in de woods and dat de bad time, 'cause most us didn't know where to turn. I wasn't raise to do nothin' and I didn't know how. Dey didn't even give us a hoecake or a slice of bacon."25

The ill treatment continued, of course, throughout the 1860s and 1870s—and far beyond, for that matter. Freedmen's Bureau agents frequently commented on the lack of sympathy for blacks among the whites in their districts. Capt. James Emerson wrote from Waco that "some of the citizens . . . have a good Feeling towards the Freedmen, while others, if it was not for the Bureau, would cheat, abuse and maltreat every man, woman or child on their plantation." Whites around Sherman, according to Capt. Albert Evans, were "generally . . . adverse to the interest of the freedmen in every particular. . . . The nigger shall not accumulate property, they must be kept poor, no schools shall be established in this part of the state for the niggers." Threats and pressure against white friends of the Negro prevented Evans from leasing a house to be used as a school, and local courts put orphans "of the colored persuasion" under indentures until they were twenty-one, after first fixing their ages in order to add four or five years to their "apprenticeship." Only those who could do a full day's work were snatched up under the state apprentice law; "small orphan children are not disturbed particularly those who need caring for." Ira Evans protested in his June 1867 report that the white people of Wharton County, "with but very few exceptions, will cheat, and swindle the freed-

people whenever they think they can do so with safety to themselves."
James Devine expressed his outrage at the "violence and swindling"
perpetrated by "planters and others" against freedmen in Anderson,
Trinity, and Angelina counties in Southeast Texas. Even "the most *reliable, high-toned gentlemen*" overcharged freedmen with whom they had
labor contracts for equipment, liquor, and other supplies.[26]

Far more brutal treatment marked the experience of freedmen in
some parts of the state. One former slave from East Texas told of how the
slaves in Harrison County were freed immediately, but those in Rusk
County were not. When slaves from Rusk tried to escape into Harrison,
"they owners have 'em bushwhacked. . . . You could see lots of niggers
hangin' to trees in Sabine bottom right after freedom, 'cause they cotch
'em swimmin' 'cross Sabine River and shoot 'em." Annie Row, who lived in
Rusk County, saw her master's family disintegrate during and just after the
war. One son, John, was killed in the army, while another, Billy, came
home from the war and slit his own throat. "A piece of paper say he not care
for to live, 'cause de nigger free and dey's all broke up." The master "starts
cussin' de War and him picks up de hot poker and say 'Free de nigger, will
dey? I free dem.' " He hit Annie's mother in the neck with the poker, then
"takes de gun offen de rack and starts for de field whar de niggers am a
workin'." Fortunately for the slaves, he collapsed before he reached the
field and died the next day. Travis County whites were also "unfriendly"
toward freedmen, and "the hope is freely expressed, that white labor may
be procured from Europe, and the colored race become annihilated or
driven out of the Country." A group of Freestone County planters resolved
late in 1865 not to hire freedmen and to whip any black who tried to
negotiate a contract with a white man. A white who violated the agreement
would be warned the first time, but whipped or hanged if he did it again.[27]

The most horrific tales of white mistreatment of blacks were the
rumors, never substantiated, that scores of freedmen died after being
poisoned by vengeful whites—a macabre irony, in that tales of antebellum
insurrection plots often included mass poisonings of white people. Ella
Washington, who had fled with her master to Texas from Louisiana during
the war, told an interviewer many years afterward that shortly after
freedom, and after the master had agreed to let the freedmen stay for a few
days to decide what to do, "somethin' funny happen dere. De slaves all
drinks out an old well. Dey'd drink water in de mornin' and dey'd have de
cramps awful bad 'bout dinner time and in de evenin' dey's dead." People
were dying so fast "dey couldn't make de coffins for dem." Some slaves
suspected their old master of poisoning them. "I don't know what kill
dem," Ella said, "but it sho' look funny." A group of slaves arrived in
Millican in the days after the war, and a storekeeper set out a barrel of

apples for them to eat. "De apples had been poisoned," according to a story told by Annie Day, "and dey killed a lot of de colored people." Teen-aged Lucy Thomas moved to the Widow Haggerty's place in Harrison County three years after the war ended. The old woman had once owned three hundred slaves and had a reputation as a harsh mistress. "When she knew the slaves was gittin' free," Lucy heard from slaves who had lived there for years, "she poisoned a lot of dem and buied dem at night. We'd hear the other slaves moanin' and cryin' at night for the dead ones." Finally, when over two thousand freedmen gathered in Marshall, Texas, in honor of Independence Day in 1867, a rumor flashed through the crowd that the well from which they were all drinking had been poisoned. Only the appearance of Mayor James Turner, who drank from the well himself, dispelled their fears.[28]

The most visible indication of the whites' hatred for blacks was, of course, the Ku Klux Klan. Begun as a fraternal society in Tennessee during the first two or three years of Reconstruction, the Klan became the unofficial enforcer of white standards of behavior on blacks. Their repertoire ranged from pranks designed to frighten gullible blacks to bloody methods of physical intimidation. As the federal military presence dwindled, groups such as the Klan, the Knights of the Rising Sun, the Knights of the White Camellia, or the Teutonic Band of Brothers sprang up in towns all over Texas, but especially in the eastern third of the state; "Ku Kluxers" became a generic name for any band of rowdies or outlaws that caused trouble for Unionists or blacks. They targeted Loyal Leaguers, black criminal suspects, Union men, employers of "uppity" blacks, federal agents and soldiers, and educators of freedmen. Fifteen hundred Marion County residents indicated their support for the Knights of the Rising Sun at a ceremony and parade celebrating the founding of a local chapter.[29]

Klansmen played sophomoric tricks on terrified freedmen and perpetrated random violence against individuals and groups of freedmen during their night rides. According to Louis Young, "it so bad de cullud folks 'fraid to sleep in dey house or have parties or nothin' after dark. Dey starts for de woods or ditches and sleeps dere. It git so dey can't work for not sleepin', from fear of dem Klux." A woman who grew up under the shadow of the Klan and other forms of white intimidation recollected, "in dem days when chillun wouldn't mind all dat I had to say was, 'All right de Ku Klux will git yo!' " and "Dey'd come right into de yard and mind."[30]

Freedmen had few options in the face of such violence and mistreatment, nor could they do much to rid themselves of poverty. Neither the racist and thinly posted United States army nor the understaffed Freedmen's Bureau could offer much protection or support. The latter agency, although it distributed rations and clothing to a few hundred black Texans

between 1865 and 1868, did not accept responsibility for indigent freedmen; counties, townships, and cities also refused to fill the support
vacuum created by emancipation. The number of federal troops stationed
in Texas dropped from over 45,000 in September 1865, to just 5000 two
years later; these were dispersed into thirty-seven posts located primarily
on the western frontier. The Freedmen's Bureau found its limited resources totally inadequate to police the state's vast interior. There,
according to the bureau's inspector general, freedmen were "beaten un-
mercifully and shot down like wild beasts, without any provocation, and
followed by hounds and maltreated in every possible way."[31]

Although intimidation of blacks continued throughout and beyond the
period of Reconstruction, many whites believed that the best way of
making sure that freedmen would not cause trouble was to make them
understand that their interests matched the interests of their former
masters. They nodded editorially when a slave here and there expressed
his or her dissatisfaction with freedom. When the Marshall Freedmen's
Bureau agent assigned a local freedwoman to work in the streets, she
purportedly said, "dis freedom, was a good deal like Confederate money;
de more you have ob it, de worse you is off." "Pretty good for Dinah,"
smiled the *Texas Republican*. The *Southern Intelligencer*, a Republican
paper based in Austin, accurately judged the "Game" of at least some
Conservatives early in 1867. Planters hoped "to secure the freedman's vote
in their interest. They appear to flatter themselves with the idea that after
four years of bloody civil war to perpetuate the enslavement of black men,
their wives and children, they can yet convince the now enfranchised
blacks that Southern secessionists are now and ever have been their best
and truest friends." The *Intelligencer* doubted that the freedmen were as
ignorant as the Conservatives apparently believed they were, and confidently predicted that the blacks "will not be caught in this trap set by their
old enemies."[32]

Nevertheless, some of those old enemies tried to outflank Texas
Republicans by turning blacks against the party of Lincoln. One way, of
course, was to scare blacks away from the Republicans. Andy McAdams
voted only once during his lifetime, when "that Federal Governor Edwin
[*sic*] J. Davis" sent soldiers to Huntsville to protect the new black voters.
McAdams claimed that "I did not know who I was voting for or even what
they was holding that election for." Afterward, the "padderrollers" got after
the freedmen who voted for Republican candidates. "I went right to the
Trinity river bottom," Andy recalled, "and stayed there until they quit
whipping negroes." Making examples out of black voters would, Conservatives hoped, create the sort of attitude evinced by young Will Adams's
father. The elder Adams told one Yankee carpetbagger, "Listen, white

folks, you is gwine start a graveyard if you come round here teachin'
niggers to sass white folks." Much later Will himself claimed that "them
carpet-baggers starts all the trouble at 'lections in Reconstruction. Niggers
didn't know anythin' 'bout politics."33

Conservatives frequently tried to turn blacks away from the Republicans with parables describing the downward slide in the lives of freedmen.
One story, which the *Dallas Herald* predicted would "disgust an honest
Southern family with Radical hypocrisy," took place in a Texas town during
the years immediately following the war. Esther had been a happy "confid-
ential servant" and nurse for one of the little community's best families.
When northern troops and carpetbaggers occupied the place, black soldiers and "a genuine Yankee family" convinced Esther to leave her old
home and work for the northerners. Soon she married a black man from
the North. Unhappily, "his brutish instincts" led to a beating that incapaci-
tated her, after which her husband and new employers cast her into the
street. Her former mistress took her home, however, "and tenderly nursed
her till death closed her sufferings." Although neither her husband nor her
"Pharisaical Yankee family" appeared at the funeral, "a whole village of
Southern white people joined in procession to inter the remains of this
faithful old servant." Esther's tragic fate was "but one of thousands of cases
in the South since the war."34

Even before freedmen cast a single vote in Texas, the *Texas Republican*
declared that similar tragedies did not have to occur. The editor assured his
white readers that "the better informed negroes in the South know well
enough that their former masters and present employers are the best
friends they have." They would, "in the first election that transpires," show
the "radical office-seekers, and would-be destroyers of peace between the
races" that "they are not so soft-headed as to throw off old, well-known, and
long-tried friends for flimsy, new, coming pretenders, and transient inter-
lopers." Southern whites and blacks "understand each other's advantages
and wants." "It will require a long line of Radical instructors to satisfy the
negro that he is a white man, or that he can prosper without his control and
guidance."35

Although some former masters supported the conservatives' efforts to
win friends and influence freedmen through kindness, they often seemed
to pursue that course out of the same desire to cling to the characteristics of
slavery that inspired the abuse of freedmen. Whites sought to retain their
authority over and to promote the dependence of their former slaves.
Some doubted that blacks could care for themselves and many seemed
unwilling to forfeit the emotional and psychological rewards of the master-
slave relationship. A few offered the use of teams, tools, and land to their
former slaves; others actually distributed property to freedmen or insisted

on caring for freedmen's children until the former were able to support their families. One former slaveowner in Waco offered to raise the children whose mothers he had sold. Whites occasionally mixed their concern for freedmen with a certain amount of contempt for their ability to provide for themselves. John Price's father moved away from his master's plantation after the war ended, but "when my li'l sister have de whoopin' cough, old massa come down in a hurry and say, 'You gwineter kill dem chillen,' and he puts my sister and brother on de hoss in front of him and takes 'em home and cures 'em hisself." Similarly, Freedmen's Bureau subassistant commissioner A.H. Mayer reported from Liberty that "the people throughout this section accept the condition of affairs as they are, and treat the freedmen with kindness." Mayer had heard of many occasions when former slaveowners "have seen the freedpeople fooling off their money" and gone "forward & advise them to save their money, that in a year or two they could purchase homes for themselves & families."[36]

Masters frequently offered paternalistic and unsolicited advice to their former slaves. Mary Overton's master encouraged his slaves to stay on his plantation for a while, for white people were "pretty much worked up and might treat us pretty mean." Another owner predicted that there "might be trouble 'twixt de whites and niggers" and advised his blacks "to stay and not git mixed in dis and dat org'ization." Nath Newman grimly told his slaves that "now de war is over and times is hard . . . and work is goin ter be hard ter get." He reminded them "you is all on your own and has got ter hustle fer yourself." They must not wait until they were hungry before they looked for employment, because as soon as they failed to get a job they would steal something, and "dat will get you in trouble jest as sho' as you is standing here in front of me." Then "you will has ter get yourself out of it er go ter jail, for remembers you don't belong ter me er anybody else any more." According to Betty Bormer, who was a child in 1865, Col. M.T. Johnson declared to his former slaves "you is now free and can go whar you pleases." Then he told them, in a demonstration of the paternal ideal that flourished among many slaveholders, that "he have learned us not to steal and to be good and we 'uns should 'member dat and if we 'uns gets in trouble to come to him and he will help us." Apparently he meant it, "'cause de niggers goes to him lots of times and he always helps."[37]

Such treatment would, many Texans believed, help them recapture their state and reconstruct their relationships with former slaves. In 1868, after reports that freedmen near Huntsville planned an arson campaign against whites, and in response to the political manipulations of the bureau agent for that area, local Democrats organized a huge barbecue for whites and blacks. Fifteen hundred freedmen showed up, white and black leaders spoke to the crowd, and good wishes were exchanged. Whites thanked blacks for their long service and faithfulness and assured them that their voting rights would not be threatened. According to one of the Democrats who attended, many blacks came over to the conservatives, and race relations improved considerably. Reports from Freedmen's Bureau sub-assistant commissioners revealed that planters in other parts of the state were also "acting in a manner to gain the confidence and good will of the free people . . . treating them in a manner best calculated to create a greater degree of harmony between the two classes." Whites near Livingston "desire to make political proselytes" of the blacks. "Much jealousy exists least [sic] the freedmen favor confiscation . . . by advice of the white unionists." Planters in other areas believed that "moral and intellectual darkness, is, and ever will be the only true status of the freedpeople . . . thinking that thus they can be the more easily controlled as laborers, and . . . perhaps, as voters." Others "poison[ed] the minds" of freedmen by threatening that if they failed to vote the planters' way, "they will all be discharged from work upon the plantations & will die of starvation." P. B. Johnson, an agent assigned to Tyler County, feared that the blacks' best character traits would cause them to go over to the planters' side. The freedman, he wrote, "in respect to *forgiveness* and *forbearance* . . . *is the best man in the world.*" In addition, "his anxiety to be favorably noticed," and his "religious disposition and fidelity . . . [to] morrall obligations" left him vulnerable to control by "his former enslaver."[38]

Conservatives naturally rejoiced whenever their strategy seemed to succeed. One hundred fifty Harrison County blacks attended a conservative meeting in December in 1868, while five years later a "Colored Convention" in Brenham refused to pass a resolution offered by Matt Gaines that endorsed the Davis administration. The *Democratic Statesman* reported that the resolution "was too much even for African blood to swallow." The gathering also gave Davis's ambassador-at-large, James Newcomb, a cold shoulder, which "shows the odor in which such men are held even by the negroes." Although significant numbers of blacks did not turn away from the party that had, in their minds, released them from bondage, some did respond to the Conservatives' carrot-and-stick tactics and rejected the Republicans. Their voter turnout plummeted 16 percent to two-thirds of all registered freedmen in the 1869 gubernatorial election. "Crazy" Jim Black of Nacogdoches gave "a decidedly practicable speech" in June 1867, when he told a Negro meeting that they were foolish and that it was God's will that they earn a living by manual labor. The *Texas Republican* commented approvingly, "If that negro was crazy, insanity should be at a premium." William M. Thomas came to Galveston in 1874 and began working as a stevedore. Soon after his arrival, his boss gave him election day off, handed him a marked ballot, and ordered him to go to the polling place. "When us comes dere, 'twas a table with meat and bread and stuff for to eat, and whiskey and cigars. Dey give us something to eat and a cup or two of dat whiskey and puts de cigar in de mouth. Us am 'portant niggers, ready to vote. With dat cup of whiskey in de stomack and dat cigar in de mouth and de hat cock on side de head, us march to de votin' place and does our duty. Fix up de way us was, us would vote to put us back in slavery."39

One agent correctly believed that the Conservatives' efforts to persuade or to bribe black voters would have little effect on the majority of ex-slaves. "The very fact that the Planters want them to vote one way," he wrote, "they say is a sufficient reason why they should not vote that way." Freedmen proved as much at the polls in 1873, when the Democrats "redeemed" Texas with very little help from black voters, despite their efforts. Nevertheless, the *Dallas Herald* celebrated with the sort of rhetoric that had been used to convince blacks of where their true loyalties lay. "The day has come," proclaimed the *Herald*, "when the Democrats are about to control the destinies of Texas, and now the colored people will, for the first time, have an opportunity of seeing how they have been deceived and misled by the Radicals." Now that the Democrats were in power, "the colored people will enjoy, in peace and security, all their rights under the Federal and State Constitution and laws." They will finally be able to "vote as they please, without the dread of anathemas or assassination by loyal leagues." The Democrats of Texas assured the freedmen that they "are not the enemies of colored men, but, on the contrary, wish them well and desire their welfare in the State." What Radical could have said it better?40

Some observers and at least a few freedmen believed that emancipation had brought little actual freedom to Texas blacks. Lt. J.A. Archer reported early in 1867 that without government protection "the Freedpeople . . . would be in a worse condition, than when Slaves, as they were then protected by their owners to some degree." Now, however, "no one takes any interest in them, except to get all they possibly can out of them." Mary Gaffney bitterly declared that "we was not given a thing but freedom. . . . Instead of being free, slavery had just begun among the negroes . . . we was a people turned loose like a bunch of stray dogs." Another freedwoman indicated one source of the blacks' helplessness during and after Reconstruction. If a white man "wanted to kill a negro he did not lose anything cause the negro was free and he could get another one without costing anything." There was a replacement "always waiting for him to say the word."41

The number of blacks in the state legislature dwindled throughout the 1870s and 1880s, and during that time freedmen and their children remained chained to menial and agricultural jobs, enjoyed few educational opportunities above a bare literacy, and rarely served on juries or participated in other civil or political freedoms. Black Texans had made one huge leap in attaining their freedom, but further gains would have to wait for another era, as Dave Byrd, a former slave, knew only too well. "You talk about slavery," he said long after he had become a free man, "it never begin until after we was supposed to be free. We had to work farms on the halves, very little to eat, and no clothes 'cept what we begged. Then after we got a crop made it would take every bit of it to pay our debts. We had no money to have Doctor's [sic] when we got sick, and from the day we turned loose we had to shoulder the whole load. Taxes to pay, groceries to buy and what did we get? Nothing."42

In many ways, blacks replaced white Unionists as the primary group of outsiders in Texas. Few freedmen resisted becoming, for lack of a better word, dissenters during Reconstruction. Their political lives and economic survival necessitated it, and their race automatically put them at odds with most white policy makers and even many white Republicans. By trying to join the mainstream society, they dissented against the plans that whites held for that society. Whites believed that freedmen had forgotten where their true interests and loyalty lay and transferred to blacks the intimidation and political pressure that they had formerly directed against white dissenters. Combined with violence inspired solely by racial antipathy, this vigilance proved effective in redeeming the South for white men. Those few whites who had sustained their dissent against the justice of slavery, the methods with which the South tried to preserve it, secession, or the mistreatment of freedmen finally found themselves unable or unwilling to continue the fight. By 1874, much of their dissent had evaporated with the support of the federal government and of the Republican party, as politically pragmatic dissenters found it uncomfortable and often personally distasteful to associate themselves with the problems of the freedmen. As a result, without white support, and burdened by their own political inexperience and limited economic resources, blacks found their struggle as unrewarding and, at least for the time being, as hopeless, as the struggle carried on by the dwindling numbers of white dissenters throughout the Civil War period. In the end, ironically, blacks—or the debates about the future of blacks—had helped to close the doors on dissent in Texas.

Epilogue:
Nothing to Regret
but Failure

When Edward King, a writer for *Scribner's Monthly*, toured Texas in 1874 researching his magazine's "The Great South" series, he found that Texas had undergone many changes since the years just before the Civil War. A San Antonian told the journalist that "it was like living in an asylum where every one was crazy on one especial subject; you never knew when dangerous paroxysms were about to begin." Twelve years before, wrote King, "it was dangerous for a man to be seen reading the *New York Tribune*, and . . . perilous for him to be civil to a slave." Now, however, those times had "passed away, and the Texans themselves are glad that they have awakened from their dreams of patriarchal aristocracy, which place such a check upon the development of the State."[1]

In many ways, Texans had awakened from a bad dream, and some of the leading dissenters during the war and Reconstruction were able to leave the violence and controversy behind them and live much as they had before the war interrupted their lives. E.M. Pease retired in peace to his Austin home, Wood Lawn, where he had lived during his voluntary exile from public life during the war. Thomas DuVal, after surviving an impeachment attempt by Radical Republicans, served on the federal bench for many years until his death in 1880, while John Haynes enjoyed a sinecure as collector of customs at Brownsville for over a decade; he ended his "retirement" from politics in 1884 for a quixotic campaign as the Republican candidate for lieutenant governor. James W. Throckmorton and John Hancock represented Texas in the United States Congress during the 1870s and 1880s. George Brackenridge overcame his unsavory reputation as a war profiteer and Unionist and rose to prominence as a merchant, banker, and philanthropic regent of the University of Texas. Thaddeus McRae, the Unionist refugee and chaplain to black soldiers, returned to Texas in early 1866 to minister to Austin Presbyterians. Even A.J. Hamilton benefited posthumously from the remarkably selective memories of the participants in the sectional crisis in Texas. When he died of tuberculosis at the age of 60 in 1875, Radicals and Conservatives alike packed the capitol for his funeral, which was held beneath the United States flag and attended by an honor guard of blue-clad former Yankees and Rebels. [2]

Although hill country Germans had suffered their share of persecution during the war, the general population's disdain for them faded as the century drew to a close. Germans nevertheless retained their reputation for Unionism; in 1866, the residents of Comfort erected over the graves of the victims of the Nueces Massacre a stone monument poignantly inscribed *"Treuer der Union*—True to the Union." Politically, they split their allegiance nearly equally between the Republican and Democratic parties and pursued a political course different from other Texans until well into the twentieth century. Despite the experiences of Texas Germans during the war, immigration from the old country also continued unabated, as more Germans entered Texas after the Civil War than before. By 1900, there were over 48,000 German-born Texans, compared with just under 20,000 in 1860. [3]

Others were not able to settle comfortably into post-Reconstruction Texas. E.J. Davis struggled for a decade trying to practice law in Austin and in Corpus Christi. He nearly missed the 1880 Republican National Convention because he could not afford the $100 train fare. Rev. Charles Gillette rejected a call from his old praish of St. David's in Austin, moving instead to Brooklyn, New York, where he died in 1868. One of his New York neighbors, S.M. Swenson, had also left Texas for the North. Taking leave of Thomas DuVal in 1865—"a friend who has stuck closer than a Brother"—the Swede sailed out of New Orleans with the fortune he had earned in the cotton trade. In New York, he opened a bank and promoted Swedish immigration to Texas. [4]

Some of the war- and Reconstruction-spawned violence between and against Anglos, tejanos, and blacks spilled into the postwar years. The Early-Hasley feud in Bell County grew out of wartime atrocities committed against Unionists and deserters by a local home guard unit. Conflicts between former Confederates, the freedmen's Loyal Union League, and Yankee officials sparked the Lee-Peacock and Sutton-Taylor feuds. The former lasted into the 1870s, and the latter simmered for three decades. Although a few Mexican-Texans continued to serve in local and county governments, they often suffered from racial violence. Lynchings in retaliation for real or imagined crimes, random assaults, and economically motivated terrorism combined to make tejanos in West and South Texas especially vulnerable. Finally, violence also marred the lives of Texas blacks for decades after the close of the sectional conflict. Twenty-five

Houston blacks were slaughtered during church services in 1875, and a horrified Houston newspaper reported that the victims were drawn and quartered. Vigilante "justice" continued for decades after the war; whites lynched perhaps five hundred blacks between 1870 and 1900. Other victims included petty criminals who found themselves behind the bars of the overcrowded and disease-ridden state prison, where blacks constituted 50 percent of the inmates, although they made up only 25 percent of the state's population.[5]

Not surprisingly, blacks suffered a startling decline in power and expectations following the end of Radical Reconstruction. Texas freedmen lost one of their most influential spokesmen when George T. Ruby left for New Orleans in 1874. Before he died of malaria at the age of forty-one, eight years later, he edited newspapers and worked in the New Orleans customs office. Ruby's colleague in the state senate, Matt Gaines, spent the last twenty-four years of his life as an impoverished preacher and farmer. When he died in 1900, he was buried in an unmarked grave in a black cemetery near Giddings, leaving behind only a faded photograph of himself, a pair of cuff links, and a gold tie tack engraved with his initials and the dates of his term in the senate. By the 1880s, the usual number of blacks in the legislature had dwindled to around three or four, and after the Twenty-fourth Legislature in 1895, no blacks served in state government until the 1960s. In their attempts to mount an effective opposition to the Democrats, black voters unsuccessfully experimented with Greenbackers and Populists. By the 1890s, "Lily Whites"—led, ironically, by the former secretary of the Loyal Union League, James P. Newcomb—had practically driven blacks out of the Republican party. That mattered little by the early years of the twentieth century, however, as intimidation, poll taxes, and white primaries blocked blacks' access to the ballot box.[6]

The rapidity with which the concepts of the Lost Cause and the New South swept the old Confederacy in the decades following the war partly explains the attitude of southern whites toward the increasingly alienated and disfranchised blacks. The subconscious goal of the literary creators of the Lost Cause was to reinstill traditional southern values—as well as to confirm the idea of white supremacy—and if they were to succeed, their formula had to apply to all southerners, even those to whom the cause had been anathema. Fortunately for southern conservatives, virtually none of the Unionists of 1861 or the Republicans of 1868 was willing to go along with the government centralization, Negro equality, and federal interference entailed in the program created by the northern Radicals. Unenthusiastic about the Yankee vision of the future, and often ignored by northern Republicans, the Lost Cause became the cause of many former dissenters, too. In fact, southern literature went through a brief period during the decade and a half after the war where the traditional Lost Cause celebration of Confederate gallantry and chivalry was mixed with stories, letters, and reminiscences that attacked trouble-making secessionists, deserters, draft evaders, speculators, undisciplined soldiers, poor officers, glory seekers, and various other species of disloyalists and unsavory southerners. By 1890, however, this brand of Civil War literature had died out; according to one historian, "the next generation would hardly know they existed." If, as another historian has argued, the Lost Cause became the civil religion of the South, the former Unionists were welcome converts to a congregation anxious to save as many southern souls as possible. The New South ideology shared this tendency to forgive and forget. There was no room in its forward-looking optimism for complaints about previous indiscretions. The southern way of life was too important to let the mistakes of the past mar this progressive vision of a united South.[7]

As a result, although the ultimate fragility of Confederate loyalty and nationalism contributed to the defeat of the Confederate nation in the Civil War, Reconstruction accomplished what nationalistic oratory and a bloody war could not: the creation of a "nation" to which southerners gladly declared their loyalty. Unhampered by Confederate demands on their lives or their treasure, southerners could once again pledge their allegiance to the South, with a much clearer notion than in 1861 of what was at stake. The North Carolina journalist Wilbur Cash wrote that Reconstruction "fused . . . the ideas and loyalties of the apotheosized past," creating a rather mythical entity "with all the binding emotional and intellectual power of any tribal complex of the Belgian Congo." With his talent for marvelous hyperbole, Cash described the effect of the system of beliefs spawned by the bitter experience of Reconstruction. If one did not think, say, and do exactly what was expected of him by southerners—whether in terms of one's racial relations, social or political attitudes, or religious practices—"one stood in pressing peril of being cast out for a damned nigger-loving scoundrel in league with the enemy." A man could be forgiven from straying from the rules once, but "let him deviate twice, three times, and men's eyes were hard and dangerous in his, women began to gather their skirts closely about them as they passed, doors . . . slammed in his face, marriage into a decent family became difficult or impossible, the children in the village street howled and cast stones, the dogs developed an inexplicable eagerness to bite him, his creditors were likely to call in the sheriff."[8]

Twenty years later, the poet, novelist, and Vanderbilt agrarian Robert Penn Warren wrote less colorfully but no less eloquently that losing the war was the best thing that could have happened to the Confederacy. "Only at the moment when Lee handed Grant his sword was the Confederacy born," Warren wrote at the beginning of the Civil War Centennial, "or to state matters in another way, in the moment of death the Confederacy entered upon its immortality." Although "there had been great and disintegrating tensions within the Confederacy" during the war—as an examination of its citizens' loyalty amply demonstrates—"once the War was over, the Confederacy became a City of the Soul," untarnished by "the haggling of constitutional lawyers, the ambition of politicians, and the jealousy of localisms." Everyone became a Confederate, regardless of his role in the late war, and as the veterans and civilians whose memories were filled with burning towns, telegraph office casualty lists, and outrageous prices gradually died off, the rolls of loyal Confederates grew inexorably longer.9

David M. Potter, an eminent Civil War historian and also a student of nationalism, believed that there was no true southern nation before the Civil War began. Southerners shared a sense of "kinship" and common interests, but lacked an "impulse toward political unity." The primary unifying factor for the southern states was "resentment . . . not . . . a sense of separate cultural identity." Potter did not assert that there never was a "deeply felt southern nationalism," but he claimed that "it resulted from the shared sacrifices, the shared efforts, and the shared defeat." The Civil War "did far more to produce a southern nationalism which flourished in the cult of the Lost Cause than southern nationalism did to produce the war."10

The overriding principle of the cause to which old rebels as well as Confederates-come-lately dedicated themselves was, of course, white supremacy. Although Greenbacker, Populist, or other minor political and social revolutions occasionally broke out in the South and threatened the loose coalition of interests that was the Democratic party, the one common denominator that united white men was their fear and hatred of the blacks among them. Whether this was reflected in brutality against individuals or in a paternal tolerance of the blacks' right to life combined with a dogmatic opposition to their right to enjoy their lives, southerners never forgot the white thread that bound together the diverse proponents of the Lost Cause.11

In Texas, as in other parts of the South, the most vivid expressions of the issue that forced dissidents into their uneasy alliance with mainstream southerners were periodic campaigns against blacks. These ranged from Comanche County's famous expulsion of all Negroes in 1886, to the intransigence, brutality, and discrimination that led up to the violent 1917 riot in Houston, to the remarkable rebirth of the Ku Klux Klan in the early 1920s, in which violence and politics combined to remind blacks and whites alike just what the war and Reconstruction two generations before had been all about. W.E.B. DuBois wrote of the Lone Star State during the Red Summer of 1919: "This is Texas. This is the dominant white South. . . . This is the thing that America must conquer before it is civilized, and as long as Texas is this kind of Hell, civilization in America is impossible."[12]

The ghostly nation to which most southerners pledged their loyalty for the rest of the nineteenth century and well into the twentieth was based on more than the violence and economic and political discrimination perpetrated on southern blacks. It also surfaced in the Democratic "solid South," in the region's conservative social system and religious fundamentalism, and in the enduring affection southerners held for their Confederate ancestors. The magnanimity of selective memory allowed the descendants of antisecessionists, conscription evaders, and cotton speculators residence in this southern "Brigadoon" that appeared out of the mists from time to time. A 1959 plaque placed in the state capitol in Austin by the Texas Division of the Children of the Confederacy pledged the loyalty of "the children of the South" to this unforgotten past. The organization promised "to preserve pure ideals," to honor veterans, to promote the teaching of "the truths of history," and to "always act in a manner that will reflect honor upon our noble and patriotic ancestors." Long before, the *Marshall Texas Republican* predicted such an outcome to the Civil War. "Men must not suppose," it declared, "that because the Southern Confederacy is dead, its memory will become odious either to this generation or to the generations that are to follow. . . . The southern people have nothing to be ashamed of or to regret except failure."[13]

Notes

INTRODUCTION: DRAWING THE LINE

1. Walter L. Buenger, "Texas and the Riddle of Secession," *Southwestern Historical Quarterly* 87 (Oct. 1983): 151–82.

2. Boyd C. Shafer, *Faces of Nationalism: New Realities and Old Myths* (New York: Harcourt Brace Jovanovich, 1972), 133–35; Boyd C. Shafer, *Nationalism, Myth and Reality* (New York: Harcourt, Brace and Co., 1955), 144–50, quotes on pp. 145–46. Leonard W. Doob offers a useful definition of patriotism in *Patriotism and Nationalism: Their Psychological Foundations* (New Haven, CT.: Yale Univ. Press, 1964), 6: Patriotism is "the more or less conscious conviction of a person that his own welfare and that of the significant groups to which he belongs are dependent upon the preservation or expansion (or both) of the power and culture of his society." Among the many works dealing with loyalism during the American Revolution, the most useful surveys are Robert M. Calhoon, *The Loyalists in Revolutionary America, 1760–1781* (New York: Harcourt Brace Jovanovich, 1973); Wallace Brown, *The Good Americans: The Loyalists in the American Revolution* (New York: William Morrow and Co., 1969); and William H. Nelson, *The American Tory* (London: Oxford Univ. Press, 1961).

3. For exceptions, see Carl N. Degler, *The Other South: Southern Dissenters in the Nineteenth Century* (New York: Harper and Row, 1974); Roger W. Shugg, *Origins of Class Struggle in Louisiana: A Social History of White Farmers and Laborers during Slavery and After* (Baton Rouge: Louisiana State Univ. Press, 1939); James Welch Patton, *Unionism and Reconstruction in Tennessee, 1860–1869* (Chapel Hill: Univ. of North Carolina Press, 1934); and Bessie Martin, *Desertion of Alabama Troops from the Confederate Army: A Study in Sectionalism* (New York: Columbia Univ. Press, 1932).

4. Randolph B. Campbell, *A Southern Community in Crisis: Harrison County, Texas, 1850–1880* (Austin: Texas State Historical Association, 1983); Vera Lea Dugas, "A Social and Economic History of Texas in the Civil War and Reconstruction Period" (PhD diss., Univ. of Texas, 1963); Walter L. Buenger, *Secession and the Union in Texas* (Austin: Univ. of Texas Press, 1984); Frank H. Smyrl, "Unionism in Texas, 1856–1861," *Southwestern Historical Quarterly* 68 (Oct. 1964): 172–95; Robert P. Felgar, "Texas in the War for Southern Independence, 1861–1865" (PhD diss., Univ. of Texas, 1935); Stephen B. Oates, "Texas under the Secessionists," *Southwestern Historical Quarterly* 67 (Oct. 1963): 167–212; Claude Elliott, "Union Sentiment in Texas 1861–1865," *Southwestern Historical Quarterly* 50 (April 1947): 448–77; Robert L. Kerby, *Kirby Smith's Confederacy: The Trans-Mississippi South, 1863–1865* (New York: Columbia Univ.

Press, 1972); Charles W. Ramsdell, *Reconstruction in Texas* (New York: Columbia Univ. Press, 1910; Austin: Univ. of Texas Press, 1970); James A. Baggett, "The Rise and Fall of the Texas Radicals, 1867–1883" (PhD diss., North Texas State Univ., 1972); Carl H. Moneyhon, *Republicanism in Reconstruction Texas* (Austin: Univ. of Texas Press, 1980).

    5. Degler, *The Other South*, 6, 9.

    6. *Brownsville Ranchero*, December 17, 1864; Drew Gilpin Faust, *The Creation of Confederate Nationalism: Ideology and Identity in the Civil War South* (Baton Rouge: Louisiana State Univ. Press, 1988), p. 7.

1. SOUTHERN VIGILANTISM AND THE SECTIONAL CONFLICT

    1. Wesley Norton, "The Methodist Episcopal Church and the Civil Disturbances in North Texas in 1859 and 1860," *Southwestern Historical Quarterly* 68 (Jan. 1965): 339.

    2. William W. White, "The Texas Slave Insurrection of 1860," *Southwestern Historical Quarterly* 52 (Jan. 1949): 259–61; *Austin State Gazette*, July 28, 1860. See also Wendell G. Addington, "Slave Insurrections in Texas," *Journal of Negro History* 35 (Oct. 1950): 408–34, and Bill Ledbetter, "Slave Unrest and White Panic: The Impact of Black Republicanism In Antebellum Texas," *Texana* 10, no. 4 (1972), 342–48. For the insurrection scare in East Texas, see Donald E. Reynolds, "Smith County and Its Neighbors during the Slave Insurrection Panic of 1860," *Chronicles of Smith County* 10 (Fall 1971): 1–8. Clement Eaton called the southern fear of servile insurrection "pathological" and believed it contributed to the suppression of freedom of thought in the South. Clement Eaton, *The Freedom-of-Thought Struggle in the Old South* (New York: Harper and Row, 1964), 89–117.

    3. White, "Texas Slave Insurrection," 262–76; Mann to Thomas Huling, August 24, 1860, Thomas Huling Papers, Barker Texas History Center, University of Texas at Austin; *Brownsville Ranchero*, August 4, 1860; *Navarro Express*, July 14 and August 11, 1860; *Seguin Union Democrat*, August 8, 1860, quoted in the *Austin State Gazette*, Septembr 8, 1860; *Matagorda Gazette*, August 15, 1860.

    4. Gideon Lincecum to D. B. and Emily Moore, August 15, 1860, Gideon Lincecum Collecion, Barker Texas History Center; White, "Texas Slave Insurrection," 276; Larry Jay Gage, "The Texas Road to Secession and War: John Marshall and the *Texas State Gazette*, 1860–1861," *Southwestern Historical Quarterly* 62 (Oct. 1958): 198; *Bastrop Advertiser*, August 11, 1860, quoted in James M. Smallwood, *Time of Hope, Time of Despair: Black Texans during Reconstruction* (Port Washington, NY: Kennikat Press, 1981), 19; Edward Burrowes to Mrs. Mary Burrowes, December 31, 1860, in Charles M. Snyder, "New Jersey Pioneers in Texas," *Southwestern Historical Quarterly* 64 (Jan. 1961): 363. Free blacks were the most frequently suspected nonslave conspirators, but white men, especially foreigners or out-of-staters, also earned the close scrutiny of vigilantes during insurrection scares. See Herbert Aptheker, *American Negro Slave Revolts* (New York: Columbia Univ. Press, 1943), 164–65, 224–25, 232–33, 303–4; Peter H. Wood, *Black Majority: Negroes in Colonial South Carolina from 1670 through the Stono Rebellion* (New York: W. W. Norton, 1974), 295, 303–6, 312; and Davidson Burns McKibben, "Negro Slave Insurrections in Mississippi 1800–1865," *Journal of Negro History* 34 (Jan. 1949): 76–79. A recent edition of Helper's book is Hinton Rowan Helper, *The Impending Crisis of the South; How to Meet It*, ed. George Frederickson (Cambridge: Harvard Univ. Press, 1968).

    5. G. L. to John Lincecum, August 18, 1860, Lincecum Collection; Norton, "Methodist Episcopal Church and Civil Disturbances," 317–41; White, "Texas Slave Insurrection," 265–67. For a recent analysis of the breakup of the Methodist Church in

1844, see C. C. Goen, *Broken Churches, Broken Nation: Denominational Schisms and the Coming of the American Civil War* (Macon, GA: Mercer Univ. Press, 1985), 78–90.

6. For an early examination of mobs as instruments of suppressing unpopular opinions, particularly those that threatened slavery, see Clement Eaton, "Mob Violence in the Old South," *Mississippi Valley Historical Review* 29 (Dec. 1942): 351–70. For northern mobs, see Michael Feldberg, *The Turbulent Era: Riot and Disorder in Jacksonian America* (New York: Oxford Univ. Press, 1980) and Leonard L. Richards, *"Gentlemen of Property and Standing": Anti-Abolition Mobs in Jacksonian America* (New York: Oxford Univ. Press, 1970).

7. Wilbur J. Cash, *The Mind of the South* (New York: Alfred A. Knopf, 1941), 68; quoted in Stephen A. Channing, *Crisis of Fear: Secession in South Carolina* (New York: W. W. Norton, 1970), 291. A recent work that emphasizes the relationship of southern religion to slavery is Donald G. Mathews, *Religion in the Old South* (Chicago: Univ. of Chicago Press, 1977). For other strong arguments in favor of the South's defensiveness as a factor in the coming of the Civil War, see Avery Craven, *The Coming of the Civil War*, 2d ed. (Chicago: Univ. of Chicago Press, 1957), 398–403; Frank L. Owsley, "The Fundamental Cause of the Civil War: Egocentric Sectionalism," *Journal of Southern History* 7 (Feb. 1941): 15–16; Charles S. Sydnor, *The Development of Southern Sectionalism, 1819–1848* (Baton Rouge: Louisiana State Univ. Press, 1948), 120–56, 222–74, 331–39; and William L. Barney, *Flawed Victory: A New Perspective on the Civil War* (New York: Praeger, 1975), 81–82, 183–84. An exaggerated description of southerners' perception of their distinctiveness and a useful summary of the evolution of southern attempts to remedy their declining power within the Union are in Jesse T. Carpenter, *The South as a Conscious Minority, 1789–1861: A Study in Political Thought* (New York: New York Univ. Press, 1930).

8. Channing, *Crisis of Fear*, 24–38, stonecutter story on p. 30; Victor Howard, "John Brown's Raid at Harpers Ferry and the Sectional Crisis in North Carolina," *North Carolina Historical Review* 55 (Autumn 1978): 396–420; Donald B. Kelley, "Intellectual Isolation: Gateway to Secession in Mississippi," *Journal of Mississippi History* 36 (Feb. 1974): 17–37. For an overview, see William L. Barney, *The Road to Secession: A New Perspective on the Old South* (New York: Praeger, 1972), 153–60.

9. John V. Mering, "The Constitutional Union Campaign of 1860: An Example of the Paranoid Style," *Mid-America* 60 (April–July 1978): 95–106, quote on p. 99; William L. Barney, *The Secessionist Impulse: Alabama and Mississippi in 1860* (Princeton, NJ: Princeton Univ. Press, 1974), 153–88; *Nashville Union and American*, October 12, 1860, quoted in Dwight L. Dumond, ed., *Southern Editorials on Secession* (New York: Century Co., 1931), 182. See also John V. Mering, "The Slave-State Constitutional Unionists and the Politics of Consensus," *Journal of Southern History* 43 (Aug. 1977): 395–410. For state-by-state summaries of the campaign, see Collinger Crenshaw, *The Slave States in the Presidential Election of 1860* (Baltimore, MD: John Hopkins Univ. Press, 1945). For an example of election abuses, see Patton, *Unionism and Reconstruction in Tennessee*, 20–21.

10. Herschel V. Johnson, "Documents: From the Autobiography of Herschel V. Johnson, 1856–1867", *American Historical Review* 30 (Jan. 1925): 319–22.

11. Hedrick to Manly, October 14, 1856, in J. G. de Roulhac Hamilton, "Benjamin Sherwood Hedrick," *The James Sprunt Historical Publications, vol. 10* (Chapel Hill: Univ. of North Carolina Press, 1910), 30–32.

12. Thomas North, *Five Years in Texas* (Cincinnati: Elm Street Printing Co., 1871), 72. In fact, as late as 1845, Texans suspected Mexican emissaries of infiltrating Texas in an attempt to incite a slave rebellion. Paul D. Lack, "Urban Slavery in the Southwest" (PhD diss., Texas Tech Univ., 1973), 135–36.

13. H. P. N. Gammel, comp., *The Laws of Texas 1822–1855*, 10 vols. (Austin: Gammel Book Co., 1898), vol. 4, 99–100; Frank H. Dugan, "The 1850 Affair of the Brownsville Separatists," *Southwestern Historical Quarterly* 61 (Oct. 1957): 270–87, quote on p. 286; Paul D. Lack, "Slavery and Vigilantism in Austin, Texas, 1840–1860," *Southwestern Historical Quarterly* 75 (July 1981): 1–20; Ronnie C. Tyler, "The Callahan Expedition of 1855; Indians or Negroes," *Southwestern Historical Quarterly* 70 (April 1967): 574–85; Alwyn Barr, *Black Texans: A History of Negroes in Texas, 1528–1971* (Austin: Jenkins Publishing Co., 1973), 8–12.

14. Frederick Law Olmsted, *A Journey through Texas; or, A Saddle-Trip on the Southwestern Frontier* (reprint; New York: Burt Franklin, 1860; Austin: Univ. of Texas Press, 1978); Laura Wood Roper, "Frederick Law Olmsted and the Western Texas Free-Soil Movement," *American Historical Review* 56 (Oct. 1950): 58–64; Denison to Sister Eliza, January 12, 1856, James A. Padgett, ed. "Some Letters of George Stanton Denison, 1854–1866 . . . " *Louisiana Historical Quarterly* 23 (Oct. 1940): 1159.

15. Harvey Wish, "The Slave Insurrection Panic of 1856," *Journal of Southern History* 5 (May 1939): 206–22, 208; *Clarksville Standard*, November 29, 1856; Ledbetter, "Slave Unrest and White Panic," 339, 336; Gammel, *Laws of Texas, vol. 4*, 499–500.

16. *Austin State Gazette*, November 15, 1856; Speech of Anson Jones delivered at Washington, Texas, on July 29, 1856, typescript in Anson Jones Papers, Barker Texas History Center.

17. *Galveston Weekly News*, April 14, 1857, in Frank H. Smyrl, "Unionism, Abolitionism, and Vigilantism in Texas, 1856–1865" (MA thesis, Univ. of Texas, 1961), 33–34; *Dallas Herald*, October 26, 1859; *Brownsville Ranchero*, April 28 and May 5, 1860; Anna Irene Sandbo, "Beginnings of the Secession Movement in Texas," *Southwestern Historical Quarterly* 18 (July 1914): 73. For the occasional harassment of travelers suspected of being abolitionists, see Marilyn McAdams Sibley, *Travellers in Texas, 1761–1860* (Austin: Univ. of Texas Press, 1967), 130–51.

18. Quoted in Marilyn McAdams Sibley, *Lone Stars and State Gazettes* (College Station: Texas A & M Univ. Press, 1983), 284; *Marshall Texas Republican*, August 25, 1860; *Paris Press*, August 18, 1860, copied by *Marshall Texas Republican*, August 22, 1860; *Austin Southern Intelligencer*, September 12, 1860; *San Antonio Alamo Express*, August 25, 1860.

19. Quoted in Sibley, *Lone Stars and State Gazettes*, 285; *State Gazette*, August 25, September 8, and September 1, 1860, and January 26, 1861. For the role of Texas newspapers during the insurrection scare, see Sibley, *Lone Stars and State Gazettes*, 276–89.

20. George Rawick, ed., *The American Slave: A Composite Autobiography* (Westport, CT: Greenwood Publishing Co., 1972), supp. 2, vol. 8, pt. 7, 2982–83. Billy Don Ledbetter argues that Texans' fears of the race conflict and chaos that would accompany emancipation led them to reject their previously strong support for the Union. The apparent increase in slave unrest during the late 1850s foreshadowed the future if the Republicans gained power. "Slavery, Fear, and Disunion in the Lone Star State: Texans' Attitudes toward Secession and the Union, 1846–1861" (PhD diss., North Texas State Univ., 1972), 36–63, 150–224.

21. *San Antonio Alamo Express*, February 16, 1861.

2. ANTEBELLUM DISSENTERS IN TEXAS

1. Amelia H. Barr, *All the Days of My Life: An Autobiography* (New York: D. Appelton and Co., 1913), 220.

2. The development of disloyalty is, in some ways, more difficult to explain than the development of loyalty. Most people are loyal to their country, either because they

heartily support its policies, because their economic or political self-interest requires their loyalty, or simply because inertia keeps them on the right side of the treason laws. Acting disloyally is hard work and attaches a terrible stigma to the actor. As Morton Grodzins writes, "By inclination or by default, most men are patriots." *The Loyal and the Disloyal: Social Boundaries of Patriotism and Treason* (Chicago: Univ. of Chicago Press, 1956), 20–35.

3. This summary and much of the discussion that follows is based on Buenger, *Secession and the Union.* The white reaction to the slave "insurrection" lent to secession in Texas an element of the passion described by Channing in *Crisis of Fear.* The "official" opinions on secession of the southern rights and Unionist factions are set out in the majority and minority reports, respectively, of the Committees on Federal Relations of the State Senate and House of Representatives. The reports dealt with the response Texas should make to the South Carolina Resolutions of late 1859, which declared the right of secession, urged a convention of southern states, and appropriated $100,000 for military protection. See State of Texas, *Journal of the Senate, Eighth Legislature* (Austin: State Printer, 1860), 516–17 (Majority report), 524–26 (Minority report) and State of Texas, *Journal of the House of Representatives, Eighth Legislature* (Austin: State Printer, 1860), 634–35 (Majority report), 636–37 (minority Report).

4. Julia Lee Hering, "The Secession Movement in Texas" (MA thesis, Univ. of Texas, 1933), 1–30; Oran Lonnie Sinclair, "Crossroads of Conviction: A Study of the Texas Political Mind, 1856–1861" (PhD diss., Rice Univ., 1975), 2–25. For the debate in Texas over the reopening of the African slave trade, see Earl Wesley Fornell, *The Galveston Era: The Texas Crescent on the Eve of Secession* (Austin: Univ. of Texas Press, 1961), 215–30, and Ronald T. Takaki, *A Pro-Slavery Crusade: The Agitation to Reopen the African Slave Trade* (New York: The Free Press, 1971), 180–85. For an early indication of Texas's unity with the rest of the South, see Randolph B. Campbell, "Texas and the Nashville Convention of 1850," *Southwestern Historical Quarterly* 76 (July 1972): 1–14. For the states' rights planks from the platforms of the Texas Democrats, see Ernest W. Winkler, ed., *Platforms of Political Parties in Texas* (Austin: Bulletin of the Univ. of Texas, no. 53, 1916), 48 (1848), 66–68 (1856), 76 (1858), 79 (1859), 82–83 (1860). For the gradual erosion of antisecession sentiment in South Carolina and Mississippi during the 1850s, see Harold S. Schultz, *Nationalism and Sectionalism in South Carolina, 1852–1860; A Study of the Movement for Southern Independence* (Durham, NC: Duke Univ. Press, 1950) and Percy Lee Rainwater, *Mississippi: Storm Center of Secession, 1856–1861* (Baton Rouge: Otto Claitor, 1938).

5. Sandbo, "Beginnings of the Secession Movement," 56–66; Hering, "Secession Movement in Texas," 30. For the importance of the threat from Indians in determining the political alignment of voters in West Texas, see Charles Ramsdell, "The Frontier and Secession," *Studies in Southern History and Politics* (New York: Columbia Univ. Press, 1914), 63–79, and Buenger, *Secession and the Union,* 106–18.

6. *Brownsville Ranchero,* November 17, 1860; Allan to D. G. Osborn, November 10, 1860, John T. Allan Letterbook, Barker Texas History Center; *Indianola Courier,* November 24, 1860; *Brownsville Ranchero,* December 1, 1860; *Navarro Express,* November 16, 1860, quoted in Felgar, "Texas in the War," 22–23; *Indianola Courier,* December 1, 1860.

7. Buenger, *Secession and the Union,* 141–58; Frank Brown, "Annals of Travis County and of the City of Austin (from the Earliest Times to the Close of 1875)," chap. 21, 8, Austin History Center, Austin Public Library; Ernest W. Winkler, ed., *Journal of the Secession Convention of Texas, 1861* (Austin: Austin Printing Co., 1912), 85; Hering, "Secession Movement in Texas," 75–116. For the long, uncertain process of secession in Virginia and Arkansas, see Henry T. Shanks, *The Secession Movement in Virginia,*

1847–1861 (Richmond, VA: Garrett and Massie, 1934) and Jack B. Scroggs, "Arkansas in the Secession Crisis," *Arkansas Historical Quarterly* 12 (Autumn 1953): 179–224.

8. *Austin State Gazette,* February 16 and February 23, 1861. For the *State Gazette's* role in the secession movement, see Gage, "Texas Road to Secession and War," 191–226.

9. Buenger, *Secession and the Union,* 2; *San Antonio Alamo Express,* March 2, 1861; Gilbert D. Kingsury, "Lectures, Reports, and Writings, Vol. 2, 1855–1867," 20, Gilbert D. Kingsbury Papers, Barker Texas History Center; Anson Mills, *My Story* (Washington, D.C.: Press of Byron S. Adams, 1918), 76–77.

10. James P. Newcomb, *Sketch of Secession Times in Texas* (San Francisco, 1863), 8; *Dallas Herald,* February 27, 1861; Hering, "Secession Movement in Texas," 139–56. For a dramatic and readable narrative of secession in Texas, see T.R. Fehrenbach, *Lone Star: A History of Texas and the Texans* (New York: Macmillan, 1968), 327–49.

11. J. Walker Austin to "Son," March 22, 1861, J. Walker Austin Papers, Barker Texas History Center.

12. *Clarksville Standard,* June 4, 1859, quoted in Sibley, *Lone Stars and State Gazettes,* 273. Useful summaries of southern Unionism appear in Eaton, *The Freedom-of-Thought Struggle,* 376–407, and Degler, *The Other South,* 99–187.

13. Walter Buenger explains the differences between secessionists and Unionists in terms of their cultural backgrounds. Men who had imigrated from the lower South or who participated in the plantation economy of southern and eastern Texas tended to be secessionists; those who came from states in the upper South and were less reliant on plantation agriculture, such as farmers or professional men in the northern and western parts of the state, tended to be Unionists. The latter group found themselves increasingly outnumbered during the years immediately preceding the war, and gradually most upper-South types accepted secession and cast their lot with the lower-South secessionists. Buenger, *Secession and the Union,* esp. pp. 62–79.

14. Houston to A. Daly, August 14, 1860, Amelia W. Williams and Eugene C. Barker, eds., *The Writings of Sam Houston, 1813–1863,* vols. 7–8 (Austin: Jenkins Publishing Co., 1970), vol. 8, 119; Andrew Jackson Hamilton, *Speech of Hon. Andrew J. Hamilton, of Texas, on the State of the Union* (Washington, D.C.: Lemuel Towers, 1861), 16. Like Houston and Hamilton, other Unionist southern Democrats believed slavery was safer within their beloved Union than outside it. See Craven, *Coming of the Civil War,* 403–7; Lillian Adele Kibler, "Unionist Sentiment in South Carolina in 1860," *Journal of Southern History* 4 (Aug. 1938): 346–66; and Channing, *Crisis of Fear,* 167–226.

15. A. B. Burleson to Capt. E. Burleson, November 19, 1860, Edward Burleson, Jr., Papers, Barker Texas History Center.

16. For a useful description of Jacksonian Democrats in Texas, see Buenger, *Secession and the Union,* 22–24.

17. An excellent definition of conservative Unionists can be found in Herbert J. Doherty, Jr., "Union Nationalism in Georgia," *Georgia Historical Quarterly* 37 (March 1953): 18–38; for their opinions on economic issues, see Robert R. Russell, *Economic Aspects of Southern Sectionalism, 1840–1861* (Urbana: Univ. of Illinois Press, 1924), 58, 85, 87, 179; for their opposition to the controversial question of reopening the African slave trade, see Takaki, *A Pro-Slavery Crusade,* 103–33.

18. Arthur Charles Cole, *The Whig Party in the South* (Washington, D.C.: American Historical Association, 1914; Gloucester, MA: Peter Smith, 1962), 277–308, 309–43; Degler, *The Other South,* 105–16; W. Darrell Overdyke, *The Know-Nothing Party in the South* (Baton Rouge: Louisiana State Univ. Press, 1950), 16–33, 73–90, 127–28, 281–95; Litha Crews, "The Know Nothing Party in Texas" (MA thesis, Univ. of Texas at Austin, 1925), 112–60; *McKinney Messenger,* September-November, 1860; *San*

Antonio Alamo Express, September 3, 1860; Buenger, *Secession and the Union,* 22–44; James A. Baggett, "The Constitutional Union Party in Texas," *Southwestern Historical Quarterly* 82 (Jan. 1979): 233–64; Smyrl, "Unionism in Texas," 172–95. For an excellent analysis of the various strands of Whig ideology and interest, see Daniel Walker Howe, *The Political Culture of the American Whigs* (Chicago: Univ. of Chicago Press, 1979), 238–62.

19. "Address to the People of Texas," Broadside, Robert H. Taylor Papers, Barker Texas History Center. Many newspapers around Texas printed the address. The men who attached their names to the document were: State Senators Martin D. Hart, I.A. Paschal, Emory Rains, and J.W. Throckmorton; State Representatives M.L. Armstrong, Sam Bogart, L.B. Camp, W.A. Ellett, B.H. Epperson, John Hancock, John L. Haynes, J.E. Henry, T.H. Mundine, A.B. Norton, W.M. Owen, Sam J. Redgate, Robert H. Taylor, and G.W. Whitmore; and Convention Delegates Joshua F. Johnson, John D. Rains, A.P. Shuford, L.H. Williams, George W. Wright, and William H. Johnson.

20. George Durham to O.M. Roberts, March 8, 1861, O.M. Roberts Papers, Barker Texas History Center; *Austin Southern Intelligencer,* March 27, 1861; *McKinney Messenger,* March 1, 1861; Barr, *All the Days of My Life,* 226–27.

21. Abraham Enloe to John Enloe, January 6, 1861, Abraham Enloe File, Civil War Miscellany, Barker Texas History Center.

22. *Corpus Christi Ranchero,* January 21, June 9, and November 10 and 25, 1860; January 19, February 2, and April 13 and 20, 1861. For a brief description of conditional unionism in the South, see Degler, *The Other South,* 124–25. Secessionists and unconditional unionists fit the characteristics of what Morton Grodzins calls *traitriots,* those persons who renounce their country because it has somehow forsaken the values for which they loved it or who remain consistent to principles or values that become more important to them than national loyalty. Secessionists withdrew their loyalty to the United States because their northern enemies had perverted the principles set forth by the founding fathers in the Constitution so that it no longer protected the property and rights of southerners. Unconditional unionists ignored the Confederate government's demands for their loyalty and remained true to the principles that they believed the United States still represented. Grodzins, *The Loyal and the Disloyal,* 208–16.

23. U.S. Bureau of the Census, *Population of the United States in 1860: Compiled from the Original Returns of the Eighth Census* (Washington, D.C.: Government Printing Office, 1864), 486. Much of the following is drawn from the excellent discussion of the ethnic element in Texas politics and secession in Buenger, *Secession and the Union,* 80–105.

24. Buenger, *Secession and the Union,* 81; A.E. Zucker, ed., *The Forty-eighters: Political Refugees of the German Revolution of 1848.* (New York: Columbia Univ. Press, 1950), 3–25, 43–78, 111–56; Zoie Odom Newsome, "Antislavery Sentiment in Texas, 1821–1861" (MA thesis, Texas Technological College, 1968), 63–64. For a recent work on German colonization in Texas, see Bobby D. Weaver, *Castro's Colony: Empresario Development in Texas, 1842–1865.* (College Station: Texas A & M Univ. Press, 1985). For the causes of German migration, see Terry G. Jordan, *German Seed in Texas Soil: Immigrant Farmers in Nineteenth Century Texas* (Austin: Univ. of Texas Press, 1966), 32–54. The small groups of Norwegians, Poles, Czechs, French, and Alsatian immigrants in Texas also tended to oppose slavery. Newsome, "Antislavery Sentiment," 68–70.

25. Rena Mazyck Andrews, "German Pioneers in Texas: Civil War Period" (MA thesis, Univ. of Chicago, 1929), 29, translation of San Antonio platform on pp. 29–31; E.R. Tausch, "Southern Sentiment among the Texas Germans during the Civil War and

Reconstruction" (MA thesis, Univ. of Texas, 1965), 1–53; Rudolph L. Biesele, *The History of the German Settlements in Texas, 1831–1861* (Austin: Von Boeckmann-Jones Co., 1930), 191–207; Ella Lonn, *Foreigners in the Confederacy* (Chapel Hill: Univ. of North Carolina Press, 1940), 417–23. A good narrative of the events surrounding the Germans' meeting in San Antonio is in Rudolph L. Biesele, "The Texas State Convention of Germans in 1854," *Southwestern Historical Quarterly* 33 (April 1930); 247–61.

26. *Austin State Gazette*, July 29, 1854; *Dallas Herald* quoted in *State Gazette*, May 20, 1854; Olmsted, *A Journey through Texas*, 328–29, 439. Despite Olmsted's observations, Terry Jordan asserts that the Germans' antisecessionism stemmed less from abolitionism and Unionism than from their lack of interest in East Texas concerns and their fear of losing federal protection from the Indians. Jordan, *German Seed in Texas Soil*, 180–85, 194.

27. Ada Maria Hall, "The Texas Germans in State and National Politics, 1850–1865" (MA thesis, Univ. of Texas, 1938), 103–08; Robert W. Shook, "German Unionism in Texas during the Civil War and Reconstruction" (MA thesis, North Texas State Univ., 1957), 31–32.

28. Walter L. Buenger, "Secession and the Texas German Community: Editor Lindheimer vs. Editor Flake," *Southwestern Historical Quarterly* 82 (April 1979): 379–402, quotes on pp. 395, 396.

29. Gideon Lincecum to D.B. and Emily Moore, August 15, 1860, Lincecum Collection; Buenger, *Secession and the Union*, 67 (the counties and the percentages against secession were Fayette, 52; Gillespie, 96; Mason, 97; and Medina, 60), 99–100. For more on the southern Know-Nothings' program of connecting foreigners to antislavery, see Overdyke, *The Know-Nothing Party*, 198–210.

30. *U.S. Census, Population of the United States in 1860*, 490; Buenger, *Secession and the Union*, 85; Bette Gay Ash, "The Mexican Texans in the Civil War" (MA thesis, East Texas State Univ., 1972), 11–36; Arnoldo DeLeón, *They called Them Greasers: Anglo Attitudes towards Mexicans in Texas, 1821–1900* (Austin: Univ. of Texas Press, 1983), 49–62, 75–86; Carey McWilliams, *North from Mexico: The Spanish-speaking People of the United States* (New York: Greenwood Press Reprint, 1968), 98–108; LeRoy P. Graf, "The Economic History of the Lower Rio Grande Valley, 1820–1875" (PhD diss., Harvard Univ., 1942), 369–76; John Denney Riley "Santos Benavides: His influence on the Lower Rio Grande, 1823–1891" (PhD diss., Texas Christian Univ., 1976), 89–100. For the early history of the religious and political conflicts between Anglos and tejanos, see Samuel H. Lowrie, *Culture Conflict in Texas, 1821–1835* (reprint; New York: AMS Press, 1967).

31. *Corpus Christi Ranchero*, September 3, 1863, quoted in Riley, "Santos Benavides," 116; Ronnie C. Tyler, "Slave Owners and Runaway Slaves in Texas" (MA thesis, Texas Christian Univ., 1966). For examples of the sorts of machinations Anglos used to defraud Mexican landowners, see U.S. Congress, House, *The Impeachment of Judge Watrous*, 34th Cong. 3d sess., 1856–1857, H. Rept. 175 (Serial 913). Watrous, a United States District Judge in Texas, had validated shady Anglo land titles that violated state law. The House did not convict him.

32. Olmsted, *A Journey through Texas*, 245, 160–65, 325; Rawick, *American Slave*, vol. 4, pt. 2, 132; Olmsted, *A Journey through Texas*, 456, 245.

33. David Montejano, *Anglos and Mexicans in the Making of Texas, 1836–1986* (Austin: Univ. of Texas Press, 1987), 26–29, 30–37.

34. DeLeón, *They Called Them Greasers*, 82–83; *Corpus Christi Ranchero*, November 11, 1859; *Navarro Express*, November 26, 1859. For a sympathetic interpretation of Cortina, see Charles W. Goldfinch, "Juan N. Cortina, 1824–1892: A Reappraisal" (MA thesis, Univ. of Chicago, 1949), in Carlos E. Cortes, ed., *Juan N. Cortina: Two Interpretations* (New York: Arno Press, 1974). For a summary of the

problems caused by white conflicts with Indians and Mexicans along the border, see U.S. Congress, House, 36th Cong., 1st sess., 1859–1860, H. Exec. Doc. 57 (Serial 1050), esp. pp. 19–23, 31–142.

35. Many Germans, who chose to be disloyal to the Confederacy because giving their allegiance to it would violate their moral principles, were, in effect, *traitriots* (see n. 22, above). Other Germans, and most Mexicans, saw no reason to actively oppose the Confederacy until wartime conscription, taxes, or hardships drove them to resistance. The "gratifications" they received for remaining loyal to Texas and the Confederacy had disappeared, thereby removing any motivation to devote their time and effort to the Confederate cause. As a result, they found other outlets for their loyalty— usually their families, or, in a few cases, the Union army. For a discussion of how "life-situations" affect loyalty, see Grodzins, *The Loyal and the Disloyal*, 132–52. See also Harold Guetzkow, *Multiple Loyalties: Theoretical Approach to a Problem in International Organization* (Princeton, NJ: Center for Research on World Political Institutions, 1955), esp. "Loyalty as Means," "Loyalties as End-Values," and "Loyalties as Conformity," pp. 19–22, 24–28.

36. Grodzins, *The Loyal and the Disloyal*, 28–30.

37. Allan to D. G. Osborn, April 19, 1861, Allan Letterbook.

3. CONFEDERATE UNIONISTS AND THE WAR

1. Fehrenbach, *Lone Star*, 344–45. See also Buenger, *Secession and the Union*, 148. The men in the photograph with Throckmorton are A.P. Shuford, Lemuel H. Williams, Joshua Johnson, William H. Johnson, George W. Wright, and Thomas P. Hughes. The eighth man to vote against secession was John D. Rains. The Austin History Center at the Austin Public Library owns a print of the original.

2. Claude Elliott, *Leathercoat: The Life of James W. Throckmorton* (San Antonio: Standard Printing Co., 1938), 5–12, 16, 42.

3. Ibid., 15–40, 41–62, 59; Buenger, *Secession and the Union*, 67; *Clarksville Standard*, May 11, 1861.

4. Elliot, *Leathercoat*, 63–98.

5. The original letter, dated January 19, 1862, is in the Benjamin H. Epperson Papers, Barker Texas History Center. It has also been published in James Marten, ed., "The Lamentations of a Whig: James Throckmorton Writes a Letter," *Civil War History* 31 (June 1985): 163–70.

6. Throckmorton to Epperson, February 5, 1864, Epperson Papers.

7. Throckmorton to Epperson, June 18, 1864, Epperson Papers; Throckmorton to Murrah, December 20, 1864, Pendleton Murrah Papers, Governors' Records, Texas State Archives, Austin, Texas.

8. Throckmorton to Epperson, November 3, 1864, Epperson Papers; Texas Legislature, *Resolutions of the State of Texas, Concering Peace, Reconstruction, and Independence* (Austin: State Printer, 1865). The published proceedings are not nearly so dramatic as Throckmorton's description of them. James M. Day, ed., *Senate Journal of the Tenth Legislature, Second Called Session* (Austin: Texas State Library, 1966), 36–37.

9. Alfred Huger to Benjamin F. Perry, November 27, 1860, Benjamin F. Perry Papers, Ramsdell Microfilm Collection, Barker Texas History Center; Vance to G.N. Folk, January 9, 1861, in Frontis W. Johnston, ed., *The Papers of Zebulon Baird Vance*, vol. 1 (Raleigh, NC: State Department of Archives and History, 1963), 81–83; May 3, 1861, John W. Brown Diary, Southern Historical Collection, University of North Carolina at Chapel Hill; Stephens to Samuel R. Glenn, February 8, 1861, quoted in Doherty, "Union Nationalism in Georgia," 38.

10. Glenn Tucker, *Zeb Vance: Champion of Personal Freedom* (Indianapolis, IN: Bobbs-Merrill Co., 1965), 107–410; Lillian Adele Kibler, *Benjamin F. Perry, South Carolina Unionist* (Durham, NC: Duke Univ. Press, 1946), 274, 347–70.

11. Rawick, *American Slave*, supp. 2, vol. 10, pt. 9, 4233–34.

12. Walter P. Webb, ed., *Handbook of Texas, vols. 1 and 2* (Austin: Texas State Historical Association, 1952), vol. 1, 861; vol. 2, 913–14; E.L. Dohoney, *An Average American* (Paris, TX: E. L. Dohoney, n.d. [ca. 1900]), 73, 123.

13. Taylor's speech appeared alongside the Unionists' "Address to the People of Texas." See "Address to the People of Texas," Taylor Papers; Taylor to Epperson, November 20, 1861, Epperson Papers; Webb, *Handbook of Texas*, vol. 2, 716. A letter from Mrs. C.G. Long to Llerena Friend in the Robert H. Taylor Biographical File, Barker Texas History Center, reveals that Taylor left few papers other than two pages of heavy paper, on one of which is written "I am against secession," and on the other "Too bad Texas out."

14. Ralph A. Wooster, "Ben H. Epperson: East Texas Lawyer, Legislator, and Civic Leader," *East Texas Historical Journal* 5 (March 1967): 29–42.

15. Buenger, *Secession and the Union*, 67; *Clarksville Standard*, April 27, June 15, and October 5, 1861; Wooster, "Ben H. Epperson," 34.

16. Webb, *Handbook of Texas*, vol. 2, 938; *Austin American*, September 2, 1954, in Thomas F. McKinney Biographical File, Barker Texas History Center; McKinney to Tom, Ballinger, and Guy, November 22, 1860, quoted in Hering, "Secession Movement in Texas," 46. Another veteran of the Texas navy, James G. Hurd, opposed secession, but remained at his home in Galveston and served as an unofficial protector of the families and property of soldiers in the service. *History of Texas, Together with a Biographical History of the Cities of Houston and Galveston* (Chicago: Lewis Publishing Co., 1895), 625–26.

17. Winkler, *Platforms of Political Parties*, 51; *Corpus Christi Ranchero*, March 30, 1861. For an overview of Houston's opinions and actions during this period, see Edward R. Maher, Jr., "Sam Houston and Secession," *Southwestern Historical Quarterly* 55 (April 1952): 448–58.

18. Houston to George W. Paschal, June 3, 1859; Speech in the Senate concerning the Pacific Railroad and Other Matters, January 12–13, 1859; Synopsis of a speech at Danville, September 11, 1858; Houston to H.M. Watkins and others, November 20, 1860; Speech at Brenham, Texas, March 31, 1861: all in Williams and Barker, *Writings of Houston*, vol. 7, 339–40, 211, 185; vol. 8, 195, 298–99. For Houston's economic arguments against reopening the African slave trade, see his Speech at Nacogdoches, July 9, 1859, ibid., vol. 7, 347.

19. Maher, "Sam Houston and Secession," 448, 458; State of Texas, *Journal of the House of Representatives, Extra Session of the Eighth Legislature* (Austin: State Printer, 1861), 25.

20. Houston's Message to the Secession Convention, January 31, 1861; Houston's Message to the People of Texas, March 16, 1861; Houston's Speech at Independence, May 10, 1861: all in Williams and Barker, *Writings of Houston*, vol. 8, 47, 275, 301–2.

21. Maher, "Sam Houston and Secession," 456–57; March 9, 1862, William Pitt Ballinger Diary, Barker Texas History Center.

22. Houston to S.M. Swenson, August 14, 1862, in Williams and Barker, *Writings of Houston*, vol. 8, 320–22; Joseph E. Chance, *The Second Texas Infantry: From Shiloh to Vicksburg* (Austin: Eakin Press, 1984), 101; Gary Wilson, "The Ordeal of William H. Cowdin and the Officers of the Forty-second Massachusetts Regiment: Union Prisoners in Texas," *East Texas Historical Journal* 23 (1986): 19; Chance, *The Second Texas Infantry*, 5.

23. Smyth to John Reagan, May 21, 1859; Smyth to McKinney, July 19, 1859; Smyth to E.H. Cushing, November 12, 1860; Harvey Allen to Smyth, April 22, 1860; Smyth to Cushing, November 12, 1860: all in George W. Smyth Papers, Barker Texas History Center.

24. Fornell, *The Galveston Era*, 148–50, 215–16, 277, quote on p. 281; September 1, 1860, Ballinger Diary; Ben C. Stuart, "Hamilton Stuart: Pioneer Editor," *Southwestern Historical Quarterly* 21 (April 1918): 386.

25. Cavitt to Andrew Johnson, September 7, 1865, Josephus Cavitt Papers, Barker Texas History Center.

26. Bellew to Hamilton, July 13, 1865, Andrew Jackson Hamilton Papers, Governors' Records, Texas State Archives; Ike Moore, ed., *The Life and Diary of Reading Wood Black* (Uvalde, Texas: El Progresso Club, 1934), 27–29.

27. Webb, *Handbook of Texas*, vol. 1, 861; Howell R. Hughes, "Life of an East Texas Pioneer, Reece Hughes," typescript, Barker Texas History Center.

28. John A. Maretta, "William Pitt Ballinger: Public Servant, Private Pragmatist" (Ph.D. diss., Rice Univ. 1985), 1–50.

29. December 31 and 30, 1860, Ballinger Diary. Ballinger knew most of the influential Texans of his time, and the typescript copy of his diary and its detailed index, both located in the Barker Center, are invaluable to historians of Texas during the late antebellum, Civil War, and Reconstruction periods.

30. August 1, 1859, August 23, September 8, November 14, November 15, December 8, December 31, 1860: all in Ballinger Diary. Ballinger's most recent biographer, John A. Maretta, inexplicably asserts in his useful dissertation that Ballinger "committed himself to doing all that was necessary to prevent the dissolution of the Union." Maretta, "William Pitt Ballinger," 50.

31. Maretta, "William Pitt Ballinger," 158–203; December 30, 1860, October 24, 1861; June 12 and February 26, 1863; January 31, 1863; all in Ballinger Diary. For the workings of the Confederate sequestration act, see T. R. Havins, "Administration of the Sequestration Act in the Confederate District Court for the Western District of Texas, 1862–1865," *Southwestern Historical Quarterly* 43 (Jan. 1940): 295–322.

32. Ballinger to Paschal, letter fragment, May 8, 1863, William Pitt Ballinger Papers, Barker Texas History Center.

33. December 31, 1860, Ballinger Diary. See also his entry for July 29, 1863.

34. James A. Creighton, *A Narrative History of Brazoria County* (Waco, TX: Texian Press, 1975), 17, 18; Webb, *Handbook of Texas*, Vol. 1, 141; *A Sketch of the Life of Hon. James H. Bell: Memorial Proceedings Had in the Supreme Court of Texas in Respect to the Memory of Hon. James H. Bell* (Austin, 1893).

35. James H. Bell, *Speech of Hon. James H. Bell, of the Texas Supreme Court, Delivered at the Capitol on Saturday, December 1st, 1860* (Austin: Intelligencer Book Office, 1860). Bell admitted in the customary letter accepting the honor of publishing his speech that he would be called a free-soiler and an abolitionist "by those who think that the greatest political offence of which a man can be guilty, is to differ from them in opinion."

36. Bell to Epperson, February 22, 1865, Epperson Papers.

37. Hebert proclaimed martial law on May 30, 1862, in order to facilitate the enforcement of the conscription act in Texas. President Davis, claiming that only the president had the power to proclaim martial law, nullified the order on September 12, 1862. *War of the Rebellion: A Compilation of the Official Records of the Union and Confederate Armies* (Washington, D.C.: Government Printing Office, 1880–1901), ser. 1, vol. 9, 715–16 (hereafter cited as OR, followed by series, volume, part [when necessary], and page numbers); Felgar, "Texas in the War," 204–6; May 24, 1862, Ballinger Diary.

38. An unsigned editorial in the March 23, 1864, *Houston Daily Telegraph* is apparently the editorial to which Ballinger refers in his March 23 diary entry.

39. *The Supreme Court of Texas on the Constitutionality of the Conscript Laws* (Houston: Telegraph Book and Job Establishment, 1863). The decision arose in response to a plea for a writ of habeas corpus from a man who believed he was illegally held when he resisted conscription. The case: *Exparte Frank H. Coapland.* His lawyers: George W. Paschal and John Hancock.

40. March 22, 1863, Ballinger Diary. Ballinger failed to note what arguments he used or to whom he sent the letter. For his personal life during the war, see his diary entries for February 3, June 12, and October 22, 1862, and January 13 and November 25, 1864.

41. February 22 and 23, 1863, Ballinger Diary.

42. February 23, 1862, Ballinger Diary. Eccles. 12:6–7 reads, "Or ever the silver cord be loosed, or the golden bowl be broken, or the pitcher be broken at the fountain, or the wheel broken at the cistern. Then shall the dust return to the earth as it was; and the spirit shall return unto God who gave it."

43. Throckmorton to Epperson, January 19, 1862, and February 5, 1864, Epperson Papers; Austin to "Johnson," September 2, 1861, Austin Papers.

44. The conservatism of these men resembles in some ways the conservative "Copperheads" of the Midwest. See especially Frank L. Klement, *The Copperheads in the Middle West* (Chicago: Univ. of Chicago Press, 1960) and *The Limits of Dissent: Clement Vallandigham and the Civil War* (Lexington: Univ. Press of Kentucky, 1970).

4. UNIONISTS AS DISSENTERS

1. Works Projects Administration (WPA), *St. David's through the Years* (Austin: Betty Gilmer Chapter of St. David's Guild, 1942), 26–31; Webb, *Handbook of Texas*, vol. 1, 691.

2. WPA, *St. David's through the Years*, 32–35.

3. Wilson Gregg, *Alexander Gregg: First Bishop of Texas* (Sewanee, TN: The University Press at the Univ. of the South, 1912), 3–4; WPA, *St. David's through the Years*, 35–37. The 1860 census reveals that Greg owned 31 slaves on the eve of the Civil War.

4. Lucadia Pease to her sister, April 20, 1861, Lucadia Pease Papers, Austin History Center; August 23, 1863, Thomas DuVal Diary, Barker Texas History Center.

5. WPA, *St. David's through the Years*, 36–39; Charles Gillette, *A Few Historic Records of the Church in the Diocese of Texas, during the Rebellion* (New York: John A. Gray and Green, 1865), 11–19, 35–36.

6. WPA, *St. David's through the Years*, 39–41.

7. For the isolated positions of Southern Whigs and for the strength of North Carolina's Whig Unionists, see Howe, *Political Culture of Whigs*, 252–55, and Marc W. Kruman, *Parties and Politics in North Carolina, 1836–1865* (Baton Rouge: Louisiana State Univ. Press, 1983), 180–221. For the commitment of National Democrats in the South to preserving the political system, see Joel H. Silbey, "The Southern National Democrats, 1845–1861," *Mid-America* 47 (July 1965): 176–90. Walter L. Buenger argues that while Whigs felt a sentimental attachment to the Union, Democrats stressed the pragmatic benefits of membership in the Union. Whig nationalism survived through 1860 and early 1861; Democrats were much more likely before that time to have decided that the advantages of staying in the Union had vanished. Buenger, "Texas and the Riddle of Secession," 151–82. It could be argued that the toughest Democratic Unionists in Texas shared the Whigs' romantic attachment to the Union.

8. Zenas R. Bliss Reminiscences, Barker Texas History Center, 41; *San Antonio*

Weekly Herald, March 3, 1862; *Austin State Gazette,* February 2, 1861; N.G. Shelley to Roberts, March 6, 1862, Roberts Papers; Alwyn Barr, ed., "Records of the Confederate Military Commission in San Antonio, July 2–October 10, 1862," *Southwestern Historical Quarterly* 70 (July 1966): 94–95.

9. *Marshall Texas Republican,* December 8, 1860. In his "Union Sentiment in Texas," 448–77, Claude Elliott subscribes to the theory that only one-third of the population of Texas was loyal to the Confederacy, one-third remained neutral, and one-third actively supported the United States. While this is probably accurate as far as it goes, it simplifies the situation. The percentage of Texans actively loyal to the Confederacy at any given time varied widely during the war, depending on how the war was currently affecting them and the rest of the South. Some Texans were quite loyal at the beginning of the war, but later found themselves opposed to one or more Confederate policies and turned against the Confederacy. Others, disliking the policies of emancipation or total war adopted by the United States, became resigned to the existence of the Confederate States and accepted their duties as loyal citizens.

10. John H. Aughey, *The Iron Furnace; or, Slavery and Secession* (Philadelphia: William S. and Alfred Martien, 1863), 145; *Parson Brownlow, and the Unionists of East Tennessee, with a Sketch of His Life* (New York: Beadle and Co., 1862), 48.

11. R.L. Abarr to "My dear Brother Joseph," *Western Journal of Commerce,* June 20, 1863, bound typescript, Barker Texas History Center. Andrew J. Hamilton, a better-known Texas Unionist, estimated in a speech in September 1862, that mobs had murdered two hundred Texas Unionists. *New York Tribune,* September 29, 1862.

12. *Clarksville Standard,* June 29, July 6, and June 22, 1861; *Marshall Texas Republican,* May 4, 1861; *Austin State Gazette,* October 28, 1863.

13. *Austin State Gazette,* March 9, 1861; *Clarksville Standard,* July 6, 1861; *Marshall Texas Republican,* June 8, 1861.

14. Dohoney, *An Average American,* 134–35; Darrell Debo, *Burnet County History,* vol. 1 (Austin, TX: Eakin Press, 1979), 35–36; J.L. Stambaugh and Lillian Stambaugh, *A History of Collin County, Texas* (Austin: Texas State Historical Association, 1958), 69; H. Smythe, *Historical Sketch of Parker County and Weatherford, Texas* (St. Louis, MO: Louis C. Lavat, 1877), 177–84; Brown, "Annals of Travis County," chap. 23, 52–53.

15. G. W. Whitmore to Hamilton, August 24, 1865; Jacob P. Halsey to Hamilton, September 14, 1865; Petition from "Loyal Citizens" of Goliad County, n.d.: all in Hamilton Papers, Governors' Records, Texas State Archives. For an anecdotal account of Unionism and conflict in the hill country west of Austin, see "Guerrilla Warfare in Hills about Austin when Sympathizers with Union Opposed Secession," Harold Preece Scrapbook, Austin Chronological File, 1862, Austin History Center.

16. Barr, "Records of the Confederate Military Commission," 70 (Oct. 1966): 289–313.

17. Ibid., 73 (July 1969): 91–104. McKean was later released.

18. "Common Sense," Clippings File, Reuben G. White Family Collection, Barker Texas History Center; September 24, 1863, DuVal Diary.

19. Felgar, "Texas in the War," 299–323.

20. Bliss Reminiscences, 59, 32; McLane to Messrs Tunstall and Howell, March 1, 1861, Warrick Tunstall Papers, Barker Texas History Center; *San Antonio Weekly Herald,* August 17, 24, and 31, and September 14, 1861.

21. Webb, *Handbook of Texas,* vol. 2, 275; *San Antonio Alamo Express,* August 25, 1860, February 6 and May 3, 1861.

22. Lois Ellsworth, "San Antonio during the Civil War" (MA thesis, Univ. of Texas, 1938), 19–22; Bliss Reminiscences, 33–34; *Indianola Courier,* May 25, 1861.

James B. Newcomb published his version of the secession movement and a travelogue of his journey through Mexico in *Sketch of Secession Times in Texas*.

23. *Austin State Gazette*, September 21, 1861; George Denison to Salmon P. Chase, May 1862, Edward G. Bourne and Frederick W. Moore, eds., "Diary and Correspondence of Salmon P. Chase, . . . " *Annual Report of the American Historical Association for the Year 1902*, vol. 2 (Washington, D.C.: Government Printing Office, 1902), 300.

24. Baggett, "The Constitutional Union Party," 253, 249; Brown, "Annals of Travis County," chap. 21, 8–14; Winkler, *Journal of the Secession Convention*, 48–49.

25. The 261 names on the petition were taken from Brown, "Annals of Travis County," chap. 21, 9–14. Of these, 162 were located in the 1860 Travis County manuscript census. Recognizing that some voters may not have had the opportunity to sign the petition, I have added ten more well-known Travis County Union men, whose names did not appear on the petition. Data on wealth-holding came from the microfilm copies of the 1860 Travis County Census, Schedule One, located in the Texas State Archives in Austin. All other information came from Alice Duggan Gracy and Emma Gene Seale Gentry, comps., *Travis County, Texas: The Five Schedules of the 1860 Federal Census* (Austin: Privately printed, 1967). The population of Travis County in 1860 numbered 4892. White males over the age of twenty-one accounted for 1263 (25.8 percent) of the county's population, while the 172 known Unionists accounted for 13.6 percent of the white adult males.

26. Travis County offers a contrasting example to recent analyses of the origins of Unionists. Michael P. Johnson's examination of Georgia's drive to form a "Republic of Slaveholders" shows that most of that state's dissenters originated among conservative, aristocratic Whigs and nonslaveowning Democrats. Most North Carolina Unionists were Whigs, according to Marc W. Kruman; they managed to keep their state in the Union for so long primarily because, unlike most southern states by 1860, they had a viable party organization and a large popular following. Mississippi and Alabama Unionists, writes William L. Barney, came out of those groups whose large or small fortunes inhibited their interest in the expansion of slavery. Johnson, *Toward a Patriarchal Republic: The Secession of Georgia* (Baton Rouge: Louisiana State Univ. Press, 1977), 66–67, 100–101; Kruman, *Parties and Politics in North Carolina*, 180–221; Barney, *The Secessionist Impulse*, 97–100.

27. H. Robinson to the *Austin State Gazette*, April 27, 1861; Austin to "Son," March 22, 1861, Austin Papers; Alexander W. Terrell, "The City of Austin from 1839 to 1865," *Southwestern Historical Quarterly* 14 (Oct. 1910): 120; Terrell to Burleson, August 1861, Burleson Papers; Brown, "Annals of Travis County," chap. 23, 53; *Marshall Texas Republican*, July 12, 1862.

28. Charles Westmoreland to Hamilton, November 1, 1862, and Chase to Hamilton, August 27, 1863, Andrew Jackson Hamilton Papers, Letters, 1850–1907, vol. 1, Barker Texas History Center; Denison to Chase, September 19, 1862, Bourne and Moore, "Diary and Correspondence of Salmon P. Chase," 314–15; Enos Woofter to Hamilton, October 8, 1865, Hamilton Papers, Governors' Records, Texas State Archives.

29. *Dallas Herald*, November 8 and December 27, 1862.

30. John L. Waller, *Colossal Hamilton of Texas: A Biography of Andrew Jackson Hamilton* (El Paso: Texas Western Press, 1968), 3–33, 34–46. (For Johnson's choices during the secession crisis, see LeRoy P. Graf, "Andrew Johnson and the Coming of the War," *Tennessee Historical Quarterly* 19 [Sept. 1960]: 208–221); *Marshall Texas Republican*, November 1, 1862; Woofter to Hamilton, October 8, 1865, Hamilton Papers, Governors' Records, Texas State Archives; Leonard Pierce, Jr., to William Seward,

August 26, 1862, Matamoros Consular Dispatches, Ramsdell Microfilm Collection, Barker Texas History Center; Webb, *Handbook of Texas*, vol. 1, 723.

31. David Donald, ed., *Inside Lincoln's Cabinet: The Civil War Diaries of Salmon P. Chase* (New York: Longmans, Green and Co., 1954), 167; Andrew Hamilton, the "Speech of Hon. Andrew Jackson Hamilton, of Texas, on the Conditions of the South under Rebel Rule, and the Necessity of Early Relief to the Union Men of Western Texas," October 3, 1862, Barker Texas History Center; Hamilton, *Speech of Gen. A.J. Hamilton of Texas, at the War Meeting of Faneuil Hall* (Boston: T. R. Marvin and Son, 1863); Waller, *Colossal Hamilton*, 34–36; *New York Times*, October 3, 1862; *New York Tribune*, October 2, 1862; *Marshall Texas Republican*, November 1, 1862; Stanton to Hamilton, November 14, 1862, OR ser. 3, vol. 2, 782–83. For more examples of the reactions of New York newspapers to Hamilton, see the *Tribune* for September 29 and October 3, 1862, and the *Times* for October 4, 1862.

32. November 28, 1864, John Hancock Diary, Texas State Archives; Banks to Stanton, January 7, 1863, OR ser. 1, vol.15, 642–43. See also Waller, *Colossal Hamilton*, 47–58.

33. Waller, *Colossal Hamilton*, 35, 56–57; *Austin State Gazette*, August 3, 1864. Hamilton's son John died in New Orleans, where the family lived for a time after the war. Obituary of John Hamilton, Scrapbook, Hamilton Papers, Barker Texas History Center.

34. For example, Hamilton's colleague as military governor, Edward Stanly of North Carolina, resigned after Lincoln issued the Emancipation Proclamation. A longtime Republican, he nevertheless believed that freeing and arming the slaves would prevent a peaceful reconstruction of the Union. Norman D. Brown, *Edward Stanly: Whiggery's Tarheel 'Conqueror'* (University: Univ. of Alabama Press, 1974), 249.

35. *Brownsville American Flag*, February 9 and March 17, 1860, John L. Haynes Scrapbook, Barker Texas History Center. For Haynes's thoughts on the Rio Grande troubles, see the Scrapbook in the John L. Haynes Papers, Barker Texas History Center, esp. pp. 12–18. Most of Haynes's articles appeared in the *Austin Southern Intelligencer*.

36. "Address to the People of Starr County," *Southern Intelligencer*, n.d., Haynes Scrapbook. A letter to the *New York Times* dated August 14, 1862, and signed "Tombigbee," presumably written by Haynes, assured northerners that the majority of southerners were not in favor of secession and would welcome reconstruction, as long as immediate emancipation did not become a war aim of the United States government. Haynes Scrapbook.

37. "*Conciudadanos Del Condado De Starr*," June 10, 1859, Haynes Scrapbook, translated by James Boyden; Brown, "Annals of Travis County," chap. 24, 64.

38. James D. Lynch, *The Bench and Bar of Texas* (St Louis, MO: Nixon-Jones Printing Co., 1885), 160–64; DuVal to James Guthrie, May 30, 1864, typescript, Thomas DuVal Papers, Barker Texas History Center; DuVal to A.J. Hamilton, March 16, 1874, Hamilton Papers, Barker Texas History Center; August 8, 1863, DuVal Diary. For DuVal's entertaining and unusually legible observations during his month-long trip from Austin to Washington—during which he discovered northern customs such as honeymoons and compared the beauty of women in the various cities in which he stayed—see his diary entries from October 10 to November 14, 1863.

39. August 3, March 30, March 20, April 25, and April 20, 1863; DuVal Diary.

40. March 28, August 10, May 11, May 26, and September 30, 1863: DuVal Diary.

41. November 21, 27, and 18, 1863, and January 20, 1864; DuVal Dairy. For DuVal's account of his stay in Washington, see his diary entries for November 14 to December 2, 1863. For his experiences during the brief occupation of the Texas coast,

see his entries for December 26, 1863, to March 3, 1864. The surviving volumes of DuVal's diary skip from March 1864 to February 1865.

42. Lynch, *Bench and Bar*, 422–26; speech at LaGrange, quoted in Felgar, "Texas in the War," 41; Hancock to E. B. Burleson, Jr., April 16, 1861, photocopy in Burleson Papers; John Salmon Ford, *Rip Ford's Texas*, ed. Stephen B. Oates (Austin: Univ. of Texas Press, 1963), 333–34; Nannie M. Tilley, ed., *Federals on the Frontier: The Diary of Benjamin F. McIntyre, 1862–1864* (Austin: Univ. of Texas Press, 1963), 34; *Dallas Herald*, February 16, 1865; John Henry Brown, *Indian Wars and Pioneers of Texas* (Austin: L. E. Daniell, 1880), 253–54.

43. February 7, 1865, December 23, 28, and 29, 1864, Hancock Diary.

44. B. H. Mills, "Elisha Marshall Pease: A Biography" (MA thesis, Univ. of Texas, 1927); June 8, 1864, Ballinger Diary; *Marshall Texas Republican*, July 12, 1862. Pease has been a favorite of Texas graduate students. See also Robert Joseph Franzetti, "Elisha Marshall Pease and Reconstruction" (MA thesis, Southwest Texas State Univ., 1970), and Roger Allen Griffin, "Connecticut Yankee in Texas: A Biography of Elisha Marshall Pease" (PhD diss., Univ. of Texas, 1973).

45. Jane Lynn Scarborough, "George W. Paschal: Texas Unionist and Scalawag Jurisprudent" (PhD diss., Rice Univ., 1972), 1–38, 39–68; James P. Hart, "George W. Paschal," *Texas Law Review* 28 (Nov. 1949): 27–28; Elizabeth Paschal O'Connor, *I Myself* (New York: G. P. Putnam's Sons, 1914), 2–5, 16–19; *Weekly Southern Intelligencer*, November 16, 1865. For more on the Paschal-Marshall "duel," see Sibley, *Lone Stars and State Gazettes*, 269–71. For an explanation of his moderate views on slavery and his reluctance to see slavery become a national political issue, see Paschal's biography of his mother, *Ninety Four Years: Agnes Paschal* (Washington, D.C.: George W. Paschal, 1871), 277–86.

46. Paschal to Smyth, April 9, 1860, Smyth Papers; *McKinney Messenger*, September 14, 1860.

47. December 8, 1860, and April 28, 1863, Ballinger Diary, *Marshall Texas Republican*, September 13, 1862; O'Connor, *I Myself*, 28–32; January 28, 1864, DuVal Diary; Scarborough, "George W. Paschal," 72–87.

48. *Austin State Gazette*, October 1, 1862; Elizabeth Paschal O'Connor, *I Myself*, 31, and *My Beloved South* (New York: G.P. Putnam's Sons, 1913), 40; January 14, 1864, DuVal Diary.

49. Paschal to Ballinger, May 1, 1863, Ballinger Papers. For a sample of Ballinger's reaction to Paschal's gloominess, see chapter 3. The second section of the first article of the Confederate Constitution stated that "no person of foreign birth, not a citizen of the Confederate States, shall be allowed to vote for any officer, civil or political, State or Federal." Paschal's letter uncovers the same feelings exhibited by the South Carolina Unionist and attorney, James Louis Petigru, who also defended southerners caught with their disloyalty showing; he wrote in 1862 that he was "the only man of my way of thinking in the state." Petigru to J.J. Pettigrew, March 7, 1862, James Petigru Carson, ed., *Life, Letters, and Speeches of James Louis Petigru* (Washington, D.C., 1920), 436.

50. Charles C. Anderson found 634,255 white and black "southern federals" from the Confederate States and Missouri, Kentucky, Maryland, and the District of Columbia. *Fighting by Southern Federals* (New York: Neale Publishing Co., 1912). Southern white men made up eighty-five Union army regiments. Frederick H. Dyer, ed., *Compendium of the War of the Rebellion* (Des Moines, IA: Dyer Publishing Co., 1908), 21–34. The only state study on southerners fighting for the North is William Stanley Hoole's *Alabama Tories: The First Alabama Cavalry, U. S. A., 1862–1865* (Tuscaloosa, AL: Confederate Publishing Co., 1960), a large part of which consists of rosters of the various units of Alabama cavalrymen.

51. "Index to the Compiled Service Records of Volunteer Union Soldiers Who

Served in Organizations from the State of Texas," Records of the Adjutant General's Office, Record Group 94, National Archives.

52. Webb, *Handbook of Texas*, vol. 1, 44; Charles Anderson, *Speech of Charles Anderson on the State of the Country* (Washington, D.C.: Lemuel Towers, 1860); Ellsworth, "San Antonio," 14–15; Col. Henry McCulloch to Brig. Gen. P.O. Hebert, October 4, 1861, OR ser. 1, vol. 4, 115; Mills, *My Story*, 57–64, 76–77; W. W. Mills, *Forty Years at El Paso* (El Paso: Carl Hertzog, 1962), especially the introduction by Rex W. Strickland, xi–xviii; Webb, *Handbook of Texas*, vol. 2, 201; Thaddeus McRae Autobiography, typescript, Thaddeus McRae Papers, Barker Texas History Center; *Houston Tri-Weekly Telegraph*, January 3, 1864.

53. H. C. Hunt, "The First Texas Cavalry of U.S. Volunteers—Its History," undated newspaper clipping, Haynes Scrapbook; Frank H. Smyrl, "Texans in the Federal Army, 1861–1865," *Southwestern Historical Quarterly* 65 (Oct. 1961): 234–50. All statistics on Texans in the Union Army have been compiled from the "Index to the Compiled Service Records." This record set consists of thousands of slips of paper on which were written a soldier's name, entering and exiting rank, company, and regiment. An effort was made to determine ethnic origins simply by looking at soldiers' surnames. This unscientific method may not guarantee exact results, but it does provide important comparisons of the wartime experiences of Anglo, German, and Mexican Unionists. One confusing characteristic of the compiled index is its proliferation of names; as various clerks tried to straighten out regimental files, they attempted to make sure that the names were spelled correctly. As a result, they filed a separate slip for every different misspelling of the same soldier's name. The problem is especially acute for Hispanic names; a name such as Rodríquez, shared by dozens of tejanos, might go through five or six different versions, creating a sea of identification slips through which a researcher must wade.

54. Ronald N. Gray, "Edmund J. Davis: Radical Republican and Reconstruction Governor of Texas" (PhD diss., Texas Tech Univ., 1976), 1–17; R.H. Williams, *With the Border Ruffians: Memories of the Far West, 1852–1868* ed. E.W. Williams (London: John Murray, 1908), 294.

55. *Corpus Christi Ranchero*, May 3, 1861; E.B. Scarborough to Edward Clark, May 8, 1861, Edward Clark Papers, Governors' Records, Texas State Archives; Gray, "Edmund J. Davis," 18–35, 36–71.

56. Hamilton to Stanton, December 19, 1863, OR ser. 1, vol. 26, pt. 1, 865–66.

57. James Steedman to Charles Steedman, January 6, 1861; Eliza to Charles, December 30, 1860; "Your Devoted Wife" to "Steed," April 1861: all in Charles Steedman Papers, Manuscript Collection, Duke University Library. Later letters to his wife reveal that Charles commanded several United States warships throughout the war and, as a rear admiral, in the South Pacific after the war.

58. James A. Irby, "Confederate Austin, 1861–1865" (MA thesis, Univ. of Texas, 1953), 118. For examples of reports of the poor treatment of relatives of Texans in the federal service, see Col. H. E. McCulloch to Francis Lubbock, March 13, 1862, Francis R. Lubbock Papers, Governors' Records, Texas State Archives, and J.P. Bethell to A.J. Hamilton, September 13, 1865, Hamilton Papers, Governors' Records, Texas State Archives.

59. Ella Lonn, *Desertion during the Civil War* (New York: Century Co., 1928), 235; Tilley, *Federals on the Frontier*, 370; Col. H.M. Day to Maj. William H. Clark, August 3, 1864, OR ser. 1, vol. 41, pt. 2, 532. At least thirty Texans in federal service died while on duty and were buried in their home state. Quartermaster General, U.S. Army, *Roll of Honor; Names of Soldiers Who Died in Defense of the Union. . . .* (Washington, D.C.: Government Printing Office, 1866).

60. See Louis S. Gerteis, *From Contraband to Freedman: Federal Policy toward Southern Blacks, 1861–1865.* (Westport, CT: Greenwood Press, 1973).

61. "Biographical Sketch," S.M. Swenson Papers, Barker Texas History Center; Lynch, *Bench and Bar,* 151–59; Webb, *Handbook of Texas,* vol. 2, 288–89; *Dallas Morning News,* May 12, 1964, A.B. Norton Biographical File, Barker Texas History Center; A.B. Norton, *Speech of Hon. A.B. Norton, in Vindication of History and the Constitution and the Union, in the Texas Legislature, January 24, 1860* (Austin: Southern Intelligencer Press, 1860); *Marshall Texas Republican,* July 12, 1862.

62. Webb, *Handbook of Texas,* vol. 2, 440; Melinda Rankin, *Twenty Years among the Mexicans: A Narrative of Missionary Labor* (Cincinnati: Chase and Hall, 1875), 97–119. Rankin was a missionary in Monterrey from 1865 to 1872; she died in Illinois in 1888.

63. Black to Stratton, October 24 and December 20, 1864, Reading W. Black Papers, Barker Texas History Center.

64. Etchison to Pile, December 7, 1864, Matamoros Consular Dispatches.

65. Noah Smithwick, *The Evolution of a State; or, Recollections of Old Texas Days* (Austin: Gammel Book Co., 1901), 331–36; Pierce to Seward, September 22, 1862, Matamoros Consular Dispatches; M. M. Kimmey to Seward, June 4, 1863, OR ser. 1, vol. 26, pt. 1, 657; Pierce to Seward, December 8, 1864, and Maj. Gen. F.J. Herron to Brig. Gen. Stone, February 2, 1864, Matamoros Consular Dispatches.

66. Tilley, *Federals on the Frontier,* 371–72. The Confederate commander in the area, Col. John Ford, refused to allow local vigilantes to confiscate the houses of Unionists in Brownsville for the use of loyal families. Ford, *Rip Ford's Texas,* 366. For the federal policy on loyalty oaths and the dangers that faced southerners who took them, see Harold M. Hyman, *A More Perfect Union: The Impact of the Civil War and Reconstruction on the Constitution* (New York: Alfred A. Knopf, 1973), 147–70, and *To Try Men's Souls: Loyalty Tests in American History* (Berkeley: Univ. of California Press, 1959), 193–96 (see pp. 139–250 for his complete discussion of the war years).

67. December 4 and 3, 1864, Hancock Diary.

68. December 25, 1863, DuVal Diary.

69. *Loyal National Union Journal,* March 5, 12, and 19, 1864; March 5, 1864, DuVal Diary.

70. F. F. Fenn, et al., to Maj. Gen. F. J. Herron, January 8, 1864, Kingsbury Papers.

71. Williams, *With the Border Ruffians,* 294–98; *Dallas Herald,* April 8, 1863; Vicki Betts, "Private and Amateur Hangings': The Lynching of W. W. Montgomery, March 15, 1863," *Southwestern Historical Quarterly* 88 (Oct. 1984): 145–66. Montgomery was a Caldwell County sheep rancher before the war, and appears to have been a former Kansas Jayhawker. A. J. Hamilton had secured his acquittal on a murder charge in Austin in 1855. *Austin State Gazette,* January 12, 1861; Waller, *Colossal Hamilton,* 35.

72. Betts, "Private and Amateur Hangings," 151–55; Leonard Pierce to William Seward, March 26, 1863, Matamoros Consular Dispatches; Tilley, *Federals on the Frontier,* 277–78. For other diplomatic correspondence regarding the incident, see J. A. Quinterro to Judah P. Benjamin, March 21, 1863, and H. P. Bee to Quinterro, March 16, 1863, OR ser. 1, vol. 26, pt. 2, 67–70. A rumor circulated shortly after the lynching that Montgomery's head had been cut off and carried to Brownsville as a trophy. Rankin, *Twenty Years,* 102. A. J. L. Fremantle's Confederate escort showed him what was purported to be Montgomery's gravesite while guiding the British tourist to Brownsville. Fremantle reported that "he had been slightly buried." His head and arms—multilated by wild dogs—were above the ground, and a rope still encircled the

body's neck. Walter Lord, ed., *The Fremantle Diary* (Boston: Little, Brown & Co., 1954), 7–9.

73. *Victoria Advocate*, March 28, 1863, copied from the *Brownsville Fort Brown Flag*, March 13, 1863; *Clarksville Standard*, April 25, 1863, copied from the *Brownsville Flag*, n.d.

74. Haynes to Hamilton, June 13, 1863, typescript in Hamilton Papers, Barker Texas History Center.

75. A. W. Bishop, *Loyalty on the Frontier; or, Sketches of Union Men of the Southwest* (St. Louis, MO: R. P. Studley and Co., 1863), 5; Abraham Lincoln to Nathaniel Banks, September 19, 1863, in Roy P. Basler, ed., *The Collected Works of Abraham Lincoln*, vol. 6 (Springfield, IL: Abraham Lincoln Association, 1955), 465–66. Harold Hyman writes that "many federal soldiers failed completely to see how swearing a Union oath made a Southerner less a rebel." *To Try Men's Souls*, 196.

5. SPECULATORS, DESERTERS, AND BANDITS

1. Bell I. Wiley, *The Road to Appomattox* (Memphis, TN: Memphis State College Press, 1956), 67; Smith to H. E. McCulloch, October 2, 1863, OR ser. 1, vol. 26, pt. 2, 285; Magruder to W. R. Boggs, April 20, 1864, OR ser. 1, vol. 34, pt. 3, 779–80; Throckmorton to Josiah Crosby, March 19, 1865, James W. Throckmorton Papers, Barker Texas History Center.

2. Frank L. Owsley, "Defeatism in the Confederacy," *North Carolina Historical Review* 3 (July 1926); 446–56; Georgia Lee Tatum, *Disloyalty in the Confederacy* (Chapel Hill: Univ. of North Carolina Press, 1934), 3–23; Charles H. Wesley, *The Collapse of the Confederacy* (Washington, D.C.: Associated Publishers, 1937), 74–104; Wiley, *Road to Appomattox*, 43–76; Clement Eaton, *A History of the Southern Confederacy* (New York: Free Press, 1954), 250–68; David Donald, "Died of Democracy," in Donald, ed., *Why the North Won the Civil War* (Baton Rouge: Louisiana State Univ. Press, 1960), 79–90; Paul D. Escott, *After Secession: Jefferson Davis and the Failure of Confederate Nationalism* (Baton Rouge: Louisiana State Univ. Press, 1978); Emory M. Thomas, *The Confederate Nation: 1861–1865*. (New York: Harper and Row, 1979), 234–35, 285–86, 297–99. A recent, controversial interpretation of how the weakness of Confederate nationalism, the peculiar nature of southern religion, and military defeats combined to sap Confederate morale can be found in Richard F. Beringer et al., *Why the South Lost the Civil War* (Athens: Univ. of Georgia Press, 1986). For information on dissent in other states, see Walter L. Fleming, *Civil War and Reconstruction in Alabama* (New York: Macmillan 1905), 113–14, 138–48; Hugh C. Bailey, "Disaffection in the Alabama Hill Country, 1861," *Civil War History* 4 (June 1958), 183–192; T. Conn Bryan, *Confederate Georgia* (Athens: Univ. of Georgia Press, 1953), 139–51; John K. Bettersworth, *Confederate Mississippi: The People and Politics of a Cotton State in Wartime* (Baton Rouge: Louisiana State Univ. Press, 1943), 188–245; Rudy H. Leverett, *Legend of the Free State of Jones* (Jackson: Univ. Press of Mississippi, 1984); Henry T. Shanks, "Disloyalty to the Confederacy in Southwestern Virginia, 1861–1865," *North Carolina Historical Review* 21 (April 1944): 118–35; John G. Barrett, *The Civil War in North Carolina* (Chapel Hill: Univ. of North Carolina Press, 1963), 181–89; William T. Auman and David D. Scarboro, "The Heroes of America in Civil War North Carolina," *North Carolina Historical Review* 58 (Oct. 1981): 327–63; and Horace W. Raper, "William W. Holden and the Peace Movement in North Carolina," *North Carolina Historical Review* 31 (Oct. 1854): 493–516; Ted R. Worley, "The Arkansas Peace Society of 1861: A Study in Mountain Unionism," *Journal of Southern History* 24 (Nov. 1958): 445–56; Wilfred Buck Yearns, *The Confederate Congress* (Athens: Univ. of Georgia Press, 1960), 171–83.

3. *Dallas Herald*, March 8, 1862; Gammel, *Laws of Texas, 1822–1897*, vol. 5, 483, 674, 684–85; quoted in Ruby Garner, "Galveston during the Civil War" (MA thesis, Univ. of Texas, 1927), 36.

4. Wiley to Edward Clark, April 4, 1861, and Carothers to Clark, April 14, 1861, Clark Papers, Governors' Records, Texas State Archives.

5. *Dallas Herald*, October 16, October 30, and November 6, 1861.

6. James Thornton to Pendleton Murrah, April 10, 1864, and Mrs. F. Cockran to Murrah, November 11, 1863: both in Murrah Papers; John Q. Anderson, ed., *Brokenburn: The Journal of Kate Stone, 1861–1868*. (Baton Rouge: Louisiana State Univ. Press, 1955), 242, 256–57, 238, 275. Another Louisiana refugee in Texas, Frances Fearn, found a much warmer reception from the people she encountered. See Fearn, *Diary of a Refugee* (New York: Moffat, Yard, and Co., 1910), 37–38. The only secondary account of white refugees in the Confederacy is Mary Elizabeth Massey's thorough *Refugee Life in the Confederacy* (Baton Rouge: Louisiana State Univ. Press, 1964).

7. For the economic background of Civil War Texas, see Dugas, "A Social and Economic History," e5p. pp. 240–323.

8. Alexander Gregg, *The Sin of Extortion, and Its Peculiar Aggravations at a Time Like the Present* (Austin: Texas Almanac Office, 1863), 2.

9. *Houston Tri-weekly Telegraph*, February 4, 1863; Gammel, *Laws of Texas*, vol. 5, 500, 657; Day, *House Journal, Ninth Legislature, First Called Session*, 62,100, 170–71; May Spence Ringold, *The Role of the State Legislatures in the Confederacy* (Athens: Univ. of Georgia Press, 1966), 73; Yearns, *Confederate Congress*, 132–33.

10. *San Antonio Weekly Herald*, November 9, 1861; Thomas C. Smith, *Here's Yer Mule: The Diary of Thomas C. Smith* (Waco, TX: Little Texian Press, 1958), 12; David G. McComb, *Houston: The Bayou City* (Austin: Univ. of Texas Press, 1969), 74; *New Braunfels Zeitung*, November 7, 1862, translation in Oscar Haas Collection, Texas State Archives; Annie C. Terrill, "A Calendar of the Memorials and Petitions to the Legislature of Texas, 1861–1877" (MA thesis, Univ. of Texas, 1936), 19; Barr, "Records of the Confederate Military Commission," 71 (Oct. 1967): 258–60, 247–52.

11. *San Antonio Weekly Herald*, April 26, 1862; *San Antonio Semi-Weekly News*, April 28, 1862; *Dallas Herald*, August 2, 1862; *Marshall Texas Republican*, January 3, 1863; *Austin State Gazette*, August 12, 1863. For a striking discussion of economic disloyalty—particularly the "Sin of Extortion"—in the context of Confederate nationalism and southern religion, see Faust, *The Creation of Confederate Nationalism*, 41–57.

12. Mattie Davis Lucas and Mita H. Hall, *A History of Grayson County, Texas* (Sherman, TX: Scurggs Printing Co., 1936), 118–21; Chance, *The Second Texas Infantry*, 143. For the best account of the most famous riot in the Confederacy, see Michael B. Chesson, "Harlots or Heroines? A New Look at the Richmond Bread Riot," *Virginia Magazine of History and Biography* 92 (April 1984): 131–75.

13. James K. Blair to Clark, May 23, 1861, and R. English to Clark, October 15, 1861: both in Clark Papers; Charles Shearn to Lubbock, December 6, 1861, and B. L. Peel to Lubbock, December 7, 1861: both in Lubbock Papers; Williams, *With the Border Ruffians*, 277–78; copied by *Arkansas Patriot*, March 5, 1863.

14. Charles W. Ramsdell, "The Texas State Military Board, 1862–1865," *Southwestern Historical Quarterly* 27 (April 1924): 253–75; Ludwell H. Johnson, "Trading with the Union: The Evolution of Confederate Policy," *Virginia Magazine of History and Biography* 78 (July 1970): 308–25. For trading with the enemy along the Mississippi River, see Bettersworth, *Confederate Mississippi*, 174–87; Lawrence N. Powell and Michael S. Wayne, "Self-Interest and the Decline of Confederate Nationalism," in *The Old South in the Crucible of War*, ed. Harry P. Owens and James J. Cooke (Jackson: Univ. Press of Mississippi, 1983), 29–45; and Gary B. Mills, "Alexandria, Louisiana: A

'Confederate' City at War with Itself," *Red River Valley Historical Review* 5 (Winter 1980): 23–36.

15. Quoted in the *Austin Tri-Weekly State Gazette*, June 25, 1863; Anne Cowling, "The Civil War Trade of the Lower Rio Grande Valley" (MA thesis, Univ. of Texas, 1926); McComb, *Houston*, 25–26; Steven Strom, ed., "Cotton and Profits across the Border: William Marsh Rice in Mexico, 1863–1865," *Houston Review* 8 (1986): 89–96. A valuable survey of the diplomatic, military, and political contexts of the southern trade through Matamoros, Mexico, is James W. Daddysman's *The Matamoros Trade: Confederate Commerce, Diplomacy, and Intrigue* (Newark: Univ. of Delaware Press, 1984).

16. Brackenridge to Alexander W. Terrell, June 12, 1912, Alexander W. Terrell Papers, Barker Texas History Center; Thomas H. Franklin, "George W. Brackenridge," *Alcalde* 8 (March 1921): 407–09; Marilyn McAdams Sibley, *George W. Brackenridge: Maverick Philanthropist* (Austin: Univ. of Texas Press, 1973), 33–84, and "Charles Stillman: A Case Study of Entrepreneurship on the Rio Grande, 1861–1865," *Southwestern Historical Quarterly* 77 (Oct. 1973): 227–40.

17. "The Fall of Brownsville on the Rio Grande, November 1863," pp. 4–9, John Warren Hunter Biographical File, Barker Texas History Center.

18. Wiley, *Road to Appomattox*, 48; Lonn, *Desertion during the Civil War*, 231.

19. *Houston Tri-Weekly Telegraph*, November 5, 1862, quoted in Chance, *The Second Texas Infantry*, 52; Rebecca W. Smith and Marion Mullins, eds., "The Diary of H.C. Medford, Confederate Soldier, 1864," *Southwestern Historical Quarterly* 34 (Oct. 1930), 120–21; William Physick Zuber, *My Eighty Years in Texas*, ed. Janis Boyle Mayfield (Austin: Univ. of Texas Press, 1971), 196; quoted in Campbell, *A Southern Community in Crisis*, 235. See also Lonn, *Desertion during the Civil War*, 3–20; Bell I. Wiley, *The Life of Johnny Reb: The Common Soldier of the Confederacy* (Baton Rouge: Louisiana State Univ. Press, 1978), 123–50; Martin, *Desertion of Alabama Troops*; and Richard Bardolph, "Inconstant Rebels: Desertion of North Carolina Troops in the Civil War," *North Carolina Historical Review* 41 (April 1964): 163–89.

20. Norman D. Brown, ed., *One of Cleburne's Command: The Civil War Reminiscences and Diary of Capt. Samuel T. Foster, Granbury's Texas Brigade, CSA* (Austin: Univ. of Texas Press, 1980), 151; Rudolf Coreth to Family, October 25 and December 24, 1863, February 4, 1864, in Minnetta Altgelt Goyne, *Lone Star and Double Eagle: Civil War Letters of a German-Texas Family* (Lubbock: Texas Christian Univ. Press, 1982), 107, 114–15, 119.

21. Ford to Edmund P. Turner, July 22, 1863, OR ser. 1, vol. 26, pt. 2, 119; McCulloch to Maj. Gen. J. B. Magruder, October 21, 1863, ibid., 344–45. For early resistance to conscription in Texas, see Fredericka Ann Meiners, "The Texas Governorship, 1861–1865: Biography of an Office" (PhD diss., Rice Univ., 1974), 123–54. The first Conscription Act of April 16, 1862, and its September amendment required all men between the ages of eighteen and forty-five to serve three years in the army, except for laborers in vital industries. The Second Conscription Act of February 17, 1864, made all men between the ages of seventeen and fifty liable to conscription. Thomas, *Confederate Nation*, 152–54, 260.

22. McCulloch to Magruder, February 3, 1864, and McCulloch to Smith, February 5, 1864, OR ser. 1, vol. 34, pt. 2, 941–43, 945; McCulloch to Capt. Edmund P. Turner, November 9, 1863, OR ser. 1, vol. 26, pt. 2, 401.

23. Lovenskold to Slaughter, November 23, 1864, copy in Murrah Papers.

24. McCulloch to Gov. Francis Lubbock, March 37, 1862, Lubbock Papers; *Austin State Gazette*, March 15, 1863; Magruder to Brig. Gen. W. R. Boggs, May 20, 1864, OR ser. 1, vol. 34, pt. 3, 833–34; *Texas Almanac Extra*, February 27 and March 3, 1863; Zuber, *My Eighty Years in Texas*, 223; Rawick, *American Slave*, supp. 2, vol. 6, pt. 5, 2125. For one reluctant Confederate's experiences as a deserter, frontier defender,

and Union scout, see L. D. Clark, ed., *Civil War Recollections of James Lemuel Clark* (College Station: Texas A & M Univ. Press, 1984).

25. Felgar, "Texas in the War," 200–225.

26. Magruder to Murrah, April 2, 1864, Murrah Papers; Governor's Message, May 11, 1864, in James M. Day, ed., *Senate and House Journals of the Tenth Legislature, First Called Session* (Austin: Texas State Library, 1965), 19; to Charles Besser from his wife, June 29, 1861, Charles Besser Civil War Biographical File, Barker Texas History Center; Kaleta Hardin to William Hardin, June 1, 1864, in Camilla Davis Trammell, *Seven Pines: Its Occupants and Their Letters, 1825–1872* (Dallas: Southern Methodist Univ. Press, 1987), 200.

27. "Instructions to Enrolling Officers," July 4, 1862, Broadside Collection, Barker Texas History Center; *San Antonio Weekly Herald*, April 26, 1862; *Brownsville Fort Brown Flag*, April 17, 1862; *Bexar County Court Journal*, vol. 2A, June 1863, Special Term, February 1864 Term, October 1864 Term, pp. 483, 515, 557, Microfilm Reel 1019358; Day, *Senate and House Journals, Tenth Legislature, First Called Session*, 63, 109, 128; *Marshall Texas Republican*, February 26, 1863; Governor's Message, November 24, 1863, Day, *Senate Journal, Tenth Legislature, First Called Session*, 104, 96.

28. *Clarksville Standard*, July 18 and November 28, 1863, and January 9, 1864; *Dallas Herald*, May 29, 1863; *Marshall Texas Republican*, February 26, 1863. North Carolina and Georgia also set penalties for aiding deserters, while the Confederate Congress dealt with the problem ineffectually. Ringold, *State Legislatures*, 28; Yearns, *Confederate Congress*, 114–15.

29. Petty to his wife, January 29, March 4, March 13, and March 15, 1863, in Norman D. Brown, ed., *Journey to Pleasant Hill: The Civil War Letters of Captain Elijah P. Petty, Walker's Texas Division, CSA* (San Antonio: Institute of Texan Cultures, 1982), 134, 145, 148, 151.

30. Quoted in Brown, *One of Cleburne's Command*, xxxix; quoted in Chance, *The Second Texas Infantry*, 94, 54–55; Zuber, *My Eighty Years in Texas*, 199.

31. Paul C. Boethel, *History of Lavaca County* (Austin: Von-Boeckmann-Jones, 1959), 81–82; Cain to John R. Hill, n.d. (ca 1863), John R. Hill Papers, Barker Texas History Center.

32. Lord, *Fremantle Diary*, 19; January 17, 1865, and December 9, 1864, Hancock Diary.

33. Copies of the Ferguson letters, dated March 10, 1862; Sweet to Lubbock, March 27, 1862; Brig. Gen. H. P. Bee to Lubbock, May 5, 1862: all in Lubbock Papers.

34. *Austin State Gazette*, October 14, 1863; Rawick, *American Slave*, supp. 2, vol. 2, pt. 1, 64; Sophia to Levi, January 24, 1864, in Davis Bitton, ed., *Reminiscences and Civil War Letters of Levi Lamon Wight* (Salt Lake City: Univ. of Utah Press, 1970), 147–48; Boethel, *Lavaca County*, 82–84; George W. Tyler, *The History of Bell County* (San Antonio: Naylor Co., 1936), 241–42; Ernst Coreth to Rudolf, May 19, 1865, in Goyne, *Lone Star and Double Eagle*, 172. For bands of outlaw deserters and disaffected southerners in other parts of the Confederacy, see John D. Winters, *The Civil War in Louisiana* (Baton Rouge: Louisiana State Univ. Press, 1963), 307, 387; Bryan, *Confederate Georgia*, 144–46; Barrett, *The Civil War in North Carolina*, 174–77, 186, 239–43; Fleming, *Civil War and Reconstruction in Alabama*, 119–21, 128; Bettersworth, *Confederate Mississippi*, 213–17, 234–41; John F. Reiger, "Deprivation, Disaffection, and Desertion in Confederate Florida," *Florida Historical Quarterly* 8 (Jan. 1970): 279–98.

35. "Address to the People of Texas," Taylor papers; Graham Landrum and Allan Smith, *Grayson County* (Fort Worth, TX: Historical Publishers, 1967), 70–71; William E. Sawyer, "Martin Hart, Civil War Guerrilla," *Texas Military History* 3 (Fall 1963): 146–47.

36. *Marshall Texas Republican.* January 29, 1863; Sawyer, "Martin Hart," 148–53; James M. Day, ed., *House Journal of the Ninth Legislature, First Called Session* (Austin: Texas State Library, 1963), 98. Later in the year officials in Hunt and Hopkins counties hanged seven of Hart's men for "robbery, murder, and treason." *Marshall Texas Republican,* April 4, 1863. The most famous outlaw guerrillas, of course, performed their deeds in Missouri. See Richard S. Brownlee, *Gray Ghosts of the Confederacy: Guerilla Warfare in the West, 1861–1865.* (Baton Rouge: Louisiana State Univ. Press, 1958).

37. Boyd W. Johnson, "Cullen Montgomery Baker: The Arkansas-Texas Desperado," *Arkansas Historical Quarterly* 25 (Autumn 1966): 229–34.

38. Al Eason, "Cullen Baker—Purveyor of Death," *Frontier Times* 40 (Aug.–Sept. 1966): 12, 67; Johnson, "Cullen Montgomery Baker," 234–39; *New York Tribune,* September 29, 1868.

39. T. U. Taylor, "Swamp Fox of the Sulphur; or, The Life and Times of Cullen Montgomery Baker," typescript, Barker Texas History Center, 58–60, 23–25, 30, 54–55; Rawick, *American Slave,* supp. 2, vol. 8, pt. 7, 3363; supp. 2, vol. 5, pt. 4, 1823.

40. Petition from residents of Collin County to Murrah, enclosed with letter from G. B. Breedlove to Murrah, November 19, 1864; Throckmorton to Murrah, December 9, 1864: both in Murrah Papers.

41. Thomas Barrett, *The Great Hanging at Gainesville* (Gainesville, 1885; Austin: Texas State Historical Association, 1961), 12; *Marshall Texas Republican,* November 1, 1862; Sam Acheson and Julie Ann Hudson O'Connell, eds., "George Washington Diamond's Account of the Great Hanging at Gainesville, 1862," *Southwestern Historical Quarterly* 66 (Jan. 1963): 344–49, 350.

42. *Marshall Texas Republican,* November 1, 1862; Acheson and O'Connell, "Diamond's Account of the Great Hanging," 360–64; Barrett, *The Great Hanging,* 13; James M. Smallwood, "Disaffection in Confederate Texas: The Great Hanging at Gainesville," *Civil War History* 22 (Dec. 1976): 349–60. Although Smallwood believes that the organization was initially formed to provide a safe forum for the expression of Unionist opinions, he gives credence to many of the more violent objectives that Confederates accused the group of planning. On February 20, 1864, *Frank Leslie's Illustrated Newspaper* printed woodcuts of "Rebel Barbarities in Texas" that were based on sketches made by a former North Texas Unionist who had barely escaped hanging in Gainesville. Included was a sketch of dozens of the "over 100" men hanged in Cook[e] County in 1862.

43. *Clarksville Standard,* November 1, 1862; Throckmorton to J. J. Diamond, May 25, 1867, Throckmorton Papers; Elliott, *Leathercoat,* 75; Roy F. Hall and Helen G. Hall, *Collin County: Pioneering in North Texas* (Quanah, TX: Nortex Press, 1975), 57–58; Ford, *Rip Ford's Texas,* 338. For Diamond's similar explanation for the organization and vigilant repression of this group, see Acheson and O'Connell, "Diamond's Account of the Great Hanging," 340–43.

44. Magruder to Smith, December 24, 1863, OR ser. 1, vol. 26, pt. 2, 528–31; Austin to Pease, July 30, 1865, E. M. Pease Papers, Austin History Center.

6. ETHNIC TEXANS AND THE WAR

1. Olmsted, *A Journey through Texas;* 440, 431, 432–33.

2. Ibid., 456.

3. Rawick, *American Slave,* vol. 4, pt. 2, 126–29. Age and time may have erased the sorrows and exaggerated the joys of southern slaves; by the same token, decades of discrimination and poverty may have deepened their resentment and affected their memories. Witin reason, however, I have taken the slaves' testimonies at face value.

4. See Benjamin Quarles, *The Negro in the Civil War* (Boston: Little, Brown & Co., 1953); Harvey Wish, "Slave Disloyalty under the Confederacy," *Journal of Negro History* 23 (Oct. 1938), 435–50; C. Peter Ribley, *Slaves and Freedmen in Civil War Louisiana* (Baton Rouge: Louisiana State Univ. Press, 1976); Clarence L. Mohr, *On the Threshold of Freedom: Masters and Slaves in Civil War Georgia* (Athens: Univ. of Georgia Press, 1986); Robert Francis Engs, *Freedom's First Generation: Black Hampton, Virginia, 1861–1890* (Philadelphia: Univ. of Pennyslvania Press, 1979), 3–79; Ronald L. F. Davis, *Good and Faithful Labor: From Slavery to Sharecropping in the Natchez District, 1860–1890* (Westport, CT: Greenwood Publishing Co., 1982), 60–73; Willie Lee Rose, *Rehearsal for Reconstruction: The Port Royal Experiment* (New York: Bobbs-Merrill Co., 1964); and James H. Brewer, *The Confederate Negro: Virginia's Craftsmen and Military Laborers, 1861–1865.* (Durham, NC: Duke Univ. Press, 1969).

5. *Marshall Texas Republican*, June 2, 1965.

6. *Marshall Texas Republican*, January 6, 1865; *Houston Tri-Weekly Telegraph*, July 30, 1862; *Texas Almanac Extra*, April 9 and 28, 1863; Rawick, *American Slave*, vol. 5, pt. 4, 209; vol. 4, pt. 1, 194–96 and 182–84; supp. 2, vol. 9, pt. 8, 3609–23.

7. Rawick, *American Slave*, supp. 2, vol. 9, pt. 8, 3561; *Houston Tri-Weekly Telegraph*, January 11, 1864; Lena Dancy Ledbetter Reminiscence, Mrs. L. D. Ledbetter Collection, Barker Texas History Center; Rawick, *American Slave*, vol. 4, pt. 2, 131–34; vol. 4, pt. 2, 189.

8. See testimony of Mollie Dawson and Andy Anderson in Rawick, *American Slave*, supp. 2, vol. 4, pt. 3, 1141; vol. 4, pt. 1, 14–16; Lack, "Urban Slavery," 305–8.

9. Rawick, *American Slave*, vol. 5, pt. 4, 140; supp. 2, vol. 10, pt. 9, 4335; supp. 2, vol. 6, pt. 5, 2213–14; vol. 5, pt. 4, 14.

10. Smyrl, "Unionism, Abolitionism, and Vigilantism," 146–60; Rawick, *American Slave*, vol. 4, pt.1, 14–16; vol. 5, pt. 3, 256; supp. 2, vol. 7, pt. 6, 2801, 2495. In Tennessee, where Union lines were always relatively close and where masters had far more to worry about than a few unruly bondsmen, slaves aggressively forced a relaxation of controls and often ran away. See John Cimprich, *Slavery's End in Tennessee, 1861–1865.* (University: Univ. of Alabama Press, 1985).

11. Rawick, *American Slave*, vol. 4, pt. 1, 141; vol. 5, pt. 4, 224; *Houston Telegraph*, December 29, 1864; Tilley, *Federals on the Frontier*, 264.

12. *Houston Tri-Weekly Telegraph*, January 24, 1865; *San Antonio News* quoted in Kerby, *Kirby Smith's Confederacy*, 401; Rufe Byler to Martha Byler, May 15, 1863, Dobie-Byler Family Papers, Barker Texas History Center; *Marshall Texas Republican*, March 5, 1863; March 30 and August 13, 14, and 16, 1864, John B. Walker Plantation Book, Barker Texas History Center.

13. Lizzie to Will Neblett, November 4 and August 13 and 18, 1863, Lizzie Neblett Papers, Barker Texas History Center.

14. May 30, 1863, Ballinger Diary; *Marshall Texas Republican*, December 23, 1864; Kerby, *Kirby Smith's Confederacy*, 257; *San Antonio Herald*, copied by the *Marshall Texas Republican*, May 19, 1865; Gammel, *Laws of Texas*, vol. 5, 601–3, 608–10, 484, 762–63; Wilson, "The Ordeal of William H. Cowdin," 16–26; *Austin Tri-Weekly State Gazette*, July 14, 1863. The law enslaving captured black soldiers was not always enforced; over thirty blacks captured at Galveston early in 1863 roamed freely about Houston for a year-and-a-half, despite complaints from residents. Andrew Forest Muir, "The Free Negro in Harris County, Texas," *Southwestern Historical Quarterly* 46 (Jan. 1943): 235–37.

15. George W. Davis to his sister, February 8, 1863, in Trammell, *Seven Pines*, 192; Rawick, *American Slave*, vol. 4, pt. 1, 108; vol. 5, pt. 4, 125; *Marshall Texas Republican*, May 19 and 5, 1865.

16. *Marshall Texas Republican*, June 16, 1865.

17. Denison to Salmon P. Chase, May 1862, Bourne and Moore "Diary and Correspondence of Salmon P. Chase," 300.

18. Stephen Schwartz, *Twenty-Two Months a Prisoner of War* (St. Louis, MO: A. F. Nelson Publishing Co., 1892), 26–27, 43–53.

19. Charles Montague to Edward Clark, July 9, 1861, Clark Papers.

20. Thomas B. White to Lubbock, March 20, 1862; McCulloch to Lubbock, March 27, 1862; Petition from Citizens of Guadalupe County, March 22, 1862: all in Lubbock Papers; Wells to Ballinger, October 27, 1862, Ballinger Papers.

21. Bliss Reminiscences, 61; Lord, *Fremantle Diary*, 18; Williams, *With the Border Ruffians*, 267.

22. *Memorial of Anthony M. Dignowitz*, 37th Cong., 2d sess., 1861, S. Misc. Doc. 9; August Schuchard to Hamilton, August 7, 1865, Hamilton Papers, Governors' Records, Texas State Archives.

23. Biesele, "Texas State Convention of Germans," 255; *Biographical Directory of the American Congress, 1774–1971* (Washington, D.C.: Government Printing Office, 1971), 843.

24. Barr, "Records of the Confederate Military Commission," 73 (Oct. 1969): 246–48, letter on 193.

25. Rev. E. M. Wheelock, "In Memoriam—Hon. Jacob Kuechler," Jacob Kuechler Biographical File, Barker Texas History Center; Hertzberg to Hamilton, June 27, 1865, Hamilton Papers, Governors' Records, Texas State Archives.

26. Barr, "Records of the Confederate Military Commission," 71 (Oct. 1967): 260–71, 253–58; 73 (July 1969): 83–90. The three men escaped together in August 1862, and made their way to Mexico. Braubach served in the Union army as a captain in the First Texas Cavalry. Maj. Gen. N.J.T. Dana to Brig. Gen. Charles R. Stone, Dec. 27, 1863, OR ser. 1, vol. 26, pt. 1, 885–86; Brown, "Annals of Travis County," chap. 24, 64.

27. Barr, "Records of the Conferate Military Commission," 73 (Oct. 1969): 266; Louis E. Brister, "William von Rosenberg's *Kirtik:* A History of the Society for the Protection of German Immigrants to Texas," *Southwestern Historical Quarterly* 85 (Oct. 1981): 161–63; Christine Schott, "Gustavus Schleicher: A Representative of the Early German Emigrants in Texas," *West Texas Historical Association Yearbook* 28 (Oct. 1952), 50–64.

28. Robert W. Stephens, *August Buchel: Texan Soldier of Fortune* (Dallas: Privately printed, 1970), 1–6; Felgar, "Texas in the War," 341.

29. Joseph Bruckmuller, "Description of the Family and Life of Joseph Bruckmuller," typewritten translation, Barker Texas History Center.

30. Rudolf Coreth to his family, December 31, 1861, in Goyne, *Lone Star and Double Eagle*, 30; biographical information on pp. 18, 127–58.

31. August Siemering, "German Immigration into Texas," 1015-D, translated typescript, Dresel Scrapbook, Barker Texas History Center; Rudolf to his family, May 10, 1863, and May 11, 1862, in Goyne, *Lone Star and Double Eagle*, 84, 56.

32. Rudolf to his family, December 23, 1864, and March 15, 1862, in Goyne, *Lone Star and Double Eagle*, 154, 47.

33. *Dallas Herald*, September 6, 1862. The factual details for this brief account of an oft-told tale come from Robert W. Shook, "The Battle of the Nueces, August 10, 1862," *Southwestern Historical Quarterly* 66 (July 1962): 31–42. For participants' accounts, see Williams, *With the Border Ruffians*, 232–51, on the Confederate side, and John W. Sansom, "Battle of Nueces River in Kinney County, Texas, August 10, 1862," Barker Texas History Center, on the Germans' side. Robert P. Felgar provides a good account of this incident and other persecutions of the Germans in "Texas in the War," 340–56.

34. Smith, *Here's Yer Mule*, 19–20.

35. Lt. C.D. McRae to Maj. F.F. Gray, August 18, 1862, OR ser. 1, vol. 9, 614–16.

36. Fehrenbach, *Lone Star*, 364; William Banta and J. W. Cadwell, Jr., "Twenty-seven Years on the Frontier; or, Fifty Years in Texas, Vol. 1: Life of J. W. Cadwell, Sr.," pp. 220, 223, typescript in Barker Texas History Center; Rudolf Coreth to his family, August 26, 1862, in Goyne, *Lone Star and Double Eagle*, 66; Barr, "Records of the Confederate Military Commission," 73 (Oct. 1969): 270–72.

37. James B. Martin, "Terror in Texas: Violence and Fear in the Hill Country during the Civil War," Seminar paper, Univ. of Texas at Austin, 1985; A.J. Bell to Maj. J.P. Flewellen, Nov. 28, 1862; Brig. Gen. William G. Webb to Maj. A.G. Dickinson, Jan. 4, 1863; Capt. E.P. Turner to Lt. Col. H.L. Webb, Jan. 12 and 21, 1863; all in OR ser. 1, vol. 15, 887, 926–28, 945–46, 955. Lord, *Fremantle Diary*, 43; quoted in J.B. Wilkinson, *Laredo and the Rio Grande Frontier* (Austin: Jenkins Publishing Co., 1975), 284.

38. Carl L. Duaine, *The Dead Men Wore Boots: An Account of the Thirty-second Texas Volunteer Cavalry, CSA, 1862–1865.* (Austin: San Felipe Press, 1966), 23–24. Historians have not agreed on the extent to which Germans were actually disloyal to the Confederacy. Rena M. Andrews argued that the Germans' antislavery tendencies and the seriousness with which they took their oath to the United States (as immigrants and new citizens) caused them to become the "nucleus" of disaffection against the Confederacy. Robert W. Shook wrote that Germans "remained loyal to the Union for the most part," while Bobby Weaver found that "most of the colonists" of a colony in Medina County left for Mexico. On the other hand, Andrews also asserts that Germans who had come to Texas prior to the 1840s generally supported the South during the war. Ella Lonn found that Germans eventually came to support secession, at least cautiously; they were characterized during the war mainly by their desire to be left alone. E.R. Tausch, maintains—in the most reasonable, if cautious, argument—that Texas Germans were no more or less loyal to the Confederacy than other Texans. Andrews, "German Pioneers in Texas," 29, 32–34, 46–54; Shook, "German Unionism in Texas," iv; Weaver, *Castro's Colony*, 135–40; Lonn, *Foreigners in the Confederacy*, 311–13 (see pp. 417–38 for Lonn's description of the persecution of Germans in the Confederacy during the war); Tausch, "Southern Sentiment among the Texas Germans," 54–70.

39. McCulloch to Lubbock, March 27, 1862, Lubbock Papers; Olmsted, *A Journey through Texas*, 456; Ash, "Mexican Texans in the Civil War," iii–v. Ash writes that "many Mexicans had no interest either in insuring the success of the Confederacy or in preserving the Union." They "were concerned primarily with promoting their own interests."

40. Ronnie C. Tyler, *Santiago Vidaurri and the Southern Confederacy* (Austin: Texas State Historical Association, 1973), 41–61, 98–156; quoted in *Austin Weekly State Gazette*, October 14, 1863.

41. "Influence of the Benavides Family," John S. Ford Papers, Texas State Archives; Jerry Don Thompson, *Vaqueros in Blue and Gray* (Austin: Presidial Press, 1976), 16–17, 22–23; Ford to Clark, April 21, 1861, Ford Papers; Brig. Gen. H.P. Bee to Don Albino Lopez, Governor of Tamaulipas, February 3, 1863, and Lopez to Bee, February 11, 1863, OR ser. 1, vol. 15, 966–67, 975–78; Nueces County Historical Society, *The History of Nueces County* (Austin: Jenkins Publishing Co., 1972), 64, 74; Wilkinson, *Laredo and the Rio Grande Frontier*, 288–89.

42. Thompson, *Vaqueros in Blue and Gray*, 81, 25–31.

43. Ash, "Mexican Texans in the Civil War," 37–71, 72–102.

44. Lt. Col. A. Buchel to Maj. Samuel B. Davis, December 5, 1861, OR ser. 1, vol. 4, 152–53; Williams, *With the Border Ruffians*, 275; Bee to Capt. Edmund P. Turner, April 27, 1863, OR ser. 1, vol. 15, 1056–57.

45. "Index to the Compiled Service Records;" Tilley, *Federals on the Frontier,*

346–47, 338; Thompson, *Vaqueros in Blue and Gray*, 89–92. In her study of desertion in the Confederacy, Ella Lonn wrote rather unsympathetically that "Mexicans seem to have been addicted to desertion." Lonn, *Desertion during the Civil War*, 273.

46. I have drawn most of the material on Benavides from John Denny Riley's "Santos Benavides."

47. N.J.T. Dana to L. Pierce, December 1, 1863, OR ser. 1, vol. 26, pt. 1, 830; M. Dolan to Maj. Gen. S.A. Hurlbut, April 3, 1865, OR ser. 1, vol. 68, pt. 2, 17–18. The Union General Dana wrote that "I am not disposed to play hide and seek with such cut-throats as [Benavides]."

48. Thompson, *Vaqueros in Blue and Gray*, 71–75; Williams, *With the Border Ruffians*, 289–91; Brig. Gen. H. P. Bee to Capt. Edmund P. Turner, October 28, 1863, OR ser. 1, vol. 26, pt. 1, 448–49.

49. *Loyal National Union Journal*, March 5, 1864; Maj. Gen. N.J.T. Dana to Brig. Gen. Charles P. Stone, December 2, 1863, OR ser. 1, vol. 26, pt. 1, 830–31; Thompson, *Vaqueros in Blue and Gray*, 75–78; Tilley, *Federals on the Frontier*, 349–50.

50. Thompson, *Vaqueros in Blue and Gray*, 79.

7. LOYALTY AND RECONSTRUCTION, 1865–1874

1. April 9, 1865, DuVal Diary; *Edwards' Annual Directory to New Orleans* (New Orleans: Southern Publishing Co., 1872), 764.

2. *Weekly Southern Intelligencer*, July 7, 1865.

3. A useful article on Texas Reconstruction historiography is Edgar P. Sneed's, "A Historiography of Reconstruction in Texas: Some Myths and Problems," *Southwestern Historical Quarterly* 72 (April 1969): 435–48. The classic study of Texas Reconstruction is Ramsdell's Dunningesque *Reconstruction in Texas*, while the most useful examination of the period is Carl H. Moneyhon's *Republicanism in Reconstruction Texas*, which is especially effective in detailing the myriad Republican factions that sprang up in the state during Reconstruction. Less satisfying is William Curtis Nunn's misnamed *Texas under the Carpetbaggers*. (Austin: Univ. of Texas Press, 1962).

4. May 30, 1865, Ballinger Diary.

5. Lucadia Pease to her sister, August 30, 1865, Lucadia Pease Papers; *Weekly Southern Intelligencer*, July 21, 1865; A. C. Greene, "The Durable Society: Austin in the Reconstruction," *Southwestern Historical Quarterly* 72 (April 1969): 494–95; Brown, "Annals of Travis County," chap. 24, 45–46; *Marshall Texas Republican*, August 25, 1865.

6. Carl H. Moneyhon stresses the importance of prewar political alliances and economic sectionalism in Reconstruction politics in Texas. He quite accurately asserts that the war did not create a new class of political leaders in Texas; rather, the traditional elite fought their political battles as "part of a continued and traditional search for power." *Republicanism in Reconstruction Texas*, xvi.

7. Hamilton to Johnson, July 24, 1865, Andrew Johnson Papers, Presidential Papers Microfilm, University of Texas at Austin Library.

8. Hamilton to Johnson, August 30, September 28, and November 27, 1865, Johnson Papers.

9. *Ibid.*, November 27, 1865, and February 26, 1866; Ramsdell, *Reconstruction in Texas*, 91–93; Waller, *Colossal Hamilton*, 78–94; James A. Baggett, "Birth of the Texas Republican Party," *Southwestern Historical Quarterly* 78 (July 1974): 9.

10. *Marshall Texas Republican*, May 5, 1866. Under the June 17, 1862 "Jurors' Loyalty Oalth" and the July 2, 1862 "Ironclad Test Oath," jurors, government officials, and others swore that they would uphold the United States Constitution and that they had never taken up arms on behalf of, aided or abetted participants in, or held office

during an insurrection or rebellion against the United States. For texts of the oaths, see Hyman, *Era of the Oath*, 157–59.

11. Hamilton to Johnson, July 24, 1865, Johnson Papers.

12. Thockmorton to Epperson, June 13 and August 27, 1865, Epperson Papers.

13. Epperson to Throckmorton, June 24 and 18, 1865, Throckmorton Papers; Wooster, "Ben H. Epperson, 35–36. Congress refused to seat Epperson and the other Texas Representatives and Senators.

14. Nov. 19, 1864, John Hancock Diary, Texas State Archives; Moneyhon, *Republicanism in Reconstruction Texas*, 33, 50, 153; *Galveston Weekly News*, December 19, 1865.

15. Throckmorton to Epperson, January 21, 1866, Epperson Papers.

16. Moneyhon, *Republicanism in Reconstruction Texas*, 44; Elliott, *Leathercoat*, 110–12, 161–78; Throckmorton to N.A. Taylor, December 4, 1866, Letter Book, James W. Throckmorton Papers, Barker Texas History Center; Throckmorton to Epperson, April 17, 1866, Epperson Papers. Throckmorton, in a reflective moment, suggested in the December 4 letter to Taylor that southerners may have been "equally intolerant" if they had won the war, "and had it in our power to have oppressed" northerners. "Our experiences at the beginning and during the war," he recalled, "shows [*sic*] that we were as intolerant as the puritans (almost) in the days of their witch-burning."

17. For examples, see Moneyhon, *Republicanism in Reconstruction Texas*, 49–52; Barr, *Black Texans*, 56–57; Gammel, *Laws of Texas*, vol. 5, 131–32, 76–81, 102–4, 1015, 988.

18. Walter T. Chapin, "Presidential Reconstruction in Texas, 1865–1867" (MA thesis, North Texas State Univ., 1979), 141; Jacob Raney and Anderson Scroggins to Throckmorton, May 3, 1867, Throckmorton Papers, Barker Texas History Center; Ramsdell, *Reconstruction in Texas*, 169; Throckmorton to Anne Throckmorton, December 27, 1866, Throckmorton Letter Book. For the role of the military in Texas Reconstruction politics, see William L. Richter, *The Army in Texas During Reconstruction, 1865–1870* (College Station: Texas A & M Univ. Press, 1987).

19. Petition of Citizens of Parker, Denton, Jack, Wise, and Stephens counties, September 5, 1865; Baldwin to Hamilton, November 7, 1865: both in Hamilton Papers, Governors' Records, Texas State Archives; *Flake's Weekly Bulletin*, May 9, 1866.

20. U.S. Congress, House, *Report of the Joint Committee on Reconstruction*, 39th Cong., 1st sess., 1866, H. Rept. 30, pt. 4: 36–37, 39, 72, 87; C. Caldwell to Hamilton, January 23, 1867, Hamilton Papers, Barker Texas History Center.

21. U.S. Congress, House, *Communication from Governor Pease of Texas, Relative to the Troubles in that State*, 40th Cong., 2d sess., 1868, H. Misc. Doc. 127. A select committee at the 1868 Constitutional Convention compiled simiar statistics. See Jesse Dorsett, "Blacks in Reconstruction Texas, 1865–1877" (PhD diss., Texas Christian Univ., 1981), 174.

22. *Communication From Governor Pease of Texas*, 6–7.

23. *Austin Tri-Weekly State Gazette*, July 6, 1868; *Flake's Weekly Bulletin*, August 1, October 3, and November 28, 1866.

24. Haynes to Pease, October 4 and November 28, 1866; DuVal to Pease, October 18 and November 20, 1866; Hamilton to Pease, November 9, 1866: all in E. M. Pease Papers, Austin History Center.

25. For a collective biography of thirty of the original Republicans, see James A. Baggett, "Origins of Early Texas Republican Party Leadership," *Journal of Southern History* 40 (Aug. 1974): 441–54.

26. *Report of the Joint Committee on Reconstruction*, xviii, xxi–xxii, 1–13. For the reasons for the radicalization of the Republican Reconstruction program, see David

Donald, *The Politics of Reconstruction, 1863–1867* (Baton Rouge: Louisiana State Univ. Press, 1965; Cambridge: Harvard Univ. Press, 1984), 57–58, and Kenneth M. Stampp, *The Era of Reconstruction, 1865–1877* (New York: Alfred A. Knopf, 1965), 83–118.

27. *Flake's Weekly Bulletin*, March 21, 1866; Andrew Jackson Hamilton, *An Address on Suffrage and Reconstruction, The Duty of the People, the President, and Congress* (Boston: Impartial Suffrage Legue, 1866).

28. Moneyhon, *Republicanism in Reconstruction Texas*, 61–81; Ramsdell, *Reconstruction in Texas*, 166–67; Baggett, "Birth of the Texas Republican Party," 14. Baggett's unpublished dissertation includes a series of useful tables containing the names and positions of Whigs, Know-Nothings, Constitutional Unionists, wartime Unionists, German Unionists, Texas Union soldiers, freedmen, carpetbaggers (who did not contribute much in numbers to Texas Republicanism), and Confederates who became Republicans after the war. Baggett, "The Rise and Fall of the Texas Radicals," 1–37, 84, 86, 89. For the origins of Republicanism in one East Texas county, see Paul D. Casdorph, "Some Early Republicans of Smith County, Texas," *Chronicles of Smith County* 7 (Fall 1968): 1–6.

29. Moneyhon, *Republicanism in Reconstruction Texas*, 82–103; Ernest Wallace, *The Howling of the Coyotes: Reconstruction Efforts to Divide Texas* (College Station: Texas A & M Univ. Press, 1979); Newcomb to Richard J. Hinton, July 10, 1871, Letter Press, Newcomb Papers. Weston J. McConnell analyzes several decades of the debate over division, placing it in its postannexation and cultural contexts, in *Social Cleavages in Texas: A Study of the Proposed Division of the State* (New York: Columbia Univ. Press, 1925).

30. Ramsdell, *Reconstruction in Texas*, 204, 308–09; Moneyhon, *Republicanism in Reconstruction Texas*, 116, 162; Mills, "Elisha Marshall Pease, 160; Ramsdell, *Reconstruction in Texas*, 264; Waller, *Colossal Hamilton*, 105–22; Moneyhon, *Republicanism in Reconstruction Texas*, 72–74,147–48. Ironically, Pease, both Hamiltons, and James Throckmorton all served as leading delegates to the taxpayers' convention. *Proceedings of the Tax-Payers' Convention of the State of Texas* (Galveston: News Steam Book and Job Office, 1871). For the decidedly un-Radical efforts of the Texas Republican delegation to Congress, see Philip J. Avillo, Jr., "Phantom Radicals: Texas Republicans in Congress, 1870–1873," *Southwestern Historical Quarterly* 77 (April 1974): 431–44.

31. Moneyhon, *Republicanism in Reconstruction Texas*, 100, 115–16, 122, 145–46, 154, 169.

32. "Mr. Newcomb's Kind of Government" (1867) and *San Antonio Weekly Express* clipping, October 22, 1868: Newcomb Papers; Dale A. Somers, "James P. Newcomb: The Making of a Radical," *Southwestern Historical Quarterly* 72 (April 1969): 449–69.

33. Ramsdell, *Reconstruction in Texas*, 209, 247, 286; Gray, "Edmund J. Davis," 72–122; Baggett, "Birth of the Texas Republican Party," 11. For a detailed narrative of the "Radical" constitutional convention, see Betty J. Sandlin, "The Texas Reconstruction Constitutional Convention of 1868–1869" (PhD diss., Texas Tech Univ., 1970). Ironically, the Radicals succeeded in incorporating into the document few of their pet projects, inluding ab initio and disfranchisement and ended up trying to block its passaage.

34. *Marshall Texas Republican*, June 9, 1868; Sandlin, "Texas Reconstruction Constitutional Convention," 81–83; G. C. Rives to Newcomb, September 7, 1869; E. J. Davis to Newcomb, September 8, 1869; *San Antonio Weekly Express* clipping, November 12, 1868: all in Newcomb Papers; Haynes to Pease, June 15 and 27, 1869: both in E. M. Pease Papers, Austin History Center; Haynes to Newcomb, November 21, 1869, Newcomb Papers.

35. Rives to Newcomb, October 19, 1869; Burnett to Newcomb, February 8,

1869; Union League Circular, August 9, 1869, and *San Antonio Express* clipping, January 10, 1869: all in Newcomb Papers.

36. Manning to Newcomb, November 27, 1870; A.R. Parsons to Newcomb, September 9, 1870; George B. Webber to Newcomb, April 25, 1870; J.J. Gossler to "Friend Hillebrand," November 1, 1871; Union League of America, State of Texas, Circular, May 19, 1871: all in Newcomb Papers.

37. Rives to Newcomb, June 11, 1869; Tracy to Newcomb, April 27, 1872: both in Newcomb Papers; *San Antonio Weekly Express*, January 11, 1868.

38. *Austin Daily Democratic Statesman*, August 1, 1871.

39. Moneyhon, *Republicanism in Reconstruction Texas*, 124–26; Gray, "Edmund J. Davis," 182–358; Moneyhon, *Republicanism in Reconstruction Texas*, 104–51; William L. Richter, " 'Devil Take Them All: Military Rule in Texas," *Southern Studies* 25 (Spring 1986): 5–29. Richter examines the degree to which federal and Confederate military authorities attempted to centralize power in Texas. See also Richter's "Spread-Eagle Eccentricities: Military-Civilian Relations in Reconstruction Texas," *Texana* 8, no. 4 (1970), 311–27.

40. *Daily Democratic Statesman*, July 26, 1871; Moneyhon, *Republicanism in Reconstruction Texas*, 164–67.

41. Quoted in Smallwood, *Time of Hope, Time of Despair*, 139; Moneyhon, *Republicanism in Reconstruction Texas*, 168–82; *Tri-Weekly Democratic Statesman*, September 21, 1871;

42. Moneyhon, *Republicanism in Reconstruction Texas*, 183–96; *Daily Democratic Statesman*, January 14, 1873.

43. Fehrenbach, *Lone Star*, 429–32; *Dallas Herald*, January 24, 1874; Joe B. Frantz, *Texas: A History* (New York: W. W. Norton, 1976), 124–25; Alwyn Barr, *Reconstruction to Reform: Texas Politics, 1876–1906* (Austin: Univ. of Texas Press, 1971), 244.

44. Degener to Pease, December 30, 1866, E.M. Pease Papers, Austin History Center; U.S. Congress, House, *Report of the Joint Committee on Reconstruction*, 39; Byron Porter to Lt. J. T. Kirkman, Acting Adjutant General, August 19, 1867, "Registered Reports of Operations and Conditions," Records of the Assistant Commissioner for the State of Texas, Bureau of Refugees, Freedmen, and Abandoned Lands, 1865–1869, Record Group 105, National Archives; *Tri-Weekly Democratic Statesman*, August 10, 1871.

45. Tausch, "Southern Sentiment among the Texas Germans," 72–74, 85–90, 97–100; E. Degener, *The Minority Report, in Favor of Extending the Right of Suffrage, with Certain Limitations, to All Men without Distinction of Race or Color* (Austin: Southern Intelligencer Office, 1866), 16; Barr, "Records of the Confederate Military Commission in San Antonio," 73 (Oct. 1969): 247–68.

46. Ann Patton Malone, "Matt Gaines: Reconstruction Politician," in *Black Leaders: Texans for Their Times* ed. Alwyn Barr and Robert A. Calvert (Austin: Texas State Historical Association, 1981), 61–62; Maj. John Hatch to Kirkman, May 28, 1867, "Registered Reports of Operations and Conditions;" Constant to A. J. Hamilton, October 18, 1865, Hamilton Papers, Governors' Records, Texas State Archives.

47. *Flake's Weekly Bulletin*, March 21 and 14, April 18, and December 26, 1866; Tausch, "Southern Sentiment among the Texas Germans," 101–2.

48. Tausch, "Southern Sentiment among the Texas Germans," 100–101; Moneyhon, *Republicanism in Reconstruction Texas*, 178–79; John Pressley Carrier," "A Political History of Texas during the Reconstruction, 1865–1874" (PhD diss., Vanderbilt Univ., 1971), 473–78.

49. Citizens of Fayette County, *People's Movement* (Fayette County, 1873). Many of the reforms mentioned in the platform of the People's Movement had also been

included in the 1854 San Antonio Platform. A large majority of the names attached to the document—of the men who issued the call for the meeting and of the men who actually wrote the pamphlet—are clearly of German origin.

50. Moneyhon, *Republicanism in Reconstruction Texas*, 164.

51. Arnoldo DeLeón, *The Tejano Community, 1836–1900* (Albuquerque: Univ. of New Mexico Press, 1982), 23–36; DeLeón, *They Called Them Greasers*, 56–57.

52. Riley, "Santos Benavides," 223–62; James Heaven Thompson, "A Nineteenth-Century History of Cameron County, Texas" (MA thesis, Univ. of Texas, 1965), 117–19; Degener to E. M. Pease, December 30, 1866, E. M. Pease Papers, Austin History Center; Newcomb to Pease, November 22, 1867, Elisha M. Pease Papers, Governors' Records, Texas State Archives.

53. *Brownsville Weekly Ranchero and Republican* clipping, September 19, 1871, translation by James Boyden, Haynes Scrapbook; DeLeón, *They Called Them Greasers*, 57–59; Evan Anders, *Boss Rule in South Texas: The Progressive Era* (Austin: Univ. of Texas Press, 1982).

54. DeLeón, *They Called Them Greasers*, 87–102, 61–62; McWilliams, *North from Mexico*, 108–111. For the border violence that continued to plague the region in the twentieth century—especially as Mexican farm laborers and railroad workers flooded into the state after 1900—see McWilliams, *North from Mexico*, 111–14, 162–88. For the connection between the postwar economic and political disruptions and tension between Anglos and Hispanics along both sides of the Rio Grande, see Graf, "Economic History of the Lower Rio Grande Valley," 590–645. Walter Prescott Webb presented a positive interpretation of the Texas Rangers' actions against Hispanics on the border; according to him, most of the Mexican-Texans and Mexican nationals the Rangers killed were rustlers, bandits, raiders, and revolutionaries, among other undesirable groups, and deserved whatever they got. Webb, *The Texas Rangers: A Century of Frontier Defense* (Boston: Houghton Mifflin Co., 1935), 231–94, 441–44, 450–51, 461–65, 473–518.

55. *Dallas Herald*, November 29, 1873.

56. Dohoney, *An Average American*, 140–45.

57. See especially Michael Perman, *The Road to Redemption: Southern Politics, 1869–1879* (Chapel Hill: Univ. of North Carolina Press, 1984), and Richard H. Abbott, *The Republican Party and the South, 1855–1877* (Chapel Hill: Univ. of North Carolina Press, 1986). For a recent analysis of how white supremacism affected the outcome of the Civil War and Reconstruction in Tennessee, see Stephen V. Ash, *Middle Tennessee Society Transformed, 1860–1870: War and Peace in the Upper South* (Baton Rouge: Louisiana State Univ. Press, 1988).

8. BLACK TEXANS DURING RECONSTRUCTION

1. The most useful works on Texas blacks during Reconstruction are Smallwood, *Time of Hope, Time of Despair;* and Dorsett, "Blacks in Reconstruction Texas." Merline Pitre focuses on black legislators in *Through Many Dangers, Toils and Snares: The Black Leadership of Texas, 1868–1900* (Austin: Eakin Press, 1985). A brief, but valuable survey of several centuries of black life in Texas is Barr's *Black Texans*.

2. Brown, *One of Cleburne's Command*, 178–79, 174.

3. *Weekly Southern Intelligencer*, August 11, 1865.

4. *Marshall Texas Republican*, June 30, 1865.

5. Rawick, *American Slave*, vol. 5, pt. 4, 181; vol. 4, pt. 1, 142; vol. 5, pt. 4, 124.

6. Ibid., supp. 2, vol. 2, pt. 1, 4; supp. 2, vol. 8, pt. 7, 2934. For the debate among whites and blacks over the parameters of freedom, see Leon F. Litwack, *Been in the Storm So Long: The Aftermath of Slavery* (New York: Afred A. Knopf, 1979), 221–31.

7. Rawick, *American Slave*, vol. 5, pt. 3, 257; supp. 2, vol. 10, pt. 9, 4130; *Weekly Southern Intelligencer*, August 11, 1865; Barr, *Black Texans*, 65–66. See also, Litwack, *Been in the Storm So Long*, 292–335.

8. James Smallwood, "Black Texans during Reconstruction: First Freedom," *East Texas Historical Journal* 14 (Spring 1976): 10; Rawick, *American Slave*, supp. 2, vol. 6, pt. 5, 1937; Theresa to Mary Polley, February 4, 1869, Joseph H. Polley Papers, Barker Texas History Center.

9. *Weekly Southern Intelligencer*, November 16, 1865; Lucadia Pease to Carrie Pease, March 2, 1866, Lucadia Pease Papers; Alton Hornsby, Jr., "The Freedmen's Bureau Schools in Texas, 1865–1870," *Southwestern Historical Quarterly* 77 (April 1973): 397–417.

10. Smallwood, *Time of Hope, Time of Despair*, 57; May 15, 1867, Eugene Bartholomew Diary, Austin History Center.

11. *Weekly Southern Intelligencer*, July 7, 1865; Dorsett, "Blacks in Reconstruction Texas," 150–51, 153–58;

12. Dan T. Carter, "The Anatomy of Fear: The Christmas Day Insurrection Scare of 1865," *Journal of Southern History* 42 (Aug. 1976): 345–64; *Tyler Reporter*, July 31, 1867, copied by *Marshall Texas Republican*, August 10, 1867; Rawick, *American Slave*, vol. 5, pt. 3, 186–87; *Marshall Texas Republican*. August 31, 1867; Rawick, *American Slave*, vol. 4, pt. 2, 289.

13. *Marshall Texas Republican*, July 10, 1868; *Dallas Herald*, September 25, 1873; *Austin Tri-Weekly Democratic Statesman*, October 5, 1871; *Marshall Texas Republican*, June 26, 1868.

14. Ann Patton Baenziger, "The Texas State Police during Reconstruction: A Reexamination," *Southwestern Historical Quarterly* 72 (April 1969): 470–91; Dorsett, "Blacks in Reconstruction Texas," 176; Otis A. Singletary, "The Texas Militia during Reconstruction," *Southwestern Historical Quarterly* 60 (July 1956): 23–35; *Austin Tri-Weekly State Gazette*, March 15, 1871.

15. *Marshall Texas Republican*, July 10 and November 27, 1868, and August 31, 1867 (copied from *Hempstead Countryman*); *Flake's Weekly Bulletin*, July 18, 1871.

16. Moneyhon, *Republicanism in Reconstruction Texas*, 79; J. Mason Brewer, *Negro Legislators of Texas and Their Descendants* (Austin: Jenkins Publishing Co., 1970), 15; Alwyn Barr, "Black Legislators of Reconstruction Texas," *Civil War History* 32 (Dec. 1986), 342.

17. James M. Smallwood, "George T. Ruby: Galveston's Black Carpetbagger in Reconstruction Texas," *Houston Review* 5 (1983): 24–33; Merline Pitre, "Richard Allen: The Chequered Career of Houston's First Black State Legislator," *Houston Review* 8 (1986): 79–80; Barr, "Black Legislators of Reconstruction Texas," 343–46; Brewer, *Negro Legislators of Texas*, 61, 65–68; Barr, "Black Legislators of Reconstruction Texas," 347.

18. George Ruby, "To the Subordinate Councils U. L. A., Texas," Newcomb Papers; Lucadia Pease to her sister, February 11, 1868, Lucadia Pease Papers; Rawick, *American Slave*, supp. 2, vol. 5, pt. 4, 1881; J. L. Randall to Lt. J.T. Kirkman, Acting Adjutant General, April 30, 1867; M. H. Goddin to Kirkman, July 31, 1867: both in "Registered Reports of Operations and Conditions."

19. *Dallas Herald*, September 27, 1873; *Marshall Texas Republican*, June 29, 1867.

20. Lucadia Pease to her sister, February 11, 1868, Lucadia Pease Papers; *Austin Tri-Weekly State Gazette*, December 3, 1869.

21. Copied by *Marshall Texas Republican*, June 22 and August 10, 1867.

22. *Marshall Texas Republican*, August 24, 1867, June 19 and June 12, 1868, October 6, 1865, and June 5, 1868.

23. *Marshall Texas Republican*, June 16, 1865 (*Houston Telegraph* copied in same issue).

24. *Tri-weekly State Gazette*, June 29, 1868. Attitudes such as these sparked early efforts to segregate the races with legal measures, coercion, and violence. See Barry A. Crouch and L. J. Schultz, "Crisis in Color: Racial Separation in Texas during Reconstruction," *Civil War History* 16 (March 1969): 37–49.

25. Rawick, *American Slave*, supp. 2, vol. 7, pt. 6, 2455; supp. 2, vol. 4, pt. 3, 1103–4; vol. 4, pt. 1, 69.

26. Emerson to Kirkman, May 30, 1867; Albert Evans to Col. William Sinclair, January 8, 1867; Ira H. Evans to Kirkman, July 1, 1867; James Devine, Annual Report, January 2, 1866; all in "Registered Reports of Operations and Conditions."

27. Rawick, *American Slave*, vol. 5, pt. 3, 78, 258–61; Lt. J. P. Richardson to Kirkman, March 31, 1867, "Registered Reports of Operations and Conditions"; Smallwood, "Black Texans during Reconstruction," 12.

28. Rawick, *American Slave*, vol. 5, pt. 4, 133; supp. 2, vol. 4, pt. 3, 1160; vol. 5, pt. 4, 90; *Marshall Texas Republican*, July 13, 1867.

29. Allen W. Trelease, *White Terror: The Ku Klux Klan Conspiracy and Southern Reconstruction* (New York: Harper and Row, 1971), 137–48; Smallwood, *Time of Hope, Time of Despair*, 142–43; James M. Smallwood, "When the Klan Rode: White Terror in Reconstruction Texas," *Journal of the West* 25 (Oct. 1986): 4–13.

30. Rawick, *American Slave*, vol. 5, pt. 4, 233–34; supp. 2, vol. 8, pt. 7, 2967.

31. William L. Richter, "The Army and the Negro in Texas during Reconstruction, 1865–1870," *East Texas Historical Journal* 10 (Spring 1970): 7–19; Claude Elliott, "The Freedmen's Bureau in Texas," *Southwestern Historical Quarterly* 56 (July 1952): 1–24; Ira Christopher Colby, "The Freedmen's Bureau in Texas and Its Impact on the Emerging Social Welfare System and Black-White Social Relations, 1865–1885" (PhD diss., Univ. of Pennsylvania, 1984), 98–133; James E. Sefton, *The United States Army and Reconstruction, 1865–1877* (Baton Rouge: Louisana State Univ. Press, 1967), 261–62; quoted in Donald G. Nieman, *To Set the Law in Motion: The Freedmen's Bureau and the Legal Rights of Blacks, 1865–1868* (Millwood, NY: KTO Press, 1979), 14. Nieman asserts that the lack of federal support for the bureau, the attitudes of agents and administrators, and the freedmen's poverty all conspired to prevent the bureau from fully protecting the legal rights of freedman.

32. *Marshall Texas Republican*, March 30, 1866; *Weekly Southern Intelligencer.* April 4, 1867. For the evolution of Reconstruction violence from an emotional outlet to a political tool, see George C. Rable, *But There Was No Peace: The Role of Violence in the Politics of Reconstruction* (Athens: Univ. of Georgia Press, 1984).

33. Rawick, *American Slave*, supp. 2, vol. 7, pt. 6, 2457; vol. 4, pt. 1, 3.

34. *Dallas Herald*, November 1, 1873.

35. *Marshall Texas Republican*, May 18, 1867.

36. Rawick, *American Slave*, vol. 4, pt. 2, 146; vol. 4, pt. 1, 222; vol. 5, pt. 3, 199; vol. 4, pt. 1, 161–62; supp. 2, vol. 2, pt. 1, 151; Mayer to Kirkman, May 1, 1867, "Registered Reports of Operations and Conditions."

37. Rawick, *American Slave*, supp. 2, vol. 8, pt. 7, 3005; vol. 5, pt. 4, 34–35; supp. 2, vol. 4, pt. 3, 1141; vol. 4, pt. 1, 110.

38. William Physick Zuber, *My Eighty Years in Texas*, 232–33; P. F. Duggan to Kirkman, June 30, 1867; M. H. Goddin to J. A. Potter, August 31, 1867; Lt. John Hutchison to Kirkman, April 30, 1867; J. L. Randall to Kirkman, May 31, 1867; Johnson to Kirkman, May 4, 1867: all in "Registered Reports of Operations and Conditions."

39. Campbell, *A Southern Community in Crisis*, 289; *Austin Daily Democratic*

Statesman. July 8, 1873; Moneyhon, *Republicanism in Reconstruction Texas,* 123–24; *Marshall Texas Republican,* June 29, 1867; Rawick, *American Slave,* vol. 5, pt. 4, 98.

40. J. L. Randall to Kirkman, May 31, 1867, "Registered Reports of Operations and Conditions;" *Dallas Herald,* December 6, 1873.

41. Archer to Gen. J. B. Kiddoo, January 10, 1867, "Registered Reports of Operations and Conditions;" Rawick, *American Slave,* supp. 2, vol. 5, pt. 4, 1454, 1568.

42. Brewer, *Negro Legislators of Texas,* 61–99; Lawrence D. Rice, *The Negro in Texas, 1874–1900* (Baton Rouge: Louisiana State Univ. Press, 1971), 151–83, 209–39, 240–57; Rawick *American Slave,* supp. 2, vol. 3, pt. 2, 570.

EPILOGUE: NOTHING TO REGRET BUT FAILURE

1. Edward King, *Texas, 1874: An Eyewitness Account of Conditions in Post-Reconstruction Texas,* ed. Robert S. Gray, (Houston: Cordovan Press, 1974), 104–5.

2. Greene, "The Durable Society," 505–6; Webb, *Handbook of Texas,* vol. 1, 529; vol. 3, 381; vol. 2, 778, vol. 1, 763–64, 202; *Weekly Southern Intelligencer,* January 11, 1866; Waller, *Colossal Hamilton,* 140–42.

3. Guido E. Ransleben, *A Hundred Years of Comfort in Texas* (San Antonio: Naylor Co., 1954), 94; Barr, *Reconstruction to Reform,* 17; Seth Shepard McKay, *Texas Politics, 1906–1944: With Special Reference to the German Counties* (Lubbock: Texas Tech Press, 1952); Terry G. Jordan, "The German Settlement of Texas after 1865," *Southwestern Historical Quarterly* 73 (Oct. 1969): 193–212.

4. Gray, "Edmund J. Davis," 362–63, 399; *Weekly Southern Intelligencer,* July 7, 1865; WPA, *St. David's through the Years,* 41; Swenson to Cora Mae Swenson, July 2, 1865, and "Biographical Sketch," Swenson Papers.

5. C. L. Sonnichsen, *I'll Die before I'll Run: The Story of the Great Feuds of Texas* (New York: Devin-Adair Co., 1962), 17–18, 21–38; DeLeón, *The Tejano Community,* 18–22; Crouch and Schultz, "Crisis in Color, 47–48; Rice, *The Negro in Texas,* 250, 246–47.

6. Carl H. Moneyhon, "George T. Ruby and the Politics of Expedience in Texas," in *Southern Black Leaders of the Reconstruction Era,* ed. Howard N. Rabinowitz, (Urbana: Univ. of Illinois Press, 1982), 388–89; Malone, "Matt Gaines," 72; Brewer, *Negro Legislators,* 81–101; Lamar L. Kirven, "A Century of Warfare: Black Texans" (PhD diss., Indiana Univ., 1974), 38–120; Paul D. Casdorph, "Norris Weight Cuney and Texas Republican Politics, 1883–1896," *Southwestern Historical Quarterly* 68 (April 1965): 455–64. One of the last of the black lawmakers was Robert L. Smith, who, as a proponent of Booker T. Washington's campaign for morality, industry, and thrift, devoted most of his time to promoting black vocational and liberal arts education. He cooperated with the Texas "Lily Whites" and refused to work for his constituents' political or social equality. Merline Pitre, "Robert Lloyd Smith: A Black Lawmaker in the Shadow of Booker T. Washington," *Phylon* 46 (Sept. 1985): 262–68.

7. Rollin G. Osterweis, *The Myth of the Lost Cause, 1865–1900* (Hamden, CT: Archon Books, 1973); Susan S. Durant, "The Gently Furled Banner: The Development of the Myth of the Lost Cause, 1865–1900" (PhD diss., Univ. of North Carolina at Chapel Hill, 1972), 72–104; Charles Reagan Wilson, *Baptized in Blood: The Religion of the Lost Cause, 1865–1920* (Athens: Univ. of Georgia Press, 1980); Paul M. Gaston, *The New South Creed: A Study in Southern Mythmaking* (New York: Alfred A. Knopf, 1970).

8. Cash, *Mind of the South,* 138.

9. Robert Penn Warren, *The Legacy of the Civil War* (New York: Random House, 1961), 14–15.

10. David M. Potter, *The Impending Crisis, 1848–1861* (New York: Harper and

Row, 1976), 448–69, quotes on pp. 461, 469. For a more recent statement of this idea, see Rable, *But There Was No Peace*, 188.

11. Robert F. Durden has traced the political importance of one of the ideas to which most southerners could be loyal—racial dominance—in *The Self-Inflicted Wound: Southern Politics in the Nineteenth Century* (Lexington: Univ. Press of Kentucky, 1985).

12. Billy Bob Lightfoot, "The Negro Exodus from Comanche County, Texas," *Southwestern Historical Quarterly* 56 (Jan. 1953): 407–16; Robert V. Haynes, *A Night of Violence: The Houston Riot of 1917* (Baton Rouge: Louisiana State Univ. Press, 1976); David M. Chalmers, *Hooded Americanism: The History of the Ku Klux Klan* (New York: Franklin Watts, 1965), 40–48; W. E. B. DuBois, "Opinion Column," *The Crisis* 18 (Oct. 1919): 283–84.

13. *Marshall Texas Republican*, May 26, 1865. One of the "most important" historical "truths" that the Children of the Confederacy intended to preserve was "that the War Between the States was not a rebellion, nor was its underlying cause to sustain slavery." The plaque is located on the west wall near the southern entrance to the capitol.

Selected Bibliography

PRIMARY SOURCES

Manuscript Collections

Austin History Center, Austin Public Library, Austin, Texas

Austin Chronological File, 1861–1865
Eugene Bartholomew Diary
Brown, Frank. *"Annals of Travis County and of the City of Austin* (from the Earliest Times to the Close of 1875)"
E.M. Pease Papers
Lucadia Pease Papers

Barker Texas History Center, University of Texas at Austin

John T. Allan Letterbook
J. Walker Austin Papers
William Pitt Ballinger Diary and Papers
Banta, William, and J.W. Cadwell, Jr. "Twenty-seven Years on the Frontier; or, Fifty Years in Texas, Vol. 1: Life of J.W. Cadwell, Sr." Typescript.
Charles Besser Civil War Biographical File
Reading W. Black Papers
Zenas R. Bliss Reminiscences
Broadside Collection
Bruckmuller, Joseph. "Description of the Family and Life of Joseph Bruckmuller." Typewritten translation.
Guy M. Bryan Papers
Edward Burleson, Jr., Papers
Josephus Cavitt Papers
Dobie-Byler Family Papers
Dresel Scrapbook
Thomas DuVal Diary and Papers

Abraham Enloe File, Civil War Miscellany
Benjamin H. Epperson Papers
Andrew Jackson Hamilton Papers
Hamilton, Andrew Jackson. "Speech of the Hon. Andrew Jackson Hamilton, of Texas, on the Conditions of the South under Rebel Rule, and the Necessity of Early Relief to the Union Men of Western Texas." October 3, 1862.
John L. Haynes Papers and Scrapbook
John R. Hill Papers
Hughes, Howell R. "Life of an East Texas Pioneer, Reece Hughes." Typescript.
Thomas Huling Papers
John Warren Hunter Biographical File
Anson Jones Papers
Jones, Mary Ruth Lewis. "Disaffection in the Austin-Hempstead Region, 1862–1864." Typescript.
Gilbert D. Kingsbury Papers
Jacob Kuechler Biographical File
Mrs. L. D. Ledbetter Collection
Gideon Lincecum Collection
Thomas F. McKinney Biographical File
Thaddeus McRae Papers
Lizzie Neblett Papers
James P. Newcomb Papers
A. B. Norton Biographical File
Benjamin F. Perry Papers, Ramsdell Microfilm Collection
Joseph H. Polley Papers
O. M. Roberts Papers
Sansom, John W. "Battle of Nueces River in Kinney County, Texas, August 10, 1862." Typescript.
George W. Smyth Papers
S. M. Swenson Papers
Robert H. Taylor Biographical File
Robert H. Taylor Papers
Taylor, T. U. "Swamp Fox of the Sulphur; or, the Life and Times of Cullen Montgomery Baker." Typescript.
Alexander W. Terrell Papers
James W. Throckmorton Papers and Letter Book
Warrick Tunstall Papers
John B. Walker Plantation Book
Western Journal of Commerce, bound typescript
Reuben G. White Family Collection

Duke University Library, Durham, North Carolina

Charles Steedman Papers, Manuscript Collection

Texas State Archives, Austin, Texas

John S. Ford Papers
Governors' Records
  Edward Clark Papers
  Edmund J. Davis Papers
  Andrew Jackson Hamilton Papers
  Francis R. Lubbock Papers
  Pendleton Murrah Papers
  Elisha M. Pease Papers
  James W. Throckmorton Papers
Oscar Haas Collection
John Hancock Diary
Schedule One, 1860 Travis County Manuscript Census. Microfilm.

University of North Carolina at Chapel Hill

John W. Brown Diary, Southern Historical Collection

University of Texas at Austin Library

Andrew Johnson Papers, Presidential Papers Microfilm.

Newspapers

Austin Democratic Statesman
Austin Weekly Southern Intelligencer
Austin State Gazette
Brownsville Fort Brown Flag
Brownsville Weekly Ranchero and Republican
Clarksville Standard
Corpus Christi Ranchero
Dallas Herald
Flake's Weekly Bulletin
Frank Leslie's Illustrated Newspaper
Galveston Civilian
Galveston Weekly News
Goliad Express
Houston Telegraph
Indianola Courier
Lavaca Herald
Loyal National Union Journal (Brownsville)
Marshall Texas Republican
Matagorda Gazette
McKinney Messenger
Navarro Express
New York Times
New York Tribune

San Antonio Alamo Express
San Antonio Express
San Antonio Herald
San Antonio News
Texas Almanac Extra
Tyler Reporter
Victoria Advocate

Public Documents

Bexar County Court Journal. Vol. 2A, 1863-1864. Microfilm Reel 1019358.
Day, James M., ed. *House Journal of the Ninth Legislature.* Austin: Texas
   State Library, 1964.
———, ed. *House Journal of the Ninth Legislature, First Called Session.*
   Austin: Texas State Library, 1963.
———, ed. *Senate and House Journals of the Tenth Legislature, First
   Called Session.* Austin: Texas State Library, 1965.
———, ed. *Senate and House Journal of the Tenth Legislature, Second
   Called Session.* Austin: Texas State Library, 1966.
"Index to the Compiled Service Records of Volunteer Union Soldiers Who
   Served in Organizations from the State of Texas." Records of the Adju-
   tant General's Office. Record Group 94. National Archives. Microfilm.
Matamoros Consular Dispatches. Ramsdell Microfilm Collection. Barker
   Texas History Center.
Quartermaster General, U.S. Army. *Roll of Honor: Names of Soldiers
   Who Died in Defense of the Union, Interned in the Eastern District of
   Texas; Central District of Texas; Rio Grande District, Department of
   Texas; Camp Ford, Tyler Texas; and Corpus Christi, Texas.* Washington,
   D.C.: Government Printing Office, 1866.
"Registered Reports of Operations and Conditions." Records of the As-
   sistant Commissioner for the State of Texas. Bureau of Refugees, Freed-
   men, and Abandoned Lands, 1865–1869. Record Group 105. National
   Archives. Microfilm.
State of Texas. *Journal of the House of Representatives, Eighth Legis-
   lature.* Austin: State Printer, 1860.
———. *Journal of the House of Representatives, Extra Session of the
   Eighth Legislature.* Austin: State Printer, 1861.
———. *Journal of the Senate, Eighth Legislature.* Austin: State Printer,
   1860.
*The Supreme Court of Texas on the Constitutionality of the Conscript
   Laws.* Houston: Telegraph Book and Job Establishment, 1863.
Texas Legislature. *Resolutions of the State of Texas, Concerning Peace,
   Reconstruction, and Independence.* Austin: State Printer, 1865.
U.S. Bureau of the Census. *Population of the United States in 1860:*

Compiled from the Original Returns of the Eighth Census. Washington, D.C.: Government Printing Office, 1864.

U.S. Congress. House. *Communication from Governor Pease of Texas, Relative to the Troubles in that State.* 40th Cong. 2d sess., 1868. H. Misc. Doc. 127.

———. 36th Cong. 1st sess., 1859–1860. H. Exec. Doc. 57. Serial 1050.

———. *The Impeachment of Judge Watrous.* 34th Cong. 3d sess., 1856–1857. H. Rept. 175. Serial 913.

———. *Report of the Joint Committee on Reconstruction.* 39th Cong., 1st sess., 1866. H. Rept. 30.

U.S. Congress. Senate. *Memorial of Anthony M. Dignowitz.* 37th Cong. 2d sess., 1861. S. Misc. Doc. 9.

War of the Rebellion: A Compilation of the Official Records of the Union and Confederate Armies. Washington, D.C.: Government Printing Office, 1880–1901.

Winkler, Ernest W., ed. *Journal of the Secession Convention of Texas, 1861.* Austin: Austin Printing Co., 1912.

Published Primary Sources

Acheson, Sam, and Julie Ann Hudson O'Connell, eds. "George Washington Diamond's Account of the Great Hanging at Gainesville, 1862." *Southwestern Historical Quarterly* 66 (Jan. 1963): 331–414.

Anderson, Charles. *Speech of Charles Anderson on the State of the Country.* Washington, D.C.: Lemuel Towers, 1860.

Anderson, John Q., ed. *Brokenburn: The Journal of Kate Stone, 1861–1868.* Baton Rouge: Louisiana State Univ. Press, 1955.

Aughey, John H. *The Iron Furnace; or, Slavery and Secession.* Philadelphia: William S. and Alfred Martien, 1863.

Barr, Alwyn, ed. "Records of the Confederate Military Commission in San Antonio, July 2–October 10, 1862." *Southwestern Historical Quarterly* 70 (July 1966), (Oct. 1966), (April 1967); 71 (Oct. 1967); 73 (July 1969), (Oct. 1969).

Barr, Amelia H. *All the Days of My Life: An Autobiography.* New York: D. Appleton and Co., 1913.

Barrett, Thomas. *The Great Hanging at Gainesville.* Gainesville, 1885; Austin: Texas State Historical Association, 1961.

Basler, Roy P., ed. *The Collected Works of Abraham Lincoln.* Vol. 6. Springfield, IL: Abraham Lincoln Association, 1955.

Bell, James H. *Speech of Hon. James H. Bell, of the Texas Supreme Court, Delivered at the Capitol on Saturday, December 1st, 1860.* Austin: Intelligencer Book Office, 1860.

Bentley and Pilgrim. *Texas Legal Directory for 1876-1877.* Austin Democratic Statesman Office, 1877.

Bishop, A.W. *Loyalty on the Frontier; or, Sketches of Union Men of the*

South-West. St. Louis: R.P. Studley and Co., 1863.

Bitton, Davis, ed. *Reminiscences and Civil War Letters of Levi Lamon Wight.* Salt Lake City: Univ. of Utah Press, 1970.

Bourne, Edward G., and Frederick W. Moore, eds. "Diary and Correspondence of Salmon P. Chase: Letters from George S. Denison to Salmon P. Chase, May 15, 1862, to March 21, 1865." *Annual Report of the American Historical Association for the Year 1902.* Vol. 2. Washington, D.C.: Government Printing Office, 1902.

Brown, Norman D., ed. *Journey to Pleasant Hill: The Civil War Letters of Captain Elijah P. Petty, Walker's Texas Division, CSA.* San Antonio: Institute of Texan Cultures, 1982.

————, ed. *One of Cleburne's Command: The Civil War Reminiscences and Diary of Capt. Samuel T. Foster, Granbury's Texas Brigade, CSA.* Austin: Univ. of Texas Press, 1980.

Carson, James Petigru, ed. *Life, Letters, and Speeches of James Louis Petigru.* Washington, D.C., 1920.

Citizens of Fayette County. *People's Movement.* Fayette County, 1873.

Clark, L.D., ed. *Civil War Recollections of James Lemuel Clark.* College Station: Texas A & M Univ. Press, 1984.

Dawson, Sarah Morgan. *A Confederate Girl's Diary.* Edited by James I. Robertson, Jr. Bloomington: Indiana Univ. Press, 1960.

Degener, E. *The Minority Report, in Favor of Extending the Right of Suffrage, with Certain Limitations, to All Men without Distinction of Race or Color.* Austin: Southern Intelligencer Office, 1866.

Devine, Thomas J., and Alexander W. Terrell, *Speeches Delivered on the 17th January, 1862, in the Representative Hall, Austin, Texas.* Austin: John Marshall and Co., 1862.

Dohoney, Eben Lafayette *An Average American.* Paris, TX: E.L. Dohoney, n.d. [ca. 1900].

Donald, David, ed. *Inside Lincoln's Cabinet: The Civil War Diaries of Salmon P. Chase.* New York: Longmans, Green and Co., 1954.

Dumond, Dwight L., ed. *Southern Editorials on Secession.* New York: Century Co., 1931.

Dyer, Frederick H., ed. *Compendium of the War of the Rebellion.* Des Monies, IA: Dyer Publishing Co., 1908.

Edwards' Annual Directory to New Orleans. New Orleans: Southern Publishing Co., 1872.

Fearn, Frances. *Diary of a Refugee.* New York: Moffat, Yard, and Co., 1910.

Ford, John Salmon. *Rip Ford's Texas.* Edited by Stephen B. Oates. Austin: Univ. of Texas Press, 1963.

Gammel, Hana Peter Nielson, comp. *The Laws of Texas, 1822–1897.* 10 vols. Austin: Gammel Book Co., 1898.

Gillette, Charles. *A Few Historic Records of the Church in the Diocese of Texas, during the Rebellion.* New York: John A. Gray and Green, 1865.

Goyne, Minetta Altgelt. *Lone Star and Double Eagle: Civil War Letters of a German-Texas Family.* Lubbock: Texas Christian Univ. Press, 1982.

Gracy, Alice Duggan, and Emma Gene Seale Gentry, comps. *Travis County, Texas: The Five Schedules of the 1860 Federal Census*, Austin: Privately printed, 1967.

Gregg, Alexander. *The Duties Growing out of it, and the Benefits to be Expected, from the Present War.* Austin: State Gazette Office, 1861.

————. *The Sin of Extortion, and Its Peculiar Aggravations at a Time Like the Present.* Austin: Texas Almanac Office, 1863.

Hamilton, Andrew Jackson. *An Address on Suffrage and Reconstruction: The Duty of the People, the President, and Congress.* Boston: Impartial Suffrage League, 1866.

————. *Speech of Gen. A.J. Hamilton of Texas, at the War Meeting at Faneuil Hall.* Boston: T.R. Marvin and Son, 1863.

————. *Speech of Hon. Andrew J. Hamilton, of Texas, on the State of the Union.* Washington, D.C.: Lemuel Towers, 1861.

Hamilton, J.G. de Roulhac, ed. "Benjamin Sherwood Hedrick." *The James Sprunt Historical Publications.* Vol. 10. Chapel Hill: Univ. of North Carolina Press, 1910.

Helper, Hinton Rowan. *The Impending Crisis of the South: How to meet It.* George Frederickson, ed. Cambridge: Harvard Univ. Press, 1968.

Johnson, Herschel V. "Documents: From the Autobiography of Herschel V. Johnson, 1856–1867." *American Historical Review* 30 (Jan. 1925): 311–36.

Johnston, Frontis W., ed. *The Papers of Zebulon Baird Vance.* Vol. 1. Raleigh, NC: State Department of Archives and History, 1963.

King, Edward. *Texas, 1874: An Eyewitness Account of Conditions in Post-Reconstruction Texas.* Edited by Robert S. Gray. Houston: Cordovan Press, 1974.

Lord, Walter, ed. *The Fremantle Diary.* Boston: Little Brown & Co., 1954.

Marten, James, ed. "The Lamentations of a Whig: James Throckmorton Writes a Letter." *Civil War History* 31 (June 1985): 163–70.

Mills, Anson. *My Story.* Washington, D.C.: Press of Byron S. Adams, 1918.

Mills, William Wallace. *Forty Years at El Paso.* El Paso: Carl Hertzog, 1962.

Moore, Ike, ed. *The Life and Diary of Reading Wood Black.* Uvalde, TX: El Progreso Club, 1934.

Newcomb, James P. *Sketch of Secession Times in Texas.* San Francisco, 1863.

North, Thomas. *Five Years in Texas.* Cincinnati: Elm Street Printing Co., 1871.

Norton, Anthony B. *Speech of Hon. A.B. Norton, in Vindication of History and the Constitution and the Union, in the Texas Legislature, January 24, 1860.* Austin: Southern Intelligencer Press, 1860.

O'Connor, Elizabeth Paschal. *I Myself.* New York: G.P. Putnam's Sons, 1914.

————. *My Beloved South.* New York: G.P. Putnam's Sons, 1913.

Olmsted, Frederick Law. *A Journal through Texas; or, A Saddle-Trip on the Southwestern Frontier.* New York: Burt Franklin, 1860; Austin: Univ. of Texas Press, 1958.

Padgett, James A., ed. "Some Letters of George Stanton Denison, 1854–1866: Observations of a Yankee on Conditions in Louisiana and Texas." *Louisiana Historical Quarterly* 23 (Oct. 1940): 1132–1240.

Parson Brownlow, and the Unionists of East Tennessee, with a Sketch of His Life. New York: Beadle and Co., 1862.

Paschal, George W. *Ninety Four Years: Agnes Paschal.* Washington, D.C.: George W. Paschal, 1871.

Patrick, Rembert W., ed. *The Opinions of the Confederate Attorneys General, 1861–1865.* Buffalo, NY: Dennis and Co., 1950.

Phillips, Edwin D. *Texas, and Its Late Military Occupation and Evacuation.* New York: D. Van Nostrand, 1862.

Proceedings of the Tax-Payers' Convention of the State of Texas. Galveston: News Steam Book and Job Office, 1871.

Ranklin, Melinda. *Twenty Years among the Mexicans: A Narrative of Missionary Labor.* Cincinnati: Chase and Hall, 1875.

Rawick, George P., ed. *The American Slave: A Composite Autobiography.* 19 vols. Westport, CT: Greenwood Publishing Co., 1972.

————. *The American Slave: A Composite Autobiography. Supplement.* 12 Vols. Westport, CT: Greenwood Publishing Co., 1977.

Schwartz, Stephen. *Twenty-two Months a Prisoner of War.* St. Louis, MO: A.F. Nelson Publishing Co., 1892.

A Sketch of the Life of Hon. James H. Bell: Memorial Proceedings Had in the Supreme Court of Texas in Respect to the Memory of Hon. James H. Bell. Austin, 1893.

Smith, Rebecca W., and Marion Mullins, eds. "The Diary of H.C. Medford, Confederate Soldier, 1864." *Southwestern Historical Quarterly* 34 (Oct. 1930): 106–40.

Smith, Thomas C. *Here's Yer Mule: The Diary of Thomas C. Smith.* Waco, TX: Little Texian Press, 1958.

Smithwick, Noah. *The Evolution of a State; or, Recollections of Old Texas Days.* Austin: Gammel Book Co., 1901.

Snyder, Charles M. "New Jersey Pioneers in Texas." *Southwestern Historical Quarterly* 64 (Jan. 1961): 348–68.

Strom, Steven, ed. "Cotton and Profits across the Border: William Marsh Rice in Mexico, 1863–1865." *Houston Review* 8 (1986): 89–96.

Tilley, Nannie M., ed. *Federals on the Frontier: The Diary of Benjamin F. McIntyre, 1862–1864.* Austin: Univ. of Texas Press, 1963.

Trammell, Camilla Davis. *Seven Pines: Its Occupants and Their Letters, 1825–1872.* Dallas: Southern Methodist Univ. Press, 1987.

Williams, Amelia W. and Eugene C. Barker, eds. *The Writings of Sam Houston, 1813–1863*. Vols. 7–8. Austin: Jenkins Publishing Co., 1970.

Williams, Robert H. *With the Border Ruffians: Memories of the Far West, 1852–1868*. Edited by E.W. Williams. London: John Murray, 1908.

Winkler, Ernest W., ed. *Platforms of Political Parties in Texas*. Austin: Bulletin of the Univ. of Texas, no. 53, 1916.

Zuber, William Physick. *My Eighty Years in Texas*. Edited by Janis Boyle Mayfield. Austin: Univ. of Texas Press, 1971.

SECONDARY SOURCES

Books and Articles

Abbott, Richard H. *The Republican Party and the South, 1855–1877*. Chapel Hill: Univ. of North Carolina Press, 1986.

Abernethy, Francis E., ed. *Tales from the Big Thicket*. Austin: Univ. of Texas Press, 1966.

Addington, Wendell G. "Slave Insurrections in Texas." *Journal of Negro History* 35 (Oct. 1950): 408–34.

Anders, Evan. *Boss Rule in South Texas: The Progressive Era*. Austin: Univ. of Texas Press, 1982.

Anderson, Charles C. *Fighting by Southern Federals*. New York: Neale Publishing Co., 1912.

Aptheker, Herbert. *American Negro Slave Revolts*. New York: Columbia Univ. Press, 1943.

Ash, Stephen V. *Middle Tennessee Society Transformed, 1860–1870: War and Peace in the Upper South*. Baton Rouge: Louisiana State Univ. Press, 1988.

Auman, William T. "Neighbor against Neighbor: The Inner Civil War in the Randolph County Area of Confederate North Carolina." *North Carolina Historical Review* 61 (Jan. 1984): 59–92.

Auman, William T., and David D. Scarboro. "The Heroes of America in Civil War North Carolina." *North Carolina Historical Review* 58 (Oct. 1981): 327–63.

Avillo, Philip J., Jr. "Phantom Radicals: Texas Republicans in Congress, 1870–1873." *Southwestern Historical Quarterly* 77 (April 1974): 431–44.

Baenziger, Ann Patton. "The Texas State Police during Reconstruction: A Reexamination." *Southwestern Historical Quarterly* 72 (April 1969): 470–91.

Baggett, James A. "Birth of the Texas Republican Party." *Southwestern Historical Quarterly* 78 (July 1974): 1–20.

———. "The Constitutional Union Party in Texas." *Southwestern Historical Quarterly* 82 (Jan. 1979): 233–64.

———. "Origins of Early Texas Republican Party Leadership." *Journal of Southern History* 40 (Aug. 1974): 441–54.

Bailey, Hugh C. "Disaffection in the Alabama Hill Country, 1861." *Civil*

War History 4 (June 1958): 183–92.

————. "Disloyalty in Early Confederate Alabama." *Journal of Southern History* 23 (Nov. 1957): 522–28.

Bardolph, Richard. "Inconstant Rebels: Desertion of North Carolina Troops in the Civil War." *North Carolina Historical Review* 41 (April 1964): 163–89.

Barney, William L. *Flawed Victory: A New Perspective on the Civil War.* New York: Praeger, 1975.

————. *The Road to Secession: A New Perspective on the Old South.* New York: Praeger, 1972.

————. *The Secessionist Impulse: Alabama and Mississippi in 1860.* Princeton, NJ: Princeton Univ. Press, 1974.

Barnwell, John. *Love of Order: South Carolina's First Secession Crisis.* Chapel Hill: Univ. of North Carolina Press, 1982.

Barr, Alwyn. "Black Legislators of Reconstruction Texas." *Civil War History* 32 (Dec. 1986), 340–52.

————. *Black Texans: A History of Negroes in Texas, 1528–1971.* Austin: Jenkins Publishing Co., 1973.

————. *Reconstruction to Reform: Texas Politics, 1876–1906.* Austin: Univ. of Texas Press, 1971.

Barr, Alwyn, and Robert A. Calvert, eds. *Black Leaders: Texans for Their Times.* Austin: Texas State Historical Association, 1981.

Barrett, John G. *The Civil War in North Carolina.* Chapel Hill: Univ. of North Carolina Press, 1963.

Beringer, Richard E., Herman Hattaway, Archer Jones, and William N. Still, Jr. *Why the South Lost the Civil War.* Athens: Univ. of Georgia Press, 1986.

Bettersworth, John K. *Confederate Mississippi: The People and Politics of a Cotton State in Wartime.* Baton Rouge: Louisiana State Univ. Press, 1943.

Betts, Vicki. " 'Private and Amateur Hangings': The Lynching of W.W. Montgomery, March 15, 1863." *Southwestern Historical Quarterly* 88 (Oct. 1984): 145–66.

Biesele, Rudolph L. *The History of the German Settlements in Texas, 1831–1861.* Austin: Von Boeckmann-Jones Co., 1930.

————. "The Texas State Convention of Germans in 1854." *Southwestern Historical Quarterly* 33 (April 1930): 247–61.

Biographical Directory of the American Congress, 1774–1971. Washington, D.C.: Government Printing Office, 1971.

Boethel, Paul C. *History of Lavaca County.* Austin: Von-Boeckmann-Jones Co., 1959.

Bragg, Jefferson Davis. *Louisiana in the Confederacy.* Baton Rouge: Louisiana State Univ. Press, 1941.

Brewer, J. Mason. *Negro Legislators of Texas and Their Descendants.* Austin: Jenkins Publishing Co., 1970.

Brewer, James H. *The Confederate Negro: Virginia's Craftsmen and Military Laborers, 1861–1865.* Durham, NC: Duke Univ. Press, 1969.

Bridges, C.A. "The Knights of the Golden Circle: A Filibustering Fantasy." *Southwestern Historical Quarterly* 44 (Jan. 1941): 287–302.

Brister, Louis E. "William von Rosenberg's *Kirtik:* A History of the Society for the Protection of German Immigrants to Texas." *Southwestern Historical Quarterly* 85 (Oct. 1981): 161–86.

Brown, John Henry. *Indian Wars and Pioneers of Texas.* Austin: L.E. Daniell, 1880.

Brown, Norman D. *Edward Stanly: Whiggery's Tarheel 'Conqueror.'* University: Univ. of Alabama Press, 1974.

Brown, Richard Maxwell. *Strain of Violence: Historical Studies in American Violence and Vigilantism.* New York: Oxford Univ. Press, 1975.

Brown, Wallace. *The Good Americans: The Loyalists in the American Revolution.* New York: William Morrow and Co., 1969.

Brownlee, Richard S. *Gray Ghosts of the Confederacy: Guerilla Warfare in the West, 1861–1865.* Baton Rouge: Louisiana State Univ. Press, 1958.

Bryan, T. Conn. *Confederate Georgia.* Athens: Univ. of Georgia Press, 1953.

Buenger, Walter L. "Secession and the Texas German Community: Editor Lindheimer vs. Editor Flake." *Southwestern Historical Quarterly* 82 (April 1979): 379–402.

———. *Secession and the Union in Texas.* Austin: Univ. of Texas Press, 1984.

———. "Texas and the Riddle of Secession." *Southwestern Historical Quarterly* 87 (Oct. 1983): 151–82.

Calhoon, Robert M. *The Loyalists in Revolutionary America, 1760–1781.* New York: Harcourt Brace Jovanovich, 1973.

Campbell, Randolph B. *A Southern Community in Crisis: Harrison County, Texas, 1850–1880.* Austin: Texas State Historical Association, 1983.

———. "Texas and the Nashville Convention of 1850." *Southwestern Historical Quarterly* 76 (July 1972): 1–14.

Carpenter, Jesse T. *The South as a Conscious Minority, 1789–1861: A Study in Political Thought.* New York: New York Univ. Press, 1930.

Carter, Dan T. "The Anatomy of Fear: The Christmas Day Insurrection Scare of 1865." *Journal of Southern History* 42 (Aug. 1976): 345–64.

———. *When the War Was Over: The Failure of Self-Reconstruction in the South, 1865–1867.* Baton Rouge: Louisiana State Univ. Press, 1985.

Casdorph, Paul D. "Norris Wright Cuney and Texas Republican Politics, 1883–1896." *Southwestern Historical Quarterly* 68 (April 1965): 455–64.

———. "Some Early Republicans of Smith County, Texas." *Chronicles of Smith County* 7 (Fall 1968): 1–6.

Cash, Wilbur J. *The Mind of the South.* New York: Alfred Knopf, 1941.

Chalmers, David M. *Hooded Americanism: The History of the Ku Klux Klan.* New York: Franklin Watts, 1965.

Chance, Joseph E. *The Second Texas Infantry: From Shiloh to Vicksburg.* Austin: Eakin Press, 1984.

Channing, Stephen A. *Crisis of Fear: Secession in South Carolina.* New York: W.W. Norton, 1970.

Chesson, Michael B. "Harlots or Heroines: A New Look at the Richmond Bread Riot." *Virginia Magazine of History and Biography* 92 (April 1984): 131–75.

Cimprich, John. *Slavery's End in Tennessee, 1861–1865.* University: Univ. of Alabama Press, 1985.

Cole, Arthur Charles. *The Irrespressible Conflict.* New York: Macmillan, 1934.

———. *The Whig Party in the South.* Washington, D.C.: American Historical Association, 1914; Gloucester, MA: Peter Smith, 1962.

Cortes, Carlos E., ed. *Juan N. Cortina: Two Interpretations.* New York: Arno Press, 1974.

Craven, Avery. *The Coming of the Civil War.* 2d ed. Chicago: Univ. of Chicago Press, 1957.

———. *The Growth of Southern Nationalism, 1848–1861.* Baton Rouge: Louisiana State Univ. Press, 1953.

Creighton, James A. *A Narrative History of Brazoria County.* Waco, TX: Texian Press, 1975.

Crenshaw, Ollinger. *The Slave States in the Presidential Election of 1860.* Baltimore, MD: Johns Hopkins Univ. Press, 1945.

Crouch, Barry A., and L. J. Schultz. "Crisis in Color: Racial Separation in Texas during Reconstruction." *Civil War History* 16 (March 1969): 37–49.

Cumberland, Charles C. "The Confederate Loss and Recapture of Galveston, 1862–1863." *Southwestern Historical Quarterly* 51 (Oct. 1947): 109–30.

Curti, Merle. *The Roots of American Loyalty.* New York: Columbia Univ. Press, 1946.

Daddysman, James W. *The Matamoros Trade: Confederate Commerce, Diplomacy, and Intrigue.* Newark, DE: Univ. of Delaware Press, 1984.

Davis, Archie K. " 'She Disdains to Pluck One Laurel from a Sister's Brow': Disloyalty to the Confederacy in North Carolina." *Virginia Magazine of History and Biography* 88 (April 1980): 131–47.

Davis, Ronald L.F. *Good and Faithful Labor: From Slavery to Sharecropping in the Natchez District, 1860–1890.* Westport, CT: Greenwood Publishing Co., 1982.

Debo, Darrell. *Burnet County History.* Vol. 1. Austin, TX: Eakin Press, 1979.

Degler, Carl N. *The Other South: Southern Dissenters in the Nineteenth Century.* New York: Harper and Row, 1974.

DeLeón, Arnoldo. *The Tejano Community, 1836–1900.* Albuquerque: Univ. of New Mexico Press, 1982.

———. *They Called Them Greasers: Anglo Attitudes toward Mexicans in Texas, 1821–1900*. Austin: Univ. of Texas Press, 1983.

De Ryee, William, and R. E. Moore. *The Texas Album of the Eighth Legislature, 1860*. Austin: Miner, Lambert, and Perry, 1860.

Deutsch, Karl W. *Nationalism and Social Communication: An Inquiry into the Foundations of Nationality*. 2d ed. Cambridge, MA: MIT Press, 1966.

Doherty, Herbert J., Jr. "Union Nationalism in Georgia." *Georgia Historical Quarterly* 37 (March 1953): 18–38.

Donald, David. *The Politics of Reconstruction, 1863–1867*. Baton Rouge: Louisiana State Univ. Press, 1965. Reprint. Cambridge: Harvard Univ. Press, 1984.

———, ed. *Why the North Won the Civil War*. Baton Rouge: Louisiana State Univ. Press, 1960.

Doob, Leonard W. *Patriotism and Nationalism: Their Psychological Foundations*. New Haven, CT: Yale Univ. Press, 1964.

Duaine, Carl L. *The Dead Men Wore Boots: An Account of the Thirty-second Texas Volunteer Cavalry, CSA, 1862–1865*. Austin: San Felipe Press, 1966.

DeBois, W. E. B. "Opinion Column." *The Crisis* 18 (Oct. 1919): 283–84.

Dugan, Frank H. "The 1850 Affair of the Brownsville Separatists." *Southwestern Historical Quarterly* 61 (Oct. 1957): 270–87.

Dumond, Dwight Lowell. *The Secession Movement, 1860–1861*. New York: Macmillan, 1931.

Durden, Robert F. *The Self-Inflicted Wound: Southern Politics in the Nineteenth Century*. Lexington: Univ. Press of Kentucky, 1985.

Eason, Al. "Cullen Baker—Purveyor of Death." *Frontier Times* 40 (Aug.–Sept. 1966): 6–12, 67.

Eaton, Clement. *The Freedom-of-Thought Struggle in the Old South*. New York: Harper and Row, 1964.

———. *The Growth of Southern Civilization, 1790–1860*. New York: Harper and Row, 1961.

———. *A History of the Southern Confederacy*. New York: The Free Press, 1954.

———. "Mob Violence in the Old South." *Mississippi Valley Historical Review* 29 (Dec. 1942): 351–70.

Elliott, Claude. "The Freedmen's Bureau in Texas." *Southwestern Historical Quarterly* 56 (July 1952): 1–24.

———. *Leathercoat: The Life of James W. Throckmorton*. San Antonio: Standard Printing Co., 1938.

———. "Union Sentiment in Texas, 1861–1865." *Southwestern Historical Quarterly* 50 (April 1947): 448–77.

Engs, Robert Francis. *Freedom's First Generation: Black Hampton, Virginia, 1861–1890*. Philadelphia: Univ. of Pennsylvania Press, 1979.

Escott, Paul D. *After Secession: Jefferson Davis and the Failure of Confederate Nationalism*. Baton Rouge: Louisiana State Univ. Press, 1978.

Faust, Drew Gilpin. *The Creation of Confederate Nationalism: Ideology and Indentity in the Civil War South*. Baton Rouge: Louisiana State University Press, 1988.

Fehrenbach, T.R. *Lone Star: A History of Texas and the Texans*. New York: Macmillan, 1968.

Feldberg, Michael. *The Turbulent Era: Riot and Disorder in Jacksonian America*. New York: Oxford Univ. Press, 1980.

Fleming, Walter L. *Civil War and Reconstruction in Alabama*. New York: Macmillan, 1905.

Flippin, Percy Scott. *Herschel V. Johnson of Georgia: State Rights Unionist*. Richmond: Dietz Printing Co., 1931.

Fornell, Earl Wesley. *The Galveston Era: The Texas Crescent on the Eve of Secession*. Austin: Univ. of Texas Press, 1961.

Franklin, John Hope. *The Militant South*. Cambridge: Harvard Univ. Press, 1956.

Franklin, Thomas H. "George W. Brackenridge" *Alcalde* 8 (March 1921).

Frantz, Joe B. *Texas: A History*. New York: W.W. Norton, 1976.

Gage, Larry Jay. "The Texas Road to Secession and War: John Marshall and the *Texas State Gazette*, 1860–1861." *Southwestern Historical Quarterly* 62 (Oct. 1958): 191–226.

Gaston, Paul M. *The New South Creed: A Study in Southern Mythmaking*. New York: Alfred A. Knopf, 1970.

Gerteis, Louis S. *From Contraband to Freedman: Federal Policy toward Southern Blacks, 1861–1865*. Westport, CT: Greenwood Publishing Co., 1973.

Goen, C.C. *Broken Churches, Broken Nation: Denominational Schisms and the Coming of the American Civil War*. Macon, GA: Mercer Univ. Press, 1985.

Graf, LeRoy P. "Andrew Johnson and the Coming of the War." *Tennessee Historical Quarterly* 19 (Sept. 1960): 208–21.

Greene, A.C. "The Durable Society: Austin in the Reconstruction." *Southwestern Historical Quarterly* 72 (April 1969): 492–518.

Gregg, Wilson. *Alexander Gregg: First Bishop of Texas*. Sewanee, TN: The University Press at the Univ. of the South, 1912.

Grodzins, Morton: *The Loyal and the Disloyal: Social Boundaries of Patriotism and Treason*. Chicago: Univ. of Chicago Press, 1956.

Guetzkow, Harold. *Multiple Loyalties: Theoretical Approach to a Problem in International Organization*. Princeton, NJ: Center for Research on World Political Institutions, 1955.

Hall, Roy F., and Helen G. Hall. *Collin County: Pioneering in North Texas*. Quanah, TX: Nortex Press, 1975.

Hamilton, Holmen. *Prologue to Conflict: The Crisis and Compromise of*

1850. Lexington: Univ. of Kentucky Press, 1964.

Hart, James P. "George W. Paschal." *Texas Law Review* 28 (Nov. 1949): 27–28.

Havins, T.R. "Administration of the Sequestration Act in the Confederate District Court for the Western District of Texas, 1862–1865." *Southwestern Historical Quarterly* 43 (Jan. 1940): 295–322.

Haynes, Robert V. *A Night of Violence: The Houston Riot of 1917*. Baton Rouge: Louisiana State Univ. Press, 1976.

History of Texas, Together with a Biographical History of the Cities of Houston and Galveston. Chicago: Lewis Publishing Co., 1895.

Hoole, William Stanley. *Alabama Tories: The First Alabama Cavalry, U.S.A., 1862–1865*. Tuscaloosa, AL: Confederate Publishing Co., 1960.

Hornsby, Alton, Jr. "The Freedmen's Bureau Schools in Texas, 1865–1870." *Southwestern Historical Quarterly* 77 (April 1973): 397–417.

Howard, Victor. "John Brown's Raid at Harpers Ferry and the Sectional Crisis in North Carolina." *North Carolina Historical Review* 55 (Autumn 1978): 396–420.

Howe, Daniel Walker. *The Political Culture of the American Whigs*. Chicago, IL: Univ. of Chicago Press, 1979.

Hyman, Harold M. *A More Perfect Union: The Impact of the Civil War and Reconstruction on the Constitution*. New York: Alfred A. Knopf, 1973.

———. *To Try Men's Souls: Loyalty Tests in American History*. Berkeley: Univ. of California Press, 1959.

Johns, John E. *Florida during the Civil War*. Gainesville: Univ. of Florida Press, 1963.

Johnson, Boyd W. "Cullen Montgomery Baker: The Arkansas-Texas Desperado." *Arkansas Historical Quarterly* 25 (Autumn 1966): 229–34.

Johnson, Ludwell H. "Trading with the Union: The Evolution of Confederate Policy." *Virginia Magazine of History and Biography* 78 (July 1970): 308–25.

Johnson, Michael P. *Toward a Patriarchal Republic: The Secession of Georgia*. Baton Rouge: Louisiana State Univ. Press, 1977.

Johnston, Angus J., II. "Disloyalty on Confederate Railroads in Virginia." *Virginia Magazine of History and Biography* 63 (Oct. 1955): 410–26.

Jones, Allen W. "Military Events in Texas during the Civil War, 1861–1865." *Southwestern Historical Quarterly* 64 (July 1960): 64–70.

Jordan, Terry G. *German Seed in Texas Soil: Immigrant Farmers in Nineteenth Century Texas*. Austin: Univ. of Texas Press, 1966.

———. "The German Settlement of Texas after 1865." *Southwestern Historical Quarterly* 73 (Oct. 1969): 193–212.

Kelley, Donald B. "Intellectual Isolation: Gateway to Secession in Mississippi." *Journal of Mississippi History* 36 (Feb. 1974): 17–37.

Kerby, Robert L. *Kirby Smith's Confederacy: The Trans-Mississippi South, 1863–1865*. New York: Columbia Univ. Press, 1972.

Kettner, James H. *The Development of American Citizenship, 1608–1870*. Chapel Hill: Univ. of North Carolina Press, 1978.

Kibler, Lillian Adele. *Benjamin F. Perry, South Carolina Unionist*. Durham, NC: Duke Univ. Press, 1946.

———. "Unionist Sentiment in South Carolina in 1860." *Journal of Southern History* 4 (Aug. 1938): 346–66.

Klement, Frank L. *The Copperheads in the Middle West*. Chicago, IL: Univ. of Chicago Press, 1960.

———. *The Limits of Dissent: Clement L. Vallandigham and the Civil War*. Lexington: Univ. Press of Kentucky, 1970.

Kruman, Marc W. *Parties and Politics in North Carolina, 1836–1865*. Baton Rouge: Louisiana State Univ. Press, 1983.

Lack, Paul D. "Slavery and Vigilantism in Austin, Texas, 1840–1860." *Southwestern Historical Quarterly* 75 (July 1981): 1–20.

Landrum, Graham, and Allan Smith. *Grayson County*. Fort Worth, TX: Historical Publishers, 1967.

Lang, Herbert H. "J. F. H. Claiborne at 'Laurel Wood' Plantation, 1853–1870." *Journal of Mississippi History* 18 (Jan. 1956): 1–17.

Lathrop, Barnes F. "Disaffection in Confederate Louisiana: The Case of William Hyman." *Journal of Southern History* 24 (Aug. 1958): 308–18.

Ledbetter, Bill. "Slave Unrest and White Panic: The Impact of Black Republicanism in Antebellum Texas." *Texana*, 10, no. 4 (1972), 335–50.

Lee, Charles Robert, Jr. *The Confederate Constitutions*. Chapel Hill: Univ. of North Carolina Press, 1963.

Leverett, Rudy H. *Legend of the Free State of Jones*. Jackson: Univ. Press of Mississippi, 1984.

Lightfoot, Billy Bob. "The Negro Exodus from Comanche County, Texas." *Southwestern Historical Quarterly* 56 (Jan. 1953): 407–16.

Litwack, Leon F. *Been in the Storm so Long: The Aftermath of Slavery*. New York: Alfred A. Knopf, 1979.

Lonn, Ella. *Desertion during the Civil War*. New York: Century Co., 1928.

———. *Foreigners in the Confederacy*. Chapel Hill: Univ. of North Carolina Press, 1940.

Lowrie, Samuel H. *Culture Conflict in Texas, 1821–1835*. Reprint. New York: AMS Press, 1967.

Lucas, Mattie Davis, and Mita H. Hall. *A History of Grayson County, Texas*. Sherman, TX: Scruggs Printing Co. 1936.

Lynch, James D. *The Bench and Bar of Texas*. St. Louis, MO: Nixon Jones Printing Co., 1885.

McCardle, John. *The Idea of a Southern Nation: Southern Nationalists and Southern Nationalism, 1830–1860*. New York: W. W. Norton, 1979.

McComb, David G. *Houston: The Bayou City*. Austin: Univ. of Texas Press, 1969.

McConnell, Weston J. *Social Cleavages in Texas: A Study of the Proposed*

Division of the State. New York: Columbia Univ. Press, 1925.

McKay, Seth Shepard. *Texas Politics, 1906–1944: With Special Reference to the German Counties.* Lubbock: Texas Tech Press, 1952.

McKibben, Davidson Burns. "Negro Slave Insurrections in Mississippi, 1800–1865." *Journal of Negro History* 34 (Jan. 1949): 73–90.

McPherson, James M. *Ordeal by Fire: The Civil War and Reconstruction.* New York: Alfred A. Knopf, 1982.

McWilliams, Carey. *North from Mexico: The Spanish-speaking People of the United States.* New York: Greenwood Press Reprint, 1968.

Maher, Edward R., Jr. "Sam Houston and Secession." *Southwestern Historical Quarterly* 55 (April 1952): 448–58.

Mantell, Martin E. *Johnson, Grant, and the Politics of Reconstruction.* New York: Columbia Univ. Press, 1973.

Martin, Bessie. *Desertion of Alabama Troops from the Confederate Army: A Study in Sectionalism.* New York: Columbia Univ. Press, 1932.

Massey, Mary Elizabeth. *Refugee Life in the Confederacy.* Baton Rouge: Louisiana State Univ. Press, 1964.

Mathews, Donald G. *Religion in the Old South.* Chicago: Univ. of Chicago Press, 1977.

Memorial and Genealogical Record of Southwest Texas. Chicago, IL: Goodspeed Brothers, 1894.

Mering, John V. "The Constitutional Union Campaign of 1860: An Example of the Paranoid Style." *Mid-America* 60 (April–July 1978): 95–106.

———. "The Slave-State Constitutional Unionists and the Politics of Consensus." *Journal of Southern History* 43 (Aug. 1977): 395–410.

Mills, Gary B. "Alexandria, Louisiana: A 'Confederate' City at War with Itself." *Red River Valley Historical Review* 5 (Winter 1980): 23–36.

Mohr, Clarence L. *On the Threshold of Freedom: Masters and Slaves in Civil War Georgia.* Athens: Univ. of Georgia Press, 1986.

Moneyhon, Carl H. "George T. Ruby and the Politics of Expedience in Texas." In *Southern Black Leaders of the Reconstruction Era*, edited by Howard N. Rabinowitz. Urbana: Univ. of Illinois Press, 1982.

———. *Republicanism in Reconstruction Texas.* Austin: Univ. of Texas Press, 1980.

Montejano, David. *Anglos and Mexicans in the Making of Texas, 1836–1986.* Austin: Univ. of Texas Press, 1987.

Moore, Albert B. *Conscription and Conflict in the Confederacy.* New York: Macmillan, 1924.

Muir, Andrew Forest. "The Free Negro in Harris County, Texas." *Southwestern Historical Quarterly* 46 (Jan. 1943): 214–38.

Nelson, William H. *The American Tory.* London: Oxford Univ. Press, 1961.

Nieman, Donald G. *To Set the Law in Motion: The Freedmen's Bureau and the Legal Rights of Blacks, 1865–1868.* Millwood, NY: KTO Press, 1979.

Norton, Wesley. "The Methodist Episcopal Church and the Civil Disturbances in North Texas in 1859 and 1860." *Southwestern Historical Quarterly* 68 (Jan. 1965): 317–41.

Nueces County Historical Society. *The History of Nueces County.* Austin: Jenkins Publishing Co., 1972.

Nunn, William Curtis. *Texas under the Carpetbaggers.* Austin: Univ. of Texas Press, 1962.

Oates, Stephen B. "Texas under the Secessionists." *Southwestern Historical Quarterly* 67 (Oct. 1963): 167–212.

Osterweis, Rollin G. *The Myth of the Lost Cause, 1865–1900.* Hamden, CT: Archon Books, 1973.

———. *Romanticism and Nationalism in the Old South.* New Haven, CT: Yale Univ. Press, 1949.

Overdyke, W. Darrell. *The Know-Nothing Party in the South.* Baton Rouge: Louisiana State Univ. Press, 1950.

Owsley, Frank L. "Defeatism in the Confederacy." *North Carolina Historical Review* 3 (July 1926): 446–56.

———. "The Fundamental Cause of the Civil War: Egocentric Sectionalism." *Journal of Southern History* 7 (Feb. 1941): 3–18.

———. *State Rights in the Confederacy.* Chicago: Univ. of Chicago Press, 1925.

Patton, James Welch. *Unionism and Reconstruction in Tennessee, 1860–1869.* Chapel Hill: Univ. of North Carolina Press, 1934.

Perman, Michael. *Reunion without Compromise: The South and Reconstruction, 1865–1868.* Cambridge: Cambridge Univ. Press, 1973.

———. *The Road to Redemption: Southern Politics, 1869–1879.* Chapel Hill: Univ. of North Carolina Press, 1984.

Pitre, Merline. "Richard Allen: The Chequered Career of Houston's First Black State Legislator." *Houston Review* 8 (1986): 79–88.

———. "Robert Lloyd Smith: A Black Lawmaker in the Shadow of Booker T. Washington." *Phylon* 46 (Sept. 1985): 262–68.

———. *Through Many Dangers, Toils and Snares: The Black Leadership of Texas, 1868–1900.* Austin: Eakin Press, 1985.

Potter, David M. *The Impending Crisis, 1848–1861.* New York: Harper and Row, 1976.

———. *The South and the Sectional Conflict.* Baton Rouge: Louisiana State Univ. Press, 1968.

Powell, Lawrence N., and Michael S. Wayne. "Self-Interest and the Decline of Confederate Nationalism." In *The Old South in the Crucible of War,* edited by Harry P. Owens and James J. Cooke, 29–45. Jackson: Univ. Press of Mississippi, 1983.

Quarles, Benjamin. *The Negro in the Civil War.* Boston: Little, Brown & Co., 1953.

Quill, Michael. *Prelude to the Radicals: The North and Reconstruction during 1865.* Washington, D.C.: Univ. Press of America, 1980.

Rable, George C. *But There Was No Peace: The Role of Violence in the Politics of Reconstruction.* Athens: Univ. of Georgia Press, 1984.

Rainwater, Percy Lee. *Mississippi: Storm Center of Secession, 1856–1861.* Baton Rouge, LA: Otto Claitor, 1938.

Ramsdell, Charles W. "The Frontier and Secession." *Studies in Southern History and Politics.* New York: Columbia Univ. Press, 1914.

———. *Reconstruction in Texas.* New York: Columbia Univ. Press, 1910. Reprint. Austin: Univ. of Texas Press, 1970.

———. "The Texas State Military Board, 1862–1865." *Southwestern Historical Quarterly* 27 (April 1924): 253–75.

Ransleben, Guido E. *A Hundred Years of Comfort in Texas.* San Antonio, TX: Naylor Co., 1954.

Raper, Horace W. "William W. Holden and the Peace Movement in North Carolina." *North Carolina Historical Review* 31 (Oct. 1954): 493–516.

Reiger, John F. "Deprivation, Disaffection, and Desertion in Confederate Florida." *Florida Historical Quarterly* 48 (Jan. 1970): 279–98.

Reynolds, Donald E. *Editors Make War: Southern Newspapers in the Secession Crisis.* Nashville, TN: Vanderbilt Univ. Press, 1970.

———. "Smith County and Its Neighbors during the Slave Insurrection Panic of 1860." *Chronicles of Smith County* 10 (Fall 1971): 1–8.

Ribley, C. Peter. *Slaves and Freedmen in Civil War Louisiana.* Baton Rouge: Louisiana State Univ. Press, 1976.

Richards, Leonard L. *"Gentlemen of Property and Standing": Anti-Abolition Mobs in Jacksonian America.* New York: Oxford Univ. Press, 1970.

Rice, Lawrence D. *The Negro in Texas, 1874–1900.* Baton Rouge: Louisiana State Univ. Press, 1971.

Richter, William L. "The Army and the Negro in Texas during Reconstruction, 1865–1870. *East Texas Historical Journal* 10 (Spring 1970): 7–19.

———. *The Army in Texas during Reconstruction, 1865–1870.* College Station, TX: Texas A & M Univ. Press, 1987.

———. " 'Devil Take Them All': Military Rule in Texas." *Southern Studies* 25 (Spring 1986): 5–29.

———. "Spread-Eagle Eccentricities: Military-Civilian Relations in Reconstruction Texas." *Texana* 8, no. 4 (1970), 311–27.

———. " 'We Must Rubb out and begin Anew': The Army and the Republican Party in Texas Reconstruction, 1867–1870." *Civil War History* 19 (Dec. 1973): 334–52.

Ringold, May Spencer. *The Role of the State Legislatures in the Confederacy.* Athens: Univ. of Georgia Press, 1966.

Robinson, William M., Jr. *Justice in Grey: A History of the Judicial System of the Confederate States of America.* Cambridge: Harvard Univ. Press, 1941.

Roper, Laura Wood. "Frederick Law Olmsted and the Western Texas Free-Soil Movement." *American Historical Review* 56 (Oct. 1950): 58–64.

Rose, Willie Lee. *Rehearsal for Reconstruction: The Port Royal Experiment.* New York: Bobbs-Merrill Co., 1964.

Russell, Robert R. *Economic Aspects of Southern Sectionalism, 1840–1861.* Urbana: Univ. of Illinois Press, 1924.

Sandbo, Anna Irene. "Beginnings of the Secession Movement in Texas." *Southwestern Historical Quarterly* 18 (July 1914): 41–74.

———. "The First Session of the Secession Convention of Texas." *Southwestern Historical Quarterly* 18 (Oct. 1914): 162–94.

Sawyer, William E. "Martin Hart, Civil War Guerrilla." *Texas Military History* 3 (Fall 1963): 146–53.

Schott, Christine. "Gustavus Schleicher: A Representative of the Early German Emigrants in Texas." *West Texas Historical Association Yearbook* 28 (Oct. 1952): 50–70.

Schultz, Harold S. *Nationalism and Sectionalism in South Carolina, 1952–1860: A Study of the Movement for Southern Independence.* Durham, NC: Duke Univ. Press, 1950.

Scroggs, Jack B. "Arkansas in the Secession Crisis." *Arkansas Historical Quarterly* 12 (Autumn 1953): 179–224.

Sefton, James E. *The United States Army and Reconstruction, 1865–1877.* Baton Rouge: Louisana State Univ. Press, 1967.

Shafer, Boyd C. *Faces of Nationalism: New Realities and Old Myths.* New York: Harcourt Brace Jovanovich, 1972.

———. *Nationalism, Myth and Reality.* New York: Harcourt, Brace and Co., 1955.

Shanks, Henry T. "Disloyalty to the Confederacy in Southwestern Virginia, 1861–1865." *North Carolina Historical Review* 21 (April 1944): 118–35.

———. *The Secession Movement in Virginia, 1847–1861.* Richmond, VA: Garrett and Massie, 1934.

Shook, Robert W. "The Battle of the Nueces, August 10, 1862." *Southwestern Historical Quarterly* 66 (July 1962): 31–42.

Shugg, Roger W. *Origins of Class Struggle in Louisiana: A Social History of White Farmers and Laborers during Slavery and After.* Baton Rouge: Louisiana State Univ. Press, 1939.

Sibley, Marilyn McAdams. "Charles Stillman: A Case Study of Entrepreneurship on the Rio Grande, 1861–1865." *Southwestern Historical Quarterly* 77 (Oct. 1973): 227–40.

———. *George W. Brackenridge: Maverick Philanthropist.* Austin: Univ. of Texas Press, 1973.

———. *Lone Stars and State Gazettes.* College Station: Texas A & M Univ. Press, 1983.

———. *Travelers in Texas, 1761–1860.* Austin: Univ. of Texas Press, 1967.

Silbey, Joel H. "The Southern National Democrats, 1845–1861." *Mid-America* 47 (July 1965): 176–90.

Singletary, Otis A. "The Texas Militia during Reconstruction." *Southwestern Historical Quarterly* 60 (July 1956): 23–35.

Smallwood, James M. "Black Texans during Reconstruction: First Freedom." *East Texas Historical Journal* 14 (Spring 1976): 9–23.

———. "Disaffection in Confederate Texas: The Great Hanging at Gainesville." *Civil War History* 22 (Dec. 1976): 349–60.

———. "George T. Ruby: Galveston's Black Carpetbagger in Reconstruction Texas." *Houstin Review* 5 (1983): 24–33.

———. *Time of Hope, Time of Despair: Black Texans during Reconstruction.* Port Washington, NY: Kennikat Press, 1981.

———. "When the Klan Rode: White Terror in Reconstruction Texas." *Journal of the West* 25 (Oct. 1986) 4–13.

Smyrl, Frank H. "Texans in the Federal Army, 1861–1865." *Southwestern Historical Quarterly* 65 (Oct. 1961): 234–50.

———. "Unionism in Texas, 1856–1861." *Southwestern Historical Quarterly* 68 (Oct. 1964): 172–95.

Smythe, H. *Historical Sketch of Parker County and Weatherford, Texas.* St. Louis, MO: Louis C. Lavat, 1877.

Sneed, Edgar P. "A Historiography of Reconstruction in Texas: Some Myths and Problems." *Southwestern Historical Quarterly* 72 (April 1969):435–48.

Somers, Dale A. "James P. Newcomb: The Making of a Radical." *Southwestern Historical Quarterly* 72 (April 1969): 449–69.

Sonnichsen, Charles L. *I'll Die before I'll Run: The Story of the Great Feuds of Texas.* New York: Devin-Adair Co., 1962.

Sparks, Randy J. "John P. Osterhaut: Yankee, Rebel, Republican." *Southwestern Historical Quarterly* 90 (Oct. 1986): 111–38.

Stambaugh, J.L., and Lillian Stambaugh. *A History of Collin County, Texas.* Austin: Texas State Historical Association, 1958.

Stampp, Kenneth M. *The Era of Reconstruction, 1865–1877.* New York: Alfred A. Knopf, 1965.

Stephens, Robert W. *August Buchel: Texan Soldier of Fortune.* Dallas: Privately Printed, 1970.

Stuart, Ben C. "Hamilton Stuart: Pioneer Editor." *Southwestern Historical Quarterly* 21 (April 1918): 381–88.

Stuart, Meriwether. "Colonel Ulrich Dahlgren and Richmond's Union Underground." *Virginia Magazine of History and Biography* 72 (April 1964): 152–216.

Sydnor, Charles S. *The Development of Southern Sectionalism, 1819–1848.* Baton Rouge: Louisiana State Univ. Press, 1948.

Takaki, Ronald T. *A Pro-Slavery Crusade: The Agitation to Reopen the African Slave Trade.* New York: The Free Press, 1971.

Tatum, Georgia Lee. *Disloyalty in the Confederacy.* Chapel Hill: Univ. of North Carolina Press, 1934.

Taylor, Joe Gray. *Louisiana Reconstructed, 1863–1877*. Baton Rouge: Louisiana State Univ. Press, 1974.

Taylor, William Charles. *A History of Clay County*. Austin: Jenkins Publishing Co., 1972.

Terrell, Alexander W. "The City of Austin from 1839 to 1865." *Southwestern Historical Quarterly* 14 (Oct. 1910): 113–28.

"Texas Abolitionist." *Washington-on-the-Brazos* 7 (Winter 1982).

Thomas, Emory M. *The Confederate Nation, 1861–1865*. New York: Harper and Row, 1979.

Thompson, Jerry Don. *Vaqueros in Blue and Gray*. Austin: Presidial Press, 1976.

Thrall, Homer S. *A Pictorial History of Texas*. St. Louis, MO: N.D. Thompson and Co., 1879.

Tiling, Moritz. *History of the German Element in Texas, 1820–1850*. Houston, TX: Moritz Tiling, 1913.

Trelease, Allen W. *White Terror: The Ku Klux Klan Conspiracy and Southern Reconstruction*. New York: Harper and Row, 1971.

Tucker, Glenn. *Zeb Vance: Champion of Personal Freedom*. Indianapolis, IN: Bobbs-Merrill Co., 1965.

Tyler, George W. *The History of Bell County*. San Antonio: Naylor Co., 1936.

Tyler, Ronnie C. "The Callahan Expedition of 1855: Indians or Negroes." *Southwestern Historical Quarterly* 70 (April 1967): 574–85.

———. *Santiago Vidaurri and the Southern Confederacy*. Austin: Texas State Historical Association, 1973.

Wallace, Ernest. *The Howling of the Coyotes: Reconstruction Efforts to Divide Texas*. College Station: Texas A & M Univ. Press, 1979.

Waller, John L. *Colossal Hamilton of Texas: A Biography of Andrew Jackson Hamilton*. El Paso: Texas Western Press, 1968.

Warren, Robert Penn. *The Legacy of the Civil War*. New York: Random House, 1961.

Weaver, Bobby D. *Castro's Colony: Empresario Development in Texas, 1842–1865*. College Station: Texas A & M Univ. Press, 1985.

Webb, Walter P., ed. *The Handbook of Texas*. Vols. 1–2. Austin: Texas State Historical Association, 1952.

———. *The Texas Rangers: A Century of Frontier Defense*. Boston: Houghton Mifflin Co., 1935.

Wesley, Charles H. *The Collapse of the Confederacy*. Washington, D.C., Associated Publishers, 1937.

White, William W. "The Texas Slave Insurrection of 1860." *Southwestern Historical Quarterly* 52 (Jan. 1949): 259–85.

Wiley, Bell I. *The Life of Johnny Reb: The Common Soldier of the Confederacy*. Baton Rouge: Louisiana State Univ. Press, 1978.

———. *The Road to Appomattox*. Memphis, TN: Memphis State College Press, 1956.

Wilkinson, Joseph B. *Laredo and the Rio Grande Frontier.* Austin: Jenkins Publishing Co., 1975.

Williams, Marjorie L., ed. *Fayette County: Past and Present.* LaGrange, TX: Marjorie Williams, 1976.

Wilson, Charles Reagan. *Baptized in Blood. The Religion of the Lost Cause, 1865–1920.* Athens: Univ. of Georgia Press, 1980.

Wilson, Gary. "The Ordeal of William H. Cowdin and the Officers of the Forty-second Massachusetts Regiment: Union Prisoners in Texas." *East Texas Historical Journal* 23 (1986): 16–26.

Wilson, Major L. *Space, Time, and Freedom: The Quest for Nationality and the Irrepressible Conflict, 1815–1861.* Westport, CT: Greenwood Press, 1974.

Winters, John D. *The Civil War in Louisiana.* Baton Rouge: Louisiana State Univ. Press, 1963.

Wish, Harvey. "Slave Disloyalty under the Confederacy." *Journal of Negro History* 23 (Oct. 1938): 435–50.

———. "The Slave Insurrection Panic of 1856." *Journal of Southern History* 5 (May 1939): 206–27.

Wood, Peter H. *Black Majority: Negroes in Colonial South Carolina from 1670 through the Stono Rebellion.* New York: W. W. Norton, 1974.

Wooster, Ralph A. "Ben H. Epperson: East Texas Lawyer, Legislator and Civil Leader." *East Texas Historical Journal* 5 (March 1967): 29–42.

Works Projects Administration (WPA). *St. David's through the Years.* Austin: Betty Gilmer Chapter of St. David's Guild, 1942.

Worley, Ted R. "The Arkansas Peace Society of 1861: A Study in Mountain Unionism." *Journal of Southern History* 24 (Nov. 1958): 445–56.

Wright, Edward Needles. *Conscientious Objectors in the Civil War.* New York: A. S. Barnes and Co., 1931.

Wyatt-Brown, Bertram. *Southern Honor: Ethics and Behavior in the Old South.* New York: Oxford Univ. Press, 1982.

Yearns, Wilfred Buck. *The Confederate Congress.* Athens: Univ. of Georgia Press, 1960.

Zuker, Adolf E., ed. *The Forty-eighters: Political Refugees of the German Revolution of 1848.* New York: Columbia Univ. Press, 1950.

Theses, Dissertations, and Seminar Papers

Andrews, Rena Mazyck. "German Pioneers in Texas: Civil War Period." MA thesis, Univ. of Chicago, 1929.

Ash, Bette Gay. "The Mexican Texans in the Civil War." MA thesis, East Texas State Univ., 1972.

Baggett, James A. "The Rise and Fall of the Texas Radicals, 1867–1883." PhD diss., North Texas State Univ., 1972.

Carrier, John Pressley. "A Political History of Texas during the Reconstruction, 1865–1874." PhD diss., Vanderbilt Univ., 1971.

Chapin, Walter T. "Presidential Reconstruction in Texas, 1865–1867." MA thesis, North Texas State Univ., 1979.

Colby, Ira Christopher. "The Freedmen's Bureau in Texas and Its Impact on the Emerging Social Welfare System and Black-White Social Relations, 1865–1885." PhD diss., Univ. of Pennsylvania, 1984.

Cowling, Anne. "The Civil War Trade of the Lower Rio Grande Valley." MA thesis, Univ. of Texas, 1926.

Crews, Litha. "The Know Nothing Party in Texas." MA thesis, Univ. of Texas, 1925.

Dorsett, Jesse. "Blacks in Reconstruction Texas, 1865–1877." PhD diss., Texas Christian Univ., 1981.

Dugas, Vera Lea. "A Social and Economic History of Texas in the Civil War and Reconstruction Period." PhD diss., Univ. of Texas, 1963.

Durant, Susan S. "The Gently Furled Banner: The Development of the Myth of the Lost Cause, 1865–1900." PhD diss., Univ. of North Carolina at Chapel Hill, 1972.

Ellsworth, Lois. "San Antonio during the Civil War." MA thesis, Univ. of Texas, 1938.

Felgar, Robert P. "Texas in the War for Southern Independence, 1861–1865." PhD diss., Univ. of Texas, 1935.

Franzetti, Robert Joseph. "Elisha Marshall Pease and Reconstruction." MA thesis, Southwest Texas State Univ., 1970.

Garner, Ruby. "Galveston during the Civil War." MA thesis, Univ. of Texas, 1927.

Graf, LeRoy P. "The Economic History of the Lower Rio Grande Valley, 1820–1875." PhD diss., Harvard Univ., 1942.

Gray, Ronald N. "Edmund J. Davis: Radical Republican and Reconstruction Governor of Texas." PhD diss., Texas Tech Univ., 1976.

Griffin, Roger Allen. "Connecticut Yankee in Texas: A Biography of Elisha Marshall Pease." PhD diss., Univ. of Texas, 1973.

Hall, Ada Maria. "The Texas Germans in State and National Politics, 1850–1865." MA thesis, Univ. of Texas, 1938.

Hering, Julia Lee. "The Secession Movement in Texas." MA thesis, Univ. of Texas, 1933.

Irby, James A. "Confederate Austin, 1861–1865." MA thesis, Univ. of Texas, 1953.

Kirven, Lamar L. "A Century of Wafare: Black Texans." PhD diss., Indiana Univ., 1974.

Lack, Paul D. "Urban Slavery in the Southwest." PhD diss., Texas Tech Univ., 1973.

Ledbetter, Billy Don. "Slavery, Fear, and Disunion in the Lone Star State: Texans' Attitudes toward Secession and the Union, 1846–1861." PhD diss., North Texas State Univ., 1972.

Maretta, John A. "William Pitt Ballinger: Public Servant, Private Pragmatist." PhD diss., Rice University, 1985.

Marten, James A. "Drawing the Line: Disloyalty and Dissent in Texas, 1856–1874." PhD diss., University of Texas at Austin, 1986.

Martin, James B. "Terror in Texas: Violence and Fear in the Hill Country during the Civil War." Seminar paper, University of Texas at Austin, 1985.

Meiners, Fredericka Ann. "The Texas Governorship, 1861–1865: Biography of an Office." PhD diss., Rice Univ., 1974.

Mills, B.H. "Elisha Marshall Pease: A Biography." MA thesis, Univ. of Texas, 1927.

Newsome, Zoie Odom. "Antislavery Sentiment in Texas, 1821–1861." MA thesis, Texas Technological College, 1968.

Rice, Lawrence D. "The Negro in Texas, 1874–1900." PhD diss., Texas Technological College, 1967.

Riley, John Denny. "Santos Benavides: His Influence on the Lower Rio Grande, 1823–1891." PhD diss., Texas Christian Univ., 1976.

Sandlin, Betty J. "The Texas Reconstruction Constitutional Convention of 1868–1869." PhD diss., Texas Tech Univ., 1970.

Scarborough, Jane Lynn. "George W. Paschal: Texas Unionist and Scalawag Jurisprudent." PhD diss., Rice Univ., 1972.

Shook, Robert W. "German Unionism in Texas during the Civil War and Reconstruction." MA thesis, North Texas State Univ., 1957.

Sinclair, Oran Lonnie. "Crossroads of Conviction: A Study of the Texas Political Mind, 1856–1861." PhD diss., Rice Univ., 1975.

Smyrl, Frank H. "Unionism, Abolitionism, and Vigilantism in Texas, 1856–1865." MA thesis, Univ. of Texas, 1961.

Tausch, E. R. "Southern Sentiment among the Texas Germans during the Civil War and Reconstruction." MA thesis, Univ. of Texas, 1965.

Terrill, Annie C. "A Calendar of the Memorials and Petitions to the Legislature of Texas, 1861–1877." MA thesis, Univ. of Texas, 1936.

Thompson, James Heaven. "A Nineteenth-Century History of Cameron County, Texas." MA thesis, Univ. of Texas, 1965.

Tyler, Ronnie C. "Slave Owners and Runaway Slaves in Texas." MA thesis, Texas Christian Univ., 1966.

Index

MOORFIELD STOREY *and the Abolitionist Tradition*

MOORFIELD STOREY
*Courtesy of the National Association for
the Advancement of Colored People*

MOORFIELD STOREY

and the Abolitionist Tradition

WILLIAM B. HIXSON, Jr.

NEW YORK   OXFORD UNIVERSITY PRESS   1972

To Vivian

Preface

This book began as a doctoral dissertation at Columbia University when, in the typical quandary of a graduate student, I found that the projects I had been considering were for one reason or another no longer possible to complete. My attention was first focused on Storey by Mark A. DeWolfe Howe's *Portrait of an Independent: Moorfield Storey, 1845–1929* (Boston: Houghton Mifflin, 1932), a book which impresses me now, as it did then, as contained a good selection of his letters but as unimaginatively organized and outdated in approach. My appetite whetted, I eventually located the various manuscripts and began the research.

Unlike other historians who have tended to approach Storey from his position as an Independent reformer in the late nineteenth century, I was drawn to him through earlier research on the history of the civil-rights movement, and saw him first as president of the National Association for the Advancement of Colored People. Work on the dissertation was begun in 1965, the year of the march on Selma, and also of the intervention in Santo Domingo and the escalation in Vietnam; and it would be disingenuous of me not to note that my interest in Storey's career was maintained by the relevance of the problems he considered, and the positions he took, to those of our own time. At the same time, as I hope the manuscript makes clear, I have been impressed by the degree to which Storey was a product of his own time, the degree to which he represented the fulfillment of the nineteenth-century reform tradition and should not be considered a harbinger of contemporary dissent.

This book is a study of Moorfield Storey's public career, because his public career is more interesting to historians and to the general public than his private life; and also because I did not have access to whatever materials portray the private side of the man. What glimpses one gets of Storey from the public record reveal him as a completely successful lawyer and give me no reason to doubt that he was a devoted husband and father as well. And his correspondence further indicates that for a man of such strong opinions he had a remarkable ability to preserve friendships with those who disagreed with him.

My deepest debt in writing this book is to Moorfield Storey's son, Charles M. Storey, who, while the family manuscripts were still in his possession, graciously allowed me to spend every day for almost a month in his library looking at his father's letters. In late 1969, Mr. Storey donated his father's papers to the Massachusetts Historical Society, and I am grateful for their permission to quote them here.

I wish also to thank the staffs of the Houghton Library of Harvard University, the Manuscripts Division of the Library of Congress, and the Massachusetts Historical Society for their courtesy in helping me through other manuscript collections. I am particularly indebted to the staff of the Williams College Library for their kindness in allowing me to use their facilities over four summers.

Research in the various manuscript collections was made possible through a Woodrow Wilson Dissertation Fellowship, and successive All-University Research Grants from Michigan State University.

Portions of Parts III and IV originally appeared, in somewhat different form, in the *Journal of American History* and the

New England Quarterly, and are here reproduced with the editors' permission. I would also like to thank the following publishers for permission to quote from copyrighted works: Case Western Reserve University Press, for Robert Cruden, *James Ford Rhodes: The Man, The Historian, His Work;* Harcourt Brace, Jovanovich, for Mary White Ovington, *The Walls Came Tumbling Down;* Harvard University Press for Robert Bacon and James B. Scott (eds.), *Latin America and the United States, Addresses of Elihu Root,* and Elting E. Morison (ed.), *The Letters of Theodore Roosevelt;* Houghton Mifflin for Edward W. Emerson (ed.), *The Early Years of the Saturday Club, 1855–1870,* Worthington C. Ford (ed.), *A Cycle of Adams Letters, 1861–1865,* Mark A. DeWolfe Howe, *James Ford Rhodes, Historian,* and Bliss Perry, *The Life and Letters of Henry Lee Higginson;* Louisiana State University Press for Robert J. Harris, *The Quest for Equality: Congress, the Constitution, and the Supreme Court;* the Macmillan Company for John P. Roche, *The Quest for the Dream: The Development of Civil Rights and Human Relations in Modern America;* and the New York *Times* for Hodding Carter, "Furl That Banner?," which appeared in the *Magazine* for July 25, 1965.

This book owes much to the late Richard Hofstadter, whose perceptive criticism and friendly encouragement were invaluable. James M. McPherson read the manuscript and I am grateful for his comments. My discussion of Storey's career in the NAACP has profited from exchanges with my fellow-scholars in that field, C. Flint Kellogg and Robert L. Zangrando. And finally the entire enterprise has been sustained, intellectually and emotionally, by my wife, Vivian, who has acted as editor and counselor, and who has been forced to hear about Moorfield Storey longer than either of us care to remember.

W. B. H.

East Lansing, Michigan
December 1970

Table of Contents

No people in the history of the world has ever
learned how to govern itself without trying.

Moorfield Storey, 1903

MOORFIELD STOREY *and the Abolitionist Tradition*

1 ❧ The Making of a Reformer

BOUND together by their conviction that they were the agents of God, the founders of Massachusetts saw themselves as the vanguard of the Reformation. They had come to the New World to construct a "holy commonwealth" of the elect, and they were made acutely aware of the responsibilities of their divinely appointed mission by their leader, John Winthrop:

> . . . we shall be as a city upon a hill, the eyes of all people are upon us; so that if we shall deal falsely with our God in this work we have undertaken and so cause Him to withdraw His present help from us, we shall be made a story and a by-word throughout the world.

Moorfield Storey's ancestors had been part of that first great wave of Puritan migration to the American continent. By the time he was born, in 1845, the theological content of Puritanism had long been weakened, but its moral imperatives remained the basis of New England life.

> The first principle I would inculcate in my children [his grandmother wrote] is independence of mind, a determination to act as a rational, accountable, immortal being un-

3

der all the circumstances of this changeful life. Under the
most favorable circumstances you can be no more than a
man, and under the most unfavorable, you need not be
less. Only determine in the strength of God that it shall
be so and His providence toward you will aid the full ac-
complishment of His high purposes.[1]

The Puritan sense of responsibility further implied not only
that an individual was accountable for his own actions, but that
he was "personally responsible for everything done on earth. If
there was a wrong, he was called to right it. . . ." It was his
mother, Storey later recalled, a woman beneath whose "serene
and friendly exterior there lurked a capacity for fierce indignation," who first inspired him to speak out against injustice. But
if it was the women in his family who formed his character, it
was Storey's father who introduced him to the men who most
forcefully presented the young Moorfield with the Puritan response to public questions.[2]

A graduate of Harvard Law School, Charles Storey had
written for the Boston *Atlas,* and during Moorfield's early childhood served as clerk of the Massachusetts House. He was, his
son remembered, "the most perfect gentleman I ever knew. . . .
He had a brilliant mind, a marvelous memory, love of good
books, and fine taste in literature." He included among his close
friends Ebenezer Rockwood Hoar, James Russell Lowell, and
John Holmes, the brother of the Doctor. Widely admired for his
wit, he frequented the more notable social gatherings of the period and was active in several distinguished clubs. Whether joining Emerson on camping trips or serving as Charles Sumner's
secretary, Moorfield Storey benefited from his father's sociabil-
ity; because of it he came to know many of the most eminent
men of nineteenth-century Massachusetts.[3]

It would be incorrect, however, to conclude from Moorfield
Storey's easy movement in the world of the Boston Brahmins
that he had been born to great wealth. On the contrary, the
economic position of the Storey family appears to have grown
increasingly insecure as he entered manhood. Both of his grand-

fathers had, it is true, made substantial fortunes shipping goods to Latin America, but both had met with reverses, and ultimately financial disaster, before he was born. And his father, while "capable of hard and sustained work when the occasion required it . . . , lacked the desire to push himself," so that when his tenure with the legislature ended in 1850 he justified his somewhat desultory practice of law with the hope that he would soon inherit a sizable bequest from an uncle in Havana. The uncle, however, uncharitably fathered two children, and the income from various minor positions in the municipal government was insufficient to support Charles Storey in his declining years. "The result," Moorfield wrote afterward, "was that I was obliged to contribute toward the expenses of my father's family" as a beginning young lawyer, and "I squeezed every copper that came into my hands until I thought I should be a skinflint." It was largely through Storey's own efforts that his economic position gradually rose. Thus, when fifteen years later, Storey was appointed counsel to the Union Pacific Railroad, and when, at fifty years of age, he was elected to the honored position of president of the American Bar Association, he must have taken considerable pride in his career.[4]

Storey's rise to the height of his profession was accompanied by a continuing involvement in public affairs. Like the men of his father's generation whom he so deeply admired, Storey believed that the greater a man's personal good fortune, the greater was his duty to enter political life. As he first argued at his Harvard graduation, "The educated men should form the crown of the state, its leaders, whose object it should be to raise the weaker and more ignorant members of the community to a higher plane." And throughout his life he continued to maintain that "a life of pure study . . . is an aimless and selfish one . . . ," criticizing those of his friends like Henry Adams, who withdrew from public affairs.[5]

Storey began his career as a reformer trying to bring back into public life the standards the men of his youth had represented: honesty, self-sacrifice, and, above all, independence. But whether because he was impressed by the difficulty of restoring earlier standards of political conduct to the rapidly changing society of the period, or because his most compelling public concerns lay elsewhere, by the beginning of the twentieth century his rhetoric had begun to change. From that time on he would argue not so much for a return to older political standards as for a return to the substantive humanitarian values of the world in which he had been raised; and like many of the men he admired he would devote the remainder of his public activity to confronting the evils of racial oppression and imperialist war.

The changes in American society during Storey's lifetime determined, too, that his reform career was to follow a pattern almost directly opposite to that of his father's generation. Typically emerging as isolated individual reformers, these men had moved to participation as Conscience Whigs in the antislavery coalition and ultimately to leadership in the new Republican party. But this was to be the peak of their power. By the time Storey entered political life, many of these same men were leaving the party, and under their influence, he moved with them into a group of Independent reformers, hoping to influence the two major parties from outside. With the disintegration of the Independent movement at the end of the nineteenth century, Storey had no alternative but to return to a career of individual agitation, the very position from which his father's generation had begun.

1. The Antislavery Coalition

The political tradition in which Moorfield Storey was raised assumed a close connection between the moral behavior of individuals and the moral level of their government: Puritan morality and Enlightenment thought both fortified the proposition that a good government could last only as long as there were good men to sustain it. When men like Storey talked about "republican virtue," they referred partly to this abstract proposition, but also to what seemed to them its historical confirmation: the actual "virtue" which sustained the American Republic, produced by the simplicity, integrity, and industry of life in New England small towns before the Civil War. Those who live in the houses of their fathers "have a stake in the community of priceless value to the public weal," Storey later maintained. "It is in towns like these that the high traditions of New England are preserved, that the spirit of ordered freedom is left alive." In such communities, his sister remembered, "there were not so many ways of spending money, nor so many amusements to be had, nor such innumerable social complications" as would develop in the latter part of the century.[6]

Such a simple yet civilized society would, naturally enough, be dominated by men who had developed the art of living well. Unlike their Puritan ancestors, who thought that the purpose of human existence was the glorification of God, and unlike their counterparts elsewhere, who saw it as the acquisition of wealth, these men formed a conception of life that was largely secular in tone yet tempered with the claims of civic duty and the demands of self-discipline. For them, as for the men of the Revolution whom they sought to emulate, the images of classical antiquity were still viable; and when Storey and Emerson's son wrote their memoir of Hoar they felt it necessary to turn again and again to Roman metaphors to describe their subject. Hoar's father "suggested a fine old Roman, and his classmates in college used to call him Cato," while Hoar himself "seemed most to resemble Cincinnatus, a man who at the call of his country, his state, or his town left the plough in the furrow, and when the emergency had passed returned to it again. . . ." His biographers further emphasized that, as with the ancients, Hoar's defense of civic virtue was associated, not with a self-righteous priggishness, but only with an avoidance of extremes:

> He kept a simple but generous table, befitting his station, retaining but adding to the old New England dishes. Grahamites never made a vegetarian out of him, nor did extreme abolitionists induce him to exclude rice, sugar,

coffee, and spice, as slave-labor products, nor temperance
lectures persuade him to confound temperance with ab-
stinence. He came "eating and drinking" but was neither
"glutton nor wine-bibber." [7]

Whatever simple dignity they radiated in person, however,
Hoar and the rest of Charles Storey's friends did not make their
historical reputations by being good citizens, and it was not their
conception of the art of living well so much as their approach to
the art of politics that decisively affected the younger generation.
The political education of Moorfield Storey was determined by
the ideas of the "Conscience Whigs," a group which received its
name the day in 1846 that Hoar rose in the Massachusetts State
Senate to remark that it was time that the legislature represented
the conscience of the Commonwealth as well as its cotton. Regardless of their particular partisan label at any point between
1846 and 1861, this was a group of men—most notably Hoar,
Charles Francis Adams, John Gorham Palfrey, and Charles Sumner—who tried to achieve abolitionist goals within the Whig
constitutional framework.

The space within which the Conscience Whigs could operate
was, of course, provided by the more radical abolitionists themselves, led by William Lloyd Garrison and Wendell Phillips. The
abolitionists hoped through moral appeals to reach the consciences of the slaveholders. But they were confronted by a
Southern society which for its own economic and psychological
reasons was already engaged in a full-scale defense of its "peculiar
institution." Identifying attacks upon slavery with threats to social stability everywhere, Southern leaders gained the support of
political, business, and religious leaders throughout the country.
The abolitionists thereupon charged that the slaveholders were
turning the churches and the government into their agents; but
whatever the validity of these charges, the abolitionists' sweeping attacks on American institutions only perpetuated their
status as a tiny minority. At this juncture, a succession of events
between 1845 and 1848—the hasty annexation of the slaveholding Republic of Texas, the war with Mexico, and the acquisition

of more territory adjacent to the slave states—raised fears about the expansion of slavery among many of the former opponents of the abolitionists, and converted them into a constituency for the Conscience Whigs. While Garrison engaged in his ritual of burning the Constitution, Adams, Hoar, Palfrey, Sumner, and others continued to argue that the restriction of slavery was constitutionally possible, and they strove persistently to confine it within the Old South.[8]

With few exceptions the Conscience Whig leaders came from middle- or upper-class backgrounds; and it was the security which their backgrounds provided, perhaps, which permitted them so completely to follow the dictates of their consciences. In both their personal integrity and their moralistic conception of politics, they remained a singularly high-minded group of public figures; but what they gained in purity they tended to lose in effectiveness. For one thing, their very determination to preserve what they saw as their principles made them fickle partners in any potential antislavery coalition. Having been manipulated by the state Whig organization of several occasions, they left the party in 1848, and, with Democrats who were opposed to the extension of slavery, they helped form the Free Soil party at both the national and state level. Two years later, the Whigs failed to receive the necessary majority in the state election, and the outcome was thrown to the legislature. There, the regular Democrats and Free-Soilers reached an agreement: they would give mutual support to a Free-Soil candidate running for senator and to Democrats running for the state offices. The bargain had a certain rationality—Sumner could attack slavery in the United States Senate, and the Democrats could attack monopolies in the state—but the Democratic candidate for governor supported the Fugitive Slave Law, and the loss of principle was too much for Adams, Palfrey, and Hoar, who thereupon abandoned the new coalition.[9]

In the second place, the preoccupation of the Conscience Whigs with the menace of slavery limited their base of support in a Massachusetts that was feeling the full impact of industrialism. In the 1840's a disastrous combination of land consolidation and the potato blight had forced hundreds of thousands of Irishmen to leave their homeland: the accidents of trade routes brought many of them to Boston. The accelerated rate of immigration after 1845 created a new labor supply and led to further industrial expansion, but it also caused the collapse of local relief and public-health institutions and the deterioration of parts of Boston into crowded, disease-ridden slums. With their peasant suspicion of radical social change, with their Church teaching that slavery was not necessarily sinful, and with their competition in the unskilled labor market adding a personal resentment of the free Negro, the Irish inevitably clashed with the abstract humanitarianism of the antislavery coalition.[10]

To some antislavery men it seemed that the way to curb this new opposition to their crusade (as well as the old opposition of the textile magnates, who were tied to Southern cotton) was to reduce Boston's representation. In 1853 widespread sentiment against the state's cumbersome election procedures had resulted in a constitutional convention: dominated by the remnants of the coalitionist Free-Soilers, the delegates redistricted the legislature in favor of the small-town bastions of antislavery sentiment. Though the convention's final product, a new constitution, was backed by Senator Sumner from Washington, it was tied too closely to devious tactics for Adams, Palfrey, and Hoar; and so they incongruously joined the Cotton Whigs and the Catholic hierarchy to defeat the constitution. The next year the same confusion of purpose reappeared. As the Whig party collapsed under the explicit repeal of the Missouri Compromise in the Kansas–Nebraska Act, Massachusetts voters rushed en masse into the new anti-immigration, anti-Catholic Know-Nothing party. Some Free-Soilers rationalized their participation in the new party on the basis that it struck at the clerical defenders of slavery. But Adams, Palfrey, and Hoar, and Sumner, in this case— partly out of a principled rejection of bigotry, and partly, one suspects, out of a distrust of coalitions—ended 1854 in political isolation.

Two years later all of these men had entered the new Republican party, and it was as Republicans that they made their impact on history. Adams, as Ambassador to the Court of St. James's, bore much of the responsibility for keeping Great Britain neutral during the Civil War. Sumner, though Chairman of the Senate Foreign Relations Committee, made his major impact as the staunchest advocate of civil rights for the freedman among American statesmen of his time. Storey, as secretary to Sumner, absorbed the humanitarian concerns and the moralistic approach to politics that characterized the Conscience Whigs of Massachusetts.

Storey's clerkship with Sumner was the result of his father's efforts. Though most of his political attitudes appear to have been identical with those of the Conscience Whigs, Charles Storey remained with the party until 1850 when, according to his son, he left it out of revulsion at Webster's support of the Fugitive Slave Law. Not having been a Free-Soiler, he was relieved of his clerkship in the Massachusetts House when the coalition gained control. By 1856, Charles Storey had become the "Sumner Republican" Moorfield remembered: in that year he introduced his son to the antislavery senator, who was recovering from a severe beating he had received at the hands of a self-appointed defender of Southern honor. Eleven years later Charles Storey was able to write his son that "Mr. F. V. Balch and Mr. Edward L. Pierce have called to see about your taking the place of secretary to Mr. Sumner, who is favorably impresed with the accounts he has received of you. . . ." Storey, who was so eager to escape from his second year at Harvard Law School that he had contemplated signing on as a ship's clerk, enthusiastically accepted the offer. In late November of 1867 he arrived in Washington.[11]

Officially, Storey was Sumner's personal secretary and clerk to the Foreign Relations Committee; in fact, the specific duties to which he had been assigned impressed him as a series of tedious chores. Beginning in January 1868, he occupied a vacant room in the senator's house, and each morning he would go downstairs to meet with the petitioners who, in those days before

congressional office buildings, filled the rooms of their congressmen's homes. Storey also answered Sumner's correspondence,
and he complained to his college roommate about having to reply to those "whose views, doubtless of importance in Los Lunas,
N. Mexico, or S. Malden, Mass., seem hardly to have the same
weight here or materially effect the national policy." But even
from that lowly position, a twenty-three-year-old and highly impressionable young man could participate in the excitement of
Washington society: one event he never forgot was a dinner
party Sumner gave for Charles Dickens, at which Storey and
Secretary of War Edwin Stanton were the only other guests.
And most of all, as the senator's secretary Moorfield Storey developed a lifelong admiration for the ideals and the career of
Charles Sumner.[12]

The major events in Washington during Storey's clerkship
were, of course, the congressional impeachment proceedings
against President Andrew Johnson. Although the argument in the
House was ostensibly over the President's violation of specific
restrictions on his power of appointment, the final break culminated two years of tension between Johnson and Republicans in
Congress. A lifelong Democrat and champion of the small farmers of Tennessee, Johnson, not surprisingly, showed neither
Lincoln's interest in the continued supremacy of the Republican
party nor his growing acceptance of the idea that some civil
rights must be granted the former slaves. During his first year,
therefore, Johnson restored self-government to the defeated Confederate states, in spite of Republican anxiety that the abolition
of the Constitution's three-fifths clause would increase Southern
representation in Congress and emerging Northern opposition to
what seemed to be attempts to return the Negro to his former
servitude. In 1866 and 1867 Johnson's attitude toward the South
and toward the freedmen turned Northern opinion against him
and pushed Republican moderates toward the most militant
members of the party, the Radicals. This resulted in the passage
of the Fourteenth Amendment, guaranteeing citizenship to all
Americans; the imposition of Negro suffrage on the Southern

states as a condition of their return to the Union; and the only impeachment proceedings ever brought against a President of the United States.[13]

When Storey arrived in Washington, he wrote to his father about the conflict between Johnson and the Congress, and he was harsh in his condemnation of the President. He termed "absurd" Johnson's refusal to recognize that the seceding states had in fact left the Union and that therefore Congress, and not the President, possessed the authority to set the terms for their return. Accusing him of usurping power, Storey particularly attacked Johnson for his constant reference to "Africanization" if civil rights were granted the freedmen, calling it "an abominable appeal to prejudice." Initially dubious about the wisdom of impeachment, he was not long in Washington before he became convinced that both the preservation of the freedmen's rights and the security of the nation required it. When, however, the long-awaited trial took place in the spring of 1868 (the House prosecuting, the Senate sitting as jury), he soon became contemptuous of the behavior of the participants on both sides of the contest.[14]

As the trial progressed, Storey felt "not a little disgusted with the Congress of the United States. . . . It scarcely becomes the House to charge Andrew Johnson with indecent harangues, while the beam in its own eye is so great." He was appalled at the conduct of the prosecution by the House managers: "Logan's speech was simply disgraceful"; Wilson and Bingham did not "touch a real point of their case"; Butler "displayed remarkable acuteness in working in apparently irrelevant testimony" but "brought the trial down to the level of a petty larceny case"; Boutwell's argument "was absolutely without plan." On the other side, of the Republican senators who voted for acquittal, Storey felt that Fessenden "has allowed his personal prejudices to warp his judgment"; Trumbull "is a cold, ambitious, narrow-minded man"; and "Fowler and Ross, especially the latter, there is too much reason to fear have been bought." [15]

Though Sumner was the leader of the Radicals in the Senate, and a major force in the fight against Johnson, as far as Storey was concerned none of the sordidness seemed to touch the senator personally. Yet it would not be correct to say that Storey idolized Sumner. Upon moving into Sumner's house, for example, he soon became aware of some of the senator's idiosyncracies:

> Mr. Sumner is not great at conversation, properly so called, I think. He can make himself very agreeable if he likes, and frequently does, but he either does all the talking himself and goes off into long disquisitions, or he simply draws out the other person and lets him do the talking, so it is a monologue on one side or the other.

As the months passed, Storey became the daily companion of a man desperately in search of friendship beyond the calculated associations of official Washington. The extent to which Sumner was friendless (and whether he was to blame for it) seems destined to be one of the permanent minor controversies of American historiography. But the senator had a genuine affection for Storey, an affection fully reciprocated by the younger man. "I recall too many instances of his kindly thought for myself and others not to feel that his essential nature has been much misrepresented," Storey wrote fifty years later. Until he died, he missed few opportunities to defend Sumner against the bitter criticism that was even then engulfing his reputation.[16]

In his own biography of Sumner, written as part of the Houghton Mifflin *American Statesmen* series, Storey conceded that the senator had important flaws:

> He was a man of great ability but not of the highest intellectual power, nor was he a master of style. He was not incisive in thought or speech. His orations were overloaded, his rhetoric was often turgid, he was easily led into irrelevance and undue stress upon undisputed points. His untiring industry as a reader had filled his memory with associations which perhaps he valued unduly. Originally modest and not self-confident, the result of his long contest was to make him egotistical and dogmatic.

He was willing to say this against Sumner, but little more; and the views of a man who lived in the same house and saw his subject day in and day out cannot easily be brushed aside. In the last analysis, Storey agreed with Emerson: "It characterizes a man for me that he hates Charles Sumner: for it shows that he cannot discriminate between a foible and a vice." For Storey, Sumner's virtues clearly overshadowed his weaknesses. "Sumner," he wrote, "was by nature essentially simple, sincere, affectionate, and kindly, and in the words of a classmate, he was possessed by a 'life-and-death earnestness.'" He may have been dogmatic, but "as you would probably be somewhat intolerant in dealing with a man who defended forgery or murder, so he who regarded slavery as the sum of all villainies was somewhat intolerant with a man who undertook to defend that, especially if he came from the North." [17]

By the time he was ready to leave Washington in the spring of 1869, Storey's preparation for a career seemed complete. From the Latin School through Harvard College he had received the best education Boston had to offer. Then, in 1870, he married Miss Gertrude Cutts of Washington, a grand-niece of Dolly Madison, and a descendant on her mother's side from Thomas Jefferson. Having already directed his preparation for the bar examination, Sumner was able to secure for Storey a position as Assistant District Attorney for Suffolk County. In 1873 Storey joined the law firm of Brooks and Ball, becoming a junior partner at twenty-eight. Twenty years before it would have seemed obvious that any man of Storey's capability and connections would be headed for a major political career. Indeed, there is every reason to think that Storey expected it. If the educated men "will assert their rightful pre-eminence and prove themselves worthy to lead," he had assured his Harvard classmates, "they will find the people ever ready to follow. . . ."

Yet by the time Storey began the practice of law, the men whom his generation had used as models, men whose placing of principle above compromise he sought to emulate, were ending their lives in political isolation. In the 1870's Palfrey retired to write history; Adams and Hoar were defeated in elections; and Sumner, at odds with the Grant administration, was denied his chairmanship by his Senate colleagues. If, as Storey indicated at his graduation, he and his contemporaries wanted to enter politics to commemorate their fallen classmates, so that "the country which they saved may be made worthy of the sacrifice they made," it was increasingly apparent that it could not be done holding office in the dominant Republican party.[18]

2. The Independent Movement

Even while the constitutional rights of the freedmen were being extended under Reconstruction, many in Massachusetts worried whether the "public spirit" that made the Union's victory possible could be long maintained. During the war some had hoped that a moral reformation would result from the crisis of the Union and that it would move the country toward traditional New England ideals. "It will depend upon the generation to which you and I belong," Henry Adams had written his brother in 1862, "whether the country is to be brought back to its true course and the New England element is to carry the victory. . . ." When "the New England element" committed themselves to the Republican party, they had assumed that others in the party shared their beliefs, among them that, as his father wrote Moorfield Storey, "it is only by the resolution of every citizen to sacrifice his immediate convenience for the general public weal" that the Republic could be maintained. But from his vantage point in Sumner's office, Storey was made increasingly aware that a sense of self-sacrifice characterized neither the Republican party nor postwar Americans.

New office-seekers look very much like old ones, and afford us no new sensations, only the same old disgust. I hate the cant of these fellows. They ask office "because they wish to serve their country and are convinced of their eminent fitness for the position they seek," "because their state deserves recognition," "because it is time the officers of the volunteer navy were rewarded"—in fact for every reason but the true one which none have the manliness to state, their own desire for the honor or emolument.[19]

If, as Massachusetts spokesmen feared, the Republican party was changing from an association of principled opponents of slavery and defenders of the Union to a group of self-interested careerists, the new President, Ulysses S. Grant, was making no effort to discourage the process. "Grant certainly shows great confidence in his own sagacity," Storey wrote shortly before returning to Boston, "and no disposition to seek advice." A self-confidence useful in winning battles proved disastrous in administering public affairs, and Grant's refusal to consider the possibility of malfeasance among his appointees allowed corrupt and ruthless men to burrow into his administration by the score. As Grant's first term progressed, Jay Gould and Jim Fisk were tapping Treasury wires to further their scheme of cornering the gold market; the Secretary of War was selling Indian trading posts; and within the White House itself, one personal aide was pocketing the proceeds from specially levied whiskey taxes while another was squandering millions on statues for Washington's parks.[20]

The local counterpart of the Grant administration was, as far as the friends of the Storey family were concerned, the organization of Representative Benjamin F. Butler. For them Butler was (and for Moorfield Storey he would remain) the careerist *par excellence,* dedicated to nothing but his own ambition. Butler had begun as a flamboyant district attorney and was widely known before the war as a staunch Democrat—indeed, as one of those who helped nominate John C. Breckenridge in 1860, a Democrat of Southern sympathies. When the war came he enlisted in the Union army, and though persistent questions were raised both as to his military capability and as to the disappearance of money in his possession, he was promoted to the rank of general. The war transformed Butler from a pro-Southern

Democrat into a Radical Republican, and as such he entered the House in 1866. He soon constructed a coalition of Union army veterans, Irish immigrants, mill-workers, and Negroes into a machine of such efficiency that he easily defeated the well-known writer and reformer Richard Henry Dana, Jr., in 1868, even though Dana was backed by the money and prestige of the community.[21]

Dana's defeat appalled his Brahmin supporters, including the Storey family, and not only because his opponent had such a dubious political past. It was Butler's program fully as much as his record that antagonized respectable Massachusetts. At the time, at least, his advocacy of civil rights for the freedmen was indistinguishable from that of other Republicans; but his support for a ten-hour day for workers and expanded veterans' pensions struck many as demagogic and socially divisive. What Butler's opponents found most unacceptable, however, was his advocacy of retaining in circulation the greenbacks, paper money issued by the government under wartime duress. Highly popular with the entrepreneurs and the farmers of the Middle States and the West regardless of party, proposals for the continued inflation of the currency were linked by Butler and many of his Radical Republican colleagues with advocacy of a protective tariff. The conjunction of these two proposals revealed the majoritarianism implicit in the Radical Republican position, for he and the others were quite willing to use the full powers of the Federal Government not only to secure rights for the former slaves, but also to secure any demands their constituents might make.[22]

The men who influenced the young Moorfield Storey had come from an era in which the sectional controversy over slavery and not interest-group dissension over economic policy had been dominant, and they were already sympathetic to the laissez-faire idea that the play of individual initiative should be limited only by the operation of the free market. They therefore argued that inflation of the currency and a protective tariff were unnecessary extensions of government power and violations of sound principle. But beyond that, they also maintained that these economic proposals would give to individuals wealth which they had not earned, and thus would weaken the moral fiber of the Republic. Storey's father summed up the position of Butler's opponents when he commended Dana on his campaign and concurred that "a republic stands on justice and the mutual confidence of its citizens. Let one class of citizens conspire openly to rob another class, and civil war has actually begun." Ever since the time of the Puritans, the leaders of Massachusetts had believed that success through individual effort reflected the moral order of the universe, and they did not now propose to abandon their convictions to accommodate iron manufacturers from Pennsylvania or indebted farmers in the Mississippi Valley.[23]

With the Republican party degenerating into a morass of graft and incompetence, with the Reconstruction regimes in the South increasingly dependent on military force for their continuance, and with men such as Butler assuming roles of party leadership, the ties which men such as Moorfield Storey might have had with the Grant administration became increasingly brittle. They were shattered by a series of events, beginning with Grant's attempt to push through a treaty of annexation with Santo Domingo, negotiated through her dictator. His efforts blocked in the Senate by Sumner, Grant retaliated by having Sumner stripped of his chairmanship. Then he decided to appease the pro-Sumner faction by giving them a place in his Cabinet; and to make room, he asked the unpopular Hoar to resign as Attorney General. This treatment of Sumner and Hoar pushed many of Storey's contemporaries (though probably not Storey himself) into open opposition, and they joined the defecting Liberal Republicans in their ill-fated attempt at coalition with the Democrats in 1872.[24]

In 1874, Henry Cabot Lodge, still one of Henry Adams's graduate students, asked Storey, Brooks Adams, and some others to join with him in "an organization intended to unite men of both parties in support of good government." Called the Commonwealth Club, it gave way in two years to a frankly partisan organization supporting for President the man who had uncovered the whiskey-ring scandals, Treasury Secretary Benjamin Bristow.

Henry Adams and Lodge made a fruitless attempt to gain the Republican nomination for Bristow and briefly toyed with independent action. Failing in both plans, and unimpressed by the man the convention eventually chose, the undistinguished Governor of Ohio, Rutherford B. Hayes, they voted for the nemesis of the Tweed Ring, the Democrat Samuel J. Tilden. Storey, less embittered by Reconstruction than the Adamses, and less concerned about the exploitation of the sectional issue than Lodge, voted Republican.[25]

For Lodge the election of 1876 was his last independent fling before settling down as a regular Republican; for both Storey and the Adamses, however, it marked their deepening involvement in the post–Civil War "Independent movement." The crusade which this movement would wage was against what the Adamses, in defending their vote for Tilden, called "the tendency of our political system for corruption." "Corruption" meant more to these men than the graft of the Grant administration, for they also referred to the economic policies—condemned by them as divisive, unsound, and immoral—advocated by men like General Butler. Beginning as a reaction to the environment of the early 1870's, therefore, the Independent movement advocated both political and economic reforms. Political reform included not only the placing of honest men in office regardless of party, but also the gradual elimination of the spoils system through the institution of a competitive civil service. Economic reform involved the reduction of government expenditure and, save for the maintenance of a single monetary standard of gold, the abstention of the government from interference with the economy. Noting the closeness of elections in the period following Reconstruction, the Independents tried to organize themselves into a bloc holding the critical balance of power between the two parties and from that position attempted to demand the implementation of their program.[26]

Drawn generally from the culturally influential, socially prominent, commercial and professional classes of the Eastern seaboard, the Independent movement was especially vigorous in

Boston, for in few other places was there more concern over the decline in political standards. And in Boston, the force behind Independent activity was an association of younger men, the Massachusetts Reform Club. It was there that Moorfield Storey began his career as an Independent reformer. Like the Conscience Whigs of their fathers' generation, Storey and the other members of the Club saw themselves as engaged in the defense of principles, and Storey, for one, bitterly resented accusations of personal ambition and political prejudice. Having already organized the successful House campaign for fellow-reformer Theodore Lyman, by 1883 the Club felt assured enough to organize against the man they had long felt was the greatest menace to their principles, and to end, once and for all, the career of Benjamin Butler.[27]

Correctly suspecting that powerful forces in the state Republican party were determined to defeat him, Butler had carried his machine into the Democratic party, and as a Democrat had won the governorship in 1882. The conflict between General Butler and his Brahmin opponents remained implacable, but the issue between them after 1882 was not without its ironies. While a member of the House, Butler had championed active government intervention in monetary, tariff, and labor affairs, and so occasioned the enmity of advocates of laissez-faire, but in his administration as governor, he was dedicated to the strict retrenchment of the state government. Thus his proposals—slashing expenditures for public education, closing the women's reformatory, and reducing funds for the state poorhouse—antagonized all those who prided themselves on the Massachusetts tradition of humanitarian reform. Butler's sensational and unfounded charges that the poorhouse was secretly selling its dead inmates to the Harvard Medical School gave his opponents the perfect opportunity to discredit his career. Together with Hoar, Storey prodded his fellow Overseers into denying Butler the honorary degree traditionally given by Harvard to the governor, and that done, moved quickly toward organizing all the opponents of Butler. He kept pleading with Lodge, now the Republican state chairman, to persuade his party to nominate a gubernatorial candidate jointly with the Independents, or at the very least, to submerge party identity on a common platform of "we are opposed to Butler and Butlerism." And as a personal contribution, Storey wrote a lengthy document cumulating Butler's misdeeds, in order to reach those voters who remained, as he put it, "entirely ignorant of Butler's previous history." The Republican-Independent coalition prevailed, and in a hard-fought campaign Butler was defeated for re-election.[28]

Fresh from their victory over Butler, Storey and his friends in the Massachusetts Reform Club looked forward to an active political role in the presidential campaign of 1884. And, from the moment the Reform Club asked those Bostonians dissatisfied with the Republican nominee, James G. Blaine, to meet on the afternoon of June 13, Storey in particular played a significant role. It was to him, for example, that James Mulligan, Blaine's voluble correspondent, came with additional letters revealing the extent of the Republican leader's previous connections with the Fort Smith and Little Rock Railroad. Storey advised Mulligan to release the letters anonymously, to prevent a repetition of Blaine's melodramatic defense of his actions in 1876, and then he proceeded to make use of their contents in a pamphlet he wrote anonymously. Later he was one of the delegates to the New York convention of Independents called to consider the endorsement of the Democratic candidate Grover Cleveland. In retrospect, the convention had a slightly ludicrous look: after solemnly agreeing that "the issue of the present campaign is moral not political," the group adjourned, only to be told of Cleveland's affair with a Buffalo widow and of his support payments for her illegitimate child. But whatever his youthful indiscretions had been, Cleveland proved to be the perfect Democrat for the Independents to support.[29]

Personally honest and a firm believer in laissez-faire, Cleveland as President would present only one problem for the Independents. For in addition to their agitation for honest men in office and for limited government, they had sought to erase the memories of Grant and Butler by imposing upon the Federal Government a classified civil service. From 1865, when a bill was introduced in Congress to create a commission to administer competitive examinations for the civil service, until 1883, when a similar proposal was signed into law, civil service reform generated an enthusiasm among these Massachusetts spokesmen matched only by the antislavery crusade. Behind the Independents' agitation, however, lay their conviction that partisan loyalty should not be a requirement for an administrative position. As soon as Cleveland was elected, therefore, they began arguing that he should make his administration a test case of the principle of nonpartisanship by keeping competent Republicans in office. Cleveland, however, as head of a party which had been out of power for a quarter-century, not surprisingly operated on the premise that "the importance of general administrative reform has appeared to be superior to the incidental civil service reform." Thus, though he extended the merit system in that part of the civil service classified under the 1883 law, he made little effort to keep Republicans elsewhere in office. Indeed, as Cleveland neared the end of his term, his record seemed so unsatisfactory to the civil service reformers that while Storey expected to support the President for re-election, he thought "it better that he should not count on our support" because "the Democrats should understand" that reformers "won't support Democrats in doing what they left Republicans *for* doing." [30]

The disappointment of the Massachusetts Independents with Cleveland's civil service record was balanced to some degree by their opportunities to obtain control of the state Democratic organization. Upon entering that organization, however, the Independents came face to face with the Irish, who had backed Butler only a few years before and were still more interested in patronage than in the principle of "good government." The confrontation undoubtedly heightened the Independents' suspicions of immigrants in general, for the Irish were among the most assimilated of the newcomers; what, the reformers wondered, would be the political consequences of the current large-scale migration from southern and eastern Europe? Almost to a man they agreed that the immigrants would certainly not help men like themselves, who were trying to maintain the highest standards in public life. Storey spoke for them all when he wrote:

> The foreigners who seek our shores know little of our society, our methods, our history, or the traditions of our government. Their prejudices, their habits of thought, their entire unfamiliarity with American questions—in a word their whole past, unfit them to take an intelligent part in our political contests, yet in a few years they become citizens and their votes in the ballot-box count as much as our own.[31]

Many Massachusetts Independents were so frightened about the prospects that they joined Republicans like Lodge, who wanted to curtail immigration, and not a few indulged in the increasingly fashionable rhetoric about the immigrants' "inherent" incapacity for American citizenship. Storey, while agreeing that large-scale immigration presented a problem, remained firmly opposed to racial arguments of all sorts, and deplored the trend toward restriction. At one point he seems to have considered an extended naturalization period, but his main emphasis, then as later, was on education, "the only cure for the evils which spring from ignorance. . . .":

> You may start with this postulate, that the majority of people of this country or any other country want good government. They desire just what you desire. They only do not know how. Now, if you have a meeting in a hall and invite none but civil service reformers who think as you do, you do not reach these men. If once a year, just before election, you go down and talk to them, even if you give them some money when they are unemployed, you do not reach them. They say, "What they want is our votes." . . . You have got to get down side by side and interest yourselves in the daily lives of these people, stand with them, understand their problems, work with

them in January, February, March and April, as well as in November, before you have any real influence.

And, he continued to remind his audience,

> it is not the poor and ignorant men who are bought,—it is not even the corrupt politicians who distribute the money,—against whom public opinion should be turned. These are the tools, and as long as there are men to use them, the supply of tools will not fail. . . . The real offenders are the rich and respectable members of society who supply the money to accomplish a desired political result, who select unscrupulous men to spend it, and then shut their eyes.[32]

Even with the best will in the world, however, a reconciliation between the Brahmin Independents and the working-class Irishmen was not so easily affected. The Independents' commitment to limited government was not at issue, for that aspect of their program was quite compatible with the political culture of the Irish, a compound of Catholic conservatism and Jacksonian laissez-faire. The division, rather, came more over the Independents' passion for civil service reform and the underlying attitudes which led them to support it. The reformers were quite correct in their assumption that the replacement of patronage with the merit system would be savagely attacked by the spoilsmen, and they were forced to expend much of their energy refuting charges that their proposals required a college education for garbagemen. Storey, for one, was convinced of the compatibility of the merit system with the democratic tradition, and he was quite as much concerned with the need to create an efficient municipal bureaucracy as he was with restoring moral tone to American politics. Yet so permeated was Independent rhetoric with the theme of an upper-class mission to redeem the political system that the workingmen soon concluded that civil service reform was a device to exclude them from public employment. And any merit system would curtail those who did not have the advantages of a middle-class background—those like the immigrants, who had to depend directly upon organizations to achieve political power.[33]

With these differences between the Yankees and the Irish, it was not surprising that the efforts of the Independents to push their own "public-spirited" candidates tended to degenerate into ethnic clashes. But in at least two significant cases they prevailed: their candidates were selected by Cleveland over Irish rivals for the positions of Secretary of War and Collector of the Boston Port. With reformers increasingly occupying key positions, the Massachusetts Democratic party began to acquire an upper-class Yankee tone. And though the Independents' aspirations were temporarily set back by Cleveland's narrow defeat in 1888, they moved on to their greatest triumph in 1890, when they succeeded in nominating the reform-minded mayor of Cambridge, William E. Russell, for governor. Russell was elected, becoming the first respectable Democratic governor in half a century, and the Independents now had new incentives for supporting the party organization. Two years later, in his third try for the presidency, Cleveland won by a handsome majority, and the Independents were at the height of their influence. In spite of a squabble between Storey and fellow-reformer Josiah Quincy over the extent of patronage in the State Department, reform of the civil service was no longer the dominant issue in Cleveland's second administration.[34]

A deepening agricultural depression provided the background for the Populist movement of the early 1890's. For various reasons that movement became identified with the unlimited coinage of silver as a panacea for alleviating economic conditions. Perceiving the popularity of this simple appeal, the Republicans had attempted to head off discontent in 1890 by passing legislation which increased the Federal Government's purchase of silver. When Cleveland returned to office in 1893, he stood firm on the gold standard, and in doing so he not only won the support of the Eastern financial community, but he also received the warm approval of those who had long considered inflation, like the tariff, a violation of the moral discipline necessary to sustain the Republic.

Cleveland and the Independents may have moved within the same moral universe, but in 1894 it was obvious that much of the rest of the country did not. As the agricultural depression spread into industry and gangs of jobless men roamed the countryside, Cleveland continued to place the highest priority on the preservation of the gold standard, successfully repealing the Republican legislation of 1890 and ultimately relying on the House of Morgan to maintain the Federal Government's reserves. While he refused to grant relief to drought-stricken farmer, he was quick to send Federal troops to Chicago when a cutback in the employment of railroad workers provoked a mass strike in the summer of 1894. In the congressional elections of that year, the conservative wing of the Democratic party was decimated as Republican swept the East, and the South and the West focused their inchoate grievances in a demand for "free silver." By 1895 the Independents had gained a President, but they had lost the Democratic party.

At first, various Independent leaders considered the possibility of a third party, but they decided to hold back in the faint hope that a pro-Cleveland Democrat like Russell might gain the nomination. After the 1896 convention, however, when the young William Jennings Bryan swept the delegates off their feet with his "Cross of Gold" speech and became the presidential candidate, the Independents abandoned their attempt to save the party. Many Massachusetts Independents were so incensed by the Democratic platform, which not only declared for "free silver," but also attacked the property-conscious Supreme Court, that they voted for the Republican, William McKinley. Others, like Storey, could not make the transition. He had written in 1892 that "the dominating issue is tariff reform" and so could hardly support McKinley, the author of the highest tariff act in American history. Repelled by both candidates and convinced that after the election "there must be some trustworthy organization to which the voters can turn," he backed former Senator John M. Palmer of Illinois, nominee of the pro-Cleveland National Democratic party. Palmer offered himself as a low-tariff, anti-inflationist reformer, but he was hardly interested in beginning a permanent third party. He made no secret of his basic purpose to defeat Bryan, and it is difficult to believe that those who voted for him did not realize that they were in effect supporting McKinley.[35]

Whether they supported McKinley or Palmer, the Independents had destroyed what remaining political influence they still possessed. With few exceptions, they had cut themselves off from the Democratic party without endearing themselves to those who had stayed with Blaine in 1884. More significantly, in pursuing their economic orthodoxies the Independents compromised their self-appointed role as moral guardians of American politics. Whatever effect the limitations of Bryan's mind or the provincialism of his supporters had on his chances of success, he remains the victim of one of the best-financed, most ruthless campaigns in American history. His opponents were at least as hysterical as his supporters, and considerably more influential: in 1896 both major parties were so obsessed with the monetary question that they missed the real problems of controlling industrial power. The Independents, who prided themselves on their rationality, indulged in as much distorted rhetoric as the Republican organization, and with far more feeling: their "Independent" judgment, it would seem, had become subservient to their economic fears.[36]

The fears of the respectable during this period were so great, in fact, that a number of their spokesmen openly questioned the capacity of the American people for self-government. This was especially true in the legal profession, where the judicial nullification of social and economic legislation acquired a sudden popularity. Lawyers looked on approvingly as the Supreme Court successively struck down a Federal income tax, then gutted the Sherman Anti-Trust Act's application to manufacturing, while construing its prohibitions on "restraints of trade" strictly against militant labor leaders. Storey, then reaching the pinnacle of his legal career, assumed a more conciliatory stance. Addressing his colleagues in the American Bar Association in

1894, he informed them that, however offensive some of its consequences might be, the current agitation sprang from a deep-rooted political crisis. The American people had lost faith in their state and national governments, he told his audience, and were particularly disillusioned with their legislatures:

> The people of the United States have been taught an implicit confidence in the power of the government. If times are hard, no matter from what cause, the party in power is held responsible. It is to the legislature that they naturally turn for relief. If ever they believe that this omnipotence is corruptly controlled by money, that their misery at any moment is the result of laws purchased by their employers or creditors, if they have lost their faith in peaceful agitation and relief within the law, they will begin to consider how they can help themselves, law or no law.[37]

It might be expected from this diagnosis that Storey's remedies for the situation would be equally bold, and in some ways they were: his call for court-enforced reapportionment, for a restriction on campaign expenditures, and for limitations on the power of the Speaker of the House anticipated the agenda of twentieth-century political reform. But as one reads on, the speech gives a growing sense of unfulfilled expectations. Its theme was that the legislature should be made more efficient and more representative so that the public's faith in its institutions might be restored—but Storey omitted any discussion of what the substantive legislative result of such reforms might be, perhaps because of his own ambivalence on the subject. In his presidential address to the Bar Association in 1896, Storey referred to "the rapid growth of the disposition to assert the general interest of the community at the expense of individual freedom, or perhaps, to put it more accurately, of individual selfishness," and he noted with approval the passage of regulatory measures in the several states. But there is no evidence that at that point he had yielded his basic conviction about the moral and economic wisdom of laissez-faire, and he lamented after

the election of that year that men like himself were now forced
to choose between two parties, one controlled by "a movement
to enhance by law the value of silver, organized and promoted
by men directly interested in the production of that metal . . . ,"
and the other "by a combination of other producers, who wish
the taxing power of the government used to increase the value of
their products." [38]

It was awkward enough to favor democracy and laissez-faire
in a time of increasing popular pressure for government intervention in the economy; it must have been even more uncomfortable to regard oneself as part of a bloc holding the balance of
power and be consistently ignored by the two major parties. The
Massachusetts Republicans had shown little enough appreciation when the Independents helped defeat Butler, and the
Democratic party only a little more after the defeat of Blaine;
but the behavior of the Republicans after 1896 revealed the
depths of ingratitude. "They took office knowing that to the
votes of Democrats they owed their triumph," Storey charged,
"and that these votes were not cast for a protective tariff." When
the McKinley administration promptly passed a new protective
tariff, Storey complained that the Independents had been betrayed; what he did not know was that McKinley's "betrayal" of
the Independents—if "betrayal" it was—had just begun. "Ah, you
may be sure," the newly inaugurated President had told one
leading Independent, "There will be no jingo nonsense under my
administration." In the next three years, however, there would be
bitter debate over the administration's expansionist policies; and
for many of the Independents "anti-imperialism" became their
final, futile effort to save the virtue of the Republic.[39]

The Spanish-American War and the annexation of the Philippines marked the end of the Independent movement; the same
crisis saw the beginning of the major phase of the reform career
of Moorfield Storey. Until that time, there seemed little in his
experience to distinguish him from other young men of his
acquaintance. A Puritan sense of responsibility, an exposure
to the principles of the Conscience Whigs, and an attempt to fol-

low their example in politics—these surely characterized the Adamses even more than they did Storey. Storey's Radical Republicanism of 1868 was no different from that of men who would later turn against even the memory of Reconstruction. Twenty years after his Washington experience, Storey still did not appear to differ from many other Brahmin Independents. But sixty years later, at the time of his death, he stood out among his contemporaries in his championship of civil equality and self-determination, and he was almost alone in Massachusetts in carrying on the pre-Civil War agitation for human rights.

3. The Survival of Humanitarianism

To understand why Storey's subsequent career differed from those of his contemporaries, it is necessary to place him more precisely in his immediate social and intellectual context. To define Storey only as an Independent during the 1869–97 period is to miss the fact that that movement, while middle-class in membership and often upper-class in leadership, nonetheless was comprised of men from different backgrounds with different interests. To concentrate on their persistent appeals for a restoration of moral tone to government, for example, is to overlook the degree to which many Independents represented the emergent social and intellectual forces of the period, forces typically associated with the establishment of industrial capitalism. As individual entrepreneurs, for example, Independents proved themselves quite competent in securing or maintaining control over many of the major corporations of Massachusetts. The movement's laissez-faire program also attracted other businessmen not dependent on government encouragement, while civil service reform appealed to a universal business interest in orderly, efficient government. Finally, with their membership of both academicians and businessmen, the Independents were often the major proponents of new intellectual trends, such as the theories of Charles Darwin and Herbert Spencer.[40]

But if important segments of the Independent constituency, whether aggressive businessmen or scientific intellectuals, were quite attuned to the values of late nineteenth-century America, the fact that some Independents did indeed yearn for the past cannot be ignored. This turning toward past values best explains the development of Moorfield Storey, but we must add two qualifications: first, that the antebellum past meant different things to different men; and second, that in Storey's circles arguments over the past and the future most often occurred among Independents.

Storey's satisfaction with the intellectual world of his youth can best be seen against the background of an informal club to which he was admitted soon after he began his legal practice. Formed by younger men as an alternative to the established Saturday Club, and called simply "the Club," it included the finest minds that late nineteeth-century Massachusetts could produce, and it soon became recognized as a center of uninhibited and brilliant discussion. ". . . I think you will agree with me," one of its members later wrote to another, "that one hears the best talk in the town at our little club."

> Certainly one hears the freest interchange of thought, for the Saturday Club is clever enough, but men do not say all that they wish to, and they do hesitate to express themselves with absolute freedom. In the old days it used to be great fun to hear William James and Wendell Holmes (the Judge) spar, or at any rate excite each other to all sorts of ideas and expressions. . . .

Holmes and James were both friends of Storey, as was Henry Adams, and a brief consideration of their careers, as the most luminous minds of their time and place, may help explain the different path Moorfield Storey followed.[41]

With all three men—Holmes, Adams, and James—it must be admitted that their attitudes were shaped in part by parental influences and personal crises. In the case of Holmes it was the testing of an acquired skepticism in a near-fatal combat ex-

perience; in the case of James the challenge to his father's strenuous optimism wrought by an emotional breakdown; in the case
of Adams, a whole series of calamities, from his father's estrange-
ment from the Republican party to the suicide of his wife. Any
discussion of thinkers of the stature of Holmes, Adams, and James,
however, must deal not only with their personal experiences but
with intellectual influences as well. The thought of all three
men took as its starting-point the image of the universe modern
science had given them. Confronting a determinist universe without transcendent purpose, subject to no laws but those of its
own evolution, their first reaction was intellectual passivity. One
could gauge the forces governing the universe, even adjust to
them, but one could not, it seemed, change them. Adams
abandoned his initial interest in Independent politics, and spent
the rest of his life shuttling back and forth between the centuries,
trying to find the points at which medieval unity had dissolved
into contemporary chaos. Holmes devoted his judicial career to
eliminating *a priori* principles from the law, allowing it to adjust
to evolving power relationships. The eloquence of his later pleas
for dissenters would come not from any sympathy for social
reform, but from a revulsion at the unfairness of repressing
dissident movements before they had a chance to compete for
political power. Of the three thinkers, James alone ended by rejecting the image of a deterministic universe, and asserted the
possibility of chance and thus of moral action. But the larger
philosophical task he set himself seems to have absorbed almost
all his energies, preventing him from applying his deep human
sympathy to public questions on more than rare occasions. It
would be for younger men like John Dewey to apply pragmatism
to social thought.[42]

With Adams, Holmes, and James among his associates, it
could not have been easy for Storey to avoid discussions of the
new science; it must have been even more difficult since one of
his most intimate friends was involved in working out some of
its intellectual implications. Thomas Sergeant Perry, like his colleagues Henry James and William Dean Howells, was one of the

founders of the "realist" school of literary criticism. Convinced that literature must be studied in the context of the evolving society from which it came, Perry tried to persuade Storey of the general relevance of evolutionary thought:

> The notion of evolution which has been spreading in Germany for a century has raised that country to the place it holds in all matters of research, and is indubitably the only way in which modern thought that is to count for anything can move. . . . And you must remember that Evolution is nothing terrible after all; it is merely the hypothesis that everything is a matter of growth, as opposed to the notion of special creations.

There is no evidence that his letter had any impact on Storey's subsequent thought. For that matter, though he lived through an intellectual revolution, one cannot find, either in Storey's published work or in his personal correspondence, any mention of the ideas (positivism, utilitarianism, Darwinism) which so profoundly influenced his contemporaries.[43]

If the intellectual quest of most men begins in their college years, it would seem plausible to blame at least part of Storey's intellectual isolation on the Harvard of the 1860's. The College which Storey entered in 1862 raised academic drudgery to the level of official policy. Though written examinations had largely replaced the notorious system of daily recitations, an ingeniously restrictive grading system remained in force under which points gained in academic performance were negated by points lost in minor infractions of discipline. With such barriers against youthful curiosity, it is not surprising that Storey enjoyed his undergraduate days chiefly for the opportunities they offered for parties, the literary Institute of 1770, and the productions of the Hasty Pudding Club. More, perhaps, because of his native intelligence than because of his devotion to work, he managed to be graduated sixth in a class of 106.[44]

Yet even in these "Dark Ages" of Harvard (preceding the "Renaissance" under President Eliot) there were outposts of brilliance in the faculty: Louis Agassiz and Asa Gray debating Darwin's theory of evolution, and Lowell beginning Dante studies in America. Henry Adams (Class of 1858), for one, was able to reach them. Storey, even in retrospect, chose not to mention his professors. In his defense of the pre-Eliot curriculum, made to an audience of undergraduates in 1896, he maintained that "studying the same books" produced a "close intimacy"; he defended "required labor" as good discipline since "every profession calling involves its own drudgery"; but he ignored every member of the faculty except Lowell—and Lowell appeared, not as Professor of Modern Languages, but as author of the "Commemoration Ode." It is understandable that remembering his years at Harvard, Storey would say, "the scenes which come most readily to my memory, undimmed by time, are all associated with the war." But his subsequent tributes, in this 1896 address, to the courage of Garrison and the wisdom of Emerson suggest priorities determined not by wartime developments but by his own choice of influences. The influences he cited may well have been the major ones on his youth; they were not, however, those of Harvard.[45]

If Storey's intellectual life while at Harvard contrasts with that of Adams, his post-collegiate intellectual career can be contrasted with that of Holmes. Recuperating from a combat wound received at the battle of Fredericksburg, Holmes began reading Herbert Spencer. In a roughly comparable period of leisure time during his clerkship with Sumner, Storey decided, not to explore the new science, but to deepen the classical education he had received at Harvard. He found himself interested, he wrote to a childhood friend, in "Finance, International Law, French, Italian, Constitutional Law, Politics, [and] American History"— a list of subjects indicating intellectual breadth perhaps, but not intellectual boldness. In the 1870's Storey succeeded Holmes as one of the editors of the *American Law Review*, but while Holmes had used the *Review* as a testing-ground for the application of anthropology to law, there is little evidence that Storey went beyond his assigned task of editing and writing case notes.[46]

As he began his legal practice, therefore, Storey had isolated himself from the scientific thought that was stirring the minds of his contemporaries. By the time he reached the height of his legal career, not only had science become remote from his own interests, but, seeing its determinist implications used to justify a whole series of social evils, he may well have congratulated himself on his lack of acquaintance with it. By that time, the prevalent idea that " 'philanthropy' and the feeling of 'common humanity' have nothing to do with any problem which involves the relations between men" had become deeply repugnant to him. And when it supported racial discrimination and imperialist aggression, so that the rights of self-government "we deny at home, we now deny all over the world," he felt compelled to reject it *in toto* and take his stand on old-fashioned humanistic values.[47]

What those values represented for Storey was first illustrated during his service from 1877 to 1907 on the Harvard Board of Overseers. Particularly in his insistence on the importance of Greek and Latin in the curriculum, but also on other issues, Storey stood with Harvard Fine Arts Professor Charles Eliot Norton against their business-minded colleagues who wanted a more "practical," more "modern" orientation for the college. Behind this voting alignment lay a similarity of perspective which Storey himself noted at Norton's death: "There was no man living with whom I felt in such complete sympathy." As a literary critic deploring the loss of cultural standards in an era of democracy, however, Norton stands pre-eminently among those Independents who wished to return to a stabler past. He never hid the fact that he thought the era of his childhood a far better time, and he would refer wistfully to "New England during the first thirty years of the century, before the coming in of Jacksonian Democracy, the invasion of the Irish, and the establishment of the system of Protection." [48]

Storey also revered the world of his childhood, and their fondness for the past may have brought the two men together. But as he wrote Norton's daughter, his past was different from her father's. That this difference represented more than the obvious fact that he was twenty years younger, Storey did not bring out; for his "golden age," the "years between 1840 and, say, 1870," were also the years of the sectional conflict and the Civil War. Like Norton, he may have wanted to return to the high statesmanship of the pre-industrial Republic; but he definitely wanted to bring back the moral fervor of the abolitionists. Storey's defense of the traditional curriculum, therefore, though shared by Norton could lead to conclusions that Norton would not have accepted.[49]

One issue in particular that came before the Board suggests the values that Storey wished to preserve. For if the years of Eliot's administration marked the institution of a flexible curriculum, they were also the years in which Harvard discovered football. Storey's attempts to bar Harvard participation in intercollegiate athletic competition had met with defeat as early as 1888, and appeared to be permanently doomed when, in 1896, Henry Lee Higginson donated a large plot of land for the construction of Soldier's Field. But Storey persisted in his opposition. Far from denying that exercise should play an important part in the lives of college men, he insisted upon it. Indeed, he remembered with some pride his own youthful exertions. By the time he had left Harvard, he wrote in his autobiography, he had "walked forty miles in a day," "had swum the longest distance across Fresh Pond without fatigue," and "could fence with any standard weapon—small sword, saber, single stick, [or] bayonet. . . ." Such healthy exercise for all Harvard students would, Storey feared, be hurt—and certainly not be helped— by the new regime of spectator sports. Intercollegiate athletic competition was also wrong, in Storey's mind, because it distorted the basic academic purpose of the university. "Today," he complained, "the brilliant scholar too often finds that his scholarship brings him little of honor or the social consideration which men prize, while both wait for the successful athlete." [50]

Storey's opposition to intercollegiate athletics—like his insistence on the importance of Greek and Latin to the curriculum

—can be seen as reflecting a loyalty to older ideals of education. But the debate over intercollegiate athletics—as Higginson's donation of "Soldier's Field" indicates—involved larger issues. America, in the late nineteenth century, was engaged in a search for national stamina. Some saw the toughness developed on the playing field as a substitute for that of the battlefield; others saw it as preparation for more violent pursuits—no one more so than Theodore Roosevelt. When Roosevelt carried his preaching of the "strenuous life" into the White House, Storey noted that the President first "divided boys into two classes, 'molly-coddle boys' and those 'who like to use their fists' . . ." and then went on to argue that "everyone who believes in a policy of justice and peace rather than of war . . . is a 'weakling and a coward.'" As a result, Storey charged, young Americans "grow up to believe that the strong warrior is the perfect type of man, and that the nation whose armies and navies make it the terror of its weaker neighbors, is the only great nation. . . ."[51]

Thus Storey's opposition to intercollegiate athletics, while it came from an old-fashioned devotion to classical education, may also signify the first indication of a deep revulsion at the prevalent glorification of physical force. Almost alone among his contemporaries, Storey did not feel compelled to establish his virility by advocating either violent sports or a violent foreign policy. And he mantaned that position with equanimity, though he had not served in what was regarded as the great testing-ground of his generation, the Civil War. He had regularly drilled with his classmates at the Boston Latin School during the first year of the war, with the intention of enlisting, but seems to have changed his mind (perhaps because of parental pressure), and spent four years at Harvard instead. In later years, he indicated no regrets about not having served, though he did not doubt that the war had afforded "opportunity for the highest patriotism, the rarest courage, the noblest self-sacrifice, and such examples appeal to us all. . . ."[52]

But these virtues, he insisted, "were not the fruit of war, but were the product of the long peace and the most perfect civilization which preceded that war." Indeed, courage and self-sacrifice on behalf of a noble cause were found in full measure among the abolitionists before the war; and theirs, Storey suggested, was the higher courage:

> The censure of neighbors, the averted faces of former friends, the shafts of ridicule, and all the thousand ways in which the community makes its disapproval felt, are practically harder to meet than bullets or bayonets, and many a man dares not encounter them who would march to his death in battle without flinching.

"The courage which will risk political death and personal obloquy . . . is the courage we want," he told his audiences, "and that is the strenuous life which some among us ought to preach." Storey had moved from championing calisthenics in the age of college football to defending William Lloyd Garrison in the era of Theodore Roosevelt. Entering public life as a defender of classical education, he emerged as one of the last champions of the ideals of the pre-Civil War humanitarian reformers.[53]

Totally opposed to the determinism of his science-minded friends, Storey continued to work for the restoration of the intellectual outlook in which he had been raised, an outlook which for him included pacifism, anti-imperialism, and racial egalitarianism fully as much as it did laissez-faire and moral tone in government. It was the breadth of this outlook which saved Storey's reputation as a reformer; had he devoted his energies solely to the defense of laissez-faire and "good government," he would deserve the oblivion into which so many other eminent Bostonians of his time have fallen. It is because Storey was less interested in defending economic principles than in defending human rights that he stands out in his time. For the early twentieth century witnessed the assertion of American "interests" in the Pacific and the Caribbean that rode roughshod over the pride of weaker peoples; and it saw a heightened ethnocentrism within America that denied acceptance to the immigrant and constitutional rights to the Negro. In the face of these evils many progressives fell silent—and some led the brutal crusade to preserve "Anglo-Saxon supremacy." If it was sympathy for the plight of little children working all day in factories that motivated the best of the progressives, it was concern over the victims of national and racial exploitation—sympathy with the Filipinos, the Haitians, the Mexicans; and with Negro and Japanese Americans—that engaged Moorfield Storey.

4. The Citizen as Agitator

Storey enjoyed a love affair with the law that lasted his entire life, but the law is notoriously a jealous mistress; and Storey was often forced to relegate reform to third place, behind his profession and his family. Even with this limitation on his activity, however, the problem remained of how to most effectively advocate the principles in which he believed. For a man of his professional stature, it was remarkable how many alternatives he had foreclosed: for example, that of entering politics. There Storey was partly handicapped by the aloofness he had acquired from his father's generation. "As a young man I made up my mind that I should never seek any office, that if my fellow-citizens who were entitled to speak wanted me to take it I should not refuse it,—in other words I meant that the office should seek me and not I the office." For someone like Storey, a political career was further foreclosed by his tenacious personal independence in national politics, which went far beyond the predictable outlook of the Independent movement to which he belonged. Disciple of the founders of the Republican party, and resident of a state carried by the G.O.P. all but twice in his lifetime, he seems to have supported its presidential ticket only four times. On the other hand, he refused to support the Democrats in two critical campaigns, rejecting Bryan on the monetary issue in 1896, and moving away from Wilson even before the 1916 Adamson Act provoked him into voting for Hughes.[54]

The consequences of those two defections highlight Storey's

political isolation. In 1900, those of his "fellow-citizens who were entitled to speak" persuaded him to run as an Independent candidate in the Eleventh Congressional District. His platform was unimpeachable—"that every man under the jurisdiction of the United States is entitled by law to no less and no greater rights than we of Massachusetts hold"—and his speeches were cogent. But he was a candidate who, as one editor wrote after the election,

> declares at the outset that he is against the Republicans on such questions as expansion and protection and against the Democrats on silver, suppression of the colored vote, reconstruction of the Supreme Court and the other populistic ideas which have found approval in the last two Democratic platforms.

However closely his linkage of a high tariff and inflation reflected his Independent past, however closely his connection of imperialism abroad and the oppression of minorities at home prefigures contemporary liberalism—at the time, in 1900, Storey's position only antagonized confirmed supporters of both parties and bewildered the mass of the voters. In the end he polled only 7 per cent of the vote.[55]

Because of its continuing advocacy of Philippine independence and a low tariff, because of Bryan's faith in disarmament, and because of its strong states' rights tradition, the Democratic party received Storey's support from 1900 through 1912. Sooner or later, however, he had to face the consequences of the victory of a party still dominated by white supremacists. When the party did not return to power in 1913, the Wilson administration made segregation in the civil service official policy. In his capacity as president of the National Association for the Advancement of Colored People, Storey threw himself into the fight against it. At the same time, however, Bryan had resigned as Secretary of State, and Oswald Garrison Villard, trying to play an active role in the NAACP and to remain a confidant of the President as well, suggested Storey as a replacement. It is doubtful that

Wilson, never particularly tolerant of those who opposed him, even considered Storey as a possibility. Once again Storey had suffered for his political independence.[56]

"If ever I had gone into public life I could not have stayed there," Storey eventually conceded, "for I have never belonged to any party, or any church, or any great organization like the Masons or the Odd Fellows, or even to any club for any length of time except small dining clubs." What, then, could one individual do? Since citizenship in a republic, Storey argued, meant that each individual became part of public opinion, the citizen's "silence, his indifference, or his thoughtless speech" is effective, "often more effective for ill than he realizes. He must be active for good or he will be counted for evil." [57]

Lowell had written that "if the politicians must look after the parties, there should be somebody to look after the politicians, somebody to ask disagreeable questions and utter uncomfortable truths. . . ." Storey took the adjuration to heart: indeed, on one occasion he almost went so far as to insist that it was *outside* the parties that the greater contribution to civic virtue could be made. "It is by enlisting for a cause, and in some organization formed to advance that cause," he said, "and making that organization so strong that parties must bid for its vote, that one really works to some purpose in politics. . . ." Plainly, the duties of responsible citizenship were for Storey strenuous ones, and at times were indistinguishable from the function of the agitator as conceived by pre-Civil War humanitarian reformers like Wendell Phillips. Storey himself admitted the resemblance: "The citizen in his political action must, as Wendell Phillips said of the agitator, have 'no bread to earn, no candidate to elect, no party to save, no object but the truth,' if he would really serve his country." [58]

If Storey's call for responsible citizenship resembles the philosophy of one of the leading abolitionists, he appears to have turned again and again to the abolitionist movement for personal guidance in his own reform career. "Though I was a boy up to the time when the war began," he wrote, "I was very familiar with some people who were prominent in that agitation and I think I knew their motives." But Storey's interpretation of the abolitionists, as revealed in his many addresses on the subject, indicates something more than personal reminiscence.

> Ah, what a time it was to live in, when "the frozen apathy" which Garrison deplored when he founded *The Liberator* was gradually yielding, and the tide of freedom was constantly rising; when the annexation of Texas with a slave constitution, the Fugitive Slave Law, the repeal of the Missouri Compromise, the expulsion of Samuel Hoar from Charleston, the return of Anthony Burns, the assault on Sumner, the outrages in Kansas and the growing insolence of the slave lords taught the North, as it were line upon line and precept upon precept, what slavery meant to freemen as well as slaves, until secession and the attack on Sumter brought the smouldering fire into fierce life and the conflagration began in which slavery finally perished.[59]

The irreversibility of the pre-Civil War "tide of freedom" was apparent only from the perspective of a half-century, if at all; it had not been obvious to those abolitionists who had supported John Brown in a last gesture of despair. Is it not possible that here Storey was not describing history, but constructing a myth, reciting not a chronology but a catechism? For someone like him, without the consolation of religion and unwilling to accept a scientific determinism, the creation of such a myth may well have been one way of sustaining faith in the possibility of meaningful human action.

> We are passing through a reaction against the great principles of freedom and equal rights to advance which Garrison devoted his life, and we need assured faith. We need to be reminded how much can be accomplished in a good cause by courage, persistence and unwavering devotion against odds which seem to be overwhelming—how certain is the triumph of right.[60]

"Men criticize his methods, complain of his violence, call him fanatic, and question how much he helped to win the victory," Storey said of Garrison; but this was clear: "He inspired the friends of freedom, he roused the defenders of slavery, he made men think and talk. . . ." Storey, unlike Garrison, was hardly about to attack the foundations of American society, but he too wanted to make men think and talk. As he assumed unpopular stands—as he tried to break the sectional compromise on the race question and bipartisan acquiescence in an expansionist foreign policy, for example—he was prepared to admit that, like Garrison's, his agitation might be disruptive. But, as he reminded his audiences, fifty years before it had been a common charge

> that the abolitionists were destructive, that they were seek-
> ing to destroy the great government of this country as it
> was then carried on and established. It is very likely true
> that the action of the abolitionists was destructive of slav-
> ery, but it was constructive of freedom. . . .[61]

2 ❧ Anti-Imperialism

THE decisive event in Moorfield Storey's public career was the Spanish-American War. In the spring of 1898, when the war began, he was fifty-three years old, a highly successful corporation lawyer, and a man whose public interests were largely circumscribed by the limits of Independent reform: free trade, the gold standard, and a classified civil service. Storey's deviations from the opinions of his contemporaries had so far expressed themselves chiefly in his reluctance as a member of the Harvard Board of Overseers to abandon the traditional curriculum. The events spanning the years from 1898 through 1902, however—a war waged to liberate Cuba from Spain, a peace settlement by which the United States acquired the Philippines, another war to suppress a Filipino nationalist movement, and the establishment of a protectorate over Cuba—produced a shift in Storey's perspective so great as to warrant being called a transformation.

Too old, and perhaps too obstinate, to abandon entirely his laissez-faire convictions, Storey nevertheless shifted his attention to entirely new issues during this period. By the beginning of 1903 he was already set on his career as an anti-imperialist critic of American foreign policy, a career which would

45

occupy much of the rest of his life and include not only the original objects of his concern, the Filipinos, but the peoples of Latin America as well. By 1903, his perception of a link between the subjugation of Filipinos abroad and the oppression of Negroes at home had brought Storey back to the egalitarian tradition of his childhood, making him a persistent foe of racial discrimination and turning his formidable legal talent to the defense of black Americans. Entering 1898 as an Independent reformer, by 1903 he was carrying on the tradition of the humanitarian agitators of his youth.

An event of that impact is surely deserving of further consideration. The Spanish-American War and the debate over the ensuing peace settlement marked the last two years of the 1890's; and it has been suggested that those events serve as a historical culmination of the decade as well. The major political fact of the 1890's was the prolonged depression between 1893 and 1897, a depression which developed against an existing slump in farm prices and recurrent labor unrest. That sizable segment of the population which even in the best of times lived close to the subsistence level now struck blindly at those they considered their oppressors. Faced with what seemed assaults on the fabric of American society, the middle class responded with a hysteria of its own. Many Americans turned to various symbolic crusades, in which the fact of social disunity "might be rationalized as a product of foreign influence, or denied by a compensatory demonstration." It is not surprising, therefore, that the decade of the most acute social tensions, 1886 to 1896—the decade of the Haymarket Riot, the Pullman strike, and the rise of the Populists— saw the beginnings of an organized movement to restrict immigration.[1]

Nor is it surprising that the same decade marked the institutionalization of patriotism as a secular religion, with its sacred object (the flag), its rituals (pledges of allegiance by schoolchildren), its saints (the Founding Fathers), and even (in patriotic organizations) its prosecutors of heresy. Because many Americans needed no encouragement to affirm their unqualified loyalty, the impact of the inculcation of this kind of obedience is difficult to measure. But it does seem that the idea expressed by Carl Schurz, "My country, right or wrong: if right to be kept right and if wrong to be set right!," though always the position of a minority was at the time of Schurz's death, in 1906, the conviction of a very small minority indeed. The idea that a citizen might see it as his patriotic duty to oppose a war his government was already waging, though widely held at the time of the Mexican War, and still supported by the anti-imperialists, had become so feeble that opposition to World War I was confined to avowedly "unpatriotic" radicals.[2]

If the proposition that a citizen should totally support any war waged by the government was gaining greater acceptance in the 1890's, so also was the proposition that the government should, on any given occasion, risk war rather than compromise "national honor." Thus Congress—still considered the institutional representative of the popular will—enthusiastically rallied behind the belligerent positions taken by the administrations in power, whether against Canada in 1888, against Chile in 1891, or against Britain in 1892. Then came the depression of 1893. Against the background of bitter strikes, violent resistance to farm foreclosures, and jobless men roaming the countryside, the vague, half-articulated assumption that an aggressive foreign policy might restore a lost national unity began to assume major political importance.[3]

In the midst of the depression, in 1895, the Cleveland administration chose to intervene in a dispute between Great Britain and Venezuela over the boundaries of British Guiana. Though Britain soon agreed to arbitrate the issue, the initial impulse of the nation—until an awareness of British economic connections produced sober second thoughts—was to support the administration's belligerence, even at the cost of war. The same year an insurrection against Spanish rule broke out in Cuba, which was to prove a more effective catalyst for the emergent popular jingoism. Though the Cleveland administration proclaimed American neutrality, Congress, in the summer of 1896, extended belligerent rights to the rebels. Throughout 1896 and 1897 reports reached America of the mass imprisonment of Cubans and scores of individual atrocities. Well-publicized by a group of Cuban exiles and sensationalist newspapers, such stories found the country in a receptive mood. A potential war with benighted Spain, with its appeal both to the prevailing doctrine of Anglo-Saxon supremacy and to reformist impulses thwarted at home, had an appeal that a war with Britain could not possess.[4]

In 1897 McKinley succeeded Cleveland as President. Like Cleveland, he offered to mediate between Spain and the Cubans, and, like Cleveland, he threatened intervention. But unlike Cleveland, McKinley would accept no settlement that did not also meet Cuban approval—and the Cubans wanted nothing less than independence. In 1897 he could afford to be patient; in early 1898 events forced him to face the consequences of his administration's pro-Cuban policies. In early February a minor diplomatic crisis ensued when the Spanish Ambassador to Washington wrote a letter that protrayed McKinley as an opportunist, and the letter was made public. Then, on February 15, under somewhat ambiguous circumstances, the U.S.S. *Maine*, stationed at Havana to protect American property, exploded and sank to the bottom of the harbor. In March, even the previously pacific Wall Street community was shaken by a lurid portrayal of Cuban conditions on the floor of the Senate. At the end of the month, under the pressure of the steadily mounting clamor for war, McKinley resolved to present Spain with an ultimatum. Calling for the end of the detention camps, an armistice, and arbitration by the United States if peace was not achieved by October 1, the ultimatum was briefly debated—and accepted—by the Spanish Cabinet on April 10, 1898. But the only kind of arbitration which McKinley felt he was able to undertake was one which would result in the independence of Cuba; and that Spain was unwilling to grant. And so the President went to Congress for authority to use the armed forces to secure a settlement giving Cuba independence. With congressional approval of his request, the Spanish-American War began.[5]

During the previous winter the United States naval planners, considering the possibility of war with Spain, had formulated a decision to strike at the Spanish-controlled Philippine Islands so as to deny the Islands to Spanish trade should war break out. Upon this basis, Acting Secretary of the Navy Theodore Roosevelt issued his well-known order of February 25, 1898: the commander of the Pacific fleet, George Dewey, was to assemble his ships at Hong Kong and prepare to sail to Manila in case of war. On April, 24, after war was declared, Secretary of the Navy John D. Long ordered Dewey to proceed to the pre-arranged destination and to capture or destroy the Spanish fleet. On the morning of May 1, in an engagement lasting only seven hours, Dewey succeeded in his mission. Within two months American troops were occupying Manila.[6]

As early as the Venezuela crisis, Moorfield Storey had expressed concern lest "demagogues go too far in the way of rousing the jingo feeling." In 1897 he took the occasion of an address to the Naval War College to condemn the politicians who were "doing their best to embroil us in a foreign war," remarking that "this has always been the method by which rulers who feel their positions in peril have sought to direct attention from the consequences of their misrule, and to reestablish their own power by an appeal to patriotic feeling." Shortly before Congress declared war in 1898, Storey pointed out that the advocates of war against Spain had brought forth little evidence that diplomatic initiatives had been exhausted, and he doubted that war would bring anything more than devastation to the Cuban people.[7]

Soon thereafter, Storey was among those speaking at a meeting at Fanueil Hall on June 15, "to protest the adoption of the so-called imperial policy by the United States." Some of their countrymen might have wondered why the speakers were so agitated, since no "imperial policy" appeared to have been adopted: the government was pledged by congressional resolution to withdraw its troops from Cuba once peace was secured. To this, Storey and the others could well have pointed out that the major event of the war had so far taken place on the other side of the world from Cuba, and they might also have asked why American troops were being deployed elsewhere in the Caribbean. The suspicions they had entertained in June were confirmed by December. Exploiting the expansionist fervor unleashed by the war, in July the administration pushed through the Senate the long-debated treaty of annexation with Hawaii. And when the peace treaty was finally signed with Spain, the Americans gained not only the independence of Cuba, but the cession of all the territory even partially occupied by American troops —not only the Philippines, but the Pacific island of Guam and the Caribbean island of Puerto Rico as well. The "imperial policy" did indeed appear to have been adopted.

From the June 15 meeting in Fanueil Hall had already come a Committee of Correspondence which, jointly with a delegation from the Massachusetts Reform Club, formed the Anti-Imperialist League in November 1898. The Senate ratification of the peace treaty in February 1899 only spurred the expansion of the anti-imperialist movement: during that year chapters similar to the one in Boston appeared in New York, Chicago, and other major cities. By November 1899, the local chapters had been federated in a new national organization, the American Anti-Imperialist League, with the stated purpose of bringing the issue of expansion before the people in the campaign of 1900.[8]

With the re-election of McKinley in 1900, the anti-imperialists lost their best chance to change the course of policy; but, contrary to the general impression, their movement did not immediately disappear. In its campaign against the conduct of American military operations against Filipino insurgents between 1899 and 1902, the Anti-Imperialist League continued to enjoy the active support of men such as Andrew Carnegie and Carl Schurz. By 1904, however, membership had declined in so many cities that the organization was substantially reduced to the New Englanders who had begun the movement six years before. Reconstituting itself as the Anti-Imperialist League, the organization then asked Storey to become president the following year, 1905. Under the leadership of Storey and of Erving Winslow, who continued as secretary, the League first turned its attention to investigating possible administrative corruption and economic exploitation in the Islands. Then, between 1912 and 1920, the League, now aided by Filipino leaders such as Manuel Quezon, devoted its major efforts to securing passage of congressional legislation pledging Philippine independence within a stated time. Only after these efforts bore partial fruition in the Jones Act of 1916, did the League formally dissolve in 1920.[9]

The acquisition of the Philippines ended a chapter in American history, for it was the last major territorial acquisition of the United States. Storey never doubted that some day the Islands would be granted independence, but he did not therefore join those historians who have since seen the events of 1898 and 1899 as simply a phase in national self-assertion, "America's imperialist adventure." His advocacy on behalf of the Filipinos turned his attention to other areas of American policy, such as Latin America, where more sophisticated techniques of control were being developed that avoided territorial annexation and relied instead on financial control and military intervention. But unlike the annexation of the Philippines, this new policy of intervention in Latin America was carried out with a notable lack of opposition. Intervention went unopposed in part because policy formulation in the area was almost totally an executive monopoly, in part because Latin America was universally accepted as an American sphere of influence, and in part because the fears behind most congressional opposition to the retention of the Philippines—the entry of hordes of colored immigrants and the competition of low wage rates and cheap raw materials—were completely inapplicable. It is significant, therefore, that one of the very few voices heard protesting the policy of intervention in the Caribbean was that of Moorfield Storey.[10]

As his concern over United States policy in Latin America would reveal, Storey was less concerned with the kind of control exercised than with the actual denial of self-government to the weaker nation. This broadly defined defense of self-determination, however, co-existed in his mind with attitudes acquired from the nineteenth-century peace movement. Faced by a war of conquest waged by the United States, anti-imperialism and pacifism could come together, and Storey could forcefully condemn American policy. But how would he react to a situation in which the United States might be called upon to intervene on behalf of those attacked? Was war, in short, a lesser evil than imperialism?

Forced after 1914 to choose between the avoidance of war and the protection of small nations, Storey had become, by the end of World War I, a proponent of collective security. His advocacy of Philippine independence—and, later, of self-determination for Latin America—had led him to champion what he now referred to as a "vital principle" of American foreign policy, that "every small nation is entitled to maintain her independence and have all her rights respected as fully as the most powerful." Only through the guarantee of joint action by the community of nations even at the risk of war, Storey would then argue, could the independence of any one nation be preserved. Yet deciding in favor of collective security solved only one of his problems, for the peace treaty of 1919, containing its embodiment in the covenant of a new League of Nations, also incorporated guarantees of American intervention in the Caribbean. It had not been easy for Storey to decide that the defeat of German imperialism had been worth a war, and he now had to ask himself (in 1919 and 1920) whether the incorporation of American imperialism into the treaty was too high a price to pay for effective guarantees of the peace.[11]

1. Philippine Independence

At the time of Dewey's victory, the Philippine Islands contained approximately seven million people, spread over 115,000 square miles of land and water. The original inhabitants, a dark Melanesian people, had long before been driven into the interior by a race of Malayan origins. Upon these conquerors had been imposed in turn the influences of India, China, and Islam— and, in the sixteenth century, the cultural and political domination of Spain. One result of these crosscurrents was a maze of forty-three separate peoples speaking eighty-seven different languages. Though supporters of annexation would argue that such a mixed group of peoples could not long sustain a viable government, beneath the apparent heterogeneity lay an underlying unity: over 90 per cent of the population was Roman Catholic in religion, and conversant in one of nine closely related languages. In addition, about half the entire population could read its own language, and of that number half could write their own language as well.[12]

As administrators of the insular school system, the members of the various religious orders deserve credit for raising the level of literacy; but their arrogant dominance over Philippine life was sufficient to drive a whole generation of native leaders into anti-clericalism. Greedy, bigoted, often openly unchaste, and seldom checked by a feeble civil administration, the friars created a feudal regime in miniature, amassing vast estates and requiring forced labor on the roads. During the nineteenth century various developments—the opening of the port of Manila to foreign trade, sporadic liberalization of the colonial administration, and the construction of the Suez Canal—brought the most educated of the Filipinos into contact with western ideas of nationalism and democracy. When, in 1872, reactionary forces within Spain ended a period of relatively enlightened rule, the stage was set for the Philippine revolution.[13]

The first nationalist leaders, like José Rizal, were middle-class intellectuals; limiting their demands to political representation, religious freedom, and the expulsion of the friars, they expressed no desire to leave the Spanish Empire. Failing to moderate the regime, however, this group lost influence, and leadership in the nationalist movement passed next to the revolutionary faction, to Andres Bonifacio and his secret society, the Katipunan. It was the Katipunan which spearheaded the insurrection of

1896, but the military exigencies of the ensuing war allowed soldiers such as Emilio Aguinaldo to assume the nationalist leadership. At the end of 1897, Spanish and Filipino forces were deadlocked, and Aguinaldo accepted the offer of an armistice.

Under the terms of the Peace of Biaknabato, the insurgents were to surrender and their leaders to go into exile, in return for a payment of 800,000 pesos and universal amnesty. Spain did not complete payment, and the insurgents did not lay down their arms, but their leaders did go into exile. And in exile Aguinaldo and his colleagues looked to the United States for aid. During the winter of 1897–98, Filipino leaders tried to obtain rifles from the American Consul, Rounceville Wildman, and to gain assurances of American support from Commodore Dewey, but were unsuccessful in both attempts. When hostilities appeared imminent between the United States and Spain, however, the American response was more favorable. In Singapore, Aguinaldo was assured by the American consul there, E. Spencer Pratt, that, as with Cuba, independence for the Philippines would follow from an American victory over Spain. Pledging the cooperation of his insurgents, but determined to have a written statement promising independence, Aguinaldo sailed to Hong Kong to meet with Dewey. Arriving there on May 1, the day of the Commodore's victory at Manila, he used his time to negotiate the arms purchase with Wildman that his agents had been unable to consummate the previous autumn. Upon hearing of Dewey's defeat of the Spanish, he returned to the Philippines. On May 19, 1898, Aguinaldo and Dewey met aboard Dewey's flagship, and agreed to coordinate their offensives, the insurgents to join forces with American troops moving up from Manila Bay.[14]

What Aguinaldo did not know was that men like Pratt spoke only for themselves and that the American forces landing on the Islands were an army of occupation, not of liberation. For the American victory at Manila Bay had created a growing demand for retention of the Islands. American businessmen, for example, had seen their markets limited by the depression, and thus had been casting hopeful glances at the Far East for almost a decade. The German seizure of Kiaochow, followed by the Russian acquisition of Port Arthur in the winter of 1897–98, had created new barriers for American imports, pushing many businessmen toward support of a belligerent foreign policy. Now, in the aftermath of Dewey's victory, the Philippine Islands suddenly appeared to be a gateway to the markets of the Far East. At the same time (and perhaps for similar reasons) the events in Manila Bay seem to have persuaded McKinley that the United States must gain complete control of the Islands. Though he did not publicly commit himself to annexation until the autumn, when the peace negotiations were already in progress, three weeks after Dewey's victory he instructed the commander of the Philippine expedition to establish the supremacy of American authority in those areas occupied by United States forces. That supremacy was to be maintained he added, by force if necessary. And the supremacy of American authority anywhere on the islands meant a denial of the aims of the Filipino nationalist revolution.[15]

Upon his return to the Islands, Aguinaldo as dictator transformed the insurgents into a regular army, and reorganized both the administration of justice and the municipal government. On June 12, as part of an attempt to gain diplomatic recognition, he proclaimed the independence of the Philippines. Two weeks later he announced the institution of a revolutionary government with himself as executive, an administrative cabinet, and a congress of provincial delegates. Those of the delegates who were able to pass through the war lines that summer convened in the town of Malolos, where they wrote the first constitution of the Philippine Republic. Their document provided for separation of Church and State (after protracted and bitter debate), freedom of speech and assembly, *habeas corpus*, the confiscation of all Church property, the abolition of all privileges, and (over the arguments of Aguinaldo's advisers) a parliamentary system of government with a unicameral legislature.[16]

On August 12, 1898, a preliminary protocol ended hostilities between the United States and Spain. In October, the American

peace commissioners arrived in Paris, still divided among themselves on whether to demand all, part, or none of the Islands. A
triumphant tour of the Midwest, in which crowds cheered his
references to expansion, appears to have definitely confirmed for
McKinley his earlier desire to retain the Islands. On October 26,
therefore, he instructed the commissioners to demand the cession
of the entire archipelago. Spain finally accepted the demand,
made palatable by the additional payment of $20 million, and, on
September 10, she transferred her title over the Philippines to
the United States. With the signing of the peace treaty, McKinley moved with such boldness as to make the Senate ratification
two months later seem almost peripheral to the course of events.
On December 21, he instructed American generals to inform the
Filipinos that American government was to be extended to all
the Islands, and that henceforth their allegiance was to be American authority. And on January 20, 1899, he appointed a commission, headed by Jacob Schurman, president of Cornell, to
outline the future plan of American control to Filipino leaders.[17]

Two weeks after Mckinley's proclamation of American sovereignty over the Islands, Aguinaldo replied that if American
troops extended their operations the two nations would be at
war. Still hoping for the peaceful achievement of independence,
he sent Felipe Agoncillo to the American government to state
the Filipino position: that sovereignty over the Islands could not
be transferred to the United States by Spain since it arose
from the Filipino people. Turned down by McKinley and unheard by the commissioners, Agoncillo ended his mission by
writing fruitless letters to Secretary of State John Hay. On February 6, 1899, the Senate—hesitantly, as the defeat of an
amendment, in a tie vote, to definitely promise independence
would indicate—gave its consent to the annexation of the
Philippines. Two days before, however, the shooting of a
Filipino soldier by an American soldier had set off the spark for
the mass insurrection of the Filipino people against American
rule.

In implementing his decision to retain control over the

Philippines, President McKinley enjoyed two immense advantages over his opponents. In the first place (and here he set a pattern for subsequent twentieth-century foreign policy), his execution of presidential policy was so fast that his critics, in the Congress and elsewhere, were rendered incapable of responding effectively. In the second place, while the electorate's attitude toward imperialism may have been uncertain, its support of the Republican party had been confirmed in 1894 and 1896; Republicans could look forward with confidence to another victory at the polls in 1900. With these advantages, it is hard in retrospect to see how McKinley could have been defeated in his policy.

Nevertheless, the confusion of the opponents of Philippine annexation did play a part in assuring McKinley's victory. The first to be heard were the politicians. As the simultaneous condemnations of annexation by both Bryan and Cleveland indicated, Democratic leaders would oppose the acquisition of the Philippines, though in taking that position they may well have reflected the long-standing prejudice of their constituents against colored peoples. On the other hand, the most prominent Republican opponent of acquisition, Senator George F. Hoar of Massachusetts, had only recently tried to protect the voting rights of the freedman. When the treaty came before the Senate, therefore, Hoar found himself on the same side as Ben Tillman, South Carolina's impassioned defender of white supremacy, Hoar's invocation of the universality of human rights jarring with Tillman's taunts that Republicans could no longer legitimately oppose the suppression of the Southern Negro. To compound the confusion, Hoar, Tillman, and other Senate opponents of the treaty found their efforts undercut by the maneuvers of Bryan, who now operated on the debatable assumption that the best way to defeat imperialism was to give the United States freedom of action through ratifying the treaty.[18]

It is not surprising, therefore, that those who had previously regarded it as their duty "to look after the politicians" (in Lowell's phrase) would soon take the initiative, or that the leadership of the Anti-Imperialist League—with the exception of a few Republicans such as George Boutwell and Erving Winslow—consisted of the Independent veterans of earlier low-tariff and civil service crusades. The initial result of Independent participation in the anti-imperialist movement, however, was to give it a strikingly defensive quality, so that idealistic appeals to the principle of government by consent were mixed with (and sometimes overwhelmed by) conservative fears of a self-aggrandizing bureaucracy and racist appeals against the incorporation of colored peoples. If the Independents' conservatism showed itself in their arguments against Philippine annexation, their political ineptitude revealed itself in their efforts to defeat it. Rebuffed by ratification of the annexation treaty in the Senate, their only hope was to ally themselves with the Democratic party, though the party was still led by Bryan, whom they had so roundly condemned in 1896. Instead, the Independents spent most of 1899 and 1900 trying to find other candidates or reviving the idea of a third party; and when the choice of McKinley or Bryan finally became inevitable, they either voted for McKinley or half-heartedly supported Bryan. Only a few decided with Storey that foreign policy was more important than economic issues and openly advocated a Democratic victory.[19]

It has become fashionable among historians to review the anti-imperialists' conservatism and political ineptitude, and dismiss their movement as a shabby charade. That it was more than this, that its rhetoric can still appeal to generations seven decades away from the event, is in no small measure the achievement of Moorfield Storey. Though he was less well known than some of those in the early stages of the movement—less well known, for example, than either of his friends, Charles Francis Adams, Jr., and William James; or than Independent leader Carl Schurz; or than industrialist Andrew Carnegie—Storey stayed with the movement longer than anyone else. Only his death in 1929 ended his connection with the cause of Philippine independence. His persistence alone gives Storey claim to be considered one of the key figures in the anti-imperialist movement; and his arguments on behalf of Philippine independence, arguments appealing to the oldest of American ideals or concerned with the desires of the Filipinos themselves, ennoble the entire movement.[20]

Privately opposed to the war against Spain from the outset, Storey soon began to condemn publicly what seemed its transformation into a war of conquest. No acquisitions the United States might choose to make could be justified by European precedents, he wrote in July 1898, for "their system of government rests on the divine right of kings and other political theories which we repudiated in 1776, and which we have been denouncing ever since." For the next thirty years of his life, Storey never deviated from his assumption that American institutions rested on other values:

> The government of the United States rests on the self-evident truths that "all men are created equal," that is, with equal political rights, and that "governments derive their just powers from the consent of the governed," or, in the words of Abraham Lincoln,—"No man is good enough to govern another without that other's consent. I say this is the leading principle—the sheet-anchor—of American republicanism."

But, in the forcible acquisition of the Philippines, "this great land, which for more than a century, has offered refuge to the oppressed of every nation, has now turned oppressor, and the guilt must be shared by every citizen who by word or silence consents." [21]

Storey's conviction that "the great principles of freedom which our fathers proclaimed when this nation was born . . . are still 'self-evident truths,'" was, as he and other opponents of imperialism agreed, the faith of an older America. Indeed, the imperialists' attack on the universality of the Declaration of Independence may have been responsible for Storey's reassertion of the values with which he had been raised. "Here I am brought up under Lincoln, Sumner, Andrew, and last and best, your father," he wrote Emerson's daughter in 1905:

My ideals are such as I have learned them, they are embodied in the Declaration of Independence, they are
summed up in your father's lines

"For what avail the plow or sail,
Or land or life, if freedom fail?"

I have read history enough to know that this is the
universal creed of man, believed in as firmly by the Greeks
in their contest with Turkey, by the Irish in dealing with
England, by the Russians today, by the Boers in South
Africa, by the Negroes whom the Germans are slaughter-
ing, by the Indians and Negroes in our own land, by the
Filipinos in the Philippines, as by the men who died at
Concord Bridge.[22]

Storey began his anti-imperialist argument by reviewing the
events leading up to annexation. He rejected the claims of the
proponents of annexation that it represented an inevitable development in the national destiny:

Senator Frye tells us that God sent Dewey to the Philippines and shut the door behind him. As I read history it
was Governor Roosevelt, then Acting Secretary of the
Navy, who issued the orders to our fleet. We may admit
all that is claimed for the Governor, but there is a distinction.

There were no impersonal forces involved, he insisted, no analogy
to the Atlantic migration or the westward movement—nothing
but the policies of the McKinley administration. And, unlike
some of his fellow-critics of the Philippine policy, Storey did
not exempt the President from his attack. "For some reason there
is a disposition to treat McKinley as if he was a very well-
meaning man," he complained, "who is deceived by wicked sub-
ordinates. . . . I am satisfied that he knows exactly what is going
on. . . ."[23]

Storey's indictment of the President's course started with what
he regarded as McKinley's betrayal of the spirit of the Congressional resolution pledging Cuban independence. "To say that

we meant only Cuba, and no other territory of Spain, is to construe a great public declaration as if it were a criminal indictment." Then, Storey charged, while planning to place the Islands under American control, McKinley permitted his agents —Pratt, Wildman, and (so Storey believed) Dewey—to promise independence to Aguinaldo and the insurgent leaders. Finally, the President extended control over all the Islands as part of a strategy to force the Senate into accepting a *fait accompli*. And then, though half the membership indicated a willingness to relinquish the Islands at the earliest possible opportunity, McKinley regared ratification as an endorsement of his policy of an indefinite period of American rule.[24]

Believing that the administration's record was deliberately deceitful and its course morally unjustifiable, Storey was outraged when its supporters appealed to the new chauvinistic mood:

> . . . Senator Lodge said at Pittsfield, "We are not going to pull down the flag while it is being shot at. We have never done it, and never will." This is a mere appeal to passion. Whether the flag is rightly resisted or not, whether some officer or agent of ours has wrongly attacked a peaceful neighbor or not, no matter how criminal our aggression, no matter how just the resistance,—if a shot is fired against us, this mighty nation in blind wrath must crush its opponents, not asking or caring whether it is right right or wrong. This doctrine dethrones God, and makes a deity of bunting. . . .

> They repeat the cry of "Our country right or wrong," demanding in the sacred name of our country that we support the party in power, right or wrong. I deny that Mr. McKinley, Mr. Hanna, Mr. Lodge, or any other politician for the day in office, or all together, are my country. I deny that they may commit us to a bloody and needless war, and then insist that those who oppose their policy are not patriots. The doctrine that the king can do no wrong has no place in a republic and no application to its servants. It has ever been a buttress of despotism.[25]

Many Republicans simply defended existing policy by appealing to party and country; a few attempted a defense of imperialism itself. After Hoar had cited the principles of the Declaration of Independence as a barrier to the acquisition of the Philippines, the more intellectually inclined among the proponents of annexation devoted their efforts to showing how limited the Declaration was in character. Lodge, for example, argued that since the principles of self-government had not been applied by the United States in its acquisition of previous territories, in its treatment of the Indians, or in its suppression of the Confederacy, there was little need to apply them to the Philippines. And, he continued, the right of self-government existed only for those who were fit to use it—which excluded the Filipinos, a racially backward people who had never constituted a nation.[26]

In his reply to this defense of imperialism itself, Storey denied that there were any precedents in American history for the Government's ruling over a people without their consent. The territories had always possessed representative institutions, he argued, and he denied that the more plausible example of the American Indian was relevant.

> We have treated the tribes throughout as independent nations. . . . When we have taken land by treaty, it has been land alone, and not inhabitants, so that we have not claimed the legal right to tax them or to govern them as our subjects without their consent.

He was the first to admit that "no American . . . can find any cause for just pride in our dealings with the Indians. . . ." But though "we have abused our power; we have not abandoned our theories of government." As far as the suppression of the Confederacy was concerned, Storey pointed out that the South had consented to be part of the United States. Our only claim upon the Philippines, however, rested on our purchase of the Islands from Spain: to argue that by a transfer of title we therefore had a right to conquer them was to say that "after Yorktown, France could properly have bought England's title to Massachusetts, and have proceeded to conquer us. . . ." [27]

It was, however, upon the imperialists' second argument, that "superior" peoples had the right to judge the "fitness" of others for self-government, that Storey concentrated his attention. At times he attempted to refute the champions of Philippine annexation on their own ground. Storey would point out, for example, that the leaders of the Filipino nationalist movement were "men who were educated at Manila University, older than any university that exists in the United States, men who were Christians. . . ." Perceiving that the plurality of cultural groups was more fearsome on paper than in actuality, he continually emphasized the ethnic and linguistic unity of the majority of the Islands' population. And impressed by the constitution written by the Malolos convention, he remained skeptical of reports that the nationalists would be unable to preserve civil order.[28]

On the whole, however, Storey proved to be uneasy over attempts to prove the ability of any nation to govern itself by American standards, in part because he believed that "it is the God-given right of a nation like the Philippines to be independent and to govern itself," but also because he had serious reservations about the universal applicability of those standards. He had already referred his audiences to the disasters wrought by the application of those standards to the native Indians:

> We began by allowing the Indians to preserve their tribal system. In this we were true to our principles. When we interfered to impose our more civilized laws upon them, think you the result was satisfactory to them? We called it better government. They knew it as fraud, violence, and death.

The peoples of Asia were different in many ways from Americans, Storey argued, and he warned against any attempt to impute inferiority to those differences. "The Chinese mandarin is an absolutely different creature from the English nobleman, but both may be equally civilized." Yet when confronting Asian civilization, America, like the European powers, reacted with the greatest arrogance, "the hideous barbarities which marked the

march of the Allies from Tientsin to Peking" during the suppression of the Boxer Rebellion having their counterpart in "the
slaughter, pillage, and torture for which we were responsible in
the Philippines. . . ." On one occasion Storey contrasted the
spiritual resources of Asians with the aggressiveness of their
white overlords; but he also exulted in the Japanese naval victory
over Russia in 1905, in which "the superstition that yellow men
are inferior to white, that Asiatics are not in every way equal to
Europeans, received its death blow." [29]

Ultimately, Storey threw the "fitness" argument back at the
imperialists. Did any of them really believe, he asked, that a
fair assessment of people's "fitness" to govern itself could be
made?

> . . . Who shall decide that such unfitness exists? Can the
> decision be safely left to the stronger nation? Shall it be
> made by men who know nothing of the weaker people,
> who never have visited the country, who do not under
> stand their language, their traditions, their character, or
> their needs? Shall it be made without hearing their repre
> sentatives and learning all they can tell about their coun
> trymen? Can we be sure that the judgment of the strong
> is not affected by appeals to national vanity, by apos
> trophes to the flag, by hopes of commercial advantage,
> by dreams of world power, by the exigencies of party
> politics, by personal ambitions?

Storey pointed out that not only was the right the imperialists
reserved for themselves to judge another people's "fitness" for
self-government unworkable in principle, but it would be disastrous in practice. When he said that "it is no man's duty to
govern another; all share an equal right to govern themselves,"
he was expressing a personal conviction; when he added "there
is no middle ground between this position and the law of might,"
he was warning the imperialists of the implications of their
ideas. And he reminded those Republicans who now championed
the rights of "superior" races of the similar arguments on behalf
of the slavery whose extension their party had been formed to
fight.[30]

It is easy to call Storey an idealist; yet his protest against imperialism also came from a pessimistic view of human nature. It was the lesson of history, he claimed, that men could not be trusted with governing others:

> Men are essentially selfish, and power is always used to benefit him who wields it. The king aims to preserve and strengthen his dynasty. The oligarchy clings to its privileges at the expense of the people. The "boss" governs in his own interest. It is only when power is in the hands of the people that the rights and interests of the people are secure, and this is the truth which the founders of this nation declared.

From this pessimism sprang not only Storey's fears of possible military brutality and political corruption, but also his attacks on American economic expansion in the Philippines. This concern is especially notable in view of the argument made by some historians that the only division between imperialists and anti-imperialists was over political control, both sides favoring economic penetration. The president of the Anti-Imperialist League and lifelong champion of Philippine independence cannot be placed in this category. Storey consistently opposed American investment in the Philippines, in part because he suspected the motives of the investors, in part because he felt the Filipinos had no political safeguards against exploitation, and in part because investment would only postpone the achievement of Philippine independence.[31]

In this connection, it would be well to consider the charge, raised even by sympathetic observers, that the anti-imperialist movement failed to offer any practical alternatives to the annexation of the Philippine Islands. In the first place, such an assessment too easily accepts the view of the McKinley administration, which, having rejected either giving the Islands back to Spain or transferring them to another power, saw the only course to lie in the extension of direct American control. Those choices, however, assumed the inability of the Filipinos to govern themselves, but that assumption was by no means universal, even within the administration. For example, after two of Dewey's aides undertook a lengthy tour of the Islands, they reported that Aguinaldo's insurgents were effectively maintaining order. The subsequent burial of that Sargent–Wilcox report suggests that it was not the situation in the Philippines but pressures within the United States—the inertia of a policy evolving since May, business hopes for Far Eastern markets, popular dreams of national glory, and the racist myopia through which Americans perceived Asian peoples—that dictated American control.[32]

If one assumes, as Storey certainly did, that the Filipinos were capable of governing themselves, the case for annexation then shifts to the argument that the Filipinos could not protect themselves from foreign aggression, aggression which would certainly destroy their self-government and possibly threaten American security. Storey's first response to this argument was to point out that no nation had offered to aid the insurgents against American authority; "it was either indifference or fear of us that prevented" them from doing so. Had the United States granted Philippine independence, "the same influences would have been effectual." And had any nation challenged that independence, "far fewer ships and soldiers could have held the islands with Filipinos as cordial allies than we need now to repress the Filipinos alone." In later years Storey moved toward the idea of an international guarantee of Philippine independence. And if, he wrote during World War I, any nation "dares to follow the German example and attack an independence which the world has guaranteed," the threat of force must be invoked by the guarantors of the Islands' independence.[33]

The anti-imperialist movement that Storey entered had been united on one point alone, that "the people of the Philippine Islands, whether they are few or many, are capable or incapable, are not ours." In practice, as he remembered some years later, this meant that many of the anti-imperialists were "more anxious to get rid of the Islands for the sake of the United States than for the sake of the Filipinos." From the outset of his participation in the movement, however, Storey remained primarily concerned with the Filipinos themselves. That the movement eventually moved toward his concerns was partly due to his leadership, but also to two other developments. As several historians have pointed out, the actions of the Filipinos themselves in setting up a new government and defending it by force made it increasingly awkward for the anti-imperialists to continue to deny their capability for self-government. A second development, which has not been generally discussed, was the impact of the Supreme Court's decision in the Insular Cases of 1901. There the Court made a distinction between "fundamental rights" (life, liberty, and property), which applied to all persons under American jurisdiction, and "formal rights" (jury trial, suffrage), which required congressional action to be extended. By implication at least, the Filipinos seemed to be excluded from participation from American government, and the decision may have diminished the protests of those whose anti-imperialism sprang from fear of such participation. On the other hand, the remaining anti-imperialists could now join Storey and say that as long as the Philippines were under American rule,

> We insist that constitutional liberty shall be the inalienable right of every man who owes allegiance to our flag; that freedom shall belong to man and not to place; that our Constitution shall be no respecter of persons, colors, or races; that it shall recognize the equal rights of all.

Storey would make that statement many times as president of the National Association for the Advancement of Colored People; it is significant that one of the first occasions he made it was on behalf of Filipinos.[34]

2. Self-determination

That Moorfield Storey's anti-imperialism would first express itself in an advocacy of Philippine independence was fortuitous, for it had been American expansion to the south—and not across the Pacific—that had shaped his political background. It had been against the war with Mexico that Emerson and Lowell had inveighed in their poetry; it had been the same war which marked the political rise of Charles Sumner; and it was Sumner's opposition to a proposed annexation of the Dominican Republic that had caused his downfall. Storey himself had been influenced by Latin-American developments: it had been the Cleveland administration's attitude in the Venezuela episode of 1895 that had produced his first major criticism of foreign policy, and it was a war ostensibly to liberate Cuba that had resulted in the acquisition of the Philippines. Although in succeeding years the various interventions in Latin America would occupy far less of Storey's attention than the cause of Philippine independence, his reaction to them would reveal the depth of his anti-imperialism, an anti-imperialism primarily concerned with the protection of the right of political and economic self-determination in the smaller nations.

As Storey had perceived, the Spanish-American War would lead to a new assertion of American power throughout the world: nowhere was this change more evident than in the traditional American sphere of influence south of the Gulf of Mexico. There three developments, all in the first years of the twentieth century, would determine the subsequent course of policy. The first was the McKinley administration's decision to oppose various pressures to annex occupied Cuba and instead to maintain dominance over the island through financial control and a legally guaranteed right of intervention. The second development was occasioned by the logistical problems of the war itself, which had led to renewed American interest in an isthmian canal. When the Colombian legislature rejected its government's treaty providing for an American lease on the isthmus of Panama, an American-supported uprising led to Panamanian independence and the acquisition of a canal site by the United States. The third development was President Roosevelt's modification of the Monroe Doctrine against a background of foreign intervention and civil war in the Dominican Republic. This Roosevelt Corollary maintained that since political and economic instability might lead to foreign intervention, instability itself warranted American intervention. With the protection of the Canal as its objective, and the techniques of financial control and military occupation (already developed in Cuba) as its implements, the Corollary would become the basic rationale for United States policy in the area for the next quarter-century.[35]

The initial decision made by President Roosevelt to formulate the Corollary reflected a particular strategic concern; but by the end of the Taft administration other influences had intruded to such an extent that even now it is difficult to point to a single motivating factor in American intervention. One such influence was the prerogative traditionally claimed by all great powers—and now firmly asserted by Washington—to protect the lives and property of their citizens anywhere in the world. While the guiding decisions in Latin-American policy might well be made in Washington, this kind of pledge was certain to ensure a close alliance betwen government officials and private investors. Finally, American policy-makers appeared to be increasingly captured by what has been called a missionary spirit to extend the lessons of stable self-government to the turbulent Caribbean republics, a spirit notably expressed by the architect of Roosevelt's policy, Secretary of State Elihu Root, when he urged upon his audience the necessity of helping those countries "up out of the discord of and turmoil of continual revolution into a general public sense of justice." [36]

In 1913 sixteen years of Republican administration came to an end, and Woodrow Wilson's initial actions seemed to indicate a break with previous policies which had led to intervention in Cuba and Panama in 1906, and in Cuba, the Dominican Republic, and Nicaragua in 1912. Heartened by the new administration's attempt to pay Colombia reparations for the loss of Panama, Storey concluded that "nine months of President Wilson's administration. . . have shown that he and his associates have a far juster appreciation of our obligations to other countries than has been exhibited by their Republican predecessors since 1898. . . ." Yet as the massive Haitian intervention of 1915 would prove, Wilson not only held to the prevalent interventionist attitude, compounded of strategic calculation, economic interest, and aggressive idealism, but he would try to implement it far more sweepingly than either Roosevelt or Taft had hitherto attempted.[37]

In Haiti, as elsewhere in the Caribbean, illiterate peasants had watched contending factions succeeding each other in periodic waves of violence, and there, as elsewhere, foreign economic interests had subsidized various contenders in the hope of gaining advantage. While total American investment in Haiti was small, it was sufficient to dominate the Haitian economy; and American interests were singularly fortunate in having as their spokesman Roger L. Farnham, vice-president of the National City Bank of New York and director of the Haitian national railroad. Watching the turbulent events of 1913 and 1914, in which four presidents were overthrown by violence, Farnham sought out State Department officials and pleaded for American control of Haitian finances. In presenting his case, Farnham skillfully framed his argument in the purest progressive rhetoric: American intervention would advance the condition of the Haitian masses. And he did not neglect to arouse fears of foreign intervention, fears which, however well-founded in the past, bore little relationship to the then existing engagement of the European powers in a life-and-death struggle on the other side of the Atlantic.[38]

The Wilson administration, led by its own desire to bring order and progress to the Caribbean, and increasingly persuaded by the arguments of Farnham, finally ordered the Marines into Haiti in July 1915. The commander of the occupying forces quickly established control and induced a compliant Haitian President to accede to a treaty giving the United States control of the nation's finances, health, agriculture, public works, and police administration. The control so easily established did not go unchallenged, for popular opposition to the American presence mounted. It culminated in an insurrection between 1918 and

1921, and that insurrection was suppressed, with 2000 insurgents killed for every 7 Americans. Even aside from the opposition of the Haitians, however, American policy, even after five years of intervention, had failed to achieve its objectives. In spite of notable improvements in transportation and sanitation facilities, the intervention had not produced economic stability: Haiti defaulted on her debt payments, foreign investment remained low, and Washington was unsuccessful in negotiating a general loan. As an attempt to ensure democratic government, the experiment was even more dismal. Believing that one key to economic improvement lay in the introduction of large-scale agriculture, the American administrators decided to push a new constitution that would permit foreigners to own land. Thwarted in their efforts by two successively elected legislatures, the administrators finally resorted to a "plebiscite": illiterate voters were given "Yes" ballots by the police, but they were forced to request "No" ballots from the same officials. This travesty resulted in ratification of the new constitution by a vote of 98,225 to 768.[39]

The military occupation of Haiti (and of the Dominican Republic in 1916, under somewhat similar circumstances) shattered Storey's faith in an administration that he had hoped would move in a new direction. As early as the establishment of Panama, he had protested against American policy both because "it is morally wrong" and because "the weaker republics of this hemisphere established with our sympathy must learn from this to regard the United States as a nation that they cannot trust but must fear." As an anti-imperialist, Storey was more impressed by what he saw as the consistent violation of national sovereignty in the Caribbean by the successive administrations than by the repeated statements of officials that they sought no further acquisition of colonies. Panama, Nicaragua, Haiti, and the Dominican Republic had become for him "all American territorial acquisitions," and as such were vulnerable to the arguments against American imperialism he had raised in connection with the Philippines.[40]

Throughout the early twentieth century, Storey remained

skeptical of the various justifications for intervention. He was, for example, suspicious of the argument that if the United States did not assert her control in a particular area, other nations would assert theirs; Secretary of State Robert Lansing's *ex post facto* fears of German intervention in Haiti, fears unsubstantiated in the correspondence of the time, could only confirm such suspicions. Nor was Storey persuaded by the justification claimed by officials—and supported by many international lawyers—that the United States had a right to intervene to protect the lives and property of her citizens. And both his past interest in "good government" and his contemporary defense of civil rights made him regard as the sheerest hypocrisy the justification that the United States had a mission to teach self-government to Latin Americans.[41]

The intervention in Haiti outraged Storey, but his initial attempts to lead a protest movement against it were hindered, he wrote in 1915, because "it is very hard to get people to consider anything except the war" in Europe. Believing that there was deliberate suppression of information about the occupation of the Haiti, he could only remark bitterly,

> We are going to restore order and going to benefit them, of course. Men stifle their consciences by saying "We are doing them good." Who knows what we are doing? No newspaper tells us, and of our self-appointed trusteeship no account is rendered to us or by us. Who shall decide what is good, the wolf or the lamb?

In this connection the Negro population of the island assumed special significance, both for Storey and for the NAACP, of which he was president. Failing in its attempt to persuade the Wilson administration to investigate conditions in Haiti in the immediate aftermath of the intervention, the Association waited until 1918 to authorize James Weldon Johnson to conduct its own private investigation in Haiti. All the leaders of the NAACP feared the consequences of American rule over a black people, and reports of brutality in the suppression of the 1918–20 insurrection heightened their fears: "knowing as we do how colored men are lynched . . . ," as Storey put it, "we must admit that our population includes many men who are capable of treating people they think of as an inferior race with great brutality." [42]

Taking heart from Harding's criticism of the occupation in the 1920 campaign, the NAACP moved quickly after his election to construct a coalition to prod the new administration toward withdrawing troops. Together with the Popular Government League and the Foreign Policy Association, the coalition concentrated on pointing out the actual conditions under the occupation and the dubious justifications for intervention. No one in the coalition was to emphasize more persistently than Storey another consequence of the policy of intervention—that the use of military force pointed to an unprecedented expansion of presidential power:

> It has of late years been too common for the President of the United States in some emergency to use the military force of the United States without the consent of Congress, against nations with which we are at peace, as when we made war on China to rescue our legation, or when President Roosevelt used both army and navy against Colombia to seize the Panama Canal, or when our forces occupied Cuba, or now when they are in Haiti; and unless some protest is made these acts become thoroughly dangerous precedents. The people through their representatives have the right to decide whether they will go to war or not; and the President not only has no power to make the decision for them, but has no right to take steps which commit this country to war, so that the people cannot deliberately decide for or against it.[43]

Skepticism about the justifications for intervention, fear of the consequences of American rule over peoples the Americans generally considered inferior, and concern over the expansion of presidential power—these summarized Moorfield Storey's criticisms of intervention in the Caribbean between 1903 and 1920.

That other arguments would enter his critique was due to his response to a far more important historical development, the response of the United States to the Mexican Revolution.

Neither of the major wars of independence fought by Mexico—against Spanish rule in 1810–21 and against French intervention in 1862–67—had changed the balance between the peasant masses and the ruling oligarchy. In fact, in the last three decades of the nineteenth century the dominant figure in Mexican life had been the conservative dictator, Porfirio Díaz. His defenders at the time claimed that he had brought political stability and economic expansion to a war-torn and impoverished land; his critics since have argued that he replaced anarchy with tyranny, and that his prosperity resulted more in gains for foreign investors and local entrepreneurs than for the majority of the people.[44]

An election dispute in 1910 provoked the various opponents of Díaz into rebellion; and his first successor was the moderate reformer Francesco Madero. But in early 1913 Madero was murdered and his government overthrown by one of his generals, Victoriano Huerta. Huerta received the support of propertied elements in Mexico and of investors in the United States, but President Wilson was so revolted by the murder that he refused to extend recognition to the new regime. With that refusal to extend recognition, Wilson began his three-year course of interference with the Mexican Revolution, a course ironically motivated by his belief that the Mexicans must be allowed to complete their revolution. Storey believed Wilson's nonrecognition policy was justified, and he endorsed the President's attempt to mediate between Huerta and the leader of the Madero forces, Venustiano Carranza. But when that mediation attempt failed and Wilson decided to bring Huerta down by a show of naval forces at Veracruz in 1914, Storey was horrified. "Whatever one's opinion of Huerta . . . ," he wrote, "our clear duty was to remain outside, and let the Mexicans settle their own difficulties."[45]

In July 1914 Huerta finally abdicated, and Carranza proclaimed the new government, but Wilson's desire to guide the course of Mexican politics had not abated. When Carranza proved unamenable to American advice, the administration was angered to such an extent that for almost a year Wilson and his advisers thought of throwing their support to the peasant leader Pancho Villa. By the end of 1915, however, much of Villa's following had gone to Carranza, and in revenge Villa decided to discredit the Carranza government by leading a series of murderous border raids into the United States. In March 1916 Carranza consented to allow the American pursuit of Villa's forces across the border, but he was unprepared for the 6000-man Punitive Expedition, or for its penetration 600 miles into Mexican territory. With skirmishes between American and Mexican forces increasingly frequent, it seemed quite probable, in the early summer of 1916, that the two countries would drift into war. Appalled by the prospect, Storey joined a group led by pacifist educator David Starr Jordan, which met privately with Mexican representatives in an attempt to bring the two sides together. Jordan's efforts appeared to be successful when, later that summer, the two governments agreed to negotiate their differences.[46]

The negotiations, from September 1916 to January 1917, halted the trend toward war but had few positive results. And, as the United States approached war with Germany, the Mexican question was momentarily forgotten. It soon reappeared, however, in a new and more significant form. Mexico was experiencing a major social revolution, not the usual Latin-American jockeying for political power, and whatever confrontations there were with the United States, such as that caused by Villa's raids, were the result of that revolution. Two of the goals of the revolution— land reform and separation of Church and State—were objectives which, with their Jeffersonian overtones, appealed to many Americans and to the progressive administration in Washington. But unlike the liberal revolutions of the previous century, whose aims Wilson so eloquently championed, in this revolution the Mexicans were determined to drive out those they considered the foreign exploiters of their country's economy.

The new path that the Mexicans were to travel was dramat-

ically revealed in the revolutionary Mexican Constitution of 1917. The Mexicans had long believed that title to all natural resources, originally held personally by the King of Spain, had passed to Mexico at the moment of independence: thus, property previously held to be a gift from the king was now held to be a gift from the Mexican nation. Driven by their conviction that their country would not be truly free until the foreign-owned concessions were reclaimed, the revolutionary leaders tried to embody their theory of property in Article 27 of the Constitution, and sucessive governments under that Constitution would argue that the gift of property was revocable at the will of the giver, the nation itself. At that time the greatest American investment in Mexican resources was in oil, which at the time of the Revolution was almost totally owned by an Englishman, Lord Cowdray, and two Americans, Edward L. Doheny and Charles A. Canfield. In attempting to implement Article 27, successive Mexican presidents therefore ran counter not only to the interests of American investors, not only to the traditional American commitment to protect the property of her nationals, but to the whole Anglo-American tradition of private property.[47]

Had the disposition of oil deposits been the only outstanding issue between the United States and Mexico the situation would have been tense enough. But far from bringing stability to Mexico, the Carranza government itself perished in violence when its leader was assassinated in 1920. Conditions in Mexico continued to be hazardous: more Americans were killed, and an American Consul imprisoned, by bandits. The rising anticlericalism of the Revolution was met by an increasingly recalcitrant Church, so that in the middle of the 1920's, the Church stopped administering the sacraments. Perceiving only the revolutionary turmoil, and ignorant of the non-Marxist rationale behind the Mexican theory of property, many Americans soon bracketed Mexico with the Soviet Union as part of international Communism. When American attention turned away from Europe in 1918, demands for intervention in Mexico grew with mounting intensity. In their preparation for the 1920 campaign, the Republicans lost little time in laying the blame for tensions with Mexico upon the preoccupied President Wilson; and at least one spokesman, Senator Albert Fall of New Mexico, called for withdrawal of recognition and preparation for war.[48]

Storey had never been persuaded by the argument that the United States had a right to intervene in other countries to protect the lives and property of her citizens. He doubted whether any such rule was just, but in any case, it was inconsistently applied. We "claim the right to make the Chinese Government pay indemnity for injuries suffered by our missionaries at the hands of a Chinese mob," he had written in 1907, but refuse "to give like indemnity for Chinamen . . . who are injured by our mob." Instead, he called for a new rule to be adopted in international law, to the effect that

> the citizens of every country understood that if they go into another they must submit themselves to the government of that country, and take the justice which that country affords, that they cannot claim in the country which they are visiting greater rights than the citizens of that country themselves have.[49]

In the case of Mexico, Storey did not find the interventionist argument, that it was necessary to protect American lives, very plausible. Your claim, he wrote one belligerent newspaper,

> that 217 American citizens have been murdered in Mexico since 1911 would give the impression that during this very disturbed period in Mexico these men have been murdered by the Mexican authorities and in every case without fault on their part. You simply take the numbers and, without investigation as to the facts, charge them all to a government which has been fighting for its life against various banditti.

The United States was hardly in a position to complain about mob violence in other countries, for in America lynchings were occuring with appalling frequency, "and the persons guilty of this have not been punished," so that "it makes it difficult to complain to Mexico because she does not catch all the bandits that have disturbed her." [50]

But as he examined the demands for intervention more closely, Storey suspected that it was not the protection of lives that was the real argument, but the protection of property—specifically, the oil holdings of American investors. And so he began to turn toward an economic interpretation of American interventionism. Even before the development of his interest in Latin-American affairs Storey had asserted that if capital "was invested in a weak foreign state, its owners seek to own the government of that state, and, failing, try to make their own government interfere and control it." Watching the Wilson administration and an officer of the National City Bank of New York jointly planning financial reorganization in Haiti helped move Storey toward an economic interpretation. Partly because of this impression, he regarded the idealistic justification for intervention in the Caribbean as hypocritical: "I do not like to have people drift along under the impression that they are doing good when as a matter of fact they are picking their neighbor's pockets." Now the actions of Senator Fall, who was simultaneously demanding intervention in Mexico and, as the Teapot Dome investigations would make all too clear, representing his good friend, Edward L. Doheny, confirmed in Storey's mind the validity of the economic interpretation. [51]

In Storey's interpretation of the Mexican situation economic pressures within the United States were in conflict with the revolutionary aspirations of the Mexican people. His fullest statement of this position came in his 1920 Godkin Lectures at Harvard. Mexico, "the frontier of Latin America," he said,

> has been passing through a revolution, which was needed to break up the enormous holdings of land and also to do away with other abuses which had grown up under the administration of Díaz and his predecessors.

There had been disorder and violence, "as there is in every civil war," but

I need only remind you of the wars between the English and the Scotch, the Wars of the Roses, the revolution in England, and the long religious contests in France with her great revolution, to say nothing of later struggles which followed the Franco-Prussian War, our own revolution and our civil war, and all that is now going on in Russia and elsewhere in Europe, to satisfy you that Mexico is in no way peculiar.

If the Mexican Revolution was a justifiable response to centuries of oppression, and its violence comparable to that of other revolutions, why then was it so heatedly denounced in the United States?

Americans have acquired property in Mexico and are making money out of it. They wish to make more. They have not thrown in their lot with Mexico, they have not become Mexican citizens, they are not taking their part as such in the attempt to govern the country from which they are taking their money, but they want us to intervene and smooth their financial path by becoming rulers of the country and governing it in the interests of themselves. . . .

These investors "do not lay before us a statement of their properties" or "how they were acquired," Storey concluded sharply. Instead, "they dwell more on the killing of Americans." [52]

Storey did not hesitate to say that he disagreed with this position, believing instead that "if foreigners elect to acquire property or engage in business there they must not ask their fellow-countrymen to make war in order to help their business." And of all possible claimants to American aid, he thought the oil investors had the weakest case. "We in our country think that oil and other valuable deposits should be under the control of the government and cannot complain if Mexico does the same thing." Reiterating his position that "the citizens of one country ought not to go into another country and there acquire land or carry on business without subjecting themselves to the laws of the country into which they go," Storey argued that if the oil properties were expropriated without compensation the owners had no claim on the public treasury, for "they should bear their own loss as they pocket their own profit." By the end of the Wilson administration, therefore, Storey's anti-imperialism was moving far beyond opposition to formal colonial status, beyond even a defense of the right of every state to govern herself without the fear of foreign intervention, to include a defense of the right of every state to determine her own economic affairs.[53]

3. The Community of Nations

Moorfield Storey's thirty-year career as a critic of American foreign policy sprang not only from his anti-imperialism, but also from his opposition to war. It is not difficult to find the source of this attitude. He had been the personal secretary of Charles Sumner, who had come as near to pacifism as any Chairman of the Senate Foreign Relations Committee ever would; and judging by the number of times he commented upon it, Sumner's early exposition of antiwar doctrine, "The True Grandeur of Nations," made a profound impression upon Storey. Sumner's arraignment of the military ethic and his opposing view that "the true grandeur of nations" lay in "deeds of justice and beneficence"; his argument that war defeated its ostensible purpose of establishing justice between nations; even his proposals for a world court and arbitration treaties—all these themes would appear throughout Storey's advocacy of peace.[54]

Yet Sumner had been able to preach the cause of peace against a background of nineteenth-century optimism: since, as he put it, "man, as an individual, is capable of indefinite improvement," war, like the slave trade and barbarous punishments, could be relegated to the benighted past. Storey, advocating peace at the end of the century, was confronted not only by deterministic intellectual trends, but by a specific glorification of physical force. As he wrote at the turn of the century,

. . . A school of thinkers—political, religious, commercial —has sprung up into being which teaches that war is in itself desirable, that it is a nursery of manly virtue without which nations must decay, the handmaiden of commerce, and the appointed means of spreading the doctrines of Christ: and that it is our duty to employ its methods religiously against our weaker and more ignorant fellow men. It is a singular return to doctrines familiar in the days of Pizarro but not accepted lately by enlightened men.[55]

The growing intensity of Storey's commitment to peace during this period is perhaps best revealed by his retrospective comments on the Civil War. After the assault on Fort Sumter, Sumner seems to have been able to place the war under his earlier category of "the conservation of domestic quiet," and thereby exempt it from his general condemnation. Storey found it difficult in retrospect to make such a distinction, though he admitted that questioning the value of "a war which freed a race" was not an easy one. Yet he seemed to imply that the act of emancipation, though necessary, said nothing in favor of the war, but much against a society which had permitted slavery to continue. "If our countrymen had foreseen the terrible consequences, if they had realized that what seemed the sin of the South was the sin of us all . . . is there any doubt that the same result . . . might have been won by peaceful means?" And what, besides formal emancipation, had the war accomplished? Could it be said that "that war freed us from the prejudice against the colored man which has been a prolific source of injustice?" On the contrary, in early twentieth-century America that prejudice appeared to be everywhere increasing. And it was being rationalized on the same basis as the suppression of the insurgents in the Philippines was, so that "we have learned to say that the brown man has no right to govern himself which the white man is bound to respect." Thus war achieved nothing, for the rights established by one war would be destroyed as a consequence of another.[56]

Storey's opposition to war led him to advocate specific measures to reduce the likelihod of international conflicts. In 1897 he lent his support to an unsuccessful effort to have the Senate ratify an arbitration treaty with Great Britain. And not only as a peace advocate, but as former Independent concerned about heavy taxation, he urged that the United States reduce its military expenditures:

> The amount this country is now spending for past and possibly future wars is altogether out of proportion to our expenditures for other purposes which, I think, seem to most reasonable citizens of vastly greater importance. We are perfectly safe from attack for every foreign power knows our reserve strength, and when we consider that since 1812 (except during the Rebellion) we have never really needed a navy except in war of our own seeking, we might safely economize now. The burden of military expenditure the world over is altogether unreasonable, and no nation can afford to set an example in economy in this respect so well as the United States.[57]

Having persistently argued for two decades against the use of force to settle international disputes, Storey was horrified at the outbreak of war in 1914:

> It is the greatest calamity that has visited the world in any time, and I shudder at the contemplation of the losses which the contending powers are inflicting on the world —a loss not only to be felt by this generation but for generations to come. They are filling up a reservoir of international hatred that will obstruct the process of civilization for a century. . . .

Not surprisingly, his initial approach to the European war reflected his earlier participation in the peace movement. He did not want the United States to enter the conflict on the side of the Allies because, he wrote, "while the world is mad there should be some great region where peace prevails, and from which an influence can come to help end the conflict on proper conditions."

He was therefore opposed to the mobilization that Roosevelt and his friends were demanding. "My feeling is that for a good many years to come there will be no power in the world that feels like attacking us," he wrote in early 1915. With others in the peace movement, he found one of the lessons of the war to be that "you get what you prepare for, and if you prepare for peace, you will get peace, while if you prepare for war . . . you are sure in the long run to get war." And he maintained that position throughout 1915 and 1916, offering his personal support to the Wilson administration when it tried, through diplomacy, to defend American neutral rights.[58]

Yet even as he urged the avidly pro-Allied Winslow not to arouse public opinion lest it impair American influence on the peace settlement, Storey left no doubt as to his own opinion on the merits of the contending alliances. "I cannot see that any outcome is tolerable," he wrote three months after the war began, "that does not result in the overthrow of the military party in Germany and the destruction of Germany's military power, so that this thing cannot be repeated." For the next three years, even while he urged American neutrality, Storey continued to describe German actions in the harshest possible terms. Sympathy for the Allied cause may well have prevailed among opponents of intervention, but few of them were so unequivocal in their condemnation of Germany. In that condemnation of Germany, Storey revealed the nature of his allegiance to the cause of peace. His had always been a qualified commitment, and after the American declaration of war in 1917 he abandoned it.[59]

In his qualified support of the peace movement, Storey reflected particular influences within his own background. Storey's colleague in anti-imperialism and civil rights, Oswald Garrison Villard, had come from a comparable background: indeed, as the grandson of William Lloyd Garrison, he had an even greater claim to the antislavery tradition. But Villard was an absolute pacifist, perhaps even more than his grandfather, and he found even indirect support of a war too great a violation of his moral values. Thus, though his grandfather finally, uneasily, gave his support to Lincoln's decision to suppress secession by force, Villard never supported Wilson's decision to enter the war against Germany.[60]

If Villard represented the extreme pacifist side of the antislavery heritage, Storey, despite his support of disarmament and conciliation, did not. For the major influence upon Storey had not been Garrison, but Sumner. In Sumner's attacks upon war he gave a copious array of legal citations and historical references, and these may have been an indication that he found the simple moral argument inadequate not only for his audiences but also for himself. Sumner's basic argument had been that war represented a gross incongruity between horrible means and prosaic (even sordid) objectives. This essentially pragmatic argument did not necessarily exclude support for any particular war, but made the central question whether the objectives of that particular war were sufficiently exalted to warrant either the cost of success or the possibility of failure.

It was this aspect of the antislavery heritage, and not that in which opposition to war itself precluded consideration of the merits of the contenders, that Moorfield Storey represented. For someone of his background, one such justifiable war was in defense of human rights; and Storey's troubled questions about the justification of the Civil War, far from contradicting this position, in fact reaffirm it. At great cost the war had succeeded in establishing the supremacy of the Union over the constituent states, but Storey remained ambivalent toward that particular objective. The other great objective of the war had been the liberation of the Negro race, a liberation (for someone of Storey's views) from the confinement of prejudice as well as from legal bondage. Yet in the early twentieth century, Southern Negroes appeared to be driven back into a position closely approaching that of slavery, and from that perspective, Storey could only conclude that the "war for emancipation" had been something of a fraud. Unconvinced that the successful first objective of the war was worth the cost, and suspecting that the second objective, while worth the cost, had never been achieved, Storey questioned the entire war. But can it be doubted that, had the war truly liberated the Negro, Storey would have endorsed it? [61]

In addition to the defense of human rights, a second possible justification for war was self-defense against aggression. As he weighed the merits of any particular contenders, Storey's judgment would go against those he believed responsible for provoking the war in the first place. Certainly this would explain Storey's hopes for an Allied victory after 1914, for in his mind "this war was brought on by Germany":

> It was she who took the initial step, it was she who gave Austria her support in making the extraordinary demand upon Serbia, it was she who was prepared down to the last point for war, and it was she apparently who desired it.

The American declaration of war in 1917 simply enabled him to say publicly what he had been writing privately for three years, that "the German people are in substance a mad dog at large in the community, and until the Hohenzollerns and their theories of government are overthrown for good and all, there will be no such thing as peace in this world." [62]

But Storey's belief that resistance to aggression constituted a justification for war can explain only a part—perhaps the less important part—of his attitude toward World War I and the peace settlement. In the rhetoric of international debate he had been more responsive to the themes of anti-imperialism and self-determination than to any others. Thus Germany's real offense in Storey's eyes probably was less her encouragement of Austria against Serbia than her invasion of Belgium, an invasion which for him represented the culmination of a long-standing German aim to dominate the smaller nations along her frontiers. And, as he continued to remind his audiences, German actions represented the logical extension of aspirations which had influenced American policy for two decades:

> The Germans are sure that their culture is the best in the world, and that they are serving mankind by extending its

areas as widely as possible, and imposing it by force upon
their weak and inferior neighbors. Is this doctrine strange
to us? Have we not occupied the islands of the Filipinos
by force? Are we not insisting that they are inferior, and
that our civilization is far superior to theirs? Have we not
. . . visited them with every extremity of war in order
that we might impose upon them our superior civilization? [63]

It was, of course, unnecessary for Storey to look back to the
annexation of the Philippines to perceive parallels between
American and German actions. He had only to look at the current
interventions in the Caribbean, equally arrogant in spite of their
cover of idealistic rhetoric:

Germany's course is atrocious, but at least she does not
pretend that she was right in breaking her treaty with
Belgium and making war on that stricken country. We in-
vade Nicaragua, Haiti, and Santo Domingo, but pretend
all the while that we respect their rights.

The case Storey would argue against Germany, in other words—
that no nation should be permitted to violate "the most solemn
national engagements, the long-established principles of international law, the precepts of religion, the rules of morals, [and]
the instincts of humanity"—he had already presented against the
United States for twenty years.[64]

And so, while admitting that in the war against Germany the
United States would be allied with "nations with varying ideals,
with varying records, and with different standards," he remained
hopeful that the defeat of Germany would "advance the standards of international intercourse and do something for the freedom of small nations." Storey would measure the achievement of
the peacemakers at Paris not by their provisions for the van-
quished (for he continued to believe that "the power of Germany should be broken"), but by the anti-imperialist criteria he
had already indicated. When he wrote of the "things in the
treaty to which I am strongly opposed," he referred to the denials

of the rights of the weaker nations, for it had been for her violation of such rights that he had condemned Germany in the first place. Storey was, for example, bitterly critical of the transfer of German-controlled Shantung to Japan instead of its return to China, and of "the refusal to recognize racial equality at the instance of Japan and China, a refusal which seems to me extraordinarily insolent and tactless. . . ." And he was most suspicious of the mandate system under which the victorious Allies would govern the former colonies of Germany and the provinces of the defunct Turkish Empire, seeing the proposal as an invitation to the extension of traditional imperialism.[65]

In spite of these qualifications, by the time President Wilson returned to America with the Treaty of Versailles, in the spring of 1919, Storey urged its ratification. For him, as for Wilson, the heart of the Treaty was the Covenant of the proposed League of Nations; and entry into the League for him, as for Wilson, seemed at the time "the only possible course to take in order to save the world from shipwreck, a disaster in which we shall share with all other countries." With all its imperfections, the League seemed to Storey to represent the best means yet discovered for preserving the peace; on this point, both his long support for international conciliation and his current fear of Germany led him to support the Treaty. Storey's support for the Treaty was ultimately determined, however, by the Covenant's embodiment of the principle that the relations of the great powers with their weaker neighbors would henceforth be controlled by the community of nations.[66]

Yet by the time the Treaty came to a vote in the Senate, in the fall of 1919, Storey had become one of its sharpest critics, going so far as to urge senators not to ratify it. Accused of inconsistency, he could argue that the Treaty to be ratified was not the Treaty signed at Paris. For during 1919 Senator Henry Cabot Lodge had succeeded in adding to the original Treaty a number of "strong" reservations, which either required further congressional assent to American actions within the League, or exempted policies (such as the Monroe Doctrine) from League jurisdiction.

Lodge's reservations struck not only at the basis of Storey's support of the Treaty, but at his entire attitude since 1914. Storey had finally accepted American intervention in the war because of two convictions: that those who broke the peace must be punished; and that the rights of all nations, great or small, must be equally respected. It was on the basis of those convictions that he had supported the product of the peacemakers. Yet Lodge's reservations appeared to him to deny the League the power to punish aggression, and seemed to violate the rights of the smaller nations. Thus Storey felt compelled to urge its rejection, for the amended Treaty seemed to violate the very objectives—collective security and self-determination—that had led him to support the war.

Storey's opposition to the Treaty with the Lodge reservations developed as part of a larger debate between him and other supporters of the League of Nations, a debate revealing different and perhaps even more profound divisions than those which separated the supporters and the opponents of the Treaty. The focus of the debate occurred among members of the League to Enforce Peace, the most influential organization advocating collective security. Founded in 1915, the League had met with initial opposition from pacifists, who objected to its implied use of force against an aggressor nation. Storey acknowledged the persuasiveness of this argument, and he pointed out that the effectiveness of the League's program in actually averting war was somewhat limited.

The program of the League to Enforce Peace, Storey wrote, called for all nations to pledge themselves to peaceful arbitration of their disputes, but he regarded it as unlikely that all nations would actually keep their pledge. What if a nation rejected peaceful arbitration? The League's program required the community of nations to compel the recalcitrant nation to accept arbitration. Since such compulsion implied the threat of war, if a nation believed she could successfully defy such a threat (and here Storey referred to what he saw as German calculations in 1914), then the international community would have to go to war

—a war to punish aggression, but a war nevertheless. Even if the League's program had been in effect, he believed, it could not have averted World War I. So his initial response was to think that the best hope of reducing the likelihood of war lay in general disarmament.[67]

What is significant here, however, is not that Storey had doubts about the League's program, but that he continued to maintain an active membership within the organization. He revealed part of the reason for his continued support in a letter to the League's secretary. "I have always questioned whether the immediate purpose of the League was feasible, but if a large number of my best fellow-citizens were starting any movement to secure peace, I felt it my duty to associate myself with them and help as far as I could." It is also true that Storey supported the League because during the war he increasingly came to believe that resistance to aggression and the defense of weaker nations were more important than the preservation of peace. But the most plausible explanation, and one which would account for his later attack upon the Treaty, seems to lie elsewhere; he was convinced that, in some situations, the program of the League would be effective. There might well arise situations in which a nation refused arbitration yet ultimately would be unwilling to risk war—though the World War was not one of them. In such situations, the threat of collective action indicated in the League's program would actually "enforce the peace." [68]

Seeing the Covenant of the new League of Nations as an embodiment of the basic program of the League to Enforce Peace, Storey logically expected his organization to support the Treaty. But while the League as an organization in fact did so, its endorsement was weakened by the involvement of one prominent member (Elihu Root) in the authorship of the Lodge reservations, and the efforts of two others (William Howard Taft and Harvard president A. Lawrence Lowell) to propose reservations of their own. Thus what had begun as the League's endorsement of the original Treaty ended up as endorsement of the Treaty with the Lodge reservations. Storey was by no means adamant against reservations, but those proposed by Lodge and accepted by the Senate Republicans brought forth his heated opposition. Further requirements of congressional consent, he reasoned, could only be perceived by other nations as weakening the role of the United States in the League of Nations, and thus weakening the effectiveness of the League in deterring aggression:

> Reservations which leave this nation "full independence and freedom of action" relieve us of the obligation to help in preserving the peace of the world which the Treaty imposes, while every other party to the Treaty remains bound. This is not ratifying but rejecting the Treaty and proposing a new one.[69]

Storey continued to stand with that faction of the League which opposed Lodge's "strong" reservations, but it was not only his specific approach to the problems of collective security that set him apart from the more prominent members of the League. What seems to have upset him the most was that men like Lodge did not want to have American actions in Latin America challenged in an international tribual. Storey had sharply attacked the American record of intervention in Latin America for over a decade, and after 1914 he did not draw back from the severest possible analogy: "we stand toward Mexico and the countries south of us as Prussia stood in Europe." He therefore remained unyielding in his insistence that "the smaller nations of this hemisphere would need to invoke the protection of the League of Nations against the Monroe Doctrine. . . ."[70]

But even before the Treaty arrived in the Senate for consideration, Lodge and others had persuaded Wilson to incorporate the Monroe Doctrine into the Treaty. Storey had opposed such a recognition as "a fortification . . . behind which we can carry on aggression against all our weaker neighbors." Not content with a recognition of the Monroe Doctrine in the Treaty, Lodge then persuaded his colleagues to accept a reservation specifically excluding United States relations with Latin America from the

League's jurisdiction. As Storey's anti-imperialism had affected his view of the origins and purpose of the war, so would it now determine his attitude toward the peace settlement.[71]

The division within the League to Enforce Peace over the question of the Monroe Doctrine, though less well known than the division over the collective security aspects of the Treaty, also served to divide Storey from other League members. The formation of the League had occurred against the background of tensions with Mexico, and Storey wanted the League to take the initiative in demanding arbitration of the dispute. "The present crisis tests the value of our scheme, and unless we act now, I think we must confess that it is impracticable." Yet when he made the suggestion to Taft, he received no reply. Three years later, however, Taft came forth with his own remedy for the solution of Mexican-American difficulties:

> I am not quite sure what we can do about Mexico until we get this League through. Then I have always thought we could amend the League so as to provide for mandatories if necessary, and have Mexico put under the mandatory of the League with an obligation to straighten out and then turn her back to her people.[72]

In the course of the correspondence, Storey challenged Taft's entire argument:

> I think you use the word "mandate" inaccurately. As I understand it a mandate is something done by a body of nations who collectively entrust some backward nation to the care of one of their number. That is a very different thing from our constituting ourselves a mandatory and proceeding for causes which satisfy us to overthrow the rights of a neighbor. I do not think the obligation to return Mexico to independence would be enforceable, or even be enforced, and I think you yourself will see that for us—on account of injury done to ourselves, very doubtful and very trifling—to insist upon conquering Mexico is an abuse of the theory of a mandate.

Storey's debate with Taft occurred at the same time as the Senate debate over the Treaty, and Taft's frank admission that he saw the League as serving the traditional ends of American diplomacy quite probably made Storey more intransigent in his opposition to the amended Treaty. It is certain that the exchange of views with Taft made him more suspicious of the League to Enforce Peace. Storey had, after all, seldom been able to differentiate the positions of Taft, on the one hand, and Lodge, on the other, on Philippine policy, and after this episode he probably saw their views as convergent on the purpose of the League of Nations as well.[73]

With the positions of the protagonists—President Wilson and Senator Lodge and, on a lesser, private level, Storey and Taft—so clearly marked, events moved to an inevitable conclusion. Initially a supporter of the Treaty, Storey had turned against ratification because of Lodge's "strong" reservations. For Storey the fight over the League of Nations was not whether America would enter the organization, but whether it would do so in a genuine spirit of international cooperation. If the United States insisted on reserving the right to intervene in the Caribbean—or to hesitate in joining to resist aggression—then, he seemed to say, it was better that the Treaty not be ratified at all. Storey's letters urging rejection of the amended Treaty were superfluous: the President's influence alone was sufficient to persuade a majority of Senate Democrats to vote against accepting the Treaty with the Lodge reservations. Combined with the "irreconcilables"—those Republicans like William E. Borah and Hiram Johnson who opposed the Treaty in any form—they thus prevented the Treaty from gaining the two-thirds majority necessary for ratification.[74]

As the issue of the League of Nations passed from the Senate debate into the presidential campaign of 1920, Storey remained firm in his position: either the Treaty should be ratified substantially as it stood, or it should not be ratified at all. When, therefore, the Republican wing of the League to Enforce Peace—Taft, Root, and Lowell—attempted to rally their party behind the

Treaty, Storey attacked their sincerity. They "have committed themselves substantially to the reservations proposed by the Republican Senators, and those reservations, it seems to me, destroy the Treaty. . . ." Wilson had agreed to accept some amendments, he wrote, yet these men continue to talk of Wilson's "obstinacy." What about the "obstinacy" of the various Republican opponents of the Treaty? he asked. A supporter of Cox partly because of the League issue, Storey could not understand why pro-League Republicans had so much faith in Harding. "As between Messrs. Taft and Lowell, on the one hand, who are not in public office, and Messrs. Johnson and Borah, whose support is vital to him," Harding would meet the demands of the latter. Storey's skepticism about Harding and the League proved correct: the twelve years of Republican administration in Washington permanently foreclosed American entry in the League of Nations.[75]

4. An Internationalist in Isolation

Storey could find few consoling features in the Republican foreign policy after 1921. Under the Harding and Coolidge administrations, American participation in two movements he had supported—disarmament and international arbitration—seemed closer to fulfillment than before. Storey's spirits were raised by the first major disarmament conference of the decade, the Naval Conference held at Washington in 1921–22, and he lent whatever influence he still possessed to the attempts of the Coolidge administration to secure American entry into the World Court in 1926–27. But for him the Republican efforts at international cooperation were not only incomplete, but in one important aspect —the war debts of the Allies—retrogressive. Believing that the wartime loans made to the Allies were "our contribution toward what seemed to us a vital need," Storey advocated that all war debts be canceled. His views were not shared by the administrations in Washington, however, and the dreary cycle of the

United States underwriting German reparations to the Allies, so that the Allies could continue their debt payments to the United States, continued until the Depression.[76]

The Republican attitude toward the American colonies and protectorates in Latin America and Asia had, as far as Storey was concerned, even less to commend it. The Harding and Coolidge administrations refused to implement even the vague pledge of Philippine independence in the Jones Act and appeared determined to carry on the colonial policies set by Roosevelt and Taft. A special Senate committee went to Haiti and returned with a report not only vindicating the American record in the suppression of the insurrection, but also supporting maintenance of the occupation, so that by the time supporters of the withdrawal of troops presented their brief against the occupation in late April 1922, Secretary of State Charles Evans Hughes felt secure enough to treat their protest with the utmost contempt. Toward Mexico the Republicans were less aggressive than they had promised to be in the 1920 campaign, but the oil question remained, for in spite of temporary agreements, Carranza's successors proved ultimately unwilling to concede the principle behind Article 27.[77]

Tensions with Mexico became critical when they became linked to the crisis in another Latin-American nation, Nicaragua. That crisis marked the end of Storey's career as a foreign-policy critic, for he fought that intervention until his death. Along with Cuba and the Dominican Republic, Nicaragua had been one of the testing-grounds for the emerging policy of intervention, with its techniques of military occupation and financial reorganization. The bitter strife between the two leading parties in Nicaragua, the Conservatives and the Liberals, had been suppressed but not eliminated by the American military ocupation between 1912 and 1925. As soon as the Marines withdrew, a disgruntled Conservative general staged a series of coups and overthrew the Liberal government. As the country headed toward civil war, the Coolidge administration first attempted to mediate between the parties, but when the United States candidate, Adolfo Díaz, a

Conservative without ties to the incumbent dictator, proved unable to bring stability, Coolidge called back the Marines.[78]

Eager for further American support to ensure his survival, Díaz charged that Mexico was sponsoring the Liberal insurgency and that behind both the Mexican government and the insurgent Liberals stood the international Communist movement. Quite possibly because of the concurrent uproar over Mexican expropriation of oil properties, officials in the administration not only supported Díaz's charges, but, with Secretary of State Frank Kellogg's presentation of the memorandum, "Bolshevist Aims and Policies in Latin America," they even tried to substantiate them. Thus, with Kellogg's appearance before the Senate Foreign Relations Committee in January 1927, the specter of Communism was raised for the first time as a justification for American intervention in Latin America.

Protesting the last intervention he would live to condemn, Storey was not impressed by the anti-Communist rhetoric. "The oil interests are undoubtedly behind the activity of the State Department," he wrote, "and would be glad to embroil us with Mexico." Storey again criticized the presidential deployment of troops: the President, he wrote, has no constitutional authority "to exercise any power not given to him, or to decide the question of war or peace which is expressly committed to Congress." Nor did he have the authority under international law, Storey argued, to send forces into a country with which the United States was formally at peace. "It is time that usurpations such as these were characterized as they deserve, and that Congress asserted the rights of the American people and protected the rights of friendly nations from abuse." [79]

On this occasion, however, Storey was no longer quite the lonely voice crying out against American intervention that he had been for two decades. Whereas the Haitian occupation had been sporadically condemned by a handful of senators, the Nicaraguan involvement apparently united the progressive bloc in Congress in criticism of American policy. And yet the political attitudes of the congressmen who most forcefully condemned the intervention and favored a conciliatory policy toward Mexico (even at the cost of American economic interests) highlight the uniqueness of Storey's own position. Surveying the debates over Nicaragua, one comes to the conclusion that the anti-interventionist attack was spearheaded by men—notably Senator Borah —who had most sharply opposed American entry into the League of Nations. The men in public life who held most closely to Storey's anti-imperialist convictions, in other words, were those who were the most opposed to his commitment to collective security.[80]

As the years passed, these progressives' belief that the Versailles Treaty had been an attempt to preserve the status quo (in the colonies as elsewhere) became combined with a growing suspicion that the 1914–18 war had been an imperialist war from the beginning; and so they turned against all efforts to involve the United States in any collective security arrangements in the 1930's. It is not surprising, in view of the struggle for American survival which followed, that historians have been less charitable toward Borah than toward someone such as Henry L. Stimson, who moved from a background in colonial administration to become an unyielding foe of fascist aggression.

For Storey, however, anti-imperialist connections led to a commitment to collective security. From his first statements in 1898 protesting the acquisition of colonies, continuing through his protests over military occupation and economic domination of other nations, he had remained a steadfast supporter of self-determination. And from his first proposals for guarantees for Philippine independence, Storey had argued that the solution to any threatened aggression lay not in unilateral intervention by the United States, but in collective action. Initially opposed to the use of force in international relations, he emerged from World War I with a more pragmatic attitude. Storey's position in the fight over the Treaty may have been short-sighted, but it was not a result of his wavering on the issue of collective security; his opposition to the Lodge reservations came partly from his fear that they would weaken the collective security principle.

Inheritor of an older view of America's role in the world, Storey had always been something of an isolated figure. His isolation after 1918 was heightened by his support of both self-determination and collective security. Yet in view of the developments within fifteen years after his death—Philippine independence, a non-interventionist policy in Latin America, and most of all, American participation in the United Nations—is it too much to suggest that Storey's isolation in his last years came from the fact that he was ahead of his time?

3 ❧ Civil Equality

AMERICAN historians who have grown interested in the development of American race relations have uncovered one of the bitterest paradoxes in our history: the final abandonment of the Negro by his Northern supporters and the appearance of systematic racial proscription in the South did not occur in the supposedly callous and corrupt 1880's; rather, they accompanied the rising tide of reform in the 1890's, and they reached their highest point at the zenith of progressivism during the administration of Woodrow Wilson. In reaction to the increasing disfranchisement, segregation, and racial violence in the early twentieth century, a number of black leaders, most notably W. E. B. DuBois, banded together to protest the trend toward racial proscription. That Negroes decided to assert their dignity and demand their constitutional rights is not surprising; what is surprising is that, at a time of virulent anti-Negro prejudice, some white men and women joined them in their struggle for equality.

The most notable expression of this common front against racism was the National Association for the Advancement of Colored People, founded in 1909 by Negroes and whites together. Two of the white founders of the Association—Oswald Garrison

Villard and Mary White Ovington—indicated in their autobi-
ographies some of the factors that impelled them toward championing the Negro's cause. Both—Villard, particularly, because
of his Garrison ancestry—had some claim to being considered in-
heritors of the civil rights tradition of the previous century. But
Ovington, a social worker trying to alleviate the condition of the
poor, and Villard, a crusading journalist and an ardent civil libertarian, both tended to sympathize automatically with the victims
and outcasts of society, a reaction more characteristic of twentieth-century liberalism than of nineteenth-century reform. It is
unclear, therefore, whether their continuing dedication to the
Negro's cause came primarily from their childhood memories of
the abolitionist movement or from the liberal environment in
which they spent their careers.[1]

The first president of the Association, however, was Moorfield
Storey who, largely adhering to the values he had acquired as an
Independent reformer, cannot be considered a twentieth-century
liberal at all. Storey's outlook on racial matters was little different
from that of Villard and Ovington, but because he did not experience the reinforcing effect of a general liberalism, the source
of his dedication to the Negro's cause is easier to discover.
Storey's legal arguments on behalf of the National Association
for the Advancement of Colored People, and his consistent advocacy of racial equality, were a direct reflection of the influence
of Charles Sumner, who made the most notable nineteenth-
century argument that the law must make no racial distinctions.

When the abolitionists found that the general statements of
equality in the state constitutions failed to change the massive
discrimination against the free Negroes of the North, they began
to demand specific legal prohibitions on racial discrimination.
In 1849, Sumner introduced into American jurisprudence this
new meaning of the phrase, "equality before the law." In that
year, he served as counsel for a black couple whose daughter was
prohibited by the rules of the Boston School Committee from attending the neighboring public school because it was restricted
to whites. Since only black children were prevented from attend-

ing the schools nearest them, and were instead sent to all-Negro schools often at a considerable distance, they were made to feel inferior, Sumner argued, and white children were made to regard them as such. The Negro schools did not have facilities equal to those attended by whites, but even if they had been equal, Sumner explained, "this compulsory segregation from the mass of the citizens is of itself an *inequality* we condemn." In view of the general principles of "equality before the law" embodied in the Massachusetts constitution, the Boston School Committee could not, in justice, make such a distinction. The state Supreme Court ruled against Sumner's clients, but several years later the Massachusetts legislature abolished the remaining segregated schools.[2]

Sumner took his commitment to civil equality with him into the Senate and, once emancipation became a certainty, he devoted the remaining years of his career to securing civil equality for all the citizens of the United States. Though directly responsible for minor gains for Negroes during the Civil War, his greater significance lies in his leadership in guiding the emerging postwar Northern sentiment that the Negro be granted the rights of citizenship. His persistent demands for universal manhood suffrage were ultimately realized in the Fifteenth Amendment; but his other goal, a bill prohibiting segregation in all public facilities for education, recreation, and transportation, remained unfulfilled at the time of his death.[3]

It was with Sumner that the young Moorfield Storey spent two of the most impressionable years of his life. Perhaps because of a self-imposed intellectual confinement that isolated him from the racist implications of the science of the time, Storey carried forward Sumner's dedication to civil equality as long as he lived. As a man of essentially conservative temperament, Storey was doubly fortunate. The Reconstruction Amendments, though stripped of their force by the Supreme Court, still existed: unlike Sumner, therefore, he did not need to soar into the realm of speculation to justify his case. And the decline of the Negro's status was so obvious by the first decade of the twentieth century that Storey could well regard an advocacy of civil equality as a return to older and better values.

Unlike some of his contemporaries—unlike Lodge, for example, who simultaneously championed free elections in the South and the restriction of immigration—Storey rejected racist attitudes toward all ethnic minorities. By the mid-1890's, Storey had ceased whatever criticism of immigrant citizenship he had made as an Independent; and on subsequent occasions he defended both the Irish Catholics and the Jews. He continued to advocate the increasingly unpopular cause of Japanese immigration, and urged the relocation of the oppressed Armenian people in the United States and Canada. For Storey, a defense of civil equality on behalf of the Negro implied a defense of all minorities: for him "the absurd prejudices of race and color" were equally obnoxious and equally worthy of attack, "whether they bar the Negro from his rights as a man, the foreigner from his welcome to our shores, the Filipino from his birthright of independence, [or] the Hebrew from social recognition. . . ." If Storey concentrated on the oppression of the Negro, it may well have been because, though other groups were subjected to discrimination, few were so completely denied civil and political rights, and none suffered the continuous brutality that marked the conditions of black Americans in the early twentieth century.[4]

1. The Establishment of "White Supremacy"

During the years in Moorfield Storey's life between his clerkship with Sumner and his assumption of the NAACP presidency, the years between 1869 and 1909, he expressed his attitudes on public questions within the framework of Independent reform. At first glance it might seem surprising that anyone from the Independent movement should emerge as a champion of the Negro, for the Independents had initially defined themselves as opposing Federal protection of civil rights. After the passage of the Fifteenth Amendment in 1870, the Reconstruction coalition dwindled to an alliance of Republican politicians, who saw in the allegiance of the Southern Negro the best means of perpetuating their party, and a small band of abolitionists led by Wendell Phillips, who saw in the supremacy of the Republican party the best protection of the rights of the freedman. During the Grant administration this alliance was increasingly opposed by men who, though often past fighters in the antislavery cause, were more concerned with the moral tone of American life than with the welfare of the Negro. Together with capitalists seeking new fields for investment and merchants interested in reopening Southern markets, these Independent spokesmen were among the main forces seeking the abandonment of Reconstruction.[5]

The Independents maintained that they had turned against Reconstruction because of the corruption of the bi-racial "carpet-bag" governments in the South. A more charitable observer might have noted that a people recently emerged from slavery, allied with the most disparate elements of the white community, had somehow managed to install public school systems for the first time in many areas of the South. The suspicion lingers that many Independents saw only what their preconceptions permitted them to see, preconceptions determined sometimes by simple racial prejudice, sometimes by disillusionment with social experimentation, and sometimes by fears of an unpropertied and illiterate electorate. Influenced by the laissez-faire premises of both the old classical economics and the new Darwinist biology, the Independents could rationalize their feelings with the argument that the freedman had to advance himself unaided by the Federal Government. For many of the Independents, the conclusion is inescapable: their abandonment of Reconstruction meant abandonment of the Negro.[6]

And yet there were Independents who maintained that their opposition to Reconstruction signified no loss of faith in the freedman: the most notable proponent of this position was Carl Schurz. Schurz's attitudes are especially significant in view of Moorfield Storey's later comment about him, that "of all the men I have ever known, there is not one . . . to whom I have turned more constantly for guidance and inspiration." Carl Schurz's evolving views may therefore indicate Storey's own position at this time. Immediately after the war, a tour of the South convinced Schurz that continued military occupation would be necessary to avert "a general collision between the whites and the blacks. . . ." Indeed, his report on Southern conditions served as part of the Radicals' brief for more stringent Reconstruction terms. Supporting the initial Reconstruction legislation, Schurz described the purpose of the Fifteenth Amendment as furthering the principle of self-government: "a political organization of society which secures to the generality of its members, to the whole people, and not to part of them only, the right and the means to cooperate in the management of their common affairs. . . ." Because of his opposition to the exclusion of any group, he claimed, he soon turned against Reconstruction. Making the common error of exaggerating the number of whites disfranchised under the Radical terms, he began to worry about the exclusion of the "intelligence" of the community, an exclusion even more dangerous "when ignorance and inexperience were admitted to so large an influence upon public affairs. . . ." In the 1870's, therefore, he persistently advocated the end of Reconstruction, believing that the restoration of "intelligence" in the South, as well as in the North, could best secure the freedmen's rights.[7]

The belief of Schurz and other Independents in the compatibility of Southern "home rule" and the protection of civil rights has never lacked critics. But in the Independents' defense it should be noted that in a significant number of cases, the triumph of the coalition of planters and businessmen which "redeemed" the South from Reconstruction was not followed by a wholesale denial of civil and political rights. Segregation had replaced slavery as a means of assuring racial subordination, but it was still largely a matter of social practice (not statutory decree) and was by no means universal. Compared with what was to develop, the color line was unevenly drawn in the 1870's and 1880's: schools, for example, had already been segregated during Reconstruction; but segregation in dining and recreational facilities varied considerably from place to place; and in many states Negroes had been successful in maintaining desegregated railroad cars. The situation of Negro suffrage was comparable: though black voting continued more as a matter of factional need than of principled support, many of the conservatives who "redeemed" the South from Reconstruction appeared to accept Negro participation as a fact of political life.[8]

When, therefore, Thomas Wentworth Higginson returned from a visit with the veterans of his all-black regiment and said that he saw in the Southern seaboard states little discrimination against them and no attempt to deprive them of their rights, there are grounds for accepting the good faith of at least some of his fellow Independents who agreed with him. Similar optimistic assessments of Southern conditions may explain Independent acceptance of Supreme Court decisions which restricted Reconstruction legislation on the basis that the Fourteenth Amendment could not be used to punish either private violence or private discrimination. Undoubtedly this acceptance signified some Independents' repugnance at the very idea of civil rights legislation, but it also may have represented the conviction of others that civil rights were already secure without further Federal interference. Some Independents helped defeat a Republican bill in 1890 which would have sent Federal registrars into the South because they saw the bill as a violation of laissez-faire; but others may have helped to do so because they believed it was unnecessary.[9]

Even as the Independents were opposing the Federal elections bill of 1890, partly on the assumption that civil rights were in fact protected, new trends within the South forced men like Storey to make a sudden re-assessment of their position. Since these events, regional and national, defined the context in which Storey's subsequent career as a civil rights advocate took place, it is well to look at them in some detail.

The decade of the 1890's, in the South as elsewhere in the nation, was a time of intense political conflict. There, Redeemer solicitude for coal, iron, and railroad interests clashed with the protest movements arising from the agricultural depression. The subsequent battles between established machines and insurgents, whether Democratic or Populist, were protracted, bitter, and sometimes violent. In some states, black voters continued their alliance with the paternalistic Redeemers; in others, they tentatively joined the insurgent farmers. In either case, the alignment proved politically fatal, for when the side they had not joined came to power its first action was to launch a campaign for disfranchisement, whether through constitutional convention, constitutional amendment, or simple legislation.

The actual devices used to "legally" disfranchise the Negro— that is, to disfranchise him while conforming to the letter of the Fifteenth Amendment—varied from state to state. But in each case, uniform literacy requirements were imposed which effectively restricted Negro participation in elections while allowing equally illiterate whites to vote, primarily under two kinds of exemptions. The first was the "understanding clause," under which the literacy requirement was waived "if the voter was able to understand or gave a reasonable interpretation" of the state constitution. The second was the "grandfather clause," in which the requirement did not apply to those who had been voters on January 1, 1867, and the descendants of such voters—or, in a later modification, to those who were veterans of various American wars and the descendants of such veterans. Having served their purpose, the exemptive clauses expired shortly after they were passed, but other restrictions on Negro suffrage were permanent. These included the institution of a poll tax, along with state-wide party rules barring Negroes from Democratic primaries. The poll tax and literacy test also disfranchised an indeterminate number of lower-class whites, but they achieved their main objective—the virtual elimination of Negro suffrage in most of the South.[10]

The adoption of a progressive reform like the direct primary as a capstone of disfranchisement was symbolic of a whole generation of Southern progressives who came to power advocating both reform and Negro proscription. The class unity which made reform possible was achieved at the Negro's expense. Conversely, "the more white men recognize sharply their kinship with their fellow whites, and the more democracy in every sense of the term spreads among them, the more the Negro is compelled 'to keep his place'. . . ." Disfranchisement was the product of many forces; the institutionalization of segregation, on the other hand, more clearly reveals the political triumph of lower-class whites. Before 1885 only Tennessee required segregated accommodations on railroads; during the next twenty years segregation statutes were passed in every state in the South. Until the Georgia law in 1891 there was no state-wide legislation requiring Jim Crow streetcars; within a decade such legislation had become all but universal in the South. In the years following, legal segregation spread to waiting rooms; to toilet and eating facilities, public and private; to parks and hospitals; and to the ultimate absurdities—the use of separate Bibles in court and a prohibition of interracial checker games.[11]

To the surprise of many Southerners, the successful campaigns for disfranchisement and segregation were followed by an even greater hostility toward the blacks. Significant in the new trend was the shift in Southern political rhetoric and literary expression from the image of the Negro as happy child to that of the Negro as savage brute. According to James K. Vardaman, reform Governor of Mississippi, "the Negro is necessary to the economy of the world, but he was designed for a burden-bearer. Six thousand years ago the Negro was the same as he is today. . . . His civilized veneer lasts as long as he remains in contact with the white man." Under similar interpretations, it was slavery that had made the Negro acceptable to civilization, but emancipation had removed both the external restraints on his "innate" savagery and the physical compulsion to work.

> He was told he was the equal of the white when he was not the equal; he was given to understand that he was the ward of the nation when he should have been trained in self-reliance; he was led to believe that the Govern-

ment would sustain him when he could not be sustained. In legislation, he was taught thieving; in politics, he was taught not to think for himself, but to follow slavishly his leaders (and such leaders:); in private life he was taught insolence.[12]

Insolence was the best description of what the New South found objectionable in the Negro; the category was broad enough to blur all individual merit into some kind of mass racial turpitude. Ben Tillman, champion of the South Carolina farmer, for example, could offer an impassioned defense of lynching on the floor of the Senate, and then attack Booker T. Washington on many of the same assumptions. "The action of President [Theodore] Roosevelt in entertaining that nigger," he said, after the famous "dinner at the White House," "will necessitate our killing a thousand niggers in the South before they will know their place again." This new temper, "not defensive, but assertive and combative," resulted in new patterns of racial violence, such as the race riot, in which all Negroes were attacked because of the "insolence" of a few.[13]

The rest of the country, or so it seemed, was indifferent toward the fate of the Negro, and there was growing evidence that it accepted the Southern view. The abolitionists had long before disappeared as a force in American political life, and by the mid-1890's the Republican party had abandoned its interest in the Negro's potential as the nucleus of party organization in the South. A series of close presidential elections between 1876 and 1888 had produced widespread party support for a Federal elections bill, but with the McKinley victory over Bryan in 1896, many Republicans discovered that since they had solid support from Maine to Minnesota, they had no need of Southern votes at all. From that time onward, it was the advocates of "lily-white" organization who determined the party's attitude toward the South; the rest of the party, already committed to taking up the "white man's burden" in the Caribbean and in the Pacific, offered little resistance.[14]

Among Republican leaders, the old verbal commitment was

still there, but the conviction had disappeared. Theodore Roosevelt, for example, proudly placed himself in the party of emancipation, and wrote that he "very firmly" believed "in granting to Negroes and to all other races the largest amount of self-government which they can exercise." Given some of Roosevelt's other attitudes, however, the "amount of self-government" he was prepared to fight for on the Negro's behalf was minimal. "The Negroes," one visitor recalled him as saying, "are 200,000 years behind," though he was willing to accept the suggestion of a million-year lag; it was obvious to him at least, he wrote one correspondent, that an "absolutely representative government in the Yazoo would bring about the condition of Haiti." At a time of widespread disfranchisement on the ostensible basis that the Negro was unfit for the duties of citizenship, the opinions of the President of the United States were of more than academic significance. At no time in his eight years of office did Roosevelt do anything to halt the growing movement toward racial proscription in the South, and only the region's hysteria on the subject allowed it to become obsessed by minor gestures—a dinner with Booker T. Washington and the appointment of several Negroes to minor offices—during his first year as President.[15]

Intellectually, Roosevelt had no trouble finding authoritative support for his attitudes. The biologists of the period, having measured the Negro brain, confidently pronounced it inferior, since "the anterior association center is relatively and absolutely smaller." In other words, "the Negro has the lower mental faculties (smell, sight, handicraftmanship, body-sense, melody): the Caucasian the higher (self-control, will-power, ethical and aesthetic sense, and reason)." The implications of scientific thought were seized upon by popular writers, one of the most skillful of whom was James Ford Rhodes. Rhodes, a friend of both Roosevelt and Storey, had been an Ohio iron manufacturer before he moved to Boston and began his massive work, a history of the United States from 1850 to 1877. For the quarter-century before his death in 1927, Rhodes was "not so much *an* authority as *the* authority, the final arbiter, on all matters relating to the Civil War and Reconstruction': for progressive historians, who challenged him on many points, did not challenge his view of the Negro.[16]

For Rhodes, "the pretty general view of ethnologists" was that Negroes were stunted intellectually at the level of white thirteen-year-olds. This inherent limitation, compounded by two centuries of slavery, meant that the extension of citizenship after the Civil War was doomed to fail: "given character and fitness as the proper tests for candidates in office, the Negroes almost always voted wrong." Any government involving their wholesale participation would be—and Rhodes never doubted that Reconstruction had been—"a sickening tale of extravagance, waste, corruption, and fraud." Rhodes was unsure whether to place more blame for this debacle on "the knavish white natives and the vulturous adventurers who flocked from the North" or the misguided idealists who "overrated their [the Negroes'] mental and moral caliber," failing to "appreciate the great fact of race. . . ."[17]

The biologists and the historians cast aspersions on the Negro's capacity for citizenship; the sociologists, progressive as well as conservative, helped rationalize racial discrimination. Franklin Giddings contributed to such a rationale—though the ideas he drew on were common—when he wrote that "the original and elementary subjective fact in society is *the consciousness of kind.*" "Our conduct towards those whom we feel to be most like ourselves," in other words, "is instinctively and rationally different from our conduct towards others, whom we believe to be less like ourselves." In fairness to Giddings, "consciousness of kind" was a conceptual tool; but he combined it with his belief that "when the higher and lower races come in contact, it is necessary for the higher in many ways to sustain the lower. . . ." The result of such a synthesis was a perceptible shift toward the idea of "consciousness of kind" as the prerogative of a "superior" race in ordering society. The effect of such sociological theories was most seriously felt when, between 1875 and 1915, the Federal courts nullified the legislative embodiments of civil equality.[18]

A weakened version of Sumner's civil rights bill, prohibiting only discrimination in public accommodations, became law in 1875. But in 1883 the Supreme Court declared it unconstitutional, reasoning that the Fourteenth Amendment did not prohibit private discrimination. Thirteen years later, the Court upheld segregation in *Plessy* v. *Ferguson*, the famous ruling over Jim Crow railroad accommodations in Louisiana. Among the precedents cited in *Plessy* was a previous Court decision, that a Mississippi statute requiring *segregated* facilities added no burden to interstate commerce. In 1877, however, the Court had already ruled that the *desegregated* facilities did add a burden to interstate commerce, and were thus unconstitutional. The two Justices who sat on both cases, Harlan and Bradley, could see no distinction between the issues presented, and for them, neither statute constituted a "burden." Though a somewhat strained argument can be made to the effect that the Mississippi law was *within* a state (and therefore not a burden on *inter*state commerce), it is difficult to avoid the conclusion that the majority in both cases assumed that segregation was "natural," and thus that contrary legislation would be undesirable, indeed a positive hindrance. Rulings such as these weakened Northern enforcement of state civil rights statutes, leaving Negro plaintiffs to face a long and uncertain litigation in civil suits. More important, in making the Southern system of institutionalized segregation the law of the land, the decisions of the Supreme Court represented the supreme example of the nation's new acceptance of the Southern view of the Negro.[19]

The marked deterioration of racial conditions beginning in the 1890's went unnoticed by most of the Independents, who had long before passed off a commitment to human dignity as another of their youthful infatuations. For a minority of Independents, however, the resurgence of racial proscription rekindled their earlier antislavery convictions. Schurz, for example, had never believed in a contradiction between honest government and equal rights: not during Reconstruction when he had worried about morality, and not now, when he worried about justice. He wrote Storey in early 1903, that "unless the reaction now going on be stopped, we shall have to fight the old anti-slavery battle again." And so Schurz began work on a lengthy article for *Mc-Clure's* on the rising tide of racial proscription; in it he warned the South against finding itself "once more in a position provokingly offensive to the moral sense and the enlightened spirit of the world outside. . . ." [20]

Schurz's increased concern reinforced Storey's views, for he was reaching the same conclusions independently. There is little evidence of Storey's attitudes on racial matters during his Independent phase: what evidence there is suggests that his views were indistinguishable from his fellow-reformers, as in his description of the 1890 Federal elections bill as attacking "the root of constitutional government . . . and parent of the grossest abuses and gravest disturbances." As a Boston man with a Virginia-born wife, Storey also had personal reasons for taking a cautious view of the subject: his wife could never bring herself to meet with Negroes on social terms, and she impeded his personal contact with them for forty years. The appearance of systematic disfranchisement and segregation in the South and its acceptance in the North, however, seems to have jolted Storey out of his earlier passivity; the change can be traced most clearly in his comments on Reconstruction, still the touchstone of a commitment to the Negro. In 1889 he addressed the subject of Reconstruction in typical Independent terms, finding its lessons to be that "intelligence is forced to regain the supremacy even by revolutionary methods" under a corrupt and incompetent government. In 1899 he still worried about the corruption of the carpetbag regimes, but now spoke of the need at the time for Federal protection so that "the rights of loyal men, black and white, might be secured against fraud and violence." Thereafter, he would pass lightly over the corruption and concentrate on the wisdom and justice of granting suffrage to the freedmen.[21]

2. A Personal Crusade for Equality

By the beginning of the twentieth century Storey had taken as his basic premise, in race relations as in foreign policy, the statement of Lincoln: "When the white man governs himself that is self-government; but when he governs himself, and also governs *another* man, that is *more* than self-government—that is despotism." He had been among the first of the anti-imperialists to see a connection between the denial of consent in the Pacific and the denial of consent in the South. As early as his speech of June 15, 1898, against "the adoption of a so-called imperial policy by the United States," Storey had warned that any attempt to rationalize the denial of self-government in colonial possession would have domestic repercussions. By the time of his independent campaign for Congress in 1900, he had firmly linked in his own mind the suppression of Negroes in the South with the suppression of the natives in the Pacific possessions:

> No man of anti-slavery antecedents can fail to regard with horror the treatment of the colored race in the South and the attempt to disfranchise them. The whole reaction against this unhappy race, both in the northern and southern states, is deplorable. While, however, the President and the Republican Party are denying the doctrine of human equality which the party was formed to maintain, and are justifying conquest and despotic methods in the Philippines and Porto Rico by the argument that the inhabitants of these islands are unfit for freedom because of their race or color, it is only to be expected that the same doctrines will be applied at home.

Four years later, as the Roosevelt administration took no action to stem the mounting tide of disfranchisement and segregation, the reasons seemed apparent. "The Philippine war has paralyzed the conscience of the Republican party," Storey said, "it cannot denounce the suppression of the Negro vote in the South by any argument that does not return to condemn the suppression of the Philippine vote in Luzon and Samar." [22]

Significantly, it was a remark attributed to the administrator of Roosevelt's Philippine policy, Secretary of War Elihu Root, that Negro suffrage had been a failure, which brought forth Storey's fullest defense of Negro citizenship. Just as no country had the right to deny national independence to another, so no race within one country had the right to deny citizenship to another. The purpose of congressional Reconstruction, he reminded his audience, had not been to establish good government, but to grant self-government to the emancipated slaves:

> The object was not primarily to secure well-tilled fields, well-ordered towns, an industrious laboring class, nor even a legislature, a bench, and an executive taken from the ablest men in the state. All these results had been secured by slavery. Had these been the object of our policy, slavery need never have been destroyed. It was because these advantages, the material prosperity of a few, had been gained by the degradation of a whole race,—because millions of human beings had been denied the rights and hopes of humanity, that slavery was abolished, and unless we carried the work through we had better never have begun it. The same reason that led us to abolish slavery forbade us to establish any legal inequality between man and man. Anything less than equality of rights was sure to be the seed of future trouble.

There had been corruption under the Reconstruction regimes, "an orgy of corruption after Negro suffrage was granted. . . ." This Storey freely admitted. "But," he asked, pointing to the current outcry against the "bosses,"

> can we insist that the color is the cause? While Pennsylvania bows to Quay; while Montana elects Clark; while Addicks owns Delaware; while the trials at St. Louis reveal the nature of her rulers, and Minneapolis is punishing Ames, are we sure that white suffrage is a success?

And the South, which was still fighting corruption, could hardly blame its present condition on the black man, for, in the broadest sense, "since 1876 Negro suffrage *has not been tried* and therefore has not failed." [23]

In his defense of civil rights Storey may have begun as one of those who, as his friend Charles Francis Adams, Jr., put it, "plant themselves firmly on what Rufus Choate once referred to as the 'glittering generalities of the Declaration of Independence.'" But in an age in which moral judgments were increasingly argued on the basis of empirical evidence, Storey found that his commitments led to factual arguments. His first debate was with historians. Consulted by Rhodes in the writing of his *History*, he nevertheless remained one of the more persistent critics of the completed work. Rhodes, Storey felt, had drawn a one-sided picture of actual conditions under the Reconstruction governments. Discussions with prominent white Southerners had led him to suspect, he wrote to Rhodes, "that we in the North have a very exaggerated notion of the trouble in the South" occasioned by the carpetbag regimes.[24]

Simultaneously, Storey carried on a somewhat more extended debate with Adams. Adams, increasingly drawn to the South through his researches on General Lee, thought that "the reconstruction policy of 1866 we forced on the helpless states of the Confederacy was worse than a crime; it was a political blunder, as ungenerous as it was gross." But, Storey wrote to Adams, it was not true "that the reconstruction policy was 'conceived in passion' and devoid of statesmanship. It is the fashion to forget that white reconstruction was tried faithfully and that Johnson's white legislatures at once passed laws which in effect reestablished slavery." Nor was it true, he argued, that Reconstruction had been engineered by a small group of "vindictive" Radicals:

> The Reconstruction policy was largely framed and was supported by the most conservative men in the Senate like Trumbull, Grimes, Sherman and the group that voted

against impeachment. . . . the policy was adopted in
view of the exigencies of the time by the sober judgment
of men who were then in control of the Republican party
and Thad Stevens was only one force.

In fact, Storey's growing conviction that the historians of his
time were distorting the record of Reconstruction led him to become one of the first white supporters of Carter G. Woodson's
Association for the Study of Negro Life and History and its
Journal of Negro History, which consistently battled against the
hostile bias of existing scholarship.[25]

But against the natural and social scientists, Storey was less sure
in his arguments than he had been against the historians. By the
time he died, he had acquired a notable collection of books on
Negro history and society; studies in psychology and anthropology, on the other hand, were absent. Storey had been isolated
too long from scientific thought to be more than vaguely aware
that a new wave of anthropologists, Franz Boas among them,
were attacking long-established notions of biological and cultural
"superiority." Instead, he used whatever arguments he could,
combining the general knowledge acquired in a liberal education, the personal experience of sixty years, and the discipline of
a sharp legal mind. In 1913, for example, he exchanged views on
"race purity" with Harvard's president, Charles W. Eliot. It was
the position of Eliot, who is currently enjoying a reputation as an
exponent of racial tolerance, that "the experience of the world
demonstrates upon an immense scale that peoples far advanced
in the scale of civilization cannot profitably mix with backward
peoples. The purer a race is kept, the more likely it is to maintain itself and prosper." Storey took the occasion to disagree, and
presented the following argument:

A *priori,* it is hard to see why the admixture of different
breeds which has produced such wonderful results in the
vegetable and animal worlds should be so disastrous to
the human race. Nature demands variety, and intermarriage between members of the same family or class long

persisted in tends to produce degenerates. Even the fact that the results are jeered at and called hard names is not conclusive. The term "cur" has long been a term of reproach, but no one who knows dogs can fail to admit that the most admirable qualities of canine nature are very commonly found in dogs of very mixed ancestry.[26]

Whatever the merits of the abstract issue, Storey never doubted the absurdity of "race purity" in a society, such as the American, in which there had been widespread sexual contact:

You wish to keep the white blood pure [he wrote a Southern correspondent] and free from contamination with an inferior strain. Let me ask you, do you? If the public opinion of the South disgraced a man who established relations with colored women, and became the parent of colored children, I should acquiesce in your contention, but it does not, and it is not the presence of a marriage ceremony which makes the contamination but the mingling of blood as a fact. From the time when the colored people were first brought into this country until now there has been no instinct which prevents the mingling of blood, and until there is I feel that it is not race pride which controls the action of the white people of the South.

Whatever the causes of the trend toward racial discrimination, in other words, a sudden awareness of "consciousness of kind" was not one of them. Storey had traveled in the South before the days of institutionalized Jim Crow, and he remembered one incident of interracial harmony on a New Orleans streetcar:

There was no trace of objection to this association of white and colored during the whole trip, but had we crossed the street and taken the railroad train these same people would have been given separate cars. Such discrimination is fashion, not instinct, and other illustrations in abundance could be given. It is a bad fashion, not an uncontrollable instinct, against which we contend.[27]

To all those—whether historians or biologists, his friends or occasional correspondents—who justified either "race purity" or "consciousness of kind" by the "inherent inferiority" of the Negro, Storey answered that their case against the Negro remained unproven:

> When the colored men have had an equal chance with the white man, and as for many years, we can form a sound opinion as to their respective abilities, but in my own time I have seen men belonging to races which were deemed inferior establish their right to be regarded as the equal of all their fellow men. A notable instance is the case of the Jews, who are treated in Russia very much as the colored men are treated in the South, are denied social equality, herded together in quarters, and generally regarded as hopelessly inferior. We know in the United States that this opinion is unfounded.

Those who wanted to subjugate the Negro were really unsure of the racial "inferiority" they tried to establish. He asked the irrefutable question, "If the Negro is so hopelessly inferior, why do the whites fear the effect of education? Why do they struggle against his progress upward?" He could only conclude: "The attempt to prevent him from rising, by violence or by adverse legislation, is a confession that the assumption of white superiority is unsafe." [28]

Storey's contention that Negroes could not be fairly judged unless they were given an equal chance is best revealed in his continual fight against discrimination in private institutions. His correspondence is full of incidents of minor indignities suffered by Negroes: a doctor barred from the staff of a public hospital, a girl refused dormitory accommodations at Smith College, a worker barred from employment by a "lily-white" union. The most notable incidents, however, involved discrimination in two organizations with which Storey had long and close associations, the American Bar Association and Harvard College.[29]

William H. Lewis was graduated from Amherst College and Harvard Law School, had served as a representative in the Massachusetts House, and, after 1910, had been appointed an Assistant Attorney General for the United States. Lewis was black, and when this fact was brought to the attention of the Executive Committee of the American Bar Association, he was expelled from the organization. Storey was furious: "If the Association sustains this action I shall resign, and I hope my example will be followed by a large number of people. The Association is not worth preserving if the color line is to be enforced." The president of the Association, Stephen S. Gregory, however, defended the Committee's action. Many of the Association's founders had been Southerners, Gregory wrote Storey, and since *they* had intended it to be a social organization, the Committee was simply carrying out their wishes once the fact of Lewis's race had been brought to its attention.[30]

Storey missed the 1912 convention; he was with his dying wife in Europe. At that convention, though the resolution excluding present Negro members was rescinded, a resolution effectively barring future applicants of that race was passed. Upon his return he sent a petition, signed by a majority of the local council for Massachusetts, to all A.B.A. members. "Such inquiry as I have been able to make among those who took part in the formation of the Association satisfies me that the idea of excluding colored men from membership was not even suggested," Storey wrote. "Had any such distinction found a place in the constitution of the Association it never would have reached its present position of influence." But the intentions of the founders were really peripheral to his main argument:

> No one can question the right of a man to admit who he will to his own table. He may, if he chooses, exclude all foreigners, all Jews, all persons who do not sympathize with him politically, or select his associates for any reasons, however capricious, but in my judgment the American Bar Association is not a social organization. It claims to represent the whole American Bar, and its recommendations are made on that basis. I think, therefore, it cannot exclude from membership persons who are in other respects entirely fit, merely because their complexion is dark, or their race different from that of other members.

The 1913 convention was held in England, and Storey decided against making an issue of exclusion at that time. At the 1914 meeting, however, he did succeed in having the color bar rescinded. Though he still faced the consequences of passage of another motion calling for full disclosure of race on applications, which tended to prohibit Negro applications on the local level, he was satisfied that at least the policy of national exclusion had ceased.[31]

With views like these, it was predictable that Storey would fight discrimination when it appeared in the institution closest to his heart, Harvard College. He had already written to the Secretary of the Harvard Club of Philadelphia in 1913, protesting the exclusion of Negro alumni from its social functions, and he refused to join the Boston club because of a similar exclusion. On no point did he bear down harder than that "the whole influence of Harvard is thrown against the prejudice of color, and graduates who are loyal to their Alma Mater should follow her example." Within the next decade, however, the policies of Harvard were to shift in the direction of greater discrimination. In the years immediately following World War I, a time of heightened ethnocentrism, it was found that the number of Jewish students had tripled: the result was renewed pressure from various sources for an arbitrary limitation upon Jewish students. Though this is less well known today, there was at the same time pressure from Southern students, who demanded that their black classmates be excluded from the campus dormitories, in which residence was compulsory for freshmen. The man who had to deal with both these demands was the president of the University, Abbott Lawrence Lowell. Lowell seems to have sincerely believed—as the "consciousness of kind" argument led many men to believe—that Harvard student life could be made more cohesive, and hence more "democratic," by restricting the "unassimilable" students. Lowell may not have been the bigot his critics made him out to be, but for those who believe that whenever the schools become "the custodians of the forces of darkness, of ignorance, of bias, bigotry, and hate" they defeat their very reason for existence, the fact that Lowell accepted the prevailing view was indictment enough. This surely was the view of Moorfield Storey.[32]

By the end of the academic year 1921–22, rumors were spreading both about an impending Jewish "quota" and about new restrictions on black students. Storey's attention was first called to these developments by Lewis Gannett, then one of the editors of the *Nation*, and Storey was outraged. "The Jews and everyone else can get on without Harvard College," he wrote a prominent Jewish leader, "but Harvard College cannot survive such discrimination."

> I think that if Harvard College caters to this unchristian prejudice of some people against Negroes and other people against Jews and perhaps in time to [Henry] Ford's feelings against Catholics, it will be responsible for more mischief in this country and the policy will do more injury to the College than the persons who favor it can possibly conceive.

And so Storey joined Gannett in a petition protesting the obvious anti-Semitic overtones to the faculty's endorsement of "racial and national" criteria in selecting students for admission. But while Storey was, as he put it, "actively engaged in undertaking to defend the Negroes and prepared to enlist on behalf of the Jews . . . ," Gannett, for reasons that are unclear, insisted on keeping the two campaigns separate. As a result, while outside attention would increasingly be drawn to Harvard's treatment of its Jewish students, Gannett's decision had the effect of directing the efforts of liberals within the Harvard community away from the plight of the Jews and toward that of the Negro students.[33]

Concentrating on the proposed segregation of the Negro students, therefore, Gannett sent Storey an open letter in June of 1922 (which Storey signed) addressed to President Lowell and the members of the Corporation, asking whether segregation was the official policy of the University. "We believe that the University owes the Southern man the best possible opportunity for education, but we do not owe him the surrender of Northern ideas of democracy and Harvard ideals of justice." By late July the letter, with its invocations to "the Alma Mater of Channing, of John Quincy Adams, of Sumner, of Robert Gould Shaw, of the 54th Massachusetts Infantry, and of the Lowells . . . ," had gathered the signatures of almost every prominent American liberal who had been graduated from Harvard.[34]

The months after the open letter to Lowell were relatively quiet, but two incidents in January 1923 drew nationwide attention to discrimination at Harvard. In that month the College refused dormitory accommodations to a Negro freshman: its intention to draw the color line, long suspected, was now confirmed. "I am sure you will understand why, from the beginning," Lowell wrote the boy's father, "we have not thought it possible to compel men of different races to reside together." At about the same time, the troubled waters were stirred still further. A Harvard graduate told reporters of a conversation he said he had had with Lowell aboard a train. According to him, Lowell said that unless Jews voluntarily renounced their culture, "within twenty years there would be outbreaks of anti-Semitic violence." Lowell flatly denied the report, but what in 1922 had chiefly concerned Harvard graduates, had now, by 1923, become an event of wider significance.[35]

The situation was a difficult one, Storey wrote, for if public attacks on Lowell and his supporters continued, "the College will be injured, and on the other hand, strong expressions of opinion from the illiberal graduates may perhaps be used as ammunition to plant the prejudice which does not now exist and to strengthen it where it does." The solution for the segregation question at least, was to allow the Corporation itself to appoint a committee to investigate the matter: ultimately, he felt, either the compulsory residence rule would be waived or exceptions to it could be made. Finally, on April 9, 1923, the Corporation did waive the rule so that "men of the white and colored races shall not be compelled to live or eat together, nor shall any man be excluded by reason of his color." The same day a faculty committee presented its report "recommending that no departure be made from the policy that has so long approved itself—the policy of equal opportunity for all, regardless of race and religion." To all appearances, at least, the trend toward discrimination at Harvard had been halted. In retrospect, the significance of Storey's private campaigns against discrimination lies not in whatever battles were won, however, but in the breadth of the struggle. In Storey's case, devotion to civil equality was based on an opposition to discrimination broad enough to include what many of his contemporaries saw as "private" associations.[36]

Whatever the incidence of private racial discrimination, however, Storey soon realized that the main problem lay elsewhere:

> I am firmly of the opinion that the most pressing political duty of every citizen today is to do what he can to secure for every citizen of the United States, whatever his race or color, equal standing before the law, equal political rights, and equal opportunity.

In the presence of mounting racial oppression, he became aware that individual gestures on behalf of civil equality would do little to turn the tide.

> The whites in the South are one party in the contest, and the interests of the other party are not safe in their hands. They had the full charge of the Negro problem for a great many years, and they made a great mess of it, so that I desire to reserve the right to bring to bear all the public opinion that we can muster in favor of the Negro in the South and elsewhere.

Storey's conviction of the urgent necessity of ending legal discrimination led him in 1910 to accept the presidency of the newly established National Association for the Advancement of Colored People.[37]

3. The NAACP: The Formative Years

The National Association for the Advancement of Colored People was the product of two converging forces. One was the intense concern over racial discrimination and violence expressed by a small group of white liberals. Though Storey was correct when he wrote that, among his white contemporaries, "the old anti-slavery sentiment has now but few representatives," the savage looting of the Negro section of Springfield, Illinois, in 1908, served as a catalyst for the few white friends the Negro had. "Either the spirit of the abolitionists, of Lincoln, and of Lovejoy must be revived and we must come to treat the Negro on a plane of absolute political and social equality," one investigator of the riots reported, "or Vardaman and Tillman will soon have transferred the race war to the North." One New York social worker, Mary White Ovington, upon reading the article was so concerned that she sought out its author, William E. Walling. Within a few months the two of them had persuaded Oswald Garrison Villard, editor of the New York *Post*, to join with them in planning a new interracial organization dedicated to reversing the tide of discrimination.[38]

Villard, the grandson of the great abolitionist, was enthusiastic about their proposal and agreed to write a statement of principle to the country. Appearing on the centennial of Lincoln's birthday and signed by a number of prominent churchmen, journalists, educators, and social workers, the "Call" cited the denials of life, liberty, and property experienced by black Americans. ". . . This government cannot exist half-slave and half-free any better today than it could in 1861," the statement concluded. "Hence we call upon all the believers in democracy to join in a national conference for the voicing of protests, and the renewal of the struggle for civil and political liberty." Storey did not sign the call, but he did participate in the resulting National Negro Conference of 1909, from which the new Association was born.[39]

The second major force behind the Association was the development of a militant black opposition to Booker T. Washington. These black leaders (notably William Monroe Trotter and W. E. B. DuBois) had initially broken with Washington in resentment at his self-appointed role as spokesman for the black community. DuBois and Trotter were able to gain influence, however, because of the jeopardy in which the growing racial oppression placed Washington's program: the new forces in the South and elsewhere increasingly precluded the possibility of self-government under white guidance on any but the most degrading terms for the Negro. As the tide of proscription developed, so did Washington's opposition: in 1903 he was savagely heckled by Trotter in Boston; in 1906 his very program was challenged by DuBois's Niagara Movement, with its demands for the abolition of segregation and the guarantee of universal manhood suffrage.[40]

Storey sympathized with both positions in the controversy among black leaders; he always recognized Washington's contribution to Negro progress, and it was chiefly through his continuing interest in Negro education that Storey communicated with Washington. At the same time, however, Storey was writing Washington's most formidable opponent in an equally cordial spirit; and he ultimately sided with DuBois for reasons he set down shortly after assuming the presidency of the NAACP.

> I am, myself, a great admirer of both Mr. Washington and Mr. Frissell, and believe that they are doing great work for the race. Their purpose is to help the Negroes to become self-supporting, to acquire property, and to become an important industrial factor in the communities where they live, and this is undoubtedly most desirable.

> But after their property has been acquired, and after the Negroes have become what Mr. Washington seeks to make them, it is very important that their rights to the property and its undisturbed enjoyment should be secured, and there is today no adequate effort made to accomplish this result. . . .

Moreover, it is true that there are many men among the Negroes who are capable of greater things than mere mechanical pursuits. The Negroes must have leaders, and the more we throw upon the race the responsibilities of taking care of its own criminal members, the more important it is that they should have good leaders. Such leadership involves good education of the highest kind. We want men of broad views, and of thorough civilization, men who can meet white men on equal terms, and not in any discussion find themselves inferior from a lack of adequate knowledge. There is, therefore, a very strong demand for such education as Atlanta can give, and there is a very sound foundation for Mr. DuBois's feeling that such education should be provided, and that nothing should be said or done to discourage Negroes who are capable of receiving such education from seeking it.

Though Storey remained in sympathy with the ideas of DuBois—the need for an aggressive defense of civil rights, and for a "Talented Tenth" to lead the Negro people—he found that working with a militant black leadership often presented unexpected difficulties.[41]

The burdens of discrimination upon intelligent and sensitive individuals, combined with a constant battle against an opponent of the shrewdness and power of Washington, tended to make the militant leaders of the time intransigent in their positions, arrogant toward their opponents, and suspicious of each other. For example, William Monroe Trotter, co-founder of the Boston Negro journal, the *Guardian,* who was for a time allied with DuBois in the Niagara Movement, was deeply committed to the advancement of his people. But his effectiveness as a leader was limited by "his inability to accept the restraints involved in working for any organization he could not wholly control." After breaking with DuBois, he refused to join the new NAACP, which, he suspected, was not firmly opposed enough to the Washington policies. From 1910 until his death, he often worked in a parallel direction with the Association toward the same end—but missed few opportunities to attack the rival organization.[42]

Storey's relationship with Trotter became strained over the seemingly minor matter of arrangements for a meeting commemorating the centennial of Sumner's birth, January 6, 1911. Storey had suggested that the Boston branch hold its meeting in Fanueil Hall, but Trotter's New England Suffrage League had already reserved the hall and after protracted negotiations he still refused to have a joint meeting with the Association. Eventually the NAACP celebration (at which Storey spoke) was held in New York, but the experience left Storey with a somewhat snappish attitude toward Trotter. "Nothing can discourage all efforts in your behalf so greatly as contests like the one just ended . . . ," he wrote Trotter, and regretted that the black leader was "disposed to continue indefinitely the warfare against men who seem to me as sincere as you could possibly be in their effort to help a race which needs all the help it can possibly get. . . ." [43]

On the other hand, Storey could never understand why DuBois, in his capacity as editor of the *Crisis,* "attacks Trotter and Washington impartially, though Trotter dislikes Washington's methods as much as DuBois does." It was because he saw DuBois as a man of great talent that he resented his indulgence in personal vendettas: "DuBois is a leader, an educated man, a singularly able writer, and he ought to feel that the cause of his race should be lifted above all these little personal allusions, and [to] avoid personal incrimination or little digs at persons that he does not agree with." Storey, however, never developed the personal animosity that increasingly characterized Villard's attitude toward DuBois, and he thought he could understand the basis of DuBois's intractability. "That he with his gifts should be treated as inferior by so many men whom he knows to be his inferiors . . . is a very hard lot." [44]

In his congratulations to DuBois on the occasion of the latter's wedding anniversary—"I hope that before you part you will see the cause for which you have been fighting victorious"—Storey paid partial tribute to the Negro contribution to the new Association. Initially, however, that contribution was less than what at least some of the white founders had hoped it would be. Storey, fond of citing the maxim, "who would be free himself, must strike the first blow," felt that "whenever it is possible, the responsibility of protecting their rights should be assumed and paid for by the colored men. The more self-reliant we make them, the more likely they are to work out their own salvation. . . ." And he worried that there was not more interest in the Association's activities. The problem, though, was not so much one of membership—since its inception, the Association has probably always had more Negro than white members—as one of leadership. Ovington later regretted that in the first seven years of the Association the only black man in a policy position was DuBois.[45]

Yet on those occasions when Negroes tried to assert leadership, further splits in the Association developed, often not from clashes of personalities but from deep disagreements on basic principles. DuBois, for example, tended to see the achievement of civil equality in America as only a stage in the world-wide assertion of the darker peoples; the whites, on the other hand, having devoted their efforts toward arguing the irrelevance of color, were dubious about DuBois's increasing glorification of négritude. On the other side, many black spokesmen saw an uncompromising insistence on civil equality as the only basis of the Association, while the whites, also concerned with Negro advancement, were more willing to accept the establishment of segregation, if necessary, to further the progress of the race. In 1911, for example, an all-Negro branch of the YMCA was proposed for Boston; Storey opposed the idea on principle. But when it was finally completed, he favored its use: "If no institution for the education or advancement of the colored people is to be tolerated," he wrote, "then Atlanta, Tuskegee, and Hampton, and many another school and college in the Southern states must be abandoned." Butler Wilson, a leader of the local black community and a friend of Storey's, strongly disagreed, telling Ovington that if segregation was the price of recreational facilities, Boston's black citizens were better off without them. Fortunately for the Association in its early years, the forces of segregation and discrimination were so powerful that clashes of individuals and disagreements over tactics were largely subdued in a common defense of civil rights.[46]

The first two years of the Wilson administration represent a kind of high water mark for anti-Negro sentiment in the United States, and it was at that time that the young Association had to prove itself a militant guardian of civil equality. In the election of 1912, the sudden downward trend was not yet apparent: "intent on removing hindrances to the free development of the individual," the NAACP had much the same program for racial questions as the Wilsonian "New Freedom" had for economic ones. Villard enthusiastically supported the Democratic candidate. Storey and DuBois also voted Democratic, but chiefly out of repugnance at the policies of Roosevelt and Taft: the racism implicit in the retention of the Philippines, the arbitrary dismissal of an entire Negro regiment because of a riot at Brownsville, Texas, and the formation, by both Republican regulars and the Bull Moose faction, of "lily-white" organizations in the South. In the campaign, Wilson promised "absolute fair dealing" to all citizens, and seemed interested in Villard's suggestion for a national commission to study economic conditions among Negroes. The majority of black voters stayed with the Republicans, but a significant minority, including DuBois and Trotter, voted for Wilson.[47]

Their hopes soon turned to bitterness, and the NAACP embarked on a full-scale program of agitation for civil equality. Wilson's administration has been rightly praised as one of the great examples of cooperation between the President and Congress, but it was made possible by the rise of congressional leaders who could say with the President, "The only place in the country, the only place in the world, where nothing has to be explained to me is the South." The consequences of this rapprochement between Southerners on both ends of Pennsylvania Avenue included heightened discrimination against the Negro. The first indication came when, after his inauguration, Wilson told Villard that he had to abandon the race commission because of congressional opposition. And almost as soon as he took office, Wilson began replacing Negro appointees with whites, ignoring the support he had received from the Negroes in the election. Here again he yielded to Southern pressures; when he tried to appoint a Negro as Register of the Treasury, a position long reserved for that race, Vardaman, Tillman, and other Southern Senators complained so loudly that the nominee quietly withdrew. Of thirty-one positions held by Negroes in 1913, only eight were retained by 1917, and Wilson appointed only one new Negro official in his first administration.[48]

In April 1913, the President offered no opposition to the decision of two of his Cabinet members, Secretary of the Treasury William Gibbs McAdoo and Postmaster General Omar Burleson, to institute segregation among their civil service employees. Whatever segregation had hitherto existed in the Federal bureaucracy now received endorsement at the highest level, and the segregation spread beyond the two departments. At the same time, discrimination in hiring increased as the requirement of photographs for applications allowed racial bias to play a larger role in selection under the "rule of three." With typical tenacity, Wilson defended his position. It was, he said, "distinctly to the advantage of the colored people themselves that they should be organized so far as possible and convenient, in distinct bureaux where they will center their work." [49]

For the NAACP this new proscription at the highest levels of government was a challenge; for Storey it was "the crowning outrage" of the national trend toward discrimination:

> Suffering at every turn from race prejudice, the colored man has felt that in the national capital at least his rights were secure. He has seen men of his race sitting in the Senate and in the House of Representatives, filling high offices in the Departments, arguing cases before the Supreme Court of the United States, representing the country in the diplomatic service, sitting at the President's table, while in the clerical force of the various departments

colored men and women have for years served side by
side with white clerks on equal terms.

An equality so established and so long recognized is
now denied, and by various underhand methods, by orders
made and in form repealed but in substance enforced,
the colored employees are set apart from others and made
to feel that they are an inferior class, while there is too
much reason to suspect that the attempt is made to dis-
place them in order that their places may be given to
white persons. In a word the national government sanctions and approves the race prejudice which is today the
greatest barrier to Negro progress.[50]

For Storey the whole issue was particularly disturbing, because he admired many of Wilson's economic and foreign policies. The President's approval of segregation, however, began
Storey's eventual disillusionment with Wilson. "He is a man of
Southern antecedents," Storey wrote to Villard of Wilson, "and I
have never really believed that he did not share the race prejudice which today is the fashion." In August 1913, Storey, Villard,
and DuBois sent a written protest to the President. Wilson,
Storey recalled, "rather objected to discussing the matter and
asked for a delay, but after waiting a good while, I made a
speech in Boston in which I attacked the segregation policy, and
from that time on I do not think he ever took any special interest
in me." The following year, Trotter, still working outside the
Association, went with some other black leaders to talk with
Wilson, and after a brief but heated exchange, was shown the
door. While Storey had often been antagonized by Trotter himself, on this occasion he supported the black leader's action completely. "I rather think he spoke plainly to the President but do
not believe he was impudent," he wrote, adding, "I fancy that
plain talk from any colored man would seem to some of our
fellow-citizens to be impudent." [51]

The Association's campaign and the ensuing publicity seems
to have temporarily halted the spread of Federal segregation,
though it did not end it completely in all departments. The Association's victories at this time, together with its concurrent pro-

test against various congressional proposals to outlaw racial intermarriage (proposals which Storey termed "deplorable"), have been regarded by at least one historian as marking that point at which public policy, while not yet moving toward civil equality, at least began moving away from racial proscription. The immediate result of successful fights against heightened discrimination, however, was to set before the NAACP—at least before Storey—the elusive goal of beginning "a new abolition movement," in which the Association could "perhaps pledge ourselves not to vote for any men who will not in advance pledge to oppose any of these segregation policies. . . ." In practice, the results of this plan were unsuccessful. In 1916, for example, though they could hardly vote for Wilson, the leaders of the NAACP were unable to elicit from Hughes a specific statement condemning either segregation in the government or even lynching.[52]

Again, in 1920, the Association was able to get few commitments from either of the candidates, though Storey had hoped for a pledge from Harding and Cox, that "if elected to the presidency, you will extend your sympathy to us and will work to relieve us of the oppression to which we are now subjected." Unlike Cox, Harding did condemn lynching and the Haitian intervention during the campaign; when in office, however, he kept the troops in Haiti and made no move to encourage passage of the Dyer anti-lynching bill through the Congress. In 1922, the Association claimed that the Negro vote had been responsible for the defeat of several Northern Representatives who opposed the bill, and it was probably correct; but it had no success in stiffening the Senate leadership against Southern threats of a filibuster. And under both the Harding and Coolidge administrations, segregated civil service facilities, though begun by the Wilson administration, were preserved and in some areas extended. Storey urged the Association to make a public protest against these conditions, and wanted to raise it as an issue in the 1926 congressional elections. Since "Coolidge has professed such interest in our cause and such anxiety that we should succeed," he wrote James Weldon Johnson, "it should embarrass him to have this particular question raised. . . ." Though the Association conducted two publicized investigations, by 1928 the situation in the government service had not changed.[53]

The sad fact was, as Storey wrote Trotter, that in the first two decades of the Association's work "as far as the Negro question is concerned, I think the parties are about equally unreliable," and they would remain so "until the Negro vote is organized and powerful enough to seriously affect the election. . . ." A point Storey did not make was that 90 per cent of black Americans still lived in the South, where they were politically powerless. If, during Storey's lifetime, the NAACP failed to realize his hope for "a new abolition movement," it did, however, establish itself as an effective pressure group. Yet the best-remembered battle of the NAACP as such a pressure group during that period involved not public policy, but artistic representation. In the early autumn of 1914, motion picture producer D. W. Griffith filmed his adaptation of Thomas N. Dixon's novel of Civil War and Reconstruction, *The Clansman*. Dixon was an exponent of Southern white supremacy whom Storey was not alone in describing as "substantially insane on the subject," and Griffith's picture, called *The Birth of a Nation*, was faithful to the spirit of the original. Great as a work of art, the picture nevertheless portrayed the freedmen as lustful brutes, and ended by glorifying the Ku Klux Klan.[54]

The picture opened in New York City, and the Association, forewarned of the film's distribution, sought to have it banned. Though the Mayor of New York limited his powers of censorship to deleting the more offensive scenes, Dixon was so afraid of possible action by the Association that he arranged for a private showing at the White House. Whether or not it was, as the Southern-born President claimed, like "writing history with lightning," it electrified the South. Hodding Carter remembers watching it as a small boy in Mississippi, and at the point where Pickett's Charge at Gettysburg flashed on the screen, "Never before or since have I heard the Rebel yell done properly. It was something to hear, a shrill yelping that rippled and cascaded in inhuman din that set me to trembling." In the North, on the other hand, men who had fought on the Union side, and particularly those who had invested their cause with moral grandeur, would hold the picture in deep contempt, a "skillful and insidious defamation of the Union cause, and an apotheosis of slavery and rebellion." It was never allowed to be shown in Ohio, and it was banned in Pennsylvania as a libel on Thaddeus Stevens.[55]

Small wonder, then, that the greatest furor over the picture occurred when it arrived, in April 1915, in Boston—the home of Garrison, Sumner, and Colonel Shaw's black regiment. The result was a series of protests not seen since fugitive-slave days, culminating in a rally of 25,000 people on the Boston Common. The Boston NAACP chapter issued a pamphlet, *Fighting a Vicious Film*, which attacked the movie not only as a false picture of Reconstruction and a justification of mob violence, but, as Villard put it, as "a deliberate attempt to humiliate ten million Americans, and to portray them as nothing but beasts." In his contribution to the pamphlet, Storey called for a tightened censorship law:

> If it is immoral to bear false witness against one's neighbor, to excite hate, to say those things which directly lead to disorder, assault, and perhaps homicide; unless, in a word, the only immorality is sexual immorality, this play tends to corrupt public morals and should be suppressed.[56]

Storey's greatest moment in the whole affair undoubtedly occurred at a joint meeting with Griffith and Mayor Curley. On few other occasions in his presidency of the NAACP did Storey so clearly reveal himself as the inheritor of the abolitionist spirit. Mary White Ovington remembered it vividly thirty years later:

> Griffith, the producer, spoke pleasantly of freedom of speech as represented by Boston, and of his pleasure at being at the cradle of liberty. The Mayor said he could censor but had no power to stop the production. With this announcement the hearing was over.
>
> Moorfield Storey had spoken for a few moments and as

he moved to leave the platform, Griffith turned to him saying, "I am glad to have the opportunity of meeting you,
Mr. Storey," and held out his hand.

Storey said quickly, "I do not see why I should shake
hands with you, Mr. Griffith."

Griffith dropped his hand and turned away, but Mrs.
Butler Wilson, standing near them both, tears on her face,
said agitatedly, "That was wonderful, Mr. Storey, that
was wonderful." And it was wonderful. It was the first
time and it might be the last time, that she or I would
ever see a northern gentleman refuse to shake hands with
a southern gentleman because he had given the country
a malicious picture of the Negro.[57]

4. The NAACP and Constitutional Law

Storey was removed from the daily organizational problems of
the Association, and had he limited his effort to participation in
its public protests, his contribution would have been financially
generous but historically negligible. He was aware of his isolation, and aware, too, of the limitations age put on his activity
(he had assumed the presidency of the Association when he was
sixty-five). On two occasions—once following the death of his
wife in 1912, and once in 1921—he offered his resignation. Both
times his offer was rejected. But any organization devoted to
securing equality before the law, as the NAACP has been devoted, is peculiarly dependent upon the processes of litigation
for the realization of its goals; and here someone with Storey's
legal skill and professional prestige was invaluable. Relying on
the careful investigations conducted by the Association's branches
and the preliminary preparations of the cases by local lawyers,
Storey appears to have determined the constitutional basis for
the NAACP arguments. In several notable cases before the Supreme Court he was thus able to halt the judicial trend of three
decades toward racial proscription. The Association's campaigns
against lynching and on behalf of guarantees of a fair trial we

will deal with in the next chapter. Our concern here is with the judicial expansion of the idea of civil equality.[58]

At the time the NAACP was formed, the effective expression of civil equality in public policy was hampered by two judicial doctrines. There was "state action," which appeared to exempt private discrimination and intimidation from the prohibitions of the Fourteenth Amendment. There was also the "separate but equal" doctrine, which required proof of actual inequality of facilities to show a denial of "the equal protection of the laws." Though opposed to segregation on principle, the Association was forced, initially at least, to work within that framework, fully aware that only those acts of government whose denial of "equal protection" were blatant would be declared unconstitutional by the Supreme Court. In the years since Reconstruction, there were but two decisions to which the Association could appeal as precedents: a West Virginia case affirming the constitutional right of Negroes to sit on juries and a California case striking down those building requirements for laundries which were framed in such a way as to effectively prohibit only Chinese establishments.[59]

The first Supreme Court case in which Storey appeared for the NAACP involved the constitutionality of the Oklahoma "grandfather clause." The precedents were not favorable, for the Court had seemed to uphold the authority of Southern states to impose restrictive suffrage requirements while at the same time passing exemptive clauses under which illiterate, unpropertied whites might vote. In a case arising in Mississippi, for example, the Court had held that the requirements themselves, by-passing as they did "race, color, or previous condition of servitude" did not violate the prohibitions of the Fifteenth Amendment; only the discriminatory enforcement of those requirements would be unconstitutional. In several other cases decided during this period the Court had dismissed suits on a variety of grounds: that the election in question had already been held, that the registration could not be enforced under provisions the plaintiff charged were invalid, that plaintiffs could not sue for damages in equity.[60]

In 1907 Oklahoma was admitted to the Union. The Oklahoma constitution provided for universal manhood suffrage, with only residence requirements. In 1910, however, an amendment was added which required a literacy test for all voters except those who were "on January 1, 1866, or at any time prior thereto, entitled to vote under any form of government" or anyone who was a "lineal descendant of such person." Obviously, few Negroes were entitled to vote in the United States of 1865, before the passage of either the Fourteenth or Fifteenth Amendments. Acting under a Reconstruction statute still viable as far as Federal elections were concerned, the United States government brought indictments against certain registrars, in part for their administration of the Oklahoma amendment. The registrars were convicted and sentenced to one year in the Federal penitentiary. They appealed to the Eighth Circuit Court of Appeals; the sentence was affirmed; they appealed to the Supreme Court. Action on the part of the government had been continued during the transition from the Taft to the Wilson administrations; when the case was finally argued, the government was represented by John W. Davis, a decade away from his presidential nomination. The role of the NAACP was limited to an *amicus curiae* brief filed by Storey.[61]

In his own attitudes toward suffrage, Storey differentiated between personal principle and legal precedent. As a matter of principle, he wrote in a private letter, "I rather agree with Clay that no people is fit for any government except self-government, though I do not feel certain that any of us are any too competent." But as a matter of law, he wrote, "The denial or abridgement of the right to vote need not be illegal or unconstitutional. An educational qualification for example, is neither. . . . The same would be true of a property qualification." But, even though such restrictions might be "constitutional," if they were used, the second section of the Fourteenth Amendment would automatically come into force:

> When any state denies to any male person who is an inhabitant of that state and at the same time a citizen of the United States the right to vote, or in any way abridges it,

except for participation in rebellion or other crime, the
basis of representation shall be reduced. [Storey's para-
phrase.]

If the Court accepted his argument on this point, and "reac-
tivated" the second section, two consequences might occur. On
the one hand, "if the South finds that it loses power because the
basis of representation is reduced, it would be a constant motive
to modify their laws and admit colored men to the polls. . . ."
On the other hand, the South just might accept such conditions
as the price of white supremacy, and if it did, the Negroes would
remain disfranchised while the North would be apt to say "that
they would not disturb the situation as so long as they profited
by it in the increased representation [for themselves]." With this
unfortunate possibility in mind, Storey dropped any idea of relying on the Fourteenth Amendment in his argument, and decided to litigate under the Fifteenth Amendment instead.[62]

Because he favored the latter approach, Storey was personally
committed to his brief in the "grandfather clause" case. "If it is
possible for an ingenious scrivener to accomplish that purpose
[of disfranchisement] by careful phrasing, the provisions of the
Constitution which establish and protect the rights of some ten
million colored citizens of the United States are not worth the
paper on which they are written, and all constitutional safeguards are weakened." Like Davis, Storey argued that the *effect*
of the Oklahoma amendment was discriminatory, and therefore,
citing the *Yick Wo* precedent, unconstitutional. In its decision,
the Court paid homage to state control over elections: "the [Fif-
teenth] Amendment does not change, modify, or deprive the
States of their full power as to suffrage except of course as to
the subject with which the amendment deals and to the extent
that obedience to its command is necessary." This case, however,
was manifestly one involving the denial of suffrage for reasons
of "race, color, or previous condition of servitude." The Court declared:

We are unable to discover how, unless the prohibitions
of the Fifteenth Amendment were considered, the slightest

reason was afforded for basing the classification upon a
period of time prior to the Fifteenth Amendment. Certainly it cannot be said that there was any peculiar
necromancy in the time named which engendered at-
tributes affecting the qualifications to vote which would
not exist at another and different period unless the Fifteenth Amendment was in view.[63]

Though the Supreme Court struck down the "grandfather
clauses," other barriers remained for those Negroes who were cou-
rageous enough to attempt to vote—among them, the all-white
primaries of a one-party South. In 1922 the Texas Democratic
State Committee passed a resolution excluding Negroes from the
party primaries. One Negro sued, and the Supreme Court on appeal ruled that no issue was presented, as the election had already
occurred. Various factions in Texas politics pushed for a more
thorough exclusion, and in 1923 the Legislature passed a bill
which prohibited Negro participation in party primaries. Dr.
L. A. Nixon, head of the El Paso NAACP chapter, brought suit
for damages; the suit was dismissed by the District Court, but it
was finally taken on appeal by the Supreme Court. Storey had
regarded the statute as "absurd," and hoped "the Supreme Court
will sustain the case." Though the case was finally argued by
Fred Knollenberg and Arthur Spingarn for the Association,
Storey made a final review of their brief. Its main points were
that the 1923 act violated the Fifteenth Amendment and the
Fourteenth, because in Texas the primary was considered, by
statute, a public election, and thus Negro exclusion violated the
prohibition of denial of the suffrage because of "race, color, or
previous condition of servitude" of the one Amendment, and the
guarantee of "the equal protection of the laws" of the other. Mr.
Justice Holmes, speaking for the Court, was succinct in declaring
the Texas statute unconstitutional: "We find it unnecessary to
consider the Fifteenth Amendment, because it seems to us hard
to imagine a more direct and obvious infringement of the Fourteenth." [64]

In addition to the more blatant disfranchising procedures, another area that seemed to the NAACP to involve discriminatory "state action" was enforced residential segregation. The original targets were municipal residential-segregation ordinances. The first of these ordinances was one applied to the Chinese in San Francisco, but it was declared unconstitutional by a Federal District Court as violating both the treaty with China and the Fourteenth Amendment. In the early years of the twentieth century, however, the device more often represented the conclusion of the trend toward racial proscription in the South. Beginning with Baltimore, Southern cities passed ordinances freezing areas with a majority of one race or another into permanent "white" or "colored" sections. The Baltimore ordinance was declared unconstitutional by the Maryland Supreme Court on the grounds that it did not adequately protect the rights of the present owners of property and that a municipality did not have the authority to issue such an ordinance. Where the rights of owners were clearly protected, however, state courts tended to uphold similar ordinances.[65]

The city of Louisville passed one such ordinance classifying certain blocks as "white" and "colored": no owner or resident of the other race would be compelled to sell his property, but if he did so the property would have to be sold to the predominant race in the classified area. Drawn as it was to protect rights of ownership, the ordinance passed a test in the Kentucky Supreme Court. The NAACP, already active in the fight against enforced segregation elsewhere, decided to test the ordinance. In the fall of 1914, therefore, William Warley, head of the Louisville chapter, arranged to buy a lot for $250 from a sympathetic white, Charles H. Buchanan. To provide a cause for legal action, Warley said he would pay the final $100 after he made sure that the transaction did not violate the ordinance. When he found that it did, he refused to pay; Buchanan then appealed to the state Supreme Court, which ruled against him. By 1916 the case was on the docket of the United States Supreme Court, where Storey, assisted by the Louisville attorney Clayton L. Blakey, presented the Association's argument. Perhaps because only seven

Justices were sitting at the time, Chief Justice Edward J. White ordered a rehearing the following term, and the case was finally argued early in 1917.[66]

The spectacle of the NAACP defending a white property-owner trying to collect payment from an unwilling Negro (even if the situation was pre-arranged) was not without its ironies. The defendant, as Storey explained, "is not complaining of discrimination against the colored race. He is not trying to enforce their rights but to enforce his own." By restricting the freedom of Louisville citizens, black and white, to buy and sell property, the ordinance deprived them of income from the sale of property without due process of law, and thus violated the Fourteenth Amendment. That, as we shall see, may have been Storey's most persuasive argument as far as the Court was concerned, but for him there were more important reasons for arguing the case. In no other case in any court of law was Storey's passionate dedication to civil equality so apparent.[67]

The law ostensibly was passed to curtail "ill-feeling between the races," but Storey ridiculed the idea that an alley could serve as an effective barrier between racially different blocks; and he then went on to challenge the whole presumption of "race purity." The defendant's counsel talked of "racial barriers which Providence and not human law has erected," Storey argued. "Had Providence in fact erected such a barrier it would have been impassable and no human law would have been needed. It is because no such divine barrier exists that they seek to establish one by human legislation." The ordinance discriminated against "the better class of Negroes" who wished to move out of the ghetto; and this discrimination, he claimed, was the purpose of the ordinance. "No one outside a courtroom would imagine for an instant that the predominant purpose of this ordinance was not to prevent the Negro citizens of Louisville—however industrious, thrifty, and well-educated they might be, from approaching that condition vaguely described as 'social equality.' " It was specious to say that the law also affected whites, for it was the Negro's advancement that was being hindered. Storey quoted Anatole

France's aphorism that the law forbids the rich, as well as the poor, from sleeping under the bridges of Paris, and added, "A law which forbids a Negro to rise is not made just because it forbids a white man to fall." [68]

With the intention of hindering the mobility of its Negro population, the city of Louisville was not only denying their property rights secured by the "privileges and immunities" clause of the Fourteenth Amendment, but was also denying them "the equal protection of the laws." Whatever the trend of decisions from *Plessy* v. *Ferguson* onward, Storey concluded, the "separate but equal" doctrine had no relevance in a case of such obvious statutory discrimination. Nor, as the city's representatives claimed, could the ordinance be regarded as a legitimate exercise of the police power. Such a power could operate only against the "injurious consequences of individuals," and not against classes. The Negro was the victim, not the instigator, of social disorder; just because white men "do not like him as a neighbor, [they] pass an ordinance depriving him of his right to live where he pleases, and they justify it on the ground that it is necessary to protect them from being tempted to assault him if he exercises that right." [69]

In his argument, Storey compared Negroes with employers, who were also victims (as he saw it) of an organized assault upon their rights as property-owners. Such analogies reflected his own view, but they no doubt also pleased the conservative Court. Indeed, some commentators have argued that it was a solicitude for property rights, and not for the victims of discrimination, that motivated the Court to rule for Storey's client. It is true that the decision made no mention of the aspirations of Negro citizens. Significantly, however, the Court did impose limitations upon the "separate but equal" doctrine and the sociological assumptions behind it:

> That there exists a serious and difficult problem arising from a feeling of race hostility which the law is powerless to control, and to which it must give a measure of consideration, may be freely admitted, but its solution can-

not be promoted by depriving citizens of their constitutional rights and privileges.

There were situations in which (under the *Plessy* precedent) it would uphold segregation legislation, the Court continued, but it would not permit such legislation to restrict the right to buy and sell property, secured under the "privileges and immunities" clause. By limiting real-estate transactions to persons of the same race, the Louisville ordinance—and all other such ordinances—restricted that right, and thus was unconstitutional.[70]

Storey, who had been worried before he argued the case ("you know how ingenious the Court sometimes is in finding a method of avoiding a disagreeable question . . ."), was overjoyed with the decision. "I cannot help thinking," he wrote Villard, "it is the most important decision that has been made since the *Dred Scott* case, and happily this time it is the right way."[71]

As Negroes began moving in large numbers to the North during and after World War I, new devices were found to keep them segregated. The most prominent was the restrictive covenant, a contractual agreement among property-owners not to sell to Negroes for a specified number of years; the courts would enforce the agreements. California and Michigan courts declared the future restriction void, but concurred with other state courts on the validity of restrictions against current purchase or occupancy. Storey denied the validity of all restrictions, and cited the *Buchanan* ruling, "that the attempt to prevent the alienation of the property in question to a person of color was not a legitimate exercise of the police power of the State." He argued that "if public policy does not justify the state in making this restriction, neither does it justify the restriction when imposed by a private citizen. . . ." The case the NAACP entered came from the Supreme Court of the District of Columbia. One party to a covenant (John J. Buckley) had successfully sought an injunction against another (Irene H. Corrigan) to prevent the sale of property to a Negro (Helen Curtis). Louis Marshall argued the case on appeal to the United States Supreme Court, but Storey played a major role in preparing the brief.[72]

In this case Marshall and Storey, as usual, attempted to counter in advance any question the Supreme Court might raise, but to a greater extent than in any of the previous briefs the Association had ever prepared for the Court. Their first point was that enforcement of the covenant by the lower court deprived Mrs. Corrigan of the right to dispose of her property without the "due process of law" guaranteed by the Fifth Amendment. Partly because both men hoped that a favorable ruling from the Court would void all such covenants throughout the United States, and partly because Storey at least seems to have believed that the Fourteenth Amendment extended to all territory under American jurisdiction, their brief also contended that judicial enforcements of those covenants violated the Fourteenth Amendment as well. Yet as far as the Court was concerned, the Fourteenth Amendment, even more than the Fifth, applied only to cases of "state action." What if the Court dismissed the case on the ground that the covenant constituted private discrimination? [73]

To counter this contingency, Marshall and Storey decided to argue that the covenant went against "public policy." "Public policy," Marshall had written to Storey, "is largely based upon constitutional and statutory definitions as to what the policy of a state is"—in this case, the common-law prohibitions on contracts in restraint of the alienation of property, statutory prohibitions on contracts in restraint of trade, and, most of all, the implications of the Court's decision in *Buchanan* v. *Warley*. There the Court had prohibited municipal governments from segregating residential areas. Since "there can be no permissible distinction between citizens based on race, creed, or color if we are to remain a harmonious nation," the Court could not now permit such segregation to be furthered through judicially enforced private agreements.[74]

As Marshall and Storey had feared, the Court could find no case of "state action" presented. But it also refused to consider their "public policy" argument and, in a somewhat opaque decision, dismissed the case for want of jurisdiction. Storey was "not surprised at the decision," but, he wrote, "I deplore it bitterly for the same rules will be tried not only against colored people but against everybody who by social position, nationality, religion, or perhaps politics is objected to by their neighbors." This, the only major case lost by the NAACP in Storey's lifetime, was only a temporary defeat. Twenty years later, the Supreme Court decided that judicial enforcement of racial covenants was indeed "state action," and therefore unconstitutional, and, in a companion case, the Court extended its ruling to the District of Columbia.[75]

Working on the restrictive covenant with Marshall was Storey's last effort for the NAACP. In the last years of Storey's life, he could look upon the Association with pride in its accomplishments and hope for its future. Negro participation in the organization was increasing at all levels, and, what must have been especially heartening to him, black attorneys were playing a larger role in handling the Association's litigation in the lower courts. Though he still felt "they ought to take a stronger interest in their own race than they do," he remained hopeful that black Americans "are acquiring rapidly the self-respect and the pride in their own race which is essential" to their progress. By the late 1920's DuBois had been replaced by James Weldon Johnson as the major black leader within the Association. Johnson left a brilliant literary and diplomatic career to become its executive secretary. Storey was deeply impressed with his intelligence and dedication, and wrote him that "I feel as if you were today rather more than anyone else the leader and inspiration of the movement." There was "no one in our army who has fought more unselfishly and more persistently than he," Storey wrote three years later. "I respect him and admire him as one of the first citizens of the United States. . . ." [76]

The warmth was reciprocated by Johnson: when Storey was unable to attend the 1925 convention, he sent "warmest greetings to its beloved and generous President whose unswerving devotion to the welfare of oppressed black America finds few parallels in the history of men." Apart from the affectionate impulses which inspired the message, that tribute underscores Storey's role, not only in the development of the Association, but in the advancement of civil equality in America.[77]

"Those who would hold the Negroes down, who would deprive them of their rights, now understand that any attempt of that sort is going to be met by proceedings in the courts backed by an adequate organization," Storey wrote prophetically in 1926, "and in the courts our rights are safer than anywhere else in this great country." The NAACP's eventual success in achieving the total destruction of the legal embodiment of "white supremacy" was launched with the victories won by Moorfield Storey. It has been said that the founding of the National Association for the Advancement of Colored People represented a "new abolitionism," a second commitment of some white Americans to join in the fight for freedom of their black countrymen. In the case of Moorfield Storey, it would be more accurate to say that it represented the culmination of the original abolitionist commitment, of Charles Sumner and his idea of "equality before the law." [78]

4 ❧ Obedience to the Law

I N the spring of 1920, Moorfield Storey was to give the
annual Godkin Lectures at Harvard, and under the rubric
"Problems of Today," he bore down heavily on what he called
"the growing tendency to ignore or disobey the law." Behind his
current strictures lay a deeply rooted belief that law was the very
basis of civilization, a belief most notably expressed in an address
on "lawlessness" he had given sixteen years before:

> It is hardly too much to say that civilization is the
> process of restraining the will of the individual by law,
> that the liberty of a people depends on its success in curb-
> ing by a written constitution the power of its rulers, and
> that the cause of justice in the world is advanced by ob-
> serving the law of nations. . . . The history of civilization
> is the record of the struggle between might and right,
> between force and law.

Storey had, therefore, already worried about the "growing
tendency" of Americans to achieve their goals through extra-legal
means; now what seemed to him the complete breakdown of
order after the Armistice of 1918 raised his interest in "obedience
to the law" to the highest level of concern.[1]

146

The 1920 census confirmed what had long been suspected: in ever-increasing numbers Americans were living in cities. But the actual loss in population meant less to the traditional America of farms and small towns than their increasing vulnerability to the cultural and political influence of the expanding urban centers. The subsequent decade, it has been said, was "the crucible, in which the value system and power structure of the old society would either adapt to the new urban realities or declare war à l'outrance and snap the bonds of community." In retrospect, it is possible to say the adaptation was made, but the initial results of the conflict—as it must have appeared to Storey— seemed to reveal only exacerbated tensions and a perceptible increase in violence.[2]

Many of the tensions had been indirectly caused by the World War itself, for it had led to an increase in status for many of the submerged groups in American society. Mobilization itself had encouraged at least 300,000 Southern Negroes to look for work in the Northern cities, and had put organized labor in the strongest bargaining position it had known. The rhetoric of a war "to make the world safe for democracy" persuaded returning black soldiers to defend their rights, and allowed immigrant groups to advocate self-determination for their people during the peace settlement which followed. But at the same time the war also engendered a demand for social cohesion, and representatives of exclusion and privilege were increasingly able to pose as champions of "the American way of life."

After 1918 the rising urban groups in American society were temporarily checked. City dwellers found their personal habits challenged by a Federally enforced Prohibition and union members saw their wage demands rebuffed by confident employers. Assertive immigrants were met with a rising tide of nativism, while dissenting intellectuals were hounded by demands for an unqualified nationalism. Many of these groups, Negroes not least, discovered their physical security to be threatened by a resurgent Ku Klux Klan. For two years after the Armistice, the country was torn by a series of bombings, strikes, race riots, and incidents of mob violence and governmental repression unparalleled in their intensity. Even after the country settled down with Harding to enjoy the pleasures of prosperity, the rise of organized crime, the restrictive immigration act of 1924, and the Scopes trial all bore witness to conflicts that continued throughout the 1920's.

Massachusetts was a heavily industrialized state with a large population of first- and second-generation Americans, and Storey forcibly felt the new assertion of urban ethnic and economic groups. Few were more assertive at this point in time than the oldest immigrant group in the state, the Irish-Americans, who used the debate over the peace settlement to voice their traditional grievances against Great Britain and to demand independence for their homeland. Storey believed that those grievances had been largely removed by the British government, and questioned Irish claims to nationhood; he tended to see the cause of Irish independence as more analogous to Southern secession than to the nationalist movements in Asia, which he supported. Before 1918 the entire problem had not occupied much of his attention, but now he was alarmed at the rising agitation among Irish-Americans, and he urged them not to "undertake to involve America in a controversy which would lead to war now when the whole world is struggling for peace. . . ." [3]

At the same time, Storey argued that the ethnic assertion of the Irish was the natural response to their "inhospitable" treatment by his fellow Yankees, for "by the prejudices of race and religion" they had been "driven together until they have become in our midst a coherent body united by racial ties." They and other immigrant groups, he pointed out to a Harvard audience, "built our railroads, settled our territories, turned our wild lands into fertile farms, and in every way speeded our growth," and there was no place in the America which they helped build for "our contemptuous phrases and our irritating stories" at their expense. Consistently an opponent of racial and religious prejudice, it was at this time that Storey involved himself in the fight against the proposed restriction of Jewish students at Harvard. He was appalled at the rebirth of the Klan, which was already spreading from the South and the Midwest into Massachusetts, and while "it is something to fight," he remained hopeful that "the alliance of Catholics, Jews and Negroes, together with the sensible people of the United States, will be too much for it." [4]

These various evidences of tension were a challenge for Storey, who had long believed that "any man who undertakes to array class against class, foreign-born against native, Catholic against Protestant, capital against labor, or black against white, is an enemy to society against whom we should all unite." What was more disturbing to someone with his dedication to social order, however, was what he saw as the steady erosion of the legal system underneath these surface manifestations of conflict. "Theodore Roosevelt's famous story of the question, 'What is the Constitution between friends?' is still told," he wrote in 1923, "but the more pressing question today is 'What is the Constitution between enemies?' " [5]

In addition to urging tolerance upon his audiences, therefore, Storey responded to what he saw as the rising tide of "lawlessness" with constant appeals "to maintain the law; to teach respect for it by speech and by example, in public and in private; and to condemn its violation whenever and by whomsoever committed." Obedience was due a law even if it was objectionable:

> If it is bad the citizen may agitate against it by pen and tongue, may write with others to educate his fellow-citizens, so that they may recognize its folly or its dangers and so secure its repeal, but he must nonetheless obey it until it is repealed. Any other course is anarchy.

"With cases so rare as to be negligible," Storey concluded, "no citizen can refuse to obey the law and justify his disobedience by appealing to his conscience." But while expressing his opposition to any philosophy "which makes each man judge for himself how far he will respect the law," he could hardly forget the abolitionist environment of his boyhood. The widespread resistance of Massachusetts to the Fugitive Slave Law may have been a rare episode in American history, but it was hardly negligible, and when

pressed on the matter (as he was by Southern audiences) Storey
seems to have maintained the position he took in his biography
of Sumner:

> When the decisions of the courts cannot be reconciled
> with the great principles of right and wrong, when they
> find no support in the consciences of men, their authority
> is gone, and a refusal to obey them may be justified by
> the same arguments that make resistance to other tyrants
> "obedience to God." In each case the question of acquies-
> cence or resistance is a question which each man in the
> last report must decide for himself according to his con-
> science, submitting to the penalties with fortitude if he
> fails to make his resistance good.[6]

It was not the most satisfactory answer in the world, but, as
Storey would have pointed out, whatever bearing the great
issues of slavery and freedom had upon obedience to the law
before the Civil War, the most flagrant defiance of the law in the
1920's involved no moral issue at all. Not a drinker himself, and
reluctant to return to the conditions of pre-Prohibition America
("You cannot get much enthusiasm out of me in favor of the
right to get drunk"), he was at first willing to give the Eighteenth
Amendment and its enforcing Volstead Act a chance. When enforcement broke down and created as many evils as it proposed
to solve, Storey declared himself willing to help "create a public
opinion favorable to repeal." But he consistently maintained that,
until repealed, it had to be obeyed, and that "everyone who
values our institutions and recognizes the importance of upholding the law should discourage this bootlegging business that is
now going on." [7]

The last decade of Storey's life is significant, however, not
because he reiterated his earlier call for "obedience to the law,"
but because within his appeal for "obedience," he was modifying
his ideas about the legal system. Originally concerned with
curbing overt defiance of existing law, he soon recognized that

many of the conflicts which disturbed him came about because there was no law under which the actions of the participants could be judged. To be meaningful in an increasingly complex twentieth-century America, "obedience to the law" had to include not only acquiescence in the law—whether legislative enactment, executive enforcement, or judicial decision—but expansion of the legal system itself to cover new situations.

Storey's advocacy of the expansion of the law challenged many of his earlier attitudes and began his gradual but perceptible reappraisal of many of them. His revulsion at industrial conflict, for example, would lead him to abandon much of his earlier commitment to laissez-faire, just as his passionate outrage at the practice of lynching would lead him to a bold and prophetic reinterpretation of judicial precedent and Federal power. While never abandoning his interest in protecting the community against the criminal, to take a third case, Storey's growing awareness of the excesses committed by law-enforcement officials brought a new concern over the importance of procedural guarantees. In a process still uncompleted at the time of his death, Moorfield Storey was trying to adapt the law to changed conditions.

1. Laissez-faire and Industrial Conflict

If the heightened social conflict following the Armistice moved Storey toward a re-examination of his conception of the law, it was primarily because it forced him to re-emphasize the basic position he had assumed as a lawyer, that of mediator. By the time he had achieved prominence in the legal profession at the end of the century, the lawyer's role had already shifted from one of mediation between groups to a tacit alliance with business interests; and the new philosophy of the profession stressed total identification with one's clients. For the majority of his professional contemporaries this meant an abdication of public responsibility; for others, like Clarence Darrow, it meant a kind of relativism, in which the importance of a fair trial outweighed the intrinsic justice of the client's claims.[8]

But Storey stubbornly adhered to the older tradition in which he had been raised: one of the functions of the lawyer, he wrote at the end of his life, was "to keep the community orderly and peaceful, and to adjust the questions or disputes which arise among its members." As he expressed it, the position of mediator further assumed that the lawyer should preserve a position of neutrality; consequently, his attacks on those who identified too closely with their clients tended to broaden into a wholesale indictment of his profession. Storey impartially rebuked those attorneys who helped their corporate clients escape public regulation and said he had "no sort of respect" for criminal lawyers like Darrow, scornfully adding, "I suppose he naturally sympathizes with the class to which his clients belong."[9]

Storey's highly personal standards of legal conduct were most notably expressed in his public opposition to the 1916 nomination of Louis D. Brandeis to the Supreme Court. Whatever the motives of the rest of the opposition, there is absolutely no evidence to suggest anti-Semitism as a factor in Storey's opposition. Nor is it easy to find political differences as a factor, because in a significant number of instances, from their common opposition to the New Haven Railroad's attempts to monopolize transportation to their common enthusiasm for Wilson's New Freedom, Storey and Brandeis were on the same side; and Storey's only comments on Brandeis as a Justice reveal support for the latter's civil libertarian position. The two men, however, had opposed each other in several cases, and from one case in particular (in which Brandeis's actual clients turned out to be different from those whom Storey, as opposing counsel, had believed he was representing) Storey was led to conclude that Brandeis "would in the interest of his client cross the line" and was therefore unfit to sit on the Supreme Court.[10]

As some of the targets of his criticism undoubtedly concluded, Storey's conception of himself as a mediator, keeping "the community orderly and peaceful," seemed somewhat incongruous with his other conception of himself as agitator, raising embarrassing questions about the plight of racial minorities and subject peoples. Storey would have replied that the conflict was more apparent than real, for in the tradition in which he had been raised, mediation between conflicting interests was possible only after the major forms of oppression had been removed. Only after the legal and institutional embodiments of discrimination had been removed could the various racial and ethnic groups within America be brought into harmonious relationship; and only after a reduction in armaments and an end to imperialism could the various nations of the world begin to settle their differences peaceably. The role of the agitator, then, was to lay bare the existence of oppression and mobilize opinion to eliminate it; the function of the conciliator was to proceed from there and adjust the remaining conflict among the participants. In this sense, Storey maintained his conciliatory position from the time he first set forth his views at the end of his Independent phase:

> To reconcile the conflict of interests, to educate the ignorant, to make the natives of other countries into true Americans, to give our colored fellow citizens their proper standing in the community, to secure labor its just rights while preventing its organizations from oppressing men who do not join them, to regulate the aggregations of capital, to control for good the socialistic movement, and to remove the causes of dangerous discontent . . . these are things which may well tax all the ability and patriotism that our country can command, and they are things which must be done, if our institutions are to endure.[11]

Without knowing it, Storey had sketched the agenda which would occupy the various groups of progressive reformers in the years between the Spanish-American War and World War I. But while middle-class constituencies increasingly turned progressive leaders toward the use of government power to moderate social conflict and restore economic opportunity, Storey proved slow to respond. While he never indulged in the hysteria with

which some of his professional colleagues greeted social legislation, his mild but persistent criticisms of many progressive
proposals placed him well in the rear of the movement. At a time
when the task of social reconciliation more and more appeared to
involve government action, Storey appeared to be left only with
moral exhortation, with urging tolerance upon his audiences and
"obedience to the law."

By the second decade of the twentieth century, Storey acknowledged that "this is emphatically an age of organization, for men
recognize that by united effort they can accomplish more for the
common good than one man can secure by his individual efforts.
. . ." But his heritage of economic individualism was too strong
for him not to remain suspicious of monopolies of either capital
or labor, and he supported progressive attempts to restore economic opportunity. He was glad that others still believed that
"the tariff is the stronghold of privilege," and while favoring municipal regulation of public utilities, he agreed with the apostles
of Wilson's New Freedom that in most cases "a regulated monopoly does not exist. What we want is competition." Similarly,
like most progressives, Storey supported "the right of workmen
to combine in order to insure the advantage of collective bargaining," but he remained a partisan of the open shop. "To say that
men shall not work unless they belong to a union is as unjustifiable as to say that no man shall work who does not belong to a
particular church or political party." [12]

As the progressive movement turned to the Federal Government for the execution of its programs, Storey, still an opponent
of Federal intervention, began to criticize the movement. He, too,
opposed the idea of child labor:

> If children are compelled to labor while they are still chil-
> dren, they lose the time which should be spent in educa-
> tion, and in almost every manufacture in which child labor
> is employed the conditions in which the labor is performed
> are such that the general growth of the child is retarded
> and his health suffers.

But he did not favor the proposed Twentieth Amendment, which would have prohibited the products of child labor from interstate commerce. Generalizing perhaps from the successful legislation in Massachusetts, he wondered why state statutes were not sufficient, and most of all, he feared that Federal enforcement would mean "the creation of a great body of officers who must keep the run of all the children of the country. . . ." For similar reasons, Storey had opposed the Sixteenth Amendment. He favored an income tax, he emphasized, as the "fairest tax," but "until I see some signs of economy I do not feel like increasing the revenue of the Federal Government"; and he therefore opposed a Federal tax.[13]

Undoubtedly influenced by Massachusetts' pioneering role in political reform, corporate regulation, and labor legislation, Storey believed that the states, not the Federal government, were the seedbeds of democracy and innovation. He gave his major statement of that view at the commemoration of the 300th anniversary of the first Virginia constitution; and though his views were probably tailored to the biases of the audience, there is no reason to believe that his statement did not also reflect his own convictions. He could not agree with those who demanded greater Federal power, Storey told his audience; for it was the states, not the Federal government, that were most effective in curbing monopolies. And in the American system, he pointed out, corruption of the democratic process was likely to begin at the top:

> Is it not quite possible that the trusts and the railroads combined may some time elect a President and Congress to exercise in their favor the very powers which are demanded now in order to curb them? Capital has before now carried a presidential election. Let us hesitate before we strengthen officers who may easily be chosen by the very interests that we wish to control.[14]

If Storey's conception of the states acting as barriers to the tyranny of economic power evokes Madison, his discussion of the advantages of local government is infused throughout with Jefferson. In his Independent phase, he had paid tribute to the New England town meeting, in which "every citizen of the town has his voice and vote, and we all know how often a man who stands alone when he begins to address his fellow-townsmen, finds himself when he ends that they are all on his side. . . ." Just so, Storey now said, at the state level "the smaller community with its identity of interests is more easily dealt with than the whole nation. A man who is entitled to lead can get the ear of his neighbors, when the whole country knows nothing of him." [15]

Often sympathetic with the purpose of progressive reform, but usually skeptical of the specific legislation proposed, and with a decided preference for state over Federal action, Storey proved unwilling during the progressive era to abandon the greater part of his earlier laissez-faire ideology. The industrial unrest which seemed to be sweeping across the country in the months after the Armistice seemed to him to be of such massive proportions, however, that he began to reappraise his former beliefs. Storey's conception of himself as mediator again came to the fore, but this time he advocated a greater degree of government action than anyone would have predicted.

In February 1919 the Seattle Central Labor Council called a general strike in support of the shipyard workers' demand for higher wages. Although essential services (food, fuel, and electricity) were continued, the city's economic life was paralyzed, and much of the country thought it saw a dress rehearsal for another performance of the Bolshevik Revolution. Storey took the occasion of a commencement speech four months later to condemn "irresponsible" labor leaders:

> The irresponsible men, who too often lead the workmen and who in order to justify their existence must agitate, usurp a power which the law gives to no one, and they cannot be permitted to set the constituted authorities at defiance and arrest the industrial life of a whole city or state. Such conditions threaten the life of a nation, and could not exist save where respect for law and its processes

was dead. We must all labor to restore the supremacy of
law in determining disputes between employers and employees or face the consequences of anarchy.

The culmination of labor disturbances came in the summer: the
steelworkers struck in August, the Boston police in September,
and the United Mine Workers in November. Storey saw his
antithesis of "peaceful" determination of disputes and "anarchy"
as proven.[16]

Already a partisan of the "open shop" before 1919, the industrial unrest of that year initially served to deepen his hostility
to unions. At times during the immediate postwar period he
seemed to deny the principle of collective bargaining itself: "If
men cannot combine to raise the price of goods, it would seem
that they cannot combine to raise the price of labor." And going
beyond even the Supreme Court, which in 1927 would uphold
damage suits against unions, Storey supported damage suits
against the individual strikers, since "every person who makes
a contract is bound to perform it." If striking violates the contract,
"the employee becomes liable for damages and escapes suit only
because the attempt to collect damages would not pay." [17]

There is no reason to doubt the depth of his feeling "that the
strike as an industrial weapon is a relic of barbarism and must be
abandoned for the same reasons which have led us to prevent
individuals from settling their disputes upon the street." But
what is interesting is that even though Storey started from
premises of economic individualism—no worker should be compelled to join a union; each worker is an economic entity and
hence liable—he did not, in the main, want to extend those
premises and apply antitrust legislation to unions. Instead he
moved toward supporting a degree of positive state action which
his laissez-faire associates of an earlier day would have regarded
as pure paternalism.[18]

In 1919 Storey was already working on the idea that "the man
who enters the employ of a corporation whose continued operation is of great importance to the public should be required to

agree that he will not strike." Within two years he was representing the state of Kansas before the Supreme Court, defending a
statute which fulfilled his idea. It "forbids strikers and compels
contestants to submit their questions to a court in cases where
the business in which they are engaged is affected with a public
interest, like the production of food, clothes, fuel, and transportation." By 1923, at the outbreak of another coal strike, Storey
had further expanded his doctrine: he hoped that the state of
Pennsylvania would pass "the necessary laws to regulate the
business of mining," but since the mining of coal was clearly a
national industry, "Congress could perhaps legislate, as it has in
the case of railroads, by fixing the price which could be charged
for the coal as the Interstate Commerce Commission fixes the
rates which the railroads may charge, and the price to be paid
the laborers as was done by the Adamson law." Yes, he admitted,
"the Supreme Court has held that the mining of coal is not
interstate commerce even though the coal is intended for export
from the state where it is mined. . . ." But, he reflected,

> The Supreme Court sometimes changes its opinions, and
> it may be that such a situation as now confronts the coun-
> try may lead them to feel that Congress has a right to inter-
> fere where the natural deposits of a certain kind are within
> the limits of a state, and the whole country or a very large
> part of it needs it.

Though he had begun with laissez-faire premises, Storey was led
by his concern over economic and social disorder to advocate
first state and then Federal regulation of a major industry through
the setting of wages and prices, and to persuade the Supreme
Court to accede to the expansion of power.[19]

But Storey's major interests did not involve economic issues,
and it is quite probable that this evolution of his thought in
economics was only the reflection of a similar development of his
thought in the area of civil rights. This was the "lawless" decade
of the 1920's, when the lynch mobs perpetrated their horrors, and
these convinced him not only that the law must be upheld and

enforced but that without a massive extension of the law to contain violence the protection of civil rights would become impossible.

2. States' Rights and the Horror of Lynching

"Lynching" is thought by many to derive its name from a Virginia Revolutionary, Judge Lynch, who administered summary trials and whipping to British sympathizers in this country. In the pioneer West, an area where there were no legal institutions, the tradition of summary justice was continued almost by necessity; but it was in the South that lynching was most widespread. There, the victims of lynch mobs were almost always Negroes— once they ceased to be valuable property. The reasons for this have been much debated. Defenders of lynching used to portray it as an act of justice, in which a group of righteous men, impatient with the law's delay, abducted the black rapist and slew the brute. The only difficulty with this model (waiving aside moral and legal considerations) is that less than a third of the victims were *accused by the mob itself* of sexual offenses against white women (and that percentage included many who were charged with considerably less than rape); and, between 1889 and 1918, at least fifty of the victims of lynching were black women.[20]

A more dispassionate analysis might point to other factors. Certainly the rise of brutal stereotypes of the Negro after 1890 and bitter competition between Negro and white farmers, intensified in economic recessions, were important. More controversial is the theory that would connect lynching with the consequences of a repressive fundamentalist religion. Southern whites were guided, this theory holds, by "an elaborate system of taboos that label as 'sinful' even relatively innocent diversions, which absorb at least part of the time otherwise given to erotic thoughts and desires. . . ." But sexual urges remain, even in a repressive culture, and as a continuing exploitative attitude toward black women was projected onto the black man's attitude toward white women, the result was a persistent sadism almost totally absent from lynching in the West, a sadism without parallel in our society.[21]

To Storey and his contemporaries, of course, the problem of lynching involved neither abstract statistics nor the finer points of social psychology. It was simply the killing of human beings in defiance of the processes of justice, and the pointless torture of those human beings in a manner that violated all the rules men make to define civilized behavior. "Lynching" did not only mean murder by a mob—it had a more immediate horror:

> Jesse Washington was an illiterate field hand for a farm family named Fryar living near Waco, Texas. In May of 1916 he assaulted Mrs. Fryar and killed her with a hammer. He was arrested, indicted, and convicted. After the jury delivered the verdict, a crowd seized the victim in the courtroom; the sheriff, running for re-election, was unwilling to interfere. The mob dragged him for a distance of between a quarter and a half a mile, castrating him en route and striking him with shovels, bricks, clubs, and knives so that "when he was strung up his body was a solid color of red." The mob then chained him to a tree, and before lighting the pile of boxes beneath him, chopped off his fingers, toes, and ears to give to the crowd of 10,000 spectators. After he was burned to a crisp, his torso was dragged through the streets, his head placed on a prostitute's doorstep, and his teeth extracted by boys and sold for five dollars apiece.

> Lation Scott was a half-witted field hand for a family near Dyersburg, Tennessee. On November 22, 1917, he bound and assaulted his employer's wife. He fled and remained at large for ten days before being captured by local authorities. The sheriff's car, however, was overtaken by the mob, which arranged a kangaroo court before which he confessed. Scott was then bound to a stake with chains, his clothes and skin ripped from his body with knives, his eyes, tongue, and genitals burned out with red-hot pokers. Hot irons which housewives had been using on their laundry were contributed and applied to his feet,

back, and body. The local paper reported that thousands of people witnessed the prolonged torture; children were lifted to the shoulders of the spectators that they might better see the agony of the victim.

After being beaten and abused, a Negro peon by the name of Sidney Johnson shot his employer near Valdosta, Georgia, in May of 1918. For a week a mob searched the countryside, killing any Negro who remotely resembled Johnson. Among those so murdered was Hayes Turner; upon hearing the news, his eight-months pregnant wife threatened to swear out warrants for the arrest of the mob. When this news reached the mob, it sought her out, hanged her from a tree, poured gasoline over her body, and set her afire: "Mister, you ought to've heard the nigger wench howl." Almost dead, someone ripped open her belly with a knife; and the mob crushed the prematurely-delivered baby with their feet. (The murderer, Johnson, died more decently, in an exchange of gunfire with a sheriff's posse.)

Mary Turner was patently innocent, but Washington and Scott were probably guilty, and the opponents of lynching had to accept theirs as the paradigm case. They would then argue, with William Graham Sumner, that "torture and burning are forbidden, not because the victim is not bad enough, but because we are too good." [22]

Though the NAACP had protested lynching ever since the Association was founded, in 1916 it decided to give its anti-lynching campaign the highest priority. In February of that year, a philanthropist offered the Association $10,000 if it could develop an effective program to eradicate lynching. By April the Association had resolved to compile statistics on past lynchings, to investigate incidents as they occurred, and to encourage Southerners to speak out against the practice. The Association's Executive Secretary, Roy Nash, prepared an extended memorandum for Storey, and in it he pointed out that while the number of lynchings had greatly decreased in twenty-five years, the remaining incidents were increasingly expressive of anti-Negro hatred, took a sadistic form, and were encompassing more and more offenses. Nash had cause for concern, for during the summer and autumn three exceptionally brutal lynchings (including that at Waco) occurred in the South.[23]

The next year the World War exacerbated racial tensions throughout the nation. Negroes moving north in search of better living conditions clashed with white workers: in East St. Louis competition for work in defense plants led to a race riot, and a white mob overran the Negro section, destroying hundreds of thousands of dollars of property and murdering more than forty innocent men, women, and children. In September 1917, provoked by the taunts of the white citizenry of Houston, a group of black soldiers retaliated with force and killed seventeen whites. Between 1917 and 1918 the rate of lynching doubled, evidence of rising tension. And all of this occurred before Negro troops, seasoned in combat, had returned from the front. "The Negroes will come back feeling like men," Storey predicted, "and not disposed to accept the treatment to which they have been subjected." As the "Red Summer" of 1919 was to prove, he understated the case.[24]

During 1917 and 1918 the Association carried on its program of investigations of individual lynchings and protests to state officials. In the summer of 1918 it began to receive support from those not previously noted for sympathy for black Americans: from President Wilson, who, in July, publicly condemned lynching, and from the American Bar Association, which, in August, went on record against mob violations of legal processes. By the spring of 1919, the NAACP was able to organize a prestigious conference on lynching in New York City. The declaration of those who attended was signed by (among others) Attorney General Palmer, Charles Evans Hughes, William Howard Taft, Elihu Root, and the governors of eleven states—including those of Georgia and Tennessee. That statement concluded:

> The undersigned . . . urge all public-spirited men and women to oppose with all their power the recurrence of

the crime and shame of mob murder; they urge the Governors of the several states to do all that is possible to prevent and punish lynchings; they pledge their support to the officers of the law, who in the face of mob excitement, discharge their duties; and they urge upon the Congress of the United States a nation-wide investigation of lynching and mob murder to the end that means may be found to end this scourge.[25]

Several congressmen had needed no urging from the Conference: as early as 1917, anti-lynching bills and resolutions calling for an investigation of racial violence were introduced in the House. The most promising of these was a bill offered by Representative Leonidas C. Dyer of Missouri. Dyer's constituency had become heavily populated with refugees from the East St. Louis outbreak, and since his general sympathies were with the Negro race, he gradually emerged as the foremost congressional advocate of anti-lynching legislation. In the fall of 1918 he introduced his bill to make lynching a Federal crime, on the premise that the repeated breakdown of the orderly processes of justice when the accused was a Negro constituted a denial of the "equal protection of the laws." His bill not only gave United States Attorneys the power to prosecute negligent law-enforcement officers, but in addition gave them the power to prosecute mob members for murder; and it allowed the Federal attorneys to initiate damage suits against the county in which the lynching had occurred. By 1918 the Association was devoting its major efforts in the anti-lynching campaign to securing passage of the Dyer bill.[26]

It was natural that Storey, with his dedication both to the Negro's welfare and to the maintenance of law and order, was revolted by the continuing incidence of lynching, for he had no faith in the myth of Negro brutality by which Southerners justified the practice. As early as 1905 he had expressed his skepticism in a letter to Charles Francis Adams, Jr. First, he pointed out, during the Civil War the women and children of the South were left with the slaves, yet "there is no record of any case in which the confidence the masters reposed in their slaves was abused." Second, beginning with the Klan of the Reconstruction period, the white South launched a campaign "to keep Negroes ignorant and poor, and it is not surprising if they have succeeded in brutalizing them to a large extent. Brutality begets brutality everywhere." In contrast, where Negroes were accorded civil rights and social recognition, as in Jamaica, a British possession, "there is no brutal crime such as the South complains of. . . ." And last, few lynchings were actually connected with rape; statistically, rape was far commoner among Chicago whites than among all the Negroes in the South. "Yet we hear no crusade amongst the whites even in Chicago, nor do we understand that it is found necessary to lynch in order to discourage it." [27]

Though Storey expressed an early interest in anti-lynching legislation, he was limited by the attitudes he had already developed as a member of the legal profession. With the majority of lawyers of his time, he tended to regard the Constitution of the United States as an unambiguous document, and "the duty of the [Supreme] Court" was simply "to declare what the Constitution means—what the law is." In the area of protection against mob violence, however, any faithful acceptance of judicial interpretation presented a fundamental problem to one of Storey's commitments. For in his past defense of civil equality, he had maintained that the United States "is the country of all its citizens, and black men have under our Constitution all the rights of white men," but when it came to security from mob violence it was difficult to say exactly what those rights were. In a series of decisions nullifying Reconstruction legislation that had provided criminal penalties for the intimidation of citizens (beginning with *U.S. v. Cruikshank*), the Court had apparently exempted private acts of violence from the prohibitions of the Fourteenth Amendment.[28]

It could well be argued that lynching, as far as the constitutional law of 1918 was concerned, was simply murder, no less but no more. Thus Storey at first convinced himself that anti-lynching legislation would be unconstitutional. He wrote John R. Shillady, who had succeeded Nash as Executive Secretary of the NAACP, that, regretfully, he had come to the conclusion that lynching was beyond the reach of Congress for two reasons:

> The attempt is made to make them punishable by the contention that they are offenses against the peace of the United States which the United States may punish. They are not more so than every crime is against the peace of the United States, and if this doctrine were to prevail, the whole criminal law which now leaves these offenses to be dealt with by the states, must be set aside.
>
> The only ground on which the Federal Government can interfere is that the states by inaction and connivance with criminals deny to the colored people the equal protection of the laws. In any given case [however,] the omission to prosecute may not be the fault of the Governor or the fault of the district attorney, but the fault of the jury.

At that time (1918 and early 1919) Storey could see only two alternative goals for the NAACP's campaign: the passage of an Amendment to the Constitution, making lynching a Federal crime, or local pressure, strengthening state legislation against lynching.[29]

Within a year, however, Storey was reaching far different conclusions and, since the provisions of the Dyer bill had not changed during 1919 or 1920, one can only speculate on the reasons that made Storey decide to support the bill. Possibly it was his declining faith in the corrective force of education. Storey, who had once hoped "to stir the best men of the South" to oppose lynching, was now doubtful of the efficacy of persuasion, in spite of such heartening developments as the growth of the Southern Commission on Interracial Cooperation and the anti-lynching campaigns of the Atlanta *Constitution* and the Charleston *News-Courier*. "The process of education is necessarily slow," he wrote philanthropist George Foster Peabody, "and I do not think this evil will await its results. Toleration of lynching by men and women all through the south is itself an educational force which is constantly setting a bad example. . . ." [30]

Possibly, too, his change in attitude was due to the events of the summer of 1919, "the greatest period of interracial strife the nation had ever witnessed." From July to September race riots occurred in Chicago, in Washington, in Tulsa, in Knoxville, in Omaha, and in other cities across the nation. The causes differed from place to place: in many cities, rumors of assaults on white women incited the mob, but in Longview, Texas, it came from white opposition to the militant mood of the local black community. In Chicago, it arose over a chance confrontation and accidental drowning on a segregated beach: the result was 38 deaths, 537 injuries, and 1000 black families driven from their homes. In August 1919 Executive Secretary Shillady went to Austin to find out why the local branch of the Association there was being investigated by the Texas Attorney General. Called before a "court of inquiry," he was beaten while local officials watched, and the physically and spiritually weakened victim severed his connection with the NAACP. Whether because of his own reflections or because of events like these, by the end of 1919 Storey was writing not only that "I want the attention of the country arrested" but that "I want such a public opinion aroused as will control the action of Congress. . . ." [31]

Storey had not completely overcome his doubts about the constitutionality of the Dyer bill when hearings were held on it in 1920. He therefore did not join James Weldon Johnson, Archibald Grimké, and Joel Spingarn in their appearance before the House Judiciary subcommittee on behalf of the Association, probably because, as he later put it, "I should not be able to answer questions as to constitutionality in such manner as perhaps to help the bill. . . ." But already convinced of the necessity for some kind of legislation, Storey began an extended search for its constitutional justification, a search that would culminate in his brief for the bill in the spring of 1922. In early 1921, for example, he rehearsed part of his subsequent argument in an exchange of letters with George W. Wickersham, Taft's Attorney General. Wickersham, while he also wanted to curtail lynching, was "somewhat puzzled to know just what line to proceed upon." [32]

The best possible constitutional basis for anti-lynching legislation, Storey replied, was the "equal protection" clause of the Fourteenth Amendment,

> that no state "shall deny to any person within its jurisdiction the equal protection of the laws [sic]." I see no reason why that denial should not come from the refusal of the executive officers to secure to colored citizens the protection of the law with the approval, tacit if not active, of the people in the state as well as though it were done by legislation.

But, Wickersham argued, in view of the limitations on what constitutes "state action" imposed by the Supreme Court, could one prove denial of "equal protection" simply "because an individual official neglects his sworn duties? Must there not be state action as distinguished from individual dereliction?" Such a distinction was often meaningless in the South, Storey replied, where Negroes were denied their rights

> not merely because individuals use violence, but because the whole community approves their violence. . . . The Governor of the state, the prosecuting officers, the grand juries, the sheriffs, and all the instrumentalities of the law refuse to operate so as to protect Negroes against lynching. . . .[33]

In a later exchange of views, the two men argued the problem of what constituted the "privileges and immunities" of citizenship contained in the Amendment, in other words, the rights of individuals, that the Federal government would be called upon to protect against mobs. Storey had reminded Wickersham that there was a Reconstruction statute still on the books which made it a crime for two or more persons to "conspire to injure, oppress, threaten, or intimidate any citizen in the free exercise or enjoy-

ment of any right or privilege secured by the Constitution or
laws of the United States." Congress could act against lynching,
therefore, simply by amending the statute to cover a conspiracy
to *deprive* citizens of those rights and privileges. Thus "an
attempt to lynch would come within the language of the act,
because it would deprive the citizen of the right to be punished according to law and not by mob violence." Wickersham
replied that the statute Storey cited had been emptied of content
by a whole series of Supreme Court decisions, beginning with
Cruikshank and culminating in a recent decision voiding the
Federal government's prosecution of men who illegally deported
radicals from Arizona. From those cases he argued that, as far as
the Court was concerned, the rights protected by statute "do not
include the rights of the individual to life, liberty, and property,
which were primary rights within the protection of the state of
which the defendant is an inhabitant." [34]

The discussion between the two men had so far revolved
around the various clauses of the first section of the Fourteenth
Amendment. But now Storey took a step which, in view of his
past attitude toward constitutional law, was little short of
revolutionary. The man who had urged his audience "to teach
respect for the law" came very close to saying that a law should
be passed even if it were unconstitutional, because of its
beneficent effect.

> I observed that after the Lever Act was declared uncon-
> stitutional the newspapers consoled themselves by saying
> that it did a great deal of good while it lasted, and if we
> can get Congress to pass an anti-lynching statute drawn
> as nearly as possible to avoid the decisions, it may do
> some good while it lasts, and even if it is ultimately de-
> clared unconstitutional, it will at least have put this coun-
> try right before the world as not supporting the atrocities
> which now go unpunished in various states of the Union.

Wickersham remained unconvinced, but Storey, led by his
humanitarian impulses to push aside his earlier doubts about its
constitutionality, now committed himself to support of the bill.

He could now write Dyer with complete self-assurance: "I am informed that you are under the impression that I am opposed to the passage of your bill to prevent lynching. Nothing is further from the truth for I am very much in favor of it, and sincerely hope that it will pass." [35]

After the hearings of 1920, no further action was taken by the Judiciary Subcommittee, but in 1921, with the implicit blessing of President Harding and the pressure of the NAACP, the bill moved into the full committee itself, and in October the bill was released for floor action. The Dyer bill now included aliens as well as citizens in its provisions, set prison terms of up to five years and fines of up to $5000 for negligent law-enforcement officers, held mob members liable to prosecution for murder, permitted a prisoner who feared a lynching to petition for the protection of a Federal marshal, and allowed damage suits of up to $10,000 against the county where the lynching occurred or against the counties through which the mob passed. On January 22, 1922, the House voted to consider the measure, and on the following day, in a melodramatic scene with Negroes cheering in the galleries and Southerners cursing on the floor, the representatives passed the bill, 230 to 119.[36]

The bill then went to the Senate, where it was referred to the Judiciary Committee. The chairman of that committee was William E. Borah, who, though he exercised his major influence on foreign policy, considered himself something of a constitutional expert. As soon as the bill had reached his committee, Borah wrote Storey, "I have only one question open for investigation with reference to the bill and that is its constitutionality." He warned Storey that, if he thought it unconstitutional, "I would have to vote against it. I have never voted for a bill here which I thought was unconstitutional with a view to letting the Court pass upon it later." So while Johnson directed the general campaign—culminating in a "memorial to the United States Senate" and a full-page advertisement, "THE SHAME OF AMERICA,"—it devolved upon Storey and another of the Association's lawyers, Herbert K. Stockton, to meet Borah's criticisms.[37]

In this climax of the Association's campaign against lynching, Storey had completely dropped his earlier doubts about the constitutionality of the Dyer bill, and he personally submitted a brief in its support to the Committee in April 1922. All the points within his brief were made to sustain his basic contention that the persistent neglect of duty on the part of Southern law-enforcement officials confronting lynch mobs was a problem upon which Congress could constitutionally act.[38]

His first argument on behalf of the bill involved, as it had with Wickersham the previous year, the Fourteenth Amendment. The Amendment "forbids the abridgement of the rights belonging to 'American citizens,'" and it places the rights of citizens as American citizens (as opposed to their rights as citizens of the several states) under the protection of the Federal government; thus Congress may legitimately legislate to protect those rights. It appeared that the protection of the Amendment was limited to state action abridging those rights; but, Storey added, the Supreme Court had also declared that such "denial . . . need not be by legislation." He cited another decision involving a Virginia judge who arbitrarily excluded Negroes from his juries:

> A State acts by its legislative, its executive, or its judicial authorities. It can act in no other way. The constitutional provision, therefore, must mean that no agency of the State, or of the officers or agents by whom its powers are exerted, shall deny to any person within its jurisdiction the equal protection of the laws. *Whoever, by virtue of public position under a State government deprives another of property, life, or liberty without due process of law, or denies or takes away the equal protection of the laws violates the constitutional inhibition.* . . . [Italics mine.]

And the Court had recently rejected the idea that the prohibition on discriminatory state action reached the states "only in their complete governmental capacity." On the contrary, it had held in 1913,

> The theory of the [Fourteenth] Amendment is that *where an officer or other representative of a State* in the exercise

of the authority with which he is clothed *misuses the*
power possessed to do a wrong forbidden by the Amend-
ment, inquiry concerning whether the State has authorized
the wrong is irrelevant. . . . [Italics mine.]

Given a reasonably broad interpretation of such precedents as
these, it could well be argued that the persistent lack of protection given to Negroes threatened by mobs was equivalent to a
positive denial both of "due process" and of "equal protection"
by a state. Stockton, the Association's other legal adviser in the
anti-lynching campaign, so regarded it, and he placed the burden
of his brief on that point.[39]

But such an approach met only half of the constitutional challenge. In synthesizing the trend of decisions from *Cruikshank*
onward, the Supreme Court had differentiated between rights
which were "recognized and declared" by the Constitution, and
rights "created by, arising under, or dependent upon" the Constitution. The first set of rights were "guaranteed" only against
"violation or abridgment by the United States, or the states" but
could not be enforced against the "unlawful acts of individuals."
The latter, however, could be enforced in any manner Congress
thought appropriate. If the Dyer bill were enacted, what if the
Court found the Fourteenth Amendment inapplicable because
lynching constituted the "unlawful acts of individuals"? Probably
because he feared some such possibility, Storey set about to
prove that life and liberty were indeed rights "created by,
arising under, or dependent upon" the Constitution, and as
such within the power of Congress to protect.[40]

He therefore based his last main argument upon the Fifth
Amendment: no person shall be deprived of life, liberty, or
property without due process of law. The Fifth Amendment,
directed against *all* denials of due process, did not raise the
question of "state action." For Storey, it was "a shield which the
Constitution throws over every person, citizen or not, within our
jurisdiction." That the authors of the Bill of Rights intended
them only as prohibitions on the Federal government, he argued,

was irrelevant, for "the courts have again and again refused to interpret an act by its purpose as disclosed by words used in [the] debate [that had taken place] when it was passed, and have insisted that its meaning is to be found in its language. . . ." The Court had ruled many times, said Storey, that the specific grant to Congress to enforce a fundamental right was not necessary: "A right or immunity, whether created by the Constitution or only guaranteed by it, even without express delegation of power, may be protected by Congress." [41]

Storey concluded his brief with a refutation of the argument that the cases from *Cruikshank* onward went against the constitutionality of the Dyer bill. He said that in the cases following *Cruikshank* the Court had narrowed the congressional function to acting only when states had clearly defaulted in their obligation to protect the rights of citizens, but that it had not otherwise limited that function—a view recently supported by one legal scholar. Since the Southern states had manifestly defaulted in their obligation to provide due process and equal protection to Negro citizens, Congress could protect those rights by punishing lynching. With this rebuttal to possible critics, he completed his brief on behalf of the Dyer bill: persistent inaction by law-enforcement officials constituted discriminatory "state action" under the Fourteenth Amendment; the rights of life and liberty "arose from" the Fifth Amendment; and since the pattern of decisions from *Cruikshank* onward did not apply, under both Amendments the Congress could constitutionally enact an anti-lynching bill.[42]

Not long removed from constitutional doubts himself, Storey seems to have been unwilling to base his entire argument on legal precedent and so turned to historical justifications. He had written in his brief, for example,

It never was the intention of the people who adopted the Fourteenth Amendment that the states so recently in rebellion should be able to nullify the amendment by simple non-action and should be able to plead that the persons who trampled on the new citizens were merely private persons for whose acts the state was not responsible.

Since it is difficult to see why Storey felt the *intentions* of the framers of the Fourteenth Amendment should be emphasized, but only the *language* of the Fifth, the possibility intrudes that he may have been speaking not as a lawyer, but as an observer. He had, after all, arrived in Washington only eighteen months after the passage of the Fourteenth Amendment, and, given his friendship with Sumner and his later acquaintance with some of the men who helped frame that Amendment, he may well have drawn on his personal memories to buttress his case.[43]

But in taking such a broad view of the Fourteenth Amendment, Storey conjured up what, for a man who had always placed his principles in a somewhat cautious framework, was an exceptionally bold view of constitutional development. Only two years after the Arizona deportation cases, and four years before the Court began its incorporation of the First Amendment into the Fourteenth, he wrote this of the *entire* Bill of Rights:

> I regard the affirmations of rights contained in these amendments, however, not simply as preventing the Federal Government from infringing upon these rights but as recognizing a power on the part of the Federal Government to see that its citizens are not interfered with by irresponsible individuals in the exercise of these rights. . . .

Seeing his position justified in some of the dissents of Brandeis, Storey admiringly quoted one such "sound" opinion affirming the "fundamental rights of American citizenship." [44]

At the beginning of the Association's anti-lynching campaign, Storey had had grave doubts about the constitutionality of the Dyer bill. As the responses of Wickersham and Borah indicate, those doubts continued to be shared by many who wanted to end the horrors of lynching. For example, Louis Marshall, attorney for the American Jewish Committee and counsel for the NAACP in the restrictive-covenant case, felt that "great as that evil [lynching] is, it would not, however, equal that which would follow the usurpation by the Congress of the United States of power it does not possess under the Constitution." Yet Moorfield

Storey's role as a legal conservative and his role as a defender of civil rights had come into conflict, and the defender of civil rights had emerged victorious. Having always believed the legislation desirable, he first convinced himself that it would be educationally useful, and then that it was completely constitutional. As his brief for the bill indicated, he felt sure that the judicial precedents supported its constitutionality. But if they did not, he wrote,

> we are not to assume that what the Supreme Court of the United States decides must be regarded as final law. The income tax decision, the legal-tender decision, and others have been overruled, and I shall not hesitate to attack the Court on the existing situation. . . .[45]

In late June of 1922, the Dyer bill was reported favorably from the Senate Judiciary Committee, though Borah voted with the Democrats against it. Senator Shortridge of California was to lead the fight on the floor, and Republican leaders assured Johnson that action would be taken on the bill in September. But the inexperienced Shortridge yielded the floor to Senator Harrison of Mississippi, and he found, once the floor was yielded back to him, that there was no quorum in the Senate to conduct further business. In November Shortridge again attempted to begin debate on the bill, and a filibuster followed. The leadership assured Johnson that the fight would continue, but under the threat of Southern Democrats to halt all business in the short session of 1922–23, they had already tacitly agreed to abandon the fight for the bill.[46]

Because neither the Dyer bill nor any of its successors ever became law, the Supreme Court never had the opportunity to pass directly upon anti-lynching legislation. The question debated between Storey and his opponents forty years ago—would the Court *of that time* have held the Dyer bill constitutional?—can never be answered with complete assurance. But if the fate of the economic legislation of the 1930's has any relevance, it might only have been by the repeated passage of constitutionally doubtful legislation that the Court would have answered the question.

Though Storey was far removed from the New Dealers in most of his attitudes, his conception of the Supreme Court as an instrument to be tested, and not as an authority to be unquestioningly followed, reveals the humanitarian sentiments that could break through his formalistic intellectual framework.[47]

3. Community Protection and Official Lawlessness

While seeking to curb "lawlessness" by bringing industrial conflict under arbitration, and by extending governmental protection against mob violence to the individual, Storey also sought to curb the rising crime rate by making, as he put it, "punishment swift and sure." From the perspective of the present, his views on criminal procedure may seem difficult to classify. In his persistent concern for due process, Storey set himself apart from the acquiescence to brutality that has characterized many of those similarly concerned with social order. But his steadfast conviction that the object of highest importance was the protection of society also sets him apart from the civil libertarian temper of contemporary reform. In the Storrs Lectures he gave at the Yale Law School in 1911, for example, Storey could say,

> Today the law as administered throws around the criminal a protecting wall which may have been necessary when the power of the English crown pressed despotically upon the subject, but which is wholly unnecessary today. It is the community that now needs protection against the criminal, not the innocent man who must be saved from unjust prosecution.

This statement reveals not only Storey's opinions on the subject; it indicates that he had developed them well before the turbulent years after 1918, when, as he put it, "no morning paper comes without news of some hold-ups or robberies or other offenses." [48]

Storey approached the problem of crime, as he approached

problems in other areas, with a set of moral absolutes: there was a "criminal class" on one side and the law-abiding majority on the other. He fully recognized that what he called "criminality" often came from environment, but he did not believe that the control of such factors, however desirable as public policy, was the problem of law enforcement. Not for him were the relativist conclusions of a Clarence Darrow, who saw criminals as twice victimized by society: first because they were made what they were, and then because they were punished for it. If, on the other hand, one assumes with Storey the existence of a "criminal class" of rational but malevolent men, then one accepts, as he did, certain conclusions. He was quite willing to improve the rehabilitative aspects of punishment, and he favored a system of "indeterminate sentencing" so that offenders could be released as soon as they could be safely employed. But he never doubted that the main purpose of punishment was deterrence:

> I think the practice of suspending sentence and putting a criminal on probation, or giving him a very light sentence has encouraged criminals and others to think now of the possibility of not being caught, the possibility of not being indicted or not being convicted, and also of the possibility of receiving some trivial sentence and then being turned loose again on the community. I think it is the business of the judge to administer justice and give an adequate sentence, leaving mercy to the governor and council. If punishment could be sure and swift, I think crime would decrease.[49]

Storey had specific proposals for the conduct of criminal trials themselves. He favored as speedy a sequence as possible between arrest, arraignment, trial, conviction, and punishment. Today, of course, what occurs between arrest and trial is what most concerns civil libertarians, and, to an ever-increasing degree since the 1930's, this is what has concerned the Justices of the Supreme Court. In the aftermath of recent Court decisions curbing the arraignment powers of the police, and the angry reaction of the law-enforcement officers themselves, Storey's concern for the rights of the defendant, coming as it did from one who placed high value on the "protection of the community" is not without current relevance. The existing system of criminal procedure, he argued, contained a monstrous inconsistency: it would "allow a man to be tortured in the police cell without counsel or any bench to protect him and refuse to allow him to be examined in court by the judge with all the protection which counsel and publicity will give him." [50]

To avoid this absurdity, Storey, as early as his Storrs Lectures, had called for "an examination [presumably before the trial, though this is unclear] by the judge or the prosecuting officer in public with the defendant's counsel to protect him." Admittedly, this would have involved a re-interpretation of the Fifth Amendment's prohibition of self-incrimination, but he would have argued that the Amendment was being violated every day "in the secret cells of the police station." As far as Storey was concerned, his plan was unarguable:

> The accused of all men in the world knows better than anyone else whether he is guilty or not, and if the object of the criminal law is to detect and punish the guilty, why should he not be asked to tell what he knows? If he criminates himself, can there be better evidence of guilt? Why shouldn't he criminate himself? Eye-witnesses may mislead, circumstantial evidence may mislead, but the testimony of the accused against himself can be relied upon in any but the most exceptional cases. [51]

Before the World War Storey's concern for procedural guarantees already qualified his commitment to "the protection of the community": his concern for due process was renewed under the impact of the war itself. The attempts after 1917 to enforce conformity upon a pluralistic society ranged from grotesque little campaigns to eliminate sauerkraut and Wagnerian opera to brutal intimidation of conscientious objectors and antiwar Socialists. The nationalist hysteria was in part the work of what Storey called "the mob," which, "ignorant of the facts, asserts its own standard of patriotism, or generosity, any deviation from which is punished by death without trial." But there was also governmental repression, exemplified by the Espionage Act of 1917, which made it a crime to "interfere" with the operation of the Armed Forces, and the Sedition Act of 1918, which made it a crime to write or speak anything "disloyal, profane, scurrilous, or abusive" about the government or its officers.[52]

Storey does not seem to have believed in an unqualified right to free speech:

> The fundamental principle of free speech and free press must be controlled during the time of war, for men cannot be allowed to excite disaffection and stir up resistance to the measures of the Government without exposing themselves to the penalties of sedition and perhaps of treason.

Perhaps for that reason he did not join the organizing committee of the American Civil Liberties Union, writing Roger Baldwin that "I do not feel that there is any emergency now for the creation of such an organization as you speak of and I think it is liable to do more harm than good." But if he was not a defender of an absolute First Amendment, Storey remained deeply involved with issues involving procedural guarantees. He had consistently maintained during the war that "we cannot allow the law to be enforced by a casual collection of hoodlums," and was appalled at the treatment of conscientious objectors at Leavenworth penitentiary. Disclosures of their being beaten, chained by their wrists, and kept in solitary confinement "should be brought at once to the attention of the Secretary of War . . . for abuses like this disgrace the American name." While he still believed the Espionage Act to be necessary, Storey wrote, he had no doubt that it "has been a cover for many unjust prosecutions, and I know that a great many sentences which seem to me preposterous have been inflicted on men for very trifling offenses." [53]

If Storey had been concerned about the violations of procedural guarantees during wartime, when he believed restrictions on freedom of speech to be necessary, he was doubly so in a period when, as far as he could see, the restrictions were totally unwarranted. The end of hostilities with Germany had not stopped the heightened impulses toward conformity; by 1919, feeding on several bombings in spring and a summer of strikes, this mindless chauvinism now turned against dissenters. In the states, growing hysteria resulted in the dismissal of public employees of suspected affiliations, the expulsion of elected Socialists from the state legislatures, and the lynching of radical labor leaders. In the Federal government, the "Red hunt" was pushed by Wilson's Attorney General, A. Mitchell Palmer, who, unchecked by an indisposed President, and goaded by his own presidential ambitions, proclaimed his intent to purge the country of subversives. On November 7, 1919, agents of the Department of Justice raided the offices of an organization of Russian radicals, and 200 of the hapless souls uncovered in the raids were summarily packed aboard a ship and sent back to Russia that December. Heartened by public approval, Palmer launched his biggest raid on January 2, 1920, in which agents herded 10,000 more aliens, many of whom had no connection with any political organization at all, into filthy, overcrowded jails and held them incommunicado.[54]

Few men tried to stop the tide of repression, but it is significant that Storey worked with at least two of them. One was George W. Anderson. As United States District Attorney in Boston, he had instituted no prosecutions under the Espionage Act; and as a Federal Judge, he had ruled that alien membership in the Communist party was not a deportable offense, thus destroying Palmer's main legal justification for the raids. In the spring of 1919, Anderson drafted a petition to the Massachusetts Legislature opposing proposed state sedition laws, and Storey, among others, signed it. "While sympathizing with every effort to prevent the growth and spread of anarchy," it began, "we do not believe that in our efforts to do something effective we should destroy American institutions." Although it compared the proposed measures to a "Russian secret police inquisition" and to

the abuses of the Stuart monarchs, the petition's main thrust
was that the bills themselves, far more than the agitation they
proposed to curtail, jeopardized the security of American institutions:

> Both bills confess a fear and distrust, wholly unwarranted,
> in the justice, sanity and health of our democratic institu-
> tions. Their passage would be evidence of hysterical,
> panic-stricken fear and weakness which would tend to
> increase the irresponsible and ineffective agitation against
> which they are on their face directed. If passed and used,
> they may become weapons of tyranny and persecution
> and thus causes of hatred of our government.[55]

A second figure, far more significant in his opposition to
Palmer, was Assistant Secretary of Labor Louis F. Post. Using
his official prerogative to review all proceedings for deportation,
he soon whittled down the 3000 arrests Palmer's agents had
made to slightly less than 600 subject to actual deportation. One
of the few men in the Wilson administration of 1919 who had the
courage of his liberal convictions, Post succeeded in convincing
an initially hostile congressional committee of the correctness of
his actions and, partly through the impact of his testimony, by the
fall of 1920 the Attorney General was becoming just another
forgotten politician. Three years later, after the dust had settled,
Post wrote a memoir of his experience, calling it *The Deportations Delirium of Nineteen-Twenty*. Though it is not clear when
Post and Storey had met—a long-time advocate of reform causes,
Post had been an official in both the NAACP and the Anti-
Imperialist League—Post asked Storey to write the Introduction
to his book. Storey took the occasion to warn against the "lawlessness" not only of mobs, but also of zealous government officials
who, "under pretense of enforcing the laws, trample on the
Constitution." In the Red raids, he charged, "some thousands of
innocent people were very cruelly treated and exposed to much
suffering and loss." He continued,

> There was no conspiracy to overthrow this government
> and no evidence was ever produced which excused the

action of the government. The safeguards of the Constitution were ignored, and any true American must blush at what was done and at the indifference with which he and all but a handful of his countrymen tolerated it.[56]

Thus, by the 1920's, Storey's initial belief in the importance of protecting society from the "criminal class" had been qualified by his awareness of the ease with which law-enforcement officials violated procedural guarantees. In two criminal trials of the 1920's, both widely believed at the time to be paradigm cases of the denial of a fair trial, his new attitude was revealed most clearly.

Some time after the Armistice, a black veteran in Arkansas had founded an organization, the Progressive Farmers and Household Union of America, for the purpose of protecting sharecroppers against fraudulent contracts. On the night of October 2, 1919, the members of the union were meeting in a church in Phillips County when there was an exchange of gunfire outside. Several people were killed, and those inside the church were arrested. The local white community became hysterical: vigilante groups patrolled the countryside, killing scores of Negroes. The governor of the state asked for United States army forces to "restore order," and appointed a "Committee of Seven" to investigate the situation: the Committee concluded that the union was planning an "insurrection" among Arkansas Negroes. The trial of the men arrested inside the church was held at the county seat of Helena in November; sixty-seven of them were given prison terms from twenty years to life, and twelve were sentenced to die on December 27, 1919. The governor stayed the sentence pending appeal, which the NAACP, now managing the defense of the sharecroppers, was planning.[57]

On March 9, 1920, the state Supreme Court reversed the conviction of six of the defendants; these six were convicted at a second trial, and they appealed again in December 1920, this time on the ground that Negroes had been excluded from their jury. Their conviction was again reversed, but a third trial, scheduled for 1921, was never held, because of the eventual fate of the other six men. These other six, known to constitutional historians as Frank Moore *et al.*, whose convictions had been affirmed by the state Supreme Court in March 1920, and who, after two denials of review by the United States Supreme Court and two postponements of their execution, were freed after a final review by the United States Supreme Court in 1923. It was these men, Moore and the others, whom Moorfield Storey defended.[58]

Against the background of the Red scare, Storey was already well aware that any attempt by Negroes to defend their rights would be portrayed by Southern politicians as a Communist plot. When there were rumors that the Department of Justice was suspicious of the NAACP, he wrote Palmer, "I am perfectly certain that there is no justification for the suggestion that we are undertaking to do anything inconsistent with absolute loyalty to the Government of the United States." Storey was less than enthusiastic about what Negro radicalism did exist (A. Philip Randolph and his Socialist *Messenger*, for example), but he ridiculed the assumption that Negroes "are preparing for a bloody revolt against the oppression of the white man."

> They are defending themselves by endeavoring to make appeals to the conscience of this country against the oppression under which they are suffering, but they are not such fools as to attempt to redress their wrongs by force, nor are they by nature disposed to any such insurrection. If they had been capable of armed resistance, slavery would not have lasted as long as it did, nor would the slaves during the Civil War have protected their masters' families and worked to support their armies by raising food as they did.[59]

Even before their first appeal reached the Arkansas Supreme Court, Storey suspected that the Phillips County defendants were innocent. Any impartial investigation of social conditions in the South, he was sure, would find

> that substantial slavery exists in large parts of the South, in that under the plan by which the colored men as tenants

divide the crops with the landlords, the landlord keeps the accounts, charges them ridiculous prices for what they buy, and allows them very much less than the market price for the cotton, which he sells, and refuses to render them any account by which they can know whether he is dealing honestly or not. When they rebel and try to leave, he seizes all their valuables and property under a claim that they are indebted to him, and they are left without the means of moving or doing anything.

The Arkansas trouble arose from the attempt of the Negroes to employ counsel for the purpose of getting accounts from their landlords, and was brought on, I think, by a determination of the planters that this movement should not succeed. I think the planters began the fight, and then said that there was a conspiracy to murder the whites.

Sympathetic though he was to the plight of the defendants, Storey doubted that his strength was up to the effort. When, on the third attempt for appeal, the defendants' counsel, NAACP lawyer Scipio Jones, finally succeeded in persuading the Supreme Court to grant review, Storey tried to avoid taking the case. After Johnson suggested that other lawyers handle the details, Storey, partly because "the Arkansas cases have always appealed to my sympathy, and that carries me a great way," relented and agreed to argue the case on appeal.[60]

The brief that Storey presented to the Supreme Court contained facts, all attested to by sworn depositions, which had been deliberately ignored at the trial. It was impossible to prove who was responsible for the deaths of October 2, because, even though the meeting had begun peacefully, the church was being besieged by a white mob. To extract confessions from the defendants, the Committee of Seven had tortured them through beatings, electrocution, and the insertion of strangling drugs in their nostrils. Local newspapers, civic groups, and the governor himself had demanded the conviction of the Negroes, and during the trial angry crowds had surrounded the courthouse. When the union's lawyer, Ulysses S. Bratton, had been subjected to various forms of intimidation which prevented him from defending his clients, the court-appointed lawyer who replaced him at the trial had not asked for a change of venue, nor had he introduced any witnesses for the defense. And, in his charge to the jury, the presiding judge had told them to find the defendants guilty only if they were present at the church and had "aided or abetted" the riot. Through the whole proceeding,

> judge, jury, and counsel were dominated by the mob spirit that was universally present in court and out, so that if any juror had had the courage to investigate said charge, with any spirit of fairness, and vote for acquittal he himself would have been the victim of the mob. . . .[61]

With such conditions prevailing, Storey argued, the violation of due process was so gross that the Supreme Court must grant a writ of habeas corpus. The Court, in a decision of major importance, accepted his contention: if a hearing in the local federal court showed that the facts were as Storey alleged, the prisoners would be freed. The hearing proved inconclusive, but in the autumn of 1923 the sentences of the six men were commuted to short prison terms; and by 1925 they—and the sixty-seven other union men still serving their sentences—had been released. Important as the immediate victory was for the Association, its greater significance lay in the fact that it marked the beginning of the Court's concern with the substance of due process.[62]

Storey's concern for due process, as it had emerged by the mid-1920's, included not only restraints on the mob attempting to execute its own verdict outside the courtroom (as anti-lynching legislation tried to exercise), but also judicial guarantees against the influence of the mob upon the trial proceedings themselves. Any discussion of his involvement with the question of a fair trial cannot be concluded, however, without some mention of his opposition to what he called "lynch-pardons as well as lynch-executions." This opposition he most clearly revealed in the Sacco-Vanzetti case. Whether these two men—one a shoemaker,

the other a fish-peddler—were or were not responsible for two
fatal shootings in connection with a payroll robbery in South
Braintree, Massachusetts, in March 1920, seems to be as controversial today as it was forty years ago. But the question of
whether they received a fair trial—our concern here—may be
more amenably settled.[63]

During the whole period, from their trial in 1921, through
their appeals, to their execution in 1927, Storey had no doubt that
Sacco and Vanzetti had received a fair trial.

> Sacco and Vanzetti were very ably defended, and the
> defense was backed by ample funds. The trial lasted
> seven weeks before a good jury taken from the people
> of Norfolk county. . . . The jury saw the witnesses, heard
> the arguments and learned all that was to be learned
> about the case. Judge Thayer presided with infinite pa-
> tience and charged the jury fairly, expressly instructing
> them not to consider the fact that the defendants were
> foreigners or held any particular belief, but whatever
> their nationality or faith, they were entitled to be tried
> precisely like anyone else, and the only question was
> whether they did the particular thing with which they
> were charged, or not.

He was convinced not only that the two men had received a fair
trial but, having studied the transcript of the trial, he was convinced they were guilty. The second conclusion, however, does
not necessarily follow from the first. It is possible, in other words,
to find the ballistics evidence against the two men unpersuasive,
or even to entertain the hypothesis that the robbery was the
work of the Morelli gang of New Bedford, and still believe that
the two men received a fair trial.[64]

The "fair trial" issue arose when the defense, in order to
explain what the prosecution had called the defendants' "consciousness of guilt" (their possession of guns and their false statements made when arrested), was forced to admit that both men
were anarchists afraid of deportation. The issue of their political
opinions, which Felix Frankfurter used as a powerful appeal on

behalf of Sacco and Vanzetti, has grown into something of a legend, in which two poor radicals were put to death by paranoid Brahmins.[65]

Against this still-prevalent interpretation, certain facts have recently been re-emphasized. First, by the 1920's the power of the Brahmins was declining with increasing rapidity, and the group that was replacing them as administrators of the Commonwealth, the Irish, were even less sympathetic to the defendants than the Brahmins were. If there was prejudice against Sacco and Vanzetti, it was held by most of the ethnic groups in the Commonwealth. Second, Massachusetts was hardly the "center" of anti-radical hysteria in 1919–20, as Frankfurter (and others since) charged. The persecution of radicals had been almost entirely the work of Federal agents, and, as we have seen, it led to the opposition of men like Anderson; in any case, the appeals for Sacco and Vanzetti from 1922 to 1926 occurred in a much quieter atmosphere. It is also odd that a state which supposedly hated anarchists so much that it executed two of them as "murderers" actually instituted only one prosecution for criminal anarchy between 1918 and 1933. Third, whether or not Judge Thayer privately referred to the defendants as "anarchist bastards," his conduct of the trial itself is a different question. And there, as Storey pointed out at the time, defense counsel made no indication that it regarded Thayer's conduct as prejudiced.[66]

With these factors in mind, therefore, it seems unfair to condemn Storey for his refusal to see a denial of due process in what, today, to ostensibly objective observers, is still an ambiguous question. What upset him the most were not the issues of the trial itself, but what he considered the attempt of those who sympathized with the defendants ("rather hysterical or carried away by their sympathies") to interfere with the constituted processes of justice:

> Now suppose in place of a jury trial you adopt the sentiment of a minority of the community, or a majority even, as to whether a man was innocent or guilty without trial.

What do you suppose would have happened during our war? How many men charged with sedition would have been railroaded to the gallows or to prison? Do you think it is safe to abandon the well-settled practice of constitutional government and substitute such loose methods?

Though this analogy of Storey's is somewhat strained, it testifies, as much as any of his statements during this period, to his deep conviction that both security and freedom were inextricably connected to popular acquiescence in the proceedings of the courts.[67]

4. ". . . So Long a Life . . ."

By the time of the Sacco-Vanzetti affair, Storey's public role had been reduced by the limitations of old age to that of critical observer. It is of course true that, though he was convinced that the case involved larger issues, his very opposition to "outside interference" precluded his taking a more active role. Nonetheless, his secondary role in the preparation of the Association briefs in the restrictive-covenant and white-primary cases indicates that, by 1926, Storey's entire public career had virtually come to an end. Except for Justice Holmes, Storey had persisted longer in public affairs than any of his contemporaries—he was president of the Anti-Imperialist League at sixty, and of the NAACP at sixty-five; he argued the residential-segregation case at seventy-two, and prepared the brief for the Dyer bill at seventy-eight—but even the energy of Moorfield Storey, so long sustained in so many different causes, had begun to wane.

"I have a great many things on my mind, and very little time to spare," he had written James Weldon Johnson in 1921. "I probably have not many more years to live, and there are things that I want to accomplish while I can." The years between 1923 and 1925 saw the culmination of two of Storey's lifelong campaigns: that for Negro rights in his defense of the Arkansas sharecroppers, and that against American imperialism in his book, *The Conquest of the Philippines*. Now, by 1926, much that Storey had wanted to accomplish had been done: he was content to let history take its course. The NAACP was already a success: it achieved victory after victory in the Federal courts, and he was happy to confine his role to an advisory one. The Anti-Imperialist League, he knew quite well, would die when he did: if younger men wanted to revive it, they would have to be willing "to assume all the burdens of working up such an organization. . . ." [68]

The slackening pull of reform interests permitted Storey to alternate more of his time between days at the office and quiet evenings at home than he had been able to before. His new leisure also gave him time for reflection, for wondering, as he wrote his friends, "whether the world is worse than it used to be, or whether [instead] I know it better." No one was farther removed from congenital pessimism than Storey: his question reflects rather his growing awareness in his last years that the America of the 1920's had little use for Boston Brahmins, less use for humanitarian reformers—and not much use at all for Moorfield Storey. He had never been euphoric about the technology of the twentieth century, and now found the shiny new automobiles that crowded the streets to be a positive menace:

> The congestion of the streets and the reckless driving of automobiles makes every street crossing a danger to your life, and as I rather enjoy walking around the streets it has taken much of the satisfaction out of my pedestrian exercise. My family will no longer let me come home by myself in the afternoon, but send a motor for me so that I may avoid the temptation of being hit.[69]

"Possibly," he concluded, "I have forgotten the doubts in the affairs of youth," but the more Storey thought about it the more sure he was that "the prospects of the country seem more uncertain" than they had before. As he had begun his reform career fifty years before as part of a movement for honest government, so, at the end of his life, "what troubles me is the very general corruption wherever we look."

The acquittal of Fall and Doheny in the face of unan-
swerable evidence, the general low tone of juries, the
corruption which has been shown at the elections for
the Senate . . . —all these things are discouraging. We
are trying to run a very complicated and difficult machine
with very inexperienced and inadequate officers, or me-
chanics, if that suits my illustration better. The people
in charge of our government, national and municipal,
seem to be peculiarly small men, and looking not at the
country but at their own personal advantage.

In the past, he remembered, there were always "MacVeagh,
Schurz, Charles Adams, and a good many others I might name
[whom] we could always count on for active assistance" in promoting good government. Where, Storey wondered, were the
reformers of today? [70]

As Harding's corrupt conviviality was replaced by Coolidge's
quiet subservience to big business, the figure of Wilson loomed
larger in Storey's mind. For all his segregation in Washington and
intervention in the Caribbean, Storey remembered more and more
"how cleanly Wilson governed the country with apparently no
thought except what the interests of the country demanded." It
was doubtful if there were any more Wilsons in America of the
1920's, but he saw some hope for the future in the candidacy of
Al Smith. But in a country in which "the states are infested with
the Ku Klux Klan and nothing is done to put an end to it,"
Storey doubted that Smith could overcome bigotry and win the
White House:

I should very much like to have Mr. Smith who has made
an admirable Governor, elected as President if it is possible to crush the anti-religious feeling which the Protestants
will attempt to rally against him, but what is possible I
do not know. The Democrats of this country are not
popular and the Protestants are, I think.[71]

By the time Smith was defeated in November 1928, Storey had
already suffered from the first of an eventually fatal series of
strokes. On January 1 of that year he had fallen down in his

room, and from that time until his death he was under constant medical care. For a time he seemed to improve, and he was writing cheerily that "My doctor tells me that nothing serious is the matter with me, and there is no reason why I should not go on for some years to come. . . ." But in early 1929 another stroke occurred, and in the summer Storey was moved to his favorite retreat on Great Cranberry Island, Maine. It was his last summer.[72]

Three years before he had written to one of his oldest friends,

> There are many respects "to which make calamity of so long a life," but the worst are the partings which take place, when the pleasant party which we formed for our life's journey sixty or seventy years ago breaks up. You and I have worn better than most of our party, and the best that we can hope for is a short and painless illness. . . . My own age is serene, and I enjoy my children, grand-children, and great-grandchildren, but, were it not for the fact that my continued existence makes theirs easier, I would cheerfully go tomorrow.

There was little in the America of the 1920's that would make a man like Moorfield Storey want to stay. Its intolerance and corruption disgusted him, its mindless technology frightened him, and its much-vaunted prosperity impressed him as a sham. But most of all, perhaps, it was the public "apathy which I have never seen equalled" that discouraged this last great pupil of the humanitarian reformers. "Sixty years ago life was simpler and better," Storey wrote to Charles W. Eliot, "and I think we may congratulate ourselves that we have known the world at its best." His heart had always been in the nineteenth century; and he had kept its faith in minimal government, self-determination, and civil equality in the first three decades of the twentieth. He died none too soon, on October 24, 1929; the day before the stock market began its calamitous downward spiral. Storey would not have understood the era which followed.[73]

5 ❧ The Abolitionist Tradition

D
URING the last thirty years of his life, Moorfield Storey concerned himself with an extraordinary number of public questions; and he embraced each position he took with such firmness that one is tempted to abandon the task of seeing him whole. His career was filled with apparent contradictions: he was a supporter of Bryan and Wilson, who fought the proscription of the Southern Negro; a professional colleague of Root and Hughes, who assailed their foreign policies as violations of international law; an advocate of decentralization, who demanded federal enforcement of civil rights; and a believer in laissez-faire, who defended social revolution in Latin America. Faced with these divergences, it would be easy to regard Storey as a political eclectic—to call him, as his first biographer did, "an independent"—and to dismiss the subject. But it is not that hard to find certain assumptions which lie beneath his attitudes on public questions and which hold them together, assumptions which can best be labeled "abolitionist."

The American abolitionists can most accurately be defined as all those who before the Civil War agitated for the immediate emancipation of all the slaves in the United States. While it is true that some of those who influenced the young Moorfield

Storey confined their public roles to opposing the extension of slavery, it is also true that his own attitude was shaped by those who condemned slavery in all its aspects and called for emancipation. By his own account, at least, Storey's mother was an outright abolitionist. And it is surely significant that the three acquaintances of his father who Storey claimed most influenced him were Sumner, the nearest to a pure abolitionist of all the Conscience Whigs; Lowell, active in the movement through his position on the *National Anti-Slavery Standard;* and Emerson, already in his abolitionist phase. In later years, of course, Storey's identification with the abolitionist movement was so intense that even the more radical leaders whom he had not known personally—men like Garrison and Phillips—became important models for his public career.[1]

The abolitionists regarded the Negro as oppressed not only by the fetters of slavery, but also by what they called "the spirit of caste." Accordingly, once emancipation was achieved, they devoted their attention to achieving complete equality for Negroes in political and civil rights. The Northern public, however, proved unable to sustain the moral fervor of the immediate postwar years, and gradually accepted the new patterns of discrimination and disfranchisement which Southern whites imposed on the freedmen. The high tide of racial proscription at the turn of the century seems to have propelled Storey back to the abolitionist tradition, and in his subsequent civil rights career, on the platform and in the courts, he attempted to persuade his fellow white Americans to implement the egalitarian goals proclaimed in the Fourteenth and Fifteenth Amendments.

Storey, whose life span connected the original abolitionists and the National Association for the Advancement of Colored People, steadily broadened his definition of civil equality. He had begun his civil rights career by attempting to end official discrimination in the South, attacking the disfranchisement of black voters. But then he turned his attention to those situations in which Negroes, while receiving a formal equality of rights, were in fact segregated by law. Confronted by one such "separate but equal" situation, he repeated Sumner's argument—that legal segregation imposed by the dominant whites in itself constituted legal inequality. And in his brief against the Louisville residential segregation ordinance, he argued that such segregation violated the equal protection of the laws guaranteed by the Fourteenth Amendment.

In the last decade of his life Storey sought ways of preventing denials of rights in areas long considered private, by broadening the conception of discriminatory "state action," which the Fourteenth Amendment prohibited. His joint argument with Louis Marshall against judicially enforced restrictive covenants illustrates part of this new development: where the state supported private discrimination through enforcement in the courts, it became a party to such discrimination, and thus the discrimination became "state action." At the same time, as his role in preparing the brief for the Dyer anti-lynching bill indicates, he eventually came to the conclusion that some civil rights—physical security and due process of law—were so important that the Federal government had a positive duty to enforce them when the states defaulted in their guarantee of protection. In a series of major victories won since Storey's death, subsequent NAACP attorneys have incorporated far more empirical data showing the demoralizing consequences of segregation, and they have gone even farther than Storey in re-defining "state action." But they have not altered the basic argument for civil equality first formulated by Storey on behalf of the Association.

Considered as the advocacy not only of immediate emancipation but of civil equality as well, the abolitionist tradition found one of its last representatives in Moorfield Storey. The original abolitionists, however, were more than simply champions of racial justice; they were also participants in the international liberal movement which so deeply influenced Western society in the century and a half between the American Revolution and World War I. While the composition of the abolitionist movement reflected specifically American conditions (such as the traditional sense of mission in New England) its initial assumptions were common to reformers on both sides of the Atlantic. Unlike their British counterparts, however, those middle-class reformers who became abolitionists in the United States were confronted with a slave society which, in political power and public support, exceeded their own strength. Before the appearance of the abolitionists, the South had shown little evidence of wanting to abandon slavery, and during their organization the South was engaged in a full-scale defense of the institution, claiming that it was a positive good. Operating from an increasingly consolidated sectional base, the representatives of the South were able to use their sizable influence in the national government to protect slavery legally.

To counter the entrenchment of American slavery, the abolitionists devised a particular strategy of agitation. Their portrayal of slavery as a sin which the slaveholder must immediately cease undoubtedly owed much to the revivalist background from which so many of them came, but what has perhaps not been sufficiently appreciated is the tactical nature of the abolitionist argument. The abolitionists may have reasoned that Southern society, religion, and law were so permeated with the belief in the necessity of slavery that only outside pressure could force slaveholders to examine their consciences. If they emphasized individual atrocities, it was not because they thought the planting class had a monopoly on sadism, but because the recital of such incidents seemed to them the only way they could remind their fellow Americans that brutality inevitably accompanied a system in which one man had absolute power over another. And if they demanded immediate emancipation it was at least partly because of the lessons learned from the British experience, where the abolitionists had far more influence and the slaveholders far less. But even there the initial Parliamentary legislation providing for gradual emancipation had been blocked by the delaying tactics of the West Indian planters; Parliament subsequently responded by legislating immediate emancipation. From the British example the American abolitionists might well have concluded that only by demanding immediate and total emancipation would there be any emancipation at all.[2]

The essence of slavery was the absolute power of one human being over another; and slavery had so dominated Southern society that otherwise decent men supported it. This was the foundation of the abolitionist argument, and the defense of their agitation. But various abolitionists extended the argument much further: slavery had not only corrupted the South but was beginning to corrupt the North. Men like Garrison and Phillips maintained that the slaveholders had turned the institutions of Church and State into their agents. Those of more moderate persuasion emphasized the pattern of events, from attempts to suppress congressional debate on slavery through the passage of the Fugitive Slave Law, and warned of a growing threat to civil liberties throughout the country. Still others believed that slavery, which had degraded the condition of Southern labor and caused the economic stagnation of the South, was challenging the status of Northern workers as well. And, perhaps most important in the long run, most of the abolitionists maintained that slavery had engendered a prejudice among white Americans which led even those residing in the free states to deny Negroes political and civil rights and to confine them to the lowest place in society.

Quite possibly it was the abolitionist attempt to attack slavery in all its dimensions, and link it to many of the prevailing values and institutions in American society, that limited their audience. If the radicals' increasingly sweeping attacks on Church and State did not repel Northern whites, the movement's protest against racial discrimination did. Not surprisingly, then, when the North did decide that slavery threatened free society, it did not follow the abolitionists. It turned instead to those who, by promising to prevent the expansion of slavery, would restrict its corrupting effects—but would also keep black people as far away from Northern whites as possible. The war between the sections thus came not over the question of slavery's evil, as the abolitionists might have hoped, but over its expansion; and the Emancipation Proclamation in turn came not as an act of humanitarianism, but as an expedient gesture to win the war. Only in the immediate aftermath of the Civil War, when they were able to link their goals with the Northern desire for Southern submission and with the Republican desire for party supremacy, did the abolitionists begin to move toward their goal of incorporating civil equality into national public policy.

In retrospect it is easy to see that party politics, wartime emotion, and, ironically, even race prejudice had more to do with the abolitionists' success in the 1860's than did their own efforts, and, considering these other factors, it is equally easy to conclude that their great dream of a racially egalitarian society was doomed at the outset. Yet at the time political observers were more impressed by the fact that what had been the argument of isolated abolitionists only a decade before had now become the assumptions on which government policy was based. The abolitionists had said that a free society and a slave society could not co-exist; they had said that slavery would not be destroyed until the caste system which had grown out of it was also destroyed; and now, in the aftermath of the Civil War, Republican politicians were saying the same thing. The abolitionists were only human in concluding from these developments that events were moving in their direction.[3]

It was in this environment—one in which the old abolitionists, finding their program carried forward, concluded that their efforts were responsible—that Moorfield Storey developed his basic attitudes. Later, whether by personal choice or by the direction his career had taken, he decided to maintain the values of his youth. Those values included not only a commitment to racial egalitarianism but, as the experience of the abolitionists would suggest, a persisting belief in the efficacy of agitation as a means of achieving social reform.

The concept of agitation developed by the abolitionists would play the greatest role in Storey's career not, as one might think, in connection with his work in the NAACP, but rather in his leadership in the fight for Philippine independence. No analogy was more popular among the anti-imperialists than that of the abolitionists of half a century before, and while it cannot be said that Philippine independence had the significance of emancipation, their analogy does highlight important similarities. Like the abolitionists, those championing Philippine independence were forced to move against the settled policy of the United States government; like the abolitionists they remained suspicious of their erstwhile political allies; so like the abolitionists they appealed to the conscience of the American people. Their repeated use of stories of atrocities committed by American troops in the suppression of the insurrection was part of this appeal, but it represented less an attempt to single out Americans as villains (for Storey and the other anti-imperialists were equally harsh on the record of other imperial powers) than an effort to show the brutalization that accompanied any denial of self-government. As the abolitionists believed slavery to be a sin, so the anti-imperialists believed the acquisition of the Philippine Islands to be a crime; but both groups of agitators made their maximum demands in the hope of gaining minimal agreement. On several occasions, for example, Storey stated his position that although Philippine independence was politically impossible, the Anti-Imperialist League should never yield the principle of independence for the Islands.

Moorfield Storey reached maturity during a period in which an important segment of the dominant political party seemed willing to act upon the analysis formulated by the abolitionists during their years of isolation. It was a period, in other words, in which the radical aspects of middle-class liberalism were the most pronounced; and however much their concept of agitation was softened over time, and to whatever degree civil equality could later be achieved within the existing legal and institutional framework, the heritage of the original abolitionists remained the dominant influence on Storey's career. Yet even to mention the term "radical" in connection with Storey is to raise the problem of his real position. Here was a man who was not even a progressive—a man who criticized Federal child-labor legislation, who fought the Brandeis nomination, and who opposed the organization of labor unions. How can this side of Storey be reconciled with the supposedly radical heritage of his youth?

One answer to this problem, of course, would be to deny the

argument presented here, to deny either the radicalism of the heritage or its influence upon Storey. Such an interpretation would emphasize Storey the Brahmin, member of a self-satisfied social elite whose political attitudes reduced themselves to a defense of his privileged position. This interpretation has a certain plausibility, if only because generations of progressive historians have exploited it. It does not, however, fit the facts. In the first place, for a man who supposedly defended privilege, Storey had remarkably few kind words for the rich. Indeed, from his first reflections on the ostentatious life-style of wealthy men in New York to his derisive comment that they hoped to buy salvation by endowing universities, he remained consistently critical. The defense of wealth as the surest evidence of personal merit, so common among spokesmen for the business community during this period, is totally absent from his thought. In his own mind Storey seems to have identified "the rights of property" far more with the small entrepreneurs of his youth than with the corporate elite of his maturity.[4]

Also absent from Storey's letters and speeches is the contempt for democratic government, either openly hostile or subtly manipulative, which one finds among a number of business spokesmen; for whatever reason, Storey moved in a different direction. His interest in reapportionment, in reform of the House of Representatives, and in proportional representation are surely atypical of a representative of business. At a time when businessmen increasingly turned to the Federal government to save them from the irregularities of state regulation, Storey persistently advocated an active role for the states. His attacks on a powerful presidency may have paralleled corporate sentiment (though this has been disputed), but it surely had more to do with the influence of the Radical Republican doctrine of congressional supremacy and his own fears of military intervention in Latin America than it did with purported fears of presidential leadership in economic regulation. His decision to vote Democratic in 1908, for example, seems to have come largely from his belief that Bryan's innovations in domestic policy would be more palatable than a continuation of Roosevelt's foreign policy. Finally, it is unquestionably true that Storey favored a strong judiciary, a judiciary which could, and did, nullify social legislation, but it would be difficult to find a civil rights attorney in the twentieth century who did not favor such judicial activism.[5]

There remains the Brandeis nomination, a drama which usually casts Storey in the role of an enemy of one of the permanent heroes of modern reform. To so portray Storey, however, one must ignore Brandeis's consistent advocacy of decentralization and turn him into a precursor of the New Deal; similarly, one must ignore Storey's enthusiastic support of Wilson's 1912 campaign and hold him fixed in time as a Cleveland supporter. Such an interpretation must conclude by making the supposed disagreement on policy the major issue between the two men, though the issue of Brandeis's substantive views appears nowhere in Storey's correspondence. When Storey disagreed with a man's position, he usually made that disagreement abundantly clear in his letters; but in the case of Brandeis, he continued to insist that his opposition was to Brandeis's ethics as a lawyer. Under the prevalent interpretation, we are therefore left with two conclusions: either Storey knew he was attacking Brandeis's substantive views but did not say so—which, if true, would be a singular example of deviousness in his career—or he was attacking Brandeis's views but did not know it—which is the most unsubstantiated kind of determinism.

And if Storey personally regarded Brandeis as a threat to the dominance of his own class, one might, given Storey's delight in taking on adversaries, expect him to meet the threat by persistently declaiming against Brandeis. In point of fact, however, the Brandeis affair took up very little of his attention. Even when connected with the larger issues raised by the policies of the Wilson administration, the total still occupied less of his attention than the exclusion of black lawyers from the American Bar Association several years before. Storey's opposition to the Brandeis nomination was not one of his finer moments, and his testimony at the hearings, that he spoke for a representative class of Bostonians, made him an easy target for the supporters of the nomination; but his opposition cannot fairly be interpreted as part of a larger effort at resisting social reform. It cannot be emphasized too often that however much Storey remained a laissez-faire Independent on certain social and economic questions, and however much this Independent side was reinforced by his personal associations, he was simply not involved very deeply in the debates of the progressive era. There were eminent representatives of the legal profession who toured the country shrilly warning of the consequences of legislative attempts at social justice, and Storey knew many of them. But whatever his disagreement with progressive programs, when he toured the country it was to speak out on civil rights or foreign policy.

Storey's consistent involvement in civil-rights and foreign-policy issues, and his lack of interest in social and economic problems, suggest another interpretation for the basis of his attitudes, one which would return to the abolitionist tradition itself. It has often been said that the great failure of nineteenth-century liberalism was that, arising as it did in the overthrow of tyrannical government, it remained preoccupied with fighting political oppression in an industrial era, when oppression more often was social and economic. This interpretation goes far toward explaining the limitations of the abolitionists, and even further toward explaining the limitations of Moorfield Storey, but it needs some important modifications.

There were, for example, important social and economic dimensions to the abolitionist argument against slavery. The abolitionists may have begun their attack on slavery out of their objection to the absolute power slavery gave the master, but they also included in their indictment the causal relationship between slavery and race prejudice. Accordingly, once emancipation became effective they used whatever influence they had to place the law, in the North as well as in the South, against discrimination. And, because they believed that the extension of political and civil rights to the freedman would be meaningless without a corresponding grant of economic power, they also supported the confiscation of the estates of the planters and their division into small farms for the freedman. The abolitionists' attempt to provide an economic base for the free blacks was unsuccessful: the military confiscation of land during the war was first nullified by President Johnson's pardons; and then, during the subsequent period of congressional supremacy, any attempt to re-institute confiscation was opposed by moderate Republicans. If the heritage of Reconstruction remained narrowly political, therefore, it was because of these pressures, not because the abolitionists failed to appreciate the necessity for social and economic reform.[6]

Nevertheless, the abolitionists must bear part of the blame for the national abandonment of the Negro's cause in the 1870's and 1880's. While they showed considerable insight into the problems of the freedman, they only dimly perceived the dimensions of the industrial society into which the freedman had emerged, and in this sense they did indeed fail. With few exceptions, the abolitionists revealed little sympathy with the efforts of working men to improve their condition by organizing into unions, and confronted by mounting cycles of industrial violence, many of these former radicals tended to link themselves to the most belligerent defenders of the status quo. Caught between an increasingly complacent middle class, which regarded the Negro as an object of charity, and an increasingly articulate working class, which regarded him with suspicion, the abolitionists found that for the first time they had nothing to say. And so they withdrew to their memories of great battles fought and won, or spent their time in working on pallid copies of their prewar agitation, such as civil service reform.

The abolitionists' radicalism remained linked to the issue which had brought them into existence. It had been the issue of slavery which had made them radicals; and confronting that issue, and its corollary, the position of free blacks, they were able to maintain their radicalism through Reconstruction. But as other problems came to the fore, their radicalism on that one series of issues became irrelevant, and in dealing with the industrial crisis the only weapons they had were the middle-class attitudes with which they had begun. The problem with the abolitionists, in other words, was not that they were insufficiently radical on the issue of slavery, but that they were not even reformist on any other issue.

The same problem characterized the career of Moorfield Storey when he dealt with reform. The dominant influences of his youth had been the anti-imperialism that first arose from the Mexican War and the commitment to civil equality of the abolitionist movement. Both traditions became linked in Storey's mind with Lincoln's statement that no man is good enough to govern another without that other man's consent. It might have been predicted, therefore, that the reform impulses of Storey's youth would be reawakened in the 1890's, when the principle of government by consent seemed most in jeopardy, for in that decade the blacks were disfranchised in the South and the Filipinos were forcibly conquered by the United States. As long as he dealt with the ensuing problems of civil rights and foreign policy, Storey could be quite perceptive in seeing relationships, whether, for example, between the segregation imposed by the majority and the lack of motivation on the part of the minority, or between social revolution in Latin America and the pressures for American intervention. But when he was forced to confront the more traditional social and economic issues in public debate, he was confined by the individualistic categories of nineteenth-century liberalism, and continued to emphasize formal relationships ("obedience to the law") which bore little resemblance to substantive reality (the efforts of labor to organize).

The failure of nineteenth-century liberalism—and thus the failure of both the abolitionists and of Moorfield Storey—was that its radicalism was directly connected with its opposition to the denial of political rights. It could perceive social and economic oppression when it was connected with political tyranny, as Storey did in commenting on the disfranchised and exploited tenant farmers in Arkansas and on the Mexican peasants under the Díaz dictatorship. But where political tyranny was absent, liberalism could not find—or did not choose to see—social and economic oppression. The nineteenth-century reformers failed to respond to the condition of the exploited but enfranchised working class; and these reformers, who had worked courageously for Negro suffrage, turned their backs on the efforts of white workers to organize for better working conditions.

Those are the criticisms that can be made against nineteenth-century liberalism. But to stop here is to make Storey's reform persuasion simply a function of a moment in history, and of a moment which passed over a century ago, at that. The succeeding decades have eroded many of the values in which Storey believed, and critics of nineteenth-century liberalism have pointed out that "equality before the law" became a mockery when faced with the realities of social stratification; that "laissez-faire" ignored tendencies toward economic concentration; that "the neutral state" assumed middle-class values; and even that "self-determination" masked the economic domination of small nations by more powerful ones. Do liberals like Storey have anything to say to an age which sees social and economic forces behind all political procedures and institutions?

Even as Storey was agitating for the implementation of the values with which he had been raised, a new group of reformers appeared who regarded themselves more as expert professionals than as free-wheeling critics of society and proved themselves to be less interested in appealing to the public than in educating the administrators of the government. As their tactics were different, so were their objectives, and defining equality of opportunity more broadly than Storey had ever conceived of doing, they placed the unmet needs of disadvantaged classes high on their agenda. Now, after half a century, it is possible to attempt some appraisal of the achievement of these twentieth-century reformers. Their accomplishments are impressive: the emerging assumption by government of responsibility for maintaining minimum levels of economic security for the entire population; the legal and institutional support for the organization of farmers and workers to counter business power; and the mobilization of the nation against threats to its national security and its democratic values.

And yet the costs of these reformers' achievements are sufficient to warrant at least a second look at the earlier liberal position. It is debatable, for example, whether, in spite of half a century of regulation, the dominance of American society by the large corporations has even been minimally challenged; and the organization of farmers and workers has too often proved less of a check on business power than additional participation in a consensus against either the consuming public or the unorganized poor. The steady accretion of power at the Federal level and weakening of state and local government have increased the distance between the average citizen and his government. And within the Federal government what was originally conceived by the Founding Fathers as a balance of powers has now become a system virtually dominated by the Executive.[7]

Most of all, of course, twentieth-century reformers have acquiesced in (and sometimes encouraged) the growth of a national-security bureaucracy, a bureaucracy which now seems less the servant of the elected officials than their master; and it is here that Storey's fear of governmental power speaks most forcibly to the present generation. If he viewed the progressive era partly from the perspective of one of the last Independents, he also viewed it from the perspective of one of the first anti-imperialists. He was thus less impressed, for example, with the differing attitudes of Roosevelt, Taft, and Wilson on Federal regulation of corporations than with the propensity for intervention on the part of both political parties. The progressive era for Storey, if not for historians, was the interlude between the suppression of the Philippine insurrection and the interventions in Haiti and the Dominican Republic. The growth of Federal power that most concerned him was not connected with domestic policy at all, and it is surely significant that so many of his criticisms of the Federal budget reduce themselves to attacks on increased military appropriations. It might even be argued that well before

Randolph Bourne had proclaimed that war is the health of the state, Storey saw that preparation for war was coming to constitute the chief governmental business of the century. He perceived that such preparation for war involved a shift of power—first from the public to the government, and then, within the government, from the elected representatives to the permanent bureaucracy. To him the whole process represented the greatest threat to republican institutions since the existence of slavery.

In an age, therefore, in which reformers have been more concerned with local threats to freedom than with that created by the expansion of bureaucratic power, Moorfield Storey does have something to say. Throughout his career his commitment was to freedom, freedom not only from the burdens of racial discrimination, but also freedom from the abuse of governmental power. His faith had its limitations, but it was neither ignoble nor irrelevant. It was the faith of the founders of the Republic, fortified by a generation of reformers, and neither Storey's respectable demeanor nor the enshrinement of that faith in traditional rhetoric can ever quite dim its radical quality. As he wrote on his eightieth birthday, in response to congratulatory telegrams sent by the NAACP,

> During my life I have seen slavery abolished the world over, I have seen serfdom ended in Russia, I have seen the emperors of France, Turkey, Russia, Austria, and Germany swept from their thrones and their places taken by the representatives of free people. Bearing these facts in mind I want you to realize that the tide of freedom is irresistible. Least of all countries in the world can the United States arrest this progress, as it was the first to announce the proposition that all men are created free and equal, and that all governments derive their just powers from the consent of the governed.
>
> We have only to stand fast, only to persevere in asserting our rights and we cannot be beaten.[8]

Notes

In the footnotes, the following abbreviations have been used:

COPY   unless otherwise indicated, a letter-press copy of a letter dictated by Storey from his law office

HL   Houghton Library, Harvard University

LC   Manuscripts Division, Library of Congress

MHS   Massachusetts Historical Society

EPIGRAPH

* Storey to John Marvin, April 16, 1903, copy in Storey MSS, MHS.

CHAPTER 1. THE MAKING OF A REFORMER

1. John Winthrop, "A Model of Christian Charity," in Perry Miller and Thomas H. Johnson (eds.), *The Puritans* (New York, 1938), p. 199 (spelling modernized); Moorfield Storey, "Autobiography" (unpublished), Storey MSS, MHS.

2. Francis Cabot Lowell, quoted in Storey and Edward W. Emerson, *Ebenezer Rockwood Hoar, A Memoir* (Boston, 1911), p. 302; Storey, "Autobiography," Storey MSS, MHS.

3. Storey, "Autobiography," Storey MSS, MHS; William R. Thayer (ed.), *Letters of John Holmes to James Russell Lowell and Others* (Boston, 1917), pp. 19, 60, 124, 158, 180, 192, 236, 258. Emerson records one example of Charles Storey's wit, Edward W.

Emerson and Waldo E. Forbes (eds.), *The Journals of Ralph Waldo Emerson* (10 vols., Boston, 1909–14), X, 4, and describes a camping party which Moorfield Storey joined, *Journals*, X, 149–53.

4. Storey, "Autobiography," Storey MSS, MHS.

5. Storey, "Class Oration," *Baccalaureate Sermon, and Oration and Poems, Class of 1866* (Boston, 1866), pp. 28, 29; Storey to Erving Winslow, January 3, 1919, copy in Storey MSS, MHS.

6. Storey, unpublished address at the celebration of the 150th anniversary of the town of Lincoln, Mass., April 28, 1904, copy in Storey MSS, MHS; Mariana Storey, *Family Recollections* (privately printed; Boston, 1925), p. 74.

7. Storey and Emerson, *Hoar*, pp. 9, 334, 307.

8. The current historical debate on the abolitionists is ably joined in John L. Thomas, *The Liberator: William Lloyd Garrison* (Boston, 1963), and Aileen Kraditor, *Means and Ends in American Abolitionism: Garrison and his Critics on Strategy and Tactics, 1834–1850* (New York, 1969).

9. My discussion of the Conscience Whigs is drawn primarily from David Donald, *Charles Sumner and the Coming of the Civil War* (New York, 1960); Martin Duberman, *Charles Francis Adams* (Boston, 1961); Frank Otto Gatell, *John Gorham Palfrey and the New England Conscience* (Cambridge, 1963); and William G. Bean, "Party Transformation in Massachusetts, with Special Reference to the Antecedents of Republicanism, 1848–1860" (unpublished Ph.D. dissertation, Harvard University, 1922).

10. Oscar Handlin, *Boston's Immigrants: A Study in Acculturation* (rev. ed.; Cambridge, 1958), pp. 124–50.

11. Storey, "Autobiography," Storey MSS, MHS; Charles W. Storey to Storey, October 17, 1867, Storey MSS, MHS; Storey to Thomas Sergeant Perry, April 1, 1867, microfilm copy in Perry MSS, Duke University; Storey to Perry, May 6, 1867, microfilm copy in Perry MSS, Duke.

12. Storey to Charles E. Stratton, Jr., November 22, 1867, Storey MSS, MHS; Storey to Charles W. Storey, February 4, 1868, Storey MSS, MHS.

13. On the split between Johnson and the Republican party, see esp. Eric L. McKitrick, *Andrew Johnson and Reconstruction* (Chicago, 1960), and W. R. Brock, *An American Crisis: Congress and Reconstruction, 1865–1867* (London, 1962).

14. Storey to Charles W. Storey, December 4, 1867; Storey to Charles W. Storey, March 3, 1868, both in Storey MSS, MHS.

15. Storey to Charles W. Storey, May 3, 1868, Storey MSS, MHS; Storey to Charles W. Storey, April 2, April 24, 1868, Storey MSS, MHS; Storey to Elizabeth Moorfield Storey, April 24, 1868, Storey MSS, MHS; Storey to Charles W. Storey, May 17, 1868, Storey MSS, MHS. Many years later Storey revised his opinion of Ross, writing that "it took great courage to vote as he did, for it meant his political end." Storey, "Autobiography," Storey MSS, MHS.

16. Storey to Marina Storey, February 2, 1868, Storey MSS, MHS; Storey, "Charles Sumner," in Edward W. Emerson (ed.), *The Early Years of the Saturday Club, 1855–1870* (Boston, 1918), p. 303. The historiographical controversy about Sumner the man and Sumner the Senator shows no signs of diminishing. In the first of his two-volume biography, David Donald stresses Sumner's weaknesses in both roles, a view which has been challenged by Louis Ruchames in "The Pulitzer Prize Treatment of Charles Sumner," *Massachusetts Review*, II (Summer 1961), 749–69; and by Paul Goodman, "David Donald's *Charles Sumner* Reconsidered," *New England Quarterly*, XXXVII (September 1964), 373–87.

17. Storey, *Charles Sumner* (Boston, 1900), p. 431; *The Journals of Emerson*, X, 294; Storey, "Sumner," in *The Early Years of the Saturday Club*, p. 301; Storey to Curtis Guild, Jr., January 9, 1911, copy in Storey MSS, MHS.

18. Storey, "Class Oration," pp. 27–28.

19. Henry Adams to Charles Francis Adams, Jr., May 22, 1862, in Worthington C. Ford (ed.), *A Cycle of Adams Letters, 1861–1865* (2 vols., Boston, 1918), I, 152; Charles W. Storey to Storey, February 6, 1868, Storey MSS, MHS; Storey to Mariana Storey, March 21, 1869, Storey MSS, MHS.

20. Storey to Elizabeth Moorfield Storey, March 7, 1869, Storey, MSS, MHS.

21. On Butler, see the two most recent biographies: Hans L. Trefousse, *Ben Butler: The South Called Him BEAST!* (New York, 1957), and Richard C. West, *Lincoln's Scapegoat General: A Life of Benjamin Butler, 1819–1893* (Boston, 1965); on his career as a Radical Republican, see William D. Mallam, "Butlerism in Massachusetts," *New England Quarterly*, XXXIII (June 1960), 186–206.

22. My discussion of Butler's economic program and its relationship to Radical ideology owes much to David Montgomery, *Beyond Equality: Labor and the Radical Republicans, 1862–1872* (New York, 1967), esp. pp. 72–89, 335–45, 360–68.

23. Charles W. Storey to Richard Henry Dana, Jr., October 6, 1868, Dana MSS, MHS; John G. Sproat, *"The Best Men": Liberal*

Reformers in the Gilded Age (New York, 1969), pp. 143–47, 172–82, 184–91.

24. Sproat, *"The Best Men,"* pp. 74–88; Ari V. Hoogenboom, *Outlawing the Spoils: A History of the Civil Service Reform Movement, 1865–1883* (Urbana, 1961), pp. 50–54, 60–64, 74–81, 96–101, 111–19. It is still not clear whether Storey joined the Adamses in the Liberal Republican movement of 1872. When he was very old, he wrote that he had been "entirely in sympathy with it," though only as a "spectator." (Storey to Annette C. Glick, February 25, 1924, copy in Storey MSS, MHS). Yet in the spring of 1872, when the national movement was being organized, he wrote that "the Administration in many respects has done extremely well while in others it is open to severe criticism," and that while he too "was anxious for a change if we can get a better candidate than Grant," he was "unwilling by an ill-considered division to bring a Democrat to power." (Storey to E. L. Godkin, March 19, 1872, hand-written draft in Storey MSS, MHS.)

25. Storey to R. R. Bowker, November 16, 1896, copy in Storey MSS, MHS; John A. Garraty, *Henry Cabot Lodge* (New York, 1953), pp. 40–50; Sproat, *"The Best Men,"* pp. 88–103; Storey to the Republican State Committee, September 13, 1876, draft in Scrapbook No. 1, Storey MSS, LC.

26. [Henry and Brooks Adams], "The Independents in the Canvass," *North American Review,* CXXXIII (October 1876), 461; Montgomery, *Beyond Equality,* pp. 379–386; Sproat, *"The Best Men,"* pp. 7–10, 60–66.

27. Hoogenboom, *Outlawing the Spoils,* pp. 190–97; Geoffrey Blodgett, *The Gentle Reformers: Massachusetts Democrats in the Cleveland Era* (Cambridge, 1966), pp. 19–31; Storey, "Autobiography," Storey MSS, MHS; Storey to John D. Long, July 28, 1881, Long MSS, MHS; Storey to Long, July 29, 1881, Long MSS, MHS.

28. Richard Hammond, "The 'Beast' in Boston: Benjamin F. Butler as Governor of Massachusetts," *Journal of American History,* LV (September 1968), 266–80; Storey to Henry Cabot Lodge, June 14, 1883, Lodge MSS, MHS; Storey to Lodge, July 10, 1883, Lodge MSS, MHS; Storey to Lodge, August 9, 1883, Lodge MSS, MHS. Storey's pamphlet was *The Record of Benjamin Butler. Compiled from the Original Sources.* (Boston, 1883). His specific charges—(a) that while posing as a champion of labor, Butler underpaid his mill hands; (b) that as a Union General occupying Baltimore, he permitted trading with the Confederates; (c) that he received part of the profits his associate John B. Sanborn made from collecting taxes; and (d) that he pocketed funds allocated for a soldier's home—are regarded

as unproved by Trefousse (pp. 166, 220, 228, 241) and are largely ignored by West.

29. Sproat, *"The Best Men,"* pp. 112–30; Blodgett, *The Gentle Reformers,* pp. 1–11; Allan Nevins, *Grover Cleveland, A Study in Courage* (New York, 1932), p. 161; [Storey], *Mr. Blaine's Record: The Investigation of 1876 and the Mulligan Letters* (Boston, 1884); Storey, memorandum to James Ford Rhodes, December 18, 1908, copy in Storey MSS, MHS.

30. Horace S. Merrill, *Bourbon Leader: Grover Cleveland and the Democratic Party* (Boston, 1957), pp. 25–43, 91–97; Blodgett, *The Gentle Reformers,* pp. 48–52, 63–65; Cleveland, quoted in Nevins, *Cleveland,* p. 215; Storey to John Forrester Andrew, August 7, 1887, Andrew MSS, MHS.

31. Storey, *Politics as a Duty and as a Career* (New York, 1889), pp. 4–5.

32. Barbara M. Solomon, *Ancestors and Immigrants: A Changing New England Tradition* (Cambridge, 1956), esp. pp. 99–119; Storey, *A Year's Legislation. The Address of . . . [the] President of the American Bar Association, Delivered at Saratoga Springs, August 19, 1896* (Philadelphia, 1896), pp. 36–37; Storey, *The Government of Cities. The Need of a Divorce of Municipal Business from Politics. An Address . . . Delivered at Buffalo, New York, September 30, 1891* (Buffalo, 1891), p. 7; Storey, *Politics as a Duty and as a Career,* p. 6; Storey, address at Harvard College, February 20, 1894, reprinted in *Civil Service Chronicle,* undated clipping in Storey MSS, MHS; Storey, *Politics as a Duty and as a Career,* p. 29.

33. Blodgett, *The Gentle Reformers,* pp. 146–47, 155–58; Richard Hofstadter, *Anti-Intellectualism in American Life* (New York, 1963), pp. 180–81; Storey, *The Government of Cities;* Storey to William H. Brown, August 13, 1907, copy in Storey MSS, MHS; Hoogenboom, *Outlawing the Spoils,* pp. 21–22, 71–72; Sproat, *"The Best Men,"* pp. 250–58.

34. On the Independents in the Democratic party, Blodgett, *The Gentle Reformers,* pp. 53–69, 82–99; on the dispute with Quincy, transcript of meeting of the Massachusetts Reform Club, October 7, 1893, Storey MSS, MHS; Nevins, *Cleveland,* pp. 517–18.

35. Blodgett, *The Gentle Reformers,* pp. 205–14, 226–29; [Storey], "The Political Situation," *Atlantic Monthly,* LXIX (January 1892), 121; Winslow Warren to Storey, July 4, 1896, Storey MSS, MHS; Storey to Carl Schurz, July 9, 1896, Schurz MSS, LC; John M. Palmer, *Personal Recollections* (New York, 1901), p. 619.

36. The hysteria of Bryan's opponents is pointed out in C. Vann Woodward, "The Populist Heritage and the Intellectual," *American*

Scholar, XXIX (Winter 1959–60), 67–69, and developed further in J. Rogers Hollingsworth, *The Whirligig of Politics: The Democracy of Cleveland and Bryan* (Chicago, 1964), pp. 69–73, 87–90.

37. Arnold M. Paul, *Conservative Crisis and the Rule of Law: Attitudes of Bar and Bench, 1887–1895* (Ithaca, 1961), pp. 229–35; Storey, *The American Legislature. The Annual Address . . . before the American Bar Association, Delivered at Saratoga Springs, August 22, 1894* (reprinted, 1894), p. 16.

38. Storey, *The American Legislature,* pp. 19–25; Storey, *A Year's Legislation,* p. 3; Storey, *Speech . . . as Chairman at the National Democratic Convention, September 30, 1897* (reprinted, 1897), pp. 3–4.

39. Storey, *Speech at National Democratic Convention,* p. 7; McKinley, quoted in Claude M. Fuess, *Carl Schurz, Reformer* (New York, 1932), p. 349.

40. Gabriel Kolko, "Brahmins and Business: A Hypothesis on the Social Basis of Success in American History," in Barrington Moore and Robert Paul Wolff (eds.), *The Critical Spirit: Essays in Honor of Herbert Marcuse* (Boston, 1967), pp. 343–63; Edward C. Kirkland, *Dream and Thought in the Business Community, 1860–1900* (Ithaca, 1956), pp. 115–43; George M. Frederickson, *The Inner Civil War: Northern Intellectuals and the Crisis of the Union* (New York, 1965), pp. 201–11.

41. Henry Lee Higginson to James Ford Rhodes, December 27, 1906, quoted in Bliss Perry, *Life and Letters of Henry Lee Higginson* (Boston, 1920), p. 402. The most accurate account of the membership can be found in Virginia Harlow, *Thomas Sergeant Perry* (Durham, 1950), p. 46. The initial members were Henry and William James, William Dean Howells, Arthur G. Sedgwick, John C. Ropes, John Chipman Gray, Charles Grinnell, William E. Perkins, Henry Adams, Oliver Wendell Holmes, Jr., John T. Morse, Jr., John R. Dennett, and Thomas Sergeant Perry. Then Storey, Wendell P. Whalley, Charles Hale, Dr. John C. Warren, and Dr. John Homans, Jr., were admitted. In later years, Higginson, Alexander Agassiz, Edward Hooper, Rhodes, Lord Camperdown, William S. Bigelow, Raphael Pumpelly, and Bliss Perry became members.

42. My discussion here is based on the three-volume biography of Henry Adams by Ernest Samuels: *The Young Henry Adams* (Cambridge, 1947), *Henry Adams: The Middle Years* (Cambridge, 1958), and *Henry Adams: The Major Phase* (Cambridge, 1964); on the two volumes Mark DeWolfe Howe was able to complete in his biography of Holmes: *Justice Oliver Wendell Holmes: The Shaping Years, 1841–1870* (Cambridge, 1957) and *The Proving Years, 1870–1882* (Cambridge, 1963); and on the two-volume study of James by

Ralph Barton Perry: *The Thought and Character of William James* (Boston, 1935).

43. Perry to Storey, July 30, 1882, microfilm copy in Perry MSS, Duke University. Storey was similarly uninterested in the work of another close friend, Dr. James Jackson Putnam, a neurologist and one of the first Freudian psychoanalysts in the United States.

44. Samuel Eliot Morison, *Three Centuries of Harvard, 1636–1936* (Cambridge, 1936), pp. 266, 298; Storey, "Autobiography," Storey MSS, MHS.

45. Samuels, *Young Henry Adams*, pp. 16–31; Storey, "Harvard in the Sixties," address before the Harvard Memorial Society, Cambridge, April 3, 1896, reprinted in the *Harvard Graduates' Magazine*, V (March 1897), 330–31, 335.

46. Howe, *Holmes: The Shaping Years*, p. 156; Storey to Helen Appleton, January 12, 1868, Storey MSS, MHS; Howe, *Holmes: The Proving Years*, pp. 149–50, 160–68.

47. Storey to Charles Francis Adams, Jr., June 23, 1906, copy in Storey MSS, MHS; Storey, address to the Twentieth Century Club, February 13, 1901, quoted in *City and State*, X (February 28, 1901), 138.

48. On Storey's defense of classical languages, Storey to Charles J. Bonaparte, March 29, 1898; Storey to Albert S. Perkins, February 3, 1917, copies in Storey MSS, MHS. On Norton, Storey to Sara Norton, November 8, 1908, Norton MSS, HL; Kermit Vanderbilt, *Charles Eliot Norton: Apostle of Culture in a Democracy* (Cambridge, 1959), esp. pp. 194–220; Charles Eliot Norton to Samuel G. Ward, July 14, 1897, in Sara Norton and Mark A. DeWolfe Howe (eds.), *The Letters of Charles Eliot Norton* (2 vols., Boston, 1913), II, 254.

49. Storey to Sara Norton, April 5, 1914, Norton MSS, HL.

50. Untitled clipping in Scrapbook No. 2, Storey MSS, LC; Storey, "Autobiography," Storey MSS; Storey, *Minority Report of the Joint Committee on the Regulation of Athletic Sports, to the Board of Overseers, Harvard University, February 27, 1907* (Cambridge, 1907), p. 28; Storey, *Address in Behalf of the Class of 1866 at the Harvard Alumni's Commencement Dinner, 1891* (reprinted, 1891), n. p.

51. Frederickson, *The Inner Civil War*, pp. 166–76, 217–25; Storey, address at the Charleston College commencement, June 14, 1904, reprinted in the Charleston *News-Courier*, June 19, 1904.

52. Storey, "Autobiography," Storey MSS, MHS; Charles W. Storey to Storey, August 3, 1862, Storey MSS, MHS; Storey, "Harvard

in the 'Sixties," p. 337. Storey was hardly exceptional: the *Roll of Students of Harvard College who Have Served in the Army or Navy During the War of the Rebellion. Commemoration Day, July 31, 1865* (Cambridge, 1865) shows that only 6 men out of Storey's class served, compared with 54 from each of the classes of 1860 and 1861.

53. Storey, "Harvard in the 'Sixties," pp. 337–38; Storey, address at the American Peace Society banquet, May 18, 1903, reprinted in *The Advocate of Peace*, LXV (June 1903), 112.

54. Storey, "Autobiography," Storey MSS, MHS; interview with Charles M. Storey, May 3, 1965; Storey to John Jay Chapman, October 3, 1923, copy in Storey MSS, MHS. Storey definitely voted Republican in 1868, 1876, 1880, and 1916. He may have supported the Liberal Republicans' Greeley in 1872, and did support the National Democrats' Palmer in 1896. He was still recuperating from a stroke during the election of 1928, but probably voted for Smith, about whom he had been enthusiastic earlier that year.

55. Boston *Journal*, November 8, 1900. Storey's platform (contained in a broadside issue by his campaign committee), the tabulation of the District vote, and his record of campaign finances can all be found in Scrapbook No. 2, Storey MSS, LC.

56. Storey to Erving Winslow, May 5, 1904, copy in Storey MSS, MHS; Storey to Herbert Welsh, October 15, 1908, copy in Storey MSS, MHS; Storey to Charles Francis Adams, Jr., August 22, 1912, in Mark A. DeWolfe Howe, *Portrait of an Independent: Moorfield Storey, 1845–1929* (Boston, 1932), p. 302; Oswald Garrison Villard, *Fighting Years: Memoirs of a Liberal Editor* (New York, 1939), pp. 277–78.

57. Storey to Chapman, October 3, 1923, Storey MSS, MHS; Storey, *The American Legislature*, p. 17.

58. James Russell Lowell, "The Place of the Independent in Politics," in *The Writings of James Russell Lowell* (11 vols., Boston, 1892), VI, 213; Storey, *Problems of Today* (Cambridge, 1920), p. 45; Irving Bartlett, "The Persistence of Wendell Phillips," in Martin Duberman (ed.) *The Antislavery Vanguard: New Essays on the Abolitionists* (Princeton, 1965), especially pp. 114–20; Storey, *Problems of Today*, p. 49.

59. Storey to John C. Hemphill, June 28, 1902, copy in Storey MSS, MHS; Storey, unpublished address to the Whittier Club, Haverhill, Mass., December 13, 1905, copy in Storey MSS, MHS.

60. Storey, unpublished address at the Garrison centennial, Boston, December 11, 1905, copy in Storey MSS, MHS.

61. Storey, address at the Garrison centennial, Storey MSS, MHS; Storey, "The Purposes of the Club," in Massachusetts Reform

Club, *Secretary's Report and List of Members for the Year Ending Dec. 1, 1900* (Boston, 1901), p. 21.

CHAPTER 2 ANTI-IMPERIALISM

1. John Higham, *Strangers in the Land: Patterns of American Nativism, 1860–1925* (New Brunswick, 1955), p. 76.

2. Wallace E. Davies, *Patriotism on Parade: The Story of Veterans' and Hereditary Organizations in America, 1783–1900* (Cambridge, 1955), pp. 215–48; Carl Schurz, quoted in Edward L. Pierce, *Memoir and Letters of Charles Sumner* (4 vols.; Boston, 1877–93), IV, 509. Though the whole subject has never been systematically studied, Merle Curti's early investigations appear to indicate rising popular hostility to opponents of foreign war—a factor perhaps correlating with the diminishing number of those opponents—in 1846, 1898, and 1917: see his *The American Peace Crusade, 1815–1860* (Durham, 1929), pp. 126–28; and his *Peace or War: The American Struggle* (New York, 1936), pp. 169–71, 249–61. Unfortunately, Peter Brock's recent study of the ideology and organization of peace groups, *Pacifism in America: From the Colonial Era to the First World War* (Princeton, 1968), does not even raise this question.

3. The most suggestive analysis of this mood of the 1890's, and one to which I am greatly indebted, is Richard Hofstadter, "Manifest Destiny and the Philippines," in Daniel Aaron (ed.), *America in Crisis* (New York, 1952), pp. 173–200.

4. Ernest R. May, *Imperial Democracy: The Emergence of the United States as a Great Power* (New York, 1961), pp. 33–42, 56–65, 69–93.

5. May, *Imperial Democracy*, pp. 112–59; H. Wayne Morgan, *William McKinley and His America* (Syracuse, 1963), pp. 340–78; John A. S. Grenville and George B. Young, *Politics, Strategy, and Diplomacy: Studies in Foreign Policy, 1873–1917* (New Haven, 1966), pp. 248–49, 262–68.

6. Grenville and Young, *Politics, Strategy, and Diplomacy*, pp. 269–82.

7. Storey to Schurz, November 11, 1895, Schurz MSS, LC; Storey, *A Civilian's View of the Navy. Lecture Delivered to the Naval War College, September 8, 1897* (Washington, 1897), p. 13; Storey, "Nothing to Excuse Our Intervention," address to the Massachusetts Reform Club, April 8, 1898, reprinted in *The Advocate of Peace*, LX (May 1898), pp. 112–14.

8. For the early organizational history of the League, see Maria Lanzar-Caprio, "The Anti-Imperialist League," Part I, *Philippine Social Science Review*, III (August 1930), 7–41.

9. The name of the New England organization changed as follows: before the national federation in 1898, it called itself the Anti-Imperialist League; under the national federation, from 1899 to 1904, the New England Anti-Imperialist League; and after 1904, the Anti-Imperialist League. It was the only anti-imperialist organization to publish the reports of its annual meetings, and it numbered them consecutively.

10. For the most recent analysis of the various factors which led to the annexation of the Philippines but which did not produce annexations thereafter, see Ernest R. May, *American Imperialism: A Speculative Essay* (New York, 1968). May, however, defines imperialism— as Storey did not—solely as the extension of territorial control.

11. Storey to Wilbur L. Cross, August 2, 1917, copy in Storey MSS, MHS.

12. These statistics, compiled at the beginning of the American occupation, are taken from J. Ralston Hayden, *The Philippines: A Study in National Development* (New York, 1942), pp. 12, 578–88, 604. Hayden compares the relationship of the major Filipino languages to the Romance languages in the West. In addition, of course, educated Filipinos were fluent in Spanish.

13. Not surprisingly, both American administrators at the time, and Filipino historians today, concur in painting a picture of Spanish oppression and incompetence: see as examples Charles B. Elliott, *The Philippines: To the End of the Military Regime* (Indianapolis, 1916), pp. 160–81; and Teodoro Agoncillo, *The Revolt of the Masses: Andres Bonifacio and the Katipunan* (Quezon City, 1956), pp. 1–17.

14. Leon Wolff, *Little Brown Brother: How the United States Purchased the Philippine Islands at the Century's Turn* (Garden City, 1960), pp. 34–35, 45–54, 66–70; Teodoro Agoncillo, *Malolos: The Crisis of the Republic* (Quezon City, 1960), pp. 73–74, 121–35, 146–55.

15. Julius W. Pratt, *Expansionists of 1898: The Acquisition of Hawaii and the Spanish Islands* (Baltimore, 1935) pp. 1–22, 230–316; Walter LaFeber, *The New Empire: An Interpretation of American Expansion, 1860–1898* (Ithaca, 1963), pp. 300–311, 352–57, 370–93, 403–6; Morgan, *McKinley and His America*, pp. 388–89, 397–98; Grenville and Young, *Politics, Strategy, and Diplomacy*, pp. 286–87.

16. On developments within the Philippines at this point, see Agoncillo, *Malolos*, esp. pp. 215–310.

17. Morgan, *McKinley and His America*, pp. 407–15.

18. Of the steadily increasing literature on the anti-imperialist movement, I have found the following the most helpful: Fred H. Harrington, "The Anti-Imperialist Movement in the United States, 1898–1900," *Mississippi Valley Historical Review*, XXII (September 1935), 211–30; Paolo E. Coletta, "McKinley, Bryan, and the Treaty of Paris," *Pacific Historical Review*, XXVI (May 1957), 131–46; Christopher Lasch, "The Anti-Imperialists, the Philippines, and the Inequality of Man," *Journal of Southern History*, XXIV (August 1958), 319–31; Richard E. Welch, Jr., "George F. Hoar and the Defeat of Anti-Imperialism, 1898–1900," *The Historian*, XXVI (May 1964), 362–80; and Robert L. Beisner, *Twelve Against Empire: The Anti-Imperialists, 1898–1900* (New York, 1968).

19. E. Berkeley Tompkins, "Scylla and Charybdis: The Anti-Imperialist Dilemma in the Election of 1900," *Pacific Historical Review*, XXXVI (May 1967), 143–62; Storey to Schurz, August 21, 1900, Schurz MSS, LC; Storey to John Jay Chapman, September 3, 1900, copy in Storey MSS, MHS; Storey, interview in the Boston *Herald*, September 15, 1900.

20. Throughout the debate over annexation, many anti-imperialists coupled their argument that holding the Filipinos as subjects violated the American tradition of government with the argument that admitting the Filipinos as citizens would demoralize American politics. Significantly, Storey seems to have used this appeal to racial fears only once, and that was *before* 1898 and in connection with the proposed annexation of *Hawaii*. Storey, *Speech . . . as Chairman at the National Democratic Convention, September 30, 1897*, p. 19.

21. Storey, letter in the Boston *Herald*, July 29, 1898; Storey and Marcial L. Lichauco, *The Conquest of the Philippines by the United States, 1898–1925* (New York, 1925) v; Storey to Edwin Burritt Smith, June 27, 1899, copy in Storey MSS, MHS.

22. Storey to Smith, June 27, 1899, copy in Storey MSS, MHS; Storey to Mrs. William H. Forbes, October 1, 1905, in Mark A. De-Wolfe Howe, *Portrait of an Independent: Moorfield Storey, 1845–1929* (Boston, 1932), pp. 238–39.

23. Storey, unpublished address at Ashfield, Mass., August 17, 1899, copy in Storey MSS, MHS; Storey to George McAneny, May 24, 1899, copy in Storey MSS, MHS.

24. Storey, letter in the Boston *Herald*, July 29, 1898; Storey, *Is It Right? An Address Delivered at the Philadelphia Conference, February 21, 1900* (Chicago, 1900), pp. 7–9; Storey, letter in the Chicago *Record*, September 28, 1900; Storey, speech at Brookline, Mass., October 26, 1900, in *Our New Departure* (Boston, 1901), pp. 23–26.

25. Storey, speech at Brookline, Mass., in *Our New Departure*, pp. 15–16.

26. All these arguments appear successively, for example, in Lodge's speech in the Senate, March 7, 1900, in *Speeches and Addresses, 1884–1909* (Boston, 1909), pp. 315–75.

27. Storey, letter to a friend, October 21, 1899, in *Our New Departure*, pp. 8–10; Storey, letter in the Boston *Transcript*, September 13, 1900.

28. Storey, unpublished address to the National Liberty Congress, Indianapolis, Indiana, August 15, 1900, copy in Storey MSS, MHS; Storey, speech at Brookline, Mass., in *Our New Departure*, p. 33; Storey, *What Shall We Do With Our Dependencies? The Annual Address before the Bar Association of South Carolina, Delivered at Columbia, January 16, 1903* (Boston, 1903), pp. 19–22.

29. Storey to Richard Henry Dana, III, October 31, 1904, copy in Storey MSS, MHS; Storey, unpublished address at Saratoga Conference, August 20, 1898, copy in Storey MSS, MHS; Storey, *What Shall We Do With Our Dependencies?*, p. 21; Storey, address to the eighth annual meeting of the Anti-Imperialist League, in *Report of the Eighth Annual Meeting . . . November 24, December 3, 1906* (Boston, 1907), p. 24; Storey, *What Shall We Do With Our Dependencies?*, pp. 8–9; Storey, address to the seventh annual meeting of the Anti-Imperialist League, in *Report of the Seventh Annual Meeting . . . November 25–27, 1905* (Boston, 1905), p. 22.

30. Storey, *What Shall We Do With Our Dependencies?* p. 6; Storey to James Bradley Thayer, November 3, 1899, copy in Storey MSS, MHS; Storey, unpublished address to the Whittier Club of Haverhill, Mass., December 13, 1905, copy in Storey MSS, MHS.

31. Storey, *What Shall We Do With Our Dependencies?*, p. 55; Thomas J. McCormick, in *Studies on the Left*, III, No. 1 (1962), 28–33, and LaFeber, *The New Empire*, pp. 412–14; Storey, *What Shall We Do With Our Dependencies?*, p. 18; Storey, *The Philippine Policy of Secretary Taft Analyzed* (Boston, 1904), p. 17; Storey to Charles W. Eliot, August 5, 1907, copy in Storey MSS, MHS; Storey to Woodrow Wilson, October 24, 1911, copy in Storey MSS, MHS.

32. For the Sargent–Wilcox report, see Agoncillo, *Malolos*, pp. 429–31.

33. Storey, *What Shall We Do With Our Dependencies?*, pp. 57–58; Storey to E. L. Ordway, December 1, 1905, copy in Storey MSS, MHS; Storey, address to the sixteenth annual meeting of the Anti-Imperialist League, in *Report of the Sixteenth Annual Meeting . . . December 7, 1914* (Boston, 1914), p. 30; Erving Winslow, report to the seventeenth annual meeting of the Anti-Imperialist

League, in *Report of the Seventeenth Annual Meeting . . . February 28, 1916* (Boston, 1916), p. 9; William E. Dodd to Storey, February 15, 1917, Storey MSS, MHS.

34. George S. Boutwell, address to the first annual meeting of the Anti-Imperialist League, in *Report of the [First] Annual Meeting . . . November 25, 1899* (Boston, 1900), p. 15; Storey to Winifred T. Denison, January 8, 1915, copy in Storey MSS, MHS; Lanzar-Caprio, "The Anti-Imperialist League," pp. 26–28; Harrington, "The Anti-Imperialist Movement in the United States," pp. 223–24; *De-Lima* v. *Bidwell,* 182 U.S. 1 (1901) and *Downes* v. *Bidwell,* 182 U.S. 244 (1901); Storey, anti-imperialist petition, written about July 1901, draft in Storey MSS, LC. To discuss Storey's continuing involvement in Philippine affairs would be beyond the scope of this book; I have tried to suggest his general approach to those problems. A full-length study of the movement for Philippine independence during Storey's lifetime—or for that matter, a study of American administration of the Islands—waits to be written. Theodore Friend, *Between Two Empires: The Ordeal of the Philippines, 1929–1946* (New Haven, 1965), covers the later period.

35. David F. Healy, *The United States in Cuba, 1898–1902* (Madison, 1963), pp. 85–92, 153–64; Dana G. Munro, *Dollar Diplomacy and Intervention in the Caribbean, 1900–1920* (Princeton, 1964), pp. 37–60, 66–77.

36. Bryce Wood, *The Making of the Good Neighbor Policy* (New York, 1961), pp. 4–5; Munro, *Dollar Diplomacy and Intervention,* pp. 12–20, 112–16; Elihu Root, address at the National Convention for the Extension of the Foreign Commerce of the United States, January 14, 1907, in Robert Bacon and James B. Scott (eds.), *Latin America and the United States. Addresses by Elihu Root* (Cambridge, 1917), p. 275.

37. Storey, "President Wilson's Administration," *Yale Review,* New Series, V (April 1916), 460; Storey, address to the fifteenth annual meeting of the Anti-Imperialist League, in *Report of the Fifteenth Annual Meeting . . . November 24, December 8, 1913* (Boston, 1913), p. 40.

38. My account of Farnham's role, and of the execution of policy generally, follows that in Munro, *Dollar Diplomacy and Intervention,* pp. 331–56, and in Arthur S. Link, *Wilson: The Struggle for Neutrality, 1914–1915* (Princeton, 1960), pp. 518–36.

39. Munro, *Dollar Diplomacy and Intervention,* pp. 356–87; Ludwell L. Montague, *Haiti and the United States, 1714–1938* (Durham, 1939), pp. 209–33; Paul H. Douglas, "The Political History of the Occupation," in Emily G. Balch (ed.), *Occupied Haiti* (New York, 1927), pp. 15–36.

40. Storey, draft of a petition to Congress on the recognition of Panama, November 1903, copy in Storey MSS, MHS; Storey to Pitman B. Potter, May 13, 1921, copy in Storey MSS, MHS.

41. Against fears of foreign intervention, Storey, speech at Brookline, Mass., in *Our New Departure*, p. 29; Link, *Wilson: The Struggle for Neutrality*, p. 535. Against the need to protect persons and property, Storey to Samuel W. McCall, August 19, 1907, copy in Storey MSS, MHS. Against the "mission" to spread democracy, Storey, address to the eighth annual meeting of the Anti-Imperialist League, in *Report of the Eighth Annual Meeting . . . November 24, December 3, 1906* (Boston, 1906), p. 32.

42. Storey to Winslow, September 30, 1915, copy in Storey MSS, MHS; Storey, "A Plea for Honesty," *Yale Review*, New Series, VII (January 1918), 275; Charles Flint Kellogg, *NAACP: A History of the National Association for the Advancement of Colored People*, Vol. I: *1909–1920* (Baltimore, 1967), pp. 284–88; Storey to Charles Evans Hughes, June 6, 1921, copy in Storey MSS, MHS.

43. On the various arguments against the occupation, Foreign Policy Association, *The Seizure of Haiti by the United States* (New York, 1922) esp. pp. 14–15. On the expansion of presidential power, Storey, "President Wilson's Administration," pp. 459–60; Storey to William E. Borah, December 4, 1916, copy in Storey MSS, MHS; Storey to Robert M. LaFollette, November 6, 1924, copy in Storey MSS, MHS.

44. Frank Tannenbaum, *Mexico: The Struggle for Peace and Bread* (New York, 1950), pp. 36–48; Howard F. Cline, *The United States and Mexico* (rev. ed.; Cambridge, 1963), pp. 51–56.

45. Link, *Wilson: The New Freedom* (Princeton, 1956), pp. 347–416; Storey to Wilson, August 28, 1913, copy in Storey MSS, MHS; Storey to Wilson, April 25, 1914; Storey, "President Wilson's Administration," pp. 458–59.

46. Link, *Wilson: The Struggle for Neutrality*, pp. 232–66, 456–94, 629–44; Link, *Wilson: Confusions and Crises, 1915–1916* (Princeton, 1964), pp. 195–221, 280–316; Link, *Wilson: Campaigns for Progressivism and Peace, 1916–1917* (Princeton, 1965), pp. 51–55, 120–23, 328–39; Storey to A. Lawrence Lowell, June 23, 1916, copy in Storey MSS, MHS; David Starr Jordan, *Days of a Man* (Yonkers-on-Hudson, 1922), II, 690–703; Storey to George M. Hunter, December 27, 1916, copy in Storey MSS, MHS.

47. Tannenbaum, *Mexico: The Struggle for Peace and Bread*, pp. 103–12; Cline, *The United States and Mexico*, p. 230.

48. Cline, *The United States and Mexico*, pp. 189–203.

49. Storey to McCall, August 19, 1907, copy in Storey MSS, MHS.

50. Storey to the editor of the Boston *Transcript,* July 24, 1919, copy in Storey MSS, MHS; Storey to Charles L. H. Wagner, January 14, 1920, copy in Storey MSS, MHS.

51. Storey, *What Shall We Do With Our Dependencies?,* p. 41; Storey to Potter, May 13, 1921, copy in Storey MSS, MHS.

52. Storey, *Problems of Today* (Cambridge, 1920), pp. 234–35.

53. Storey, *Problems of Today,* p. 236; Storey to Wagner, January 14, 1920, copy in Storey MSS, MHS; Storey to Guy Stevens, April 8, 1926, copy in Storey MSS, MHS; Storey to Stevens, May 4, 1926, copy in Storey MSS, MHS.

54. Charles Sumner, "The True Grandeur of Nations," address of July 4, 1845, in *The Works of Charles Sumner* (15 vols., Boston, 1870–83), I, 9–10, 18, 51.

55. Sumner, "The Law of Human Progress," oration of July 25, 1848, in *Works,* II, 115; Arthur A. Ekirch, *The Idea of Progress in America, 1815–1860* (New York, 1944), pp. 258–59; Storey, unpublished introduction to Sumner, "The True Grandeur of Nations," apparently written in 1899, copy in Storey MSS, MHS.

56. Storey, "Sumner's Argument Against War Corroborated by Subsequent Events," address before the American Peace Society banquet, May 18, 1903, reprinted in *The Advocate of Peace,* XV (June 1903), 111. In his "True Grandeur" speech, Sumner had announced that he would not "throw doubt on the employment of force in the administration of justice or the conservation of domestic quiet," but would limit the object of his concern to war between nations. Sumner, *Works,* I, 15–16.

57. Statement of National Arbitration Committee, January 25, 1897, copy in Storey MSS, MHS; Storey to W. Murray Crane, January 29, 1909, copy in Storey MSS, MHS.

58. Storey to Henry F. May, November 16, 1914, copy in Storey MSS, MHS; Storey, "President Wilson's Administration," p. 461; Storey to R. M. Thompson, January 27, 1915, copy in Storey MSS, MHS; Storey to Wilson, October 7, 1915, copy in Storey MSS, MHS; Storey to Alexander Sedgwick, April 18, 1916, copy in Storey MSS, MHS.

59. Storey to Winslow, November 4, 1914, copy in Storey MSS, MHS; Storey to May, November 16, 1914, copy in Storey MSS, MHS.

60. I find more persuasive the discussion of Villard's position in Michael Wreszin, *Oswald Garrison Villard: Pacifist at War* (Bloom-

ington, 1966), pp. 38–74, than Link's inclusion of him in the "pro-Ally moderate" category in *The Struggle for Neutrality*, pp. 9–19. The category of "pro-Ally moderate" fits Storey far better than Villard, because the latter's pro-Ally sympathies were more than offset by his opposition to war.

61. Note, for example, Storey's comment in a letter to Charles Francis Adams, Jr.: "I cannot help thinking that you state the case of Lee with great fairness, and for myself, I never doubted that if the Massachusetts of my youth had seceded, I should have followed the flag." Storey to Adams, February 4, 1914, in Howe, *Portrait of an Independent*, p. 307.

62. Storey to Emil Ahlborn, January 18, 1915, copy in Storey MSS, MHS; Storey to Charles E. S. Wood, October 17, 1917, copy in Storey MSS, MHS. His major wartime statement of this position was *The Right Ethical Attitude of the American People Towards the German People. Address Delivered before the Twentieth Century Club, May 9, 1918* (Boston, 1918).

63. Storey, address to the Anti-Imperialist League, in *Report of the Sixteenth Annual Meeting*, p. 26.

64. Storey, address to the eighteenth annual meeting of the Anti-Imperialist League, in *Report of the Eighteenth Annual Meeting . . . December 18, 1916* (Boston, 1917), p. 26; Storey, *The Right Ethical Attitude of the American People*, p. 1.

65. Storey to Wood, October 17, 1917, copy in Storey MSS, MHS; Storey to the editor of *The Public*, May 10, 1919, copy in Storey MSS, MHS; Storey to Bryce, June 4, 1919, copy in Storey MSS, MHS; Storey to Bryce, March 13, 1919, copy in Storey MSS, MHS.

66. Storey to Frank B. Kellogg, June 19, 1919, copy in Storey MSS, MHS.

67. Storey to Bryce, March 3, 1917, copy in Storey MSS, MHS; Ruhl J. Bartlett, *The League to Enforce Peace* (Chapel Hill, 1944), pp. 69–72.

68. Storey to William H. Short, August 11, 1916, copy in Storey MSS, MHS.

69. Bartlett, *The League to Enforce Peace*, pp. 132–156; Storey to the editor of the Boston *Herald*, September 19, 1919, copy in Storey MSS, MHS.

70. Storey, *Problems of Today*, p. 247; Storey to Winslow, January 9, 1919, copy in Storey MSS, MHS.

71. Storey to Bryce, March 13, 1919, copy in Storey MSS, MHS. The reservation concerning the Monroe Doctrine, the fifth in Lodge's fourteen, could not have been phrased more offensively as far as someone of Storey's persuasion was concerned: "The United States will not submit to arbitration or to inquiry by the assembly or by the council of the league of nations . . . any questions which in the judgment of the United States depend upon or relate to . . . the Monroe Doctrine; said doctrine is to be interpreted by the United States alone and is hereby declared to be wholly outside the jurisdiction of said league of nations. . . ." Reprinted in Thomas A. Bailey, *Woodrow Wilson and the Great Betrayal* (New York, 1944), p. 389.

72. Storey to William Howard Taft, June 23, 1916, copy in Storey MSS, MHS; Storey to Short, August 11, 1916, copy in Storey MSS, MHS; Taft to Storey, August 14, 1919, Storey MSS, MHS.

73. Storey to Taft, December 29, 1919, copy in Storey MSS, MHS.

74. My conclusions as to why Storey urged rejection of the Treaty, rather than acceptance with the Lodge reservations, are admittedly speculative. But there is no doubt that he did move from initial support to opposition during 1919, as is revealed by his letters to Senator Gilbert M. Hitchcock, October 27, 1919, and Senator Frank B. Kellogg, November 11, 1919, copies in Storey MSS, MHS.

75. Storey to Crane, November 26, 1919, copy in Storey MSS, MHS; Storey to A. Barr Comstock, October 20, 1920, copy in Storey MSS; Storey to Fabian Franklin, October 9, 1920, copy in Storey MSS, MHS; Storey to Ralph DaVol, October 21, 1920, copy in Storey MSS, MHS. By the election of 1920 Storey had joined Irving Fisher's dissidents within the League to Enforce Peace, who called themselves the Pro-League Independents. This group supported ratification with only the "clarifying" amendments agreed to by Wilson and Senate Democratic leader Hitchcock, and they urged the election of Cox. Bartlett, *The League to Enforce Peace*, pp. 197–99.

76. Storey to Hughes, November 15, 1921, copy in Storey MSS, MHS; Storey to James Ford Rhodes, December 17, 1925, copy in Storey MSS, MHS; petition in support of the continuation of U.S. negotiations to enter the World Court, some time in 1927, copy in Storey MSS, LC; Storey to Princess Salm-et-Dyck, December 1, 1924, copy in Storey MSS, MHS.

77. Carel Grunder and William A. Livesey, *The Philippines and the United States* (Norman, Okla., 1951), pp. 162–83; Storey to W. Cameron Forbes, January 2, 1924; Storey to Calvin Coolidge, March 6, 1924, copies in Storey MSS, MHS; Montague, *Haiti and*

the United States, pp. 234–37; Judson King to Storey, May 1, 1922, Storey MSS, LC; Louis Marshall to Storey, May 11, 1922, Storey MSS, MHS; Cline, *The United States and Mexico,* pp. 203–10.

78. My discussion of the Nicaraguan intervention follows the accounts in Isaac J. Cox, "Nicaragua and the United States, 1909-1927," *World Peace Foundation Pamphlets,* X (Boston, 1927), 783-89; and Wood, *The Making of the Good Neighbor Policy,* pp. 13–23.

79. Storey to Borah, January 8, 1927, copy in Storey MSS, MHS; Storey, "Nicaragua and the Policy Our Government Has Pursued," *Century Magazine,* CXV (February 1928), 446; Storey to F. B. Livingstone, May 3, 1927, copy in Storey MSS, MHS.

80. The anti-imperialism of "isolationists" such as Borah was suggested by William A. Williams, in "The Legend of 'Isolationism' in the 1920's," *Science and Society,* XVIII (Winter 1954), pp. 10–13; and is developed further in Barton J. Bernstein and Franklin A. Leib, "Progressive Republican Senators and American Imperialism, 1898–1916: A Reappraisal," *Mid-America,* L. (July 1968), esp. pp. 167–68, 204–5.

CHAPTER 3   CIVIL EQUALITY

1. Oswald Garrison Villard, *Fighting Years: Memoirs of a Liberal Editor* (New York, 1939); Mary White Ovington, *The Walls Came Tumbling Down* (New York, 1947).

2. Charles Sumner, "Equality before the Law: The Unconstitutionality of Separate Colored Schools in Massachusetts," in *The Works of Charles Sumner* (15 vols., 1870–83), II, 364; *Roberts v. City of Boston,* 59 Mass. (5 Cush.) 198 (1849). For the abolitionist re-definition of equality, see particularly two articles by Louis Ruchames: "Race, Marriage, and Abolition in Massachusetts," *Journal of Negro History,* XL (July 1955), 250–73; and "Jim Crow Railroads in Massachusetts," *American Quarterly,* VIIII (Spring 1956), 61–75.

3. Edward L. Pierce, *Memoir and Letters of Charles Sumner* (4 vols., Boston, 1877–93), IV, 175–83; W. R. Brock, *An American Crisis: Congress and Reconstruction, 1865–1867* (London, 1962), 78–79; Ronald B. Jager, "Charles Sumner, the Constitution, and the Civil Rights Act of 1875," *New England Quarterly,* XLIII (September 1969), 350–72.

4. On the Japanese, Storey to Robert L. O'Brien, April 15, 1924, copy in Storey MSS, MHS; Storey to Charles Evans Hughes, April 16, 1924, copy in Storey MSS, MHS. On the Armenians, Storey to Augustus P. Loring, November 20, 1922, copy in Storey MSS, MHS.

Quotation, Storey, address at the Sumner memorial meeting, January 6, 1911, quoted in *The Crisis*, I (February 1911), 5.

5. On the post-1870 Reconstruction coalition, James M. McPherson, "Grant or Greeley? The Abolitionist Dilemma in the Election of 1872," *American Historical Review*, LXXI (October 1965), 48–61. On the emerging opposition, Patrick W. Riddleberger, "The Break in the Radical Ranks: Liberals vs. Stalwarts in the Election of 1872," *Journal of Negro History*, XLIV (April 1959), 136–57; Riddleberger, "The Radicals' Abandonment of the Negro during Reconstruction," *JNH*, XLV (April 1960), 88–102; and William B. Hesseltine, "Economic Factors in the Abandonment of Reconstruction," *Mississippi Valley Historical Review*, XXII (September 1935), 191–210.

6. For evidence of the various motivations listed above, see Charles Francis Adams, Jr., to Charles Francis Adams, letters of July 28, 1862, and November 2, 1864, in Worthington C. Ford (ed.), *A Cycle of Adams Letters, 1861–1865* (2 vols., Boston, 1920), I, 171–72; II, 215–17; James Russell Lowell to Mrs. Charles Russell Lowell, September 14, 1876, in Mark A. deWolfe Howe (ed.), *New Letters of James Russell Lowell* (New York, 1932), p. 221; E. L. Godkin to Charles Eliot Norton, letters of February 28, 1865, April 13, 1865, in Rollo Ogden, *The Life and Letters of Edwin Lawrence Godkin* (New York, 1907), II, 45–49. The connection between laissez-faire and the abandonment of Reconstruction is pointed out in Guion G. Johnson, "The Ideology of White Supremacy, 1876–1910," in Fletcher M. Green (ed.), *Essays in Southern History* (Chapel Hill, 1947), pp. 128–30; and in George M. Frederickson, *The Inner Civil War: Northern Intellectuals and the Crisis of the Union* (New York, 1965), pp. 192–94.

7. Storey, quoted in Claude M. Fuess, *Carl Schurz, Reformer* (New York, 1932), p. 389; Carl Schurz to Charles Sumner, August 2, 1865, in Frederick Bancroft (ed.), *Speeches, Correspondence, and Political Papers of Carl Schurz* (6 vols., New York, 1913) I, 268; Schurz speech in the Senate, May 19, 1870, ibid., I, 496; Schurz, speech in the Senate, January 30, 1872, ibid., II, 327; Schurz to Rutherford B. Hayes, February 4, 1877, ibid., III, 389.

8. The argument that segregation arose out of slavery as a means of racial subordination is developed by Richard C. Wade, *Slavery in the Cities: The South, 1820–1860* (New York, 1964), pp. 266–78, and Joel Williamson, *After Slavery: The Negro in South Carolina during Reconstruction, 1861–1877* (Chapel Hill, 1965), pp. 274–99; but they do not seem to me to invalidate the general thesis of C. Vann Woodward in *The Strange Career of Jim Crow* (2nd rev. ed., New York, 1966), pp. 11–109, that there was a significant difference between previous patterns of segregation and the institutionaliza-

tion of Jim Crow after 1890. Woodward's thesis has been supported by a number of state studies: see Charles E. Wynes, *Race Relations in Virginia, 1870–1902* (Charlottesville, 1961); Frenise A. Logan, *The Negro in North Carolina, 1876–1894* (Chapel Hill, 1964); George B. Tindall, *South Carolina Negroes, 1877–1900* (Columbia, 1952); and Vernon L. Wharton, *The Negro in Mississippi, 1865–1890* (Chapel Hill, 1947).

9. Thomas Wentworth Higginson, "Some War Scenes Revisited," *Atlantic Monthly*, XLII (July 1878), 1–9; *U.S. v. Cruikshank*, 92 U.S. 542 (1875); *U.S. v. Harris*, 106 U.S. 629 (1883); *Civil Rights Cases*, 109 U.S. 3 (1883); Stanley P. Hirshson, *Farewell to the Bloody Shirt: Northern Republicans and the Southern Negro, 1877–1893* (Bloomington, 1962), pp. 123–42.

10. Gilbert T. Stephenson, *Race Distinctions in American Law* (New York, 1910), pp. 299–310; V. O. Key, Jr., *Southern Politics in State and Nation* (New York, 1949), pp. 617–20.

11. Thomas P. Bailey, *Race Orthodoxy in the South* (New York, 1914), p. 40; Woodward, *Strange Career of Jim Crow*, pp. 49–51, 116–18.

12. James K. Vardaman, quoted in Heber Ladner, "James Kimble Vardaman, Governor of Mississippi, 1904–1908," *Journal of Mississippi History*, II (October 1940), 177; Thomas Nelson Page, "The Negro, The Southerner's Problem," *McClure's*, XXII (April 1904), 624.

13. Benjamin Tillman, quoted in Mark Sullivan, *Our Times: The United States, 1900–1915* (6 vols., New York, 1926–35) III, 136; Edgar Gardner Murphy, *The Basis of Ascendancy* (New York, 1910), p. 27.

14. Hirshson, *Farewell to the Bloody Shirt*, pp. 251–52.

15. Theodore Roosevelt to Henry Lee Higginson, February 11, 1907, in Elting E. Morison (ed.), *The Letters of Theodore Roosevelt* (8 vols., Cambridge, 1951–54), V, 585; James Ford Rhodes, memorandum of conversation with Roosevelt, May 16, 1908, in Mark A. De-Wolfe Howe, *James Ford Rhodes, Historian* (New York, 1929), pp. 168–69; Roosevelt to Sir Harry Johnson, July 11, 1908, in *Letters*, VI, 1126; Rhodes, memorandum of conversation with Roosevelt, November 16, 1905, in Howe, *Rhodes*, p. 120; Roosevelt to Lincoln Steffens, June 5, 1908, in *Letters*, VI, 1052; Seth M. Scheiner, "President Theodore Roosevelt and the Negro, 1901–1908," *Journal of Negro History*, XLVII (July 1962), 168–82.

16. R. B. Bean, quoted in Charles S. Johnson and Horace Mann Bond, "The Investigation of Racial Differences Prior to 1910," *Journal*

of *Negro Education,* III (July 1934), 331; Robert Cruden, *James Ford Rhodes: The Man, The Historian, His Work* (Cleveland, 1961), p. 224.

17. James Ford Rhodes, *The History of the United States from the Compromise of 1850 to the Final Restoration of Home Rule at the South in 1877* (8 vols., New York, 1893–1906), V, 556; VII, 149, 104, 168, 75.

18. E. Franklin Frazier, "Sociological Theory and Race Relations," *American Sociological Review,* XII (June 1947), 265–71; Franklin Giddings, *Principles of Sociology* (New York, 1903), pp. 17–18, 328.

19. *Civil Rights Cases,* 109 U.S. 3 (1883); *Plessy v. Ferguson* 163 U.S. 357 (1896); *Louisville, New Orleans, and Texas Rail Road v. Mississippi,* 133 U.S. 587 (1890); *Hall v. deCuir,* 95 U.S. 485 (1877). See the careful analyses of Barton J. Bernstein: "Case Law in *Plessy v. Ferguson," Journal of Negro History,* XLVII (July 1962), 192–98; and *"Plessy v. Ferguson:* Conservative Sociological Jurisprudence," *Journal of Negro History,* XLVIII (July 1963), 196–205.

20. Schurz to Storey, June 26, 1903, in Storey MSS, MHS; Schurz, "Can the South Solve the Negro Problem?", in *Speeches, Correspondence,* VI, 343. For a parallel interpretation to this discussion see James M. McPherson, "The Antislavery Legacy," in Barton J. Bernstein (ed.), *Towards A New Past: Dissenting Essays in American History* (New York, 1968), esp. pp. 145–48.

21. [Storey,] *To the Voters of Massachusetts* broadside by the Independent Cleveland Headquarters (Boston, 1892); interview with Charles M. Storey, May 3, 1965; Storey, *Politics as a Duty and as a Career* (New York, 1889), p. 5; Storey, unpublished address at the 70th birthday dinner of Carl Schurz, March 2, 1899, copy in Storey MSS, MHS.

22. Abraham Lincoln, speech at Peoria, October 16, 1854, in Roy P. Basler (ed.), *The Collected Works of Abraham Lincoln* (9 vols., New Brunswick, 1953–55), II, 266; Storey, address, in *Anti-Imperialism: Speeches at the Meeting in Faneuil Hall, June 15, 1898* (Boston, 1898), p. 22; Storey, interview in the Boston *Herald,* September 19, 1900; Storey, *The Importance to America of Philippine Independence. Address Delivered before the Harvard Democratic Club at the Harvard Union, Cambridge, October 28, 1904* (Boston, 1904), p. 9.

23. Storey, *Negro Suffrage Is Not a Failure. Address before the New England Suffrage Conference, March 30, 1903* (Boston, 1903), pp. 7, 16.

24. Charles Francis Adams, Jr., *The "Solid South" and the Afro-American Race Problem. Address in Richmond, Virginia, October*

28, 1908 (Richmond, 1908), p. 17; Rhodes, *History,* VI, vii; Cruden, *Rhodes,* p. 95; Storey to James Ford Rhodes, May 12, 1906, copy in Storey MSS, MHS.

25. Adams, The *"Solid South,"* p. 19; Storey to Charles Francis Adams, Jr., February 4, 1914, in Mark A. DeWolfe Howe, *Portrait of an Independent: Moorfield Storey, 1845–1929* (Boston, 1932), p. 307; Storey, *Charles Sumner* (Boston, 1900), pp. 287, 300, 322; Storey to Adams, February 11, 1914, copy in Storey MSS, MHS; "Notes," *Journal of Negro History,* XVI (January 1930), 123.

26. Storey's first exposure to Boas seems to have occurred when he was already president of the NAACP. He wrote to DuBois that "there was a course of Lowell Lectures . . . on the so-called 'inferior races' in which the lecturer [probably Boas] reached conclusions most favorable to our cause." (Storey to W. E. B. DuBois, November 22, 1910, copy in Storey MSS, MHS.) Charles W. Eliot, letter to the editor, Springfield *Republican,* February 26, 1913; Storey, letter in the *Republican,* February 17, 1913. I do not wish to demean Eliot's championship of either immigrants in general or Jews in particular, but his defense of minorities—like that of Theodore Roosevelt, a very different man—seems to have been confined to the white race and its "assimilable" ethnic groups. Unlike Storey, Eliot accepted the "necessity" both for the retention of the Philippines and for segregated facilities in the South: see Henry James, *Charles W. Eliot* (Boston, 1930), II, 53–54, 118–19, 166–68, 210–11.

27. Storey to Alexander Lawton, June 25, 1923, copy in Storey MSS, MHS; Storey, unpublished draft of a speech, possibly of that given before the Boston branch of the NAACP, December 1, 1913, copy in Storey MSS, LC.

28. Storey to N. F. Lamb, February 16, 1913, copy in Storey MSS, MHS; Storey, letter to an unnamed newspaper, clipping in Scrapbook No. 2, Storey MSS, LC.

29. Storey to A. Shuman, March 25, 1913; Storey to Marion L. Burton, October 14, 1913, copy in Storey MSS, MHS; Storey to DuBois, June 1, 1917, copy in Storey MSS, MHS.

30. Storey to Albert E. Pillsbury, March 4, 1912, copy in Storey MSS, MHS; Stephen S. Geogory to Storey, March 25, 1912, Storey MSS, MHS. The irony is that Gregory, like Storey, had a sense of social responsibility far beyond that of his colleagues: in 1894, for example, along with Lyman Trumbull and Clarence Darrow, he had defended Eugene Debs against prosecution by the Federal government. (James G. Rogers, *American Bar Leaders: Biographies of the Presidents of the A.B.A., 1878–1928* [Chicago, 1932], pp. 167–68.)

31. Storey, petition to the members of the American Bar Association, some time in 1912, copy in Storey MSS, LC; Storey to

Chauncey Hackett, April 12, 1913, copy in Storey MSS, MHS; Storey to E. Furness, April 30, 1913, copy in Storey MSS, MHS; Storey to Lucien H. Alexander, February 11, 1914, copy in Storey MSS, MHS; Storey to James C. Crosby, October 24, 1919, copy in Storey MSS, MHS.

32. Storey to Richard Haughton, February 27, 1913, copy in Storey MSS, MHS; Storey to F. Chauncey Stowell, April 6, 1925, copy in Storey MSS, MHS; Harry Starr, "The Affair at Harvard," *Menorah Journal,* VIII (October 1922), 263–76; Henry A. Yeomans, *Abbott Lawrence Lowell* (Cambridge, 1948) pp. 165–75, 209–17; Dan W. Dodson, "College Quotas and American Democracy," *American Scholar,* XV (Summer 1946), 275.

33. Storey to Julian W. Mack, June 6, 1922, copy in Storey MSS, MHS; Storey to Charles C. Jackson, June 20, 1922, copy in Storey MSS, MHS; Lewis Gannett to Oswald Garrison Villard, June 2, 1922, Villard MSS, HL; Storey to William D. Foulke, June 16, 1922, copy in Storey MSS, MHS; Gannett to Storey, August 2, 1922, Storey MSS, LC.

34. Open Letter to the President and Fellows of Harvard College, attached to letter from Gannett to Storey, June 2, 1922, copy in Storey MSS, LC. Among those who signed the petition were Heywood Broun, Herbert Croly, Ernest Gruening, Walter Lippmann, Robert Morss Lovett, Samuel Eliot Morison, and Oswald Garrison Villard.

35. New York *World,* January 11, 1923; *The New York Times,* January 15, 1923.

36. Storey to John B. Olmstead, January 20, 1923, copy in Storey MSS, MHS; Storey to John Jay Chapman, January 18, 1923, copy in Storey MSS, MHS; Henry W. Holmes, "The University: Spring Term," *Harvard Graduates' Magazine,* XXXI (June 1923), 531–34.

37. Storey to Charles E. Ward, March 30, 1906, copy in Storey MSS, MHS; Storey to Adams, November 19, 1908, copy in Storey MSS, MHS.

38. Storey to DuBois, September 21, 1910, copy in Storey MSS, MHS; William English Walling, "The Race War in the North," *Independent,* LXV (September 3, 1908), 534.

39. "Call," quoted in Mary White Ovington, *How the National Association for the Advancement of Colored People Began* (New York, 1914), p. 2; Charles Flint Kellogg, *NAACP: A History of the National Association for the Advancement for Colored People,* Vol. I: *1909–1920* (Baltimore, 1967), pp. 9–45.

40. August Meier, *Negro Thought in America, 1880–1915: Racial Ideologies in the Age of Booker T. Washington* (Ann Arbor, 1963), pp. 100–118, 171–206; Francis L. Broderick, *W. E. B. DuBois, Negro Leader in a Time of Crisis* (Stanford, 1959), pp. 62–92; Stephen R. Fox, *The Guardian of Boston: William Monroe Trotter* (New York, 1970), 49–80.

41. Storey to Booker T. Washington, December 12, 1902, copy in Storey MSS, MHS; Storey to DuBois, October 24, 1907, copy in Storey MSS, MHS; Storey to Ellen F. Mason, March 17, 1911, copy in Storey MSS, MHS.

42. Charles W. Puttkammer and Ruth Worthy, "William Monroe Trotter, 1872–1934," *Journal of Negro History*, XLIII (October 1958), 304; Fox, *The Guardian of Boston*, pp. 127–41.

43. Storey to DuBois, September 14, 1910, copy in Storey MSS, MHS; Storey to DuBois, October 20, 1910, copy in Storey MSS, MHS; Storey to DuBois, November 19, 1910, copy in Storey MSS, MHS; Storey to William Monroe Trotter, December 1, 1910, copy in Storey MSS, MHS; Storey to Trotter, January 11, 1911, copy in Storey MSS, MHS.

44. Storey to Horace Bumstead, March 10, 1914, copy in Storey MSS, MHS; Storey to Villard, October 17, 1911, copy in Storey MSS, MHS; Kellogg, *NAACP*, pp. 94–115; Elliott M. Rudwick, "W. E. B. DuBois in the Role of *Crisis* Editor," *Journal of Negro History*, XLIII (July 1958), 214–40; Storey to Villard, November 21, 1914, copy in Storey MSS, MHS.

45. Storey to DuBois and Mrs. DuBois, December 29, 1921, copy in Storey MSS, MHS; Storey to May C. Nerney, August 27, 1913, copy in Storey MSS, MHS; Storey to Villard, November 3, 1911, copy in Storey MSS, MHS; Ovington, *The Walls Came Tumbling Down*, p. 111.

46. Broderick, *DuBois*, pp. 100–105; Storey to Francis B. Sears, May 6, 1911, copy in Storey MSS, MHS; Storey to Bumstead, March 10, 1914, copy in Storey MSS, MHS; Ovington, *The Walls Came Tumbling Down*, pp. 21–24.

47. Broderick, *DuBois*, p. 94; Storey, Open Letter to Colored Voters, October 1912, copy in Storey MSS, LC; Arthur S. Link, "The Negro as a Factor in the Campaign of 1912," *Journal of Negro History*, XXXII (January 1947), 81–99.

48. Wilson, quoted in Ray Stannard Baker, *Woodrow Wilson: His Life and Letters* (Garden City, 1927–39), I, 54; Oswald Garrison Villard, *Fighting Years: Memoirs of a Liberal Editor* (New York, 1939), pp. 236–38; Kathleen H. Wolgemuth, "Woodrow Wilson's

Appointment Policy and the Negro," *Journal of Southern History*, XXIV (November 1958), 457–71.

49. Wilson to H. A. Bridgman, September 8, 1913, in Baker, *Wilson*, IV, 223; see, in general, Wolgemuth, "Woodrow Wilson and Federal Segregation," *Journal of Negro History*, XLIV (April 1959), 158–73, and August Meier and Elliott M. Rudwick, "The Rise of Segregation in the Federal Bureaucracy, 1900–1930," *Phylon*, XXVIII (Summer 1967), 178–84.

50. Storey, unpublished draft of a speech, possibly of that given before the Boston branch of the NAACP, December 1, 1913, copy in Storey MSS, LC.

51. Storey to Villard, September 11, 1913, copy in Storey MSS, MHS; Storey to Ray Stannard Baker, May 26, 1925, copy in Storey MSS, MHS; Storey to William A. Ketcham, November 16, 1914, copy in Storey MSS, MHS.

52. Wolgemuth, "Woodrow Wilson and Federal Segregation," p. 171; Meier and Rudwick, "The Rise of Segregation in the Federal Bureaucracy," p. 181; Storey to Andrew J. Peters, April 4, 1914, copy in Storey MSS, MHS; Rayford W. Logan, *The Betrayal of the Negro: From Rutherford B. Hayes to Woodrow Wilson* (New York, 1965), pp. 363–64; Storey to Villard, March 30, 1915, copy in Storey MSS, MHS; *Crisis*, XIII (November 1916), 12.

53. Storey to Mary White Ovington, July 8, 1920, copy in Storey MSS, MHS; Richard B. Sherman, "The Harding Administration and the Negro: A Lost Opportunity," *Journal of Negro History*, XLIX (July 1964), 151–68; James Weldon Johnson, statement in NAACP press release, December 8, 1922, copy in Storey MSS, LC; Storey to Johnson, November 16, 1922, copy in Storey MSS, MHS; William T. Andrews and Walter White, memorandum of 1928 investigation, copy in Storey MSS, LC; Storey to Johnson, December 2, 1924, copy in Storey MSS, MHS; Storey to Johnson, April 12, 1926, copy in Storey MSS, MHS; Storey to Johnson, September 14, 1927, copy in Storey MSS, MHS.

54. Storey to Trotter, November 1, 1920, copy in Storey MSS, MHS; Storey to Kelly Miller, September 25, 1905, copy in Storey MSS, MHS. On Dixon and the film made from his book, see Raymond A. Cook, "The Man Behind *Birth of a Nation*," *North Carolina Historical Review*, XXIX (Autumn 1962), 519–40.

55. *Crisis*, X (May 1915), 40–42; Wilson quoted in Cook, "The Man Behind *The Birth of a Nation*," p. 530; Hodding Carter, "Furl That Banner?," *The New York Times Magazine* (July 25, 1965), p. 13; Albert E. Pillsbury, statement in *Fighting a Vicious Film* (Boston, 1915), p. 23.

56. *Crisis*, X (June 1915), 87–88; Villard, Statement in *Fighting a Vicious Film*, p. 20; Storey, statement in *Fighting a Vicious Film*, p. 22.

57. Ovington, *The Walls Came Tumbling Down*, p. 129.

58. Storey to Villard, October 17, 1912, copy in Storey MSS, MHS; Storey to Johnson, December 28, 1921, copy in Storey MSS, MHS; Johnson to Storey, December 30, 1921, Storey MSS, LC. The Association estimated that by 1923 Storey had given $6000, as well as his legal services. William Pickens, statement in "The Moorfield Storeys, the Ovingtons, and the Jews," NAACP press release, January 1923, copy in Storey MSS, LC.

59. *Strauder* v. *West Virginia*, 100 U.S. 303 (1880); *Yick Wo* v. *Hopkins*, 118 U.S. 356 (1886). The NAACP was prepared to work within the "separate but squal" framework until its final onslaught against school segregation after *Sweatt* v. *Painter*, 339 U.S. 629 (1950). A case within that framework, which distantly involved Storey, was *McCabe* v. *Atchinson, Topeka & Santa Fe Railway Company*, 235 U.S. 151 (1914). The effect of the decision, which involved the constitutionality of an Oklahoma statute limiting Pullman accommodations to whites, was weakened, however, because the Negro plaintiffs had not actually sought accommodations and could not point to any denial of their rights. The NAACP participated in the case, but Storey did not, because, as he put it, "it seemed to me that the petitioners did not state a case which would justify the Court in granting the relief and deciding the question." Storey to Trotter, December 2, 1914, copy in Storey MSS, MHS. See also Charles S. Mangum, *The Legal Status of the Negro* (Chapel Hill, 1940), pp. 203–7. The Court did decide that equal accommodations must be provided in all interstate Pullman facilities in *Mitchell* v. *U.S.*, 313 U.S. 80 (1941).

60. *Williams* v. *Mississippi*, 170 U.S. 213 (1898); *Mills* v. *Green*, 189 U.S. 475 (1903); *Giles* v. *Teasley*, 193 U.S. 146 (1903); *Jones* v. *Montague*, 194 U.S. 147 (1904); Mangum, *Legal Status of the Negro*, pp. 394–405.

61. The Court had held that the government had the power to prosecute denials of the suffrage in Federal elections in *Ex parte Yarbrough*, 110 U.S. 651 (1884).

62. Storey to Bolton Smith, March 11, 1921, copy in Storey MSS, MHS; Storey to Trotter, January 7, 1921, copy in Storey MSS, MHS; Storey to Nerney, August 6, 1915, copy in Storey MSS, MHS. Storey thought action to enforce the second section of the Fourteenth Amendment could be brought either by a state, "to ask the Supreme Court by mandamus to compel a statute making a new apportion-

ment," or by a citizen's suit, "that the officers of a state be restrained from acting under the current apportionment." He acknowledged that the second section, if enforced, might also restrict the representation of those Northern states with literacy tests. Storey to Turner M. Hackman, September 20, 1916, copy in Storey MSS, MHS.

3. *Brief for the N.A.A.C.P. in Frank Guinn and J. J. Beal* vs. *the United States, in the Supreme Court, October Term, 1913* (Washington, 1913), p. 4; *Guinn* v. *U.S.*, 238 U.S. 347, 362, 365 (1915). The following year the Oklahoma legislature enacted a statute allowing all those who had voted under the old amendment to re-register in a sixteen-day period; others (i.e., Negroes) could enroll only with the approval of registrars. This statute was finally declared unconstitutional by the Court in *Lane* v. *Wilson*, 307 U.S. 268 (1939).

64. *Love* v. *Griffith*, 266 U.S. 32 (1924); Mangum, *Legal Status of the Negro*, pp. 405–16; Storey to Walter White, January 10, 1925, copy in Storey MSS, MHS; Storey to Johnson, April 20, 1926, copy in Storey MSS, MHS; *Brief for Plaintiff in Error, L. A. Nixon against C. C. Herndon and Charles Porres, in the Supreme Court, October Term, 1925* (Washington, 1925): *Nixon* v. *Herndon*, 273 U.S. 536, 540–41 (1927). Following the decision the state legislature repealed all primary legislation and allowed each party to set its own qualifications. This, the Supreme Court said, was still "state action," therefore unconstitutional: *Nixon* v. *Condon*, 286 U.S. 73 (1932). Then the state Democratic convention adopted an exclusionary policy; this, the Court said, could be permitted: *Grovey* v. *Townsend*, 295 U.S. 45 (1935). A decade later, using a decision involving election frauds in Louisiana (*U.S.* v. *Classic*, 313 U.S. 299) which stated that primaries were an integral part of the election process, the Court ruled unconstitutional all primaries excluding any citizen because of his race: *Smith* v. *Allwright*, 321 U.S. 649 (1944).

65. *In re Lee Sing*, 43 Fed. 359 (C.C.N.D., Cal., 1890); against municipal segregation, *State* v. *Gurry*, 121 Md. 534, 88 Atl. 228 (1913); *State* v. *Darnell*, 166 N.C. 300, 81, S.E. 338 (1914); upholding such segregation, *Hopkins* v. *City of Richmond*, 177 Va. 692, 86 S.E. 139 (1915); *Harris* v. *City of Louisville*, 165 Ky. 559, 117 S.W. 472 (1915); *Harden* v. *City of Atlanta*, 157 Ga. 248, 93 S.E. 401 (1917). See also Mangum, *Legal Status of the Negro*, pp. 140–46.

66. *Harris* v. *City of Louisville*, 165 Ky. 559; Roger L. Rice, "Residential Segregation by Law, 1910–1917," *Journal of Southern History*, XXIV (May 1968), 179–99.

67. *Brief for the Plaintiff in Error on Rehearsing, in Charles H. Buchanan* vs. *William Warley, in the Supreme Court, October Term, 1916* (Washington, 1916), pp. 11–12.

68. Ibid., pp. 22, 17, 33.

69. Ibid., p. 45.

70. Mangum, *Legal Status of the Negro*, p. 139; Jack Greenberg, *Race Relations in American Law* (New York, 1959), pp. 277–78; *Buchanan* v. *Warley*, 245 U.S. 60, 80–81 (1917).

71. Storey to Wells Blodgett, September 15, 1916, copy in Storey MSS, MHS; Storey to Villard, November 5, 1917, copy in Storey MSS, MHS.

72. Mangum, *Legal Status of the Negro*, pp. 149–51; *Buchanan* v. *Warley*, 245 U.S. 60, 82 (1917); Storey to W. Hayes McKenney, November 23, 1922, copy in Storey MSS, MHS.

73. My conclusions about the use of the Fourteenth Amendment in the brief is a deduction from two pieces of evidence. Marshall was hesitant about arguing that the Fourteenth Amendment applied to the District. Louis Marshall to Storey, September 24, 1925, in Charles Reznikoff (ed.), *Louis Marshall, Champion of Liberty: Selected Papers and Addresses* (Philadelphia, 1957), pp. 461–62. But in the brief, nine pages were spent arguing this very point, placing heavy emphasis on the implication of the Court's decision in the Insular Cases of 1901, *deLima* v. *Bidwell*, 182 U.S. 1. *Brief for Appellants, in Irene Hand Corrigan and Helen Curtis vs. John J. Buckley, in the Supreme Court, October Term, 1925* (Washington, 1925), pp. 17–26.

74. Storey to Marshall, December 3, 1924, copy in Storey MSS, MHS; Marshall to Johnson, September 25, 1924, in *Selected Papers and Addresses*, pp. 459–60; Marshall to Storey, December 12, 1924, ibid., pp. 460–61; *Brief for Appellants, Corrigan and Curtis* vs. *Buckley*, p. 40.

75. *Corrigan* v. *Buckley*, 271 US. 323 (1926); Storey to Johnson, May 26, 1926, copy in Storey MSS, MHS; *Shelley* v. *Kraemer*, 334 U.S. 1 (1948); *Hurd* v. *Hodge*, 334 U.S. 241 (1948). Many commentators on the *Shelley* case have been misled by the Court's assertion that it was not considering the "validity" of the covenants—as supposedly it had in *Corrigan*—but only the constitutionality of their enforcement. However, as we have seen, it was precisely the issue of their enforcement in the courts that Storey and Marshall had emphasized in their brief. It would be more accurate to say that a different Court, two decades later, had reinterpreted the concept of "state action" to include such judicial enforcement. In any case, five years later, in *Barrows* v. *Jackson*, 346 U.S. 349 (1953), the Court deprived covenants of whatever legal "validity" they still possessed by ruling that damage suits against the sellers were also unconstitutional.

76. Storey to Katharine C. Ireson, March 10, 1924, copy in Storey MSS, MHS; Storey to Alice H. Frye, February 19, 1923, copy in Storey MSS, MHS; Storey to Johnson, March 20, 1925, copy in Storey MSS, MHS; Storey to George L. Paine, February 9, 1928, copy in Storey MSS, MHS.

77. Johnson, telegram to Storey on behalf of the Association, June 29, 1925, Storey MSS, MHS.

78. Storey, statement in NAACP press release, December 20, 1926, copy in Storey MSS, MHS.

CHAPTER 4. OBEDIENCE TO THE LAW

1. Storey, *Problems of Today* (Cambridge, 1920), p. 60; Storey, *Address on Lawlessness. Read at the Ninth Annual Meeting of the Maryland State Bar Association, April 28, 1904* (Baltimore, 1904), p. 1.

2. John P. Roche, *The Quest for the Dream: The Development of Civil Rights and Human Relations in Modern America* (New York, 1963), p. 107.

3. J. Joseph Huthmacher, *Massachusetts People and Politics 1919–1933* (Cambridge, 1959), pp. 23–28; Storey to Richard Henry Dana, III, October 31, 1904, copy in Storey MSS, MHS; Storey to John Morton, June 26, 1919, copy in Storey MSS, MHS.

4. Storey to Michael J. Jordan, October 17, 1919, copy in Storey MSS, MHS; Storey, *Problems of Today*, pp. 131–32, 148; Storey to William D. Foulke, December 19, 1922, copy in Storey MSS, MHS.

5. Storey to Raymond Calkins, May 1, 1915, copy in Storey MSS, MHS; Storey, introduction to Louis F. Post, *The Deportations Delirium of Nineteen-Twenty* (Chicago, 1923), x.

6. Storey, *Problems of Today*, pp. 100, 58, 60; Storey to Charles Francis Adams, Jr., February 11, 1907, copy in Storey MSS, MHS; Storey, *Charles Sumner* (Boston, 1900), pp. 120–21.

7. Storey to R. D. Weston, November, 18, 1924, copy in Storey MSS, MHS; Storey to William R. Stayton, January 13, 1921, copy in Storey MSS, MHS; Storey to Julian Codman, April 6, 1923, copy in Storey MSS, MHS.

8. Joseph Katz, "The Legal Profession, 1890–1915. The Lawyer's Role in Society: A Study in Attitudes," unpublished M.A. thesis, Columbia University, 1953, pp. 47–55.

9. Storey, "The Advantages of Law as a Profession," *Harvard Crimson*, May 1, 1921; Storey to Arthur K. Reading, December 15, 1927, copy in Storey MSS, MHS.

10. Storey to Austen G. Fox, March 2, 1916, copy in Storey MSS, MHS; Storey to Raynal C. Bolling, February 2, 1916, copy in Storey MSS, MHS; Storey to William A. Ketcham, January 31, 1916, copy in Storey MSS, MHS. The case which seems to have first turned Storey against Brandeis occurred in 1892. At that time the New York and England Railroad, which Storey represented, was faced with suits by ten stockholders who, represented by Brandeis, were ultimately successful. The following year, in a somewhat different connection before a hearing of the Massachusetts legislature, Storey charged that Brandeis's actual clients, from whom he had received his fees, were agents for the New York, New Haven, and Hartford Railroad, then attempting to destroy all competition within New England. Brandeis admitted that he knew his real clients were not the stockholders he was ostensibly representing, but he maintained that his real client was a former president of the New York and New England Railroad, who was attempting to place the road in receivership. Storey's testimony (and a transcript of his exchange with Brandeis before the Massachusetts legislature) is in the Senate Judiciary Subcommittee, *Hearings on the Nomination of Brandeis,* 64th Cong., 1st sess. (Washington, 1916), 263–81, 415–52. For a critical assessment of Storey's account, see Alpheus T. Mason, *Brandeis, A Free Man's Life* (New York, 1946), pp. 229–32.

11. Storey, *A Civilian's View of the Navy. Lecture Delivered to the Naval War College, September 6, 1897* (Washington, 1897), p. 15.

12. Storey, presidential address to the fifth annual meeting of the Massachusetts Bar Association, in *Fifth Annual Meeting . . . at Worcester, October 10, 1914* (Boston, 1914), p. 1; Storey to Ketcham, April 3, 1912, copy in Storey MSS, MHS; Storey to Sidney Story, December 2, 1907, copy in Storey MSS, MHS; Storey, *Massachusetts vs. Monopoly. The Argument . . . before the Committee on Railroads of the Massachusetts Legislature on March 28, 1912 in Support of a Bill to Allow the Grand Trunk Railway to Extend Its Lines in Massachusetts* (Boston, 1912), p. 32; Robert H. Wiebe, *Businessmen and Reform: A Study of the Progressive Movement* (Cambridge, 1962), pp. 157–58; Storey, *The Labor Question. Address before the Phi Beta Kappa Society of Tufts College, May 8, 1918* (Boston, 1918), p. 9.

13. Storey to Sidney Story, December 2, 1907, copy in Storey MSS, MHS; Richard M. Abrams, *Conservatism in a Progressive Era: Massachusetts Politics, 1900–1912* (Cambridge, 1964), p. 286; Storey to Alice P. Tapley, October 20, 1924, copy in Storey MSS, MHS; Storey to Sophonsiba B. Breckenridge, February 3, 1925, copy in Storey MSS, MHS; Storey to David Greene Haskins, January 3, 1911, copy in Storey MSS, MHS.

14. Abrams, *Conservatism in the Progressive Era*, pp. 1–13; Storey, *The Federal Government and the States. Address Delivered at Norfolk, Virginia, on June 29, 1907, at the Celebration of the Adoption of the First Virginia Constitution* (Boston, 1907), p. 23.

15. Storey, in *The Emancipation of the Voter. The Free List and Proportional Representation. Speeches . . . at the Dinner of the Municipal League of Boston, December 19, 1894* (Boston, 1895), p. 22; Storey, *The Federal Government and the States*, p. 23.

16. Storey, *Obedience to the Law. An Address at the Opening of Petigru College, Columbia, S.C., June 9, 1919* (Boston, 1919), p. 8.

17. Storey, *Problems of Today*, p. 65; *Coronado Coal Co. v. United Mine Workers*, 268 U.S. 295 (1927); Storey, "The Right to Strike," *Yale Law Journal*, XXXII (December 1922), 99–100.

18. Storey to William M. Hargest, December 23, 1919, copy in Storey MSS, MHS.

19. Storey, *Obedience to the Law*, p. 9; *Howat v. Kansas*, 258 U.S. 180 (1922); Storey to James Bryce, January 16, 1922, copy in Storey MSS, MHS; Storey to Allen T. Treadway, September 18, 1923, copy in Storey MSS, MHS; Storey to John J. Rogers, October 29, 1923, copy in Storey MSS, MHS.

20. Walter White, *Rope and Faggot: A Biography of Judge Lynch* (New York, 1929), pp. 83–84, 93–94; National Association for the Advancement of Colored People, *Thirty Years of Lynching in the United States, 1889–1918* (New York, 1919), pp. 10, 33.

21. White, *Rope and Faggot*, p. 59.

22. The descriptions are paraphrased from the following sources: the Waco lynching, from *Thirty Years of Lynching*, pp. 23–24 and "The Waco Horror," supplement to the *Crisis*, X (July 1916); the Dyersburg lynching, from the *Crisis*, XV (February 1918), 178–83; the Valdosta lynching, from *Thirty Years of Lynching*, pp. 26–27 and White, *Rope and Faggot*, pp. 27–29. Sumner is quoted in White, *Rope and Faggot*, pp. 27–29.

23. Charles Flint Kellogg, *NAACP: A History of the National Association for the Advancement of Colored People*, Vol. I: *1909–1920* (Baltimore, 1967), pp. 209–21; Roy Nash, memorandum to Storey, May 18, 1916, in Storey MSS, LC.

24. Elliott M. Rudwick, *Race Riot in East St. Louis, July 2, 1917* (Carbondale, Ill., 1963), p. 217; Storey to John R. Shillady, January 10, 1919, copy in Storey MSS, MHS.

25. Shillady, statement in NAACP press release, August 1, 1918, copy in Storey MSS, LC; Shillady to the president and members of the Executive Committee of the American Bar Association, August 17, 1918, copy in Storey MSS, LC; statement of the Executive Committee, copy in Storey MSS, LC; declaration of those who attended National Conference on Lynching, May 6, 1919, copy in Storey MSS, LC.

26. Robert L. Zangrando, "The Efforts of the N.A.A.C.P. To Secure Passage of a Federal Anti-Lynching Bill," unpublished Ph.D. dissertation, University of Pennsylvania, 1963, pp. 63–64. At about the same time Dyer introduced his bill, Joel Spingarn of the Association's Board of Directors, then a Major with the War Department Intelligence Bureau, devised a bill which would have made the lynching of servicemen and their families a Federal crime. No action was taken on his bill, however, and the Association dropped his proposal after 1918. At the time of the Dyer bill, some state laws existed: North Carolina and West Virginia, alone among Southern and border states, held cities and/or counties where lynchings occurred liable; Alabama, Georgia, South Carolina, Tennessee, and West Virginia held sheriffs liable; and Alabama, Kentucky, South Carolina, and Tennessee permitted the removal of a sheriff when his negligence had been proven. But no state provided for the prosecution of members of a lynch mob. See, in general, Charles S. Mangum, *The Legal Status of the Negro* (Chapel Hill, 1940), pp. 290–308.

27. Storey to Adams, August 14, 1905, copy in Storey MSS, MHS. During the campaign against lynching, Storey reiterated the first point in *Problems of Today*, pp. 114–16; and the second in *Legal Aspects of the Negro Question. Address to the NAACP Annual Convention, Atlanta, Georgia, May 20–June 2, 1920* (New York, 1920), p. 5.

28. Storey to Samuel W. McCall, February 29, 1912, copy in Storey MSS, MHS; Storey, address to the eighth annual meeting of the Anti-Imperialist League, in *Report of the Eighth Annual Meeting . . . November 24–December 3, 1906* (Boston, 1907), p. 33; Storey to Bolton Smith, February 24, 1921, copy in Storey MSS, MHS; *U.S.* v. *Cruikshank*, 92 U.S. 542 (1875); *U.S.* v. *Harris*, 106 U.S. 629 (1883).

29. Storey to Walter White, July 11, 1918, copy in Storey MSS, MHS; Shillady, report to the Board of Directors of the NAACP, September 9, 1918, copy in Storey MSS, LC; Storey to Shillady, April 3, 1919, copy in Storey MSS, MHS.

30. Storey to John M. Whitehead, January 8, 1920, copy in Storey MSS, MHS; Storey to Nash, October 9, 1916, copy in Storey

MSS, MHS; Storey to George F. Peabody, June 26, 1919, copy in Storey MSS, MHS.

31. John Hope Franklin, *From Slavery to Freedom: A History of Negro Americans* (3rd ed.; New York, 1967), p. 480; Storey to William N. Rice, November 26, 1919, copy in Storey MSS, MHS.

32. Storey to White, May 28, 1921, copy in Storey MSS, MHS; George W. Wickersham to Storey, January 7, 1921, Storey MSS, MHS.

33. Storey to Wickersham, January 15, 1921, copy in Storey MSS, MHS; Wickersham to Storey, January 20, 1921, Storey MSS, MHS; Storey to Wickersham, January 22, 1921, copy in Storey MSS, MHS.

34. Storey to Wickersham, March 17, 1921, copy in Storey MSS, MHS (the statute under discussion is now Section 241 of the United States Code); *U.S.* v. *Cruikshank,* 92 U.S. 542 (1875); *U.S.* v. *Wheeler,* 254 U.S. 281 (1920); Wickersham to Storey, March 18, 1921, Storey MSS, MHS.

35. Storey to Wickersham, March 21, 1921, copy in Storey MSS, MHS; Wickersham to White, May 11, 1921, Storey MSS, LC; Storey to Leonidas C. Dyer, August 4, 1921, copy in Storey MSS, MHS.

36. Copy of bill enclosed in letter from James Weldon Johnson to Storey, October 22, 1921, Storey MSS, LC; Johnson, report of the Executive Secretary, February 1922, copy in Storey MSS, LC.

37. William E. Borah to Storey, February 9, 1922, Storey MSS, LC. Their task was complicated by tension between Borah and Lodge, the Senate Majority Leader. Lodge, running for re-election, hoped for a quick vote on the bill to improve his image among Massachusetts Negroes. Borah, on the other hand, was annoyed at having to hurry his consideration of the bill to meet Lodge's deadline, and second in line for the chairmanship of the Foreign Relations Committee, he was in no great hurry to assure Lodge's re-election. See Johnson's impressions of Borah in his autobiography, *Along This Way* (New York, 1933), p. 368.

38. Storey to Johnson, March 27, 1922, copy in Storey MSS, MHS.

39. Storey, *Brief in Support of the Dyer Anti-Lynching Bill. Submitted to the Committee on the Judiciary of the United States Senate* (reprinted; New York, 1922), p. 12; *Saunders* v. *Shaw,* 244 U.S. 317, 320 (1917); *Ex parte Virginia,* 100 U.S. 339, 347 (1879); *Home Telephone and Telegraph Co.* v. *Los Angeles,* 227 U.S. 278, 287 (1913). In his brief, Storey quoted from preceding passages in

this decision, but the passage given here seems to me the most succinct. See also Herbert K. Stockton to Borah, June 5, 1922, Storey MSS, LC.

40. *Logan* v. *U.S.*, 144 U.S. 263, 293 (1892). Between his argument under the Fourteenth Amendment and his argument under the Fifth, in his brief Storey interpolated a defense of the Dyer bill on the basis of "the peace of the United States," though he had attacked exactly this argument three years before (see above). This concept appeared most notably in *In re Neagle*, 135 U.S. 1 (1890), a case involving the authority of a Federal marshal to shoot a citizen who threatened the life of a Supreme Court Justice on circuit duty. *Neagle*, in turn, drew on the precedents of two other cases: one, *Ex parte Siebold*, 100 U.S. 371 (1879), involving the prosecution of a Baltimore judge for election fraud, the other, *Wells* v. *Nickles*, 104 U.S. 244 (1881), involving the recovery of timber stolen from a Federal reserve. But while these cases clearly indicate that authority to maintain "the peace of the United States" inherently reposes in agents of the Federal government and need not be specifically granted by Congress, it is questionable (Storey's second view notwithstanding) whether the "peace" in question refers to anything more than the operation of the United States government.

41. Storey to Dyer, August 4, 1921, copy in Storey MSS, MHS; Storey, *Brief in Support of the Dyer Bill*, p. 24; *Strauder* v. *Virginia*, 100 U.S. 304, 310 (1879). Storey's other main reason for this argument, as his phrasing indicates, was the protection of aliens, to avoid a repetition of incidents such as "the notorious case in New Orleans when Blaine was Secretary of State, and the United States paid damages for the Italians who were killed." Storey to Albert E. Pillsbury, August 13, 1921, copy in Storey MSS, MHS.

42. Storey, *Brief in Support of the Dyer Bill*, pp. 27–29. See Laurent B. Frantz, "Congressional Power to Enforce the Fourteenth Amendment against Private Acts," *Yale Law Journal*, LXXIII (July 1964), 1353–84.

43. Storey, *Brief in Support of the Dyer Bill*, p. 12. Today a majority of commentators would appear to confirm Storey's judgment on this point. The framers of the Fourteenth Amendment believed that it vested Congress with "a secondary power to afford protection to all persons in their enjoyment of constitutional rights when the states failed in the primary responsibility to do so either by neglecting to enact laws or by refusal or impotence to enforce them." Robert J. Harris, *The Quest for Equality: The Constitution, Congress, and the Supreme Court* (Baton Rouge, 1960), p. 53.

44. *Gitlow* v. *New York*, 268 U.S. 652 (1925); Storey to John J. McSwain, January 9, 1922, copy in Storey MSS, MHS; Storey to

Borah, May 19, 1922, copy in Storey MSS, MHS. The dissent quoted was in *Gilbert* v. *Minnesota*, 254 U.S. 336 (1920).

45. Louis Marshall to Stockton, July 17, 1922, in Charles Reznikoff (ed.), *Louis Marshall, Champion of Liberty: Selected Papers and Addresses* (Philadelphia, 1957), p. 423; Storey to Pillsbury, April 10, 1922, copy in Storey MSS, MHS. In 1926 Storey wrote of the Dyer bill that "my opinion has always been that it is constitutional. . . ." Storey to Johnson, February 12, 1926, copy in Storey MSS, MHS. But so gradual was the evolution of his opinion that Walter White always thought Storey doubted the bill's constitutionality. White, *Rope and Faggot*, p. 219.

46. NAACP press release, September 29, 1922; Johnson; report of the Executive Secretary, December 1922, copies in Storey MSS, LC.

47. When the Department of Justice decided to create a section dealing with civil rights violations in 1939, its legal arsenal consisted of what is now Section 241 of the U.S. Code (the statute Storey cited to Wickersham), making it a felony to conspire to injure citizens in the exercise of various rights; and what is now Section 242, making it a misdemeanor "to wilfully deprive" a citizen of his rights "under color of law." In the most notable case involving Section 241, *U.S.* v. *Williams*, 341 U.S. 70 (1951), the Court voted to void a Federal indictment brought under it but did not restrict the application of the statute. In the most notable case involving Section 242, *Screws* v. *U.S.*, 325 U.S. 91 (1945), the Court upheld the statute but ordered a new trial on the grounds that the government had failed to prove "wilfulness." It is significant, however, that the leading Court critic of the use of either section to prosecute violence was Justice Frankfurther. Frankfurter was also the leading Court exponent of "judicial restraint," and it is difficult to imagine him striking down an anti-lynching law, just passed by both Houses of Congress and signed by the President, no matter how sweeping its prohibitions against the deprivation of civil rights.

Any doubts that the Court might now declare anti-lynching legislation unconstitutional have been removed by two cases, both decided in 1966. In one, *U.S.* v. *Guest*, 383 U.S. 745, the Justices divided on a number of points, but a majority appeared to agree that Congress may legislate to punish *all* conspiracies to deprive citizens of *any* right secured by the Constitution or the laws of the United States. In another, *U.S.* v. *Price*, 383 U.S. 787, the Court held that life and liberty are rights secured by the Constitution against deprivation under "color of law." It would appear that Storey's arguments on behalf of the constitutionality of the Dyer bill are now vindicated.

48. Storey, *The Reform of Legal Procedure* (New Haven, 1911), p. 203; Storey to John M. Gibbs, March 15, 1924, copy in Storey MSS, MHS.

49. Storey to Daniel Buckley, March 11, 1926, copy in Storey MSS, MHS; Clarence Darrow, *The Story of My Life* (New York, 1932), pp. 78–83; Storey, "Some Practical Suggestions for the Reform of Criminal Procedure," *Journal of the American Institute of Criminal Law and Criminology*, IV (November 1913), 512; Storey to L. H. Barney, December 16, 1925, copy in Storey MSS, MHS.

50. Storey to William C. Loring, December 16, 1925, copy in Storey MSS, MHS.

51. Storey to the editor of the *Journal of Criminal Law and Criminology*, September 22, 1925, copy in Storey MSS, MHS; Storey, *The Reform of Legal Procedure*, pp. 215–16. For a recent re-statement of Storey's position, see the note, "Procedural Protections of the Criminal Defendant—A Re-evaluation of the Privilege Against Self-Incrimination and the Rule Excluding Evidence of the Propensity to Commit Crime," *Harvard Law Review*, LXXVIII (December 1964), 427–35, 445–49.

52. Storey, *The Negro Question. An Address Delivered before the Wisconsin Bar Association, June 27, 1918* (Boston, 1918), p. 27; Horace C. Peterson and Gilbert C. Fite, *Opponents of War, 1917–1918* (Madison, 1957), pp. 14–17, 214–21.

53. Storey to Elizabeth Gilman, November 14, 1922, copy in Storey MSS, MHS; Storey to Roger Baldwin, March 12, 1918, copy in Storey MSS, MHS; Storey to Thomas Sergeant Perry, July 6, 1917, copy in Storey MSS, MHS; Storey to Charles F. Dole, November 22, 1918, copy in Storey MSS, MHS; Peterson and Fite, *Opponents of War*, pp. 260–62; Storey to Norman Thomas, February 6, 1919, copy in Storey MSS, MHS.

54. See Robert K. Murray, *Red Scare: A Study in National Hysteria, 1919–1920* (Minneapolis, 1955), esp. pp. 170–238.

55. *Colyer* v. *Skeffington*, 265 Fed. 17 (Mass., 1920); Zechariah Chafee, Jr., *Free Speech in the United States* (Cambridge, 1940), pp. 205–8; George W. Anderson, petition to the Massachusetts Senate and House of Representatives, May 1919, copy in Storey MSS, MHS. The other signatories were Charles W. Eliot, John F. Moors, Joseph Walker, and David Walsh.

56. Murray, *Red Scare*, pp. 246–51; Storey, introduction to Post, *Deportations Delirium*, ix, xiii.

57. Kellogg, *NAACP*, pp. 242–43; Arthur I. Waskow, *From Race Riot to Sit-In: 1919 and the 1960's* (Garden City, 1965), pp. 121–40.

58. Waskow, *From Race Riot to Sit-In*, pp. 143–63.

59. Storey to A. Mitchell Palmer, February 5, 1920, copy in Storey MSS, MHS; Kellogg, *NAACP*, pp. 286–90; Storey to William E. Walling, April 2, 1920, copy in Storey MSS, MHS; Storey to Mary Gwynn, April 4, 1921, copy in Storey MSS, MHS.

60. Storey to Pillsbury, January 5, 1920, copy in Storey MSS, MHS; Storey to White, October 25, 1921, copy in Storey MSS, LC; Johnson to Storey, November 2, 1921, Storey MSS, LC; Storey to Johnson, November 3, 1921, copy in Storey MSS, MHS.

61. *Brief for the Appellants, Frank Moore, Ed. Hicks, J. E. Knox, et al., in the Supreme Court, October Term, 1922* (Washington, 1922), p. 8.

62. *Moore* v. *Dempsey*, 261 U.S. 86 (1923); Kellogg, *NAACP*, pp. 244–45; Waskow, *From Race Riot to Sit-In*, pp. 164–74. Eight years before, in *Frank* v. *Mangum*, 237 U.S. 309 (1915), the Court had refused to grant habeas corpus in another case involving "mob influence," and there is some disagreement as to whether the two decisions were consistent.

The background of the *Frank* case was, in some ways, even more sensational than that in the *Moore* case. It concerned the conviction of a Northern Jew, Leo Frank, for the sex-murder of a poor-white girl in Georgia, where economic discontent was expressing itself in violent anti-Semitism. Frank, unlike Moore and the others, had a competent defense, and his formal rights were protected; but he, too, had been faced with a mob surrounding the courthouse, in his case screaming "Hang the Jew, or we'll hang you." Afraid that Frank would be lynched on the spot (he actually was lynched two years later) his counsel waived his right to be present at the sentencing.

Louis Marshall, hired to appeal the case to the Supreme Court, argued that due process had been twice violated: first by the "mob spirit" which infected the jury's decision, and second by counsel's waiving Frank's right to be present at sentencing. The Court, however, ruled against Frank, Justices Holmes and Hughes dissenting. The chief basis for its ruling was that Georgia supplied its own corrective process: the Georgia State Supreme Court could have reversed the decision on proof of mob intimidation, but it did not. The Arkansas Court, on the other hand, had no such power; and in that sense, Storey was justified in arguing that the two decisions were consistent. Storey to the *Harvard Law Review*, December 18, 1923, copy in Storey MSS, MHS.

Against Storey's interpretation, as well as the fiction that the Court never overrules itself, three facts need to be considered. First, Marshall felt that the *Moore* decision vindicated his arguments in *Frank* (Marshall to White, March 12, 1923, in *Selected Papers*, pp. 316–17). Second, the majority decision in *Moore*, written by Holmes, seemed to say that when "the whole proceeding is a mask —that counsel, jury, and judge were swept to the fatal end by an irresistible wave of public passion, and that the state courts failed to correct the wrong . . . perfection in the machinery for correction" (as in *Frank*) was immaterial. Third, only two Justices (McKenna and Van Devanter) voted for Moore and against Frank; Holmes voted for both defendants; McReynolds voted against both; and the five other Justices who had ruled on *Frank* had been replaced.

63. Storey to the editor of the Boston *Globe,* June 8, 1906, copy in Storey MSS, MHS. He had made the same argument even earlier: see Storey to the editor of the Boston *Transcript,* January 4, 1897, copy in Storey MSS, MHS.

64. Storey to Dole, November 3, 1921, copy in Storey MSS, MHS. For a review of the ballistics controversy and the Morelli hypothesis, see Herbert B. Ehrmann, "Sacco and Vanzetti: The Magnetic Point and the Morelli Hypothesis," *Harvard Law Review,* LXXIX (January 1966), 571–98.

65. Felix Frankfurter, "The Case of Sacco and Vanzetti," *Atlantic Monthly,* CXXXIX (March 1927), 409–32.

66. David Felix, *Protest: Sacco-Vanzetti and the Intellectuals* (Bloomington, 1965), pp. 187–88; Storey to Robert L. O'Brien, November 3, 1926, copy in Storey MSS, MHS; Chafee, *Free Speech in the United States,* pp. 164–65; Storey to O'Brien, November 1, 1926, copy in Storey MSS, MHS.

67. Storey to Dole, November 7, 1921, copy in Storey MSS, MHS.

68. Storey to Johnson, November 3, 1921, copy in Storey MSS, MHS; Storey to Charles Edward Russell, March 15, 1927, copy in Storey MSS, MHS.

69. Storey to James Ford Rhodes, December 17, 1925, copy in Storey MSS, MHS.

70. Storey to Rhodes, January 15, 1926, copy in Storey MSS, MHS; Storey to John Jay Chapman, December 29, 1926, copy in Storey MSS, MHS; Storey to Wickersham, May 21, 1928, copy in Storey MSS, MHS.

71. Storey to Chapman, December 29, 1926, copy in Storey MSS, MHS; Storey to Mrs. Frederick Marshall, December 5, 1927, copy in Storey MSS, MHS; Storey to Wickersham, May 21, 1928, copy in Storey MSS, MHS; Storey to Mrs. Bellamy Storer, February 28, 1928, copy in Storey MSS, MHS.

72. Storey to Henry F. May, October 17, 1928, copy in Storey MSS, MHS.

73. Storey to Mrs. John Graham (Helen Appleton) Brooks, October 31, 1926, in Mark A. DeWolfe Howe, *Portrait of an Independent: Moorfield Storey, 1845–1929* (Boston, 1932), p. 356; Storey to Wickersham, May 21, 1928, copy in Storey MSS, MHS; Storey to Charles W. Eliot, March 23, 1926, copy in Storey MSS, MHS.

CHAPTER 5. THE ABOLITIONIST TRADITION

1. For similar definitions, see Aileen Kraditor, *Means and Ends in American Abolitionism: Garrison and His Critics on Strategy and Tactics, 1834–1850* (New York, 1969), p. 8; and James M. McPherson, *The Struggle for Equality: The Abolitionists and the Negro in the Civil War and Reconstruction* (Princeton, 1964), p. 3.

2. The most cogent statement of this tactical aspect of the abolitionist argument is Donald G. Mathews, "The Abolitionists on Slavery: The Critique Behind the Social Movement," *Journal of Southern History*, XXXIII (May 1967), 163–82.

3. This point is forcefully made by W. R. Brock in *An American Crisis: Congress and Reconstruction* (London, 1962), pp. 10–12.

4. To obtain a sense of the thought of business spokesmen during this period I have used George E. Mowry, *The Era of Theodore Roosevelt and the Birth of Modern America, 1900–1912* (New York, 1958), pp. 38–45; Robert H. Wiebe, *Businessmen and Reform: A Study of the Progressive Movement* (Cambridge, 1962), pp. 179–93; and Gabriel Kolko, *The Triumph of Conservatism: A Reinterpretation of American History, 1900–1916* (Glencoe, 1964), esp. pp. 161–64. Storey's comments on the wealthy are indicated in a letter to Thomas Sergeant Perry, February 18, 1867, microfilm copy in Perry MSS, Duke University; and in an address at the Charleston College commencement, June 14, 1904, reprinted in the Charleston *News-Courier*, June 19, 1904.

5. Storey's interest in legislative reform is most notably indicated in *The American Legislature. The Annual Address . . . before the American Bar Association, Delivered at Saratoga Springs, August 22, 1894* (reprinted, 1894), pp. 19–25; his interest in decentralization in *The Federal Government and the States. Address delivered at Norfolk, Virginia, on June 29, 1907, at the Celebration of the Adoption of the First Virginia Constitution* (Boston, 1907); his criticisms of a powerful presidency at several points: *Charles Sumner* (Boston, 1900), p. 348, letters to Charles Francis Adams, Jr., August 16, 1907, and to William A. Jones, March 25, 1912, copies in Storey MSS, MHS; his support of Bryan, in letters to Herbert

Welsh, October 15, 1908, and William A. Ketcham, May 1, 1912, copies in Storey MSS, MHS; and his attitudes toward the courts in *Problems of Today* (Cambridge, 1920), pp. 94–95, and "The Recall of Judicial Decisions," *Annals of the American Academy of Political and Social Science,* LII (March 1914), 13–24.

6. McPherson, *The Struggle for Equality,* pp. 249–59, 407–16.

7. The current reassessment of the centralizing tendencies of twentieth-century reform is widespread. Especially significant is the statement of the former special assistant to Presidents Kennedy and Johnson (and speechwriter for Senators Kennedy and McCarthy in 1968), Richard N. Goodwin, "The Shape of American Politics," *Commentary,* XLIII (June 1967), 25–40.

8. Storey to the branches of the NAACP, March 23, 1925, copy in Storey MSS, MHS.

Bibliographical Guide

The secondary works I have used in writing this book are indicated in the notes to the chapters. I have also listed there those of Moorfield Storey's published books, articles, and addresses upon which I have relied; in any case, a complete list of them may be found in the bibliography of Mark A. DeWolfe Howe, *Portrait of an Independent: Moorfield Storey, 1845–1929* (Boston: Houghton Mifflin, 1932), pp. 365–71. The major problem facing scholars who desire to study Storey has, however, been the difficulty in locating his letters and unpublished addresses. Instead of the usual bibliography, therefore, let this serve as a guide to the various collections in which Storey manuscripts may be found:

The most important collection of Moorfield Storey's papers, and that upon which this book has been substantially based, was donated by his son, Charles M. Storey, to the Massachusetts Historical Society in late 1969. The basis of this collection consists of thirty-two volumes of letter-press copies of every letter dictated by Storey from his law office between March 1894 and his death in October 1929. These letters thus include his entire correspondence with others in the Anti-Imperialist League and in the National Association for the Advancement of Colored People, as well as correspondence with strangers and friends on a wide variety of subjects. This collection does not include those letters hand-written by Storey himself before 1894 (except for those to his family during his clerkship with Sumner), or notes to close friends between 1894 and 1929; they are to be found in the manuscript collections of the various recipients. This collection does, however, include several volumes of incoming

247

correspondence, most notably from the Adamses, Holmes, the Jameses, Rhodes, Schurz, and Villard. Finally, the collection includes two drafts of Storey's unpublished autobiography, a copy of his sister Mariana's privately printed *Family Recollections*, four scrapbooks, and bound volumes containing all of his speeches, whether published in pamphlet form, reprinted in newspapers, or typed unpublished copies.

The other collection of Storey manuscripts is in the Manuscripts Division of the Library of Congress. Most of this collection consists of government documents, Filipino newspapers, anti-imperialist tracts, and multiple copies of Storey's pamphlets. Several of the boxes of correspondence are, however, of great importance to a student of Storey's career. This collection, for example, includes all the incoming correspondence (except from Schurz) relating to anti-imperialism and Philippine independence. Of equal importance are the boxes containing incoming correspondence on the Dyer anti-lynching bill, on Haiti, and on the attempted exclusion of Negro students from Harvard dormitories. In the Library of Congress there are also four scrapbooks, three of which are important: the first, 1876–1896, material on his Independent career; the second, 1899–1901, material on anti-imperialism; and the third, 1901–1907, material on the suppression of the Filipino insurrection.

There are surprisingly few hand-written letters by Storey in other manuscript collections. In the papers of the men who influenced him in his youth, for example (all in the Houghton Library, Harvard University), there are no letters from him at all in the Ralph Waldo Emerson MSS, and only a handful in the James Russell Lowell MSS and in the Charles Sumner MSS. Storey's Independent activities are indicated in scattered letters in the John Forrester Andrew MSS, the Henry Cabot Lodge MSS, and the William E. Russell MSS (in the Massachusetts Historical Society); in the Carl Schurz MSS (in the Library of Congress); and in the Herbert Welsh MSS (in the Historical Society of Pennsylvania). Letters written by Storey himself after 1894, in the papers of various correspondents, are almost without exception less important than those dictated from his office: this is true of the Storey letters in the Charles Francis Adams and Henry Adams MSS and in the James Ford Rhodes MSS (both in the Massachusetts Historical Society); and of those in the William James MSS and in the Charles Eliot Norton MSS (both in the Houghton Library). There are some interesting Storey letters in the papers of his intimate friend, Thomas Sergeant Perry (on microfilm in the Duke University Library), though surprisingly few from the years emphasized in this book.

Index